New Nations and Peoples

China

China

LOIS MITCHISON

with 108 illustrations and 4 maps

New York
WALKER AND COMPANY

To Guy with much gratitude

Library of Congress Catalog Card Number: 66-21174

First published in the United States of America in 1966 by Walker and Company, a division of Walker Publishing Company.

Printed in Great Britain

Contents

1   A New Nation?

CH'IN SHIH-HUANG-TI, so they say, built the Great Wall of China with men's bones as bricks and men's blood as mortar. His critics were boiled alive in a cauldron placed conveniently in one corner of his audience chamber. He burnt the Confucian books, and buried the Confucian scholars alive. His taxes, his conscription, his iconoclasm, and his cruelty made him the most hated man in China. For more than 2,000 years he was the classic example given to schoolboys of the strong wicked emperor.

However today Ch'in Shih-huang-ti is getting a new face. He was, in his way, 'progressive', the new Chinese leaders say. He fulfilled the needs of the China of his time. He was a unifier, and he suppressed 'corrupt elements' in his society. The Great Wall is 'a proud achievement of the Chinese working classes' even if they were 'somewhat exploited' in its making.

Ch'in Shih-huang-ti is not alone in the new light of respect accorded him. Since the break with the Soviet Union there has been a particular revival of interest in the 'strong' emperors of the past, and a new defence of the unique excellence of China's history. In their speeches and writings the older generation of communist leaders quote the classics of Chinese literature, philosophy and history. One of the first acts of the communists after they came to power was to re-furbish China's museums and historic buildings. Ancient Chinese culture and learning has once again become the serious study and a source of inspiration for the new generation. China's national claims to have done most things in the world first and better have been re-emphasized. Russian scholars recently quoted ironically the Chinese historians who believed that Confucius

7

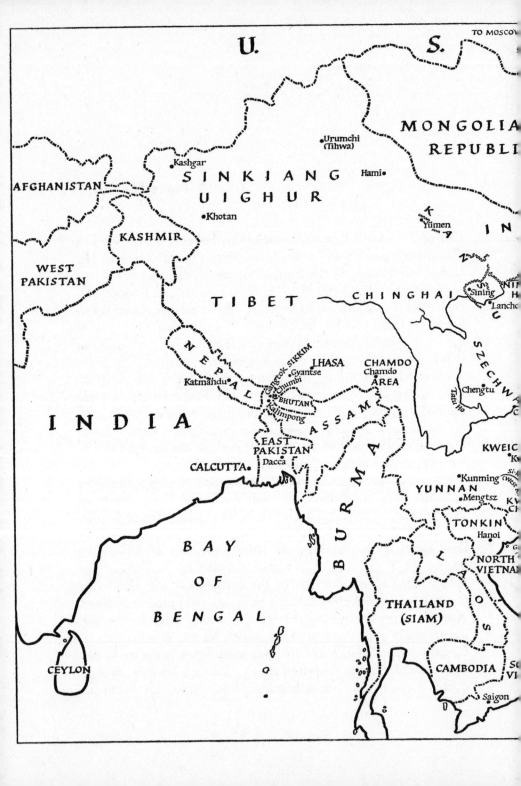

Political map of China

had been a formative influence on the French Encyclopaedists, and on the eighteenth⁄ and nineteenth⁄century German philosophers; and that the even more remote and ancient *Book of Changes* inspired some of Liebnitz's mathematical ideas.

If their past continues to be so important to the Chinese, what claim has China to call herself a 'new nation'? Are the established traditions of over 3,000 years of civilized, centralized, government simply continuing into the present? In Chinese history good rulers have always emphasized the national heritage and the virtues of their predecessors. Is this what is happening now? The fourteenth⁄century novel, *The Three Kingdoms*, begins with the words: 'If the kingdom has long been divided, it must be united again; if it has been united, it must be divided again.' Were the years between the Nationalist revolution of 1911 and the establishment of the communists in 1949 only another of the classic periods of disorder? Civil war, foreign invasion, famine, and floods are as characteristic of all the historic interregnums as they were of the period between 1911 and 1949. By Chinese standards it was, if anything, a short interregnum, but perhaps the 50 years of decaying Chi'ng rule before 1911 should be counted with it. Then, like the strong emperors who ended disorder and founded new dynasties, Mao Tse⁄tung and the Communist Party have re⁄established internal order and morals, reformed the system of taxation, extended Chinese rule over rebellious frontier peoples, and put China back almost in her old place as the im⁄ portant nation, the central country, of the world. In return the Chinese people have given Mao the adulation due to the imperial Son of Heaven. Even the simplicity of his life, his insistence on the warts painted into his portraits, has good precedents behind it. This was how Liu Pang, the rough peasant bandit who founded the great Han dynasty, behaved 2,000 years ago.

The other communist leaders, austere, uncorrupt, and, within reason, efficient, have been compared to the Mandarins, the civil servants who governed the Chinese Empire from the time of the Han dynasty onwards. Communist education and their way of recruiting officials are close to the old methods, if Marxist set books are substituted for Confucian ones.

It is not an unflattering comparison, and it is often made by liberal well-wishers of the Chinese communists; but they themselves reject it utterly. The Confucian world was static, looked backwards. The Marxist world is dynamic, and looks forward. Mencius, Confucius' greatest disciple, said that those who work with their hands always support those who work with their heads. In communism those who work with their hands are in theory, if not in practice, the natural leaders of society. In Chinese communism, particularly, intellectuals and officials can only think rightly and govern rightly if, as well as working with their minds, they also work with their hands. Prime Ministers, pianists, and philosophers volunteer for their Sundays spent digging or earth-carrying on the latest dam or road project.

The communists are, they insist, New men in a New China. The old emperors and their servants were sometimes 'progressive' within the framework of their times; but because they were not Marxists they could not even know whether they were on the side of progress, and they were not and could not have been aiming at communism. To know that they are on the side of history, progress and virtue (although this last word is only implied, not used, by the present Chinese leaders, in contrast to their predecessors) is reserved for the communists; and because only they are communists, truly one with the people and the people's interests, only they are in sight of the final goal for China, the millennium of the communist society.

If historical comparisons have to be made the proper people to compare to communists are the leaders of the peasant revolts. The more recent the revolts were, the nearer in time to the appearance of communism, the closer the peasants could get to communist ideas. The most honoured historical figures in China today are the leaders of the Taipings and the Boxers, two of the great peasant rebellions of the nineteenth century.

In science, art, the technique of farming and crafts, much, the Chinese communists said, could be learnt from the Chinese past. But it was essential, in their view, to pick out the right bits of the past. The achievements of the 'oppressing' class, 'decadent' painting and poetry, as well as 'feudal' philosophy or history had nothing, particularly in the first years of the new government, to teach the newly re-born Chinese people. Later the régime could afford to relax a little. Even Mencius could be rehabilitated. But it is always easier and safer for the scholar to praise works of learning, or works of art, like the Buddhist sculptures, made by men of working-class origins, admired by the ordinary people, and, on the whole, despised by the gentry of the past. Chinese technology is politically popular: the inventions of the working class to make working-class daily life easier. Archaeology is popular too; and the articles in the foreign-language press describing the newly discovered Neolithic village houses did not fail to point out how fortunate the archaeologists were to be able to work on sites already partially dug to make the foundations of new towns and factories. (Neolithic village sites, about 7,000 years old, have recently been excavated over much of North and Central China. Chinese Neolithic villagers were particularly skilled potters, and among the most magnificent of their artefacts are the great painted burial urns of the Kansu sites.)

Under the communists, however, China's past could not outshine its future. Part of their pride was that what they did had no parallel in their country's history or even in the world's history. In particular, they claimed, the rural and urban communes and the way of life built round them were the beginning of actual communism, something never seen anywhere at any time before. There had been rule in China in the past that was comparatively good. Other countries, like the Soviet Union, were 'socialist', an improvement on capitalist. But only China had seen the dawn of absolutely good government. China, her leaders alleged, was new born; and, in her new birth, a model for all other new nations.

2 Colonizing China

SHEN NUNG, WHO WAS THE FOUNDER of the Hsia dynasty more than 4,000 years ago, was also a great farmer. He taught the Chinese, it is said, what crops to grow, when to sow, when to reap, how to clear the land, and how to ditch and drain. Among his successors was the Yellow Emperor, Huang Ti. At his court, so they say, men wrote on strips of bamboo, studied the stars, and made a calendar. The Yellow Emperor's wife, Lei-tsu discovered the silk culture; and in their joint reigns peace and virtue so abounded that a unicorn roamed the imperial park and a phoenix nested on the palace roof. The communists have restored the supposed site of Huang Ti's tomb in Shensi, and re-dedicated it to 'the father of the Han people . . .'.[1]

Some centuries before the first millennium B.C. the Hsias and their legends merge into the Shangs and known, written, and dated history. The Shang used inscribed bones to register the questions put to their state oracle and its decrees. The state, these writings describe, was ruled by priest kings who were buried in tombs of Egyptian splendour with their wives, servants, animals, and worldly possessions around them. It is from the excavation of these tombs that archaeologists have discovered the range of Shang skills. They inlaid bone with turquoise, carved jade and ivory, used musical instruments, and went to war in chariots. The serpentine Chinese dragon, longer and less massive than its European counterpart, and with a lion's head, makes its first appearance in the Shang carvings.

These Chinese contemporaries of Crete and later Mesopotamia and Egypt lived in one of the world's least comfortable cradles of civilization. The north Chinese climate is like Canada's. The summer is hot; but in the long cold winters temperatures drop to ten degrees below freezing for months at a time. There is a low rainfall of about 20 inches a year, fortunately most of it falling in the spring. The Hwang Ho (Yellow River), that flows through the rolling northern hills, and then out to sea over a broad coastal plain, floods or dries up frequently and unpredictably. One of the Hsia legends is of the Emperor Yu and the work he did when the Yellow River flooded in his time. He was, the legend says: 'eight years away from his home, and though he thrice passed the door he did not enter'.

In spite of the stories about the Emperor Yu the main Yellow River valley and the coastal plain was too great a challenge for the early Shang state. Just as Egyptian civilization began in the easier, if potentially less fertile, lands above the Nile Delta, so the Shang kings set up their first capital at Anyang in the loess hills to the northwest. These hills are more easily worked than the land near the river, and fertile enough to produce a wheat and millet surplus sufficiently large to support a court and cities. The loess dust of which they are made is unwooded (another advantage for early settlers who have, throughout world history, avoided forests). The villagers today, like their ancestors of Shang times, hollow themselves out cave homes and buildings, sometimes working under the cliffs, sometimes burrowing under their own fields, so that no land is wasted. The only sign of a family can be smoke from a kitchen chimney blowing up through apparently deserted growing crops.

From these open grass-covered hills and the tributary valleys the early settlers gradually moved down to the main Yellow River valley, the coastal plain, and the further lowlands of North China. For thousands of miles there were no impediments to the pioneer farmers before they reached the mountains and deserts of the far west and north, the sea, and the forests of the Yangtze valley.

Unfortunately, to the north, the country was equally easy for nomadic horse-riders to move over. For centuries they raided the settled lands and towns, and retreated back to what was to be called Mongolia before the slow-moving foot-soldiers of the plain could close with them. In time along the northern frontier the settled farmers intermarried with the barbarians and learnt some of their war skills. It was from among these frontier people that the Chou dynasty came to overthrow the Shang in 1027 B.C. They fought with crossbows and elaborately carved short swords, and their first king claimed to have conquered because the last Shang ruler had 'despised the commands of heaven . . . was lazy and slothful, slighted the labours of government'.

The strength of the new Chou state, however, was quickly undermined by the independence of its nobles on their fiefs. From the ninth century until the final conquest of all settled China by Ch'in Shih-huang-ti in 221 B.C. the Chou Emperor kept only priestly power over what had by now become independent small states. Their rulers set up different systems of government, and there were constant wars between the states. Nevertheless, to the Chinese this is the classic period of their history.

The centuries of the decline of the Chou became to China much what ancient Greece was to later Europe. There were the same early heroic deeds and legends; and the same intellectual, political, and practical froth and experiment.

It cannot have been a comfortable period for a Chinese to live in. Plundering armies and unpleasant deaths were over-common. Yet, under the communists, just as it was before, it is the most often quoted period of Chinese history. At the end of the Chou, China, in all but details, is the country she remained for the next 2,000 years. The farms have become familiar. Hens, buffaloes, and wet rice cultivation had been introduced, probably from India or Burma. A late Chou text describes ploughshares, hoes, and scythes as farm tools. Houses and gardens are designed as they were to be for future centuries. Women wear gold, silver, and jade ornaments. Lacquer is used on furniture. Even chopsticks, the most character-istic of Chinese refinements, are first mentioned in the third century B.C.

Most of the ideas that have influenced the Chinese trace back to this period (and so do many more soon discarded by ordinary Chinese thinkers). It was the age of the philosophers. Confucius (Kung Fu-tzu – his name, like Mencius, was latinized by the

Jesuits), the most famous of them all, was born in 551 B.C., and spent much of his life travelling from state to state looking for a prince who would adopt his theories and found utopia. Later, Confucius' ideas were added to and tidied by Mencius during the period of '100 Schools of Philosophy'. (Typically Mencius included an arithmetically logical tax system.) The rulers of the time encouraged philosophers as ornaments to their courts and tutors to their sons and their nobles' families. As long as their views were not too outrageous, most of them said what they liked, and the ruler had no need to listen to them. Yang Shih, a cynic and an Epicurean, wondered 'if cosmically an idea is more important than the bowels', and preached that after death all men are equal in their 'rotten bones'.

The philosophers who had the most immediate influence on the rulers of the time were the Legalists.[2] They believed that man's nature was bad (a belief much less commonplace in China than in Europe) and could only be restrained by severe laws, rigidly enforced. Han Fei-tzu, the founder of the school, believed that major crime would be prevented if all minor crimes were, without exception, punished by death. In Legalist theory the state was supreme, its aim was conquest, and its ruler absolute.

The Lord Shang, a practical Legalist and one of the early advisers of the semi-barbarian state of Ch'in in the northwest, ordered that all trades and crafts should be suppressed as distractions from the main occupations of soldiering, farming, and weaving. Nobles who failed to distinguish themselves militarily were demoted; and the clothes, land, and servants allowed to those of different ranks were laid down in detail. The Lord Shang conquered the state of Wei, where he had been born, by asking the Wei prince to a parley and there taking him prisoner. In the end the Lord Shang was too much even for the Ch'in ruler who ordered him to be torn to pieces by chariots. (Typically – most of the Legalists came to unpleasant ends.) But the Ch'in state had started on its expansion over North China. The final conquest of the independent princes and the Chou overlord was completed in 221 B.C. by Ch'in Shih-huang-ti, advised by another Legalist, Li Ssu.

Li Ssu encouraged Ch'in Shih-huang-ti to massacre the 400,000 soldiers who had surrendered to him, and scatter the ashes of minor criminals in the streets of his capital. He and his imperial master broke the power of the great feudal families, and for the first time the emperor ruled through civil and military officers appointed by him to govern for a term of years.

The most famous of all the Ch'in achievements is the Great Wall: the mark of the northern boundary between China and the barbarian steppe. The wall stretched 2,000 miles east to west, over mountains and desert, rock and shifting sand dunes. It took Ch'in Shih-huang-ti 12 years to build, his best administrators and troops, and most of the resources of the newly united country. Heavy taxes were raised to pay for the wall, and anyone who crossed the emperor's pleasure was sent to labour on it. One of the most famous legends in China is about the princess from one of the newly conquered states whose husband was sent to work on the wall. He died, and she set out to find him. A spirit told her to cut her finger, hold it before her, and follow the trail of blood. It took her to her husband's body.[3]

Most of Ch'in Shih-huang-ti's wall was constructed by joining together and strengthening the older walls which had protected the small Chou states. Garrisons were stationed behind the wall, and there were defensive watchtowers every few hundred yards where archers could fight off horsemen's attacks.[4] After Ch'in Shih-huang-ti other emperors rebuilt and repaired the wall; and on the best known section near Peking today a troop of horsemen can ride abreast on the broad ramp between the side walls.

Part of Ch'in Shih-huang-ti's purpose when he built the wall was to end frequent barbarian raids on the plains people. Another aim, however, less generally acknowledged by his contemporaries and successors, was to keep the Chinese in as well as the barbarian out. The wall was built roughly along the line of the rising Mongolian plateau where rainfall becomes too scanty for intensive cultivation by hand on the orthodox Chinese model. Settlers beyond the wall needed bigger farms, animals and ploughs, not hoes. They were more thinly scattered than farmers in China proper, and more difficult to control and protect. They were also likely to ally with the

barbarian and shelter politicalmal contents – generally an admini/
strative problem for which there was no room in a tidy Legalist
state.

The Great Wall was never particularly successful at keeping the
barbarians out of China. Pushed back beyond the Wall the bar/
barians built up their own political structure independently of the
Chinese, and in times of dynastic weakness went round the Great
Wall or through its less guarded points. (Its whole length was,
naturally, seldom kept in repair.) Barbarian kingdoms set up in the
northern plains after great slaughter and destruction were to punctuate
Chinese history.

The Wall was, however, more successful as a boundary to Chinese
settlement. There continued to be scattered farms beyond the
Wall and strong emperors sent out military expeditions into the
Steppe country. But the protection given the outlying settlers
was sporadic, and the imperial court at most periods disapproved
of them. Similarly the far/flung military expeditions were not the
first step in the eventual Chinese colonization of new country, but
sorties to show the Chinese flag, revenge raids, and enlist new allies.

The main tide of Chinese colonization set south and west, away
from the danger of barbarian raids. This was approved of and
encouraged by the imperial court. Ch'in Shih/huang/ti, like other
strong emperors after him, needed settled new lands to feed his large
army. In his search for them he sent a military expedition over the
hills to the south of the Yellow River to conquer the Szechuan basin
in the middle reaches of the Yangtze valley. Szechuan is one of the
richest regions in China. In Ch'in Shih/huang/ti's day it was
already irrigated, and had a large grain surplus.

Later Ch'in Shih/huang/ti sent expeditions over most of what is
now China. Ch'in armies conquered the region around what was
to be Canton, and moved into Vietnam. But the unification and
settlement of the whole of China was not completed for another
thousand years. From Peking to Canton, north to south through
China, is farther than from Moscow to Paris. East–west, across the
width of the country, it is 1,400 miles up the Yangtze from Shanghai

to Chungking, and beyond Chungking there are hundreds of miles of mountains before the present western border. After the USSR and Canada China is the third largest country in the world.

In this continent of a country the main areas of modern settlement were to be the old northern centre of the Yellow River valley and its coastal plain; the Yangtze valley, particularly Szechuan and the delta of the river; and the West River valley and delta in the south, with the other surrounding valleys among the lower southern hills. These hills do not reach the coast on the southeast, and along the sea here there was more good arable land. The last settled farming area in China was the Yunnan plateau in the far southwest. Between these centres of farming and settlement there still are vast stretches of barren mountainous country. Less than a seventh of the Chinese countryside can be used for arable farming.

For more than a thousand years after the first Ch'in expeditions the imperial armies pushed their way over this inhospitable land. Little was known about the country and local tribespeople were often hostile. The south and the Yangtze valley was densely overgrown with forest, where tigers were the most feared wild beasts.[5] Most of the Chinese farmers who settled in the new country were soldiers from the armies. They married local women whose existing families were either killed or driven into the less fertile country. Sometimes tribal chiefs were given Chinese titles and offices, and they and their peoples, after a few generations, forgot their tribal origins. Sometimes the soldiers were backed by imperially encouraged migrants.

Farmers around Canton (now known as Kwangchow) still call themselves 'T'ang People' after the dynasty that arranged their settlement; and still speak, in the extreme south, a variant of the dialect common round Peking. A contemporary poet, at the time of this T'ang migration, wrote of the strangeness of the south:

> 'In the Southern Land many birds sing;
> of towns and cities half are unwalled.
> The country markets are thronged by wild tribes;
> the mountain villages bear river-names.

Poisonous mists rise from the damp sands;
strange fires gleam through the night-rain.
And none passes but the lonely seeker of pearls
year by year on his way to the South Sea.'[6]

At the end of the thirteenth century Marco Polo described China as two lands. The north he called 'Cathay', and the south 'Manji'. Even now, although every inch of arable land in the south is settled, it is still a strange country to the northerner.

The very languages of the south are incomprehensible in the north. The same written language is used all over China. (One of the common sights of any city used to be the traveller writing out wants he could not talk about in an alien dialect.) And over the last decades schoolchildren throughout China have also been taught the Peking dialect whatever their mother tongue was. But in the south and far southwest, particularly, many farmers still cannot speak anything other than their local language. This may not be properly understood even in the next village. In the province of Fukien alone there are 108 different dialects. Cantonese itself is a lighter language with more tones in it than the Peking dialect. A particularly good language, Chinese say, for intrigue—political or amorous.

Southern village houses are built of straw and wattle rather than the bricks of the north. There is no need for the ovens and heated bedplaces which make the northern winter tolerable; and because the southern hills are better wooded than the north, wood, rather than dried dung, is used for fuel. The farmers grow rice, not wheat or millet, and, where the country and markets are suitable, tea, tropical fruits and vegetables. Farm animals and transport differ to the north and south of the Yangtze. In the north farmers use small donkeys and wheelbarrows; in the south men's (and women's) backs or buffaloes on the farms are used. In the southern cities the rich at one time were carried in sedan chairs.

The south is above all a different-looking country. Chinese landscape painters have seldom been interested in the flat, dusty northern plains where only the villages, and the groups of trees

20

around surviving grave plots break the monotony of endless fields. Northern roads and village streets are wide and straight, so are the irrigation canals, and even the high dykes banking the much worked rivers of the plain. Some artists have drawn the Shantung hills of the northeast in their wild descent to the sea; but Shantung has a reputation as a dour province, something like the lowlands of Scotland, not given to the fine arts. Many more landscape painters have drawn the southern hills, the groves of bamboos there, and the terraced valleys. The most painted country of all is the curious karst landscape of the far south round Canton. Old limestone there has weathered into overhanging cliffs, caves, and the perpendicular, sugar-loaf type mountains which are characteristic of one sort of Chinese landscape picture. Southern streams, faster-flowing and more romantic than the great rivers of the north provide what the accepted masters of the classic painting taught was a necessary part of a balanced picture: wild country, rocks, water and trees.

As the armies and settlers pushing down from the north explored the country that was to be China, they were halted to the east by the Pacific Ocean, and to the west by the Himalayas, the other mountain ranges, and the deserts. In the northeast Korea, off and on, was a Chinese province; and there was trade with Japan. But beyond Japan the Pacific, for 2,000 years, was the end of the possible world. To the west, however, even the Himalayas could be crossed over the high passes, and for 1,500 years there was a limited exchange of ideas and trade with north India through the mountains. Tibet, off and on like Korea, acknowledged Chinese suzerainty.

North of the Himalayas better developed trade routes through the desert oases linked China to central Asia and the West. Some evidence suggests that 2,000 years ago the central Asian climate was wetter than it is now, the oases bigger, and the region more important. Through the oases China sold silk to the Roman Empire. The Roman economists worried about the export of Roman bullion to China to pay for this silk, and the Roman moralists thundered at the women who deserted honest, heavy homespun in favour of the soft transparencies from the 'Seres' (the Chinese: the silk makers – the only silk makers of the time). But the trade went on through intermediaries, and the two empires knew only rumours about each other.

However, it is in the south that Chinese border provinces merge most easily into what are now neighbouring states. North and central Vietnam were, for most of 2,000 years, governed as Chinese provinces. To the rest of Southeast Asia it is a short and relatively easy sea journey from South China. There is evidence of Han dynasty trade with Indonesia and Malaya in the second and first centuries B.C. There was probably some trade even earlier than that, from northern ports, before the south coast of China had been colonized by the Chinese.

At the beginning of our own millennium when the Sung dynasty were pushed south by the advancing Mongols, fleets were sent out to explore the southern seas. In 1178 Chou Ch'u-fei described the ships of the time as 'like houses. When their sails are spread they are like great clouds in the sky. Their rudders are several tens of feet long. A single ship carries several hundred men.' These ships carried Chinese ceramics as far as the east coast of Africa; and there was a well established sea trade with Ceylon, India, and Southeast Asia. The Indian rajahs particularly valued the Chinese green celadon plates because they believed the plates would change colour if poisoned food was put on them.

Under strong emperors, like Kublai Khan, part of the trade which came back to China was theoretically tribute from subordinate states. What came from China was then, again in theory, not equal trade but gifts to loyal subjects. Sometimes these claims to suzerainty were backed by governors, sent by the Chinese court, and naval or military expeditions; but how effective the empire was varied immensely from decade to decade. Sometimes even the pretence of tribute, although not the actual trading was dropped altogether.

Officially there was no Chinese settlement overseas. Special, and rarely given, imperial permission was needed for any Chinese to live outside China. But the groups of illegal settlers grew. Nearly all of them came from the four southern, and overcrowded provinces of Kwangtung, Kwangsi, Fukien, and Hainan Island. Chinese skill was valued in Southeast Asia and Chinese artisans settled in the major towns. After them came men to be local shopkeepers and to manage the internal trade of the south Asian countries; and in the nineteenth century some of the emigrants were farmers and unskilled labourers. There are now about 14 million Chinese settlers all over Southeast Asia. In most countries they are a sizeable and commercially important minority, and in the old Malaysia, with Singapore, there were more Chinese than indigenous Malay people.

As immigrants the disadvantage of the Chinese has been that they did not take the nationality of the country they settled in. Until the recent communist treaties, China did not acknowledge that a Chinese or the descendant of a male Chinese could ever stop being Chinese. Similarly territory that had once been Chinese was, in Chinese eyes, always Chinese. This means that Chinese maps and historians have always made very grand claims. There were recent shocked protests when Chinese communist maps showed parts of the Indian mountains and much of Southeast Asia as Chinese; but these maps could be paralleled by Ming, Sung and T'ang claims, and by maps published more recently by the Kuomintang. In the 1940s geography textbooks for Overseas Chinese schools marked most of Southeast Asia as Chinese provinces.

Nevertheless the Chinese do not think of these provinces as part of the Central Kingdom, China proper. To a Chinese 'his native place' is where he or his family originally came from. In Southeast Asia, and to some extent in the much later settlements in Manchuria and Sinkiang, the Chinese have taken a very British view of their empire. They live there temporarily, making their fortunes, and bringing 'the benefits of civilization' to the natives, and then they retire 'home'. A typical, pre-communist, emigrant pattern was for a young man to marry in his native village, leave his wife with his family, either pregnant or with a small baby (preferably, of course, a boy), and go to make his fortune overseas or in the empty northern lands. He might stay away ten, twenty or thirty years without his wife joining him, but he would send her and his family money. Ideally he returned with enough savings to buy a farm, support an honoured old age, and be buried in the family grave plots. In Chinese tradition it was a deplorable accident if the settler had to remain outside China; no other country could properly become his home, be a place where he could with full self respect leave his bones and establish his family worship.

3   The Order of Society

To the educated upper class of eighteenth-century
Europe, particularly eighteenth-century England, Chinese Society
seemed almost wholly admirable. Chinese art, architecture, and
gardening were admired and copied. The state was orderly; far
better ordered than parts of Europe. The common people were
industrious and skilled. They were governed by an effective civil
service and a despot, all of them made benevolent (at any rate in
their professed sentiments) by their regard for the Confucian system
of law and learning.

'Li', propriety, the Chinese gentleman's control and balance,
was achieved through education and maturity. Its outward expressions were good manners, a concern for the structure and formality
of human relations, and a desire to arrive at the right course of
action – the narrow path between two wrongs. As in eighteenth-
century England, over-enthusiasm and excessive piety were
condemned as suitable only for women and servants.

Yet it was a mistake, one made by many of the eighteenth-century
sinophiles, to see Confucius, the sage of this society, as a more
prominent, Chinese Lord Chesterfield. Confucius himself insisted
that he was a historian rather than a religious innovator or a meta-
physician. 'I have transmitted and do not create anew', he wrote in
the *Analects*. 'I am faithful to the men of old and love them.' (The
men of old were the god-kings of the Hsia and Chou dynasties and
their subjects.) By proper behaviour – the emperor and the officials
to the people, the people to their superiors and to each other – this
old Utopia could be re-created. It is a belief that the English and
French eighteenth century could parallel by reference to Greece and
Rome, or to the more primitive golden age discussed by Rousseau

among others. (Like the Chinese Rousseau believed that the conduct necessary to re-create this golden age would come 'naturally' to the properly educated.)

However, where the eighteenth-century view of this admirable, rational China went wrong was in forgetting that the Utopian Golden Age was partly magical. In their regulations about conduct, family, and state life, Confucius and his most influential follower, Mencius, included rites and sacrifices. Books on astrology, geo-mancy, and the appeasement of the gods were part of the Confucian classic (although most of them described traditions established long before Confucius' time); and these books became a respectable part of the examination syllabus of the scholar officials. By the standards of contemporary Europe, Chinese society of every rank was extremely superstitious.

It was an earthy sort of superstition. Chinese in a position to be moderately comfortable in this world were seldom concerned with the perils or rewards of the next. What was aimed at was the placating of forces which could make life uncomfortable in this world for those who accidentally crossed them; and the enlistment of magic on one's own side for one's own earthly advantage.

The most likely magical powers to do an injury to people were ghosts, demons, and dragons. Most villages boasted their own haunted places; and dragons, as well as broken dykes, were held responsible for floods. Moreover just as it was the official's duty to see that dykes were kept repaired, so he should placate local dragons by appropriate ceremonies. Proper rites were also needed to lay the evil ghosts of women who had died in childbirth, and the fox fairies who killed men with the importunity of their love-making.

Geomancy was the study of the proper placing of buildings so that the spirits of earth and heaven would be favourable to them. Geomancers were consulted during the nineteenth century, not only about the placing of tombs and palaces, but also about roads and military defences. It was better, orthodox Chinese officials con-sidered, to have a gun ineffectively placed, than one that was mili-tarily effective, but offensive to the spirit of the harbour it guarded. Geomancy was one of the most respectable of the magic sciences.

The proper balancing of earth forces – wind, direction, outlook, and soil – was closely allied to the ethical balances of propriety.

In the home magic and religious belief were more important to peasant families and to women than to men of rank. The most important of the minor deities of the household was the hearth god. He watched over the amity of family life and could be offended, not only by quarrelling, but also by such breaches of etiquette as a woman combing her hair in his sight. His paper image was burnt each year as part of the celebration of the greatest of the Chinese holidays, the New Year; and to sweeten the report he then made to heaven he had honey smeared on his mouth. In the village temples the gods charged with bringing rain could be recalled to their duties by being ducked, head first, into a pot of water. Similarly in times of too much rain the god's image would be left out overnight to appreciate for itself how much water there was about.

Much of the popular magic and rites in Chinese life came from Taoism. Taoism was formulated during the same period of philo‑ sophic speculation and political disorder as Confucianism; but it was a religion for the individual, not for society. The Tao is 'the way' of natural harmony; and if an individual could place himself on the way, in tune with nature, he was assured of happiness, long life, whatever he most wanted. Sometimes this search for natural har‑ mony could be for evil ends, achieved by magic. Taoist priests assured their early imperial converts that their spells could offer them unlimited power (who could successfully oppose him if the emperor had the forces of nature on his side), or immortality. Chinese mythology abounds in Taoist sages mixing the elixir of life. Yet equally Taoism could lead to a religion of great kindness to men and animals who were fellow‑travellers on the way. Or Taoism could be the religion of hermits who must be undistracted by the world in their search. However, in most educated men, Taoist principles of natural harmony merged imperceptibly into Confucian balances of propriety.

Buddhism, the only alien religion to become popular in China, established itself in another, later period of civil disturbance, 'the

Three Kingdoms', between the Han and the T'ang dynasties in the third century A.D. It was brought over the Himalayas from India; and one group of the Sutras was translated by six or seven men. There was a Hindu who knew no Chinese, but did know the scripture, a Parthian who could speak Hindi and Chinese, and four or five scholarly Chinese who spoke only their own language.

Buddhism and Taoism both became important religions for artists, writers, and artisans. Only educated men, or occasionally women, so the Chinese thought, could understand poetry or paint/ ings. Philosophical historical, and religious education was needed to understand the allusions of poetry and painting and fill out the shorthand notes of the artist into his finished vision. Education was even more necessary for anyone wanting to write or paint themselves with the admired conciseness and restraint. In a painting of bamboos, or a literary mention of them, the educated saw wise gentleness swaying with the wind of change but not breaking. In the imagery of tossing willows sensitive artists described beautiful and changeable women.

In painting it was particularly important to know the Taoist mysteries and to be in tune with the natural scene. One should, said the Sung pundits, be able to chose a path, take a walk through a painting, and lose oneself. During the Sung dynasty particularly the great painters claimed that they needed the Taoist vision of natural harmony before they could work, a miraculous revelation of the path and picture they must paint. Taoist magic and spells were used in studios to induce this miracle. Even retired officials of the period who had been orthodox Confucians during their working life, were converted to Taoism when they turned to the arts in their old age.

However, in the centuries after the Sung dynasty the education needed fully to understand or to paint a picture became formalized. Inspiration and magic were partly replaced by pattern books of trees, mountains and lakes painted by the old masters. Court painters chose and carefully copied those appropriate to the emotions they desired to convey, and assembled them in their pictures accord/ ing to the rules laid down in the book. Other painters, determined to show themselves amateur, made deliberate mistakes of technique.

A picture which was too perfect became the mark of the insincere artisan rather than the genuinely inspired scholar artists.

Buddhism's contribution to the Chinese artistic tradition was more popular, less acknowledged by Confucian scholars. When the first Buddhist monk from India, according to legend, arrived at the oasis of Tun-huang, on the western border of China, he had a vision in which he was told to dig a cave and establish a monastery. Later, as the monastery became one of the richest in China, the caves were painted in a curious mixture of Indian and Chinese tradition. Chinese-dressed T'ang courtiers standing around the T'ang emperor were edged by Indian demons. The Buddha on his lotus, as in thousands of Indian paintings, has around him Chinese dragons, Chinese-robed maids and a dark-skinned Indian groom.

The decoration of the caves continued for a thousand years from the Wei period of the fifth century A.D. to the later Sung. Most of the work was done by journeymen monks who travelled from the caves to other Buddhist temples painting and carving for their keep. The ideas they took with them from their contacts with India influenced painters, potters, and sculptors throughout China.

It was the duty of the Buddhist religious artists to show the Buddhas and scenes from their lives so that they were understood by the ordinary people; and the new skills spread from the models, carvings, and paintings of the gods to artistic work concerned with ordinary and court life, animals, and country scenes. At the end of the T'ang period the southern painters were producing the delicately detailed, botanically and zoologically accurate, paintings of insects and flowers which has since been one of the most enduring schools of traditional painting.

Buddhist priests played a large part in most funerals; and the transmigration of souls was the most comforting doctrine of life after death that the Chinese had. A Taoist hermit was a valued ornament to the country estate of a retired official with literary leanings. But both religions' most ardent followers were among the poor, and their influence grew in times of natural troubles. In the third century B.C., after a drought in Shantung, the Taoist crowds drifted in disorder over the province, singing and dancing to the Mother Queen of the West. (There were similar scenes during the Black Death in east Europe. However, on that occasion the starving dancers invoked the Virgin Mary as Queen of Heaven.)

By the eighteenth century it was rare for Buddhism or Taoism to play a major part in the religious sense of an educated man. Taoism had become above all the religion of bandits, and of semi-criminal secret societies. The members were bound to each other by magic oaths, and protected, so they believed, by Taoist spells. Both Buddhism and Taoism were associated with sexual licence in their monasteries and nunneries, and petty extortion from the poor.

However, in spite of the scandals of the past, for the last centuries of the empire the two religions were a tolerated and tolerating part of Chinese village life. Their gods shared the villagers' devotion with the ancestors authorized by the Confucian classics, and the yet older gods and ghosts of the particular neighbourhood. Buddhist, Taoist, and Confucian temples existed happily side by side; and people took a little of each doctrine to formulate their individual philosophies, so that they were able to regulate the ordinary details of their daily lives.

Most people, particularly the educated, used the balanced system of Confucian ethics. Confucius had laid down five personal relationships on which, he said, the welfare of the state depended. They were: subject to ruler, parent to child, husband to wife, older brother to younger brother, and friend to friend. Four of the relationships concerned Chinese private not public life, and three of them defined precisely the duties and obligations within the family.

In practice the most important relationship to a Chinese came to be that of parent and child, particularly father and son. A married woman (and it was a parent's duty to ensure the marriage of his daughter), lived with her husband's family. But for a son nothing could be too much to show his reverence for his parents.

A man who lost a leg or an arm in an accident might, in the Confucian examples, properly kill himself, because he had injured the body his parents gave him. It was a son's duty to sacrifice his life not only for his parents' safety, but also for their comfort or whims. His duty to them took precedence over any public duty. If the father of a good official should commit a crime, the son must take his old father on his back and they must both flee the state together.[7]

Ideally the Confucians envisaged a large joint family. Recent research has exploded the myth that this large family living under one roof was common.[8] (The average size of a twentieth-century, pre-communist, Chinese household was five, and so it probably had been in past centuries.) But the large joint families that did exist were important as a goal to which many Chinese aspired.[9]

These large families could consist of as many as 100 people living in connected courtyards surrounded by high walls. Most of the courtyards had several rooms built round them, including a living-room furnished with heavily carved tables, chairs, and chests. The rooms, if the courtyard was a pleasant one, opened on to an enclosed garden. The Chinese do not have the British passion for lawns; but where possible they plant small trees, often pines or bamboos, and they dig pools and divert streams to bring water into their garden. A 'full moon' bridge, high-arched, so that it and its reflection in the water make a perfect circle, is an admired garden ornament; so are curiously shaped rocks, and large pots of the flowers of the season.

The largest room in the joint family's house would be the hall in which hung the names of the ancestors and, if possible, their portraits. On feast days it would be the duty of all the family to watch the grandfather light incense on the central altar, and offer food and wine. Then, in order of family seniority, everyone present would bow to the ancestors and then to the older living members of the family.

The best and sunniest courtyard, where the grandparents lived, was generally close to the ancestral hall. Remaining courtyards housed married sons or male cousins, each with their own wife, children, and servants. Except on feast days each small family lived very much its own life, cooking and working separately. Each wife took her turn at attending her parents-in-law. The children played together, and shared a tutor. They were taught to call their cousins 'brother' or 'sister', and to honour their grandparents, uncles and aunts.

The least comfortable place in the family belonged to the youngest wife. Traditionally she had been married without seeing her husband, and she was under the strictest obligations to her parents-in-law. Her husband would have to divorce her if his parents complained seriously about her manners to them or her conduct. (It is perhaps not surprising that J. Lossing Buck discussing the population figures for Chinese villages in the 1930s, notes comparatively few women in their twenties and thirties. This was due, he concludes to the dangers of child-bearing and the number of suicides.)[10] But, if she survived, a grandmother became a matriarch, generally more concerned than her husband in the day-to-day ordering of the household, and honoured, rather than obedient to her sons and grandsons.

Very few of these large households lasted more than one or two generations. Even in rich families the death of the grandparents generally released each son to a separate house. But, like even the poorest of ordinary Chinese families, these households stayed part of a larger clan organization. These clans were for the majority of Chinese the bottom and most important layer of Chinese government. In the southern villages, particularly, one or two clans included all the villagers. The clan head was the senior man of the senior branch of the family; and there was also a clan council to govern the village. The clan cared for a joint ancestral hall, and kept genealogical books. It often provided for the education of able boys with poor parents. It ordered the farming of land, maintained local irrigation canals and paths, and collected taxes. All minor disputes between its members were settled by the clan elders.

Outside the clans the law was purposefully harsh. It was meant to punish only the most terrible crimes, to impress the people with the majesty of the state, and to discourage frivolous litigation. Plaintiff and defendant knelt throughout the case between a line of armed constables. Witnesses, whose evidence the magistrate doubted, were beaten on the spot. Chinese law refused to condemn a criminal except on his own confession. Torture was therefore used to extract these confessions. 'Severe' executions could be both cruel and prolonged.

Too many law cases were, moreover, a condemnation of the magistrate in charge of the district. Theoretically he governed by force of his own good example, rather than through his legal powers. He was exhorted to take a father's benevolent interest in his people, admonish rather than punish minor wrong-doing, and reward the virtuous. It was a much prized mark of honour for an official tablet to be placed outside the door of a house where a large family lived in noted amity.

The good official, concerned with the order and happiness of his district, worked with the clans. He apportioned taxes and responsibilities among them; but he interfered as little as possible with their internal affairs and with individual quarrels. Reliance on the clans was necessary because there were anyway not enough officials for detailed administration. A population of about 100 million during the great dynasties was administered by 20,000 or fewer officials. (The Indian Civil Service under British rule had the same very low proportion of administrative officials to the total population. They were also encouraged to take a benevolent interest in the people they governed, but not to interfere in minor matters.)

The country was divided into provinces which were sub-divided into prefectures, sub-prefectures and counties. To avoid corruption officials were not allowed to work in their native provinces; and in principle they were moved into new districts every three years. The better the official the more often he was moved.

At the centre the emperor's ministers were there to advise him, and to be responsible for the different departments. There were dossiers on the whole civil service, reporting on their health, the good order in their districts, their characters, and their morals – particularly on their filial piety. An official could be executed for peculiarly shocking acts, like patricide, in his district even though he had had nothing to do with the crime. His example, it was argued, must have been bad.

Traditionally officials (foreigners called them 'Mandarins') were recruited through examinations of increasing difficulty in the Confucian classics. Each candidate was given two or three sentences from a classic to comment on, and a subject for an essay taken from

33

classical times. By the eighteenth century acceptable comment had become stereotyped. Candidates were expected to produce 'eight-legged' essays with the approved divisions, links, and summary of subject matter. In order to pass the examination candidates had not only to know most of the classics by heart so as to recognize quotations, but also to be so soaked in classical analogy and ethics that the proper Confucian sentiments came naturally to them when they were thinking fast and under stress.

The idea of a civil service recruited on merit through examinations dates back at least to the Han dynasty. Almost as ancient are complaints that the examination was too remote from the actual needs of government. Under the Sungs, in the twelfth century, the Prime Minister, Wang An-shih, tried to include in the syllabus questions on astronomy, law, philosophy and government, which candidates could not answer simply by classical quotations. But his reforms were not permanent. Nor were similar attempts at reform at the beginning of the Ming and Ch'ing dynasties.

China had no hereditary nobility on the scale of Europe's. During the interregnums, and in periods of imperial weakness, powerful families would increase their landholdings, their power over the tenants and the smaller people of the neighbourhood, and their central influence. But it was part of the policy of each new strong founder of a dynasty to break this sort of power. New nobles might be created from the new emperor's own supporters, but their ascendency was often limited to themselves or to the next few generations. The Ch'ing nobility, typically, operated on a descending scale, each generation declining one rung in privileges and rank. The same process happened automatically to those whose power was based on ordinary wealth or landholding. China, in striking contrast to Europe, had no custom of primo-geniture; or even of particular priority to the immediate family. A man's destitute brothers, cousins, and nephews might customarily claim part of his land equally with his sons.

Even in times of imperial decline, when a neighbourhood had both rich men and nobles, the local officials were more respected and, if any imperial power at all remained, more powerful.[11] A saying current during the decline of the Ming dynasty was 'The poor should never antagonize the rich and the rich should never antagonize the officials.'[12] Officials were even legally privileged, they were liable to different sorts of punishment, generally less severe, and they were exempt from forced labour. (This was the particular hardship that an energetic emperor inflicted on ordinary peasants.)

Wealthy landlords naturally had social advantages over their poor neighbours. They could hire substitutes for forced labour or army conscription. If the central government was too weak to exercise proper control, they could bribe, not so much the district magistrate himself, as his Yamen clerks. These small officials who were natives of the districts, unlike the magistrate, knew local conditions and were subject to local pressures. Their corruption was the constant complaint of their superiors. (Again compare British India: with the foreign, if uncorrupt, magistrate seldom aware of all the intricacies of the law suits he tried; an easy and frequent dupe for his corrupt local clerk.)

Under the Ch'ing the rich themselves became small local officials, and leaders of the '100 family' groupings with some legal power. They could also buy minor official standing; but only in the last and worst days of the empire did most of these bought offices carry any real government power with them.

In better times a family spent its money on buying education for its children. Those sons who could profit by it passed the official examinations and entered the bureaucracy. The stupid brother, incapable of passing the examination, was left to look after the family estates. If he could, he ran them from the neighbouring town, only going out into the country when he needed to collect his rents. Except in parts of Szechuan there was no Chinese tradition of resident squirearchy, interested in their tenants' lives, and withheld by ethical and neighbourly considerations from pressing them too hard. Nor was it part of Confucian ethics to be particularly sparing of tenants. A stupid brother or a land agent's first duty was to extract enough from the tenants, at whatever cost to them, to support the old and the official members of the family.

The prolonged schooling and the private tutors the rich could afford for their sons gave them an advantage in the examinations, but never an overwhelming one. Under the early Sung 46·1 per cent of officials were classed as coming from 'humble' families[13] (although how 'humble' and poor they actually were is not clear). The majority of officials at all periods came from comparatively prosperous families where their fathers, grandfathers, or uncles had also been officials.[14] The very highest officials were even allowed to enter a son into the bureaucracy without his passing the proper examinations. But the clan system and the encouragement of free or cheap schools meant that there was an opening for very poor boys. 'The blacksmith Chu-jun', 'the shoe-repairer scholar', were the nicknames of good Ming officials. Once in the system the poor boys would be given at least equal opportunity of advancement with the rich man's son. If the empire was at a peak of strength and order, possibly they were given even more opportunities. The poor boy who makes good is a hero very much in the Chinese tradition. Mere wealth and idleness were not considered to produce good characters (a belief in contrast to the common English assumption that gentle birth and rearing produce some merit even in the most stupid). A hard-working peasant's family, on the other hand, was, the Chinese thought, an admirable nursery for incorruptible virtue. Moreover most emperors considered it greatly in their own interest to encourage the scholar from the poor home. The rich and noble had other sources of power, the poor scholar depended entirely on the government.

Servants, who were absolutely dependent on him – poor officials without the ordinary connexions of the scholar gentry class, eunuchs, even men who had failed to pass the official examinations – were needed by a strong Chinese emperor. The emperors were isolated. In theory their power was absolute. The classics laid down that a supreme ruler was a necessity for good government. A concept, like that of medieval Europe, of the king as only the first among his equals would have been as shocking to Confucian Chinese as later concepts of kings restrained by Parliament or the popular will. Moreover a weak emperor endangered the position of the officials and exposed their estates to the raids of bandits and rebellions of the peasants.

Yet to the orthodox Confucians the strong emperors were dubious figures. In theory the emperor was a Confucian, yet it was not uncommon for a ruler restoring order to kill or exile most of his family. It was also in the imperial interest to reduce the inflated power of the gentry by tax and land reforms. Most of the emperors could, and did, quote Confucian and Mencian precedents for what they were doing, but their officials were still doubtful. The emperor was acting with un-Confucian forcefulness, and it was the estates of the officials themselves which often suffered.

The established channel for official criticism and reproof of the emperors was the Board of Censors. This was made up of distin-guished and elderly officials, many of them men whose courage stands out in the contemporary accounts. The emperors were likely to reward unwelcome advice with flogging, exile, or an unpleasant death. Less courageous junior officials could show a polite disagree-ment with imperial policies by resigning on one of the numerous grounds of bereavement or pressing family duties sanctioned by the Confucian code. Or an official could commit suicide after sending a letter of reproaches. (This had the additional advantage that his ghost would haunt the erring emperor.) But the official's own reputation and his family would be compromised, if he made no protest, tacit or open, about mistaken policies. He also endangered the peace of the country and the continuation of the dynasty.

Misrule could upset the balance of heaven and earth, and cause the emperor to lose his Mandate from Heaven: his right to rule. This mandate was conditional – very unlike the seventeenth-century European Divine Right of Kings to rule badly and still retain their thrones. While the emperor held it he was, whatever the practical tensions between him and his bureaucracy, the Son of Heaven. Rebellion was blasphemy. But once his mandate had been lost, whether by misrule or natural calamity, rebellion was justified and sure to succeed. (As in Europe, of course, the test of whether the emperor had lost his mandate was whether the rebellion succeeded.) Individually a servant of the fallen emperor might with honour remain faithful to him and to his family personally. (Many of the Ming officials refused to serve the first Ch'ing emperor.) But the duty of the scholar class as a whole was to secure the throne as an institution and re-establish earthly order. This meant that even the sons of an official, who had resigned when a dynasty fell, could with propriety and family approval serve the new emperor.

As Son of Heaven the emperor had a son's duties to sacrifice to his god-ancestors. If he neglected his religious duties, just as surely as if he neglected his civil duties, the balance would be upset, heaven's wrath would fall upon the country, and he would lose his mandate. For these religious duties the Ming emperors built the blue-tiled Temple of Heaven in Peking. At the winter solstice the emperor sacrificed a perfect young bull there to safeguard the farmer's year. In this, as in his other religious duties, he claimed ancestry from the Hsias, the imperial god-farmers. Like them theoretically, he grew his own grain for the imperial rites from a sacred field of god. It was ploughed ceremonially by the emperor himself and his ministers at dawn in winter. (They were dressed in traditional silk robes and high white court boots.) Each season he went to the appropriate city gate to welcome the new change in the farm year: the north gate for winter, the east for spring, the south for summer, and the west for autumn. In theory, during the spring, the empress gathered her own mulberry leaves from the palace sacred grove for her own silkworms. She wound the silk from them, spun it, and wove it. Then she embroidered the sacrificial robes herself, as the legendary Empress Lei-tzu had, and as a good farm-wife should. (In practice this time-consuming part of the ritual was delegated by busy empresses, like the nineteenth-century Empress Dowager, Tzu Hsi, to the junior concubines.)

From Chou times onwards there are records in Chinese literature of these rites, and of the way the emperors lived. There were great imperial palaces with walls enclosing gardens, lakes and hunting forests. Chinese building, however, is mainly of wood and mud brick. When a dynasty fell the old emperor's palace was generally sacked and burnt, often with the rest of his capital city. There was no traditional capital in China. The later Ming, and the Manchus (the Ch'ing) used Peking because it was close to their homelands and the centre of their power. But other dynasties had their capitals at Loyang, Sian, Hangchow, Kaifeng and Nanking.

Sian still has the remains of a small imperial palace. But the great Ming-built, Ch'ing-restored, palace at Peking is what both travellers and Chinese now think of as the heart of China. Traditionally, administrative buildings were within the palace or close to it. Under the Ch'ings, the Imperial palace, 'the Forbidden City', was surrounded by the Manchu city of Peking. Outside this city's walls was yet another city for possibly rebellious Chinese.

The Peking palace itself, behind walls of ochre red, is of paved courtyards, contained by marble steps and terraces. Each terrace leads into an open hall with pillars lacquered red, gold, green, and blue. The roofs are of shining yellow tiles, whose upcurves end in carvings of the dragons, unicorns, and phoenixes who guard the buildings. Until the most recent office blocks were put up, the palace was the highest building in Peking. Nobody could overlook the emperor. Even now its huge walls and gates still dwarf the people who walk through them. The lines and colours are sharpened and heightened by the clear, dry air during most of Peking's year.

The emperors furnished this most beautiful of palaces according to their very varied tastes. The halls were the living quarters of the imperial families as well as offices and audience chambers. They were heated by charcoal braziers, and hung with carpets, tapestry, and the imperial choice of pictures and objects of art.

The present Chinese government has turned the old palaces into museums for the imperial collections. These vary from the symbolic, poetic Sung landscapes, and the delicately detailed Ming court and hunting scenes, to the great bulk of knick-knacks amassed by Tzu Hsi in the nineteenth century. This formidable old lady professed a great admiration for her contemporary, Queen Victoria, and shared many of her artistic tastes. Tzu Hsi's clocks, statuettes, vases, and mechanical toys from home and abroad are now the much admired centrepieces in several of the Forbidden City museums, and in the Summer Palace, which she herself built just outside Peking.

There she was well served by her landscape gardeners who sited her halls, and the pillared walks linking them between hills and the lake, with twisting paths, bamboos, and flowering bushes round them. It was the last built and most romantically gardened of all the surviving historic buildings.

1 The tomb of Huang Ti (the Yellow Emperor), who ruled China in about 2000 B.C., has today been restored and re-dedicated to 'the father of the Han People'. This conjectural drawing of the emperor dates from the Chou dynasty (second–first centuries B.C.).

2 The Great Wall of China built during the Chou dynasty by Chi'n Shih-huang-ti is now considered a 'proud achievement of the working classes'. The primary reason for its construction was to prevent barbarians from entering Chinese territory.

氏 轅 軒 帝 黄

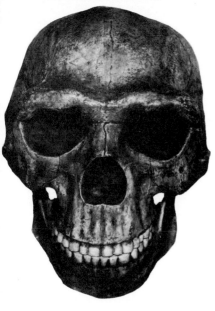

3 A reconstruction of the skull of Peking Man, who lived half a million years ago, represents the earliest known human-type in China.

4 This Neolithic Kansu pot discovered in China is about 7,000 years old and reflects the skilled craftsmanship of the Neolithic villagers.

5 The Shang dynasty produced many beautiful bronze objects including this ritual axe or jüeh which dates from the twelfth or eleventh centuries B.C.

6 This bronze bull's-head inlaid with gold and silver belongs to the Chou dynasty (c. 1027–256 B.C.).

7 Under the communist régime China's tradition and culture are respected by the young and old. Places of historical interest such as the dragon pavilions in Peihai Park, Peking are well maintained and much visited.

8 A modern young student copying a T'ang mural (sixth–ninth centuries A.D.).

9 Confucius (550–478 B.C.) formulated a philosophy which had a profound influence on the attitudes and beliefs of China's people. This nineteenth-century drawing shows Confucius with a disciple.

10 (*Below left*) By the time of the Han dynasty (206 B.C.–A.D. 220) Confucianism was the established Chinese philosophy. A tomb painting – 'Guests arriving at a funeral feast' – from Liao-Yang, Manchuria, dates from this period.

11 Within a Chinese Confucian society a gentleman's propriety, his control and balance, was achieved primarily through education. This early photograph shows a scholar at home studying for his examinations.

12 To be successful at examinations was essential for social advance. These private examination cells are relics of a system which lasted for many hundred years.

13 The South is a region of impressive scenery such as this landscape on the Lichiang River, Kwangsi Province.

14 The topography and climate of the different regions of China vary greatly. Cultivation on this land, in the West outside Chungking, follows natural terraces.

15 A principally Buddhist shrine shows an amalgam of symbols from other Chinese religious traditions including Taoism and Confucianism.

16 The local theatre has long been part of the tradition of Chinese village life.

17 Traditional observances such as the dragon-boat festival are still respected.

18 These Tibetan peasants are voting for their People's Deputies. Tibet has been part of the Chinese People's Republic since 1956.

19 Two languages, Chinese and Uighur, are used in the autonomous region of Sinkiang.

20 Livestock-breeding is a principal occupation among the inhabitants of Sinkiang. This is in the Ili River valley.

4   Rotting Tradition

'HEAVEN IS HIGH, and the emperor is far away', says one of the most often quoted Chinese proverbs. For over 3,000 years the dynasties came and went. Their collapse brought great misery to the countryside. After the fall of the Ming dynasty in 1644, over a million people were killed in the province of Szechuan alone. The killing and chaos were worse still when there was a long interregnum between the dynasties. Provincial barons struggled for overlordship while most of them were unable to suppress banditry and the violence of their soldiers within their own domains. It was a well founded Chinese tradition, however, that such periods of disorder did not last, any more than did periods of good order.

Even the foreign dynasties did not mark drastic changes of direction in Chinese history. 'China is a sea that salts all the rivers that flow into it', says one proverb.[15] The wife of the Mongol emperor, Kublai Khan, wept, according to the tradition, as she looked at the luxurious, imperial palaces of newly conquered Hangchow. 'It came to me just now,' she said, 'that the empire of the Mongols will end in this manner.' There were only small changes even in ordinary life. The Mongols introduced trousers, wide, brimmed hats, horse-riding and the blue and white pottery glazes first developed in Asia Minor. Under the Manchus Chinese men were made to wear their hair in long queues. There was always some Chinese feeling against barbarian rule; yet, when a well-established foreign dynasty was threatened by popular revolt, the loyalty of most Chinese officials stayed with the Chinese-speaking, Chinese-educated, only theoretically foreign, emperor and his court.

49

Much would be forgiven any government that did not interfere with the people. There are several versions of one of the oldest of the peasant songs:

> *I plough my ground and eat,*
> *I dig my well and drink;*
> *for King or Emperor what use have I?*

It was the government's duty, however, to maintain order that left the farmers free to drink from their own wells and eat the crops from the land they had ploughed. It was often better maintained order than in contemporary Europe. There were no dark ages of the length and destructiveness of those that followed the fall of the Roman Empire in Europe. While travel in the West was still dangerous and difficult the Chinese had good roads on which valuables could safely be moved, an excellent canal system, fast posts and well-maintained inns. Apart from bandits in times of trouble there was little crime or violence in imperial China. Laws were observed, and taxes collected, and remitted to the capital.

During the dynasties in which the civil service worked smoothly, notably the Han, the T'ang, the Sung, and the Ming, the arts flourished. Under the Sung, in their beautiful doomed capital of Hangchow, all of Chinese culture from poetry to cooking reached a new height. Confucian philosophy was debated, synthesized with parts of Taoism and Buddhism, and set in a form that was not to be broken until the end of the empire. The Sung built gardens, high houses, and temples round the lakes of Hangchow. The government was efficient, the court splendid. The Sung, however, despised war and military thinking. The emperors ignored the advice of their generals, provoked the northern barbarians, and made no sacrifices of their comforts or their city's magnificence to avert the Mongol menace which hung ever more threateningly over them.

Yet Sung art was in no way decadent. Since Shang times the Chinese have seen jade as a half magic stone: the symbol of purity and unbending virtue. Under the Sung the jade carvers were skilled enough to make realistic jokes: a miniature jade camel biting its own tail, an equally small tiger growling like a playful St Bernard's puppy. But, as in the other arts, technical skill had not under the Sungs become an end in itself. (Ming and Ch'ing artisans used jade, as they used lacquer and ivory, to show scenes of meticulous detail cut in deep relief. A bow string, the tie of a woman's dress, the separate corn stalks in a sheaf, were all separately carved out into a picture, often of greater interest in its parts than in its general shape and pattern.)

The Sung potters were as restrained as the jade carvers. The new glazes they used included celadon, a pure white, and a black glaze from Honan with brown markings. The potters used raised ornament on some of their work; but again the most ornate shapes, the dishes and bowls of several colours, the pictures on the bowls appearing as more important than basic form, were to be Ming and Ch'ing developments.

Lacquer work and embroidery were the two arts in which later technical skill showed to particular advantage. The carved lacquer of the Ch'ing is at its most impressive on a large scale, as it was used for the great imperial throne of Ch'ien Lung. Its red lacquer is inlaid with green and yellow, the imperial dragons writhe about the seated emperor, and a small elephant supports his back.

The Ch'ing textile workers used their skills both for woven and embroidered pictures; and for the robes of the emperor, his family, his servants, and his court. Only the emperor himself could wear the imperial yellow dragons on his long top coat (worn, according to Manchu custom, over high white boots), his nobles had a right to small dragonheaded roundlets on their clothes, his generals' robes were studded with brass dragon's heads. The women's clothes, like the men's in shape but not in colours or subjects of the ornament, were woven or embroidered with butterflies, flowers, or portraits of leisurely people.

By the time of the last Ch'ing emperors and the Empress Dowager, Tzu Hsi, nineteenthcentury China still appeared on the surface much as it had always been; peaceful, orderly, and traditional. Outside the few big coastal towns the country looked as it had for millennia. Every yard of arable land was handtilled; 'manicured', a visitor to China later commented. Villages centred every 20 miles or so on a small walled town. This was the market centre, the home of most of the local gentry and officials. It held the state granary for the grain offered as taxes. The town's narrow streets were lined with open-fronted craftsmen's shops where the goods were made by time-honoured methods. (A taut bowstring still powered the jade carver's drill.) Most of what the local people wanted was produced locally; but rare or foreign goods could often be copied or repaired. Some markets even had a stall which specialized in replacing the bristles of toothbrushes. Within their walls most towns had public baths, at least one good restaurant, and a number of teahouses. These served bowls of light amber-coloured Chinese tea, melon seeds and gossip. Many Chinese gentlemen, who were too educated to live on their own estates, but were not state-employed, spent a large part of their days in them.

Yet below this smooth surface of tradition nineteenth-century China was boiling with poverty and bitterly wounded pride. There were six major rebellions in the middle of the nineteenth century. The most serious, the Taiping ('the Heavenly Kingdom of Great Peace'), lasted 14 years from 1850 to 1864. For some of the time the imperial government lost control of South and Central China to the rebel administration. The Taipings only failed to topple the dynasty because the Chinese officials remained loyal to the Manchu emperor.

The Taipings killed thousands in every county and town that offered any opposition to them, and their suppression was equally bloodthirsty. The Viceroy Tseng executed all rebels in surrendering armies who spoke the dialect of Kwangsi where the Taipings had originated. Both sides massacred, and burnt villages and crops, for revenge and in order to hinder the movement of the opposing armies. In the northwest millions more Chinese lost their lives in the Moslem rebellions there. Barely a tenth of the population survived in some counties. Walled cities were left empty and ruined, and rivers polluted by corpses.

Partly because the rebellions and their suppression killed so many people the Chinese peasant's life was a little easier for a few decades in the later nineteenth century. The government encouraged peasant families to move into the devastated counties, and the grow﹨ing pressure on the limited land of China slackened temporarily.

As early as 1740 the great Emperor Ch'ien Lung wrote: 'the population is constantly increasing while the land does not become any more extensive'. In the late fourteenth century there were about 65 million Chinese, under Ch'ien Lung about 200 million, and in the middle of the nineteenth century 450 million.

The government, in the classic Chinese phrase, 'lived off the backs of the peasant', and during the nineteenth century it became an increasingly expensive government. The tentative experiments at modernization, the foreign wars, and the foreign indemnities, as well as the increasingly corrupt and extravagant court with its hierarchy of privileged eunuchs, had to be paid for out of farms growing smaller as each generation was more numerous. The farms had also to pay the expenses of a tax system which encouraged corruption. Tax collecting was let out to the local gentry who were allowed to squeeze as much as they could out of the peasants under them, remit what was forced out of them to the central treasury, and keep their profit.

Taxes were made more oppressive by the balance of trade against China at the beginning of the nineteenth century. Silver was used to pay for imports; and its value rose in proportion to the copper coins which most peasants used to pay their taxes. Later in the century the world price of silver dropped, and the whole Chinese currency depreciated in terms of European currency. Between 1864 and 1874 the value of the Chinese tael halved.

There was no margin for even minor natural disaster in this economy. Landless and indebted peasants were driven into banditry. By the end of the nineteenth century dykes and irrigation canals were not being properly repaired because the treasury was empty, and local officials weak. The results of droughts and floods were magni﹨fied. In North China between 1877 and 1879 nearly 15 million people died during a drought, and were buried in what are still known locally as 'ten thousand men' holes.

In Europe similar population increases in the eighteenth and nineteenth centuries and similar rural poverty and discontent were part of the cause of industrial as well as political revolutions. In Asia itself Japan, China's neighbour just across the sea, had taken her first startled look at Western power when the American warships appeared off her coast in 1853. In the next 50 years Japan changed from a society more hide⁄bound and more medieval than China to one of the powerful, industrialized new nations. Her first major international appearance in this new role was her over⁄ whelming victory in the Sino⁄Japanese war of 1894-5, and the Chinese humiliation in the Treaty of Shimonoseki which ended it.

China had a better supply of the raw materials needed for in⁄ dustrialization than Japan. Her people have, over the last ten years, proved able to learn industrial techniques faster than previously untrained Europeans. In the early⁄ and mid⁄nineteenth century she had a government administration which could have encouraged and enforced change. Among the rich there were periods of prosperity and men with spare money for investment. Oddest of all – until about the seventeenth century she had been the most advanced technically, as well as politically and culturally, of all the nations in the world. Through conquests by the Steppe peoples and the Arabs Europe had probably learnt Chinese skills as different as the use of stirrups and variolation (the predecessor of vaccination), and the techniques of using cranks, piston bellows, and water wheels. The Chinese printed their books, steered by the compass, made elaborate clocks, and used gunpowder centuries before Europe. (The myth, sadly, is wrong. Gunpowder was used in guns as well as in fireworks.) Chinese science, however, had no Roger Bacon. It was a matter of practical, empirical discovery to solve particular problems. Because men of education were not interested in scientific philosophy there was no working out of the principles from which scientific advance is made. There was thus no upsurge of knowledge re⁄thought and curiosity about the new in Ming[16] or Ch'ing China to correspond with the European Renaissance. China fell behind in scientific theory particularly. The first Jesuit missionaries to China were allowed to preach and hold official court positions because they made themselves useful as astronomers and mathematicians. 'As for the Western Doctrine which exalts the Lord of Heaven', the

54

Emperor K'ang-hsi wrote, 'it is opposed to our traditional teaching. It is solely because its apostles have a thorough knowledge of mathematical sciences that they are employed by the state.' (In the end K'ang-hsi expelled the missionaries and banned Christianity.)

During the eighteenth and nineteenth centuries the technological gap between China and the West widened. At first the Chinese did not even take seriously the new gadgets carried by this white-faced and foul-smelling[17] race of barbarian pirates. When Lord Macartney, George III's ambassador, arrived at the court of Ch'ien Lung, the old emperor saw his gifts as suitable tribute from a subordinate, but well-meaning, princeling. He examined the ingenious mechanical toys, the planetarium, the sprung coach, and the telescope. But the embassy's request that ports other than Canton should be opened to foreign trade was firmly refused. So also were Macartney's other requests for the regular exchange of ambassadors between Britain and China and the entry of Christian missionaries.

Ch'ien Lung might have listened with more interest to Macartney if he had been a less successful man. He had just defeated the Mongols in what was to be the last of the frontier wars. China's ancient enemies no longer menaced her, even the problem of the land shortage was temporarily relieved by settlement on the northern borders. Danger had never come to China from across the sea, Ch'ien Lung saw no reason to think this embassy marked a new epoch in China's history. 'We possess all things', was part of Ch'ien Lung's answer to George III. 'We are not interested in strange and costly objects and we have no use for your country's products.' His ministers assured Ch'ien Lung that if the strange embassy gave trouble the Europeans could easily be disciplined by stopping the rhubarb trade. Without rhubarb, it was believed in China, the Europeans would perish of constipation within months.

Even without rhubarb, there was much the Europeans, particularly the English, wanted from China. The fashion for Chinese silks, porcelain, and lacquerware had reached its height in the eighteenth century. Many of the Ch'ing potters worked entirely on orders for the new market, making dinner services ornamented with the crests of British, French, and Dutch families. Chinese bowls and vases were painted with copies of European prints: harvest scenes, Prince Charles Edward in highland dress, Venus and her attendant nymphs.[18]

As always, foreign taste was unsure of itself in a new sphere. Foreign buyers encouraged the over-ornamentation and the sentimentality of Ch'ing potters and considered the multiplication of dragons, birds, and flowers to be desirable and typical of Chinese ware.

As the fashion for Chinese art waned towards the end of the eighteenth century, a new necessity, tea, took the carrying capacity of all the ships that could make the China run. In Ch'ien Lung's day the ships were allowed to load only on their built-up mud flat outside Canton where they could buy their goods through specially accredited merchants. They were guarantees to the officials for the foreign merchant's behaviour; and chosen for their own high character, supposedly, so as to stand between the population and the corruption of barbarian manners.

Meanwhile the European economists issued solemn warnings about the trade in Chinese luxuries and tea. The ships to China went out almost empty. The Chinese were paid with silver. Bullion, the economists complained, as the Romans had done before them, was being drained West to East. But the Chinese insisted that they wanted none of the products of Europe.

A few decades later the foreign merchants discovered opium, a commodity for which they could make a growing market in China. It was a particularly profitable trade for the British, because opium was widely grown in their new Indian empire. Ships could carry cloth and other British-made goods to Calcutta, load opium there, sell the opium in Canton, and then buy tea, porcelain and silk for the home run.

The fashion for chinoiserie was, however, ebbing. Chinese porcelain and lacquerware did not mix well with the fashions of the French Empire, with their stress on classical design and simplicity. Nor were the heavy, embroidered, Chinese silks as useful for the high-waisted, sheer dresses of the early nineteenth-century lady of fashion as they had been for her full-skirted, eighteenth-century mother. Tea continued to be a necessity in the West. But the

Chinese growers were increasingly undersold by the new planters in India and Ceylon. The introduction of opium into China was to tip the balance of trade even further against China.

In China the new drug rapidly gained addicts; and the Ch'ing dynasty prohibited the import of opium into China. The foreign merchants at first ignored the prohibition, and bribed the officials to let their cargoes in. In 1839, however, the special Imperial envoy, Lin, threatened to cut off the food supplies of all foreigners if they did not surrender their opium. He then burnt 20,000 chests of the drug. A few months later English warships in Canton harbour fired on Chinese junks. Other ships captured the ports of South China, and naval parties landed and took Nanking.

Both sides were astounded by the ease of the foreign victories. The British made very large demands in return for peace: the cession of Hongkong island, the opening of five ports to foreign trade, the payment of a large indemnity, and foreign officials to be given the same respect as was accorded to Chinese of similar rank. It was to be a model for wars and treaties throughout the next 70 years.

One European power after another, joined in time by Japan, fought China on flimsy pretexts. Chinese towns were sacked, Chinese armies were defeated. Chinese apologies for the war were tendered, and large indemnities promised. More concessions were then extorted about where foreigners could live and what special protection they should be given. In 1858 the countries concerned in the Treaty of Tienstin imposed 'most favoured nation' clauses on China, so that any concession made to a foreign country automatically applied to them.

Comparatively little Chinese land was ceded outright. But it was the heyday of imperialism, and each major power collected its own sphere of influence in China where its traders and missionaries were pre-eminent. The old expression of Chinese superiority over the outer barbarians was now balanced by European righteousness. In the mid-nineteenth century British merchants of Tienstin memorialized Lord Elgin. Europe possesses a mission, they said, 'to develop the vast resources of China, and to extend among her people the elevating influence of a higher civilization.'[19]

It is part of the communist argument now that the foreigners were largely responsible for the Chinese failure to industrialize during the nineteenth century. One of the most damaging concessions the Chinese were forced to make was foreign control of their customs. Foreign manufactured goods sold more cheaply in the interior of the country than those that could be produced in China itself. The old handicrafts died. Foreign silk, cotton, bowls, spoons, pictures and lamps were all cheaper and more popular in their imported forms. Artisans without work were then thrown back on the resources of their overcrowded farm families. Peasant poverty was added to as the handicrafts died. The old source of winter income, money earned, by the women of the family, spinning and weaving cloth vanished because imported Lancashire cotton from Britain cost less. Then, without the old skills, the farm families were no longer self-sufficient, they borrowed for their shop-bought cloth and lights, and the villages grew still poorer.

Meanwhile, in the cities, Chinese industries could not compete against the cheap imported goods. Most countries protect new industries by high tariffs until they can stand against competition. The Chinese could not do this. By the 1890s, after the Treaty of Shimonoseki, they were not even allowed discretion to tax goods made in foreign factories built in China.

Imperialism, so the communists argue, also encouraged a geographically unbalanced development of China. Foreign trade came into the seaports, and foreign factories were set up there, particularly in Shanghai and Tienstin. But there was little Chinese transport, east to west, linking the interior to the coast. Instead much of it, like the Grand Canal, ran north to south. The industrial coast was isolated from the main part of the country, and easier for foreigners to control.

Yet without the foreigners the technical and educational advances China made in the nineteenth century would have been even smaller than they were. Some Western institutions were deliberately copied. In the reforms of 1864 after the suppression of the Taiping, the only major administrative change of the century was made when a Foreign Office, the Tsungli Yamen, was grafted on to the old central bureaucracy. At the same time the first of the Chinese government modern schools were ordered to teach Western sciences and mathematics as well as languages. Chinese arsenals, and a shipyard were started, and ironworks and better transport planned.

The very wars against the foreigners forced the Chinese to consider the reasons for the easy foreign victories, and what they needed to copy in self-defence. After the 1879 and 1880 crisis with the Russians over the frontier post of Ili, when Chinese negotiations were made almost impossible by the rudimentary transport on their side of the frontier,[20] the Chinese started the North China telegraph line. Less directly militarily useful institutions, like the first Chinese-owned Shanghai cotton mill and the Imperial Bank of China, were set up partly with government capital to lessen China's dependence on foreign goods and foreign loans.

In spite of these efforts at reform, however, China continued to lag behind the West and Japan. She continued to be defeated with humiliating ease by foreign expeditions. In the eyes of the rest of the world she gradually became a comic-opera country whose armies carried umbrellas instead of guns, and where nothing worked properly. Her new industries often failed or produced shoddy and expensive goods. There was no large scale industrialization or adoption of scientific ideas, and peasant poverty worsened as the century went on.

Part of the trouble was that the nineteenth-century leaders (like Ch'ien Lung) could not believe that Western techniques were more than clever tricks: not connected with real education or a different scientific mode of thinking. 'Chinese learning as the basis; Western learning for practical use', was the quoted tag of the century. The good official or the good teacher, it was thought, needed a thorough grounding in the Confucian classics to which he could then add the necessary items of scientific technique or business management. Even in war the qualification for army command was still passing the examinations in the Confucian classics. 'The conduct of war rests with men not materials.' But it did not help Chinese resistance to foreigners when commanders in charge of the guns had had no artillery training.

It was almost impossible for a man educated in the Confucian tradition to accept another system of thought. In the reform period after the Taiping attempts were made to 'revive the ancient virtues', and make the examination system and the education leading to it less stereotyped. There was more emphasis on a candidate's general moral character and his grasp of contemporary affairs. But he still had to consider contemporary affairs in the light of classical precedent and precept; and qualifying papers demanded detailed knowledge of the classics. The serious candidate anyway had no time during his education to devote to reading outside his syllabus. Moreover most teachers regarded innovations in government or thought as in themselves wrong and impious. The natural balance existed. The Golden Age had existed. It was man's duty to find this balance and to re-create the Golden Age of the past, not to try for something new.

Towards the end of the nineteenth century more of the classically educated were showing some interest in Western learning; and their interest was reinforced by graduates from government modern schools and missions schools which made no concessions to Confucian ideas. But even these new men while they urged reform on the government were not themselves principally interested in science or mathematics, far less engineering or business techniques. They studied Western philosophy with interest, and to a lesser extent literature, history, even painting. But they were, even as rebels, still tied to the literary, unscientific, tradition of classical China. It was still unthinkable for an intellectual to work with his hands, or make the amassing of a great fortune of money his first interest.

In the West it had been the growing middle class which had directly or indirectly brought about most of the educational and economic changes of their countries' industrialization. In Europe, particularly in Britain, this middle class was a powerful and very self-confident group. Ever since the seventeenth century English plays and, later, novels contained references to the rich merchants who wanted their daughters to marry into commercial wealth not the decadent aristocracy. Equally they wanted their sons educated for trade and industry not as politicians or landed gentry. In nineteenth-century China these were impossible sentiments. There was a middle class of artisans and merchants in all the cities. But it had little political or social power, the wealth of its members was disapproved of, and in a way they disapproved of themselves.

There was in China no channel, like the English parliament or even the city governments, by which merchants could govern or even offer advice to the government. Their advice anyway would have been considered impertinent and likely to be tainted by the evils of their calling. In the official Confucian hierarchy the merchant ranked lowest of all – below the scholar, the farmer and the artisan. 'Exalt agriculture, disparage commerce', said the classic Confucian tag on the treatment of merchants, and it was faithfully followed by good governments from the Han to the reformers of the mid-nineteenth century. Commercial taxes were heavy and complicated and the official clerks expected bribes and presents from local merchants.

The despised merchants were not even considered the men best able to manage new commercial enterprises. As these were established in the late nineteenth century the typical form was a business jointly owned and capitalized by the state and a private merchant. (A pattern partially repeated by the communists' state-private businesses.) 'Official supervision and merchant management' was the phrase used; and the local magistrate and his office were expected to watch the merchant and control the low practices expected from him. The customs and caution of bureaucratic government were extended to these businesses; salaries and employment within the firm had to be found not only for the merchant's family, but also for official families.

Nevertheless, commercial fortunes were made in nineteenth-century China; first by Chinese compradores working with the foreign merchants, then by men who founded the first Chinese trading firms and commercial enterprises in the late nineteenth century. But the money these men made went, not as in the West into further commercial investments, but into enterprises which were, from the Chinese point of view[21] more established and respectable:

buying land or pawnshops, founding libraries or poetry societies. The sons of these rich men were educated not for commerce, but for official careers, and so for greater social esteem and power than their fathers had had.

By the 1890s the Empress Dowager, Tzu Hsi, had presided over 30 years of national humiliation and the decay of internal good government. The attempt, after the suppression of the Taiping, to revive the Confucian state had foundered. A modern industrial-ized state had not taken its place. In the provinces power was passing from the officials into the hands of local strong men. The state was almost bankrupt. The empress decided to resign in favour of her well-meaning, but not very astute, nephew, the Emperor Kwang Su.

A group of young men became Kwang Su's advisers, and in the summer of 1898 they carried through the Reforms of the Hundred Days. The literary examinations for the bureaucracy were to be replaced by examination in Western knowledge. Western-type schools and universities were set up in every province. The army and judicial system were reformed on Western lines. Machinery was to be imported and Western books translated. What roused particular opposition was the decree that officials, whom the reformers decided were useless, were to be dismissed. It was too much, too fast. The senior ministers petitioned the empress. She descended on the palace, stormed at the emperor, and had him imprisoned on a small island on the Lake in the Summer Palace. The Reforms of the Hundred Days were rescinded, and six of the young reformers executed.

Meanwhile a more popular protest movement was rapidly spreading among the peasants of Shantung, where a famine was attributed to the magic of foreign missionaries. The Boxers[22] at first included leaders who condemned the Ch'ing misrule as much as they condemned the foreign exploitation of China. But the move-ment of guards for the foreign Legations sparked-off riots, and the particular targets of the Boxers became 'the Primary and Secondary Hairy Ones'; the missionaries and their Chinese converts.

These missionaries of all churches had, by now, rejected completely the tolerant aristocratic ideals of the early Jesuits. They entered the country to convert the heathen masses, not the *élite*. They made no concessions to despised Chinese customs, and had, most of them, as little respect for Chinese law. Their converts were forbidden to join in the ancestral rites, and so broke their Chinese family ties. Away from the treaty ports the general ignorance about foreigners increased the unpopularity of the Christian doctrines. The stories that convents cared for unwanted babies in order that the nuns might kill and eat them, and that Chinese eyes were taken by foreign hospitals so that they might be used in Christian magic, long ante-date the communists. Most of the educated did not believe these stories, but they knew that the demands of missionaries, or the killing of a missionary living illegally in the interior of the country, were often the pretexts for foreign wars. In these wars missionaries acted as spies for their fellow countrymen.

It was, then, easy for the Boxers to gather recruits and support. They moved into Peking, almost unopposed, and the foreigners were besieged in their Legations. The Boxers depended on magic drills to protect them against bullets; but these were not efficacious against the foreign armies marching to the relief of Peking. About 15,000 Chinese and 475 Europeans were killed during the Boxer troubles, and the largest indemnity in history was agreed on. The sum of £67½ million was to be paid in 39 annual instalments.

Meanwhile, as the Boxers' fortunes had risen, the policy of the empress's government had wavered from condemnation to tacit and then open support. When the Boxers were defeated the empress fled from Peking to the ancient capital of Sian. On her return, in a desperate attempt to placate the foreigners and restore the popularity of her dynasty, she enacted most of the Reforms of the Hundred Days. Men were sent abroad to study. Legal torture was forbidden. Some of the useless officials were dismissed. At court the empress allowed talk of Western subjects, and received Western ladies. She was herself, she said, particularly interested in their underclothes and corsets. She thought they must be excessively uncomfortable.

It was, however, too late. The south particularly was alive with plots, secret societies and scurrilously treasonable rhymes on every-thing from the empress's dubious morals to the need to restore pure Chinese government and expel the Manchu usurpers.

The most prominent of the rebels was by now Sun Yat-sen, a young man from the district where the Taiping had started. He had been educated in the Western tradition, partly by missionaries and partly abroad. Many of the Confucian reformers who had survived the Reforms of the Hundred Days at first despised him, because of his extremism, the failure of his early attempts at rebellion, and because of his lack of any Chinese classical education. But his ideas were increasingly popular among the Overseas Chinese. Their communities sheltered Sun, and provided him with money for new plots to overthrow the Ch'ing government. Several amateurish attempts were unsuccessful, and Sun barely escaped with his life. Then, almost accidentally in the autumn of 1911, another rebellion was precipitated by the discovery of plotters in one of the houses on a Russian concession. There were soldiers' mutinies, provincial revolts, and widespread killing of Manchus. A republic was proclaimed in Nanking, and Sun Yat-sen elected its first president.

Some months after Sun and his new ministers went to the tomb of Hung-wu, the first Ming emperor, and made an offering of food, candles, and incense to him. His ghost was solemnly assured that the soil of China had been won back from the Manchus, just as the first Ming won it back from the Mongols. Chinese history was still, officially, continuous.

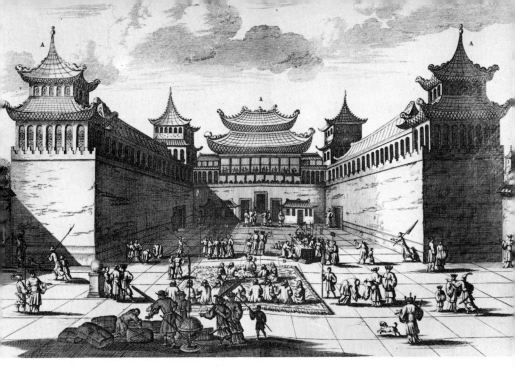

21 The Manchu Ch'ing dynasty ruled China from 1644 to 1911. This seventeenth-century engraving of the Ch'ing Emperors' palace in Peking reflects the eminence of his imperial position.

22 The administration of the Manchu Empire was in the hands of civil servants or Mandarins. This is a local magistrate's court of the period.

23 (*Above*) The religious activities of the Jesuit Matteo Ricci and his missionary colleagues were tolerated by the Chinese emperors because of their knowledge of Western science and astronomy. They helped found this Peking Observatory.

24 (*Below left*) Father Ferdinand Verbiest, a colleague of Ricci, was one of many Jesuits who emphasized the relationship between science and Roman Catholicism.

25 Ch'ien Lung who was Emperor from 1700 to 1799. He rejected proposals for alliance and trade made by George III of England.

26 Tea was an important export for China in the eighteenth century and became increasingly popular in the West. A nineteenth-century engraving of a tea plantation.

A. Humblot del. Baquoy Sculp.

27 (*Left*) The Mandarins who were the backbone of imperial administration lasted until the Revolution of 1911. The house of a Mandarin from a nineteenth-century coloured aquatint.

28 (*Below left*) The importance of imperial China as an Asian trading country is reflected in this eighteenth-century vignette.

29 The passion for Chinoiserie reached a peak in the eighteenth century. This plate inscribed with an English coat-of-arms was made for export only.

30 Lacquer work was an art in which the Ch'ing craftsmen excelled. A Ch'ing table top dating from the eighteenth century.

31 The enforcement of the Chinese prohibition on the import of opium precipitated the war of 1840 fought against Britain. This nineteenth-century engraving of the capture of Chumpei by the British dates from this period.

32 The war ended with the signing of a number of agreements which established the 'treaty ports'. Shanghai was one of these. A nineteenth-century anonymous oil painting.

33 The narrow streets of old Chinese towns were lined with craftsmen's shops.

34 Missionary zeal towards China reached a peak in Britain during the nineteenth century. This Protestant missionary was one of many who attempted to evangelize the heathen masses as distinct from the *élite* – the earlier aim of the Jesuits.

35 (*Above left*) Traditional methods of coal mining in about 1900; this crude winch was operated by man-power only.

36 (*Above*) Silk-spinning in the open air. The manufacture declined in the nineteenth century because Chinese silk was undercut by foreign silk.

37 (*Below left*) Between 1877 and 1879 nearly 15 million Chinese people died during a drought. Primitive irrigation systems like this man-run wheel were not adequate for the growing rural population in times of poor rainfall.

5   The Communists

SUN YAT-SEN'S GRAVE is a place of pilgrimage in today's communist China; and his widow, Sung Ching-ling, is one of the vice-presidents of the state. But how close to a communist Sun was himself is doubtful. Like many of his left-wing contemporaries in Europe, Sun admired the new communist state in Russia, was curious about its social experiments, and thought it had much to teach the world. He saw, however, the most pressing of Chinese problems as those of the land and the peasants, not of factories and workers; and communism, before Mao, had small place for agricultural societies.

Nevertheless, when Sun died in 1925 the Kuomintang was officially a coalition. The small Chinese Communist Party, born in the post-revolutionary turmoil, had Russian advisers who urged cooperation with the Kuomintang to bring about Chinese unity and independence. Bourgeois revolution in China, the Russian theorists argued, must necessarily precede communist power. However, Sun's successor, as leader of the Kuomintang, was Chiang Kai-shek. Chiang had been reared in orthodox Confucianism (although after his marriage to Sun's sister-in-law, Sung Mai-ling, he became a Methodist). He was determined to establish a strong, unified, and non-communist China. North of Canton, the centre of the Kuomintang's power, the country was divided among warlords. Chiang led a successful army north. In Shanghai in 1927 he turned on the communists. Those who did not escape into the deep country of central China, were killed, sometimes after torture. Communist and left-wing provisional governments were suppressed; and Chiang and the new right-wing Kuomintang were both powerful and very popular.

The young communist agitators who had followed Chiang's first army, or struck out on their own, had alienated popular feeling. They had mocked the old, and shouted 'Down with Cannibal Confucianism'. Landlords had been killed without the formality of trials, or finding out whether they were good or bad of their kind. Peasants had watched these killings without taking part in them. Even the subsequent redistribution of land had been ill-organized and ineffectual. In this young rabble there was little to appeal to the moderate or scholarly Chinese.

Chiang on the other hand had unified the country. His government was more orderly and more in accordance with tradition than that of the warlords; and there were promises of yet better government to come. In return for his break with the communists he had the support of Chinese and foreign businessmen, foreign loans, and the hope of extracting further solid concessions from the foreign powers.

Less than 25 years later only a handful of Chinese followed Chiang to Taiwan (Formosa). Most of his army had deserted him without even fighting. As well as the Chinese peasants, the great majority of the rich, the scholars, and even the civil servants who had once worked for him, preferred to welcome the advancing communists. Chiang, his relations, and the rump of his party were bitterly, and personally unpopular. The last days of his government were compared to the worst periods of the classic interregnums. The Kuomintang was condemned for failing to fulfil its promises of reform, failing to understand or help the needs of the country, and failing to fight the Japanese.

The promises the Kuomintang made in its early days were based on the three principles of government Sun Yat-sen had written into the testament he left his party. They were Nationalism, that is national unity and independence; Political Democracy, not immediately but in three stages; and the People's Livelihood, or economic reform. Specifically Sun had called for land reforms and state investment in industrialization.

Economic reform, at the time of Sun's death, was urgent. The increase in peasant debts and the pressure of population on land which had been partly responsible for the troubles of the later empire and its fall, had grown worse under the warlords who had taken power over most of the country after 1911. Paper money had been issued recklessly and the peasants forced to accept it. Savings had lost their value, or been looted by bandits, or official and semi-official soldiers. Army pay was generally months in arrears, and in order to live the soldiers had to rob the countryside. Taxes, however, continued to be collected years in advance.

Even after the Kuomintang had established itself over the warlords as the lawful government of all China, the peasants enjoyed only some of the benefits of peace and order. There continued to be local bandits. Those Kuomintang officials and troops who did reach the villages, demanded bribes, conscripted boys, raped and murdered. 'You do not take good iron to make a nail, or a good man to make a soldier', said one of the traditional proverbs. It is often quoted in accounts of life in the Chinese country under the Kuomintang.

In the 1930s China had some of the worst floods and consequent famines of her recorded history. The landlords' holdings and rents increased as families sold their land in the effort to keep alive. Interest rates went up. R. H. Tawney noted that 40 to 80 per cent was common, 150 to 200 per cent not unknown. A moneylender who charged only 25 per cent was known as 'a blessing' to his village.[23] Where they could the peasants crowded into towns already plagued by the world wide unemployment of the time. They could not beg effectively because the professional Guild of Beggars was more skilled, and adept in discouraging competition. Instead they sold their younger children for household slaves or prostitutes. Then they sat on the edge of the pavement, keeping their clothes and feet politely out of the way of passers-by, until either the police moved them on, or they died of cold and hunger. The Shanghai municipality hired carts to go round the streets at dawn picking up the night's tally of dead from the gutters.

Yet, during the 1930s, the Kuomintang was not the government without all hope that it was to become. After the break with the communists and the economic troubles of the time, the Kuomintang had lost most of what working-class and peasant support it had ever had. But its members still included representatives of the numerically small, but growing, new middle class of the eastern towns: missionary and foreign-educated technicians, business and professional men. James Sung, Chiang's father-in-law, had been one of these new businessmen with an interest in such untraditional ideas as educating his daughters. Chiang's brother-in-law, T. V. Sung, was a powerful financier, no radical, but interested in a more powerful and modern China. Partly under his influence the Kuomintang set up reform commissions. Bright young men, Chinese and foreign, were employed as advisers and public relations officers, some welfare legislation modelled on Western prototypes passed, and even a few model factories opened.

It all resulted in very little. Too many people had to have too many cuts from each new scheme. Chiang is said personally to have been incorruptible. This was not true, however, of those close to him. It was too easy to bribe one's way out of inconvenient new welfare schemes, and government-sponsored investigations. It was not even as if Chiang himself had put reform at the top of his list of priorities. His main interest, whatever other schemes the Sungs persuaded him to agree to, remained his army, placating the rich men who paid for his army, and the suppression of his opponents in China, particularly the communists.[24]

Yet with all its difficulties, economic and personal, avoidable and unavoidable, the Kuomintang would have made a more respectable government without the external menace of Japan. After Japan had enthusiastically and successfully accepted Western techniques during the nineteenth century, she also wanted an empire, and an assured market for her new industries like the Western powers. She chose China as her colony.

In 1931 the Japanese army took over Manchuria. Japanese troops were moved, more or less with Kuomintang consent, into North China; and in 1937 Japan had a reason for open war there, when Chinese troops shot back on the Marco Polo bridge outside Peking.

Long before 1937, however, Chinese young people of any education were in no doubt as to who was their national enemy. There were

incidents in the cities when students organized anti-Japanese boy-
cotts, and attempted to burn the entire stocks of shopkeepers who
displayed Japanese articles. In the clashes with the Kuomintang
police some of the students were killed, and feeling against the
Kuomintang policy of appeasement mounted.

Yet Chiang continued to say that it was necessary to achieve
internal unity before attacking the Japanese. After the first fighting
around Peking, the Japanese met only token resistance in their
conquest of northeast China. Shanghai was bravely defended; but
after its fall the Kuomintang was driven back, over the mountain
ranges, into the far interior to make their wartime capital in
Chungking.

There were Chinese who wondered whether the Kuomintang,
like the old dynasties before them, had lost the Mandate of Heaven.
But the men who still thought in these Confucian terms were
outmoded. The early communists shouting 'Down with Confucius'
had shocked the villagers of the early 1920s; but 15 years later the
breach with the Confucian past, the ideas that had inspired China
for over 2,000 years, had widened.

The beginning, in the late nineteenth century, had been the
gradual whittling down of Confucianism before the new ideas, the
success, and the self-confidence of the West. Confucianism, instead
of being the one and only system of ethics and government, the
universal truth for all civilized men everywhere, shrunk to being
only the Chinese truth. Confucianism, its partisans asserted, was
the Chinese contribution to the wisdom of the world; an equal
partner with other great truths like Christianity or Islam. Chinese
thinkers desperately searched the classics for proof that the scientific
and cultural ideas of other continents were to be found in China
too. Alternatively Confucianism was defended as the national essence
of China. Without it the Chinese would be disorientated, a people
without historical roots.

These were half-way positions; they were still further eroded
by the rejection of Confucian education as the qualification for
government administration. The young men, educated at modern
schools, blamed the old ideas for the humiliation of their country;

but they did not know what to put in their place. In the intellectual ferment after 1911, educated Chinese considered most of the world's philosophies. Christianity failed to fill the vacuum because of its associations with Western imperialism. John Dewey and Bertrand Russell lectured to enormous and enthusiastic audiences during their visits to China; and there were many adherents of the new rule of rationalism and liberal humanism. Yet, as with Christianity, the political precepts associated with these beliefs suffered from association with the West. Moreover, the Chinese did not relish being other countries' pupils. They wanted a set of beliefs and practices they could make their own.

To this intellectual hunger Chiang's Kuomintang offered a warmed-up hash of muzzy Western ideas and the discredited past. The Confucian virtues, Chiang said, could save China. His official hero was Tseng Kuo-fan, the Viceroy who had suppressed the Taiping and attempted to restore the old order in mid-nineteenth century China. Ladies in silk dresses urged modesty, austerity, and restraint. But it was only possible to warm the Confucian flesh, not to make the whole skeleton walk again. Confucian education could not be revived. Kuomintang China needed technicians, not philosophers. Nor did the old examination system for the appointment of officials replace nepotism, bribery, and the degrees of Western-style universities. The intellectual promises of the Kuomintang in China were as empty as their promises of practical reform.

The communists had more satisfying fare to offer. Their intellectual origins in China were with the New Tide discussion groups of Peking University around 1919 and 1920. The professors who led these groups were attracted to Marxism partly because the orthodox West had rejected it as a workable political idea. Moreover, the only country which then proclaimed itself Marxist, the Soviet Union, was only partly European. The communist revolution had already led to more emphasis by the Russian leaders on their Asian role, and the brotherhood in this new society of Asians and Europeans. Just after the revolution, the Soviet Union, the only European country to have done so, had voluntarily renounced its concessions in China.

78

Communism, as it developed in China, grew recognizably less German and Russian, more Chinese, closer to Chinese problems, and phrased in Chinese idioms. The architect of this Chinese communism was Mao Tse-tung, the son of a moderately prosperous Hunanese peasant. As a boy Mao had insisted on going to a modern college in Changsha, the provincial capital, and at that period a seed-bed of young revolutionaries. Several of his fellow students were to become leaders of the Kuomintang or the Communist Party. Many of them planned to study abroad, but Mao was too poor. Instead he found himself work in the National University of Peking. (In 1949 when the triumphant communist armies entered Peking the University hung out a banner 'Welcome back to our Assistant Librarian'.) He joined a New Tide discussion group, and in 1921 he was one of the dozen delegates who founded the Chinese Communist Party.

Mao was well read. Chinese history and novels provided him with analogies he used constantly in later books and speeches. But with his shambling, untidy appearance, his loud laugh, and the voice and many of the tastes of a Hunanese peasant (he still likes the fiercely peppered food of his native province) he did not seem like an educated, influential man. The part he played in the foundation of the early party was less than that of the slicker, city-bred young men who were friends of the first Russian advisers.

After the Kuomintang killing of most of their leaders in 1927, the Central Committee of the party continued to try and bring about a revolution on orthodox lines through strikes and revolts in the cities. In 1928 Li Li-san, the then leader of the party, voiced the danger that Chinese communism might become 'contaminated' with 'peasant mentality'. But city revolts were bloodily suppressed, and their leaders took refuge, when they escaped, in the villages. Even there embattled but untrained peasants were easily defeated by regular soldiers. Mao Tse-tung organized the Autumn Harvest Rising in his own province of Hunan in 1927; and he only just escaped after its failure to the mountains of Chingkangshan in South China between Kiangsi and Hunan provinces. In these mountains, and in similar inaccessible strongholds throughout the country, communist troops were trained, and communist methods devised.

In his 1927 *Report of an Investigation into the Peasant Movement in Hunan*, Mao had already stressed the dominant part he thought peasants must play in the Chinese revolution. He wrote:

'The force of the peasantry is like that of raging winds and driving rain. It is rapidly increasing in violence. Every revolutionary comrade will be subject to their (the peasants) scrutiny and be accepted or rejected by them. Shall we stand in the vanguard and lead them, or stand behind them and oppose them?'

In Chingkangshan and the neighbouring soviets, Mao's position was strengthened, as the old city leaders of the party were killed, fled to Moscow (as Li Li-san did in 1931), or forced to take refuge with him and agree to his ideas. One of Mao's earliest recruits was the reformed warlord, and ex-opium addict, Chu Teh. He became the commanding general of the Red Army, and he and Mao remained unbreakably loyal to each other through the early leader-ship crises. To the surrounding peasants and foreigners the com-mander of Chingkangshan was known as Chumao: one man, an undefeatable new kind of political bandit.

It soon became clear that Chumao headed a formidable army. In striking contrast to the Kuomintang army Chu Teh and his officers wore the same uniform as their troops, ate the same rations, and did not ride when their men had to go on foot. From the begin-ning political officers were attached to each unit. It was their duty to see that the soldiers understood the army's part in the revolution, teach them to read so that they could follow Marxist pamphlets, and impress on them the importance of good relations with the sur-rounding villagers. The soldiers were forbidden to take a needle from a peasant's house without paying for it; and they were ordered to help with farm work anywhere they were billeted.

Political education was not confined to the army. The local peasants were encouraged to kill their landlords, and redistribute the land under communist guidance. There were mass literacy cam-paigns. Opium, prostitution, child marriage, and forced betrothals were forbidden. In return the peasants provided recruits for the Red Army, supplied them, and when it was necessary hid, spied, and fought with the soldiers. Because of this peasant support Chu Teh and Mao worked out guerrilla tactics which enabled the soviets to survive four major offensives planned by Chiang Kai-shek's German military staff. 'The enemy advances: we retreat. The enemy halts: we harass. The enemy tires: we attack. The enemy retreats: we pursue.' Mao wrote about Red Army tactics.

However Mao's military tactics were over-ruled by other leaders in a Fifth Campaign. A Kuomintang army of 900,000 troops blockaded the soviet and moved inwards under heavy artillery and air cover. All villages that could supply the communists were burnt; and all peasants – men, women, and children – found in areas friendly to the communists were killed. (At least a million civilians are believed to have been killed or starved to death during this white offensive.)

In the autumn of 1934, in the face of their defeats, the communists decided to retreat. They broke out of central China, westwards, into country that was not heavily garrisoned. Then, during the Long March that followed, their goal became the only surviving large soviet in north Shensi. Their route lay along the borders of China, through country almost impassable, and inhabited by tribespeople who, before, had fought any Chinese army impartially because they saw all Chinese as aggressors.

In October 1934, the Long March began with 90,000 men and a handful of women. During the next year this army walked about 6,000 miles. (There were a few horses reserved for the most important leaders and the wounded – Chu Teh's peasant wife carried extra wounded on her back.) They took, temporarily, 62 cities that lay in their path, crossed 18 mountain chains and 24 large rivers. Hostile tribes, notably the Lolos, shot at Red soldiers but were converted to helpful allies by the promise of favoured treatment when the revolution was successful. On the whole the Red Army moved faster than the Kuomintang and so avoided pitched battles, but there was fighting, in north Kweichow and over some of the river crossings.

At the Tatu river, in the far west, the bridge had been destroyed by the Kuomintang army; but soldier volunteers swung themselves, hand over hand, across the chains which still hung above the river gorge. The pass over the Great Snowy Mountain farther to the north was 16,000 feet high, and the army had no warm clothes with them. Many of them were barefoot. On the marshland, on the Shensi border, men who strayed from the path were sucked under, and died before they could be dragged out. Others died there from exhaustion and fever. But the organization of the Red Army was not broken, even though only a tenth of the men who had set out, about 7,000 of them, and 30 women, arrived in Yenan, Shensi.[25]

The whole epic of the Long March became a source of pride, not only to communists, but to other Chinese looking for some national achievement, to place against the Japanese victories. For the communists in power after 1949 the Long March became a major inspiration for all arts. Mao himself wrote several poems about it.[26]

There are now exhibitions of Long March paintings; a museum map of the route with illuminated buttons to highlight the sites of heroic incidents; and children learn to read from simplified *Stories of the Long March*. A recent opera, *The East is Red*, included a ballet of soldiers miming in semi-traditional dance style the obstacles in the way of the Long March army.

Politically Mao's position was greatly strengthened by the Long March. Shensi was a more secure and a bigger base than the southern soviet had been. On the march north Mao, by political intrigue and out-arguing his rivals, established himself as supreme leader, not only of his own soviet and its army, but also of the delegations and reinforcements from other smaller soviets along the way.[27] After the march the survivors were united by particular loyalties to each other and to Mao. 'A Comrade of the Long March' has been one of the few reasons accepted for sentimental actions in communist China.

The avowed aim of the Long March had been to bring the Red armies into fighting proximity to the Japanese. The outspoken hostility to the Japanese (and of the Japanese to the communists),

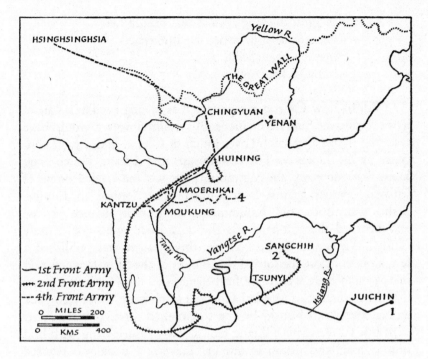

The route of the Long March

had become a major attraction of the movement for young Chinese. But the new Shensi soviet was soon surrounded by the Kuomintang; and Chiang ordered his generals to give top priority to wiping out the 'bandit remnants', not to fighting the Japanese. One of the armies he sent to the Shensi front was Manchurian soldiers under the command of the young Marshal, Chang Hsueh-liang. Chiang, however, was warned of the discontent in this army, sown by communist agents, and added to by patriotism and the stories of Japanese atrocities in their Manchurian homelands. He flew up to the Shensi front on a surprise visit of inspection, and, in what is still one of the most disputed incidents of the civil war, was taken prisoner in Sian by Marshal Chang in 1936. On the walls of the pavilion where he was held, someone wrote later:

A great thieving animal was caught here
but it was let off when we discovered
that it was no wolf,
but a jackal.[28]

In China now Chiang is represented as having been in a state of
terror during the Sian negotiations. His death, however, would have
been the signal for anarchy over much of China, and a swift conquest by the Japanese. The communists and Chang Hsueh-liang
knew this. Moreover, the communists knew of the United Fronts of
left-wing parties against fascism then being formed in Europe.
Stalin wanted the old Kuomintang-communist alliance revived
and believed that Chiang was the only leader who could unify
China. An agreement between the three leaders was published a
few months before the formal declaration of the Sino-Japanese war
in 1937 and there were to be further negotiations. (Chiang insisted
that the Manchurian Marshal Chang Hsueh-liang should go back
to Nanking with him to be court-martialled there. It was a secret
trial; but 12 years later Chiang took Chang Hsueh-liang with him
from a mainland prison to one on Taiwan. Chang was released
after 24 years in 1960. He had served a year for every day of Chiang's
imprisonment.)

The Sian agreement had only a limited value. After less than a year
of war the swiftness of the Japanese victories ensured that the Kuomintang and communist front lines were cut off from each other
by a large area of Japanese-held territory. The communist and
Kuomintang both organized their own, separate, anti-Japanese,
resistance movement among the peasants. The communists had a
particularly effective system of underground tunnels in North
China, so that Japanese troops could be taken by surprise, and
villagers hidden from Japanese revenge. Towards the end of the war,
over most of North and Central China, the Japanese held only their
forts and the main towns, while the communist underground controlled the country.[29]

As the war went on communist resistance officers complained that
Kuomintang agents preferred to betray them to the Japanese rather

than to help them. Both the Kuomintang and the communists accused the other side of intriguing against their armies, and no Kuomintang supplies were passed to the communists. Nor did the communists receive supplies from Russia. Stalin told visitors that he considered the Kuomintang the proper government of China.

The Chinese communist armies used wooden cannons they had made themselves, wound round with telephone wire stolen from Japanese country. The villagers in the resistance made their own mines filled with stones. The army wove its own clothes from the wool of Shensi sheep. What medical supplies there were were improvised; microscope slides from broken window panes, eye droppers from old rubber hoses, and a surgical instrument sterilizer from an old gasoline container.

There was the same sort of improvisation throughout the communist areas. In Yenan, the communist capital, everybody, including Mao himself and the rest of the leaders, lived in roughly furnished caves hollowed out of the loess cliffs of Shensi. There was a university in the caves with home-made and shared equipment, and books, schools, hospitals, administrative headquarters, and a clothing factory. (The stolen telephone wire again: this time used for looms.)

The foreign reporters invited to Yenan, and smuggled in despite Chiang's prohibitions, reported the improvisations, the atmosphere of equality and comradeship, the fervour with which the war against Japan was talked of and fought. There was, too, little but good to be reported about communist methods of government. Land had been re-distributed in Shensi, but without the violence and killing of the landlords that had gone on in the southern soviets. The new peasant owners generally lived better than the government officials. The army was disciplined and apparently popular, the leaders spoke gently of gradual plans for China, and of coming to terms again with the Kuomintang.

It was all a marked contrast to Chungking. Foreign supplies were brought into Kuomintang China at great cost in lives and money. For most of the war they had to be flown in from India over the Himalayas. These supplies were duly labelled 'medical' or 'ammunition', but when the boxes were accidentally opened too often they contained cosmetics or imported clothes for the wives of officials with most influence in the government. Meanwhile the hospitals were as short of supplies as those in the communist areas, and the ordinary soldiers worse armed and clothed. There was corruption everywhere, growing worse in the introverted atmosphere of wartime Chungking. The most moderate critics of the régime were imprisoned, or, if they were better known, assassinated by undetected criminals. The Kuomintang leaders were remote, arrogant, and lived in great comfort and grandeur.

Behind the mountains in Szechuan Chiang and his government were dependent on the taxes and food brought in by local landlords. These landlords were naturally implacably opposed to any reform of the system of landholding or lowering the rents; and the Kuomintang was now removed geographically from the possible reforms the more modern common sense of the seacoast businessmen had once suggested. Policy and promise for the future grew even more conservative, and more closely allied to the landlords' interest.

The contrast between the corrupt, ill-administered, and unhopeful Kuomintang, and the moderately-spoken, efficient, and egalitarian communists, was obvious to all Chinese who read the foreign reports, heard rumours, or were able to see for themselves. Young Chinese, particularly students, who were able to escape from Japanese-held towns increasingly went to Yenan not to Chungking. Other Chinese, who were not communists, and who as landlords, businessmen, or Western-oriented teachers, had interests that seemed to conflict with communism, nevertheless saw the communists as the new hope of their country.

For a few months after the end of the Japanese war in 1945 Chiang appeared to control the major part of the Chinese mainland with the communists shut up in an unimportant northern area. But it soon became obvious that, as with the Japanese, the Kuomintang controlled the towns, but the communists the country, at any rate in North China. Meanwhile, further Chinese sympathy was alienated from the Kuomintang by the rapidly spiralling inflation brought on by their simple economic policy of paying for rising war costs and the equally rising cost of corruption by printing more, and yet more, money. Housewives carried suitcases filled with the almost worthless paper dollars to pay for their day's marketing. Salary earners rushed out with their month's pay to convert it, preferably within the hour, into durables with fixed values, gold or American dollars.

Chiang himself apparently saw no need to make more than paper promises of reform and token changes in his government. He resigned as president, only to accede to the popular clamour he himself noticed for his own recall. His American advisers and associates were more and more outspokenly critical of him. They advised peace, conciliation, and immediate land reform; but their government continued to supply the Kuomintang with arms to use against the communists. After 18 months of uneasy peace Chiang started a new offensive and Yenan fell. It had, however, already been evacuated by the communist armies following Mao's old guerrilla policy of retreat in the face of head-on force. But it was the last time he was to use these guerrilla tactics.

In the communist counter-offensive of 1948 Manchuria collapsed in a few days and the Kuomintang armies there either surrendered, together with their new American equipment, or retreated south beyond Mukden to be reinforced by the best troops Chiang could send. They were defeated in the three weeks battle of Hsuchow, and in February 1949 Peking fell.

Chiang boasted that the communists could never cross the Yangtze, and in the spring of 1949 there was a short pause for further fruitless negotiations. On the night their ultimatum expired communist armies crossed the river without more than token resistance from the Kuomintang. In May they entered Shanghai. All over China Kuomintang armies surrendered without fighting. Canton fell. Chiang, his family, some of his army, the contents of the museums at Nanking, and a great deal of money went to Taiwan. The museum treasure, some of the most beautiful pictures and ceramics in the world, were lodged for a number of years in damp caves. The money went into American securities. The Formosans found themselves with a government of mainlanders of whom it was later said that they 'had learnt nothing and forgotten nothing'.

In Peking on 1 October, Mao read out the proclamation of the People's Republic of China from the Gate of Heavenly Peace: the entrance to the imperial palace of the Mings and the Manchus. 'Our nation will never be an insulted nation', Mao said. 'We have stood up.'

38 China suffered severely during the China War in the 1860s against Britain and France. The Taku forts were (wrongly) believed by the Chinese generals to be impregnable.

39 The Boxer Rebellion of the 1890s was primarily against foreigners, but the movement gained some of its strength from the general discontent. In 1900 the rebels besieged the foreign legations in Peking, leaving them in ruins.

40 (*Left*) Sun Yat-sen is acclaimed as a hero by both the Nationalists and the communists. He founded the Kuomintang and was the progenitor of the 1911 revolution.
41 (*Right*) His successor was Chiang Kai-shek who is still President of the Kuomintang in Taiwan.

42 The Second World War was for China the continuation of a war with Japan which had started in 1937. The city of Chungking after Japanese bombing.

43 Western influence and Japanese troops during the Second World War.

44 A haphazard civil war raged between the communists and the Kuomintang during the Sino-Japanese war. The communist centre was at Yenan. This capital with its simplicity, improvisation, and leaders who hollowed out cave dwellings of the Loess hills, captivated the imagination of many young Chinese and visiting Westerners.

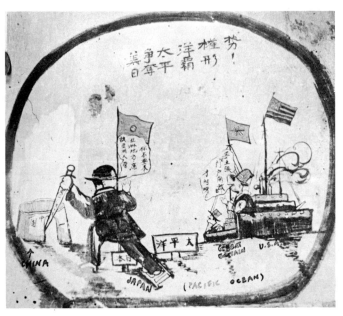

45 This wall drawing was part of the anti-Japanese propaganda promulgated by the communists.

46 The civil war went on after the end of the Second World War. In 1948 these trenches were manned by Nationalists who had temporarily forced the communists to withdraw.

47 Some of the results of the civil war: homeless refugees and defeated Nationalist soldiers.

48 During the Sino-Japanese war the communists and Kuomintang had formed a United Front. The symbols of both parties hang either side of a village theatre demonstrating anti-Japanese tactics.

49 Volunteers of the People's Liberation Army receive their orders.

50 There was an outward expression of enthusiasm and contentment among the younger communist factory workers. This is at Wu-Chi-Cheng in North Shensi.

51 A Kuomintang school of the period.

52 A Chinese Soviet workers' club room in the 1930s dominated by rough portraits of Marx and Lenin.

53 Anti-Kuomintang feeling was expressed in communist propaganda posters.

54 The civil war lasted until 23 April 1949, when Nanking was liberated by the People's Liberation Army. Nanking waits to greet the victors.

55 (*Below right*) The last session of the Nationalist government in July 1949 before the People's government took over on 1 October.

56 Chiang Kai-shek, his superior officers and the rump of the Kuomintang fled to Taiwan. These are some of the officers waiting to leave.

57 In July 1949 General Chin-yi dominated by a portrait of Chu Teh, one of the leaders of the Red Army, inaugurates a celebration of liberation.

6   The New Men

IN THEIR TRIUMPHANT SWEEP SOUTH the communists marched through crowds whose cheers, flags, and appropriate slogans had been carefully organized for weeks beforehand. But the enthusiasm was partly genuine. Nothing could be worse than the past; and the discipline and efficiency of the Red Army and the new local governments made a most favourable first impression.

The Red Army contrived to pay for its stores. Its officers were not arrogant towards the civilian population, and stayed in full control of their men, even after the fighting. The first local officials were often these officers, or the political commissars attached to all army units. If they were civilians they were trained to be equally humble in their first approaches towards the civilian population. A Shanghai presbyterian minister told me, six years later, that his first co-operation with the communists had been secured by a hiking expedition, organized for his Church Youth Group, and led by some of the new officials (cadres). What had particularly impressed him, he said, was that the cadres had washed the feet of the youngest members of the party every night.

The civilian officials had a uniform as functional and as un-splendid as the army's khaki. Their high-collared blue tunic was originally Sun Yat-sen's uniform for his followers; but most of the Kuomintang had dropped it years before or wore it in a well-cut woollen form. The uniforms of most of the young men from Yenan were patched and faded. They were meant to look poor, and like the poor, they wore padded tunics with cotton waste in winter not wool.

The new women cadres wore the same uniform as the men. Their hair was cut straight in severe bobs or swung in long pigtails down their backs. None of them wore make-up. They worked with the men, and lived in the same barracks. A few cadres married each other; and in theory, and very largely in practice, there was no sexual activity of any kind outside marriage. If two cadres of opposite sex walked back alone in the dark from a meeting, or were seen to be holding hands, they would be publicly criticized, and one of them would probably be posted away to another administrative centre. It was a matter for restrained boasting, particularly in front of Western visitors, when one of a married cadre couple could say that he or she had been separated from their spouse for several months or years. They worked in different towns, and they were glad to make this 'sacrifice for the revolution'. Besides, a conscientious official had little time for married life. Every hour of the day had its allotted activity; and periods for sleep were severely restricted. It was part of the ethos, encouraged by novels and newspaper articles of the period, that a cadre should cut into these hours yet further for his work or study. The communist myth was that it was a mark of the really good cadre to be able to do without sleep altogether for several nights on end.

Adultery, fornication, sloth, and drunkenness have continued to be among the least favoured vices of the communist society. Gluttony in recent years has been less frowned on. Officials say that Chinese cooking is part of their national inheritance, and so it is ideologically correct for good restaurants to continue; and for official banquets to be sumptuous with traditional Chinese cooking.

In the early days, however, the men and women cadres ate in communal dining halls which served food of varying qualities – the best and the most meat for the highest officials – but even for them less good and less varied meals than the town middle class were still able to afford. Junior officials swept and scrubbed for themselves and kept all their personal possessions in small unlocked cupboards. They were scrupulously clean: unhealthily so, many of the poorer Chinese thought. One of the least understood of the Red Army's propaganda lessons in Yenan had been that peasant mothers should wash their children, all over, every day.

It was extremely difficult to bribe these austere young people.

Even if they had wanted to be corrupt they had no private place to keep the bribes offered them, and no leisure to enjoy luxuries. Most of them were anyway well trained by the schools and universities of Yenan, and were high-minded to the point of priggishness. A Shanghai father told a foreigner that he and his family had prepared the most magnificent meal they could assemble for their son, return-ing with the Red Army from years of hardship in the north. They had made up his bed in his room, and asked his old friends to meet him. Only under orders from his superior officer would the young man agree to visit his family at all; and then he refused to eat the meal prepared for him, or sleep on his old bed. 'Rice and bare boards,' he said, 'are all I need now.'

The government these new men and women brought was to begin with, moderate. At first, in the conquest of Manchuria, unpopular Kuomintang officers, landlords, and factory owners had been publicly beaten or summarily executed. But this open, random violence was soon clamped down on when the communist leaders saw the damage it was doing to their image of national unity. The new government, Mao declared, was to be a 'People's Democratic Dictatorship'. There was to be 'democracy for the people, and dictatorship for the reactionaries'. The reactionaries were the land-lords, the closest associates of the Kuomintang rulers, and 'bureau-cratic capitalists'. (One definition of the bureaucratic capitalists later given to me was that they were Chiang's relations.) The petty bourgeoisie (that is the small shopkeepers), the national bourgeoisie (for instance factory owners), and the intellectuals (including those in professional occupations) were grouped with 'peasants' and 'workers' as part of the 'people' whose unity the new state should secure, and whose rights would be safeguarded. In the Chinese People's Consultative Conference which met in September 1949, the bourgeoisie were represented by members of the established political parties, including a dissident branch of the Kuomintang. But the leaders of the new society, it was said, were to be workers and peasants; and their official representative party in the Conference were the communists.

In practice this meant an amnesty for most ex-members of the

Kuomintang. Army units who had deserted during their retreat were incorporated into the Red Army, sometimes together with their officers. Members of the Kuomintang civil service were told to report to the local government centres, and then carry on with their old jobs. In the towns the first concern of the new government was to make life as normal as possible. Public services were got going again after the considerable damage done by the retreating Kuomintang. The local radio stations broadcast a continuous stream of reassurance and orders aimed at civil peace and security. Shops, banks and factories re-opened quickly. Businessmen continued to run their old businesses, except that the central government was now producing long lists of regulations for them about working conditions, welfare, and minimum wages. The most resented of the new regulations restricted an employer's right to dismiss workers without union agreement and heavy compensation. But the restrictions did prevent unemployment and destitution in the slump that, in Shanghai particularly, followed the government's first months in office.

This slump, and the government's control of monetary inflation, made life in many ways easier for townspeople. A new, more stable, currency replaced the old. The sale of gold and dollars except through a bank became illegal. Taxes were high and efficiently collected; and great pressure was put on everyone with surplus money not to spend it, but to buy victory bonds. Some of the first well-publicized executions in the towns were of black marketeers; but with exit permits rigidly controlled, there was no longer the same point in sending money out of China, or holding it in a form, like gold, which was easily transportable. In Shanghai, however, where groups of foreigners stayed on, there were to be small black-market transactions in currency for several years to come.

What struck visitors to China under the new government was how quickly the communist officials had put their own impress on what were supposed to be the ineradicable customs of China. For ten years to come visitors from China were to tell stories about what they had seen, which the 'old China hands', the businessmen who had lived in Shanghai and the treaty ports, contradicted flatly as 'impossible'. It was 'impossible' that begging, theft, and prostitution should have vanished from the Chinese city streets. But prostitutes, beggars, and petty thieves were rounded up into special camps on the city outskirts, officially sympathized with as victims of society, and trained in new occupations. The most distinguished guests of the new state found, sometimes to their indignation, that there were no prostitutes at all available. Unlocked trunks were left untouched on crowded railway stations. Hotel servants ran after departing guests with old socks, discarded into wastepaper baskets, and zealously retrieved. Tips for this, or any other service, were proudly refused.

It was only possible for the government to stamp out crime because they had also stamped out the old secret societies. By now these societies, common to every town in China, had become associations of gangsters tied together with a certain amount of Taoist magic and rites which were supposed to secure their members against the police. The old China hands, however, were sure that, where the British and French had been unsuccessful in stamping out secret societies in their far eastern empires, the communists could not have succeeded.

They were equally incredulous about the physical cleaning up of the Chinese cities. After the first months the contrast between the dirt and litter of the Hongkong streets, and the somewhat drab cleanliness of Shanghai and Peking, was remarked on by most travellers. In the new China the cadres had formed associations of local women whose job it was to be responsible for sweeping the pavement outside their homes and keeping the neighbourhood generally tidy. One of the first officially sponsored campaigns was to get rid of flies, rats, mice, and sparrows. (But the campaign had to be hurriedly backtracked when crops were eaten by field pests whose numbers were no longer kept down by the sparrows.)

The drabness many visitors complained about in the cities was added to by the general adoption of the cadre's blue uniform by both men and women. Blue cloth, for a time, was the only sort available in the shops. Even for those whose old clothes were still good, the revolutionary blue was useful protective colouring when silk or patterned cloth might otherwise have been picked out as evidence of counter-revolutionary sympathies. Women also adop- ted the female cadre's hair styles. Not having permanent waves or lipsticks was officially said to leave them more time to devote to Marxist study and revolutionary work. Only the wives of the capitalists, the factory owners of the big towns, were encouraged to go on curling their hair. Their husbands were expected to wear Western dress with a collar and tie when talking to officials or foreign visitors. These were slightly derogatory marks of the capitalists' class status.

By 1950, however, the towns had not changed radically. Without inflation and with the new social legislation, there was no longer the starvation and destitution among the very poor that there had been. But the people who had managed the towns continued, by and large, to manage them, and stayed betteroff than the people who were and had been their workers. There had been few arrests or executions for political reasons as yet, and below the surface the changes were not dramatic.

In the country it was different. There were fewer surface changes. Country peoples' clothes did not change, and there was little crime or prostitution in the villages to get rid of. But from the very beginning of the revolution landlords were outside the national partnership. The first job of the new cadres as they moved into each of the villages was to decide who were the landlords, and to group everyone else in the village into the officially defined classes.

Landlords, even if their holdings had been no larger than a suburban garden, were those who had let their land without working it themselves. Rich peasants worked their land with the help of hired labour. Middle peasants had smaller holdings which they worked almost entirely themselves with, perhaps, occasional help. Poor peasants had the smallest holdings, probably rented; and they might supplement their income from their own land by working for rich peasants or landlords. At the bottom of the old pyramid, or at the top of the new communist social structure, were the hired labourers.

It mattered immensely into which class an individual fell. Landlords not only lost their own land and their personal possessions to the poor peasants (although they might, if they were not judged guilty of some other offence, keep the same amount of land as the poorest villager for their own use); but they also lost their civil rights, and their children were discriminated against in schools and in selection for the universities. Rich peasants kept their land, but were officially disapproved of, and likely to be suspected of crime in any period of government repression. Poor peasants and hired labourers, like the skilled workers in the cities, were the official beneficiaries of the revolution. (Eight years later, at the time of the Hundred Flowers, there were bitter complaints that the cadres had misjudged individuals' class status.)

The poor peasants did benefit from the first land reform. At the end of it their holdings were slightly larger, and many of them had an extra quilt or cooking pot from a landlord's house. But there was an overall land shortage in most of China. The landlords' holdings, however they were divided, were not enough to raise the poor peasants to anything like the level of the rich peasants, or to what, in Europe, would be regarded as a reasonable standard of living.

The cadres' teams moving into the villages were instructed to live in the houses of the poorest peasants, if possible; identify themselves with their sufferings; and rouse them against the landlords. Land reform was not to be carried through until the majority of the whole village demanded it, and the peasants were encouraged to deal with the details of re-distributing the landlords' property themselves. Among the advantages of this, from the point of view of the communist leaders, was that more of the Chinese population played a positive part in the revolution, and therefore would be in danger if the Kuomintang returned.

After his property had been re-distributed, the cadre encouraged the peasants to bring the landlord to trial before a 'People's Court'. This was a crowd of local people who denounced the landlord for real, or partly real, or wholly imaginary, crimes, and shouted for his death or imprisonment. No evidence was heard except the yelled denunciations; and the landlord was pressed with blows and curses to confess to his crimes. 'Dig, dig the bitter roots. Vomit the bitter water,' was the slogan the cadres shouted as the people remembered old grievances. Some executions took place immediately. The trials were broadcast and heard in Hongkong where they made an extremely bad impression. But ever since the time of the trials there have been disputes about just how many landlords were involved, how many tens of thousands were shot, and how many of these were men whose oppression of their tenants had been truly criminal. The communists have since acknowledged that 'mistakes' (in other words wrongful executions) were made at this period; but ex-landlords, concealed landlords, and fugitive landlords, are still today the popular villains of Chinese communist mythology.

7 The Unified State

THE VISITOR FROM HONGKONG hears his first Chinese slogans come over the loudspeakers of the border station, and then over the loudspeaker piped to every compartment of his train to Canton and Peking. The station staff, says the loudspeaker, 'under the inspired leadership of Chairman Mao and the Communist Party of China' have raised their production level by 3·8 points. Their five-year plan will now be fulfilled in three years, ten months and five days. In the visitor's hotel the room stewards do not at first answer their bell because they are just finishing their meeting on raising their production levels. They have each of them unanimously agreed to clean 3·4 extra rooms a day. They were, the steward tells a visitor, 'inspired by the glorious example of Chairman Mao and the Communist Party of China'. He is speaking half-forgotten English without any witness present to report what he says to his questioner.

Elsewhere university professors, pedicab drivers, businessmen, a few of them again speaking without a witness or an interpreter present, have also raised their production levels, thanks to the same, identically inspired, leadership. The few visitors to China who have friends they knew before the revolution, find that they too quote the raised production levels, the same slogans expressed in exactly the same pattern of words.

Suddenly the pattern changes. There is a new slogan. The station staff, the room steward, the professor, are all 'walking on two feet', or 'consulting the experts', or 'exercising Red economy and thrift to safeguard the national heritage'. By traditional methods, and consulting their oldest staff member, an elderly porter of impeccable peasant ancestry, the station staff reveal that they are making an excellent substitute for axle grease out of swamp mud. The room stewards, by the same methods, have found out how to make reed brooms that clean the rooms with a minimum of expense. The university professor has been told about a neglected, effective, and cheap drug from the pharmacopoeia of traditional Chinese medicine. There is the same quotation of exact, decimal-pointed, statistics, and the same leadership thanked for the new inspiration they have given. In the past raised productivity was introduced into every conversation, however unlikely the opening seemed. Now inquiries about a parent's health, the working of a machine, the popularity of a picture, all produce the same references, ingenuously worked round to the new dominant themes of economy and traditional knowledge.

This uniformity, this absence of any individual point of view, far less complaint, is overpowering to most Westerners. It has been achieved by a national pattern of life in which there is nothing that is outside politics. Correct political attitudes and changes in political attitudes are taught in classes at schools and colleges, and at meetings for adults. In the autumn of 1964 *Small Friends*, a Shanghai publication for very young children published a song it thought apt for the times and suitable for the age of its readers. It went:

> *There is an evil sprite,*
> *The name is Johnson.*
> *His mouth is all sweetness*
> *But he has a wolf's heart.*
> *He bombs Vietnamese cities*
> *and kills the people.*
> *Chinese and Vietnamese are all one family.*
> *We will certainly not agree to this.*
> *I wear a red scarf*
> *and join the demonstrations with Daddy.*
> *With small throat but large voice I shout*
> *'US pirates get out, get out, get out.'*

Older children have classes occupying up to a quarter of their schooltime on the political theories and philosophy of Marx, Lenin, Stalin, and Mao; and on the history and achievements of the

Russian and Chinese communist parties. Bad reports of a student's political attitudes can prevent him getting the sort of work his qualifications merit; and make him or her into an object of permanent suspicion and surveillance from local political officials.

Adults attend meetings for political 'study'. These meetings may take several hours every evening, or be held only once or twice a month. It depends on the status of the individual; (the more intel-lectual his work the greater the number of meetings); and whether the period is one of political change. At their simplest these meetings consist of readings from newspapers and official handouts explaining policy. Everyone at the meeting is expected to listen carefully enough to report back the substance of the article, and to learn by heart the important slogans contained in it. The slogans are echoed in loud-speaker announcements, piped out not only at railway stations but in workshops, restaurants, or the stairway and lavatories of a block of flats. Banners with the same slogans are put up everywhere. Films and novels, as well as newspaper articles, are hurriedly produced to repeat the slogans and illustrate their practical application.

A play I saw in Shanghai was about a scientist horrified at the misuse of some of his work to support American germ warfare. He finally departed in a blaze of music and strong light to fight with the Chinese volunteers in Korea. But much of the interest of the play lay in its illustration of how political vice or virtue appeared in every aspect of life. The wicked College Dean showed his wickedness, not only in his actual treason, but in his long old-fashioned Chinese gown, reactionary in contrast to the heroic cadres' blue uniform. He had long, and again reactionary, finger-nails. His furniture was reactionary, Western style with lace antimacassars; so was his food, Western again; his wife's dresses; his abrupt manners to his servants; his own traditionally devious conversation. The play drew its biggest laugh from the audience when the hero, misled by the wicked dean, said, puzzled, 'surely science is more important than politics?'

The communist political lesson is not only that nothing is more important than politics, but also that political considerations must decide every action of life . . . and dominate every second of one's time. 'He who believes that spare time is private time lacks the correct attitude towards the revolutionary cause', said the Peking *People's Daily* 14 years after the establishment of the revolution. 'One must spend one's leisure hours strengthening one's ideology and improving one's work.'

It is wrong to scold a child in any but political terms, to lay out a garden for any but political reasons, or to enjoy a poem, picture, or film for qualities unconnected with the political lessons it teaches. This is a totalism reminiscent not only of Confucius and the laws of proper behaviour that must underlie every action of the gentleman; but also of the character training of a good girls' boarding school in England. In the boarding school, as in communist China, every action has its iceberg of political or ethical content. The girl who eats extra sweets, like the Chinese who buys black-market sugar, has committed not only a minor breach of the regulations, but also an ethical or political sin of magnitude. It could not have been committed if the Chinese, or the girl, had been in tune with the régime, or the Spirit of the School, and had fully accepted its teaching. Therefore the crime is as potentially revolutionary as throwing a bomb at the Mayor of Shanghai, or knocking down the headmistress. It must be analysed, preferably in public to rub home the lesson, in order that the criminal may seriously and sincerely repent, and others take warning from his or her example.

Public and private scolding is at least as effective in the Chinese state, as it is in an expensive English school, in producing the desired uniformity of action and thought. In the streets of Chinese towns it is the traffic policeman's duty, not to summons offenders, but to lecture them before a growing crowd until they acknowledge their faults. Young red-scarved Pioneers on buses reprove their elders for spitting. Cadres at public meetings scold those who have failed to read the right books or voice the right thoughts.

People who refuse to go to meetings (or refuse publicly to acknowledge their minor political faults) are likely first of all to be visited by delegations from their colleagues. They will be asked why they will not go, what is wrong with the meetings, what suggestions they have to improve them. The delegations will be patient, humble, and persistent. Listening to them and answering them will take more time than actually going to meetings.

A girl who had recently left college in Shanghai told me that when one of her fellow students failed to attend political meetings, and allowed his work to lapse generally, a group of his former friends were told by the cadre to go and see him. 'We stayed from supper until dawn with him once,' she said. 'When he told us to go away, we went, of course, but we always came back.' The young man finally agreed to attend meetings in future, and made a public confession of the faults in his general attitude which had led to his recalcitrance. 'His father had been a mill owner,' the girl told me. 'He had been unable to escape from his bourgeois background.'

Most Chinese from time to time have to make public criticisms of their past lives, and public confessions of their faults. For anyone with a pre-revolutionary middle-class background the confession is expected to include a denunciation of parents, teachers, and family habits, and an analysis of mistaken views at work, in their marriage, and towards their children. The audience of this self-criticism is expected to help the man or woman making it by pointing out faults he has omitted or the full seriousness of which he has failed to understand. Anyone who fails to emphasize a friend's faults to him publicly is himself liable to public criticism as a hidden enemy of his so-called friend and of state security. The traditional importance the Chinese have put on 'face', on a man's public image, make these public criticisms particularly painful; and the public denunciation of parents and teachers are outrageous by Chinese traditional standards. To the authorities the pain and outrage are a necessary part of the criticism. They mark the subject's decisive break with the past. He can no longer be the same man with the same standards as he was before. His only future is with the new, communist, standards.

Many of these public self-criticisms are made during one of the periodic campaigns against groups of people the authorities considered were, at that time, particularly vulnerable to non-communist thought, incorrect communist thought, or even counter-revolutionary thought. These campaigns have sometimes been called purges by the outside world. But the word 'purge' with its under-tones of physical brutality and mass murder is misleading. Since the government established itself in the early fifties there have been very few political (or criminal) executions in China.

In later campaigns those successfully denounced have often not even been imprisoned. The aim of the campaigns, the communists say, is not only to safeguard society but also to correct wrong thinking and to reform a section of the people – the mistaken individuals exposed by the campaign. Even for those imprisoned the state's first aim is reform. Death sentences since the early fifties, have generally been commuted for two years, to be carried out then only if the individual has not reformed. Reform in prison is shown, as it is out of it, by hard work in the prison factory, attention in political study groups, thorough self-criticism, and a denunciation of past associates and crimes. Few of the commuted death sentences, visitors to Peking and Shanghai prisons are told, need to be carried out.

Torture, in the ways in which it was used in Nazi prisons, in Stalinist Russia, and in Kuomintang China, is rare, if it is used at all. But the communists, and most of the prisoners they have released into the Western world, do not count 'physical methods of reform' as torture. Prisoners may be chained to encourage them to recant. One of the American women who were imprisoned in China had been kept in chains for most of two years. 'But they were light chains', she said on her release, 'and it was for my own good.' Other prisoners are kept short of sleep during their interrogations, and they may be beaten by their cell-mates whose duty it is to 'help' them recant and make a full confession.[30]

In the later campaigns, particularly the campaign against the intellectual critics of the Communist Party after the Hundred Flowers period, sentences to Labour Reform, or Labour Surveil-lance, were more common than prison sentences. There are Labour Reform camps attached to some state farms, and to some public works like the big irrigation schemes or new buildings in the far west. The people serving sentences work under guard. As in prisons the length of sentence and the severity of working conditions varies according to how genuine a prisoner's repentance is believed to be.

Some Western newspaper stories, particularly in America, say that forced, unpaid labour has built most of the new public works in China. The existence of Labour Reform camps on an enormous scale, involving millions of prisoners, is implied. No traveller in China has found evidence supporting these stories. Public work is to be seen all over the new state, but prisoners under guard working on it are a rarity. Probably these stories of the vast slave camps are founded on the difference between the Chinese and the Western interpretation of 'voluntary work'.

Peasants and townspeople are expected to work on public build/ings or irrigation schemes in their neighbourhood. The work is voluntary. Sometimes it is not paid, or badly paid; and very often the people who do it are expected to carry on with their ordinary farm work or city jobs in the time they have left over. People could refuse to do the extra work in theory. In practice a refusal to volunteer would involve whoever made it in the same sort of unpleasant, time/consuming and shaming process a refusal to attend a meeting involves.

Apart from Labour Reform those judged guilty in the 1958 and 1959 campaigns of a lesser degree of 'rightist thought' were often sentenced to work under supervision, sometimes in country com/munes, and sometimes in a menial capacity in their old town work/places. During these campaigns large groups from town offices, who were volunteers, not those individually denounced, were in any case sent to the villages to work on the land. They were expected to live as the peasants lived, eat the same food, and not try to clean or tidy up their rooms beyond the peasant standard.

The theoretical reasons for this enforced, but often temporary, migration are that townspeople are thus given an opportunity to learn from the doctrinally purer peasants and 'reform their work styles' by ennobling physical labour.

Sentences to Labour Reform and Labour Surveillance follow meetings of great bitterness: 'struggle meetings', where the accused are shouted at, sometimes hit, and denounced by their closest friends and relations. The confessions following these meetings in 1958 and

1959 were published in detail in the Chinese press. They were couched in abject and humiliating terms, particularly considering the former status and age of the men and women confessing. In the session of the National People's Congress, at the height of the campaign, the former ministers and their followers, who had criticized the Communist Party, confessed. A Western witness saw one of them, an elderly ex-minister weeping, and noticed that Prime Minister Chou En-lai, on the Praesidium pointedly ignored him, and went on talking and laughing with his neighbours.

Recent reports from China suggest that the campaign against the critics who had availed themselves of the Hundred Flowers was concluded in 1960. Afterwards the pendulum of permitted opinion swung a full-length back and forth. There was first a campaign against 'leftist' over-enthusiastic Communist Party members, and then, recently, a new campaign against rightists. This time they are called 'Revisionists', after Krushchev, and they are those who advocate softer policies and the weakening of class war.

Earlier campaigns and propaganda drives were aimed at groups whose thinking and organization fell outside communism. The family itself, the most potent group in pre-communist China, was never the subject of a direct campaign after 1949. Instead Chinese communist youth newspapers urged on young people their duty to support their old parents. *King Lear* was quoted in all seriousness by one young people's magazine as an example of decadent Western family life of the sort that would not be found in China.

Yet the family was weakened. After 1911 it had lost most of its legal powers, and now its members were encouraged to take disputes short of the law to the new welfare organizations rather than to the arbitration of senior relations. Moreover the prestige of the old in the family was inevitably lessened by the rapidity of technical as well as political change. Experience of the China of 40 years ago was a disadvantage, not an advantage, in the new state. What was wanted now was youth, and quickness to learn, politically and technically.

Much of the intensity of old-fashioned Chinese family life had depended on the utter absorption of women by their families. This was attacked by one of the first laws of the new government. Women were given equal legal rights with men, including rights to refuse a distasteful arranged marriage and rights to divorce. For a time the courts were crowded with women victims of the old system. Meanwhile women cadres urged other women to free themselves from 'feudal shackles' to their husbands or mothers-in-law. They encouraged them to learn to read, speak at meetings, and to go to work.

In the new China no adult and few children were without an organization which overlooked the details of their political education. Women were members of neighbourhood committees or sometimes trade unions or special women's organizations. The teaching of the new organizations was that a woman's first duty was to be a good citizen. A ground for divorce was that one's husband or wife was a counter-revolutionary. Wives were expected to denounce husbands at struggle meetings, and to report suspicious conduct to government cadres. Failure to do so would involve the wife herself in accusations of counter-revolution. Young children had the same duties. Children's comics published strip features showing daring, resourceful children who had detected their parents in counter-revolutionary activity. In the final picture the children are being congratulated by the local officials, while the police lead the criminal parents away.

Partly for economic reasons, and partly for reasons of doctrinal equality, factories and offices have been encouraged to set-up nurseries and crèches. When the urban and rural communes were first formed it was stressed that the many new nurseries, and the communal dining halls, and facilities for washing and mending clothes would 'free' women. They would reach new stature when they were full citizens working outside their homes. But Western stories of the total abolition of ordinary married life, are mistatements. Husbands and wives, particularly if both were cadres, students or emigrants to a new industrial area, were sometimes housed in separate dormitories. But it was never a policy to separate ordinary established married couples in towns or villages. Where new flats and houses are built they are always designed for family units often including space for old parents.

Like the old-fashioned family the Christian churches offered a mental escape from the communist system. Their Western connexions and ministers encouraged Western ideals in their converts. They might even have become centres of anti-communist thought and perhaps action. Communist pressure was put on the churches, first of all to get rid of their foreign funds and foreign connexions. The Western missionaries were pressed to leave; and those who did not became the victims of sometimes fantastic accusations.

The all-Chinese churches were then expected to adapt themselves to the niche prepared for them in the new society. There was official religious toleration, and in many cases the government was generous over tax rebates and other financial concessions. In return the churches had to act as patriotic organizations, and form their own pressure groups to support new government policy. Most of the Protestant churches and their million members did not find this incompatible with Christianity. Their main complaint was that their members were illegally discriminated against by over-enthusiastic cadres and schoolteachers.

The three million Roman Catholics were in a more difficult position. Many of their priests thought that it was impossible for them to cut their connexion with the Vatican. But the communists found this continuing and direct link with a foreign power suspect. Roman Catholic churches and their organizations, particularly the Legion of Mary, were accused of harbouring spies and saboteurs. The Bishop of Shanghai, Monseigneur Ignatius Kung, was arrested, together with several hundred other Shanghai Catholics. The Vatican excommunicated those priests and lay Catholics who tried to make their peace with the new state, thus adding to communist suspicions. In the resulting uneasy compromise most Chinese Catholics ended neither trusted by the communists, nor in full communion with Rome.

Buddhism and Islam are more compatible with the new state. Buddhist temples and monks are on the whole left alone. But, like the Protestants, the Buddhists complain that their influence drops steadily among the young. The Moslems had the advantage of being most numerous in border areas where the communists are careful not to cross the feelings of non-Chinese people needlessly. Their foreign friends also are in countries China is anxious not to offend. Islam is not only tolerated, but in Sinkiang and in the north-west there were sometimes generous government grants for the repair of mosques, and to subsidize Mullahs' schools and training colleges.

Even after 70 years of decline many more Chinese were influenced by the Confucian system of ideas (even if they only accepted parts of it) than any foreign importations. The communists, of course, denied the universal validity of the Confucian system; and they were concerned to fit Confucius and Mencius into their Marxist place as products of their time and class. They themselves and what they wrote was 'feudal'. Much of it was explicitly condemned as incompatible with the Marxist view of a good society. Confucius' concepts of the family and the social structure were explained as the ideology of a ruling class bent on the subjection of the 'people'. Mencius' view of history as 'now order, now chaos' was also singled out for particular condemnation as denying the existence of progress and the Marxist synthesis. But Confucius, as the teacher who had set once and for all the standards of proper behaviour, had been displaced long before 1949. The new government had only to give a final kick to some of the ideas they condemned most vigorously. Thereafter they could afford to resurrect Confucius and the classical books as historical phenomena: an interesting achievement of the Chinese people's great past. Since the mid-fifties new editions of the Confucian classics have been published in Peking, and Confucian scholars are allowed to continue their work and to teach.

The communist leaders, naturally more daring than their subordinates, used quotations from the classics in speeches and pamphlets as early as the 1930s and 40s. Liu Shao-chi quoted Mencius as well as the less condemned classics in an address published as *How to be a Good Communist*. But Liu's quotations, like the recent introductions and editorial notes in the new editions of the classics, are permissible only if they support the communist message. What Confucius or Mencius says is no longer true by its own virtue; it is true by virtue of its agreement with Marxism and Maoism.

To most Chinese townspeople disturbances during the reform of the churches were minor compared to the dislocation of government and business in 'the three anti' and 'five anti' campaigns of 1951 and 1952. The three antis were anti-bureaucracy, anti-waste, and anti-corruption in government offices. The chief sufferers in the campaign were the civil servants who had previously served the Kuomintang. But, as in later campaigns, any communist cadre against whom one of the current sins was proved was likely to be more severely punished than a non-party member. Government officials were kept locked in their offices, sleeping and eating there, until each of them had traced their working history back and proved that they had never been implicated in bribery or bad work. The better the office the more difficult this justification would be, as cadres were given percentages of the officials they were expected to bring to justice, and might themselves suffer if they failed to find their full quota of criminals.

The five antis of the campaign against businessmen were bribery, tax evasion, stealing government property, cheating on contracts, and stealing state secrets. As in the campaign of the three antis, there were genuine evils to be eradicated in the structure of Chinese business. But the campaign suffered, even more than the three antis did, from over-enthusiastic cadres, anxious to fulfill their quota of wrongdoers and ignorant of how complicated town government and business worked. 'Stealing state secrets' was interpreted to mean discovering government intentions by whatever means, however accidental or licit, and using that knowledge to make profits.

Businessmen were in any case an anomaly to many communists. Mao had said they were to be tolerated for a time in new China. But their background made them natural objects of suspicion to the less sophisticated cadre. Like the government officials, business-men were locked in their offices and exhorted to confess. When they asked what they were accused of, and what they should confess to, they were told to think and examine their account books. Special cadres called 'Tiger Beaters' were sent from office to office to rout out 'the tigers of bourgeois thought and action', bully the businessmen, and rouse their offices against them. Office managers were accused at public meetings by their workpeople; and, if they confessed humbly and if their sins were not too grave, they were sentenced to pay large fines. There were few executions; but those there were, were filmed, so that groups of recalcitrant businessmen could be shown what could happen to them. It was at this time that the grim joke circulated in Shanghai that it was unsafe to walk on the main streets because of the suicides plummeting from the upper office windows.

Later on the cadres' excesses particularly in the five anti campaigns were officially condemned. It was said that in the early campaigns against counter-revolutionaries some of the innocent had even been shot. But campaigns have continued: against the business community again; against corruption and bureaucracy in the Communist Party; against writers and those who had supported Hu Feng in his heresy that art could be separated from the interests of the state; against all intellectual and prominent critics of the Communist Party. Following all these campaigns there is tacit or open acknow-ledgement that the innocent have been punished, or that punishment has been over-severe. Accused people are allowed to slide back quietly into their old jobs. Cadres are reproved or sent elsewhere. Life is generally easier for most people for a few months. Then there is a new editorial in the Peking *People's Daily* denouncing a new group. It is copied in local newspapers. New directives are sent to local cadres, new meetings held, and a new campaign is under way.

The Chinese communists allege that these constant campaigns have been necessary. The pressure of revolutionary change must be kept up; and the roots of bourgeois thought must be dug out for the sake of the individual as well as for the health of society as a whole. Even more serious, they say, are the constant activities of saboteurs paid by the twin paper tigers of the Kuomintang in Taiwan and the American Imperialists in the West.

In Taiwan the Kuomintang do their best to add substance to communist claims by boasting of their continued war against the régime, and the activities of their guerrillas on the mainland. But the activities of all possible Kuomintang and American-trained saboteurs have to be stretched very thin indeed if they are to account for all the accusations of foreign-inspired counter-revolution.

An argument put forward by some critics of the communist government is that these constant claims of sabotage are caused by the Chinese leadership's paranoia. The Chinese leaders, so the argument goes, have been maddened, much as Stalin was in his last years, by the contradictions in their own doctrine and by unquestioned power. Because their doctrine must be faultless and they themselves are faultless in following it, state difficulties and disputes must come from outside enemies or from internal treachery.

However, the case for the Chinese leaders' paranoia or a comparison of them with Stalin is weak at several points. They have, in fact, not claimed to be faultless, although faults in policy and the execution of policy are generally blamed on cadres below the top ranks of the party. In marked contrast to what happened to the Russian leadership in the 1930s there have been no spectacular trials or accusations of treason among the heads of the Chinese Communist Party. On the few occasions when the top leadership has been seriously divided the split has been belittled, and has not been followed by any vendettas against the fallen leaders' personal followers.

In 1959 there were doubts among some of the top leaders about the policies of the Great Leap Forward (the rapid introduction of communes, and the forced pace of industrialization). Some of these doubts may have been communicated to the Russians. Among those who were involved were Chen Yun, who was senior deputy premier, and Marshal Peng Teh-huai, the then Minister of Defence, one of the most respected of the civil-war veterans, and the commander of the Chinese volunteers in Korea. Both men disappeared temporarily from public life. Chen Yun after a few months reappeared on state occasions in, apparently, positions of accustomed prestige. In 1965 he was again appointed deputy premier, but this time to rank second not first in their hierarchy.

Peng Teh-huai has not, at the date of writing, reappeared in public life (in 1960 he attended a colleague's funeral). In 1965 he was not re-elected as a deputy premier, but he has also not been publicly deprived of his party offices, his parliamentary membership or his defence council post (he was dismissed from the Ministry of Defence in 1959). His quarrel with official policy may have been as much about the army changes at the time of the Great Leap Forward as about strictly economic policy. Attempts to make the army more democratic, by having officers serve part of the time in the ranks, and to increase party control of the army were not popular among soldiers. There was also professional criticism of the arms given to the peasant militia instead of to the regular army, the cessation of military supplies from the Soviet Union, and the diversion of soldiers on to farm work. The Chinese communist leaders have always been particularly sensitive to the dangers of an army coup; or even an over-professional army attempting to manipulate policy so as to secure better military supplies and strategy. In the summer of 1965 military over-professionalism was again hit when all badges and titles of office were abolished in the Chinese army.

Neither the paranoia alleged against the Chinese leaders or their own allegations of sabotage are as convincing reasons for the continuing purges as the historical and psychological background of the Chinese people. There were national characteristics which made them initially welcome their particular brand of communist moral uplift; and national characteristics which seemed an unlikely foundation for a continuing communist state. Until 1911 the Chinese had been governed by emperors who not only told people what to do, but told them in terms of great moral superiority how they should behave and think.

People were used to being organized into small groups and letting officials know the details of their households. (The Mongols, after their conquest of Hangchow in the thirteenth century, had the names of the inmates posted on every house door.) Meetings to explain proper conduct and the politico-moral education of schoolchildren were familiar. The rebellious peasants of the Yellow Turbans in the second century A.D. had even encouraged the public confession of sins. Above all the idea that there is one, and only one correct line of conduct, is central to Chinese thought.

On the other hand many of the old traditions of Chinese family strength were inimical to any efficient modern government. The first loyalty of the good communist citizen, the communists had to emphasize, was to the state not to his family. It was illegal and improper to enrich one's family while robbing the state by bribery and corruption. They then added that it might be right to leave one's small children in a nursery or one's parents in an old people's home if the work one was then free to do was of national importance.

In the towns Chinese shopkeepers and craftsmen had developed one of the most competitive traditions in the world. Acute poverty made small differences in prices very important; and there were no effective restrictions on conditions, hours of work, or the quality of goods produced. Shopkeepers and businessmen were used to evading legislation designed to impress rather than to be universally enforced. They were used also to negotiating their own conditions with local and central governments, and to buying or by-passing the official sanctions needed.

Westerners who knew China in the 1920s and 1930s called the Chinese the most individualist people in the world. Many of these Westerners have been quite unable to accept that the new govern-ment in which individualism is a major sin, stays in power by any-thing except the most rigid repression of the majority of the people. (Their view is important, because some of 'the old China hands' with this background are now advisers on Chinese affairs to Western institutions and governments. More of them, ex-businessmen largely from Shanghai, work in Hongkong where their advice is freely given to those reporting or visiting communist China.)

The evidence commonly quoted to show that many of the Chinese people are opposed to their government is the outburst of the Hundred Flowers Movement in 1957.[31] This remarkable episode followed the post-Stalin thaw in the Soviet Union. Mao Tse-tung made a speech to communist leaders, and extracts from it were then leaked to the Chinese public. The most picturesque quotations referred back to the Golden Age of Chinese philosophy: 'let a hundred flowers blossom, let a hundred schools of thought contend'. It was interpreted as an invitation to criticize government policies; and after an initial hesitation the criticisms mounted to fill every newspaper, notice board, and discussion meeting in the country. Those who were backward with their criticisms were told that it was unpatriotic and uncommunist not to speak out now.

There were complaints about living conditions and bureaucracy from town workers. But the bulk of the Hundred-Flowers criticisms were from businessmen, politicians outside the Communist Party, and people who in the West would be classed as holding pro-fessional jobs. Most of the criticisms were about communist privileges, methods and personnel rather than about the basic aims and exis-tence of the communist state. A constant note in the complaints was that Communist Party officials were arrogant, or usurped all power for themselves and other members of the party in contrast to the principles they professed. 'Feudal princes and stinking charlatans,' said one professor complaining about communist officials in the university administration.

Most of the universities copied Peking's 'Democratic Wall' on which were pinned critical notices, and student meetings fanned the mounting excitement. Krushchev's speech denouncing Stalin, which had been kept secret in China, was first published by Peking University; and students drew dangerous morals. The more extreme statements were not published until after the Hundred Flowers Movement had been officially ended, and the process of 'pruning the dangerous weeds' had begun. The rightists of the Peking Geological Institute were then reported to have called for the killing of all Communist Party members; and at Nankai University the slogan 'Exterminate the Communist Bandits', was published and Mao's writings condemned as designed to mislead the people. At Hanyang the senior schoolchildren rioted, ransacked educational offices, and took unpopular cadres prisoner.

It has been said that the more extreme student statements were invented by the government after the Hundred Flowers Movement to enlist popular support for the suppression of the critics. This sup-pression was carried out by confessions, self-criticisms, public condemnations, and sometimes the exile or demotion of those concerned. The only executions reported were those of three of the leaders of the Hanyang school riot. Undoubtedly the Communist

121

Party leaders took a serious view of their unpopularity with at least a section of the student population. They blamed the bourgeois background of the rightist students; but even the students from the most bourgeois backgrounds had had eight years of communist schooling, classes in Marxism, and meetings to denounce the sins of their parents. They were, moreover, as students a privileged and selected class. Student food and dormitories seemed drab to Western visitors, but they were better fed, housed and clothed than the majority of the population. One of the results of the Hundred Flowers was that the party leadership apparently decided that students were over-privileged, and over-separated from the trials of the rest of the population. There was new stress on 'learning through labour'. Students were expected to spend longer periods during their vacations, and immediately they graduated, on manual labour, generally in village communes. Half-work half-study schools became an increasingly important part of the educational system. In May 1965 the Peking *People's Daily* stated in an editorial that: 'the system of study combined with factory or farm work will remove an important breeding ground for the restoration of capitalism.'

An argument about China is whether the Hundred Flowers Movement represented a basic and general discontent with the communist government; a discontent that was only just showing its full extent when the campaign ended; or whether it showed a more surface discontent with bureaucracy, some specific complaints, and the general excitability and idealism of all students. How far has this discontent, whether on the surface or deeper, survived the renewed political thought moulding which followed the campaign? Does it still exist in much the same forms today?

Most visitors to China now receive the impression of a united and indoctrinated country. No one, or scarcely anyone, complains openly to them. Many of these visitors are anyway well disposed towards communism. The sort of Chinese they come into contact with are, indeed, likely to be firm supporters of the government: interpreters or the chairman of village communes, or presidents of women's associations – official spokesmen of all kinds. Discontent would have to be officially approved, before they would voice it.

Popular unrest, however, beyond a certain point would be difficult to hide, and lead to rebellion. Diplomats, visiting businessmen, even the evidence of Chinese refugees in Hongkong agree that rebellion is very unlikely. Most of what they say supports the view that only a minority of Chinese are still hostile to communism; and only a very small number would prefer the present alternative government of the Kuomintang.

58 'Make our economy prosperous' reads a communist poster of the 1950s; this was one of the primary aims of the new communist government and a principle of the People's Democratic Dictatorship.

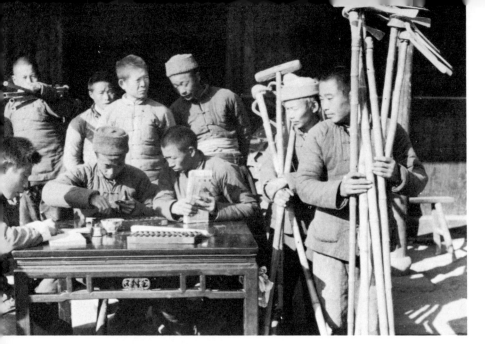

59 Land reform in China was confiscation of land from the landlords and its redistribution among the peasants. In this photograph new title deeds and farm implements are being distributed.

60 These capitalist businessmen 'voluntarily' surrendered their enterprises to the state in 1956. Previously, however, there had been considerable economic and personal pressure on all capitalists by the communist régime.

61 In 1958 the year of the 'Great Leap Forward' People's Communes which aimed at collective farming were established. Harvesting at the Hochang People's Commune.

62 Traditional terraced cultivation continued on a massive scale. This is in the Barian Hills, Kwangsi-Chuang Autonomous Region.

63 Squalor and untidiness were repugnant to the cadres of the new régime who were sometimes over-zealous in their enthusiasm for cleanliness and good order.

64 Scrupulous cleanliness extended to daily sweeping of the roads. This is in 1960 in the suburbs of Peking.

65 Women cadres of the new régime encouraged all women to free themselves of their 'feudal shackles' and go out to work. This is a meeting of women dockers.

66 Women take a lead in encouraging cotton-growers to use progressive methods.

67 (*Above*) At a communist court this woman is trying to obtain a divorce. A ground for divorce is for one of the parties to be a counter-revolutionary.

68 (*Below left*) The régime insisted that the only way was that of communism; any expression of counter-revolutionary activity was suppressed by imprisonment. A communist political prison cell.

69 (*Right*) Roman Catholicism is officially tolerated by the new government; but only at the expense of Catholics severing their ties with Rome.

70 (*Far right*) Buddhism and Islam are more compatible with communism. This is at the Buddhist University in Peking.

71 (*Below right*) Peking Moslems celebrate the Bairam Festival.

72 The people have the right to vote for their Deputies who sit in the National People's Congress. This is at Anshan in 1950 where the list of Deputies is displayed.

73 The annual commemoration of Liberation is celebrated on 1 October. This display outside the National People's Congress in Peking represents the industrial output in 1959.

8   New Scholars and Artists

THE CHINESE TRADITION of the official who retired to his native province, because he disagreed with the policy of the government of the day, was at least as strong and as admired as the tradition of the protesting censor. By 1949 students had got used to rioting against government they disapproved of. Most of their elders, the class who had once been the emperor's scholar officials, had withdrawn in disgust from government. It was better, the scholars of the interregnum thought, not to risk one's own corruption or one's family's ruin by trying to clean out the Augean Stables of the administration. They retired mostly to the universities, but country estates or even Western business were preferable to the new civil service. They remembered, however, that as the educated and civilized men of their generation it was still the government's proper duty to listen to them; and their's to admonish and advise, even if not actively to commit themselves.

This superior withdrawal was as obnoxious to the communists as the students' rioting. No admonition, it was soon made clear, was possible or tolerable to those to whom absolute MarxistMaoist truth had already been revealed. Anyone who retired to their native province would be expected to take part in productive work by joining the local agricultural cooperative, and submitting to the political education organized for them by the local cadre.

There has, however, been some rethinking about advice from those outside the party. Very useful advice, tactfully wrapped up in Maoist language and designed to further the longterm ends of the revolution, has at times been acceptable from members of certain professions, even when they were not party members. Engineers, and a few other specialists, in practical sciences have been allowed this liberty. But, during the early periods of political pressure even engineering advice was only acceptable from the politically pure, and the quoted slogan was about the need to be both 'red and expert'. Red first, but the order of importance was reversed when times got, politically, easier.

However, this was never a concession for the less immediately useful professions: artists, writers, university and school teachers, doctors, and most research scientists – the people who appeared to themselves, and to much of the rest of the world, as the direct custodians of the traditions of Chinese culture. The communist view of their proper place in the new society has always been clear. As early as 1942 Mao Tse-tung endorsed for China the classic Marxist subordination of art and literature to the interests of the proletariat. One of the best known of the authors then in Yenan, Ting Ling, criticized herself, and the editor who had published her articles, for adverse comments, not about the basic tenets of communism, but about the arrogance of party members. Young authors, dramatists, and artists in Yenan were instructed to concentrate on work showing party members and Red Army soldiers as flawless heroes, and exhorting people to further sacrifices on their behalf. The intellectuals were told to be 'educational and popular'. The audience they were to aim at were 'workers, peasants, soldiers and cadres'. (Some at least of their work had close parallels to articles in wartime Britain which were equally designed to increase public support for the war effort.)

In 1949 the pressure on the intellectuals was not at first heavy. They were encouraged to visit the villages, watch the peasants rejoice in their new landholdings, and hear about their grievances against the landlords. Like the rest of the population they went to meetings, and were expected to master Marxist doctrine.

All artists, however, became members of a big union: the All-China Federation of Literary and Art Circles. This Federation has nine branches: literature, drama, painting, music, dance, folk arts, vocal music, films, and photography. Between them the Federation and its branches control teaching institutes for the arts, studios, theatres, and most outlets for book and picture publication. If an artist wants his work to appear it is only sensible for him to follow any suggestions the Federation makes about themes or alterations. In return the recognized members of these unions found that they were guaranteed regular salaries even if considerable time passed during which they did not produce new work. Writers received about £15–£30 ($42–$84) a month in 1964, less than an engineer but more than most skilled workers. They also received small fees on each printing of their books: the author of a best seller makes £1,000–£2,000 ($2,800–$5,600) from it. Successful Chinese writers are nowhere near as financially well-off as Russian writers.

In 1954, in the first ideological thaw following Stalin's death, a literary critic, Hu Feng, published a long justification of the idealist position in literature. His article was heavily attacked as 'subjective'; supporting the writers' withdrawal into 'Ivory Towers', instead of their immersion in the life and problems of peasants and workers. The literary attacks on him were reinforced by accusations of sabotage, and past and present intrigues with the Kuomintang.

Meanwhile Hu Feng's article and his crimes had been made the occasion for a tightening of controls over intellectuals generally, and over writers particularly. Countrywide meetings were called at which intellectuals were expected to criticize not only Hu Feng's views, but also what they themselves had said in the past which might be construed as 'subjective thinking'.

Once again the pressure slackened, this time culminating in the Hundred Flowers Movement. Throughout the country intellectuals voiced their discontent with heavy-handed party control, not only of what they wrote or the research they did, but also of what they read. All Western books and the ideas in them, they complained, had been automatically bad, all Russian ones good.

In the reaction from the Hundred Flowers Movement, the mass recanting of the rightists whose criticism had been too outspoken, and the punishment among others, of Ting Ling, many of the old rules about what could be written, painted, produced, read, or said, were re-introduced, but not with quite the same fervour as in the mid/fifties. Another period of relaxation followed. Most of the rightists (but not Ting Ling), were allowed to slip back into their old employment. Once again there was limited freedom of work, and, after the Sino/Soviet breach, Western learned periodicals and books were more freely available. Then, in the autumn of 1964, an article in *Red Flag* called for renewed class struggle. Creative writers particularly were rebuked for their frivolity. The example was quoted to all intellectuals of the amateur workers and peasants who painted, wrote film scenarios, novels or poems in their spare time. Group writing, under the leadership of local Communist Party Committees, was noted with particular approval as likely to be doctrinally pure and correct.

Yet whatever doubts they might have about Marxism, most Chinese intellectuals supported the government's new political nationalism: its independence of foreigners, and its reassertion of China's tradi/ tional place in the world. Cultural nationalism, however, was less acceptable. They had been warned about it. Just as the Marxist limits on intellectuals had been defined at Yenan, so had the nationalist. They must work, they were told at Yenan, within 'national' forms and use 'national styles'. Later on communists, throughout China used the slogan 'walk on two legs'. It was a useful multipurpose slogan. It could mean the combination of industry with agriculture (communes and rural factories); but it was also used to stress the combination of Chinese and Western traditions of learning.

For a time there was see/sawing with the emphasis sometimes on Western learning, sometimes on the Chinese heritage. After the break with Russia, however, the see/saw came decisively down on the side of national tradition because there was now no doctrinally pure source of Western expertise. Nationalism appeared in unexpected places. In 1964 it was revealed with horror that in the National Orchestra 70 per cent of the musicians played instruments of foreign, Western origin. The orchestra was reformed so that Chinese instruments predominated. But the orchestra continued to have, as the major part of its repertoire, stirring marches and accompaniments to patriotic songs which sounded closer to the international brass band than to Chinese tradition.

The results on Chinese civilization of the restraints of Marxism and nationalism were very variable. The Chinese intellectuals were fortunate that nationalism did stop the wholesale adoption of everything in the communist West. On the other hand, the need to learn Marxism and the stress, at first, on learning from Russian experience, broke some of the old rigid Chinese cultural patterns, and, particularly in specialized scientific fields, stimulated new research.

No field of Chinese culture has been so disputed over as medicine. The first Western doctors to practise in China despised traditional medicine, and they taught their Chinese students that it was little but quackery. Some of the drugs of the traditional pharmacopoeia, however, notably ephedrine from the Chinese MaHuang, had been known and valued in the West for many years.

What seemed pure black magic to most Westerners were Chinese methods of treatment, particularly acupuncture and the theories of anatomy and psychology on which it was founded. In acupuncture hot, cold, or, nowadays, electrically stimulated, needles are stuck into the body at various key points generally far from the site of the pain. Cirrhosis of the liver is classically treated by a needle stuck an inch or so into the flesh just below the knee. The theory is that the internal organs and the external parts of the body are connected by twelve channels, most of which are unknown in Western medicine.

Psychologically, traditional Chinese medical practitioners lay great stress on tailoring their medical prescriptions to the needs of the individual. Illness, they say, is caused by a disturbance of the natural balance. But this balance is different for different people. To treat somebody successfully traditional doctors have to know about their family relationships, where they come from, what worries them, and, in the present society, their doctrinal and class background. In the course of treatment psychological, as well as physical disturbances, should be healed.

Acupuncture is not painful. Even when needles are pushed with some force far into the flesh, all that the patient feels is what is generally described as 'a gathering sensation'. It is very suitable for outpatient work. Its practitioners will treat anything from brain tumours to appendicitis, and there is no need for expensive surgical techniques. Besides its cheapness, the drugs and instruments needed for traditional medicine are easily available in China, and there are many more of its practitioners already at work than there are Western doctors. Doctrinally Chinese medicine complies with the communist argument about 'the wisdom of the masses'. Many Chinese, particularly the older peasants, prefer traditional to Western medicine.

Since 1949 traditional medicine has achieved a new respectability among the educated Chinese. New hospitals have been established devoted entirely to Chinese medicine, and some of the best town hospitals are mixed, offering both Western and traditional treatment. The Chinese naturally claim good results from traditional medicine; and its failures (like the official advocacy of live tadpoles swallowed after intercourse as a contraceptive) have been conveniently buried. Most Westerners are doubtful about the efficacy of widespread use of acupuncture. But, even the doubtful, like Western journalists, when they try acupuncture in China for ailments like colds or indigestion, often claim to have had some benefit from it; and it seems to work better than most other known treatments for rheumatism. At present there are clinics of acupuncture in the Soviet Union and in France, and several qualified specialists in its use in London.

In the meantime there have been indisputable advances in Western medicine in China. By 1959 nearly 50,000 fully qualified doctors had been trained, and four times that number of partially trained medical auxiliaries. The campaign for cleanliness, the building of new hospitals and new country clinics, mass vaccinations and inoculations, and new housing in cities with lavatories linked to efficient town sewage systems, have greatly raised Chinese health standards. Childbirth and the care of small children has been one of the priorities for medical help, and infant and maternal mortality has fallen dramatically.

At the time of the Hundred Flowers Movement there were relatively few complaints about medicine: except the universal one of

138

bureaucratic Communist Party meddling. The only mistake constantly alleged against the responsible ministries was too great reliance on Soviet methods. Russian doctors taught their methods of 'painless childbirth'; and preached, doctrinally so effectively, that in the Peking hospitals women were referred to as having a 'painless but sore parturition'.

Concerning the other sciences Professor Mikhail Klochko, one of the visiting Soviet experts, has published a somewhat discouraging report.[32] Professor Klochko, who is a chemist, found competent senior scientists, promising juniors, and reasonably well-equipped and spacious laboratories in the institutes he visited. But there was doctrinaire control of scientific projects, inadequate graduate training, too much research secrecy (in Kunming he found a girl working on a problem already solved in a Peking laboratory), and above all scientists' time was wasted on endless political meetings. He visited laboratories which, during working hours, were denuded of all responsible scientific staff. He also found that the higher the grade of the scientist the more meetings he had to attend and the less time he had for research.

Professor Klochko visited China during the Great Leap Forward and its aftermath. It was a time of particular political pressure on Chinese intellectuals. Two years later when conditions in China were generally easier and more relaxed, the Royal Society delegation reported in more optimistic terms. Like Professor Klochko they found laboratory standards varied greatly. But, in the opinion of most of them, senior scientists were not unduly worried by political pressures and time wasted on meetings. In the main laboratories they found research work of a high standard on both 'pure' and applied subjects.

The high standard of Chinese physics, anyway, is supported by the evidence of the Chinese atomic bombs, made without Russian help. Nuclear physicists are said to be subjected to less political harassment than other Chinese; and their work is helped by the pressure on students to specialize in the physical rather than the biological sciences.

Building, and the decoration of buildings, was one of the traditional glories of China. But when the communists took power it had be, come a neglected glory. In Peking, in the Forbidden City, just before 1949, weeds were growing in the imperial courtyards, rubbish piled up in pavilions, walls were falling down, roofs were falling in, and nothing was painted or swept. The new government had an immediate spring clean. The palace was meticulously restored on the advice of historians and architects. The pillars of the great pavilions were gilded and re-lacquered in colours to match pictures of their original painting. The marble balustrades were re-carved, and golden coloured tiles baked for the roofs.

There was a similar reconstruction of temples and palaces outside Peking. The palaces at Sian, the lakeside pavilion at Hangchow, even the monstrous nationalist monuments to Sun Yat-sen at Canton, were tidied, repaired, and used for appropriate displays. At Hang, chow they even replaced the carp the Kuomintang had killed in one of the temple pools.

New town planning and the new buildings, particularly those built in Peking, have been less successful. Under the emperors the great gates and the Imperial palace dominated the city's small grey houses and narrow streets. The imperial prohibition on buildings able to overlook the palace was little breached by the Kuomintang, partly because their capital and therefore most of their new building was at Nanking. But the communists moved the capital back to Peking. New main roads, considerably larger than the amount of traffic yet makes necessary, were driven through the old complex of lanes; and large blocks of offices, new flats and hotels were built, overshadowing the old palace and walls.

To begin with much of the detail of several of the new Peking buildings were modelled on the old imperial palaces. Their roofs were curved up in the way the emperors had hoped would cheat the stupider flying devils who could only manage straight lines. The roof tiles had to be specially baked, and sometimes offices and hotels had porches or halls of carved and lacquered pillars. These buildings were expensive, and during the mid-fifties increasingly condemned as extravagant and tasteless. Newer buildings were starker, but still often ornamented with statues and pillared entrances. The style was similar to that adopted for Stalin's new buildings in Moscow, and throughout the communist world. Many foreigners and some Chinese have regretted the changing of old Peking, and the absence of any new local style in the building of the new city.

There have also been doubts in China, although of a rather different sort, about the restoration of the old palaces and their use to display the imperial collections. The buildings had undoubtedly been used for 'feudal' and 'imperialist' purposes. A young Intourist guide told me that it was for these reasons that she did not like showing foreigners round them. She thought they gave 'a wrong impression of modern China'.

This girl, a Shanghai college graduate in her early twenties, had also reluctantly followed me round an exhibition of early paintings from the Imperial collections. Most of them were of court scenes: imperial children at play, an empress embroidering surrounded by her maid-servants, an emperor hunting.

'These pictures,' the girl said, 'are not interesting to me. They do not teach any moral lesson.' She preferred, she said, an exhibition of Russian paintings which had recently toured China. They were in the Socialist Realist (or Pre-Raphaelite) style: a young Pioneer rebuking his drunken grandfather; heroic portraits of Stakhanovites; two girls leaning eagerly out of the window of a model village house when the soldier's letter arrives from the front.

The classic Chinese tradition of painting and the classic communist one have in fact co-existed since 1949. Traditional Chinese ink and brush-work scrolls of great beauty and delicacy are still being painted in China by men tolerated by the state and even state-subsidized. Subjects are classic: lotus and plum blossom, willows, wild geese, cormorants, boats, mountains, waterfalls and lakes. Fu Pao-shih, one of the most admired artists in China today, in 1962 painted a picture he called 'Sitting Beside the Tai Lake After Playing the Ku Chin'. The painting, like the musical instrument it refers to, has a Sung dynasty ancestry. Its subject is one of the classic formulae – lapping water and mist with on the hill above one solitary white-robed figure. Fu Pao-shih has students and colleagues who follow the same austere and scholarly tradition of the classic imperial

painters. But even they are expected always to keep political considerations in mind. One of the other pictures Fu Pao-shih exhibited in
1962 was called 'The Yellow River Runs Clear', and was officially
pointed out as evidence of the artist's admiration for the achievements
of the state and the river control workers.

The Chinese paintings, however, which are easiest for most
Westerners to like and understand are livelier and more frivolous.
The men painting them are successors, the Chinese say, to the icono-
clast, and often politically revolutionary, artists of the eighteenth
century. Chi Pai-shih until his death in 1957 was a painter in this
tradition whose works figured largely in every exhibition for
foreigners. He ran a studio of artists painting all the types of pictures
he had made famous, mostly small animals and flowers, and in
his last years the master did little more than add an approving
blossom to a picture he liked, or a pair of bees, or a laudatory
inscription. A younger man in the same popular style is Li Ko-jan
whose buffaloes and cheerful southern children have been extensively reproduced.

The more austere traditional Chinese paintings, with their
economy of line and sentiment, have been greatly admired by some
Western abstract painters. Li K'u-ch'an's eagle or Wu Tso-jen's
camel caravan are very close to modern Western painting. Wu
Tso-jen studied in Europe, and he has been particularly drawn to
the spaces of China's far north and west rather than to crowded,
traditional, mountain and water landscapes. But modern Western
painting, even non-abstracts, is condemned in China. Very few of
the paintings in an exhibition of modern British art taken to China
were much liked by the people who saw them or by the artists
charged with their official criticism. Abstracts and many of the other
paintings were 'decadent'. The Chinese particularly disliked the
Western use of yellows and greens. 'The colours of a decaying
corpse', one of them said about a still life.

The exhibitors had wondered whether 'kitchen sink' paintings
would be popular. They had included a portrait of a miner in his
home, and a working-class kitchen interior. But the kitchens, the
Chinese said, were untidy and squalid. The miner looked small,

overwhelmed, and tired. These pictures were, if anything, more disapproved of than the abstracts. The worker heroes of Chinese pictures (like the many portraits of Mao Tse-tung himself) are expected to be larger than life, confident, perhaps smiling, and posed against a perfect field of corn or a smoothly running, tidy and modern factory.

In accordance with the dictum of the Yenan Forum artists paint for the people, and to further their cause; so the sort of subject commonly chosen will be 'Girls Bringing in the Commune's First Harvest', 'An Old Woman (but not a toothless or ugly old woman) Learns to Read', or 'The First Steel Ingot is Forged'. Among the Western style paintings those with most originality are likely to be the landscapes and portraits of the great epic – the Long March.

It is perhaps unlikely that the two traditions of painting will survive for ever running parallel but entirely separate courses. At one period it looked as if traditional painting was considered second best except for its power as a foreign money-getter. In the Peking Central Institute of the Fine Arts, in the mid-fifties, all the paintings on the walls were of the Socialist Realist school. The Director reluctantly acknowledged to me that he did have Chinese traditional painters on his staff; but, he said, the students (like my interpreter) were 'not interested' in their work.

At the time of the Hundred Flowers Movement several well-known traditional-style painters complained of the neglect of their art, and the contempt with which students and teachers of the new style treated them. But since 1960 and the break with the Soviet Union, visitors' accounts suggest that there has been more emphasis on the importance of both historical and new, traditional-style paintings. One third of the paintings in the 1962 national art exhibition in Peking were officially described as 'traditional'; and the exhibition was accompanied by publicity about the studios of traditional artists and the training of their successors.

The Yenan precept about artists learning from the people has resulted in the official adoption and fostering of some arts which were previously confined to peasant amateurs. One of the pleasantest

143

of these are the red and multi-coloured paper cutouts which peasant women make to stick on windows and doors at the New Year. The women base their ideas on a mixture of traditional design, local news, and what they think would be funny or suitable for the time of year. They have now been organized in commune work teams, and are sometimes provided with patterns. Their work is bought from them for general sale in China and abroad. The new designs for these cutouts have on the whole been agreeable; and the heroic subjects not too intimidatingly inhuman. Cheerful young women with corn sheaves, even a squarish version of Chairman Mao, fit well into the traditional patterns.

More sophisticated decorative art has suffered in much the same way as painting has done. Many craftsmen have been organized into co-operatives and emphasis has been placed on their political education. Bourgeois art-forms, they are told, should be avoided, and all should work for the good of the state. Classic pottery, silk hangings, carved ivory and jade are still produced, much of it for sale abroad. But there is less of a living tradition than with painting, and even less independence of thought among the designers for the crafts.[33] Much of the craftwork is debased, although still painstaking, partly because so much of it was aimed at the Soviet market. Soviet buyers admire lavishness and colour, and the Soviet technicians in China and their wives shopped for the usual sort of souvenir. Silver and gilt dragons embroidered on black silk were particularly popular, so was ivory and jade carved into ornate ashtrays.

In literature, as in art, there was the same difference between the traditional forms and the new 'educational' poems, novels, plays, and operas. The political direction of poetry developed complications because Mao Tse-tung's own poetry was written in the most allusive and compressed, classic Chinese style. The Foreign Languages Press' official translation of his poem on Loushan Pass reads:

Cold is the west wind;
Far in the frosty air the wild geese call in the morning moonlight.
In the morning moonlight,

the clatter of horses' hooves ring sharp,
and the bugle's note is muted.
Do not say that the strong pass is guarded with iron.
This very day in one step we shall pass its summit
We shall pass its summit!
There the hills are blue like the sea,
and dying sun like blood.

It is true that Loushan Pass was one of the strategic positions of the Long March, as explained by the official press in a footnote. The poem is, however, written in the classical *Tz'u* metre perfected in the Sung dynasty. When his poems were published in 1957 Mao suggested that this metre was unsuitable for young poets because 'these forms would cramp their thought and are difficult to master'. More straightforward metres and a more straightforward approach to their subjects were recommended to the young. Some of the results were translated in 1961 in *Songs of the Red Flag*:

I am past sixty but I can still work,
And I find it as easy as when I was young.
It's not that I am boasting about my strength,
but here in my heart I have Mao Tse-tung.

The vote of thanks customary to Mao and the leadership of the Communist Party is not always easy to work happily into songs or more seriously intentioned poetry. The government is, predictably, not particularly sympathetic to complaints of technical difficulty or the need for the right mood or right inspiration. There are poetry drives for a higher output of poetry, just as there are drives for higher agricultural and industrial output. (During the Great Leap Forward cadres boasted that Szechuan had produced a million new verses.)

The new poetry, conforming with the Yenan formulae, is expected to excite enthusiasm for the current official drive, describe in orthodoxly flattering terms the peasants or workers lives and achievements, and 'learn from the people' by imitating peasant verse.

Some of the poetry, however, produced under these conditions translates well, and has been received with genuine pleasure by Chinese outside communist control. The poets are helped by the similarity of most of the metres used in peasant verse to the classical forms. They use allusions to peasant myth and magic instead of the less approved classical allusions; and, as the more distant emperors of the Chinese heroic past are rehabilitated, references to their lives have become as acceptable in the new poetry as in the old. The correct moral is now, often rather loosely, attached in a couplet tacked to the end of a poem. Otherwise the poems are very like those written by Chinese outside China. In 1962 four poems by Ko Pi-chou were published. The first ends:

> New forest grows all round the Hill of Shou-Yang,
> Water below the dam of the Golden Valley is swelling, flowing,
> Behold where are the ruins of old Loyang city?
> I see only clouds and water, and oceans of trees densely without limit.
> The old dies, new life is born – life, life, never to end,
> Today the evening glory of the nimbus – tomorrow, the morning sun.[34]

Novels, at any rate in translation, have been less successful under the communists. Like the paintings of the Socialist Realist artists the most popular recent novels have a strong family resemblance to English Victorian literature. The strength of communist conviction has to be substituted for the strength of Christian conviction; but there is the same purposefulness working itself out through the same complicated plot, and at much the same (by Western standards), inordinate length. In the novels of the English Victorian writer, Miss C. M. Yonge, it would be useless to expect to find a bad sailor or a good Guards' officer. Similarly, in the successful Chinese novels, landlords and Kuomintang officials are always bad; poor peasants, industrial workers, and, above all, communist cadres are always good. Instead of defeating the school bully, a classical prize at Oxford, and ordination; the typical Chinese hero has defied the local wicked landlord, fought the Japanese, and unearthed a counter-revolutionary agent. His girl friend is at least as pure as her Victorian counterpart. Engaged couples in modern Chinese (and in Victorian) fiction do not touch. They gaze into each other's eyes and talk about ethical doubts (Victorian) or increased production (Chinese) – agricultural or industrial, not, of course, human.

Most Victorian novelists were, however, able to allow more latitude to their characters than their Chinese counterparts. Mao Tun, the then Minister of Culture and Chairman of the Writers' Union, told the All-China Federation of Literary and Art Circles in 1960 that 'signs of weakness in a hero going to his death are intolerable distortions of a hero's character and not a matter of human interest at all'. The author of *Let Life Become More Beautiful* was severely reprimanded because his flirtatious heroine induced her village friends to volunteer for the army when the local cadres had failed to find new soldiers. The author was imputing improper motives to soldiers, who elsewhere are correctly shown worrying about their overdue Party subscriptions, or crawling with hideous wounds and important despatches upheld by the inspiration of Mao and the Communist Party.[35]

Both the government and the novelists, however, deplore the dullness of the work that these pressures produce. During the Hundred Flowers Movement Liu Shao-tang, writing about the mechanical situations and characters the official guide lines had produced, asked: 'Do we mean that in writing about peasants we can only use the following type of subject matter: Ahem! Ahem! Ahem! Let's exert ourselves and work with renewed vigour, so that the produce will be an inch taller?' Some of the work produced during the Hundred Flowers Movement was freer and more interesting than anything that had preceded it since 1949. But this overfree writing was soon censored. The answer to Liu Shao-tang became again that that was indeed the only permitted form of dialogue; and as yet neither the government nor the novelists had found a way of presenting it with much novelty or excitement.

Opera was by far the most popular branch of the arts in pre-communist China. Small clay medallions of the famous actors are collected by Chinese young people with something of the same adoration as pop singers rouse in the West. ('Yellow' pop music is far more stringently outlawed, as decadent and degrading, in China

147

than in the Soviet Union. The young are officially encouraged to dance: preferably peasant rounds, but, if not these, approved waltzes like the Blue Danube. Boy generally dances with boy, and girl with girl, or if the sexes mix, they hold each other at arm's length.) Popular actors in the Peking opera are paid the highest salaries in China: about twice what a factory manager or engineer is paid, five times a civil servant's pay, and eight or ten times a factory worker's.

There are different local branches of opera in China with different traditions of dress, singing, and acting. Opera, like that of the Shanghai school, which in the old days was considered crude though popular, has received heavy state subsidies and a general lift in its prestige. But the most elaborately staged and dressed opera, that of Peking, is performed by Chinese troupes abroad and is highly esteemed by educated Chinese. Many of its conventions date back several centuries. The actors wear Manchu court dress. Their characters are drawn on their face with make-up so that the red stripes on the hero's chin proclaim him before he has opened his mouth. Men act women's parts. There is little scenery or stage properties, and the themes are taken from Chinese history or myth.

As with classical painting there were early suggestions from the young communists that traditional Peking opera was 'dull' and could be enlivened by modern stage conventions, costumes and stage properties. These suggestions were not, however, taken very seriously; and the conventions and costumes of the opera have been conserved with some minor alterations. Spitting is no longer allowed on stage. The blocks actors wore to symbolize the bound 'lotus feet' of well-brought up women have also been banned.

Opera themes, however, have been extensively reformed. There were even attempts to write entirely new plays for Peking opera, but the new plays never became popular. As part of the 'walking on two legs' policy the Peking opera actors were allowed to cite the greater popularity of the old themes with traditional backgrounds as reasons for reviving them. Some operas, however, were drastically re-written. Faithful servants, over-subordinate wives, the glorification of emperors not in present favour, were all weeded out.

It has been easier to write new plays for Shanghai opera where modern dress and modern themes had been customary before the revolution. Operas with titles like *The Wanton Woman Repines* and *The Amorous Lady Thief*, were replaced by *Reunion*, *The Life of a Peddicab Driver in the New Society*, and *It Can Be Done*, officially described as about a 'primary-school teacher's patient work with a backward child who has a discipline problem'.

In several of the arts the most successful of the models has been inspired by the revolutionary wars before the communists finally gained power. One of the most exciting new films (and a new opera) was based on the legend of the 'White-Haired Girl'. She fled from the cruel landlord's family, hid in a cave in the mountains, raiding the village temple for food. Her hair turned white, and only with the return to the village of the Red Army could she come out, singing her woes, and calling for vengeance.

So far operas and films – and pictures, poems, and novels – about the successful communists have lacked the imaginative drive and excitement of those about their struggle for power. The communists maintain, with some reason, that the building of the new society should be as exciting as the revolutionary wars. However, up until now the rules they impose about character and subject matter have made it impossible for artists to capture this excitement.

9   Building Perfection

FOR MANY YEARS the great Western myth about the Chinese communists was that they were 'nothing but agrarian reformers'. It owed much of its currency to the Western observers accompanying the communist armies in Yenan during their days of anti-Japanese compromise, conciliation, and moderation. But its origins went back to the disputes among the Communist Party leaders in the 1930s, the victory of Mao's policy of moderation, and his reliance on peasants for his army recruits, party members, and popular support.

Mao recognized peasant backing as essential for the first stage of the revolution; but he never departed so far from Marxist orthodoxy as to fail to acknowledge 'the advanced thinking' of the industrial workers, and the part they had to play in the later stages of the struggle towards communism. After the communists left Yenan, there was a drive to recruit industrial workers, and, later, intellectuals into the Communist Party. In the mid-sixties out of a total party membership of 18 million, a third were of non-peasant origin.[36]

The perfect Chinese communist society was thus never planned, except by Western wishful thinking, to be one of small independent peasant proprietors living according to their ancient ways in a country traditionally without heavy industry. On the contrary the ultimate aim of the Chinese leaders was to make every Chinese a worker. There were to be no more capitalists, no more bourgeois intellectuals, and, in a way, no more peasants. Since China was to be a modern country, capable of taking her rightful place as the leader of the world, many of her citizens would be workers in new heavy or skilled industries. Others would be worker-directors or worker-intellectuals. On the land the former peasants would work partly in rural factories. Even when they were farming their methods and hours would be as regulated and methodical as if they were working in a factory.

In this utopia there would be no need for money. With everyone working there would be enough for everyone's needs. Personal greed and selfishness would be banished. With workers directing their own work, and managers and intellectuals also working with their hands, as well as with their minds, the evils of status and bureaucracy would go. It would be the perfect, the true communist society realized on earth; and it would be universally copied. Once more China would give civilization to the known world.

The Chinese tragedy of the moment is that for a short time the leaders were within touching distance of their ideal. At the height of the communes they talked about the realization here and now of communism in China. But the high dream failed. Recently Chou En-lai has insisted that China is only a socialist, not a communist, society.

Communism – perfection – has been the unconcealed aim of the leaders all along. But they thought it politically advisable to start with compromise. In Yenan even the landlords were tolerated. In China, as a whole, there was at first peace for everyone except landlords and bureaucratic capitalists.

As a start to socialism the new state had inherited from its predecessors certain businesses like the railways, the steel-mills and the coal-mines of the pre-revolutionary centre of heavy industry, Manchuria. The capitals of private enterprise were the coastal towns, particularly Shanghai and Tientsin. Here some industry and commerce came to the state by direct confiscation from the bureaucratic capitalists who had gone to Taiwan. Other firms were foreign owned. These were gradually squeezed out of business by large fines for breaches of the suddenly numerous new regulations, and also fines for breaches of the regulations under the Kuomintang.

The same sort of pressure was exerted on Chinese firms to become 'state-private' enterprises. In addition to financial difficulties Chinese directors were also liable to more direct personal persuasion through meetings they had to attend, and from their families. Their adolescent children, in several cases, decided it was their duty to denounce their fathers loudly and repeatedly in their offices before their embarrassed staff.

In state-private enterprises the state bought a certain share in the business. Generally the price paid was approximately the same as the firm's debts to the state. The state then took the profits from its share of the business, and the former owner from his share of the business. A state manager was put in and worked in uneasy collaboration with the old private directors and with the local Communist Party secretary. How much the state manager interfered depended on how much he knew about the technicalities of the business. Generally he was not expert in them.

The next step was for the private owners to agree to surrender their businesses altogether to the state. They were guaranteed seven to ten years interest on the capital invested in their business. Some of them were retained, on salaries, as technical advisers in their former factories or offices. A few years later there were reports that the former private owners had in many cases appealed to the state to surrender the remaining interest to be paid on their capital, so that they could be reclassified immediately as workers not capitalists. Nevertheless businessmen and former businessmen remained a relatively wealthy section of Chinese society. Some of them could afford to run large and luxurious households. The greatest pressure for social conformity and surrender of their capital was maintained on the smaller men, the least on those who had formerly been the most wealthy. In 1965 there were still a handful of millionaires left in Shanghai, ready to testify about their support of the communists to visiting Westerners.

On the whole the state made good use of its new possessions. In 1949 China was, compared to the West or to Japan, an unindustrialized country. In the next decade she went through a sizeable industrial revolution. Outputs of established industries, like the cotton spun in Shanghai or the steel produced at Anshan in Manchuria, climbed back to the level they had been at before the Japanese war. They then doubled and trebled. New sources of raw materials were found. China was short of oil and petroleum; and the new oil fields in the northwest, in Sinkiang and Tibet, were particularly important discoveries.

New factories were opened to make most of the world's known goods. Trucks and lorries came from the factory at Changchun; scientific instruments and machine tools from Harbin; and most products of light industry – plastics, bicycles, clocks, and fountain pens – from Shanghai. Some of the new factories were inefficiently run and workmen made elementary mistakes because they were unfamiliar with any machinery. The Changchun car-works, particularly, looked at one time more like a vast technical school, than a factory. But the teaching seems to have been efficient, and the factory's output and standards have both gone up.

Meanwhile the new government encouraged a strategically and economically healthier pattern of industrial development. The northwest, notably around Lanchow and Taiyuan, became an important new heavy manufacturing centre. It was closer to the new oil-fields than the old coastal industrial areas: close to coal, iron, and planned new hydro-electric development; and farther from the possibility of Western sea and air based attacks. But there were also smaller industrial centres – cotton-mills and light industry – set up all through the interior of the country from Canton to Inner Mongolia.

In contrast to the decline in working-class living standards during the European industrial revolution, the standards of most Chinese working people rose steadily during their country's rapid industrialization. In the Chinese industrial areas during the 1950s, people stopped dying on the streets from cold, hunger, or anything else. Wages, while low by European standards, were enough for a family to live decently, if both husband and wife worked; and the provision of nurseries and crèches made this generally possible. Safety regulations and rules about work conditions, although again below the minimum acceptable in Europe, were enforced and by Asian standards were reasonable. All over the industrial areas new government housing blocks are going up fast. They are drab looking, providing no more than one or two rooms for a family, with communal kitchens and bathrooms. They are, however, an improvement on the tin and sacking shacks of the past.

It is a constant sport for foreign journalists, touring these blocks, to try and pick a room where they are not expected. But even the families most surprised by the sudden incursion of a large party of journalists, interpreter and officials appear to be living with a modicum of furniture, blankets, clothes, and crockery. By Asian standards, again, the families are comfortable and well-housed.

Most visitors acknowledge that industrial workers and towns-people generally are better-off under the new government. But what is often said is that the towns are living off the country; and their relatively high standards are maintained at the expense of increasing poverty among the four out of five Chinese who live in villages.

In the villages, after the landlords' holdings had been redistribu-ted, peasants were left for a few months to enjoy their individual holdings. There was, however, increasing emphasis on traditional co-operation. Before communism Chinese villagers had often built houses together, sowed or harvested co-operatively. This tradi-tion was formalized and strengthened in the 'Mutual Aid Teams' of families doing most farm work together. 'Magic mats to fly towards Socialism', said one of the English-language magazines of the time. Meanwhile the cadres and national newspapers publicized stories of the unfairness of all private landownership: poor peasants whose holdings, even after land reform, were too small to give them a living; or rich peasants buying up their neighbours' holdings to make themselves into a new class of landlords.

Around 1954, the exact date varied from one part of China to another, the first village co-operatives were set up. In these the peasants farmed collectively. Profits from the land were divided – part for the owners of the land in proportion to the amount they had put into the co-operative, part for those who had laboured on the land in proportion to the labour they had put in. Co-operatives also took into account a family's needs and its political good standing when the labour profits were distributed.

In 1955 and 1956 the Chinese said that 'the high tide of Socialism' had led to the grouping of almost all peasants into 'higher form co-operatives'. Western writers called them 'collectives'. Most of the collectives included two or more villages, and they were organized either on the basis of the old co-operatives, or from two or three Mutual Aid Teams if the village had not had co-operatives. The peasants continued, theoretically, to own the land they farmed collectively. But profits were distributed only on the basis of the amount of labour put in, not on the basis of land (or tools or animals) contributed to the collective. The peasants were also allowed to keep small garden plots for their own private cultivation, and to keep private hens and, sometimes, pigs. In theory the peasants were allowed to withdraw both from the co-operatives and the collectives if they so wished; but few even tried to exercise this right.

By 1956 and 1957 no collective any Westerner visited failed to quote figures of greatly increased production and higher living standards. Nationally, large surpluses were being saved, mainly from agriculture, for export and investment in industry. But the government claimed that the peasants' consumption of grain, cloth, and small luxuries like new basins and thermos flasks was also steadily rising.

The cadres and newspapers had been right in the early 1950s when they had preached the impossibility of living with any margin on the average plot of a Chinese farmer. After land reform this varied from a fraction of an acre in the crowded Shanghai and Canton deltas (where, however, market gardening was very profit-able), to 3 to 4 acres in the emptier lands of the north and west. The average was under 2½ acres (in contrast to a European small-holder's 20 or 30 acres). Inevitably on the minute Chinese holdings much land had to be wasted on paths and boundary ditches, and it was not feasible to use large tools.

The new village collectives were least successful in the south where the growing of rice on small hillside terraces had to be done by hand.[37] In the north, however, on the flatter land there the collectives were able to use ploughs which were quicker and more efficient than the old hand tools. The leaders of the collectives were encouraged to buy better seeds and fertilizers, and to raise money to pay for this by low interest state loans. Lecturers from state agricultural colleges were sent round the villages to explain new methods to the peasant leaders. Meanwhile schemes of irrigation, drainage, re-afforestation and the ploughing of former pasture brought more land into cultivation.

These benefits were quoted by the Chinese authorities when they were asked how the cadres had overcome the Chinese peasant's traditional reluctance to surrender land he had or could have owned. Chinese novels of the late 1950s show other pressures similar to those exerted against recalcitrant businessmen. Peasants who refused to join co-operatives were not imprisoned but they could not get the new loans, fertilizers or seeds. Their marketing became difficult. Neighbours who had formerly helped them in their work now refused.

After the peasant holdings had once been surrendered to the collectives there was comparatively little feeling in most villages against the formation of the communes: the next stage in farm organization. The first commune is said to have started in Loyang (Honan) in April 1958, and news of it spread spontaneously around the country. The formation of new communes was officially approved in August 1958. The communes were organizations of sometimes 100 or more villages; at one time 25,000 to 26,000 of them covered the whole of China. They had their own administra-tions whose duty it was to organize farmwork, commune schools, hospitals, dining-rooms, and entertainments. The communes were encouraged to set up their own rural factories, and commune mem-bers were expected to spend part of their time working in them, or on public works such as irrigation schemes or dams.

Members were paid partly in wages, and partly by the 'free supply' system, in which they obtained food, clothing, housing, and other necessities, according to their needs and without paying. In most communes wages under this system were naturally very small. The women members of the commune were expected to work much the same hours as the men, and communal dining rooms, crèches, and centres for household jobs, and clothes making and repairing, were set up. There were no private gardens in many of the com-munes – the members did not have time to cultivate them. But there was time everywhere for the new militia units where commune members were drilled and trained after their day's work.[38] Military words of command and drills were sometimes used even in the fields, where units of the commune labour force were marched out in formation shouldering their rakes and hoes like rifles.

The communes were an experiment on an enormous scale, and in the end they were not a success. It is still not clear why they were set up so quickly in the first place, without giving the government time to learn from initial mistakes. 'Popular enthusiasm', the communists say, and the order recognizing the communes in August 1958 stressed the importance of official support not lagging behind the will of the people. That way lay the political sin of 'tailism'.

All reports suggest that there was in China in the summer of 1958 a spirit of great excitement among numbers of people, official and otherwise. It was fed by every possible means; and used as the motive force for what was called 'The Great Leap Forward'. It was to be the Great Leap from socialism to communism. There would be no need for money or central authority in this new perfection. The communes were to be locally administered, and in them the necessities of life would be given, in the classic Marxist phrase, 'to each according to their needs'. In the communes, the peasants as well as being peasants, would be promoted to workers, preferably workers in heavy industry. In most of the communes, along with the factories for bicycle parts, textile mills and the like, steel furnaces were set up: 'backyard steel furnaces'. Sometimes there was one in every village. They were to use iron cooking pots, collected from village housewives who would no longer need them now that their families could be fed at the new communal dining halls.

Millions of people left the country to help the Great Leap Forward in the town. Urban communes were formed although they were never as universal as the country communes. But, in Peking and Canton particularly, small factories were organized and run by local women, together with communal dining rooms, crèches, and mending centres. It had to be the women, as their husbands were too busy. The Great Leap had meant overtime and increased 'norms' (standards of what should be produced in a working day) in most offices and factories. Everywhere people pledged themselves to produce 20, then 50, then 100 per cent more than they had produced the year before.

There were sober economic arguments for the Great Leap. Its leaders hoped that a few years' intensive work, powered by the enthusiasm of the movement, would free China from her perpetual economic embarrassment. This was, and is, an ever-growing population with ever-rising standards of living chasing dwindling industrial and agricultural surpluses. One way out of the Chinese economic problem was for industrialization to be more rapid and thorough than it was being. For this a greater national investment was needed in industry, and it could only come from greater agricultural profits. By overtime for men, freeing women for work outside their homes, and organizing all labour on as large a scale as possible, the Chinese hoped to have enough manpower, not only to increase the production of existing farms and factories, but also to build enough dams, irrigation works, and canals, to make it possible to set up new and more efficient farms and new factories.

With all the enthusiasm behind it, and the efforts and overwork of the Chinese, the Great Leap slipped. A part of the difficulties was sheer bad luck. 1959, 1960, and 1961 were years of natural disaster: drought in the north, floods in the south, and typhoons in the east. Before 1959 natural disasters on this scale had produced famines in which millions died. In the rural communes the natural shortages were increased by bad local administration. The new government had not enough efficient cadres to run the communes smoothly; to organize the suddenly much complicated working life of the tens of thousands, order the factory and farm raw materials, market, and, above all, estimate production accurately enough for central planning and taxes. Agricultural taxes in China are a percentage of the year's expected harvest. Another percentage, again of the estimated crop, has to be sold to the state at fairly low fixed prices. If the crop is much below the local officials' estimates there will not be enough for the peasants to eat and also for the state quotas.

During the first enthusiasm of the Great Leap Forward, the cadres overestimated the crops and the peasants underproduced. There seems to have been a number of reasons for this underproduction. The one at first most commonly given to the West was that the peasants missed their private gardens and would not work wholeheartedly in the communal fields. What seems, in fact, to have been more important was that the peasants, like everybody else involved in the Great Leap Forward, were muddled and overworked. They wasted time marching about because no one was sure which of the myriad jobs suddenly springing up in the new communes was the most important. They did not know how they were going to be paid: whether on the basis of the hours they worked, what they actually did, the needs of their families, or their political status.

Meanwhile the cadres got the priorities wrong. Work in the fields, and on the more feasible small-scale factory and public-works projects, suffered because they concentrated on producing steel of a uselessly poor quality, bulky goods for which there was no transport, and impressively large scale, but not very useful, dams and canals.

The chaos was cumulative. At the centre, as over-optimistic production figures poured in, the more cautious and realistic local cadres were rebuked or dismissed for the obvious failure their figures showed. The state statistical office, in normal times truthful and sober, could not cope.[39] State investments in heavy industry were made on the basis of inflated promises of agricultural production. Local cadres were unwilling to break local crop failures to the centre, and the centre refused to believe the first reports. Of the 375 million tons of cereal promised for 1959, 125 million tons failed to materialize.

There was, however, no mass starvation or large-scale breakdown of government. Grain, oil, and cotton cloth were strictly rationed; the more expensive foods and most consumer articles were also on a points system of rationing. An individual's ration varied according to the region. He or she was also often asked to set his own eating 'norm'; and it was then a matter of pride and political duty to keep it low. Certain categories of people – housewives, street hawkers, and shopkeepers were expected to eat least. Others – writers, artists, students, and heavy manual workers – had extra rations. In 1960 and 1961 most people were hungry. Few ate fish or meat. The grain ration provided less than the minimum calories needed to maintain normal health. Malnutrition diseases were said to be widespread, particularly in the south. There was some black-marketing and profiteering, and a considerable increase in crime in the big cities; but on the whole rationing worked.

It was not, however, liked. Peasants were increasingly reluctant to give up their grain. There was discontent, and rumours of mutiny in the army. The soldiers, while relatively well fed themselves, had news of bad conditions in their home villages. The number of refugees trying to enter Hongkong increased. Consequently there were unfavourable reports about China in the world press. Even the top communist leadership was not united about the wisdom of the Great Leap Forward policies. And, probably most serious of all, there was an open revolt in Honan in 1961 when militia officers and junior officials turned bandit.

Under these pressures industrial targets were drastically revised. Hundreds of small projects in inaccessible areas were shut down. No more was heard of the backyard steel furnaces, and in the towns most of the urban communes were allowed to wither, and transmute into ordinary cheap restaurants and factories. Most of the street hawkers and small artisans ceased to work within any sort of collective framework. The towns emptied dramatically. It was said, in 1962 that one million had already left Peking, and another two million were due to go back to the country.

In the villages much of the commune organization broke up. What remained varied from place to place. A general pattern was for most of the commune's functions to be passed to the dozen or more brigades that were its constituent units. The brigades were generally the same size as the old cooperatives, roughly one large village or several small ones. The brigade is made up of several teams of a few families each, and either the brigade or the team allots work to the families. Again, either the brigade or the team, can be responsible for the general farm plans, marketing, and for the division of the group's profits and the payment of tax and state quotas. The original commune often retains some sort of authority over the brigades, and may be responsible for remaining public works and factories, schools, hospitals, general welfare services, and perhaps the buying of large equipment or another investment of small surpluses. But the commune was discouraged from trying to take more than a small percentage for investment. The major profits were to be distributed by the teams to individuals.

The payment of team members was to be entirely for work done, not according to political reliability. Military commands and drills were not to be used in field work. There were to be no standard issues of necessities. Much of the communal set-up of dining rooms, mending rooms, and nurseries was dissolved, or kept only for rush periods like harvesting. The cadres were told to concentrate on field work, rather than extraneous projects, and not to encourage the peasants to overwork. They were also instructed to avoid rash agricultural schemes, and too much experiment. Within the teams the older peasants were to be consulted, and have their advice taken seriously. 'The Wise Old Peasant', restraining the hotheaded youngsters, or the over-ambitious bureaucrats, suddenly became the popular hero of Chinese plays and newspaper articles. Finally, against the wishes of many cadres, something under ten per cent of the land was returned to individual ownership, and peasants were again encouraged to cultivate their own gardens, and keep their own animals. They were allowed to sell what they had grown in local markets.

The new economic policy was officially defined as investment in agriculture, then light industry, and, last, heavy industry. The central government asked for less grain from the villages. Less machinery was imported, and the growth of heavy industry stopped. Output figures and targets for steel and coal declined for the first time in a decade. What national investment there was in industry in 1961 and 1962 was largely in factories producing goods needed by the peasants – fertilizers and agricultural implements.

There were Western observers who doubted, some with more than a touch of pleasurable anticipation, whether the Chinese economy could recover from the Great Leap Forward. Mr Joseph Alsop in particular received widespread publicity in the United States, and even in Britain, for his theory of 'the declining spiral' in which the Chinese economy was involved.

Fortunately these prophets of famines and disaster were wrong. The 1962 harvest was good, and that year there was an increase in

161

consumer goods and some rations. By 1964 the economic slogan was still 'readjustment, consolidation, filling out, raising standards', and there was still continued emphasis on the need for plain living, hard work and sacrifice. But the shops were full again, most of the queues had gone, and the rice ration had doubled. Fish and fruit were no longer rationed, and were cheap and plentiful. There was more meat and cooking oil.

The Chinese leaders acknowledge that there had been mistakes during the Great Leap Forward. But they deny that the commune movement has been a failure. The economy, they say, is on a sounder basis than it had been in 1957; and the figures support this.

In his *Report on the Work of the Government* given to the Third National People's Congress in December 1964 Chou En-lai claimed that 1962, 1963 and 1964 had all been years of economic recovery and steadily increasing production. 'In 1964', Chou said, 'the total value of industrial output is expected to increase more than 15 per cent over 1963 and to be far higher than in 1957.'[40]

Prices, the Chinese leaders claimed elsewhere, had gone down, and foreign trade up in the mid-sixties. Even the backyard steel furnaces had not been a total loss. They had provided valuable technical training for thousands.

In the country there are solid benefits from the communes. The Chinese villages have more schools, clinics, hospitals, and old people's homes, than any other country in Asia. Many small factories are left, still running, to use local products and provide useful, alternative employment. Above all some of the public works, created at great cost during the heyday of the communes, are on such a scale and of so much agricultural use, as to make a repetition of the disasters of 1959 and 1960 unlikely.

In 1960 the amount of irrigated land was double the 1949 figure. The San Men dam, with the world's third largest reservoir behind it, was finished just too late in 1960 to help the northern drought that year. It will now provide irrigation and prevent drought on 6,600,000 acres. With the San Men and other dams planned for the sixties, or already built on the Yellow River, China's electrical power output will be four times her pre-war figure.

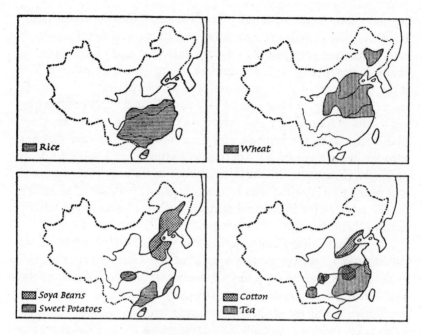

Maps showing principal crops

Nor do the leaders want to discredit the theory of the communes. In 1961 and 1962 cadres were warned to consult the experts, and not to try to make engineering and agricultural decisions on the basis of political theory only. But a few months later correct theory was again all-important. In Kwangtung villagers were told to keep the former rich peasants under constant surveillance. There were official fulminations against the rise of capitalism and hoarding in the countryside. (It was notable that the large increases in food were of vegetables, fruit, pork, eggs and chicken: the products of the peasants' private plots rather than the communally grown cereal crops.)

Chinese leaders have said that the whole commune system will be restored sometime in the future. It must be. It is an essential part of the Chinese government's official reason for existing – the coming of communism. But how soon in the future? Will the leaders be rash enough to try restoring the full communes before there are many more better educated officials to administer the countryside, before China is rich enough to afford substantial investments in each commune (not just the officially favoured and visited ones) to assure a reasonably high standard of living for all members? Yet, if the restoration of the communes is to be postponed to the distant future, how long can the present very complicated system of farming last? The responsibility for farm work is divided between three bodies: the team, the brigade, and the commune. The consultations between these three bodies are time consuming, and some students of China (but never, of course, a Chinese in China) have suggested that future development may be towards greater freedom of planning for the team or for individual families with the government leasing land to them through the commune.

At present Chinese farms cannot feed many more people or afford investments in industry on the scale of the Great Leap Forward without the danger of repeating the economic and civil disturbances. But existing farms could be considerably more efficient than they are. There is still less than half as much fertilizer used on Chinese fields as on Japanese. Because total farm profits are so small there has been little experiment with new methods of rearing stock or new crops. There is not much mechanization. Part of the plan for the communes was that they should be large enough to have their own machinery. But farmers in capitalist countries have co-operative schemes for buying and running machinery. Yet mechanization is unlikely to be successful without education and campaigns for the proper maintenance of machinery. Visitors to Chinese communes have commented on the pieces of machinery left out to rust, and the number of tractors out of order for lack of proper care. Possibly the small rural factories maintained by the communes may teach the elementary rules for the care of machines to a village society which has never had anything to do with them before.

Slightly less than 12 per cent of China is now used for crops. Some of the land is hopeless – desert, mountain, or swamp. But there is land which can be developed, particularly on the western and northern limits of the country. In Sinkiang, around Urumchi, farms run by ex-soldiers on military lines, are very fertile once the

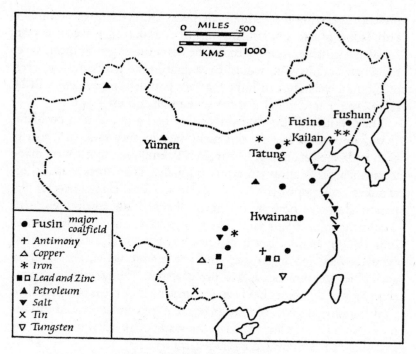

Map showing mineral resources

land is irrigated; and in this new country the fields can be laid out on a large enough scale to make mechanization easy.

Industrially China has adequate but not generous amounts of most metals, coal, and oil (except for aviation fuel). She still needs to import machinery and some manufactured goods. The biggest shortage in China is of good workmen and engineers with modern skills. But among recent testimonies to what the Chinese can achieve are both the atomic bomb and the aircraft instrument landing systems installed in time for the Pakistani airlines to use it.

If China is to survive, both industry and agriculture will have to expand rapidly. This is necessary not only to raise the peoples' living standards to a point at which the communist utopia will have a chance of success; but also just to keep alive a population rapidly increasing beyond the limits of the number who can be fed by present agricultural methods. Recent estimates give China a population of 650 million, increasing at about 2½ per cent a year. Modern medicine, introduced by the communist government, saves babies and adults who would have died in the past; and few, even of China's enemies, can hope that her population problem will be solved in the traditional manner by famine and civil war.

The Chinese at first denied that they had a population problem. It was impossible to have too many people, they said, in a society with a planned economy. Outspoken Peking economists were made to recant their Malthusian errors publicly. Then there was a short campaign to popularize contraceptives. (The explicitness of the posters showing how to use them shocked the foreign visitors.) The campaign, it was said, was to protect women's health, not to limit the population. But it was not very successful. Rubber contra-ceptives were too expensive, and the cotton waste, the Chinese authorities recommended, was not effective. The new birth control campaign of the sixties has been accompanied by the most outspoken explanations yet given of the dangers of overpopulation. But still the most common argument used is the waste of parental time and the maternal ill-health caused by large families.

Apart from contraception there are propaganda attempts to limit the population. 'Love between men and women', said one of the save-time slogans in 1963, 'is a psycho-somatic activity which consumes energy and wastes time.' Norms are now set for family size. They vary from place to place. Soldiers' wives are generally allowed four children, officials' wives only two. Mothers who exceed their norms are not automatically given maternity benefits or ration books for the new baby. This family limitation is accompanied by moral stories of the prosperity brought by late marriage, and the ruin of good students who married young. In the autumn of 1964 a young toolmaker received nation-wide publicity when he postponed his marriage for the third time to take the opportunity of more technical training offered him. His fiancée, a medical student, wrote that 'she too wished to devote all her energies to her work, and that postponing the wedding would be good for themselves and for the state'.

The right age for a woman to marry is said to be between 23 and 25, and 25 to 29 for a man. (Much later than has been customary in China.) A woman, it is recommended, could have her first baby three or four years after her marriage, but she would be well advised to wait five to eight years for the next. For the father of an overlarge family, sterilization is suggested. Abortion, however, is not encouraged except on medical grounds.

How far these methods of limiting the population will succeed is a key question for China. Most of the developing countries have found it as difficult as Europe did during the Industrial Revolution to make any method of curbing population growth work. But China has means of appealing to her people of a proved effectiveness, and which no other country has or has had.

74 A less than usually fierce expression of China's anti-Americanism. This cartoon of 1963 mocks President Kennedy's 'Strategy for Peace'.

75 Mao Tse-tung, chairman of the Central Committee of the Chinese Communist Party and founder of the Chinese People's Republic, figures in all aspects of culture even the traditional scissor cut.

76 Contemporary painters like Fu Pao-shih do not always have to represent political subjects in their pictures. This landscape at Nanking was painted in 1953.

77 (*Below left*) Contemporary literature, particularly poetry, although written in classic style usually pays allegiance to the party. These peasants are having poetry read to them in their lunch-hour.

78 (*Above*) Every New Year paintings with a distinctively communist flavour are hung in public places; this one is to demonstrate the fervour of urban people for the support of agricultural production.

79 (*Right*) These reservoir builders at Miyun are entertained by acrobats.

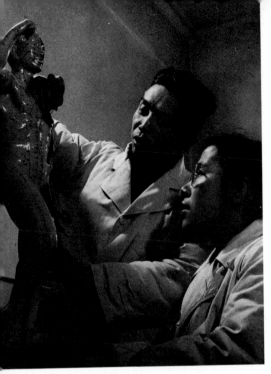

80 (*Left*) Traditional medicine such as acupuncture is still practised in China. A student is taught the various points of the body in which to insert the needle.

81 There have been great advances in Western medicine. This is a medical technician at Shanghai.

82 (*Right*) The Chinese traditional theatre is still performed and respected as an important part of China's culture.

83 The modern theatre performs propaganda plays and operas. This is the first act from the *East is Red* which tells the story of communist victory over capitalism and Nationalist government.

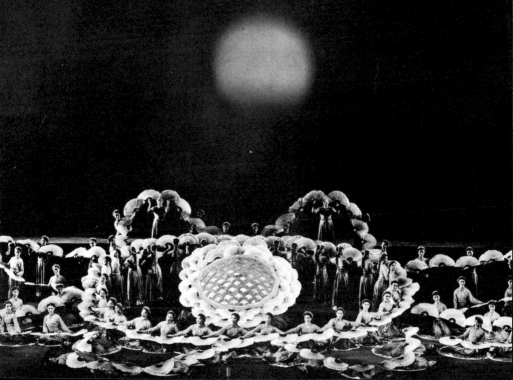

84 Because both their parents are full-time cadres these children board at their nursery, and go home on alternate weekends.

85 The poverty of South China in particular forced the emigration of Chinese to other Asian countries. Some of them made strictly capitalist fortunes, but still want their children educated in China. This school is for Overseas Chinese Children.

86 One of the aims of the 'Great Leap Forward' in 1958 was the raising of the peasant's educational standards. These peasants are being taught to read and write.

87 These working housewives of Peking are being taught the alphabet.

88 When the people are not attending lectures or public meetings in their spare time a visit to the cinema involves further propaganda indoctrination.

89 (*Above*) Outwardly the streets have not changed since pre-communist days. This is at Canton.

90 (*Left*) A shopping arcade at Peking.

10   The New Evangelists

IN 1949 MAO TSE-TUNG MADE HIS FIRST JOURNEY outside China to arrange Soviet aid for the country he now led. When they became ministers of newly communist China, Chou En-lai, Chu Teh, and Liu Shao-chi had last travelled abroad when they went to Europe as students in the 1920s. After 15 years in Yenan, isolated in the interior of China, the communist leaders were ignorant of and prejudiced about the world outside their borders.

From Yenan there had been a possible air and caravan route to the Soviet Union through the Mongolian desert; but it was little used. Until a few months before they entered Peking, Stalin continued to look on the Chinese communists as heretical adventurers without much hope of success with whom he wanted as little to do as possible. Few foreigners of any nationality had been to Yenan. (There was an American military observer group there in the last years of the war, but no diplomatic corps.) It was physically difficult to get there through the Japanese or the Kuomintang lines; and those who did make the journey were often well-wishers with no desire to contradict any part of the Chinese communist vision.

The less committed journalists, like Edgar Snow,[41] noted the carefully cultivated foreign sympathies of the Chinese communists and their irrelevance to what was happening in China. The atrocities and the heroism of the Spanish civil war were debated with rather more heat than the good and bad of the Chinese civil war. Franco was utterly condemned, but Mao, at the time of Edgar Snow's visit, was arranging a United Front with Chiang. There was an air of unreality in the completeness with which the Yenan communists condemned what they saw as evil foreigners; and the Chinese virtues with which good foreigners were endowed.[42] Only Chou En-lai, among the top leadership, had had some practical experience of the mixed and un-Chinese qualities of other peoples. He was the communist plenipotentiary who negotiated with the diplomats of Chiang's wartime capital of Chungking. Chou spoke good French and some English. Liu, it is said, spoke Russian. But Mao knew no foreign language.

The communists, including Mao, were, however, well read in Chinese history and literature; far better educated in terms of their own culture than their contemporaries in the Soviet Union, and indeed in much of the rest of Europe. They knew the traditional Chinese picture of China as the centre, or the good governess of the world; the flowery kingdom at whose borders barbarism began. Classically this kingdom was benevolent. Insolence, insubordina-tion and wrong conduct must be rebuked. But barbarians could be civilized by instruction in Chinese custom and by Chinese example.

The Empire's ill-defined boundaries included the now rebellious states of Tibet and Mongolia. Tribute was traditionally due from most of the small, neighbouring countries of South Asia. Tributaries, ambassadors and their trains of merchants might also be received from farther afield. Once they had acknowledged Chinese supremacy, the barbarians ought to be treated with the utmost courtesy and generosity: loaded with gifts and hospitality and sent back to their own uncivilized countries to tell the tale of Chinese superiority. Naturally, however, it was China's duty to decide which of the outer barbarians merited Chinese notice and approval, and which ought to be snubbed or openly rebuked. Great Britain might recognize the Chinese government within days of the communists coming to power. But the long drawn out and humiliating refusal of the Chinese to exchange diplomatic missions[43] would have caused less surprise in London if the Foreign Office had consulted the records of Ch'ien Lung's eighteenth-century dealings with Lord Macartney.

In Yenan, according to Edgar Snow, Mao read every night until the early hours of the morning. His books were partly the Chinese classics and partly the new classics of Marxism. There was little contradiction between them about the world outside China. Marxist orthodoxy reinforced the rigid division into good and evil. It was more than ever China's duty to admonish, and spread the truth. It was even true that many of China's friends and enemies were the same whether they were seen through the leaders' national or through their communist spectacles. The United States particularly had opposed the Chinese communist rise to power; and the Americans were then anxious that Chinese influence should be confined as narrowly as possible.

The major contradiction, perhaps the only contradiction, between the classic and the Marxist Chinese view of their place in the world, was the Soviet Union's claim to be the world's senior Communist Party. To begin with the Chinese did not dispute it. Mao confirmed that the new China would 'lean to one side', the Russian side of world politics. Soviet advice and aid were sought, and Soviet examples quoted.

Reliance on the Soviet Union can never have been an easy policy for the Chinese. From the beginnings of the alliance there were small personal strains. The Russian technicians were highly paid by Chinese standards, and spent freely. The Chinese nickname for them was 'ricebuckets'. Russian drunkenness and their boisterous advances to their girl interpreters were deplorable in the eyes of the puritan communist Chinese. They were similar strains to those between the English and the American servicemen during the Second World War; and as with Britain and America this added up, not to a breach of the alliance, but to the sort of surface irritation which could reinforce less friendly policies if conditions changed.

The Korean War was more serious. It is possible that Stalin encouraged North Korea to invade the south without first consulting China, and perhaps with a view to weakening China's position in Asia. If so, this policy was not entirely successful. Economically China was weakened. Her debt to the Soviet Union and her dependence on Soviet trade was increased by the war; and her industrialization was set back. She was never officially a belligerent. But semi-official 'volunteers' from the Chinese army fought well in Korea. Their courage and their technical skill finally defeated the old picture of the cowardly comic Chinaman current a few years before. After the Korean War the Chinese army was recognized as a most important factor in the East Asian balance of power, with out-of-date equipment perhaps, but with high morale and a well trained officer corps.[44]

In Korea China's principal adversary was the United States: the war confirmed both countries' paranoia about each other. Partly because of Korea the Americans committed themselves with increasing firmness to the policy of the cold war in Asia, anti-communist bastions, and also to the support of Chiang Kai-shek in Taiwan. Military and general aid was poured into the island, and the American fleet patrolled the straits between Taiwan and the mainland. At the height of the cold war it was foolhardy for an American, or a European or Asian in American employ, to question even the standards of Kuomintang government in Taiwan, far less the whole question of whether that government should be there or not. Mainland China, in American eyes, became the Antichrist nation. It was morally impossible that evil, in its Chinese guise, could be recognized by the United States or seated in the United Nations. As late as 1954 Mr Dulles, during the Geneva negotiations that ended the Franco-Vietnamese war, pointedly refused to touch Chou En-lai's outstretched hand.

Mr Dulles was supported by a vocal section of American public opinion, some of it convinced by the views of the late Senator Macarthy, and some of it lulled by the extensive advertising and semi-advertising in the United States on behalf of Chiang Kai-shek and Taiwan. The picture drawn by this advertising of mainland China was of a very weak and a very menacing country. There were American soldiers, politicians, and journalists who alleged both that only an immediate nuclear attack on the relatively defenceless mainland could save the world from total war, and also that the Chinese people were opposed to their government, ripe for rebellion, and would welcome back Chiang's forces. Many Americans (scholars concerned with far eastern affairs and State Department officials) who knew better were restrained by their fear, not only of American public opinion, but also of Asian public opinion. If the United

180

States abandoned Chiang, so the argument went, her friends in Asia would cease to trust her, and there would be no further confidence in American promises to stem communism. (A similar argument is now used by many Americans in defence of their country's Vietnamese policy.)

Meanwhile the solid Chinese reasons for their enmity with America were similarly increased by the same moral fervour.[45] America had interfered in Chinese affairs. Taiwan was a province of China; only American power sustained it in rebellion. The American fleet, and the American bases in Japan, Okinawa, Taiwan and the Philippines encircled China and menaced her. American intrigues stopped China taking her rightful place as the leader of Asia.

America, in Chinese eyes, was the enemy of all the people in all nations, the supporter everywhere of counter-revolution and foreign domination. She was also 'a paper tiger'. She might seem strong; but if she was firmly resisted she would crumble. Much of the later world anxiety about Chinese aggressiveness and seeming willingness to risk nuclear war goes back to Mao's attempts to reassure his people that America need not necessarily conquer China because she had the more terrible weapons. In support of the same view, Peking Radio broadcast after the Chinese had their own first nuclear explosion, 'The atom bomb is a paper tiger. It is people who decide the outcome of a war, not any weapon.'

Internally, just as it is a common American article of faith that the Chinese hate their government, so it is a Chinese belief that the American people are really China's friends, and only wait for the day when they will be finally delivered from their oppressive bourgeois government. Chinese cartoons show the American worker, dungaree clad, seizing the machine gun from a thin, cowardly, top-hatted Uncle Sam, and leaning over him to shake hands with his beaming Chinese opposite number.[46] Neither the Chinese picture of America nor the American of China is in much danger of contradiction. No Chinese Embassy exists in America. No delegations visit there. Few American reporters are allowed to work in China.

China's view of other countries than America moved closer to reality after the Korean War. China now saw the world as more complicated than it had seemed from Yenan. Not all capitalist countries were equally committed to the cold war. At first Britain was China's favourite European capitalist country. British delega, tions were received in China, and politely told that China had much to learn from Britain.[47] Later France, after the end of the Vietnamese and Algerian wars, became China's example of a tolerable capitalist country. Franco,Chinese trade increased. Delicate compliments are paid to General de Gaulle.

Even more important was China's discovery of the neutral nations. Like the contemporary United States the Chinese were slow to believe that neutrality could exist. For some years the Chinese rejected Indian advances as coming from a country of British stooges. A peaceful, but genuine, dissolution of empire was impos, sible. It is said that the behaviour of India as chairman of the Korean Neutral Nations Commission finally convinced the Chinese that the Indians were independent.

The culmination of China's new policy of friendship towards India and her Asian neighbours was the Bandung Conference of 1955, with Chou En,lai beaming at the representatives of nearly every Asian and independent African nation. China's parade of equality with the smallest and brashest of the new nations may not have been altogether convincing. But the newly reasonable China was prepared to negotiate with any of her neighbours about any problems. Burma and China agreed on a settled frontier. Overseas Chinese in most of Southeast Asia were exhorted to learn the language of the country they lived in, send their children to its schools, and take its citizenship. (There continued, however, to be special facilities for Overseas Chinese who wanted to be educated or to retire to the mainland.) With India China negotiated the five principles of co,existence. Chou and Nehru were photographed smiling and clasping each others' hands. Chinese and Indian friendship was to endure a thousand years.

It was not only in Asia that China was freshly seen as a moderate, friendly nation. As the East European states struggled for growing independence after Stalin's death, China intervened against rigid Soviet control; and in particular Chou En-lai's influence was exerted against a Russian military conquest of Gomulka's Poland.

There are Chinese who say now that it was not China who changed after Bandung but the rest of the world who fell out of step with her.[48] Poland was legitimately independent. But Hungary, in China's eyes, was in danger of counter-revolution; and so, rightly re-occupied by Russian forces. Suez, co-incidental with Hungary, sharply reminded China of her old view of treacherous imperialism.

Meanwhile, at home in China, the Hundred Flowers Movement had bloomed, and sharp criticisms of the communists had mounted. This, in the Chinese leaders' eyes, was a warning against lack of zeal in any sphere. As the Hundred Flowers were weeded, and the critics suppressed, Chinese energies were harnessed to the Great Leap Forward. In the dispute about the Great Leap economic policies, moderation led by Chou En-lai was defeated by Liu Shao-chi's zeal and energy.[49] Was there equally a dispute and a victory for zeal over moderation in foreign policies early in 1958?

In the autumn of 1958 the world picture of moderate China was rudely shattered by the Taiwan crisis. Matsu and Quemoy, the islands between Taiwan and the mainland, were shelled, invasion armies were massed on the southeast coast, and communist denunciation of the Nationalists mounted. So did promises for Taiwan's protection by the United States and counter threats of invasion of the mainland.

As the shelling and threats to Taiwan gradually diminished, Nehru's India emerged as a sideways victor of the crisis. The West, particularly Britain, had for a long time pointed to India as the alternative model for Asia. In India parliamentary democracy worked, more or less. The state was stable, in marked contrast to other new Asian countries; and the economy, although weak, had suffered no major crisis. The British-trained Indian Army was commonly held to be the best in Asia. India's international prestige benefited, almost equally with China's, from the Bandung Conference. After the Taiwan crisis increasing numbers of Asians saw India as the continent's new strong leader, whose gradual socialism and moderate reforms were better models for Asian revolution than Chinese violence and the exertions of her Great Leap policy.

It was galling for China. It threatened her view of herself both as the historical head of Asia, and as the new model whose revolution was the pattern for all under-developed states in Asia, as in Latin America, and in Africa. There were also solid reasons of national interest to impede the Bandung friendship of Nehru and Chou. While China was weak the British in India had seen Tibet as a usefully independent buffer state. India had accepted the Chinese annexation of Tibet as the re-establishment of Chinese power over a province historically part of the Chinese Empire. But the Western indignation over this conquest found some echoes in India. Tibetan refugees poured into Kalimpong, and Tibetan rebels bought supplies, more or less clandestinely, in India. By 1959 provinces of Tibet were in open revolt, their suppression by the Chinese was bloodthirsty, and the Dalai Lama, the godhead of the Tibetan state, fled with his court to India. Indian sympathies with Tibet mounted. Chinese indignation over the Indian reception of their rebel subjects also mounted.

The Chinese were now firmly established on the borders of India. But the actual frontier with India was still remote from Delhi. It ran through desolate country following the Macmahon line, fixed as an administrative convenience by British civil servants, but never officially agreed to by the Chinese state. Where China did not border India directly, her new neighbours were, to the east, the small, semi-independent Himalayan states: Nepal, Sikkim, Bhutan, and to the west, Pakistan and the state of Kashmir, claimed by both India and Pakistan.

Historically tribute had come to Peking from the Himalayan states. But more recently British India had controlled all their foreign policies. The new India was weaker. Chinese embassies visited the Himalayan states, aid was promised, and treaties of alliance concluded. The first was with Nepal in 1956, although most of the Chinese aid promised then did not materialize.

Meanwhile over the Aksai Chin plateau, in the far north of Indian-controlled Kashmir, the Chinese had built a road linking

Sinkiang and Tibet and running over the Macmahon line into Indian territory. The plateau was so inaccessible from the Indian side that Indian army patrols did not discover the road until several months after its completion. There were then Indian protests, and Chinese claims not only for the Aksai Chin plateau, but also for hundreds of square miles of Indian territory in the Northeast Frontier Province. In the autumn of 1961 the Chinese army broke through the eastern sector of their boundary with India and swept down over the Himalayas to within easy striking distance of the rich plain and cities of Bengal. The Indian army was apparently routed. But the Chinese stopped suddenly, and retreated back almost to their old posts.

There is still speculation about why the Chinese turned back when they did. Its defenders point out that the Indian army had been fighting uphill, and unprepared against the Chinese. Their equipment and their fighting habits were better suited to the plains. There were promises of support for India, possibly nuclear support, from Britain and America. The Chinese may have been misled by Indian Communist Party promises of a rising in Calcutta to coincide with their invasion.

The Chinese had anyway done what they wanted to do. The prestige of the Indian army was shattered. The Indian economy was severely shaken, not only by the losses in the actual fighting (where much equipment had been captured by the Chinese) but also by the consequent popular demand in India that their government should now devote more of its resources to defence. India's position as a rival leader in Asia was further damaged by the new reliance on the West, forced on her by her need for modern armaments. In conferences of neutral nations, Afro-Asian meetings, there was no longer a non-communist great power whose leadership was uncontestable, and whose position privileged her to rebuke and exhort China. India also now 'leant to one side'.

China's first ally, the Soviet Union, had, however, given her little active aid or even diplomatic support over either the Taiwan crisis or the invasion of India.[50] The causes of the growing split between

185

the two communist countries are differently emphasized by every writer on the subject. Some of them at least are personal. After Stalin's death Mao Tse-tung saw himself as the elder statesman of the communist movement: the doctrinal heir of Marx and Lenin. Far from acknowledging his leadership or seeking his advice the new Russian leaders, small men and newcomers in Chinese eyes, denounced Stalin, and so much of the communist past, without even informing the Chinese beforehand.

However, just after Stalin's death the alliance to the outsider had never seemed stronger. Krushchev visited Peking. More credits, more Soviet plans, and Soviet technicians were promised to staff a large number of Chinese enterprises. Three-quarters of China's trade was with the Soviet Union or with other communist countries in the block. There were immense rejoicings in China over the Russian sputnik, and the apparent victory of Russia over the United States in the space race. 'The East wind', said Mao, 'prevails over the West.'

What Mao apparently meant was that now world communism could triumph. Every effort should go into fostering revolution in every country in the world. The final defeat of the United States, imperialism, and capitalism, was at hand. In China itself the Great Leap Forward was to achieve communism in one generation.

In the Soviet Union Krushchev and his advisers had changed the state's economic policy to an increased production of consumer goods. Soviet living-standards went up. The whole country wanted butter not guns, to relax, to live in peace. The Great Leap Forward, the smug Chinese claims, were not only profoundly irritating, but also threatened the Russian position as the world leader of the communist block, and so indirectly her guarantee of the peace of the world.

In 1960 when the Chinese were in the throes of the economic crisis after the Great Leap Forward, the Russians asked for the repayment of all their credits to China, and withdrew their technicians. When the Soviet technicians went they had instructions to take the blueprints for half-built factories and dams with them. One of the reasons given for the withdrawal of the technicians was that the

Chinese were trying to indoctrinate them by making them read Mao Tse-tung.

It was a body blow from which Chinese industry is only just recovering. But for three years, until July 1963, the Chinese and Russians kept an official skin of friendship stretched over the growing breach. The only overt signs of trouble were the clashes on the Sinkiang joint frontier in 1962, and the Chinese reminder to the Soviet Union that the nineteenth-century treaties by which Russia had acquired Chinese-claimed Asian territory were 'unequal'. (The term used for the treaties with the imperialist powers which had been abrogated.) But there were still state references to China and Russia's 'eternal friendship and alliance'. In the months that followed, as the situation deteriorated, China attacked 'right-wing revisionism' in the Russians, but under the thin disguise of attacking Yugoslavia. Similarly the Russians attacked 'left-wing revisionism' in the Albanians, but meant the Chinese.[51]

The Chinese called for no further support for bourgeois nation-alists or negotiations with the West. The Russians quoted the Western retreat at Suez as an example of successful pressure on the West. The Chinese quoted Cuba, and the withdrawal of the Russian missiles there, as an example of unsuccessful Russian negotiation.

Several of the world communist countries and parties tried without success to mediate, or at least to preserve their own neutrality. Many of them benefited from the quarrel. Rumania used the breach to further her economic independence. In Asia rival subsidies poured into North Vietnam, North Korea, and Mongolia. Mongolia, hemmed in by the two states, eventually opted for Russia, but continued to receive Chinese aid. North Vietnam has been driven closer to the Soviet Union by the pressure of the war. She continues, however, to receive Soviet arms and Soviet diplomatic support. Over most of the world the greater economic resources and the peaceable-ness of the Soviet side won over opposition or governing com-munist parties. But China continued to have considerable internal support in these parties. The Russians angrily accused her of 'splittism'.

By the end of 1963 Russia and China were reviling each other openly. They published long lists of their grievances; and in 1964 there were official Chinese calls for Krushchev's 'liquidation'. For a few months after Krushchev's fall there was a lull in the vilification campaign. The Russian tone continued moderate, but by May 1965 the Chinese were likening Brezhnev to 'that clown Krushchev'. A month later the Soviet leaders were jointly accused of 'practising a more covert, more cunning, and more dangerous revisionism' than Krushchev's.

An important part of the quarrel with the Soviet Union has been over the future of the under-developed world in Africa, Asia, and South America. The Russians are anxious to avoid conflict with the West over these countries. They are also doctrinally convinced that before most of peasant Asian and African countries can become socialist they must have bourgeois and capitalist revolutions. The whole process will take time. For the Russians the new, under-developed nations were of marginal interest before the Chinese forced the competition for their friendship.

To the Chinese immediate revolution ought to be possible in the ex-colonial countries, particularly in Africa, if they know about and follow the Chinese model. China, the message went, was an under-developed country, and had achieved revolution. So could other under-developed countries if they did what China had done. To achieve this end in Africa Sino-African cultural societies are set up throughout the continent. Delegates are invited to Peking, and to tour China. Magazines are distributed, long hours of broadcasting undertaken in the local languages.

The Chinese believe this is essentially educational work, and that it is a sign of contempt to try to sugar the educational pill. The African audience are told about the detailed working of the Chinese revolution. A typical broadcast contains an unshortened leading article from the Peking *People's Daily*, a speech given by the local chairman of the Sino-friendship society, an account of the setting up of a new commune in Inner Mongolia, and the methods used by the third tool factory in Harbin to increase production and cut machine maintenance. The Russians (and the Americans) sweeten their broadcasting with music, cookery hints, and items of local news. The Chinese do not, and their audience has not been large.

For some years the Chinese believed that revolution would come to Africa through local communist parties. One disagreement with the Russians was about the importance of the national bourgeoisie. The Russians wanted to work with them, the Chinese despised them as imperialist dupes. It has, however, not proved easy for the Chinese to find genuine communists in most African countries.

Algeria, on the edge of the Arab and European worlds, has more developed political ideas than most of Africa. For a time Algerian leaders did quote China as a model for their country, and the young Algerian rebels carried (and sometimes read) the works of Mao Tse-tung. But after Algeria won its independence from France the country's leaders and young people became if anything more conventionally nationalist, and less inclined to flirt with world communism and Chinese-type reforms.

In the Congo the Chinese back the rebels against the established government. Here the difficulty was to disentangle communism and class struggle from tribalism and savagery. Elsewhere small opposi-tion parties all over Africa quickly discovered the free-gift system operated by the various ideologies. It is particularly difficult for the Chinese, without the Russian or the American training in anthro-pology and African custom, to disentangle those who want a land-rover bought to forward the cause of international proletarianism, from those who just want a landrover.

The buying of landrovers, the leasing of office premises, and the training of soldiers and politicians is carried on in Africa by the Chinese embassies. But some promising students are sent back to China, although here again the Chinese have been bad pickers. A good many of those chosen for further education in Peking are young men whose academic qualifications are not high enough to get them a scholarship in the West or even in Moscow, and who are anxious for more education from any source available. They are better lodged and fed than their Chinese contemporaries. Some of them, however, have been scornful of Chinese poverty. They have also been critical about the college teaching, the attempts to indoctrinate them, and the refusal of Chinese girls to respond to their advances.[52]

Recently the Chinese, in practice although not in theory, have moved a little away from their goal of immediate communist revolution in Africa. In June 1965 Chou En-lai was heavily snubbed when he announced, during his visit to Tanzania, that 'an exceedingly favourable situation for revolution prevails today not only in Africa but also in Asia and Latin America'. The Kenyan government, which a few weeks before had seized Chinese lorries and arms on their way across its territory, replied, 'the Kenyan government intends to avert all revolutions irrespective of their origins...'. Contrary to previous expectations Chou was not invited to Kenya, Uganda, Zambia, Congo (Brazzaville), or the Central African Republic. On his return to China his speeches talked of Africa as 'ripe' only for 'anti-imperialist revolution'.

China was, at the same time, beginning to realize that few African countries had left-wing oppositions capable of seizing power. Chinese support for ineffective local communists only drove the new African governments into world support for Russia or the West. Increasingly, Chinese friendship is offered to any new country ready to declare itself hostile to imperialism.[53] Today to qualify for Chinese aid, a country need not cut its ties with the West or cease to receive Western aid.

In Tanzania during the reception of Chou En-lai in June 1965 a correspondent noticed that the guard of honour was armed with Chinese rifles; but the salute accorded Chou was fired from British 25-pounders. The purpose of Chinese aid to countries like Tanzania is to win unexclusive friendship, and leave the heads of the government thinking, in the words of President Nyerere at the time of the Commonwealth Peace Mission to Vietnam, 'we believe that the Chinese are people too'.[54] It is a policy that is likely to become more successful as China's past reputation for backing impractical hotheads fades.

Between 1960 and 1965 China promised about $150 million as aid to Africa, only a quarter of which was actually disbursed. This is a considerable sum in terms of Chinese revenue, but much less than Western or even Russian credits to the countries concerned. But China has shown more imagination in the distribution of her aid than she does in her verbal or written propaganda. Earlier China sent 15 tons of grain to Guinea just as her difficulties after her drastic break with France were at their height. Chou En-lai is believed to have offered over £75 million to the governments of Tanzania and Zambia to build a railway linking the Zambia copper belt to the sea, thus freeing Zambia from her present dependence on the transport system of the white Rhodesian government.

The Chinese claimed at a recent meeting of the Afro-Asian People's Solidarity Organization that they were 'coloured, and your blood brothers in the struggle' (against imperialism). They have attempted to exclude the Russians from Afro-Asian meetings, and the Russians retorted that the Chinese are 'backward, poor, chauvinist and racialist'. Nor has the Chinese assertion of fraternity with Africans always rung quite true in countries where the smiles of a touring Chou En-lai or Chu Teh were backed by the grim disapproval of their aides and their rejection of all local friendly advances. Chinese technicians, helping with Chinese financed projects in Africa and Asia have orders to live as the local people do and eat local food. Their puritanism, however, makes less appeal in Africa than in Asia; and orders have recently, it is said, gone out to Chinese embassies in Africa to give more parties of a type that are popular locally.

In Asia, Chinese aid to non-communist, as well as the communist, states has been on a larger scale than her aid to Africa. The Chinese model is particularly applicable to Asian conditions (the Vietcong have been encouraged to fight a guerrilla war closely, and not always appropriately, modelled on the Chinese civil war). Chinese puritanism, Chinese university conditions, and heavy-handed Chinese propaganda are less inappropriate in Asia, where most Asians share some of the Chinese sentiments, than they are in Africa. On the other hand Southeast Asia was traditionally part of the Chinese tributary empire. There is an historic distrust of China added to by fear of the use China might make of the Overseas

Chinese communities. Much of this fear was allayed at Bandung; and, since Bandung, while Chinese policy has hardened in the rest of the world, it has stayed in general conciliatory and friendly to her smaller, south Asian neighbours. There has been no reversal of the Peking policy of gradual disassociation with the south Asian Chinese. It would probably be an even less gradual dissociation if China did not need the money sent her by these communities, and if she was not faced by the nationalists' insistence on Taiwan as an alternative focus for Overseas Chinese loyalties.

Yet, in the 1960s, South Asia was the most explosive region in the world. In its unhappy countries the United States and China fought out what was both their crusade against the other's ideology, and the battle for territories both nations thought essential for their national security. Their allies: western Europe, Britain, and the old dominions behind the United States; the Soviet Union behind China, gave some verbal support and occasional practical aid. Their main con-cern, however, was to moderate the ardours of their champions short of total war.

China, even more than the United States, hindered rather than helped her cause by the ferocity of her language, and the occasional ineptness of her diplomacy. Yet the Chinese, like the Americans, were eager for any allies in the region including those who did not support either Chinese communism or American capitalism as the guiding light for their countries.[55] Cambodia did particularly well out of aid given her by every power with interests or ambitions in the region.

Of the Asian battlegrounds Indonesia has been one of the bloodiest and least publicized. These rich islands, where the central government never succeeded in controlling the outlying provinces, were the victims of a series of right- and left-wing army coups. In the early 1960s the Indonesian Communist Party was the world's largest outside the countries with communist governments; and its leaders accepted the Chinese, not the Soviet, view of communism. The party's influence was, however, severely damaged by the reprisals during the suppression of Colonel Untung's attempted coup in the autumn of 1965. Over 100,000 communists, suspected communists and locally unpopular villagers were shot, and those Indonesian communist leaders who survived went into hiding. The triumphant generals were pro-Western in their sympathies. Chinese consulates were sacked, Chinese nationals killed, and Chinese policy and advice derided.

Further to the West China's alliance with the military dictatorship of Pakistan was a diplomatic triumph. Pakistan had been one of the allies the West took most for granted, and her new alliance became the showpoint for Chinese spokesmen eager to demonstrate to the world China's ready friendship for any non-imperialist nation whatever the colour of its internal government. The alliance was founded on both countries' enmity to India. The Sino-Indian border dispute was still unsettled; and over Kashmir Pakistan had been able to obtain no solid support for her claims from the West or from the Soviet Union. For China her new friendship had the additional advantage of weakening the Western organized military alliances of which Pakistan was a member.

In the 1965 Indo-Pakistani war over Kashmir the alliance was of more practical value to Pakistan than to China. Chinese threats kept Indian troops away from the Kashmir fighting, and contributed to Indian readiness to negotiate. But China did not occupy the remaining territory she claimed on the Tibet border, probably because she was afraid of provoking a major war if her troops entered India.

The danger of a major Asian war was at its most acute in Vietnam. The Chinese were naturally afraid of the establishment of a possibly hostile state on their vulnerable southwestern border; and they gave verbal and some material aid to the North Vietnamese communists. China and Vietnam, the Chinese said, are bound together as 'the lips and teeth'. On the other side the Americans too could not accept the total loss of Vietnam to their camp. It would, they claimed, damage their prestige throughout the world, and jeopardize those Asian bases which (since Pearl Harbour) many Americans had seen as the front line closely guarding San Francisco.

Chinese statements on the Vietnamese war stressed China's readiness for immediate war with the United States. Southwestern

Chinese cities were prepared for air raids, and the army warned of the likelihood of war . . . and the impossibility of China's defeat in her just cause. But China's actions were less belligerent than her leader's speeches. The North Vietnamese were urged not to negotiate; but Chinese 'volunteers' were not sent to fight in Vietnam as they had been sent to Korea. North Vietnam was kept short of weapons China could have supplied. The Chinese airforce in particular could have made a considerable difference to Vietnamese defence against air raids; but neither its planes nor its pilots were used.

In the short term perhaps the best that Southeast Asia can hope for is a more rigid division between the Chinese and the American spheres of influence and so a more limited scope for local wars and coups. The long-term prospects are more hopeful. Given time, some of the region's specific problems will solve themselves. In Taiwan, one of the region's powder kegs, Chiang Kai-shek is an old man. His successors, it is said, have their plans to make peace with Peking ready. Taiwan will be recognized as an autonomous region (like Sinkiang-Uighur or Tibet), controlling its own internal policies, but with its external policies subject to mainland Chinese control. Hints from Peking, from Taiwan itself, and most of all from Hongkong, add supporting details to this story. There is even a version, hopefully told, which sees Taiwan as continuing to receive American economic aid, although the American Seventh Fleet will no longer be needed for its protection.

If the Chinese really believe that the Americans, in the present state of the world, will be happy to go on contributing large sums of money to a Chinese autonomous region, it is one more example of their dangerous ignorance of other countries. It is the sort of mistaken thinking that increases world danger of war; and it is heavily contributed to by the isolation that the West has forced on China.

However, it seems unlikely that United States' diplomacy can continue indefinitely (even if it wishes to do so), to reserve China's seat in the United Nations to the Taiwan government; and when China becomes a member of the UN her representatives will also serve on a number of associated international bodies. Some of the present denigration of the United Nations, and the drawing up of unacceptable terms on which China would be prepared to join the UN, may be due to the Chinese leaders' reluctance to allow their junior diplomats this experience of practical international co-operation. But the Chinese are prepared to allow delegations and students to visit Britain, learn English, and study British institutions. This practical demonstration to both Chinese and Britons that neither side corresponds to the stock caricatures of communism or imperialism could be enlarged by scholarships, inviting more delegations of skilled adults, and by official and unofficial hospitality.

Contact with younger Chinese is of particular value now because there is evidence that (like the Nationalists on Taiwan) the second generation of Chinese communists may be more open to compromise settlements than their elders. And the elders are now very old men. (A part of the present critical situation in Asia has been the natural impatience of the old who want to see the millennium revealed in their own time.) The present Chinese leaders are certainly afraid that their successors will be less ardent in the cause of world revolution than they are themselves. No propaganda theme since 1949 has been as stressed for so long as the lesson on continuing revolution. Communism, the Chinese young are told, may take tens, hundreds of years, but it is their duty to continue to strive for it. They must live all their lives austerely, and resist both the blandishments of the Russian Revisionists, and the tricks of the West. Yet the young at one level still show an inclination for easy living, nylon suits and jazz; and at another for the moderate arguments of the Soviet Union and peace in their time. Are the elders going to win, and the young continue to be pledged to the crusade for world revolution? Or will the next generation follow the path of all previous second generation revolutionaries towards compromise, caution, and the subordination of their elders' dangerous enthusiasms to more soberly considered national interests? No one outside or inside China, seems certain of what the outcome will be and what Mao's successors will be like.

91 The example and leadership of Mao Tse-tung has inspired China's people. Here he is inspecting health work at Hangchow in 1958.

92 The 'Great Leap Forward' of 1958 instigated by Mao forced the pace of industrialization. This coking plant at a rural steel centre established a daily output of 1,000 tons.

93 Sung Ching Ling is the vice-chairman of the People's Republic of China and widow of Sun Yat-sen. 94 Chou En-lai, the Premier of China was one of the founders of the revolution.

95 China claims a People's Army of 120 million strong.

96 An enthusiastic army of peasant workers during a spring afforestation campaign.

97 The Yangtsze bridge is one of the proudest achievements of the present government. China, however, is only partially a modernized nation, and the traditional junk is still the commonest form of water transport.

98 At this commune iron smelting is carried out by primitive methods.

99 (*Above*) Traditional industry continues and is not always replaced with modern methods. This is salt-mining at Tseliutsin.

100 (*Below*) The communists have developed new oil wells. This oil refinery employing modern techniques still uses mule transport.

101 In 1958 the emphasis in the commune was on militarized discipline. At the Weising Commune the peasants obey the bugle call.

102 Everyone must participate in industrial production. Women workers at a factory canteen.

103 During their leisure hours these commune members relax at a rural cultural centre.

104 (*Left*) A poster in Peking urges the liberation of Taiwan the seat of the banished Nationalist government in 1956.

105 In the 1958 hostilities between mainland China and Taiwan (which was supported by the United States), this pilot who had been doing reconnaissance on Chiang Kai-shek's orders was captured and arrested by the communists.

106 (*Right*) Relations between the Soviet Union and China were outwardly friendly in 1957 when Mao Tse-tung and Krushchev met in Moscow. A rift developed between the two countries from the late 1950s over the leadership of world communism.

107 In 1955 at the Bandung Conference China adopted a peaceful and benevolent attitude to India and her Asian neighbours. Her later claims of Indian territory precipitated the war of 1961. The Chinese withdrew after a few months; these Indian prisoners were allowed to observe their religious festivals.

避孕方法介绍

108 An important challenge to China's future is the control of her population. A new move advocating family planning was instigated in 1962 with the publication of a series of posters. This is the first of the series and the caption reads: 'An introduction to the avoidance of pregnancy'.

Notes on the Text

1 But the title of the first Chinese of all must go to Peking Man, whose bones, the earliest of human type found in China, are about half a million years old.

2 After Ch'in Shih-huang-ti's death legalism became a dirty word in China. Confucianism was the respectable code. Legalist ideas, however, continued to influence later emperors and their advisers. A Legalist ancestry has been claimed, by its enemies, for Chinese communism.

3 See Cottrell, L., *The Tiger of Ch'in*, London, 1962.

4 The military strategy, however, was less to try and stop the barbarians breaking through than to pin them back against the wall once they had broken through. It was a similar theory to that which the Romans had about the use of their British wall against the Picts and Scots.

5 Even in the parts of the country where all tigers have long been exterminated, they are the wild animals of legends, proverbs and fairy stories – like wolves in Western Europe.

6 Wang Chien, c. 756–835. Translated A. Waley, *Chinese Poems*, London, 1946.

7 An un-Roman administrative tradition: more human but less convenient for the central power.

8 Fried, M. H., *The Fabric of Chinese Society*, London, 1956.

9 Mostly of course, it was an aspiration for the middle aged and settled. The revolt, passive or active, of young Chinese against their large families is the theme of a line of novels from the eighteenth-century *Dream of the Red Chamber* to the modern novelist Pa-chin's *The Family*. In both novels cousin lovers, brought up together, are forced apart by the tyranny of their family elders.

10 J. Lossing Buck, *Land Utilization in China*, Chicago, 1937.

11 Apart from the emperor and the members of his immediate family, the only Chinese given any hereditary respect were the descendants of the philosophers, particularly the Kung family, the descendants of Confucius. But even the Kung family had none of the powers of the aristocracy in Europe.

12 Quoted, Ho Ping-ti, *The Ladder of Success in Imperial China*, Columbia, 1962.

13 Op. cit.

14 Like Chou En-lai's family.

4 ROTTING TRADITION

15 The classic view of foreigners was given by Mencius. 'I have heard of men using the doctrines of our great land to change barbarians, but I have never yet heard of any being changed by barbarians.'

16 The Ming was a particularly and consciously conservative dynasty: a national reaction to the foreign Yüan dynasty and its international con-nexions through the other countries conquered by the Mongols. Ming scholars, painters, poets, as well as the government, tried to return, not altogether successfully, to the all-Chinese culture of the Sung and T'ang.

17 We are sometimes said to smell so revolting to the Chinese because we eat butter and cheese and drink milk, which they do not. We also nowadays wash ourselves and our clothes considerably less.

18 The Chinese craftsmen faithfully reproduced the details of dress, even the shockingly low necklines and bare feet of European peasant women and goddesses. (Dresses were, and are, cut high in China; and even when their feet are unbound and the rest of their clothes are rags, Chinese women always wear shoes. Female throats and feet are erotically stimulating in China.) But what the Chinese craftsmen could not bring themselves to believe in were the foreign eyes. Prince Charles Edward, the rose and gold Venus, and the buxom peasants all have narrow, slightly slanting eyes.

19 Quoted D. E. T. Luard, *Britain and China*, London, 1962.

20 Riders carrying official letters, made excellent speed for horsemen, over the post roads. But it was still a matter of weeks from the western frontiers to Peking.

21 Feuerwerker, A., *China's Early Industrialization*, London, 1959.

22 The name given them by foreigners at the time. Their proper Chinese

name is still much disputed. The most generally accepted translation is
'the Fists of Righteous Harmony'.

5 THE COMMUNISTS

23 *Land and Labour in China*, London, 1932. In this most prescient and readable
of economic surveys of China Tawney noted that 'the revolution of 1911
was a bourgeois affair. The revolution of the peasants has still to come. If
their rulers continue to exploit them, or to permit them to be exploited as
remorselessly as hitherto, it is likely to be unpleasant. It will not, perhaps,
be undeserved.'

24 To contemporary Westerners sympathetic to the idea of a strong reformed
China, the communists were a distraction and a nuisance. They did not
appear to outsiders as a serious problem, far less an alternative government.
But, while they existed, they stopped plans for reform by absorbing
Chiang's attention, and using men and money in the expensive civil war.

25 See 'The Long March' by Anthony Garavente in the *China Quarterly*,
No. 22. Mr Garavente argues convincingly that the figures for the army
losses show that the Long March was a communist defeat.

26 See the translations of some of Mao's poems in an appendix to Jerome
Ch'ên's and Michael Bullock's *Mao and the Chinese Revolution*, London,
1965. This is the most recent and authoritative history of the communists
and biography of Mao up to 1949.

27 At the beginning of the Long March there was probably no intention of
taking the Red Army as far as the remote and poverty-stricken province of
Shensi. It was part of Mao's political victory during the March that he
took the major part of the army northwards, instead of trying to establish
a base in the far west.

28 Quoted Pannikar, K. M., *In Two Chinas*, London, 1955.

29 This was to be a pattern repeated several times in Asia, notably in Vietnam, where other foreign armies (French and then American) relied again
on strong-points and the control of the cities. And again were unsuccessful
in holding the country against a hostile peasantry.

7 THE UNIFIED STATE

30 Lifton, J. R., *Thought Reform*, London, 1961. This is a detailed and
interesting study of brain-washing in Chinese prisons and outside by a
professional psychiatrist.

31 Another piece of evidence much quoted some years ago is the behaviour of
the 21,000 Chinese prisoners-of-war in Korea. They were offered the

choice of returning to their homes and families in China, or going to Taiwan. 14,000 chose exile in Taiwan. It has been argued that two-thirds of the Chinese people would similarly welcome the return of the Kuomintang in place of the communists.

It is a shaky argument because it is not clear just what the reasons were which sent the 14,000 to Taiwan. They may have been ex-Kuomintang soldiers from the armies which had surrendered to the communists, and who did not take their new loyalties more seriously than their old. Another, more sinister, explanation was, in part, put forward by the Chinese at the time of the peace negotiations. The prisoners in camps in South Korea had been roughly, and probably inaccurately, grouped according to whether they were communist or non-communist. The majority were grouped as non-communist. The administration of all the camps was very independent of the American guards; and the non-communist camps were partly staffed by Chinese Nationalists. (There were too few Chinese-speaking UN soldiers.)

When an International Commission was sent to interview soldiers from both sides who refused repatriation, the majority of the Chinese never saw the Commission. (Mostly because of UN procedural delays.) Those who did see it are said to have been carefully selected by the Nationalists. The tortured bodies found in the camps (both communist and non-communist) and the 'suicides' were of those unfortunate prisoners who had dissented from the camp's political direction.

8 NEW SCHOLARS AND ARTISTS

32 *Soviet Scientist in China*, London, 1964. Professor Klochko asked for political asylum in Canada in 1961, and his book was first published in New York.

33 Seemingly innocent classical designs are as dangerous to craftsmen as they are to writers or artists. The *Ta-Kung Pao* newspaper reported in October 1964 that the Ceramic Research Centre of the Kantan Pottery Company had a decorative design on some of their products called 'Fishing, Tree-Felling, Tilling the Land and Reading'. The drawing shows 'a scholar reading a book in a pavilion on the upper side of the picture and fishermen, woodcutters and peasants toiling in the foreground'. At a workers' discussion group on the subject, it was claimed that the picture 'sought to promote the reactionary idea of Mencius' that 'the scholastic pursuit is above all other callings', and 'those who do mental labour rule the people and those who do manual labour are ruled by others'.

34 George Orwell in *The Prevention of Literature* first noticed that totalitarian‚ ism need not be 'so deadly' for poetry as for prose. 'Bureaucrats despise poets', he said, 'and so do not bother about them.' Secondly, what the poet says, 'That is what his poem means if translated into prose – is relatively unimportant . . . a poem is an arrangement of sounds and associations, as a painting is an arrangement of brushmarks . . . it is therefore fairly easy for a poet to keep away from dangerous subjects and avoid uttering heresies.' This is more applicable to the relatively inefficient Russian totalitarianism of the 1930s and 40s than it is to China today; but poetry still remains far livelier and freer in China than prose.

35 There is an interesting collection of papers on modern Chinese literature in the *China Quarterly*, No. 13.

36 *Political Quarterly*, July–Sept. 1963.

37 Jan Myrdal in his book *Report from a Chinese Village*, London, 1965, describes the formation of collectives and a commune in the north Shensi village where he worked. In this village clearly the most dramatic and difficult step for the revolutionary peasants was the formation of the first collective.

38 There are two sorts of militia units in China. The roughly trained groups to which all adult young men and many women belong; and the better equipped, more highly trained special militia units for party members and volunteers.

39 The value of Chinese statistics has been much disputed. Most of them always have been in comparative form; and sometimes the comparison has been with pre‚war years when production generally, or of the particular item cited, was notably low. Up to 1957 most economists accept the Chinese figures as accurate. Thereafter there is a period of muddle, followed by a great scarcity of any figures at all. More plentiful economic data is now available about the Chinese economy; but some economists are still doubtful about the accuracy of all the figures given.

40 Philip L. Bridgham discussing Chou En‚lai's report in the *China Quarterly* (April–June 1965, No. 22) points out that on a *per capita* basis China in 1965 would continue to lag behind 1957 because of the large population increase (eight to one hundred million) in the eight‚year interval. Mr Bridgham also has doubts about Chou's claims for cotton and pig pro‚ duction, for the great increase in steel production, and for the 15 per cent rise in total industrial output. He accepts Chou's other claims.

41 His book *Red Star over China* published in 1937, still contains not only one of the most vivid of the pictures of contemporary Yenan, but also a description of the communist aims and methods, and biographies of the leaders which are still of great value.

42 This popular involvement with foreign countries has continued. Travellers testify to their astonishment on finding in remote interior villages posters expressing sympathy with the Algerians, and demonstrations in support of the Dominican left wing. Students in Lanchow and Chungking are eloquent about the Congolese or the Cubans. It is in some ways a major change from imperial China where most Chinese were both ignorant and uncaring about foreigners. But present-day Chinese knowledge sees (and even, on the posters, draws) the foreigners as unfortunate Chinese domiciled in the harsh outside world. Any idea that the foreigners may have different systems of thought is completely missing from the Chinese picture of them.

43 The Chinese still refuse to exchange ambassadors. The British Mission in Peking and the Chinese mission in London are each headed by a Chargé d'Affaires.

44 Probably still a fairly true picture. Apart from their atomic bomb Chinese arms and aeroplanes are old fashioned by the standards of other Asian countries, like India, which have been armed by the West. Chinese soldiers are conscious of themselves as an *élite*, however, and are well-trained and disciplined. Staff work, movement of supplies, intelligence, all appear to be good if somewhat hidebound by the traditions of the good old days of the Long March and Yenan.

45 There is a suggestion that some of the peculiar bitterness of the two countries' relationship is because modern China is, in a way, America's child. For 20 years before 1949 China had been the favourite target of American good works. American missionaries set up schools and hospitals in China; American diplomats, at any rate in theory, protected China against the excesses of the imperialist powers. American students took Chinese past and present civilization seriously when the rest of the world jeered. The Americans could have been sympathetic, helpful, and generous to a Chinese revolution they approved of. They were snubbed.

46 To begin with the Chinese saw much of the world in terms of wicked governments and good people. They believed that they could appeal effectively over the heads of the governments through the various 'peace' organizations. When it became clear that these peace organizations were

not truly popular, the Chinese used them less; and in all major countries, except the United States, strengthened their knowledge and ties of the government and the official hierarchy.

47 Although as late as 1954 when a British Labour Party Delegation toured China, they were firmly told by Chinese officials that the British National Health Service could not exist.

48 This is a Hongkong view. Chinese in Hongkong, whether communists or Nationalists, will make general statements about their leaders' policies with a freedom lacking on the mainland or in Taiwan. They are often well-informed statements; semi-official, inspired at a high level, and very useful to governments whose totalitarian structure makes it difficult for them otherwise to try out opinion; or air internal differences.

49 See Roderick MacFarquhar 'Communist China's Intraparty Dispute', *Pacific Affairs*, December 1958.

50 Over the invasion of India, China later criticized the Soviet Union's failure to support her as 'a betrayal'; and, in his long speech on the quarrel in 1964, M. A. Suslov talked of the 'pernicious consequences' of the Chinese invasion; and the 'grave harm' it inflicted on 'the national liberation movement, the progressive forces of India and the entire front of the anti-imperialist struggle'. But neither side was so outspoken in 1961.

51 'Revisionism', revising or altering the sacred text of Marx, Lenin, and Stalin is a cardinal sin in the communist world. It is difficult for a Westerner to know just how much weight to attach to the doctrinal quarrels of communism. Because the founders of communism were prolific, texts can be found to back most points of view. Non-communists are tempted to the belief that the point of view is arrived at, and the text to back it then searched out. But this is probably an over-cynical view of, at any rate, the Chinese side of the quarrel. (Educated Moslems presumably said much the same about the Christian struggles of the Thirty Years War.)

52 See E. Hevi, *An African Student in China*, London, 1965.

53 This policy received doctrinal backing in June 1963, when in 'A Proposal Concerning the General Line of the International Communist Movement', the Chinese analysed the four 'fundamental contradictions in the contemporary world'. They were between the communist and non-communist worlds, between classes in capitalist countries, between 'oppressed nations' and imperialism, and among imperialist countries. Of these the conflict between the imperialists and the oppressed nations was said to have most importance at present.

54 To mark his friendship with the Chinese people President Nyerere constantly wears the uniform of a Chinese cadre. Or this is what he says. The suits are indeed blue; but open necked and made of silk.

55 Even that bastion of old-fashioned free enterprise, Hongkong, notched into the mainland of South China, has been growled at from Peking. But it continues to be supplied with food and water from the mainland; and its existence (for good reason) is not seriously threatened. Many Chinese trade agreements with the West are arranged through the branch of the Bank of China in Hongkong. Dollar and pound foreign remittances to China from the Overseas Chinese are also sent through this Bank. Visas are commonly issued in Hongkong; and the colony serves as an economic safety valve for the province of Kwangtung. (Most of the Hongkong refugees are fleeing from poverty rather than political persecution.) Communist and Western publications are both freely available to students of either block. Macao has similar uses. The colony is less officially tolerant; but the police are less efficient.

Select Bibliography

Harris, R., *Modern China*, National Book League, London, 1961. This is an excellent introductory bibliography with short notes on the books suggested. Among the books either not mentioned or since published I found the following particularly interesting:

Ch'ên, J., *Mao and the Chinese Revolution*, London, 1965

Cottrell, L., *The Tiger of Ch'in*, London, 1962

Dawson, R. (ed.), *Legacy of China*, London, 1964

Fitzgerald, C. P., *China: A Short Cultural History* (rev. ed.), London, 1950

Fu-Sheng, M., *The Wilting of the 100 Flowers*, London, 1962

Gernet, J., *Daily Life in China on the Eve of the Mongol Invasions*, London, 1962

Greene, F., *The Curtain of Ignorance*, London, 1965

Greene, F., *The Wall Has Two Sides*, London, 1962

Grousset, R., *The Rise and Splendour of the Chinese Empire*, London, 1952

Klochko, M. A., *Soviet Scientist in China*, London, 1964

Lundquist, S., *China in Crisis*, London, 1965

Mehnert, K., *Peking and Moscow*, London, 1963

Myrdal, J., *Report from a Chinese Village*, London, 1965

Needham, J., *Science and Civilization in China*, London, 4 vols., 1954–62

Newman, R. P., *Recognition of Communist China*, New York, 1961

Prodan, M., *Chinese Art*, London, 1958

Roy, C., *Into China*, London, 1955

Snow, E., *The Other Side of the River*, London, 1963

Sullivan, M., *An Introduction to Chinese Art*, London, 1962

Swann, P., *Chinese Painting*, London, 1958

Swann, P., *The Art of China, Korea and Japan*, London, 1963

Waley, A. (trs.), *Chinese Poems*, London, 1961

Watson, W., *China*, London, 1961

Wint, G., *Communist China's Crusade*, London, 1965

Wood, S., *A Street in China*, London, 1958

The China Quarterly is the leading non-communist journal devoted to Chinese affairs.

Among the journals published in Peking and available in Britain, *China Reconstructs* is the liveliest and most easily obtainable.

Acknowledgements

The author wishes to thank Mr Guy Wint for having read this book in manuscript.

Photographs were supplied by the following: from W. Alexander, *Costume of China*, London, 1805, 27; from T. Allom and G. N. Wright, *China Illustrated*, London, 1943, 26; by courtesy of the Ashmolean Museum, Oxford, 4; Associated Press, 42, 46, 47, 48, 59; by courtesy of The British Council for the Promotion of International Trade, 108; by courtesy of the Trustees of the British Museum (Natural History), 3; by courtesy of the Trustees of the British Museum, 5, 6, 9; Camera Press Ltd (China News Service), 7, 8, 13, 14, 17, 18, 20, 40, 41, 49, 60, 61, 62, 64, 65, 66, 67, 68, 69, 70, 71, 72, 73, 74, 75, 77, 78, 79, 80, 86, 87, 88, 89, 90, 91, 92, 93, 94, 95, 96, 98, 101, 102, 105, 106, 107; Cartier Bresson, 53, 54, 55, 56, 57, 58, 82; China Inland Mission, 15, 16, 36, 43, 51; China Missionary Society, 12, 34; from J. B. de Halder *Description de l'Empire de la China*, Paris, 1735, by courtesy of the Trustees of the British Museum, 23, 24, 28; S. Farnell, 97; Imperial War Museum, 38; Lois Mitchison, 19, 63, 81, 84, 85, 100, 104; National Army Museum, Camberley, 31, 39; New China News Agency, 44, 83, 103; by courtesy of the Parker Gallery, London, 32; by courtesy of the Royal Academy of Arts, London, 30; from G. Staunton, *An Authentic Account of the Embassy to the Emperor of China*, London, 1797, by courtesy of the Trustees of the British Museum, 21; 25, Photo the *Sun*, 45, 50, 52; from J. Thomson, *Illustrations of China and its People*, London, 1873, 11, 33; from P. van Hoorn, O. Dapper (ed.), *Gedenkwaerdig Bedryf der Nederlandsche cost Indische Maetschappye op de Kuste en in Lef Keizernijk van Taising von Sino*, Amsterdam, 1670, by courtesy of the Trustees of the British Museum, 22.

Acknowledgement is also made to the following publishers whose books are quoted: George Allen and Unwin Ltd, from A. Waley (trans.), *Chinese Poems*, 1946 on pp. 19, 20; from K. M. Pannikar, *In Two Chinas*, 1955 on p. 84; Chatto and Windus, from D. E. T. Luard, *Britain and China*, 1962 on p. 57; Columbia University Press, from Ho Ping-ti, *The Ladder of Success in Imperial China*, 1962 on p. 35.

Who's Who

CHEN YI, b. 1901. Became Foreign Minister in 1958. His previous reputation was as a military leader against the Japanese and the KMT, and as administrator. He is Chairman of the National Defence Council, and has accompanied Chou En-lai on several foreign tours. He is a keen chess player, interested in football, and writes poetry.

CHEN YUN, b. 1905. China's leading economist, and a member of the Politbureau, a deputy premier, and Deputy Chairman of the CCP (Chinese Communist Party) Central Committee. He criticized the more extreme of the Great Leap Forward policies in March 1959, and suffered some political reverse as a result; but he is now largely reinstated except that he ranks second, not as before first, among the deputy premiers.

CHIANG KAI-SHEK, b. 1887. The President of the Republic of China (Nationalist). The head of the Kuomintang government in Taiwan (Formosa) which claims also to be the rightful government of mainland China. After Sun's death and the Kuomintang split Chiang was the ruler of China from the 1920s to his defeat in 1949.

CH'IEN LUNG (1711–99). The 4th Emperor of the Manchu (Ch'ing) dynasty. Conquered Sinkiang. With China at its zenith of external security and internal prosperity Ch'ien Lung rejected the proposals for alliance and trade made him by George III of England.

CH'IN SHIH-HUANG-TI (259–210 B.C.). Completed Ch'in conquest of Chou feudatory states of North China. By ruthless methods unified a larger empire in China than any of his predecessors. Built the Great Wall, burnt the Confucian books, and killed protesting scholars.

CHOU EN-LAI, b. 1898. Prime Minister, the third man in the CCP hierarchy (after Mao and Liu), and until 1958 Foreign Minister. Chou has been critical of proposals for the more extreme Chinese policies, particularly during the Great Leap Forward, but his criticism has been combined with complete loyalty in the execution of party policy once it has been agreed on. He is an able negotiator – cautious, persistent, and urbane – and his speciality has been foreign affairs.

Chou was born into a Kiangsu upper-class family with official connexions. He attended Nankai University, Tienstin, and was imprisoned after he took part in the student demonstrations of 4 May 1919. He studied in Japan, Paris, and Germany, and paid a short visit to Britain. During the period of co-operation between the later Nationalists and the Communists in the KMT, Chou became head of the political department of Whampoa Military Academy (whose Director was Chiang Kai-shek), and he organized a successful strike which opened Shanghai to Chiang in 1927. Chou was later identified within the Communist Party with the Li Li-san line of continued strikes and armed risings, but successfully confessed his errors and went to Kiangsi to join Mao in 1931. He was Political Commissar to Chu Teh during the Long March. In the civil war Chou took a leading part in negotiations with the KMT, and is credited with the decision to release Chiang after the Sian agreement.

Since 1949 he has, during his constant travels, led Chinese delegations to the Geneva Conference over Vietnam, to the first Afro-Asian conference at Bandung, to the Soviet Union during the Hungarian crisis, and recently on tours gathering allies in Africa and Asia. His wife, Teng Ying-chao, is also a member of the CCP Central Committee, and an important political figure in her own right.

CHU TEH, b. 1886. The grandfather figure of the Chinese Communist state – conciliatory, portly, and benign. Chu Teh is the oldest of the major Communist Party leaders, and takes a less active part in state affairs than he did. He is, however, still the Vice-Chairman of the CCP Central Committee, and Chairman of the standing Committee of the National People's Congress.

Chu Teh was born in Szechuan into a rich peasant family. In the first half of his life he himself became a rich, corrupt, and many-wived warlord according to the conventional pattern. After he had reformed he went to Europe in 1922, where he became a member of the CCP, and then studied in Moscow. He joined Mao in Kiangsi in 1928. He was the main Chinese army leader through-out the Chinese civil war. Since 1949 Chu Teh has encouraged the army to accept party civilian control; and he has taken a particularly prominent part in

Politbureau discussions on agriculture and foreign policy. He has also led important Chinese delegations abroad.

CONFUCIUS (551–479 B.C.) (Kung Fu⁄tzu). The most famous man in China's history. His precepts dominated Chinese education and government for over 2000 years. Much to his disappointment he himself never held important political office, and the major part of his life was spent teaching disciples.

DALAI LAMA DANTZEN JALTSO, b. 1935. The Tibetan ruler in exile. Recog⁄nized as 14th reincarnation of the Dalai Lama in 1938. He attempted to work with the Chinese, in the interests of his people, after the conquest of Tibet, but fled to India in 1959. In a press interview he later accused the Chinese of starting 'a reign of terror' in Tibet.

HUNG HSIU⁄CHUAN (1814–64). The Heavenly King, the leader of the Taiping rebellion against the Ching dynasty. He claimed to be a Christian, Christ's younger brother, who had been called by God to rule China. In the 14 years of the rebellion he conquered much of South and Central China.

HUNG WU (1328–98). Founder of the Ming dynasty. The son of a poor peasant family, Hung Wu defeated the last servants of the Yüan (Mongol) dynasty, and re⁄established a Chinese state with a legal code and administrative system based on that of the T'angs.

KANG YU⁄WEI (1858–1927). Confucian scholar. Leader of the reform move⁄ment of 1898. Blamed Chinese weakness on misinterpretation of Confucianism. Remained loyal to the idea of limited monarchy, dismissed as reactionary by younger generation of the 1920s.

KAO KANG (d. 1955). Leader of pre⁄Long March revolution in northwest China. After 1949 he was Vice⁄Chairman of Central People's government, Chairman of the State Planning Commission, and Chairman of Northeastern People's Government. Committed suicide in prison 1955. Reason for fall not yet known. Possibly plotted independence of Manchuria, with or without connivance of the Soviet Union.

KUBLAI KHAN (1215–94). The grandson of Genghis Khan, and the founder of the Yüan dynasty in China. While Kublai made China part of the vast

Mongol empire, he did not interfere with basic Chinese social or economic institutions, or alter the content of traditional Chinese education.

KUO MO-JO, b. 1891. President of the Chinese Academy of Science, and Chairman of the All-China Federation of Literary and Art Circles. Kuo has been the leading government spokesman in dealing with the Chinese intellect-uals and the various peace movements abroad. Before his complete absorption in politics, Kuo wrote poems, plays, and novels and did outstanding research on China's Bronze Age.

LAO-TZU (c. 600 B.C.). The probably mythical founder of Taoism. He is said to have advised Confucius, compiled the Book of the Tao, and departed westwards to India where he converted Buddha. The book attributed to him was probably compiled by several authors, not earlier than the 4th century B.C.

LI FU-CHUN, b. 1901. Chairman of State Planning Commission, Vice-Premier, member of CCP Politbureau, Central Committee and Secretariat. Economic specialist. Gained in influence from his support of Great Leap Forward policies.

LI LI-SAN, b. 1896. Studied in France. Became Secretary of Central Commit-tee of the Communist Party in late 1920s. Criticized for 'blind actionism' (e.g. promotion of strikes and open revolt in towns – the course of action opposed by Mao). Since returning from Soviet Union in 1946, he has held minor government offices.

LIN PIAO, MARSHAL, b. 1908. A veteran of the southern soviets and the Long March. Became Minister of Defence 1959, is at present Vice-Chairman of the Politbureau and the Central Committee of the Party. He has recently taken an increasingly prominent part in national and international receptions and delega-tions; and his portrait is displayed in public places together with those of the other top leaders. (Mao, Liu, Chou, Chu Teh, Chen Yun, and Teng Hsia-ping.)

LI PO (701–62). Considered by many critics to be the greatest of China's poets. Despite his frequent drunkenness he was a favourite of the T'ang Ming Huang Emperor, but quarrelled with the emperor's favourite concubine. He was drowned when he fell from a boat trying to kiss the reflection of the moonlight.

Li Ssu (c. 280–208 B.C.). The prime minister of Ch'in Shih-Huang-ti; a Legalist; and held responsible for many of the ruthless and totalitarian innova-tions of the Ch'in emperor. Under Ch'in Shih-Huang-ti's successor Li Ssu was involved in a court intrigue and executed.

Li Ta-chao (1888–1927). One of the founders of CCP. As President of Peking University and Chief Librarian, organized study cells there in 1920. Executed for opposing militaristic ambitions of northern warlords.

Liu Pang (248–195 B.C.). Posthumously known as Kao-tsu. Founder of the Han dynasty. Reigned from 202 to 195 B.C. The son of a peasant who became a bandit chief, Liu Pang unified China after centuries of civil strife.

Liu Shao-chi, b. 1898. Since he succeeded Mao as Chairman of the Republic in April 1959, Liu has been recognized as Mao's most likely successor as general leader of the country. His previous importance had been particularly as a theorist, and as a party organizer.

Like Mao, Liu is a Honanese, partly educated at Changsha Normal School. As a young man he studied in Moscow. He joined the CCP in the year of its foundation, 1921, became a specialist in labour organization, and joined Mao in Kiangsi in 1932. He took part in the Long March, and thereafter he was largely concerned with party organization underground in KMT and Japanese-controlled China, and Party training in Yenan. Many of his pamphlets and speeches, like Mao's, have become communist classics, studied throughout today's China. The most famous, *How to be a good Communist*, was delivered to the Party training school in Yenan.

Since 1949 Liu has taken a prominent part in all major political decisions, particularly over state and party administration and over negotiations with the Soviet Union and other foreign communist countries. He is thought to have urged some of the more extreme measures of the Great Leap Forward, and to take a generally leftist view of Chinese policies.

Lu Hsun (1881–1936). Author. In spite of his opposition to materialism and to authoritarianism, Lu Hsun has been posthumously adopted by the commu-nists as the great exemplar of a socialist-realist writer. His most famous work is *The True Story of Ah Q*. It is a satire on the old order of Chinese life and a classic portrayal of national psychology.

LU TING-YI, b. 1907. Born into a Kiangsu landowning family. China's propaganda chief, also alternate member of Politbureau, a vice-premier, and Minister of Culture, Lu was prominent in the post-Hundred Flowers Movement and later Communist Party Rectification Campaigns.

MA YIN-CHU, b. 1882. Chinese economic theorist of international standing. President of Peking University 1951 to 1960. During 1958-9 Ma defended himself publicly against newspaper attacks alleging that he was a neo-Malthusian (connecting poverty with population growth), supported Keynesian economic theories, and denied the need for a class struggle in China.

MAO TSE-TUNG, b. 1893. The accepted leader of the CCP since 1935; but not a dictator according to the Stalinist pattern. Mao has consistently asked for and apparently considered advice from other Chinese leaders. Top level personal relations seem to be good, and Mao's influence is believed to be against vendettas of a defeated side or of the advocate, within the party, of a defeated policy. He is also believed to dislike unnecessary bloodshed.

Mao was Chairman of the Republic of China from 1949 until he resigned in 1959, in order, it was officially said, to devote more time to theoretical work. His prestige and popularity appear to be undiminished, and he continues to be Chairman of the CCP's Central Committee and of the Politbureau. His books and published speeches are required reading for all Chinese students of politics; and in China are given equal authority with the communist classics of Marx, Engels, and Lenin.

Mao was born into a prosperous Hunan peasant family. His father sent him to school to learn to do the family accounts; but Mao insisted on continuing his education to a modern school and then to college in Changsha, the provincial capital. Several of Mao's fellow-students became leaders in the Kuomintang or Communist parties. Mao himself found work in the library of the National University at Peking, where he met some of the leaders of the New Tide movement. In the collapse of the old imperial institutions the New Tide men stressed China's need for a new birth, based on Western knowledge. The study groups they formed provided much of the theoretical background for both the Nationalists and the communists.

In 1921 Mao was one of the delegates who founded the CCP. He organized the Autumn Harvest Rising in Hunan in 1927; and, after its failure, fled to the mountain stronghold of Chingkangshan. From there Mao organized a Chinese soviet on the borders of Kiangsi, Fukien, and Kwangsi provinces. He urged communist reliance on peasant support and guerrilla warfare rather than on open revolts in towns; and during the late 1920s and early 1930s, as the town revolts failed and their leaders were hunted down, Mao's views were accepted. In 1934 Mao led the Long March from the southern soviet to Yenan in North China. On the March, at a party conference at Tsunyi, Mao's leadership of the Party was confirmed. Thereafter Mao's public history has been the history of the Chinese Communist Party, and after 1949 of the Republic of China.

MAO TUN, b. 1896. Chinese novelist, playwright, critic. Long association with communism. Former Minister of Culture. Vice-Chairman of All-China Federation of Literary and Arts Circles.

MARCO POLO (c. 1254–1324). The Venetian traveller who became Kublai Khan's friend and servant. His account of his travels was disbelieved by his contemporaries, but, although modern scholars have found it inaccurate in occasional details, it is, in the main, true.

MATTEO RICCI (1552–1610). Italian Jesuit missionary who (with his companion Michael Ruggieri) opened China to Christian evangelization. Ricci was allowed to settle in Peking, where he attracted converts among the Chinese intelligentsia and gained general respect by his tolerant attitude to Chinese customs and his personal erudition.

MEI LAN-FENG, b. 1893. China's most famous actor, specializes in women's parts in traditional Peking opera. First went on stage at the age of 13, his father and grandfather also being actors. Sometimes government spokesman on opera, drama, or general cultural policy.

MENCIUS (371–289 B.C.) (Meng Tzu). Confucius' most influential follower. Like his master he failed to hold important state office, and became a teacher. His particular contribution to Confucianism was his stress on practical reform and the natural goodness of human nature.

MING HUANG (684–712) (the Brilliant Emperor). His reign is the high point of T'ang prosperity and culture. Administrative abuses were corrected, and the emperor made an unsuccessful attempt at fiscal reform. Military expeditions were sent outside China, but their expense and their defeats helped provoke rebellion.

PENG CHEN, b. 1899, Shaensi. Ranks among top dozen leaders. Mayor of Peking, First Secretary of the Peking Party Committee, member of CCP's Politbureau, Secretariat and Central Committee. He also receives foreign delegations, and heads Chinese delegations abroad.

PENG TEH-HUAI, MARSHAL, b. 1905. China's leading soldier and Minister of Defence until his dismissal in 1959. His fall was probably due to his disagreement with the Great Leap Forward policies and the breach with the Soviet Union.

PU YI, HENRY, b. 1906. Ex-emperor of China. Succeeded 1908, abdicated 1912. Restored for seven days in 1917. Japanese puppet emperor of Manchukuo 1934–45. Imprisoned in China 1949 to 1959. Worked in botanical gardens, Peking, 1959–63. Now engaged on research for autobiography.

SUNG MAI-LING (Madame Chiang Kai-shek), b. 1901. Educated at Wellesley College, USA. Sister-in-law of Sun Yat-sen. Married Chiang Kai-shek in 1927. Politically active. Rallied support for Chiang abroad, particularly in tours of the United States of America.

SSU-MA CH'IEN (c. 145/135–90 B.C.). The earliest and most influential Chinese historian. Travelled widely as a young man, then spent most of life as courtier of Emperor Wu of the Han dynasty. His *Records of the Historian (Shih Chi)* cover 2000 years of Chinese and East Asian history from the earliest time.

SUN YAT-SEN (1866–1925). The leading figure in the Chinese revolution of 1911, and a hero of both the Nationalists and the communists. Educated mainly outside China, he drew much of his early backing from overseas Chinese communities. He was ousted from power in 1913, and never regained full control of North China.

SUNG CHING-LING, b. 1890. The widow of Sun Yat-sen, is also the sister-in-law of Chiang Kai-shek, and a vice-chairman of the Chinese People's Republic. She is chairman of the Sino-Soviet Friendship Association, and of several welfare organizations. She was born into a wealthy, Western-orientated, Shanghai business family. She was educated partly in the United States, and assisted her husband in the foundation of the KMT.

Tao Chu, b. 1907. The most prominent party leader in South China. Took office in the south immediately after 1949. Member of the CCP Central Committee and First Secretary of its central south bureau.

Teng Hsia-ping, b. 1904. Probably the most important of the younger CCP leaders. He has been Secretary-General of the CCP Central Committee since 1954, and since 1956 a member of the Politbureau Standing Committee. He is a deputy premier, and during Chou En-lai's tour of Africa in 1963 was acting premier. He has negotiated with Asian communist leaders visiting Peking, has been a member of recent key delegations sent to Moscow to put the Chinese view on world communism, and he led the delegation to the Soviet Union sent in 1965.

Ting Ling, b. 1907. Authoress of considerable reputation. First joined with the communists in Yenan. She was arrested in the 1958 purge of rightists, and has not reappeared in public life.

Tseng Kuo-fan (1811–72). Mainly responsible for the defeat of the Taiping rebellion. Thereafter he tried, without lasting success, to revive the Confucian virtues and institutions, and subordinate to them enough Western science to make China a powerful, independent nation.

Tzu Hsi (1835–1908). 'Old Buddha'. Virtual ruler of China as co-regent and regent from 1861 until her death. Ambitious and able but without the education or imagination to grasp the full weakness of China confronted by the Western imperialism, and the far-reaching reforms the country needed.

Ulanfu, b. c. 1903. The Chairman of the Inner Mongolian Autonomous Regional government; and the only non-Chinese on the Central Committee of the CCP. He is also Chairman of the Nationalities Affairs Commission (concerned with the administration of the autonomous regions of non-Chinese peoples living inside China's boundaries).

Wang Wei (698–759). Scholar, poet, and painter. His landscapes mark the beginning of mystical nature painting with a strong literary background.

Wu Hou (625–705) (The Empress Wu). The most infamous woman in Chinese history; but an able and forceful ruler of the T'ang Empire. She was a concubine of the Emperor Tai Tsung, dominated his successor, and after she bore him a son, obtained the rank of empress. In 690 she deposed her son and had herself enthroned as empress.

YUAN SHIH-KAI (1859–1916). A viceroy of the Empress Tzu Hsi. Became President of the Republic after 1911. In 1915 he had himself proclaimed as the new emperor; but he postponed his enthronement and surrendered his civil authority when the provinces revolted against him.

Index

Numbers in italic refer to illustrations

INTEGRATING
SCHOOL
RESTRUCTURING
AND
SPECIAL
EDUCATION
REFORM

INTEGRATING SCHOOL RESTRUCTURING AND SPECIAL EDUCATION REFORM

JAMES L. PAUL
HILDA ROSSELLI
DONNIE EVANS
University of South Florida

Harcourt Brace College Publishers

Fort Worth Philadelphia San Diego New York Orlando Austin San Antonio
Toronto Montreal London Sydney Tokyo

Publisher	Ted Buchholz
Senior Acquisitions Editor	Jo-Anne Weaver
Project Editor	Elke Herbst
Production Manager	Tom Urquhart
Senior Art Director	Don Fujimoto
Electronic Publishing Coordinator	Jill Stubblefield

Copyright © 1995 by Harcourt Brace & Company

Address for Editorial Correspondence: Harcourt Brace College Publishers, 301 Commerce Street, Suite 3700, Fort Worth, TX 76102.

Address for Orders: Harcourt Brace & Company, 6277 Sea Harbor Drive, Orlando, FL 32887–6777. 1–800–782–4479, or 1–800–433–0001 (in Florida).

ISBN: 0–15–501222–3

Library of Congress Catalog Card Number: 94–79438

Printed in the United States of America

5 6 7 8 9 0 1 2 3 4   039   9 8 7 6 5 4 3 2 1

FOREWORD

James J. Gallagher

I am pleased to have the opportunity to provide a foreword for this adventurous volume by Jim Paul and his many colleagues. These chapters take the general ideas about educational restructuring and reform and put them in a practical context focusing on special educational programs. This collection of proposed changes extends from reform of personnel preparation to a different approach to research design, to the proposed changes in the geography of special education (inclusion). It deals with reforms beginning in general education (e.g., site-based management) as well as reforms begun in special education (e.g., inclusion).

This volume represents an impressive series of accomplishments—the efforts of an entire faculty of a university school of education to create a future for personnel preparation and service delivery to exceptional children. The authors of these various chapters not only talk about change, they demonstrate its happening through their own efforts. Nor are the changes that they describe modest ones. They are describing structural changes that must take place between school systems and higher education, between various components of higher education with each other, and—above all—a changed relationship between general education and special education. Such structural change will require multiple personnel to learn different roles. Perhaps the most difficult task is to put aside a role with which one has become comfortable and adopt a new way of doing a job. It is never a welcome idea for oneself, though we may earnestly wish it for others. There must be powerful forces at work to convince large numbers of people that these changes have to come about.

Are these reforms that are being discussed *revolutionary*, overturning the very assumptions upon which the status quo is based, or *evolutionary*, keeping most of the present assumptions but increasing the efficiency of operation? There are many reasons to conclude that, although the intent of many reformers is revolutionary, the effects of the present movement will be evolutionary. There are many existing institutions, professional associations, and certification and credentialing groups that will be affected by these proposed changes. These groups can be counted on to throw sand in the wheels of change to slow down and modify the intended changes if they appear too radical or seem to have too strong a negative effect on the self-interests of those institutions. Nevertheless, the changes being suggested here will change the educational landscape from what we now know into something clearly different.

One of the major themes of the chapters is that of *collaboration*. This involves the recognition of the fundamental principle that no person, or cluster of persons, can do the job of educating exceptional children alone, nor can one person alone do the task of preparing professionals for such educational tasks. One of the significant areas of educational service delivery lies in the potential collaboration of many different disciplines to an organized program for children with disabilities and their families. When we see the importance of ecological factors in the development of young children, we instantly recognize that we need social workers, sociologists, and a whole range of service personnel from the health area in order to provide a comprehensive program. If one is going to drastically change the professional roles that are being played, then these new roles must be demonstrated in some tangible and believable fashion. The integration of programs of higher education with the six school systems reported in this text provides an impressive base for that demonstration.

Let there be no mistake, however, about the difficulties and barriers that we will encounter before we have reached the new territory to which we aspire. For those in the educational reform movement, fascinated with the potential for structural change and the redefinition of professional roles, it often comes as a surprise and a shock to be reminded by events that these systems and institutions are composed of human beings with their own psychological dynamics to be dealt with.

In moments of enthusiasm for something new (and hopefully better), we can sometimes forget a fundamental law of psychology: that self-interest is one of the primary motivators for an individual to take a particular action—or to oppose a particular action. If our proposed restructuring means that power and authority will be redistributed, we must realize that somebody, and more likely some groups of somebodies, will lose power and authority that they now hold. One group that seems certain to lose power and authority in this new situation is institutions of higher education. Therefore, it is doubly remarkable that this group from the University of South Florida has been able to institute a new series of partnerships with the public schools as detailed in Section Two of this report.

As we move forward to our new and different future, there are a number of questions and answers that must be confronted. It is to the credit of the writers in these many chapters that they have made a strong start in trying to confront these issues.

> 1. *How can higher education be encouraged to accept public school personnel as true partners in this personnel preparation model?*

Notice how this question is framed. It does not deal with the merits of the partnership, nor of the value that would come to the students because of that partnership. Rather, it addresses the psychological dynamics of status and position. This will involve more than merely giving parking privileges to the public school personnel, but will require a recognition that those who are competent in their positions and roles in the local school system are as genuine a partner in the personnel preparation efforts as many full professors in their university departments. Giving up status, even if it is illusory, is never an easy task, and it will be interesting to see how that effort progresses.

> 2. *How can we help the professional disciplines that have, in the past, jealously guarded their own turf to move into a truly multidisciplinary service delivery and personnel preparation program?*

Again, note the way the question is framed. It does not address whether it would be a good thing for the children and parents to have the professional groups collaborate, nor even whether it would bring manifest benefits to the various disciplines. Once again, the psychological issue is, What are the reasons why one should give up status? There is, in addition, a practical matter—that the personnel preparation programs in each of these many disciplines are filled to overflowing with courses considered to be essential to the well-trained professional. Yet, if we are to create a truly interdisciplinary personnel preparation, and keep the length of the program reasonable, then many of these courses will have to be abandoned or substantially changed. It does not require a rocket scientist to figure out that such proposed changes or omissions will not be received with overwhelming joy by the professionals who often have fought long and hard to have the courses inserted into the existing personnel preparation program.

3. *We will also need substantial help from the general education community to carry out many of our aspirations. The silence that we hear from that community on these issues is eloquent.*

The silence that we have heard from the general education community began with the Regular Education Initiative. The REI is misnamed, as many people have already noted. The REI is really a special education initiative designed for regular education. This is not to say that there aren't many professional educators willing and eager to try new ways of incorporating exceptional children into the general program; the various collaborative efforts described in these chapters illustrate there are. But the agenda of general education is already overflowing with issues of multicultural education, violence, sex education, etc. It is not hard to project that many general educators will have limited enthusiasm for the special education community bringing yet another problem to their doorstep. The call for the incorporation of exceptional children into the regular education program will be greeted with predictable restraint by general educators. The experienced educational administrator will understand that the problems connected with such a move toward inclusion will arise substantially before the arrival of the resources necessary to cope with the problems.

4. *If inclusion of the vast majority of children with disabilities into the regular education program is the future, then how does the special program of differentiated curriculum for many exceptional children fit into the general education program?*

We already know that physical inclusion is not the same as psychological inclusion into a group, and we also know what a sensitive and complex issue it is preparing teachers and students, currently in the general education program, for such inclusion. Again, this change calls for changing roles on the part of regular education teachers. That, too, will be one more issue to be sorted out and overcome.

Note that the four issues posed here do not, in any way, suggest that what is being proposed may not bring major benefits to our clients, exceptional students, and their families, although the proof of that outcome remains to be demonstrated.

We now have almost three decades of experience with attempts to create major reform in education, beginning with Lyndon B. Johnson's War on Poverty. We need to avoid the problems created by the destructive sequence of

Idealism ⟶ Disappointment ⟶ Despair

The fact that we often do not live up to our most enthusiastic projections does not mean that "nothing works." What it means is that change is difficult to engineer, and improvement may be even a little more difficult to obtain. We should take seriously the wise counsel of the philosopher Santyana, who reminded us that, "Those who do not remember the past will be compelled to repeat it."

There are several reasons why these reforms are likely to turn out to be episodic and uncertain, beyond that of professional self-interest (noted above). One deals with the size of the educational enterprise itself. Few people understand that educational reform means the personal change of habits of an astonishing number of people. Not many are aware that there are two and one-half million elementary and secondary school teachers in this country. This means that one out of every one hundred people in our country is an elementary or secondary school teacher. Education is, by far, the largest enterprise in our society, and each of these people is employed in one of some 14,000 independently operated school districts or separately operated private schools. What are the chances that these millions of people will give up their self-interest and march united, and in step, behind a single banner of educational reform—even assuming they can agree on which reforms to support? As Dizzy Dean used to say, that idea has two chances: "slim" and "none."

There is the continuing problem of implementing desired change once we have agreed on what the change should be. We are in the beginning stages of understanding how human organizations and institutions can be rationally changed. Michael Fullan, in his fine book *Change Forces*, makes the point that while *top down* doesn't work for effective change, neither does *bottom up*. There must be a complex mix of both strategies if significant change is to result. This is not to be taken as a counsel of despair. Rather, it is a plea for persistence, constancy of efforts, and a realization that the roads through the wilderness of change are not smooth—nor should we expect them to be. It is the philosophy of the long distance runner, not the sprinter, that will be required.

There are many places in this book, in many different chapters, that show how enthusiasm and commitment can overcome some of the barriers and, through such demonstration, the rest of us are encouraged that the job can indeed be done. This book deserves to be studied carefully by all who are embarking upon similar ventures into the wilderness of change, toward the goal of improving education for exceptional children.

PREFACE

JAMES L. PAUL

Classroom teachers, special educators, principals, special services personnel, parents, legislators, and other public officials are deeply involved in attempting to change the public education system. The debate about how to change the system, whether to improve it or to reconstitute it, is colored by different views of what is wrong with schools, the role of schooling in the future, and how public education should be managed. The rhetoric is rich with metaphors and slogans that trouble the complacent and incite enthusiasm in those seeking change.

The complexity of change in public education is amplified by several fundamental realities. One is the increasing diversity in our society, and the interdependence of the social and moral systems in which children are reared, the culture of schooling, and the agenda of public education. Second are the changing lenses through which we view child development and education. Philosophical shifts in understanding the nature of knowledge, for example, and the technologies now reconstructing our understanding of the process of learning have uprooted traditional theories of curriculum and pedagogy. Third is the changing perception of nurture and the role of public policy in constructing it. For example, demographic changes in the role of women in the work force and the concomitant change in child care have brought the government into closer proximity to the social and moral development of children.

These and other realities frame the social and political contexts in which policy debates about the education and care for children with disabilities are occurring. The "spend more, do more" policy momentum of the last three decades has created systems of services for children who were unserved prior to the 1960s. As the "lid has been lifted" off the general education system revealing a top-down bureaucracy with schooling practices, characterized by many as being inferior, sexist, and racist, seriously flawed "special" systems of education and care have also come into wider public view. Part of the complexity of the current policy debates about education reform lies in the fact that racism, sexism, and quality of instruction are issues of public accountability embedded in the general and special systems of education.

Questions about what is special education—a familiar question to special educators—have been replaced by questions of the moral and pedagogical defense of the special education project. Some would end the project which has been in place for more than a century and has had strong public and legal support in the last quarter of the century. Their argument is that both general and special education must be radically changed and an inclusive system created in which no children are marginalized or symbolically devalued. Others would change parts of the "special" system and improve its relationship to the changes in the general education system.

There is a lack of consensus on the nature of the changes needed and how to accomplish those changes. There are many debates between inclusionists and those supporting the regular education initiative, between behaviorists and holistic educators, and between post-positivists and contructivists, among others. These are serious debates within as well as between groups. The plethora of articles on reform reflects the various strongly held positions on changes needed to assure an appropriate education for all children.

The focus of this book is on change in public education as it relates to the needs and interests of children with disabilities. The book is divided into two parts. The first addresses the question, What is the nature of the reform of general and special education? The second part addresses the question, What can be done at the grass roots level of public schools and universities to understand and respond to the challenges of reform?

The first part of the book provides an historical perspective on the different forces that created the current reforms in general and special education. This part addresses the myriad of professional, political, legal, ethical, and technical issues now facing educators and policy makers seeking to effect major changes in public education. The second part describes approaches to effecting changes in special education services and the education of teachers. There are three sections in this part. The first includes a discussion of changes in the College of Education at the University of South Florida as it sought to address the issues in reform described in Part One, especially as reflected in the philosophy of teacher education. The second section describes experiments in collaboration between the University of South Florida and public school systems on the west coast of Florida seeking to construct alternative approaches to collaboration and the education of teachers. The third section addresses the future from the perspective of some who have participated in the South Florida experiments and have reflected on the meaning and implications of the difficult work of serious collaboration and change for the reform of public education. Chapters in this section include discussions of changes needed in the philosophy of special education and paradigm changes now forming the intellectual horizon of education reform.

The book raises and addresses several major questions about restructuring, inclusion, collaboration, the philosophy of special education, and the future. The unique feature of these questions is the context in which they were raised, that is, a partnership context that involved a university and school districts working on the practical problems of reform. Among these questions are the following:

- What are the dual reforms of education—restructuring and inclusion—and how did they come about?
- What are the major arguments driving the two reforms and what is the research supporting those arguments?
- Why should the reforms be integrated and how can that be achieved?
- What are the legal and ethical principles and issues raised by the reforms and how might they be addressed?

- What are the specific responsibilities of educators to families and young children resulting from a changing sociopolitical landscape?
- In what ways can a university teacher education program participate in the reform at the school level?
- What are the systemic changes needed in the university in order to participate as partners in school reform?
- What are the challenges, politics, and dynamics encountered in serious university-school partnerships?
- How are teachers's and faculties's roles changing and what potential do these changes hold for their more active participation in reform?
- What major changes are needed in the philosophies, beliefs, attitudes, and practices of general educators, special educators, and other professionals working in schools in order for the reform to occur?

This book offers no easy answers to these difficult questions. Rather, looking carefully and reflectively at our experiences with change, we share the lessons we have learned and are learning about how to go about the difficult day-to-day business of changing ourselves—habits, beliefs, goals, valued practices, traditions—as we work in partnership with others going through a similarly difficult process.

The book is not about teaching methods or curriculum reform to create an inclusive school. Rather, it is about the complex social ecology of schools and of any university. It examines the personal, professional, ethical, and technical challenges to those who would establish professional solidarity around the principles of reform within and between schools and a university.

The book is written for those involved in partnerships aimed at school reform and a wide audience that includes teacher educators, doctoral students, student interns and their supervisors, researchers, administrators, policy makers, teachers, and pupil personnel services staff. Because of the historical, philosophical, social, ideological, and ethical issues that saturate the reform process, the authors hope social foundations faculty will also find the book useful.

The principles and insights shared come out of intense reflective dialogue over a period of four years. One of the most fundamental understandings we have about our work is that it continues to inform us as we invest and risk ourselves in the process. When do we know enough and when should we be confident enough to draw conclusions, however tentative, about where our experiences have taken us in our values and our ways of thinking about our work and ourselves? It is so much easier to introduce a treatment, conduct controlled experiments, and test hypotheses. While the authors believe there continues to be an important need for experimental and quasi-experimental research, we are also convinced that we need the "thickness" of experience with imaginative trials and thoughtful consideration of real dilemmas to build a body of understanding about the nature of collaboration for serious change in schools and universities.

This book brings together those who are more inclined to shape and adapt the traditional epistemology of educational research with those much more interested in the interpretive accounts and lessons of reformers at work. Our differences on issues of the philosophy of educational science have been one of our ongoing struggles which, respectfully, we continue. The debates among ourselves, our differences about what is real, interesting, useful, and meaningful, and our conflicts over the nature of the research process have made our work invigorating and instructive for all of us. We do not seek a common path of research. Rather, we believe the pluralism that is so central to the reforms in education should be valued and nurtured in our philosophies and methods as a community of researchers.

Central to this book is the belief in a concerned, caring, thoughtful, and diverse community. We have learned that continuity of caring in a collegial community is a necessary condition for those seeking to effect major changes. We have found it essential to become a learning community in order to understand and respond to the complexity of reform.

ACKNOWLEDGMENTS

This book is about collaboration in bringing about change. The decision to write this book came out of a collaborative research group on restructuring which has been functioning now for over four years. The book reflects the university-school partnerships developed over that time. Most of the chapter authors work collaboratively on a daily basis.

In writing any book, much of the hard work is done by individuals who do not appear as chapter authors. This is especially true in an edited work involving 45 authors. From the beginning communications about the shape of the book and the memoranda that must be circulated, to the schedules that have to be coordinated for meetings, the copying, and managing data files, to the final editing of page proofs, many caring, patient, and extraordinarily competent people helped. While it is not possible to mention all who contributed to the final production of the book, we want to recognize and thank publicly those who made major contributions.

The Dean of the College of Education provided the leadership and support needed to develop and sustain the initiatives described in Part Two. The collegial environment in the College, the commitment of the leadership support team of chairs, and the deep conviction of the faculty in the Department of Special Education that the work of special educators and teacher education must be rethought and reformed made this work a reality.

Lasting partnerships have been formed with schools. The support, encouragement, and generous collaborative spirits of the leaders of exceptional student education programs in local schools helped form the foundation on which this total project rests. Those who provided particularly strong support are Ms. Liz Argot, Director of ESE Programs in Hillsborough County; Dr. Ray Ciemniecki, Director of Student Services in Manatee County; Dr. William Delp, Executive Director in Sarasota City Schools; Dr. Jack Lamb, Assistant Superintendent in Pinellas County; Ms. Oma Pantridge, Director of ESE Programs in Pasco County; and Dr. Cathy Wooley-Brown, Director of Instructional Services in Polk County.

There are approximately 68,000 students with disabilities identified for special education services in these six districts. School leaders at all levels in these districts have provided outstanding opportunities for the collaborative learning and program development reflected throughout the book. These collaborations continue with an experimental spirit and many of the trust barriers that separate schools and universities are already behind us.

Doctoral students and faculty who have participated in the collaborative research group over time, most of whom share chapter authorship, have worked hard and creatively on all of the issues addressed by the chapter authors.

A major task with so many authors and chapters constantly undergoing revision was managing the disk files. Sara Good made a major contribution to this project by helping us manage this aspect of our work. Nannette Putnam and, later, Beverley Harrison, secretaries for the senior editor, were information centers for the project and helped immensely with communications and documents. Their patience with us and their willingness to continue helping to the end made the practical work possible.

Drs. Linda Patriarcha, Wayne Sailor, and James Gallagher gave generously of their time in reading and reacting to drafts of the book. While we take responsibility for the many decisions that went into shaping the final product, their knowledge of the issues and their fresh perspective on our work were of enormous value.

While he shares authorship on two chapters, acknowledgments would be incomplete without recognizing the special role of Dr. William Morse. His careful reading of and feedback on drafts and the care with which he helped authors work through issues in their texts made a substantial contribution to the content of the book and the process of writing it.

A special debt is owed to Jo-Anne Weaver, senior acquisitions editor, and Elke Herbst, project editor, at Harcourt Brace, for their support throughout the writing and editing process.

All of the authors contributing to this work have kept their sense of humor with deadlines and endured the process of rewriting and responding to edits of many drafts. To all of these individuals we express our deepest gratitude and credit with whatever value this project may have to those working to integrate restructuring and inclusion agendas in local schools, state departments and universities.

LIST OF AUTHORS

Maria Adiegbola
Department of Special Education
University of South Florida
Sarasota, FL 34243

Fran Archer
Orange Ridge Bullock School
400 30th Ave. W.
Bradenton, FL 34205

Dr. Joanne Arhar
College of Education
Kent State University
Kent, OH 44242

Kathleen Berg
Florida Mental Health Institute
University of South Florida
Tampa, FL 33620

Dr. Cathy Wooley-Brown
Programs for Exceptional Students
Polk County Schools
P.O. Box 391
Bartow, FL 33830

Ray Ciemniecki
Exceptional Student Education
Manatee County School District
P.O. Box 9069
Bradenton, FL 34206

Kass Claggett
Thomas E. Weightman Middle School
30649 Wells Road
Zephyrhills, FL 33544

Dr. Karen Colucci
Department of Special Education
University of South Florida
Tampa, FL 33620

Dr. Lynne Cook
Department of Special Education
California State University
Northridge, CA

Dr. Scot Danforth
Department of Special Education
University of South Florida
Tampa, FL 33620

Dr. William Delp
Exceptional Student Education
Sarasota County School Board
3550 Wilkinson Road
Sarasota, FL 34231

Dr. Albert Duchnowski
Department of Special Education
University of South Florida
Tampa, FL 33620

Dr. Glen Dunlap
Florida Mental Health Institute
University of South Florida
Tampa, FL 33620

Dr. Betty Epanchin
Department of Special Education
University of South Florida
Tampa, FL 33620

Dr. Donnie Evans
Hillsborough County Schools
Department of Special Education
P.O. Box 3408
Tampa, FL 33601

Dr. James Gallagher
Keenan Professor
University of North Carolina
Chapel HIll, NC 27514

Dr. Cynthia Griffin
Department of Special Education
University of Florida
Gainesville, FL 32611

Wilma Hamilton
Exceptional Student Education
Sarasota County School Board
3550 Wilkinson Road
Sarasota, FL 34231

Dr. Deborah Harris
Department of Special Education
University of South Florida
Tampa, FL 33620

Dr. Constance Hines
Associate Dean
College of Education
University of South Florida
Tampa, FL 33620

Dr. Ann Hocutt
Department of Special Education
University of Miami
Coral Gables, FL 33124

Linda Houck
Department of Special Education
University of South Florida
Fort Myers, FL 33919

Luanne Panacek-Howell
Florida Mental Health Institute
University of South Florida
Tampa, FL 33620

Dr. Howard Johnston
Department of Secondary Education
University of South Florida
Tampa, FL 33620

Dr. Philip Jones
Department of Educational Leadership
Virginia Commonwealth University
Richmond, VA

Dr. William Katzenmeyer
Director of the Anchin Center
University of South Florida
Tampa, FL 33620

Dr. James King
Department of Early Childhood,
Language Arts, and Reading
University of South Florida
Tampa, FL 33620

Dr. Jeffrey Kromrey
Department of Education
University of South Florida
Tampa, FL 33620

Dr. Lynn Lavely
Director of the At-Risk Institute
University of South Florida
Tampa, FL 33620

Dr. Yolanda Martinez
Department of Special Education
University of South Florida
Tampa, FL 33620

Dr. Jan McCarthy
Department of Early Childhood,
Language Arts, and Reading
University of South Florida
Tampa, FL 33620

Dr. Don McKinney
Department of Special Educaton
University of Miami
Coral Gables, FL 33124

Dr. William Morse
Department of Special Education
University of South Florida
Tampa, FL 33620

Dr. James Paul
Department of Special Education
University of South Florida
Tampa, FL 33620

Susan Perez
Department of Special Education
University of South Florida
Tampa, FL 33620

Dr. Marlene Pugach
University of Wisconsin–Milwaukee
End Hall 299
Milwaukee, WI 53201

Dr. Shirley Raines
Department of Early Childhood,
Language Arts, and Reading
University of South Florida
Tampa, FL 33620

Dr. William Rhodes
Department of Special Education
University of South Florida
Tampa, FL 33620

Dr. Hilda Rosselli
Department of Special Education
University of South Florida
Tampa, FL 33620

Dr. Wayne Sailor
Department of Special Education
University of Kansas
Lawrence, KS 66045

Barbara Seidl
Department of Special Education
University of Florida
Gainesville, FL 32611

Dr. Paul Sindelar
Department of Special Education
University of Florida
Gainesville, FL 32611

Dr. Tom Skrtic
Department of Special Education
University of Kansas
Lawrence, KS 66045

Dr. Lee Smith
Department of Special Education
University of South Florida
Sarasota, FL 34243

Terry Smith
Department of Special Education
University of South Florida
Tampa, FL 33620

Dr. Kim Stoddard
Department of Special Education
University of South Florida
St. Petersburg, FL 33701

Dr. Brenda Townsend
Department of Special Education
University of South Florida
Tampa, FL 33620

Dr. Fred Weintraub
Department of Governmental Relations
International Council for Exceptional
Children
1920 Association Drive
Reston, VA 22091

Dr. Arthur Yang
Department of Special Education
University of South Florida
Tampa, FL 33620

TABLE OF CONTENTS

I

THE NATIONAL CONTEXT OF REFORM IN GENERAL AND SPECIAL EDUCATION
Reshaping the Agenda

JAMES L. PAUL AND DONNIE EVANS

T IME was when schooling seemed relatively straightforward. Schools were orderly, the curriculum was clear, the teacher was in charge and supported by parents, children who could learn did and those who could not dropped out, children of upper-class parents were in private schools and the rest were in public schools, and—you know the rest of the story. Schools then were segregated and diversity was not an acknowledged issue. Test bias and discriminatory placement were not public policy issues. Children with mild to moderate mental retardation were placed in special classes. The needs of children with learning disabilities were less obvious. They were at the lower end of the distribution of achievement scores, made poor grades, and were often viewed as lazy or strange. Some of them managed to get through school but believed they were "dumb" and exited school with low opinions of themselves. Many of them dropped out. Children with emotional and behavioral problems, on the other hand, were viewed as mean, poorly parented, or victims of the influence of bad kids. These children were often spanked, kept after school or sent home, and many of them were expelled from school. Many of those who were not expelled found school such an unpleasant place that they dropped out. Often these same children had difficulty getting along in the community and ultimately became involved with the correctional system.

Schools were different then—and that was not so long ago. Now there is a law guaranteeing all children the right to a free and appropriate public education in the least restrictive environment. The best of laws and the worst of laws, according to which special educator you ask. As a result of the law, there are now policies protecting the rights and interests of children and their families, including, for example, the right to nondiscriminatory assessment, an individual education plan, and parent participation in placement decisions. These rights were earned by many parent and professional groups who lobbied legislators, worked closely with the executive branches of government at the state and national levels, and ultimately went to court to secure the right to an education for all children, including those with disabilities.

We now know there is much more to the story. Schools are different places now. Child-rearing practices and family support systems have changed, communities are more diverse, and the children attending school come from different racial, ethnic, and religious groups. The curriculum has been viewed as flawed by cultural insensitivity and bias. Some critics wish to reform the curriculum to make it more open, inclusive, and reflective of national standards. Others see the control of the curriculum to be a matter of cultural agency and inclusion as a 1990s version of the melting pot metaphor that diminishes the place and negates the identity of all groups—except, perhaps, those who are in charge of the standards. The question of whether or not schools work is not new. Whether one argues that educational institutions in their present form are unresponsive to the diversity of our society, that they inadequately supply appropriately educated and trained person power, or that they are often not safe places, the intensity of the question and the constituencies that now embrace the possibility that our schools need reform may augur deeper changes than in the past.

Education science, on which rational changes were to be based, has turned out to be not as objective, reliable or, in some instances, even as valid as has been supposed. Education science has been challenged not only by those who seek to improve it with better definitions and more objective measures, but by those who question the basic premises of empirical science. While the cultural complexity of testing and teaching children in publicly supported institutions is generally recognized, the problematic assumptions of education science are beginning to come into focus.

In addition to the cultural and philosophical challenges, there are enormous problems with the top-down bureaucratic system of schooling today. During the past 10 years there has been a major attempt to shift authority as well as responsibility to the teacher and, in the process, to professionalize the teacher's role. This has met with mixed success. Questions of control of the curriculum, the relative legal responsibilities of schools and school boards, the role of parents, and a plethora of instructional and management issues within schools have shaped the policy discussions since the early 1980s. The educational mainstream is at once both the environment of choice for children who have not been there, including children with moderate to severe disabilities, and a failing system, where cultural interests are compromised by a common curriculum and educational needs are unmet.

The apparent paradox of negative data on school environments and student performance prompt many parents to seek another solution for educating their child. The strong inclusion movement with parents demanding access to the regular classroom presents an ethical challenge to policymakers and architects of the reform. It is in this context that the specification of outcomes for students is as necessary as it is problematic. What divides parents on the matter of today's schools as desirable has to do with differences in vision. What is the purpose of schools and what role(s) should they serve in society in the future? The necessary political, cultural, and economic perspectives that inform the different visions of schools require moral as well as empirical and rational analyses.

Since business and political leaders and policy makers have awakened to the serious problems in the public education system with the publication of *A Nation at Risk* in 1983, every state education system in the country has been involved in working on a vision for public education and a strategic plan to realize that vision. Among the many challenges to these planners are the persistent questions: How do we repair a large and dysfunctional bureaucracy? What standards should we establish, at what level of the educational system should they be established, and how can/should they be monitored and guaranteed? How should we position ourselves on the process of education if accountability is to focus on outcomes? How can we define and specify outcomes in ways that are realistic and not trivial? What kinds of data do we need? How can teachers be educated as leaders in schools of the future that are not yet envisioned? How can public education be financed? What roles should communities play? How can excellence be guaranteed? How can equity be guaranteed? How do we address diversity? How do we educate *all* children? What constitutes an appropriate education? What are the social, moral, and economic consequences of choice?

These and other basic questions comprise the changing agendas of school board meetings and shape the public debate about reinventing the public education system. Some argue we are in a period of transition with significant shifts in instruction and in the management and funding of schools. Others argue that the system of schooling no longer meets the needs of a knowledge-based society and that a transformative change in the very conceptions of education and schooling must occur.

The ongoing debate of these political, social, ideological, moral, and technical issues forms the substance of the school reform movement. The stakes are high for our society and for all children who will continue to attend our public school system, whatever form it will ultimately take. The stakes are, perhaps, amplified for those children who find their interests on the margins of the debate. These include poor children, children from ethnically diverse families, and children with disabilities.

The rhetoric of school reform plumbs the public imagination about our intentions for all children and the priority we place on their personal welfare and development. The realities of policy development, when we are required to define the terms of schooling, the conditions of classrooms, and the values to guide the allocation of resources, define the public priorities. We are, at present, involved in debates of public policy conundrums where our rhetoric does not fit our priorities. These issues implicate every aspect of public education.

The future of school reform and its impact on children with disabilities is uncertain. One of the few things about which we can have some confidence is that the models we have used in the past have little validity for predicting the future. The future is not simply a change of course, redirecting what is now in place. Rather, we are situated in between fundamentally different and often contradictory understandings of what we consider to be true and what we regard as worthy. The paradigm of knowledge is changing and this has a profound impact on how we understand and go about our work, including the work of research, teaching, and policy development. The shift in the paradigm of knowledge both reflects other changes of enormous significance in our thinking about the future of education for all children, including those with disabilities, and contributes to them. These changes include, among others, massive demographic shifts in our society which are producing dramatically different cultural profiles of students attending school, the creation and diffusion of adaptive and instructional computer technologies in all aspects of education, changes in the nature and composition of family support systems and child rearing practices, and the emergence and public validation of a diversity of moral perspectives.

Some argue that policy science is becoming more sophisticated and that, while the political and financial necessity of using existing data bases and conducting short-term studies necessarily constrains the knowledge available for policy development, the problem is in political expediency and not in the science. Others argue that the tools available for studying and describing the realities we are seeking to understand and address are inadequate and often inappropriate. The meaning and moral status of events are masked by observational tools that render the events as objective data. From this perspective, there are no prediction equations, no linear plot lines with trajectories that will aid us in anticipating the future. The progression of events does not appear to follow an orderly or lawful course and, interestingly, perhaps the more objective and personally detached from the issues we become, the less likely we are to discern where we are or the course we ought to pursue.

In this book we are primarily concerned about the policy issues and the programs involving children with disabilities and their families. Part One addresses the context of school reform and inclusive schooling. The first three chapters describe the historical and philosophical context of the broad reform of general education and the specific reform of special education.

The first chapter by Paul, Yang, Adiegbola, and Morse discusses the nature and meaning of the current educational reform in the context of educational philosophy. The authors characterize the discourse on education during the past decade as being shaped by two issues: 1) the nature and purpose of education, and 2) the nature of science and its relationship to education, which has focused on epistemological and ethical issues. The thesis of this chapter is that the policy dilemmas facing education reformers are created by a lack of consensus on the nature and mission of education. The lack of consensus on the nature and methods of education is then found to be rooted in the changing paradigm of knowledge and teaching practice. The need for a new philosophy of special education is described, and necessary features are presented.

Chapter two offers an overview of components and strategies being used to restructure the nation's schools. The reviewed restructuring components include changes in governance structures (site-based management, school improvement teams, etc.), work redesign (personnel roles and responsibilities), and core technology (the way instructional services are delivered). Then, utilizing a nested systems perspective, factors influencing the success of efforts to restructure schools at the federal, state, district, and school levels are presented. Among those examined are a vision and leadership for change, policy waivers, fiscal considerations, a culture and climate for change at the building level, collaborative planning and partnerships, and pressure at the local level.

Chapter three offers a description of the Regular Education Initiative and Inclusion initiatives; how the two initiatives are different and how they are similar; activities of the U.S. Office of Special Education Programs connected to the two initiatives, and the context in which they have evolved. The authors conclude that the Inclusion initiative is an extension of the REI and note the following similarities: 1) both come from the special education community and are not discussed much by the general educators; 2) both are touted as goals, quite apart from student outcomes; and 3) both are reflective of a desire for a unitary rather than a comprehensive educational system. Significant differences include the context in which they have evolved and a greater focus on student outcomes associated with inclusion.

A chapter on law then details the legal context in which restructuring is now occurring. This chapter reviews federal special education law, the influence of federal courts on the law, and the development of state responsibility for special education. Federal laws and amendments reviewed include the Education of All Handicapped Children Act (P.L. 94-142), the Handicapped Children's Protection Act (P.L. 99-457), the Individuals with Disabilities Education Act (P.L. 101-476), Section 504 of the Rehabilitation Act of 1973, and the Americans with Disabilities Education Act (P.L. 101-336). The influence of parent groups, such as the Association for Retarded Citizens, on the development of the Education of All Handicapped Children Act, its amendments, and related state legislation is also discussed. The author concludes by noting that the federal special education law is clearly written and interpreted by the courts and, as intended, the beneficiary remains individual children.

These background chapters are followed by a chapter on the impact of reform on the education of young children and implication for children entering school. Chapter five discusses the philosophical, programmatic, professional education, and policy issues and concerns associated with early intervention/early education in the context of reform in general and special education. It begins by establishing the legal case for early intervention programs, particularly for students with disabilities, and policy commitment at the federal level.

The authors then argue in support of merging early childhood special education and early childhood education. In support of this union are arguments that the differences among young children are less, the expectations of institutions that serve them are not limiting their measures of success to cognitive functioning, and family involvement is a hallmark of both groups. They further argue that for integration of the two fields to truly happen, several challenges and understandings must be acknowledged and openly discussed. These include: 1) what we know about young children and how they learn; 2) what we need to know about the major forces that have driven program development for early childhood education and early childhood special education and 3) what attitudes or barriers need to be addressed, including program availability, attitudes, turfdom, teacher preparedness, communication, and awareness.

The chapter ends with a discussion of the need for teacher education reform and suggestions for addressing the challenge of serving young children with special needs. The authors suggest that reform is needed to address the practice of separateness between and among special and regular education students, professors, and programs. Recommendations for addressing the challenges include broad-based involvement of constituents, rethinking teacher preparation, and assuring that lines of communication are open.

Chapter six presents the case that school restructuring provides an opportunity to reconceptualize the roles of families, particularly those who have children with disabilities, in the overall education of children as well as in general school improvement plans. It begins with a discussion of how schools need to understand and assist in meeting the needs of families by making available training, information, planning and assistance, case management, and social/emotional support.

Then it explores the role of parents as partners and decision/policy makers and ends with a discussion of five strategies for improving family involvement. They include outreach, training for partnerships, participatory research, neighborhood focus, and professional training.

The next three chapters of this section address the implications of school reform for the education of teachers with particular attention to the education of teachers of children with disabilities. Chapter seven discusses the ethical issues special educators face as their roles and responsibilities change with school restructuring. The authors highlight aspects of the restructuring movement in general and special education that will impact the role of educators. Within that context, they argue for a redefinition of the role of the special educator as a teacher leader in the ethical deliberation and collaborative decision making. The discussion is framed by the consideration of the roles of all education professionals in restructured schools. A more specific focus on education professionals serving students with disabilities or special needs is then provided.

The authors also present a framework for ethical decision making that includes policy, values and facts, and standards of professional practice. The framework is illustrated with dilemmas that will face special educators in restructured schools. The selection of dilemmas, based on CEC standards, include responsibilities to individual children and their parents, responsibilities to fellow professionals, and responsibilities to attain and maintain appropriate qualifications.

An emphasis on the study of ethics and the development of skills in ethical decision making in professional preparation and continuing education programs is also described. In addition, a strong discussion of accountability is included with a focus on: Who is accountable? To whom is the special educator accountable? And for what is special education accountable?

Chapter eight argues for a reconceptualization of teacher education for classroom teachers and teachers of children with disabilities in programs which are fully integrated. It begins by considering the characteristics of traditional special education teacher preparation, the context in which it exists, and how these factors affect the likelihood of serious reform. The authors argue that in traditional models, special education begins where general education ends and that the two are not well integrated.

Similarly, traditional teacher education in special and general education may be viewed as complementary, but not integrated.

The authors describe forces that have exerted influence on teacher education, including changing conceptions of teaching and learning to teach, general and special education reform, and marketplace and demographic changes. On the basis of their analysis, the authors argue for a union of programs that prepare classroom teachers, teachers of students with disabilities, and specialists who work with students in such areas as sensory impairments, severe disabilities, and severe emotional disturbances.

The focus of chapter nine is on the implications of the current educational reform for research in teacher education and methodological and ethical issues pertinent to educational research. Noting the fundamental paradigm issue that is currently dividing educational researchers and shaping the debate on epistemology the authors support a multi-paradigmatic perspective. They indicate the value of both the paradigm rooted in the natural sciences and the paradigm rooted in the humanities to educational research. The authors use the framework for research on teacher education developed by Yarger and Smith (1990).

The authors examine philosophical and technical issues in conducting the "right" study, conducting the study well, and interpreting and communicating the results. The final section addresses ethical issues in research. Each of the issues is illustrated with studies in teacher education.

The focus of chapter ten is the integration of parallel reform in special and general education. An examination of political, professional, and policy issues associated with the two reforms provides a foundation for understanding national research, policy and programmatic initiatives aimed at their integration. Within a historical context, reform traditions are highlighted with emphasis on what we have learned and how the traditions have influenced research on teaching and teacher training. The authors suggest that we move beyond concern about the effectiveness of instructional programs and environments to a deeper analysis of culture, etiology, and epistemological issues. They conclude by arguing that the time is ripe for a debate about education and that there are new ideas and a new sense of power in deciding how and what we teach.

Chapter eleven by Rhodes, Danforth, and Smith, focuses on the paradigmatic and political challenges to policy makers in inventing the future of a restructured inclusive educational system. The authors discuss differences between modern and postmodern thought and implications for school reform. Three directions of postmodern thought are presented: 1) hermeneutic or interpretive; 2) critical-political and deconstructive; and 3) scientific revolution. Each leads to a different path in constructing the future of education. The focus of the chapter is on a different vision for the future of education. The authors discuss the implications of new pedagogies that would reorder the priority of education which has focused primarily on content knowledge and secondarily on human development and learning. They describe liberation and hermeneutic pedagogies and their implications for a new inclusive educational philosophy.

This chapter concludes Part One on the national context of reform in general and special education. The context described reflects both modern and postmodern views which accurately characterizes the current intellectual and political culture of school reform. The chapters that follow in Part Two describe experiments in reform aimed at impacting university and public school programs addressing Goals 2000.

1

RETHINKING THE MISSION AND METHODS
Philosophies for Educating Children and the Teachers Who Teach Them

JAMES PAUL, ARTHUR YANG,
MARIA ADIEGBOLA, & WILLIAM MORSE

THE STAGE

EDUCATION is not alone: All segments of our society are struggling with massive changes. Many of those segments, such as private industry, can move on their own to formulate new philosophies and procedures. Education is more complex and has accountability to many and diverse stakeholders.

Education is being rethought and reformed. What is not clear is the depth and extent of the changes being sought. The lack of clarity about the nature of the reform is not so much a question of strategies for changing the existing education establishment as it is the challenge of reaching useful understandings of how future educational systems will meet the needs of our social and economic system in the information age. A major policy question and pedagogical challenge for general and special educators is how the interests of *all* children will be included in those understandings.

The need for changing public schools in basic ways has been a recurrent theme in the modern history of education (Sarason, 1983, 1990). Important changes have occurred in curriculum, assessment practices, teacher education, teaching methods, delivery systems for alternative and compensatory programs, and other parts of the educational system. These changes, however, have been made within the general operational patterns and structures of public schools as we have known them, not in the patterns and structures themselves (Bacharach, 1990).

NOTHING SACRED IN THE CURRENT DEBATES CONCERNING EDUCATION

The unsettled concerns about education in the current debates reach deeper into the nature of the enterprise than was characteristic of the undulations of change in past reform movements. This is not, "Shall we have middle schools or junior high schools?" It is open season on the very nature and purpose of public education, even to experiments in privatizing public education.

An overarching issue in restructuring the public school system is reaching some agreement on the purpose of education. School reform turns on the assumptions we make about the kind of education that will be required to match the demands and reflect the sciences, technologies, and values of the twenty-first century. The "openness" of general education to *all* children is predicated, in large part, upon what is understood to be the purpose of education. Until there are shared understandings of what education is supposed to accomplish, we cannot address how it is to occur. We will reach meaningful understandings of the outcomes of education and develop appropriate implementation policies when, and only when, we have reached a workable consensus on the purpose of education in schools of the future.

The purpose of education has been viewed in different ways. Young Pai (1990), discussing the importance of the cultural foundations of education, notes that some view it as "a process by which individuals become the best they can become on the basis of their ability and personally envisioned possibilities" (p. 3). Others view it as "the development of the intellect through which learners acquire essential cognitive and social skills and perennial knowledge (truths)" (p. 3). Still others, he notes, see education as "a process, fundamentally similar to that of industrial production, in which certain human behaviors are shaped and maintained so that they may become useful to the individual and others at some future time" (p. 3). Pestalozzi viewed the purpose of education to be preparation for life. Sarason espouses the view that schools should "produce responsible, self-sufficient citizens who possess the self esteem, initiative, skills, and wisdom to continue individual growth . . . (and) . . . pursue knowledge" (1990, p.163). Schlechty and Cole (1991), discussing the nature of education in a knowledge-based society, argued that education is knowledge work and that teachers are knowledge workers.

These and other views of education exist in the minds of policy makers, parents, and educators, and are embedded in current policies. Visions of the schools of tomorrow reflect these different perspectives. Each of these understandings of the purpose of education represents an ideological perspective and has implications for how we proceed with the reform of public education.

The central focus of schooling, whatever the particular ideological orientation, Pai argues, is to "transmit and perpetuate its notion of the good life" (p. 4). Cultural norms are reflected in the social organization and structure of schools. If the society is egalitarian, then relationships within the school (teacher-student, able student–disabled student) are likely to be viewed more as equals, whereas a hierarchy is more likely to exist in the school when hierarchy exists in the social order outside of school.

Pai further argues that, in addition to reflecting the society, schools must meet societal and cultural needs. In our culturally diverse society, for example, schools must address issues of dominant and minority cultures. "In sum, no part of the educative process, neither its contents nor products, is free from cultural influence. Educators need to realize that the processes of teaching and learning are influenced by the core values, beliefs, and attitudes as well as the predominant cognitive and communication styles and linguistic patterns of a culture" (p. 4). Bringing such matters from a covert to overt state is frequently disconcerting to professionals.

During the past 10 years, there have been hundreds of studies of public education, each with its own program of reform. Articulate visionaries, in the true spirit of a social movement, are crafting images of what is wrong with the public education system and scenarios for possible alternative futures. Many dysfunctional features of the public education system have been described in a plethora of publications. Top-down administration, truculent educational bureaucracies, exclusionary policies, outdated curriculum philosophies, and process accountability are among the frustrations experienced by most educators, and they are the major foci of school reform.

The goals of policy and structural reform—including site-based management, decision making that minimizes rules and bureaucracy, inclusive educational philosophy, and outcome accountability—have a strong "ring" of relevance to many educators, parents, and political leaders. Even here the challenge is how to translate these concepts of reform into reality.

It is important to make a distinction between *reform* (improving the schools of today) and *transformation* (inventing a different kind of educational system for tomorrow). So much is dependent on the choice that we pause to explicate this issue.

REFORM

Once one leaves the broad generality of goals, such as those stated in Goals 2000, specific differences in values and operations begin to have an impact. A major point of contention is the equity versus excellence debate. As reforms raise the demand for excellence (standards), special education cries foul and stresses equity. The difficulty with many of the debates on reform is that they seek to accommodate incompatible goals and values. We will need to include new strategies to resolve differences since choices are made on the basis of divergent value priorities.

Much reform rests upon the redistribution of power. In fact, Sarason (1990) holds that the real reason the many proposals for change in the present reform will fail is because they do not confront the need to redistribute the power in the system. He notes that the reason P.L. 94-142 made such a significant impact was that it empowered parents. It is possible to change curriculum and standards and avoid any significant reform because it does not change the power base. Sarason argues that pupils as well as teachers must be empowered to accomplish reform.

First generalized as open-ended empowering of all stakeholders (usually not including children to any great extent), the democratizing of power increases diversity and produces trauma in the original holders of power. Reform not based on profound and deep fundamental evolution of new premises for action will produce such seesaw actions, giving and taking back of power. This is illustrated in the following example of power exchange and veto.

A district school board in Florida refused to approve a school improvement plan developed by the advisory council of a local school. The plan was developed in accord with the state's school improvement plan which places program planning responsibility with the local school. The plan in this case, however, called for adding a sex education program and for developing a prekindergarten program. The board, with three fifths of its members taking a conservative stand on the role of the family and the possible interference of the school's proposed new programs with family rights, refused to support the plan. It went to court, and the legal authority of the board prevailed in an out-of-court settlement.

The legal implications of policies intended to reform public schools can be very complex institutionally. That complexity is amplified when it is viewed in the context of the moral, cultural, and religious interests that form the social platform upon which public policies for educating and rearing children are built. Power boundary changes, therefore, must be carefully and clearly considered in advance.

In special education, the final arbiter of "what is the right thing to do" rests with courts and the buildup of case law. Parent power was increased, school power decreased: Parents can now sue via IDEA or 504 and the outcome is resolved by the court's evaluation of Free Appropriate Public Education (FAPE). Court support of inclusion reflects a change from academic to social values. In general, court decisions are favoring regular classroom placement. The child does not have to be able to master the curriculum to be "included," and superior academic benefits of a segregated placement will not justify exclusion (*The Special Educator*, 1993, vol. 9, issue 7). The value of the acculturating influence of normal peers is seen as a potent factor. The critical issue is whether or not FAPE can be met in the regular classroom with supplementary services and cost considered not relevant.

Teachers and school leaders are having difficulty translating reforms into reality. Some focus on the *practicality* of the changes being sought; how do you make both systemic and workable changes in the way we conduct the business of educating children? How do you give teachers the power to make decisions, in consultation with parents, about what and how to teach children in their classroom? Professional programs to educate and train teachers and school leaders do not prepare them for this responsibility.

Special education has an interface with the various elements of general educational reform, but with a focus on equity. Many special educators, parents, and policy makers, focusing more on the issue of equity than on excellence, have viewed the right of children to be educated with their age peers as the central issue in reforming special education. In fact, Heumann has called segregated special education immoral, reflecting the strength of the commitment to inclusion as defined in IDEA (*The Special Educator*, 1993, Vol. 9, issue 6, p. 86). From this point of view, the moral perspectives and educational philosophies of teachers and school leaders as well as their sophistication in curriculum and pedagogical science are intimately implicated in the reform. The technical, professional, ideological, and ethical foundations are being challenged.

We are moving away from familiar ideas and educational practices in schools toward different approaches to understanding and supporting public education. Some see this as a deep transition, incorporating major corrections in the system of public education as we have known it. Others see it as a transformation requiring fundamental systemic changes that necessitate a different system.

At still another level state school reform has incorporated financial equity for student support. The changes in support for all children has frequently been prodded by the courts to equalize resources available in various districts. In like manner, the courts have ruled that crying poor is no escape from FAPE by a school district.

Whether changes now underway constitute a serious reform of schools or adjustments in obviously flawed components remains to be seen. Popkewitz (1991) points out the value of distinguishing between change and reform. He sees changes as possibly superficial quantitative differences (e.g., we add computers, teacher satisfaction goes up). Reform implies bringing the institution back in line with traditional norms and goals. What we are calling transformation, Popkewitz sees as more profound—new forms created to "respond to our hopes, desires and aspirations" (pg. 82).

Soltis (in Bacharach, 1990) offered an interesting and instructive distinction between reform and reformation. Reform, he suggested, is the change to which we are accustomed in education, even when serious and far-reaching policy redirections are involved. Unknown in the history of the modern school, however, is a reformation which involves a change of the perspective or mind-set of educators. Soltis illustrates this with the Protestant Reformation in the sixteenth century when Martin Luther led the break from the Catholic tradition of the Papacy. The idea that God was available to individuals without intercession was a radical change in belief about spiritual reality and self. A reformation in schools would involve a similarly transforming change in perspective about the role of teachers. The idea that the teacher can really decide what, how, and even whom to teach would change the nature of the educational system.

TRANSFORMING EDUCATION

Even when the same element of change is proposed by reform and transformation, the significance differs because the rationale differs. Inclusion is a case in point. Education advocated in most school restructuring plans focuses on the pupil's civil right to be educated in company with peers. In those schools aiming at transformation, inclusion is part and parcel not only of civil rights, but of different concepts regarding the purpose of education, the way children learn, the celebration of diversity, and an expanded notion of human potential. This implies deeper and more profound changes in the whole system rather than in selected components. As noted in chapters one and two, since 1983 with the publication of *A Nation at Risk* by the National Commission on Excellence in Education, there has been an increased sensitivity to the complexity and *systemic* nature of the issues that would-be reformers must face. Moral and philosophical, rather than managerial and technical, issues now characterize much of the discourse on reform aimed at transformation.

Both the mission of schooling and the methods utilized are being examined with an inclination toward rethinking the nature of education. Is the purpose of schools to *transmit the culture?* If so, which culture? Is it *preparation for life?* If so, what is the nature of the world for which children are being prepared? Is it *knowledge work?* If so, which epistemological perspective will or should prevail? These and other fundamental questions form the core of reform which resonates the cultural discontinuities in our society, the revolution in the social sciences (see chapter twenty-two), conflicting self-interests (see chapter six), and the troubled economic system upon which the reform depends and which the reform is ostensibly designed to save.

The flame of transformation is fanned by the rhetoric of change and a growing awareness of the inconsistencies within an "old system" seeking to embrace and embody "new system" ideology and practices. Transformation is like theater in the round. Often the boundaries between the players and the audience blur. Audience participation in an engaging story creates a surreal, dynamic, and suspended reality for the players and the audience. In transformation, there is a certain chaos which drives many back to more limited reforms.

Most of the stage of reform is occupied by political luminaries. The performances and contributions of educational philosophers have been disappointing. Few of the contemporary crafters of visions and missions for schools of the future have come from the ranks of philosophy. Fewer still have contributed to the translation of missions into plans for constructing educational systems to meet the needs of children in the next century. Fortunately, however, leaders are emerging from a wide variety of disciplines, including educational sociology and educational anthropology, to help create credible storylines for the reform. New scripts are being written without the benefit of a common vocabulary and without the rules that guided "playwrights" who wrote the social and cultural texts for schooling in the past.

While there is general agreement that the changes in schooling wrought by the reform in general and special education during the past decade are significant and will continue to change the way the business of education is conducted in public schools, the nature and depth of the reform is not yet clear. The sonar soundings of some reformers find no familiar foundation upon which to erect schools of the future. They argue that the paradigm of education must change to incorporate new constructive understandings of knowledge and learning (Heshusius, 1988, 1989, 1992; Poplin, 1988b; Rhodes, 1990, 1992). The philosophical task of construction in education is coextensive with the political task of inventing new kinds of schools. The process-product–oriented post-positive knowledge tradition of educational research and the collaborative strategies applied in educational practice to integrating the different political and moral interests of a diverse student population, while admittedly flawed, provide bases for the continued improvement of schools. The focus, they argue, should be on the practical process of improving (reforming) schools of today, rather than a more abstract and hypothetical process of inventing (transforming) schools for tomorrow.

PARADIGMATIC SUPPORT STRUCTURE FOR TRANSFORMING EDUCATION

Underlying the complex effort to transform schooling are many emerging social and intellectual understandings and value orientations. Various stakeholders are at different points in adopting new paradigms as bases for action. We review some of these new ways of perceiving behavior within the context of education.

- The epistemological distinction between knowledge as *discovered* and knowledge as *constructed* is of fundamental significance to theories of teaching and learning. Knowledge, understood as our awareness of objective reality discovered through the systematic and disciplined application of scientific methods of inquiry, provides an epistemological foundation for studying teaching that is very different from a view of knowledge as socially constructed and, thus, created in context and in relationship with the known.

  Traditional psychological theories were predicated upon an epistemology of knowledge as objective, external, and discovered. This view drives theories of measurement and assessment. An epistemology of knowledge as constructed, on the other hand, focuses on a different understanding of human learning. More attention in the constructivist perspective is given to the teacher as a theorizer, meaning maker and, thus, a researcher who makes those theories and meanings explicit (Stone, 1992). The teacher is viewed as a facilitator of constructive learning or a co-constructor of knowledge. This is in contrast to a view of teaching as designing and managing student learning of objective knowledge.

- Alternative paradigms of knowledge now make problematic the traditional and prevailing philosophies of education and the perceived role of school in society. One of the major issues is the appropriateness of applying the epistemology of the natural sciences to the study of human behavior. Advocating a "philosophical anthropology," Taylor (1985) argues:

  against the understanding of human life and action implicit in an influential family of theories in the sciences of man. The common feature of this family is the ambition to model the study of man on the natural sciences. Theories of this kind seem to me to be terribly implausible. They lead to very bad science: either they end up in wordy elaboration of the obvious, or they fail altogether to address the interesting questions, or their practitioners end up squandering their talents and ingenuity in the attempt to show that they can after all recapture the insights of ordinary life in their manifestly reductive explanatory languages. (p. 1)

- Since the 1920s there has been the strong influence of behaviorism in the science of education. The experimental methods of psychology and the perspective of behaviorism led to a knowledge base on learning, correlates of learning, operant procedures for modifying behavior, behavioral therapies based on principles of respondent conditioning, instructional methods such as precision teaching, and so forth. The science of teaching and learning, the process-product knowledge base for practice, has developed robust methods in the past 20 years. The grounding assumptions of these behavioral perspectives have been challenged by the growth of cognitive science and by the emergence of postmodern philosophy.

- One of the fundamental limitations of empirical "scientific" discourse is its inability to deal with any significant problem of values, meanings, and the like. The separation of the objective from the emotive, or the collective from the individual leads to the stance that values are merely psychological and that value conflicts cannot be adjudicated by rational criticism or modified by rational persuasion (Benne, 1990, p. 181). The dichotomy between fact and value greatly oversimplifies the issue of morality for the social scientist. This problem is illustrated by Means (1969) in the case of sociological studies of deviant behavior:

    The deviant behavior approach has to assume the validity of traditional morality, any variation from which is automatically called a problem of "deviant behavior." The study of ends, goals, and the values of society is decidedly secondary. For the . . . behaviorist, there is no objective theory of social values by which he may judge values and goals per se. (p. 53)

- The flawed assumption of modernism that knowledge was objective, value-free, and universal in nature has contributed to the confusion about the relationship between knowledge and culture. This quantitative research paradigm that formulated present education practice is no longer accepted by postmodern science, where results are seen as "through the eyes of the researcher."

    Until recently there was little challenge to the research base. The philosophical positions and normative assumptions of researchers are rarely made explicit in their work, and the processes of knowledge construction, authorization, and institutionalization are usually hidden from the culture consumers. The three foundations of "modernity"—certainty, formal rationality, and the desire to start with a clean slate (or the claim of detachment from any historical and cultural context), have shaped intellectual and social patterns that had the virtue of being stable and predictable in earlier times but turned out to be unadaptable, sclerotic, and unable to meet the fresh demands of novel situations (Toulmin, 1990, pp. 183–184). Dysfunctional bureaucracies are examples (Skrtic, 1991a). As the assumptions of science have changed (Rhodes, 1990), and the work of researchers has begun to reflect those changes (Heshusius, 1988, 1989; Skrtic, 1991a), the implications for the reform of educational practice are becoming clear.

    Postmodern philosophers, feminist theorists, and others argue that science is not value-free or value-neutral but contains human interests and normative assumptions which should be identified and examined. People of color, such as African Americans and Native Americans, have been frequently victimized by negative depiction in the mainstream social sciences (Ladner, 1973). Diversity has been viewed as deviance and differences as deficits. Women still have to struggle to gain equal status in all walks of life. Postmodern perspectives have brought the need for an ethic of care into focus as a basic need in school reform.

- There are different views of child development and human capacities. A specific example in special education is the redefinition of the concept of mental retardation by AAMR, which is *not* a shuffling of words but a change of context. The cognitive revolution (Gardner, 1985) in the 1980s helped focus on the reality of different human capacities. Cognitive science drew heavily on the humanities as well as the social, behavioral, and neurosciences. It led to a renewed emphasis on inner psychological states, lost to the positivism of behavioral psychology. It helped focus attention on, and has developed a knowledge base about, different forms of intelligence (Gardner, 1983), critical thinking skills (Halpern, 1988), and reflection (Schön, 1989). This knowledge base is growing in mass and in complexity as we think our way through the implications of shifting our basic epistemological stance in the social and behavioral sciences and applying different kinds of knowledge to the science and/or art of education.

• The agency of teaching is moving from a compending of isolated competencies to a holistic view of teaching as interactions of the life stories of teachers (values, views of diversity, personal histories of being cared about and taught), and the perceived expectations of their office (curriculum, methods for teaching and behavior control, classroom culture, performance requirements, and so forth). These are fundamentally paradigmatic issues which challenge the values and the grounding assumptions of educational practice.

IMPACT OF THESE ISSUES ON REFORM AND IMPLICATIONS FOR SPECIAL EDUCATION

The paradigmatic issues have significant implications for how school change is understood and managed. For example, the specification of educational outcomes as something other than measurable performance objectives is problematic for those who require valid and reliable measures of achievement. There is a major philosophical struggle between those who see the need for a holistic approach to educational accountability and those who believe measures of the performance and achievement of students in academic subjects must continue to be the bottom line of educational accountability. Another example is in the organizational philosophy applied to the management of public schools. A constructivist perspective would emphasize site-based management, believing that a top-down system of standards and curriculum imposed and managed by state, and even district, bureaucracies precludes a constructivist educational philosophy. Fixed standards and accompanying measures tend to regiment the system and make it static and bureaucratic. To date, the practical business of managing schools and the problem of leaving to a community the right to develop policies that run counter to more commonly held values has made the implementation of site-based management problematic.

Changes in paradigms in the culture at large have implications for education, as has been illustrated above. These same changes may influence special education directly or indirectly through modifications in regular education that infringe on students with handicaps. Regular and special education are inextricably bound together. For example, when regular education raises standards in requirements for graduation (excellence), the fates of many students with disabilities are put at risk (equity). In reverse, with inclusion, special education cannot use exclusion (regardless of its merits and demerits) as a disciplinary process. This can have an impact on the mainstream.

Several basic issues have impacted the development of special education practices and the ideologies that now form the complex corpus of "the field." Some of those issues are discussed in the next section.

SALIENT ISSUES IN THE EVOLUTION OF CURRENT SPECIAL EDUCATION PHILOSOPHY

In the 1960s special education grew as a field, in part, as a function of the human rights movement. There were strong advocacy voices in the courtrooms and in the Congress speaking on behalf of children with disabilities. Legal theories and moral arguments were used to obtain a guarantee of the right to a free and appropriate education for all children. "The right thing to do" became law. With 94-142, FAPE as written in the federal regulations, and as interpreted by case law, became the central force overriding matters of available resources.

The right of all children to a free appropriate education, when translated in practical terms for children with disabilities, meant the right to special education services. When P.L. 94-142 was passed in 1975, special educators were doing what they did best—employing the principles of applied behavior analysis. The science of behavior, rooted in the epistemology of logical empiricism and in behavioral psychology which had gained support in this country in the 1920s and 1930s, had been developed to a sophisticated level of application. The philosophy of measurement had been refined to correct for some of the basic flaws that characterized the early measurement of intelligence, and there was a growing awareness of the need to address some of the ethical issues raised in the study and management of behavior.

Two closely related factors were beginning in the 1970s to challenge the hegemony of applied behavior analysis that had developed in special education practice. One was the emergence of other paradigms of knowledge which challenged the fundamental assumptions of behaviorism. The other was the emergence of interest in other theories of human functioning, especially those focusing on social and cognitive development. Since the mid-1970s, there has been a dynamic dialogue between and among those applying theories of child development and those applying theories of behavior and learning to education. In some instances, new theories have been developed that seek to integrate different perspectives.

Two important philosophical issues provided a focus for much of the educational discourse for the past decade: 1) the nature of science and its relationship to values and ethical decision making in education; and 2) the nature and purpose of education. In the mid-1980s, the debate about "appropriate education" turned away from a primary concern with developing the most promising theory of behavior to concern with reforming the educational system.

The discourse on science and values addresses the fundamental epistemological arguments about knowledge and inquiry. While antipositivist arguments resulted in a more explicit relativism in science, alternative paradigms questioned the basic ontological as well as epistemological and methodological assumptions of knowledge. Critical theory and constructivism especially offered *alternatives*, not just modifications of the post-positive worldview. These bear upon the differences between reform and transforming education and special education.

Increasingly, many researchers in special education are thinking "outside the familiar box" of post-positivism. They are finding themselves in company with other researchers in education, anthropology, sociology, and philosophy who are pursuing different genres of inquiry. While qualitative research had gained some limited acceptance in special education by the mid-1980s, the broader epistemological framework of interpretive inquiry, especially the narrative genre, represents a more radical departure from the well-established research orientations in special education. Qualitative methods such as ethnography, borrowed from anthropology, came to be valued in a quantitative context as a useful way to collect data to "inform" hypotheses or to help interpret experimental findings.

Interpretive research is based on a different view of knowledge. Interpretive researchers in psychology, education, and special education now are incorporating the epistemological perspectives and methods of the humanities, as well as other social sciences. Some are using critical perspectives that focus on the implicit values in decisions about what to study, how to study it, and the value-mediated interpretations of findings. This is becoming a powerful tool for researchers in special education, which is a socially constructed field rooted in value premises, ranging from the nature of our practices to the justification of our existence. Constructive methods, such as hermeneutics, and deconstructive methods are opening new understandings of the nature and cultural functions of our work. Skrtic's deconstruction of special education (1991a) is an excellent example. Informed by the work of Dewey, Rorty, Derrida, and Foucault, among others, Skrtic develops the argument that special education emerged in the twentieth century as an institutional practice to address the conflict between the democratic ends and bureaucratic means of public education. This position is in contrast to the view that special education grew as a rational and moral response to the problems of students with disabilities.

Several special educators are opening up the conversation among their colleagues and others about the paradigmatic bias underpinning our understanding of special education and the work of special educators (Poplin, 1988a, 1988b; Heshusius, 1988, 1989, 1992; Rhodes, 1990, 1992; Skrtic, 1991a). The current dialogue is leading to different understandings of the nature and mission of special education practices.

Challenges to the traditional epistemology of science applied to the study of human behavior is accompanied by challenges to the moral stance reflected in educational policies and practices. An example of this is the familiar debate on the relative importance of equity and excellence in education. Establishing a priority of one over the other in educational policy is a moral rather than an epistemological position. Such a position communicates what is believed to be most important and the interest most valued.

The social and neurosciences have created the conceptual and empirical foundations for our current understandings of the nature of intelligence and learning. Powerful technical programs for teaching and interventions to change behavior have been developed. As we anticipate changes in special education, such new knowledge is not sufficient to guide those changes. The directing force lies within the values we espouse. Unfortunately, a comparable moral foundation for policy making and educational practice has not been developed. Philosophical tools such as ethical reasoning have had limited applications. Given the diversity in these matters, resolution of ethical differences is often necessary for coherent change. One could argue, conversely, that the philosophical base, including the moral foundation, exists but it has not been applied systematically to decision making in education. Advances and applications in behavioral and pedagogical science have not been balanced by advances and applications in social philosophy and ethics.

However, there is now more attention being given to critical theory, focusing attention on the values guiding the selection of research questions, methods of investigation and analysis, and the values embedded in interpretations of data. There are several important critiques of child development, learning, and educational pedagogy. One of the most extensive and significant critiques has come from feminist theory. The feminist critique has articulated a vision of moral development and education predicated on an ethic of care (Gilligan, 1982, Noddings, 1988, 1991) in contrast to the traditional ethic of justice (Kohlberg, 1969) which is predicated on a more rational, objective, linear view of knowledge.

Closely related to the changing epistemological perspectives of general and special educators is an increasing interest in ethics. A great deal of the literature in special education carries a moral voice about what we "ought" or "ought not to" be doing. While there have been occasional articles addressing the ethical issues in different practices and/or policies, there has been very little attention to the systematic study and application of ethics. This is especially important when we recognize that the end of the twentieth century is bringing together moral injunctions—commitments we have made to care for all of our citizens—with serious economic problems that force our attention to limitations on our resources. With endless demands, we select even what resources shall be replenished and which diminished by give and take in the seats of power where practicality dominates principles. On what basis will we make policy decisions in the future when neither our data nor the traditional logic of Western science will suffice?

Special education policies embed some of the most complex ethical issues in caregiving and in the education of children. P.L. 99-457 illustrates this well. Decisions about who would be served and, therefore, who would not be served, were made in defining the population. This included deciding whether to commit resources to the most needy, that is the most disabled and the most expensive to treat and care for, or to those who could make the most use of the resources in returning material value to the society, that is the least disabled and those at risk for disabilities. And who should make these excruciating decisions? In the implementation of policies do professionals have the right to make decisions when their judgments are at odds with the views and wishes of the family? How are the family's rights, including their rights to privacy and to religious convictions, balanced with the rights of their infant with degenerative neuromuscular disorders, for example? These and other ethical issues in the implementation policies for P.L. 99-457 and a framework for ethical reasoning are discussed by Paul and others (1992).

School policies and practices reflect ethical stances. Typically, however, those stances have not been made explicit, and the competing ethical stances have not been considered. Kauffman (1992) has discussed the lack of an ethical foundation for our decisions about inclusion, for example. Howe and Miramontes (1992) have developed a systematic, case-based work on ethics applied to the broad clinical, pedagogical, and policy issues in special education. They present an excellent deliberative framework for ethical decision making.

While culture and education are inextricably connected, the study of this relationship has not always been a focus for educators. The psychological dimensions of education have traditionally received greater emphasis in education and teacher education. Spindler, an educational anthropologist, observed:

> Educational psychology has clearly dominated the scene, partly because of a historical accident that institutionally wedded psychology and education rather early in America and partly because the need for tests and measurements and applied principles of learning have been particularly obvious in the educational milieu of American schools and have been appropriate for psychological applications. (p. 101; quoted in Pai, p. 5)

The history of special education illustrates this emphasis. Psychology played a major role in formulating views of human capacity, individual and group differences, and the philosophy of measurement that were used in schools in addressing the needs of the immigrant populations in the late 1800s and early 1900s. The abuses that occurred in intellectual measurement are well documented (Smith, 1985). According to the commonly held construction, special education, grounded in psychological principles, grew as a field to provide education and care for children who could not benefit from the general education curriculum. Behavioral and intellectual variables were defined and measured in the context of the prevailing philosophy of knowledge and behavioral science.

In recent years there has been much more emphasis on contextualizing the study of education. In his political sociology of educational reform, Popkewitz (1991) observes that "psychology is no longer a central domain, nor is individualism a central ideology"(p. 24). His analysis focuses on the sociology of knowledge, the discontinuities of power relations in institutional practice and knowledge. One of the major challenges for school reformers is to incorporate phenomenological and critical perspectives in understanding the nature of learning and the role of education in the twenty-first century.

HOW THESE MATTERS PLAY OUT IN THE TRANSFORMATION OF SPECIAL EDUCATION

It is difficult to develop meaningful policies when there is not basic agreement on the nature and purpose of education. This is clearly illustrated by the policy conundrum in special education related to the placement of children with disabilities. Since the 1970s in special education, there has been a commitment to mainstreaming, which has been understood and labeled in different ways, including least restrictive environment, regular education initiative, and, most recently, inclusion. The disagreement centers on whether the now-popular slogan "all means all" means that all children are placed in regular classrooms, or whether a continuum or cascade of services is to be in place to meet the different needs of children at different times.

The "best interests" of the child is the goal and the claim of both positions. Both psychological and moral arguments are employed in building a case for or against full inclusion. However, neither our theories of behavior nor our beliefs about what is morally right to do constitutes a sufficient case. More broadly, the nature of education and of our work as educators in current sociocultural context must also ground our policy decisions.

The lack of consensus on the nature of education, knowledge, and learning currently reflected in the broader discourse on education and psychology in the social sciences and the humanities makes special education policy choices extraordinarily difficult and different from those we have made in the past. The professional and political challenge is to reach an understanding of the educational interests of special children that does justice both to our understanding of children's development and learning and to an understanding of the nature and role of education in the twenty-first century.

The current mission discussions in special education illustrate the more general discourse on the nature and role of education. While few arguments about goals have a singular focus, some argue that we must help individuals become the best they can become, considering social as well as academic goals (TASH). Others focus more on the skills and behaviors that must be taught in settings most supportive of learning that will provide an increasingly strong foundation for later success in life (LDA).

The differences on this issue can be further illustrated by the policy statements of professional groups. The Association for Persons with Severe Handicaps (TASH), for example, has taken the position that "quality services and quality of life could only be considered mutually in environments that are integrated with the community" (Snell, 1988). The TASH deinstitutionalization policy and resolution on the redefinition of the continuum of services (1986) takes the position that students with severe disabilities should have the right to attend the same school he or she would attend if s/he did not have a disability and to receive at that school the individualized educational services which are appropriate for his or her needs without compromise to the development of interactions with peers (whether or not those peers themselves have a disability) throughout the school years . . .

. . . the right to daily interactions with peers and other citizens (without regard to disability) that are oriented toward developing a variety of relationships, social support networks, friendships, and the ultimate goal of a normalized social status for individuals with disabilities. *[this requires]* The systematic shifting of service delivery design and services away from a categorical, homogeneously grouped, and separate model to one which requires integration and thrives on a variety of grouping arrangements (quoted in Snell, 1988). This is the policy of full inclusion.

The TASH position is remarkably different from that of the Learning Disabilities Association of America (LDA), which has taken the position that it

does not support 'full inclusion' or any policies that mandate the same placement, instruction, or treatment for *ALL* students with learning disabilities. Many students with learning disabilities benefit from being served in the regular education classroom. However, the regular education classroom is not the appropriate placement for a number of students with learning disabilities who may need alternative instructional environments, teaching strategies, and/or materials that cannot or will not be provided within the context of a regular classroom placement.

LDA believes that decisions regarding educational placement of students with disabilities must be based on the needs of each individual student rather than administrative convenience or budgetary considerations and must be the results of a cooperative effort involving the educators, parents, and the student when appropriate.

LDA believes that the placement of *ALL* children with disabilities in the regular education classroom is as great a violation of IDEA as is the placement of *ALL* children in separate classrooms on the basis of their type of disability.

The Council for Exceptional Children (CEC), in an attempt to structure a policy position that would satisfy the interests of such discrepant views and values, took the position that

a continuum of services must be available for all children, youth, and young adults. CEC also believes that the concept of inclusion is a meaningful goal to be pursued in our schools and communities. In addition, CEC believes children, youth, and young adults with disabilities should be served whenever possible in general education classrooms in inclusive neighborhood schools and community settings.

A major difficulty with our reading of these policy statements is that they proceed from different views of the purpose and process of education and different understandings of the interests of children with disabilities. In the absence of a workable philosophy of education, including both the goals and the principles to be employed in reconciling differences in perspectives about competing interests, there is no basis for a coherent discourse. This situation creates the rather vague statement by CEC which attempts to integrate the policy positions of TASH, LDA, and others that are based on such deeply discrepant premises. In the absence of agreement about the premises of the arguments which concern the purpose of education and the interests of children with disabilities, there is no basis for a coherent discourse about public policy.

TOWARD THE CONSTRUCTION OF A PHILOSOPHY OF INCLUSIVE EDUCATION

Special education has been guided and supported largely by a social philosophy and a particular moral stance in the education of children with disabilities. In our society, all children have a right to a free appropriate education (FAPE). The knowledge base for providing that education, however uneven in its quality and depth, has grown. Neither the publicly sponsored philosophy nor the science of practice required serious critical analysis until the moral vision of education and caregiving that guided public policy and the philosophy of science that supported the implementation of policy were seriously challenged. During the past decade, changes have occurred in the foundations of both the vision of care and the epistemology and value premises of science. These changes have opened new opportunities to think about the nature of education and, in particular, the education of children with disabilities. They have also called attention to the assumptions about professional practice and the research and values that guide it. This has created a context in which the development of a philosophy of special education that incorporates changing ideologies and paradigmatic perspectives is necessary.

A philosophy of special education that will work in the interest of *all* children in schools of the future must position educators to include the wide diversity of students in the basic instructional program of the school. It must also position policy makers to address the competing interests of students in the allocation of resources for instruction. What our schools should be held accountable for accomplishing, that is, what all students should expect from them, must be reasoned ethically with principles and values that most accurately reflect the kind of society we believe ourselves to be and the kind of educational system we most want to support. Our ability to develop such a philosophy depends on the understandings we reach about the matters discussed above.

As we work to resolve differences and find a workable consensus or create a more open dialogue among those with differences that cannot be resolved, the following are what we believe to be necessary features of a new philosophy of special education.

1. A new philosophy of special education should create a context for a coherent discourse on general education and special education within which to incorporate both moral and empirical arguments. Policy debates in the literature, such as those focusing on the regular education initiative, involve both empirical and moral arguments, neither of which is definitive.

2. A new philosophy of special education should develop a vocabulary with shared meanings that is sensitive to the depth of differences between paradigmatic orientations. Only then can a discourse be coherent and lead to common understandings of the goals, values, moral perspectives, and knowledge base for a philosophy of special education.

3. A new philosophy of special education should connect the personal and professional aspects of teaching and caregiving both in the content (culturally embedded accounts) and in the methods (reflective practice) of special education.

4. A new philosophy of special education should reconnect theory and practice through a reflective integration of knowledge, ethical reasoning, and personal experience. The ability to reason ethically is essential to balance technical, procedural and logical thinking.

5. A new philosophy of special education should incorporate a broader interest in the knowledge and methods of the humanities. A philosophy is needed that leads professionals beyond the clinical accounts of children to broader cultural and spiritual understandings. This requires a deeper appreciation for the nature of knowledge, ethics, narrative, and ethnic and cultural traditions.

6. A new philosophy of special education should address the political, social, and moral agency of special educators. Special education is neither apolitical nor amoral. The agency of special educators must, therefore, be a major concern in developing a philosophy of special education practice.

7. A new philosophy of special education should incorporate a critical perspective on traditional hegemonies, such as behavioral philosophy, and professional practices, such as an exclusive focus on the geography or physical circumstances of a child's education. The issue is not simply whether a view is valid but the social meaning of its uncritical application in specific lived contexts. Neither arguments about "good science" nor defense of traditional practice alone will suffice in the current environment which requires a critical stance on the ethics and politics of educational interventions.

8. A new philosophy of special education should incorporate a shift from a preoccupation with individuals to a broader focus on community. A central issue in an inclusion philosophy is the relationship of children with disabilities to the larger school community. The community itself must become a basic unit of reflective analysis on the nature of schooling.

9. A new philosophy of special education should acknowledge and open possibilities for transcending the limitations of Western science. A wider and deeper discourse on treatment and healing is needed. The classic ethnographies of Katz on the !Kung (1982) and the Fiji Islanders (1993), the current efforts to generate a discourse linking American and Buddhist psychologies

(Goleman & Thurman, 1991), and the work in different disciplines on the new scientific paradigm (Sperry, 1993) reflected in the last chapter of this section are examples.

10. A new philosophy of special education should facilitate ownership of the legitimate issues in inclusion by general educators and by those who develop and teach the foundations of education. The interests reflected in the "regular education initiative," which as all special educators know was in fact an initiative by special educators and little known to "regular" educators, cannot be debated and advocated exclusively in and by the community that fundamentally agrees on the moral philosophy—"*all* children have the right and all should mean *all*." While special educators debate definitions and data, the larger community of educators and policy makers are engaged in a reform to construct a different educational system. The interests of children with disabilities were overlooked in the larger discourse on school reform until the late 1980s.

11. A new philosophy of special education should use language more judiciously and be more cognizant of the different levels of discourse functioning in the parallel reforms of general and special education. Slogans are useful in bringing about change. They are used to stake out a position, and, at times, positions are overstated in order to get some bearing on the issues. "All means all" is an example of a slogan of the current reform. It is being debated on empirical grounds relative to efficacy and practicality, and on moral grounds relative to the rights and interests of all students. Such a slogan is useful in defining the perspective of the reform but of less value in developing policy.

CONCLUSION

The policy conundrums in special education accurately reflect the discontinuities of thought, knowledge, and values that occasioned those policies. There is no integrated national policy in special education. Rather there are different voices reflecting fundamentally opposing views of the nature of education and its role in the lives of children with disabilities. Some view the purpose of education as the teaching of academic skills and the transmission of knowledge which results in measurable achievement and performance. They believe schools should be accountable for best practices and uniform standards. They argue for procedural compliance as well as accountability for specific measurable instructional objectives. Others emphasize socialization goals in education as being at least as important as academic goals. They advocate the social integration of all children into age-grade appropriate classrooms. Still others take a position somewhere in between, believing that only children with moderate to severe disabilities should be served in pull-out programs. Some take a systemic perspective and believe that schools should be accountable for broad educational outcomes, and that variability in educational procedures, organizational patterns of service delivery, and even curriculum should be flexible to the decision of school-based educational leaders.

There are equally dissimilar views of the knowledge base for practice. Some view the knowledge informing special education practice as valid and reliable and being systematically improved and increased. Others question the science of practice, viewing all education as socially constructed. Some view teachers as instructors, conveyors of knowledge according to well-established pedagogical principles, and managers of behavior according to principles of behavioral science. Others see teachers as coaches, reflective practitioners, and facilitators of learning who nurture and assist children in constructing meaningful knowledge. These views reflect different epistemological stances and paradigmatic orientations.

At present there is a kind of time warp reflected in special education policy. There are voices for inclusion, resonating the child rights and equity agenda that led to the passage of P.L. 94-142 in 1975. There are voices for quality instruction, believing that it is impractical to provide an appropriate education for all children in the regular classroom. The full inclusion advocates remind their critics of the negative effects of pull-out programs. The continuum of services advocates remind their critics of the lessons of history, especially the lessons of the value-driven deinstitutionalization movement in which resources did not follow persons with disabilities into the community, and hard-earned resources for care and education were effectively reduced for some.

Special education is viewed by many as a service delivery system for providing an appropriate education for children with disabilities. Others view it as a system to care for casualties of the regular education program in schools and as an organizational mechanism for de facto segregation. Most would agree that ample evidence for the value of special education and for its negative effects exists in the literature. The challenge, then, is to determine what special education ought to be and how it should function in the 1990s and beyond.

The development of a philosophy for twenty-first century special education practices must address the basic argument about the art, science, ethics, and politics of educational services for children with disabilities. Depending on the era, special education was guided more or less by advocates with a social equity agenda or by professionals with a knowledge-oriented excellence agenda. Neither is sufficient, and the simple view that "both are required" will not lead us to the understandings needed for practice in the future. Special education practice must be placed in historical and current social and political context and be responsive to the moral perspectives of the 1990s, which are different from those of the 1960s and 1970s. It must accommodate the paradigmatic shift in knowledge that has taken substantial root in the sciences and the humanities during the past decade. A deeper and more integrated analysis of the grounding principles, values, knowledge base, and cultural meaning of special education practices is needed than has characterized our typically fragmented efforts in the past. Both humanistic and epistemological interests must be reflected in an integrated analysis. We need new allies in the analysis and new coalitions for constructing the art and science of practice and integrating new understanding into public policy.

Eleven features of a new philosophy were suggested. While not sufficient, the authors believe these are necessary features of a philosophy of special education for restructured schools of the future.

REFERENCES

Bacharach, S. B. (1990). *Education reform: Making sense of it all.* Boston: Allyn & Bacon.

Benne, K. D. (1990). *The task of post-contemporary education: Essays in behalf of a human future.* New York: Teachers College Press.

Gardner, H. (1983). *Frames of mind: The theory of multiple intelligences.* New York: Basic Books.

Gardner, H. (1985). *The mind's new science: A history of cognitive revolution.* New York: Basic Books.

Gilligan, C. (1982). *In a different voice.* Cambridge, MA: Harvard University Press.

Goleman, D., & Thurman, R. (1991). *Mind science: An east-west dialogue.* Boston: Wisdom Publications.

Halpern, R. (1988). Action research for the late 1980s. *Journal of Community Psychology, 16,* 249–260.

Heshusius, L. (1988). The arts, science, and the study of exceptionality. *Exceptional Children, 55,* (1), 60–65.

Heshusius, L. (1989). Curriculum-based assessment and direct instruction: Critical reflections on fundamental assumptions. *Exceptional Children, 57,* (4), 315–328.

Heshusius, L. (1992). The Newtonian mechanistic paradigm, special education, and contours of alternatives: An overview. *Journal of Learning Disabilities, 22,* (7), 403–415.

Howe, K. R., & Miramontes, O. B. (1992). *The ethics of special education.* New York: Teachers College Press.

Katz, R. (1982). *Boiling energy: Community healing among the Kalahasi !Kung.* Cambridge: Harvard Univeristy Press.

Katz, R. (1993). *The straight path: A story of healing and transformation in Fiji.* New York: Addison-Wesley.

Kauffman, J. M. (1992). Foreword. In K. R. Howe & O. B. Miramontes, *The ethics of special education.* New York: Teachers College Press.

Kohlberg, L. (1969). Stage and sequence: The cognitive-developmental approach to socialization. In D. A. Goslin (Ed.), *Handbook of socialization theory and research.* Chicago: Rand McNally.

Ladner, J. A. (Ed.). (1973). *The death of white sociology.* New York: Vintage.

Means, R. L. 1969). *The ethical imperative.* New York: Doubleday.

Noddings, N. (1988). An ethic of caring and its implication for instructional arrangements. *American Journal of Education, 96,* (2), 215–230.

Noddings, N. (1991). Caring and community in education. *Scandinavian Journal of Educational Research, 35,* (1), 3–12.

Pai, Y. (1990). *Cultural foundations of education.* New York: Macmillan.

Paul, J. L., Gallagher, J. J., Kendrick, S.B., Thomas, D.D., & Young, J.F. (1992). *Handbook for ethical policy making.* North Carolina Institute for Policy Studies.

Pestalozzi, J. H. (1969): *The education of man; aphorisms.* New York: Greenwood Press.

Popkewitz, T. S. (1991). *A political sociology of educational reform: Power/knowledge in teaching, teacher education, and research.* New York: Teachers College Press.

Poplin, M. S. (1988a). The reductionistic fallacy in learning disabilities: Replicating the past by reducing the present. *Journal of Learning Disabilities, 21,* (7), 389–400.

Poplin, M. S. (1988b). Holistic/constructivist principles of the teaching/learning process: Implications for the field of learning disabilities. *Journal of Learning Disabilities, 21,* (7), 401–416.

Rhodes, W. C. (1990). From classic to holistic paradigm. In P. Leone (Ed.), *Understanding troubled and troubling children*. Newbury Park, CA: Sage.

Rhodes, W. C. (1992). Navigating the paradigm change. *Journal of Emotional and Behavioral Problems, 1*, (2).

Sailor, W. (1991). Special education in the restructured school. *Remedial and Special Education, 12*, (6), 8–22.

Sarason, S. (1983). *Schooling in America: Scapegoat or salvation*. New York: Free Press.

Sarason, S. (1990). *The predictable failure of educational reform*. San Francisco: Jossey-Bass.

Schlechty, P. C., & Cole, R. (1991). Creating a system that supports change. *Educational Horizon, 69*, (2), 78–89.

Schön, D. A. (1989). Professional knowledge and reflective practice. In T. J. Sergiovanni & J. M. Moore (Eds.), *Schooling for tomorrow: Directing reforms to issues that count*. Boston: Allyn & Bacon.

Skrtic, T. M. (1991a). *Behind special education: A critical analysis of professional culture and school organization*. Denver: Love.

Skrtic, T. M. (1991b). The special education paradox: Equity as the way to excellence. *Harvard Education Review, 61*, 148–206.

Smith, D. (1985). *Minds made feeble*. Rockville, MD: Aspen Systems Corporation.

Smith, H. (1989). *Beyond the post-modern mind*. (2nd ed.). Wheaton, IL: The Theosophical Publishing House.

Snell, M. E. (1988). Curriculum and methodology for individuals with severe disabilities. *Education and Training in Mental Retardation, 23*, (4), 302–314.

Sperry, L. (1993). Health counseling strategies and interventions. *Journal of Mental Health Counseling, 15*, (1), 15–25.

Stone, L. (1992). Philosophy, meaning constructs and teacher theorizing. In E. W. Ross, J. Cornett, and G. McCutcheon (Eds.), *Teacher personal theorizing*. Albany, NY: State University of New York Press.

Taylor, C. (1985). *Human agency and language: Philosophical papers 1*. Cambridge, England: Cambridge University Press.

Toulmin, S. (1990). *Cosmopolis: The hidden agenda of modernity*. New York: Free Press.

2

RESTRUCTURING EDUCATION
National Reform in Regular Education

DONNIE EVANS & LUANNE PANACEK-HOWELL

INTRODUCTION

THIS book is about the reform of special education within several contexts, including a massive movement to restructure the very schools in which services to students with disabilities are provided. This chapter offers a description of components and strategies being used to restructure schools and presents factors influencing local and state educational reform efforts. Restructuring components reviewed include changes in organizational and governance structures; changing roles and responsibilities of school personnel and local, state, and federal education agencies; and changes in curricula and the way instructional services are delivered. Factors influencing the success of restructuring are examined at the federal, state, school district, local school, and classrooms levels. Demographic changes in the nation's child population offer challenges to educational leaders as the year 2000 approaches. It is estimated that as many as a third of the nation's school-aged children, in their current circumstances, are at-risk of either failing in school, dropping out, or becoming a victim of crime, alcohol or drug abuse, or teenage pregnancy (Hodgkinson, 1991; Woodside, 1988). Additionally, one fourth of all children in the United States live below the poverty level, two million children of school age are not supervised by an adult after school, and up to 200,000 children have no place to call home (Hodgkinson, 1991).

This rise in at-risk children is being attributed, in part, to societal changes, including changes in the structure of the American family and in the ethnic distribution of the nation's population (Hodgkinson, 1991). Hodgkinson notes that between 1980 and 1990 the number of traditional families (married couples with children) decreased by 1% while single-female-headed families increased by 35.6% and single-male-headed families increased by 29.1%. Approximately 50% of children will live in one-parent homes before they reach age eighteen.

During the 1980s, the nation's white population increased by 8% or 15 million while the nonwhite population increased by 14 million (Hodgkinson, 1991).

Hodgkinson also projects that the nation's nonwhite child population will increase from 30% of the total cohort of children in 1990 to 38% by 2010.

Since the early 1980s, much support has existed for the professionalism of teaching and teachers, strengthening performance standards for high school and postsecondary students, and altering the structure of schools and classrooms (National Commission on Excellence in Education, 1983; Carnegie Forum, 1986). Spurred on by debate that evolved from the publication of *A Nation at Risk*, first wave educational reform in the 1980s called for centralized controls and higher standards (Murphy, 1991a). Prevailing assumptions of the day included: 1) poor student outcomes were attributable to poor quality teachers and teaching methods, and 2) mandated top-down initiatives, particularly from the state, could improve teacher quality.

Wave two reform, which began to emerge in the late 1980s, called for restructuring the education system (Murphy, 1991a). This represented a shift from focusing on strategies for structural change to approaching reform systematically and a shift from regulation and compliance monitoring to the mobilization of institutional capacity (Murphy, 1991a). These changes have aided in the creation of expectations for new forms of schooling to be invented at the individual school site which are based on a vision of success for all students.

SCHOOL RESTRUCTURING

Much ambiguity exists over the definition of school restructuring and its impact (Lewis, 1989). Some educators view it as simply a reorganization of schools and school districts. Others see it as an extension of state-legislated curriculum reform initiated in the 1980s. The concept is viewed as a threat by some and is welcomed by others. The newness of the term in education and the wide range of changes being proposed or instituted (Lewis reports more than 40) account for this confusion.

Lewis describes school restructuring as "those actions that allow and encourage higher expectations of both teachers and students." It is both teacher centered and student centered; alters the way teachers teach and students learn; is applicable to all students, including those at risk of failure; affects both organization and curriculum; requires that everyone within a school subscribe to a central vision; and is supported by all segments of the community.

Murphy (1991b) provides a framework that seems useful for examining educational restructuring. He suggests that restructuring generally encompasses systemic changes in organizational and governance structures, work redesign, and/or core technology. It also involves changes in relationships among those involved in the educational process.

Organization and Governance Structure

The challenges resulting from demographic changes as well as various other forces are propelling schools toward decentralized governance structures (Murphy,

1991b). Classical arguments supporting the decentralization of schools are grounded in political theory and economic competitiveness. Politically, the closer governance is to the people it serves, the greater the likelihood it will be responsive to their interests and demands. It is believed that in decentralized units there is increased knowledge about, access to, and participation in governance; organizations are easier to change; and undue consolidation of power at distant locations and hierarchically remote organizational levels are prevented (Murphy, 1991b). Economically, it is argued that devolution fosters competition among monopolies. The result is a wider variety of consumer services, greater operational efficiency, and more effective production techniques (Murphy, 1991b).

Schools and school districts are substantially altering their governance structures to facilitate school improvement (Van Meter, 1991; Ingwerson, 1990; David, 1991; Lally, 1991). Alterations in organizational and governance structures refers to the political and administrative decentralization of school systems (Murphy, 1991b). Common strategies for restructuring school governance include site-based management, shared decision making at the school site, waivers from state regulations, modification of union agreements, school choice, and changes in the relationship between the school and its larger community (David, 1991; Harrison, Killon, & Mitchell, 1989; Daniels, 1990; Clune & White, 1988; Murphy, 1991b). Each is founded on the premise that those closest to the point of service impact are more knowledgeable of the needs of their students and are in a better position to develop site-specific solutions to meet those needs (Fernandez, 1991).

In many states and districts, the call for school reform is resulting in the institution of school or site-based management models. School-based management represents a realignment of power and responsibility from the central office to local schools (David, 1991). Responsibility for decisions traditionally made by district level administrators is being shifted to the building level. Decisions made at the school site generally include personnel, budget, and curriculum content (Clune & White, 1988; David, 1991).

School-based teams or committees are commonly used to facilitate site-based decision making (Clune & White, 1988; Van Meter, 1991; David; 1991). Committee composition generally includes teachers, students, community leaders, parents, and building administrators. Extensive training in the sharing process and a willingness to share responsibility for decisions is required of teachers and administrators (Daniels, 1990). Preliminary research suggests improvements in morale and professionalism among participants (David, 1991).

An obvious barrier to school restructuring has been state and federal controls and restrictions that are inconsistent with the principles of the movement (Murphy, 1991b). The use of waivers of state constraints is rapidly becoming a key policy to effect change. Legislation passed by many states enables schools or districts to seek waivers of laws or regulations that impede the accomplishment of their goals or objectives. However, some criticize their use as an ineffective means of accomplishing school reform because it tends to support the status quo (Murphy, 1991b).

The involvement and support of teacher unions is also vital to the development and institution of restructuring efforts, particularly site-based management (Tornillo, 1991). Unions are renegotiating contracts with districts to promote collaborative, rather than adversarial, relationships. For example, in Dade County, Florida, the union's contract specifies that they and district management will work collaboratively in all things including personnel hiring, recruitment, site-based decision making, and administrative reorganization. Union staff and district personnel jointly provide training and technical assistance, participate on task forces, and build credibility for restructuring. In other districts, waivers of certain union contract requirements are being negotiated on a school-by-school or districtwide basis (Murphy, 1991b).

Choice is as often overlooked a strategy for improving student performance (ASCD, 1988). Plans for choice always involve parents' influence or control over the selection of the school their child will attend. Choice plans include districtwide magnet schools, controlled choice schools, and voucher plans (tuition tax credits can be considered a variation of this plan). A few states (Arkansas, Iowa, Minnesota, and Nebraska) have recently instituted statewide systems of choice. In these states, parents can seek enrollment for their children in any school in any district, and state funds will follow the student to the receiving school.

Public schools' partnerships with private businesses and communities have evolved as an important component of current reform efforts (AASA, 1988). They offer a means for all those who have a stake in schools to make a contribution to them. At the state level, business leaders have been active in developing state education legislation and are appointed to serve on state-level committees to monitor and evaluate the impact of the laws. They are also among the strongest advocates of education reform efforts. At the local level, partnership programs support a wide range of curricular and extracurricular activities from enrichment programs to programs for the educationally disadvantaged to programs designed to support teachers and administrators. Parental or community involvement in local school restructuring efforts is often facilitated through such partnerships. Increases are also being observed in the establishment of school partnerships with universities, government agencies, churches, and other nonprofit organizations.

Work Redesign

Murphy (1991b) describes work redesign as major changes in roles, responsibilities, and relationships between district office administrators and building administrators and between building administrators and teachers. In restructured schools, traditional roles and responsibilities defined by bureaucratic models are being replaced by the tenets of professionalism (Murphy, 1991b). Among the new metaphors of restructuring are superintendents as enablers, principals as facilitators, and teachers as leaders. Central offices become service centers and provide support, technical assistance, and training to schools (Fernandez, 1991; Murphy, 1991b).

Principals become "facilitators-leaders" or "coordinators of professionals" for their schools (Murphy, p. 26). Teacher's roles and responsibilities expand structurally and conceptually and they become decision makers and "leaders of learners" (Murphy, p. 35).

The role of the federal government is also undergoing change. Previously, federal influence on education was accomplished through antidiscrimination or entitlement legislation to meet the needs of special populations, such as The Education of All Handicapped Children Act of 1975 (PL 94-142) for children with disabilities. America 2000 (now known as Goals 2000) represents a significant shift in emphasis at this level in that it advances national goals for education. The foci of these goals are readiness to start school, school completion, student performance, safe schools, adult literacy, and lifelong learning (Howe, 1991). Major recommendations of the plan offer: 1) strategies for helping teachers, 2) choice as a strategy for school improvement, 3) a New American Schools Development Corporation, and 4) new standards for achievement (Howe, 1991; Bush, 1991).

The "state as facilitator" has become the new metaphor for many state education agencies (Murphy, 1991b). The major focus of reform at this level is on accountability and restructuring mandates by legislatures. Also, state departments of education are engaged in substantive discussions of reorganization to support school restructuring (Lally, 1991; Van Meter, 1991). Consideration is being given to changing their role from regulatory to supportive and facilitative for local districts. Provisions are also being made for: 1) changing state formulas for distributing funds among public schools, 2) supporting the development and institution of collaborative programs and partnerships, 3) the use of technology for school improvement (instructional and administrative), and 4) new certification standards for teachers.

For example, in Florida, legislation has been enacted requiring a system of school improvement and education accountability by the year 2000. The intent is to provide clear guidelines, or a Blueprint 2000, for achieving this aim and for returning the responsibility for education to the schools, teachers, and parents (Florida Department of Education, 1991). Components of the accountability system are: 1) broad goals at the state level that parallel America 2000 goals; 2) student outcome measures; 3) core learning proficiencies; 4) school needs assessments; 5) training and staff development; and 6) improvement strategies that influence behavior.

Core Technology

Restructuring core technology suggests changes in the teaching and learning processes, an area receiving much less attention in reform efforts (Murphy, 1991b). Spurred on by reports calling for change, first wave reform efforts of the 1980s saw schools undergoing significant curriculum revisions and increases in high school graduation requirements (AASA, 1988). Many states, and the District of Columbia, not only increased course requirements for graduation, but lengthened their school year as well. Also emerging from early accountability initiatives was the issue of specific content of required courses.

More recently, Outcome-Based Education has received much attention as a means for restructuring what we teach and the way we teach it. As defined by William Spady, an outcome is a culminating demonstration of "what students can do when they exit the system" (Brandt, 1993). It is based on four principles: 1) outcome-driven curriculum, instruction, credentialing, and assessment; 2) expanded opportunity for students to learn and demonstrate what they are expected to learn; 3) high performance expectations for all students; and 4) curricula designed from what students are expected to demonstrate upon exiting the system (Spady & Marshall, 1991).

As put forth by Spady, transformational Outcome-Based Education is grounded on the premise that schools exist to prepare students for success when they leave school (Spady & Marshall, 1991). School districts and states utilizing this strategy abandon all preexisting notions of schooling and embrace a paradigm based on their vision of what students will need to be good citizens in the future. Planning or design teams begin by developing mission or vision statements reflective of their view of the future. Exit Outcomes that evolve from these statements provide the framework for all curricula and evaluation in the schools (Spady & Marshall, 1991). A growing number of school districts have committed to Transformational Outcome-Based Education including Jefferson County and Aurora, Colorado; Syracuse, New York; Birmingham, Michigan; and states such as Pennsylvania.

The jury is still out on the impact of school reform on student performance and the effectiveness of restructured schools in meeting the needs of their diverse child population. However, preliminary research suggests improvements in morale and professionalism among teachers (David, 1991). Now let us focus attention on factors that can influence successful school restructuring.

FACTORS THAT INFLUENCE THE SUCCESS OF RESTRUCTURING

Since the mid to late 1980s, local districts and state and federal education agencies have engaged in an increasing number of activities in the name of school restructuring. It would be naive to assume that all of these restructuring efforts have been successful, or that they have been embraced with the same degree of enthusiasm from one geographic area to another, or even from person to person within the same school site. A close look at the history of education reform shows that even well-planned, systematic interventions for school improvement have not always been successful in form or in outcome (Purkey & Smith, 1983). The reason for the lack of predictable success of restructuring efforts is that these efforts are dependent not only upon the effectiveness of the strategy(ies) employed, but also upon other factors (people, personalities, policies and procedures, atmosphere, and so on), that often serve as barriers or facilitators to implementing change. These factors may or may not fall within the control of school personnel implementing change, but by becoming familiar with these potential barriers and facilitators, those considering restructuring activities may be better prepared to deal with them and may, therefore, increase the probability of their success.

There are a number of ways to examine the factors that influence the success of school restructuring efforts. One way which might be useful to this discussion is to use a nested systems perspective, as outlined in Figure 1, in which the classroom (teacher and students) is nested within the school, while the school lies within the district and community, which is nested inside of the state education authority (SEA), which lies inside of the federal education authority. Although each level is influenced by the other, the further away a level is located, the lesser the influence that level has on any other. And, although it is not unheard of for a classroom to influence the school, or the school to influence the district, generally the influence moves in the opposite direction, from the outside levels inward with the federal level influencing the state, the state influencing the district . . . and so on.

Factors at the Federal Level

At the *federal level*, policy mandates can and have set the stage for restructuring activities to occur at the state and local levels. As discussed earlier, Goals 2000 has provided us, at the very least, with a common rhetoric in promoting current reform efforts. One of the primary roles played by the federal education authority in facilitating change at other levels occurs through the funding of various demonstration and training grants which are awarded to states and local districts. These grants provide opportunities, not otherwise available, to experiment with certain innovations and create avenues for needed training and technical assistance to state and local school personnel.

Factors at the State Level

Within the *state education authority* (SEA), there are a number of factors which can either assist or obfuscate local restructuring efforts. The availability of waivers, which was discussed earlier in this chapter, is one common way the SEA can support local districts in testing out new ideas by bypassing existing state policy and procedure. One of the single most active areas in which SEAs are providing assistance to local districts for restructuring is in revamping state funding formulas and providing fiscal incentives to districts that are actively engaged in providing services in new ways to various school populations (Policy Brief, 1991). Pipho (1990) indicates that litigation can also serve to promote change emanating from the state level, although this is not always a preferred option. Many of the restructuring efforts that have been mandated by court order seem to be less effective than those occurring as a result of responsiveness to incentives.

Two important factors to consider in implementing a restructuring effort are the availability of appropriate experience at the local level to learn from and draw upon,

FIGURE 1   Factors that Influence the Success of School Restructuring

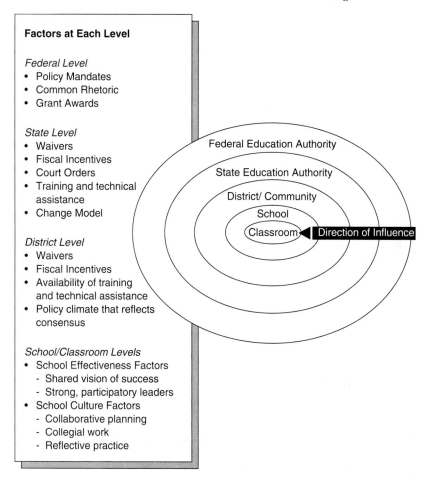

and the degree to which there is pressure at the local level to conduct school business in traditional ways (Timar, 1989). In these areas, SEAs can have a tremendous influence on districts and schools by creating the right climate for change to occur and providing an appropriate change model to follow. The tone set at the state level, the language used in state policy, the availability of creative funding and meaningful fiscal incentives for change, and the provision of timely technical assistance are all powerful tools that the state can provide to promote effective reform efforts.

Factors at the District Level

Leadership and vision at the *district level* are critical factors in creating a ripe climate for successful restructuring. Like the SEA, district-level administrators can provide waivers and fiscal incentives to demonstrate their support of school-level restructuring activities. The ability of district personnel to identify technical assistance and training needs, and then establish technical assistance linkages with state office personnel and other qualified individuals is another area in which the district can support site-based changes. Timar (1989) indicates that because schools are actually a direct product of the state and district political cultures, there must be a common denominator of agreement across the three entities (state, district, school) regarding the overall purpose of schooling and how the restructuring effort is connected to student outcomes. Therefore, establishing a policy climate within the district that reflects consensus regarding what restructuring efforts are intended to accomplish and how they are related to student outcomes is one of the most important ways in which the district can assist individual schools in making positive changes (Murphy, 1991; Timar, 1989).

Factors at the School and Classroom Levels

Factors that influence the success of school restructuring at the *school and classroom levels* can be discussed in terms of what we know about school effectiveness and school culture.

School effectiveness research indicates specific characteristics necessary for school improvement and successful restructuring efforts. Some of these characteristics include:

- a vision of success with clear goals and a plan for accomplishing them;
- a strong, visionary leader attuned to cultural differences and needs;
- an atmosphere that encourages collegiality, participation, collaboration, and consensus building;
- a restructuring plan developed by all the stakeholders in the process;
- an environment that encourages and supports ongoing staff development, life-long learning, friendly criticism, and reflective practice;
- high-quality teachers and other instructional staff;
- effective, ongoing communication with all partners (teachers, students, school administration, parents, district-level personnel);
- a focused program of instruction with high expectations for achievement within an environment that maximizes learning time;
- an ability to cope, actually thrive, with complexity and change; and
- strong parent and community involvement (Brophy, 1990; Florida Department of Education, 1990; Hirsch & Sparks, 1991; Lewis, 1988; McAffee, 1990; Mulkeen & Cambon-McCabe, 1991; Reavis & Griffith, 1991; Shroder, 1989; Slezak, 1984; Snyder, Anderson, & Johnson, 1992).

Although these characteristics are helpful in guiding us in the right direction, Purkey & Smith (1983) promote caution when applying these "recipes" for effective schools because we cannot assume that the same "ingredients" used at different schools will have even remotely similar results. In fact, they make a good case for considering *school culture* as the most useful way to approach promoting successful school-based restructuring efforts. Their point is that if schools are truly "loosely coupled" systems (Weick, 1976), in which the linkages between the classrooms and administration are weak at best, then we shouldn't put our energy and resources into creating strong leaders, but instead focus on creating the best culture for change.

Although we are still learning about creating the optimum school culture for change, it makes sense that putting the emphasis on the behavior and attitudes of all the people within the school, and attempting to create consensus regarding what issues need to be addressed and what might be the best way to address them, would certainly enhance the probability that the effort would be successful. According to Purkey & Smith (1983), studies of implementation of school change reinforce the validity of school culture in that they demonstrate that change will not occur without the support and commitment of the teachers who need to "own" the idea.

Creating the optimum culture for change is an evolutionary process within the school environment where collaborative planning and partnerships, collegial work, and reflective practice increasingly become the method by which all school business is done (Snyder, Anderson, & Johnson, 1992; Katzenmeyer, 1991; Purkey & Smith, 1983). In this setting, the quality of interpersonal relationships and the nature and quality of the learning experience become the priorities, and the role of the principal shifts from consummate leader to "head learner," coach, and facilitator (Barth, 1991; Mojkowski, 1991).

Collaborative planning and partnerships as factors in promoting the success of school restructuring are more complex issues than they appear at first glance. It has become increasingly clear that progress toward improved (educational) service delivery will only be possible when we move beyond mere cooperation to genuine collaboration (Melaville & Blank, 1991). However, collaboration means a joint understanding of the need, a willingness to establish common goals, openness to blending fiscal resources, and the relinquishing of a good deal of administrative control (MDC, 1991; National Commission on the School and Adolescent Health, 1991). It also means a commitment to and responsibility for joint program planning, implementation, and outcome evaluation. Major advantages of collaboration over cooperation, according to Melaville and Blank (1991), includes the possibility it offers to restructure the expertise, resources, and roles of partners, and the opportunity it allows the collaborative group "to design and deliver services that are developmental rather than remedial in philosophy, preventive rather than corrective in approach, and centered on the total needs of the child and family" (p. 18).

To assist those of us attempting true collaboration for the first time, Bruner (1991) identifies seven points to keep in mind: Collaboration

1. is never a quick fix;
2. is a means to an end, not an end in itself;
3. is painfully time consuming and process intensive;

4. does not guarantee that the services developed will be in sync with the philosophy you want to promote without careful monitoring;
5. occurs among people, not institutions;
6. must rely on creative problem solving and dispute resolution; and
7. is too important to be trivialized.

Creating collaborative partnerships, within the school site and from one system level to the next, is a critical feature in enhancing the success of school restructuring activities. Evans, et al. (1993) found that the most important factors influencing the success of a school site attempting restructuring are often complex and include a number of philosophical, political, policy, procedural, and logistical issues. Although some of these issues have been touched upon in this chapter, the reality is that entire books have been devoted to understanding the factors which promote or obstruct school restructuring. The purpose of offering this glimpse into the factors influencing the success of restructuring is to underscore the complexity of introducing change within our schools and to identify some of the most important variables that we know contribute to the success or failure of current school reform efforts.

SUMMARY

In this chapter we have reviewed the components and strategies of school restructuring as well as the demographic and political factors giving impetus to the changes. Site-based management represents the major strategy for changing schools' organizational and governance structures. Associated with this change is shared decision making, waivers of state regulations and policies, school choice, and the use of school improvement teams.

Changes in work redesign are changes in roles and responsibilities of school personnel and district, state, and federal education agencies. The trend among state and federal agencies has changed from compliance monitoring to a supportive and facilitative role. Restructuring core technology includes changes in the way we teach and the way students learn. Outcome-Based Education is representative of recent technology impacting on teaching and learning.

We have also suggested factors that can influence the success of school restructuring at all levels. These include policy mandates at the federal level; the availability of waivers, fiscal incentives, technical assistance, and pressure to continue conducting business in traditional ways at the state level; visionary leadership, the provision of training and technical assistance, waivers of district policy, and fiscal incentives at the district level; and school culture and collaborative planning and partnerships at the building and classroom levels.

As schools have moved toward restructuring, parallel reform efforts have been underway in special education. Chapter 3 will review the history of special education reform and related initiatives and issues that have given rise to *inclusion*.

REFERENCES

American Association for School Administrators (1988). *Challenges for school leaders.* Arlington, VA.

Association of Supervision and Curriculum Development (1988). *ASCD issues analysis: Public schools of choice.* Reston, VA.

Barth, R. (1991). *Improving the schools from within: Teachers, parents, and principals can make a difference* San Francisco: Jossey-Bass.

Brandt, R. (1993). On outcome-based education: A conversation with Bill Spady. *Educational Leadership. 50* (4), 66–70.

Brophy, J. E. (1990). *Toward effective instructional strategies and classroom management.* Contract LC88054001.

Bruner, C. (1991). *Thinking collaboratively: Ten questions and answers to help policy makers improve children's services.* Washington, DC: Education and Human Resources Consortium.

Bush, G. (1991). *America 2000.* Washington, DC: U.S. Department of Education.

Carnegie Forum on Education and the Economy (1986). *A nation prepared: Teachers for the 21st century.* New York: Carnegie Forum on Education and the Economy.

Clune, W. H. & White, P. A.(1988). *School based management: Institutional variation, implementation, and issues for further research.* New Brunswick, NJ: Center for Policy Research in Education.

Daniels, C. T. (1990). Personal reflections of shared decision making—A principal's view: Giving up my traditional ship. *The School Administrator, 47* (8), 20–24.

David, J. I. (1991). Restructuring and technology: Partners in change. *Phi Delta Kappan, 73* (1), 37–40, 78–82.

Evans, D., Harris, D., Adeigbola, M., Houston, D., & Argott, L. (1993). *Restructuring special education services., 16* (2), 137–145.

Fernandez, J. A. From the superintendents' perspective. In Hansen, J. H. & Liftin, E. (1991). *School restructuring: A practitioner's guide.* Swampscott, MA: Watersum.

Florida Department of Education (1990, June). *Hot topics: Usable research: Comprehensive school improvement.* Tallahassee, FL.

Florida Department of Education (1991). *Blueprint 2000.* Tallahassee, FL.

Harrison, C. R., Killon, J. P., & Mitchell, J. E. (1989). Site-based management: The realities of implementation. *Educational Leadership, 46* (8), 55–58.

Hirsch, S., & Sparks, D. (1991). A look at the new central-office administrators. *The School Administrator, 48* (8), 16–19.

Hodgkinson, H. (1991). Reform vs. reality. *Phi Delta Kappan, 73* (1), 9–16.

Howe, H. (1991). America 2000: A bumpy ride on four trains. *Phi Delta Kappan, 73* (3), 122–203.

Ingwerson, D.W. (1990). Personal reflections of shared decision making—A superintendent's view: Learning to listen and trust each school faculty. *The School Administrator, 47* (8), 8–11.

Katzenmeyer, W. (1991). *Inventing the schools of tomorrow.* Tampa, FL: College of Education, University of South Florida.

Lally, K. (1991). Changing the old guard: States turn toward helping rather than regulating. *The School Administrator, 48* (3), 8–12.

Lewis, A. (1989). *Restructuring America's schools.* Arlington, VA: American Association of School Administrators.

McAffee, A. L. (1990). *The importance of twelve dimensions of effective supervisory practice derived from educational literature as perceived by selected principals.* Doctoral dissertation. University of Georgia.

MDC, Inc. (1991). *Let's do it our way: Working together for educational excellence.* Chapel Hill, NC: Charles Stewart Mott Foundation.

Melaville, A. I., & Blank, M. J. (1991). *What it takes: Structuring interagency partnerships to connect children and families with comprehensive services.* Washington, DC: Education and Human Resources Consortium.

Mojkowski, C. (1991, August). *Developing leaders for restructuring schools.* Washington, DC: U.S. Department of Education, Office of Educational Research and Improvement.

Mulkeen, T. D. & Cambon-McCabe, N. (1991, Winter). Rethinking the curriculum. *AASA Professor, 13* (3).

Murphy, J. (1991a). Helping teachers to prepare to work in a restructured school. *Journal of Teacher Education, 41,* 50–56.

Murphy, J. (1991b). *Restructuring schools: Capturing and assessing the phenomena* New York: Teachers College Press.

National Commission on Excellence in Education (1983). *A nation at risk: The imperative for educational reform.* Washington, DC: U.S. Government Printing Office.

National Commission on the Role of the School and the Community in Improving Adolescent Health (1991). In A. Melaville and M. Blank, *What it takes: Structuring interagency partnerships to connect children and families with comprehensive services.* Washington, DC: Education and Human Resources Consortium.

Pipho, C. (1990, May). Reflecting on the Kentucky state court decisions. *Education Week.*

Policy Brief (1991). *Fiscal incentives in school finance: An assessment of alternative approaches* University of Southern California.

Purkey, S. C., & Smith, M. S. (1983). Effective schools: A review. *The Elementary School Journal, 83* (4), 427–452.

Reavis, C. A., & Griffith, H. (1991). *Schools: Theory and practice.* Lancaster, PA: Technomic.

Shroder, H. M. (1989). *Managerial competence: The key to excellence.* Dubuque, IA: Kendall/Hunt.

Slezak, J. (1984). *Odyssey to excellence.* San Francisco: Merritt Publishing.

Snyder, K. J., Anderson, R. H., & Johnson, W. J. (1992). A tool kit for managing productive schools. *Educational Leadership, 49,* 76–80.

Spady, W. G., & Marshall, K. J. (1991). Beyond traditional outcome-based education. *Educational Leadership, 49* (2), 67–72.

Timar, T. (1989, December) The politics of school restructuring. *Phi Delta Kappan,* 265–275.

Tornillo, P. From the perspective of the Teachers Union. In Hansen, J. H., & Liftin, E. (1991). *School restructuring, A practitioner's guide.* Swampscott, MA: Watersum.

Van Meter, E. J. (1991). The Kentucky mandate: School-based decision making. *NASSP Bulletin, 75,* 52–62.

Weick, K.E. (1976). Educational organizations as loosely coupled systems. *Administrative Science Quarterly, 21,* 1–19.

Woodside, W. (1988). Leadership for at risk students. *Challenges for school leaders.* Arlington, VA: American Association of School Administrators, pp. 61–70.

3

MOVING BEYOND THE REGULAR EDUCATION INITIATIVE
National Reform in Special Education

ANNE HOCUTT & JAMES D. MCKINNEY

INTRODUCTION

THE purpose of this chapter is to discuss the recent history of educational reform as it pertains to special education. Essentially, educational reform in special education has had two major, closely related phases: the Regular Education Initiative (REI) followed by its successor, the Inclusion Initiative. We begin with the REI, the reform effort of the 1980s with roots that can be traced back to the deinstitutionalization movement and early criticism of the efficacy of special education programs. We end in 1993 with the Inclusion Initiative and the Senate Report language accompanying S. 1150, the Goals 2000: Educate America Act, stating that the needs of children and youth with disabilities will be considered in the current general education reform movement.

Our discussion will include: a) a description of these two initiatives (the REI and Inclusion); b) the activities of the Office of Special Education Program (OSEP), U.S. Department of Education, linked to the two initiatives; and c) the context: the general education reform effort and its changes in focus over the last decade, in which the special education reform effort has taken place. Additionally, our discussion will focus on how these two initiatives are similar and how they are different.

THE REGULAR EDUCATION INITIATIVE

The Regular Education Initiative, or REI, is the nomenclature given to various loosely connected proposals developed during the first half of the 1980s. These involved changing the relationship between general and special education to create more of a partnership. The goal was to increase the extent to which students with disabilities are educated in general education classrooms (Hocutt, Martin, & McKinney, 1991; Kauffman, 1991). The various proposals were developed by professionals who believed that general educators should assume more responsibility for educating students with disabilities (Ysseldyke, Algozzine & Thurlow, 1992).

Special education has never been without its critics, and the roots of the REI go back to the concerns of some individuals a quarter of a century ago. Even prior to enactment of the Education for All Handicapped Children Act (P.L. 94-142) in 1975, some professionals (Dunn, 1968; Budoff, 1972) questioned the effectiveness of a different system for educating students with disabilities. As noted by Weintraub (1991), Reynolds and Balow, in their testimony before the Select Subcommittee on Education of the U.S. House of Representatives, opposed H.R. 70 (which became P.L. 94-142) on the grounds that the legislation moved toward separate general and special education systems, not toward the integration of the two systems.

The REI also had roots in another movement at the time, deinstitutionalization and accompanying normalization. Pictorial essays (Blatt & Kaplan, 1966; Rivera, 1972) had graphically drawn attention to the dismal facilities in which many individuals with severe mental and/or behavioral problems had been placed. The impact of the photographs on the public, probably more than analyses of the effects of institutionalization on the inmates, led to the development of the deinstitutionalization movement. Essentially, the movement focused on returning those with serious mental/behavioral problems to the community and supporting them (e.g., providing group homes in various communities) so that they could enjoy lives as normal as possible (Nirje, 1969; Wolfensberger, 1972).

Thus, many of the assumptions underlying the REI, e.g., that separation of individuals with disabilities from the mainstream was harmful and that inclusion was beneficial, existed during the late 1960s and early 1970s. However, the force of these assumptions was relatively weak when compared with the larger issue of the access of students with disabilities to a free appropriate public education—the central theme of the Education for All Handicapped Individuals Act, P.L. 94-142. Therefore, it was not until this landmark legislation had been implemented and there was clear evidence that individuals with disabilities did have access to educational services—primarily through special education—that individual criticism of special education changed into a movement that became known as the Regular Education Initiative, or REI.

In 1981 the Wingspread Conference was held to address a number of issues concerning the relationship between public policy and the education of students with disabilities, including the effectiveness of current practices and the integration of special education with other systems (Reynolds, Brand, & Copeland, 1983). At this meeting, Reynolds and Wang (1983) stated that the current educational service delivery system had been fragmented by the proliferation of separate programs for students who had special needs, referring to this phenomenon as "disjointed incrementalism" (p. 191). They further identified several concerns that became central to the REI, including the inappropriate labeling of students, the development of "bureaucracies" to serve students in specific categories of exceptionality, and the adaptation of general education to meet the educational needs of exceptional students (Lloyd & Gambatese, 1991).

The impetus provided by the Wingspread Conference gave rise to a number of critiques of special education, most notably the 1986 article by Madeline Will, then Assistant Secretary of Education for the U.S. Department of Education. Will (1986) criticized the "pull-out" approach to delivering educational services to students with disabilities through special education programs. She argued that general educators should share the responsibility of teaching students with learning problems by educating such children in the regular classroom, with assistance provided by the special education teacher. Similarly, Wang, Reynolds, and Walberg (1986) recommended the development of a "coordinated educational delivery system. This system would combine methods that have a strong research record of effectiveness with comprehensive systems of instruction that have evolved from both general and special education" (p. 28).

In October 1986 the Teacher Education Division (TED) of the Council for Exceptional Children issued a statement describing attempts to "revise instructional program options for low-performing students" (p. 1) as the Regular Education Initiative. This position paper, perhaps the first major criticism of the REI, stated that the various proposals making up the REI were quite complex in terms of their implications, and included more than 250 questions regarding the potential effects of the REI on educational practice and on students.

The TED position paper was one of the first of many criticisms of the REI, and it may be an understatement to say that the subsequent professional debate was rancorous. As noted by Keogh (1988a), "differences in perspectives, in beliefs, and in professional investment have resulted in a serious polarization . . . Special educators are defensive; critics overstate and exaggerate problems. The published literature on special education–regular education issues is steeped in rhetoric and over-generalization, and is affectively loaded" (p. 19).

The debate over the REI has centered around a number of issues, including:

- the extent to which existing efficacy studies demonstrate that special education is effective, and for whom (Carlberg & Kavale, 1980; Madden & Slavin, 1983; Biklen & Zollers, 1986; Hallahan, Keller, McKinney, Lloyd, & Bryan, 1988; Keogh, 1988a; Lipsky & Gartner, 1991);
- the extent to which classification of children is reliable/valid, relevant to instruction, and leads to stigma (Ysseldyke & Algozzine, 1990; Ysseldyke, Algozzine, & Epps, 1983; Reynolds, 1991);
- the extent to which students identified as mildly handicapped, especially learning disabled, are in fact handicapped and thus in need of special education (Bryan, Bay, & Donahue, 1988; Kauffman, Gerber, & Semmel, 1988; Keogh, 1988a; Ysseldyke & Algozzine, 1990);
- the extent to which students' failures can be attributed to systemic problems, e.g., the shortcomings of teachers (Biklen & Zollers, 1986; Kauffman, Gerber, & Semmel, 1988);

- the extent to which the REI was a "gross oversimplication of a complex problem . . . of significant differences that exist between the organizational structures, curricula, and other features of elementary and secondary schools" (Schumaker & Deshler, 1988, p. 36);
- the extent to which the Adaptive Learning Environments Model (ALEM), the empirical model associated with the REI, was in fact effective in educating disabled students in mainstream classes and had valid, reliable data to support its claims of effectiveness (Fuchs & Fuchs, 1988; Bryan & Bryan, 1988; Hallahan, Keller, McKinney, Lloyd, & Bryan, 1988; Kauffman, Gerber, & Semmel, 1988);
- the extent to which general education is capable of serving all students effectively (Wang & Birch, 1984; Wang, Peverly, & Randolph, 1984; Kauffman, Gerber, & Semmel, 1988; McKinney & Hocutt, 1988a; Keogh, 1988a,b; Bryan, Bay, & Donahue, 1988; Walker & Bullis, 1991); and
- the extent to which the existence of parallel systems of education, i.e., general and special education, is a defensible use of limited fiscal and personnel resources (Reynolds & Wang, 1983; Reynolds, 1991).

One of the more interesting aspects of the debate was the nature of the existing research base relevant to the REI and the use of the research by both sides. First, the research—particularly that relating to the efficacy of special education—was often contradictory, enabling some to attend selectively to only that research which bolstered their arguments. Second, many professionals reviewed the research base and found it seriously flawed, especially the research concerning the ALEM (Hallahan et al., 1988; Bryan & Bryan, 1988). Fortunately, in recognition that educational research needed to become more relevant to the educational reform movement, the Office of Special Education Programs (OSEP) in the U.S. Department of Education developed a high-quality research program that was relevant to the REI debate (Fuchs & Fuchs, 1990; Kaufman, Kameenui, Birman, & Danielson, 1990).

EFFORTS OF THE OFFICE OF SPECIAL EDUCATION PROGRAMS RELATED TO THE REI

Beginning in 1985, OSEP initiated a five-year program of research designed to "systematically investigate instructional, organizational, and administrative issues related to educating children with disabilities in the general education environment" (Kaufman, Kameenui, Birman, & Danielson, 1990, p. 12). Through this systematic program of research, OSEP staff hoped to become the "masters, not the victim" of educational reform through the production, management, and refinement of high-quality, school-based knowledge relevant to educating difficult-to-teach students in mainstreamed settings (Kaufman et al., 1990). The central focus on the research effort was to gather data which would assist in obtaining "better educational and postschool results for children with disabilities" (Kaufman et al., 1990, p. 109).

The 41 projects funded by OSEP over several competitions in this research program addressed the following priorities:

Enhancing instructional program options (1986). This priority funded seven projects to investigate teacher and school effectiveness in general education for mainstreaming students with disabilities. The research focused on: a) the effects of different instructional environments and assessment procedures on referral and placement for special education (e.g., Cooper & Speece, 1990); b) collaborative consultation as a strategy for enhancing the benefits of mainstreaming (e.g., Fuchs, Fuchs, & Bahr, 1990); and c) a social skills intervention program (e.g., Vaughn, Zaragoza, Hogan, & Walker, 1992).

Increasing teaching/learning efficiency (1986). This priority focused on attributes of special education services for students with disabilities in schools that were identified as effective (e.g., Semmel, Abernathy, Butera, & Tesar, 1991; Gersten, Walker, & Darch, 1988). It also focused on studies of general and special education teachers' effectiveness (e.g., Hallahan, McNergney, & McKinney, 1986; Nowacek, McKinney, & Hallahan, 1990).

Educating students with mild disabilities in general education classrooms (1987). Nine projects were funded under this priority to identify and evaluate alternative administrative and organizational strategies for delivering special education services in regular education classrooms. Some of these projects focused on alternative curricula for individualizing instruction (e.g., Deno, Maruyama, Espin, & Cohen, 1990); the relative effectiveness of different models of consultation (e.g., Schulte, Osborne, & McKinney, 1990); and the accommodation of students with learning disabilities within general education environments (e.g., Zigmond & Baker, 1990).

School building models for educating students with disabilities in general education settings (1988). Six projects were funded under this priority, which supported the development of integrated approaches for delivering special education services for all classrooms in a given school building. The projects were to provide integrated strategies for assisting teachers with: a) problem solving concerning instructional and behavior problems (e.g., Jenkins & Leicester, 1992); b) managing classrooms to maximize academic learning time for all students (e.g., Ysseldyke, Christenson, & Thurlow, 1993); c) providing appropriate instruction for students with disabilities at different academic levels within the regular classroom (e.g., Gersten & Taylor, in press); and d) continuously monitoring students' programs and classroom instruction accordingly (e.g., Fuchs & Deno, 1992; Fuchs, Fuchs, Hamlett, & Ferguson, 1992; and Whinery & Fuchs, 1992).

Research on general education mathematics, science, social studies and language arts (1989). This priority supported four projects in each academic area to:

a) analyze K–8 curricula; b) describe the alignment of general education curricula with the characteristics and needs of students with disabilities; and c) develop guidelines for their adoption for special education.

Research on general education teacher planning and adaptation for students with disabilities (1989). The purpose of this priority was to expand current knowledge about methods general educators use to plan and adapt instruction, the barriers to planning for effective instruction, and the design of strategies and interventions to enhance teacher planning to better meet the needs of students with disabilities in mainstream settings (e.g., Fuchs, Fuchs, & Bishop, 1992; Schumm & Vaughn, 1992).

In addition to the research projects funded under these priorities, OSEP also funded the Center for Educating Students with Handicaps in Regular Education Settings (CESHIRES) at the Research Triangle Institute in 1988 (Alberg, 1991). The purposes of this Center were to: a) devise a conceptual framework for organizing the major educational approaches and models for serving children with disabilities in general education settings; b) describe the key features, assumptions, and efficacy of model programs that exemplified each approach; c) specify the requirements of various models for effective implementation; and d) develop a decision-making framework that could be used by schools to select and implement the approaches and models that best meet their needs with respect to the inclusion of children with disabilities.

Some of the results of this research effort were published in the 1990 special issue of *Exceptional Children*. The findings and conclusions from the projects featured in that issue included the following:

- Specific instructional arrangements in general education first and second grade classes increased the probability of special education placement for children identified as "at-risk" in kindergarten (Cooper & Speece, 1990). Specifically, using unsupervised individual seatwork for at-risk children while other children were in reading groups significantly increased the likelihood of placement. On the other hand, small group work was related to nonplacement for children classified as "at-risk" for learning disabilities.
- Special education consultant involvement in prereferral intervention improved general education teachers' perceptions of their hard-to-teach students (Fuchs, Fuchs, & Bahr, 1990).
- More effective general and special education teachers (i.e., those who maintained higher levels of participation) provided effective transitions, made assignments, and approved of students' verbal responses more often than less effective teachers; both teaching behaviors and teacher interactive behaviors differed as a function of grade level and teacher type, i.e., special or general education teacher (Nowacek, McKinney, & Hallahan, 1990).
- Low-achieving students and those with mild disabilities performed better in integrated settings, but special education students did poorly in both integrated and resource rooms when compared to their low-achieving classmates (Deno et al., 1990).

- Learning disabled students in general education receiving a combination of consultation and direct services showed small, but statistically significant, gains in achievement compared to students placed in resource rooms (Schulte, Osborne, & McKinney, 1990).
- Students with learning disabilities in less individualized and more demanding mainstream classes made no significant progress in reading or math and received lower grades than their classmates, suggesting that students with LD will not succeed in the mainstream if teachers continue "business as usual" (Zigmond & Baker, 1990).

In essence, the results of these studies showed that some practices and some teachers could help students with disabilities remain in general education, but that there was a limit to the extent to which outcomes for the students with disabilities were improved. The major conclusion which can be drawn from the studies mentioned above and others not discussed in detail here (e.g., Ysseldyke, Christenson, & Thurlow, 1993) is that designing and implementing interventions for students with disabilities in general education settings is a difficult and complex undertaking, and one that may have limited results.

The Context of the REI: Reform in General Education

As noted by Keogh (1988a), one of the ironies of the REI was that it occurred at the same time that criticism of general education was becoming more widespread and intense. A number of major reports calling for educational reform appeared in the early 1980s, including *A Nation at Risk* (National Commission on Excellence in Education, 1983), *High School: A Report on Secondary Education in America* (Boyer, 1983), *A Place Called School: Prospects for the Future* (Goodlad, 1984), *Horace's Compromise: The Dilemma of the American High School* (Sizer, 1984), and *A Nation Prepared: Teachers for the Twenty-first Century* (Carnegie Forum on Education and the Economy, 1986). The impetus for these reports stemmed from a deep concern regarding the current nature and quality of general education and, consequently, America's ability to compete in world markets in the coming years (Hocutt, Martin, & McKinney, 1991).

These various concerns culminated during the 1989 education summit at the University of Virginia, at which the National Governors' Association Task Force on Education worked with the President's designees to recommend specific national educational goals. These goals became America 2000, a national education strategy based on six goals:

1. All children in America will start school ready to learn.
2. The high school graduation rate will increase to at least 80%.
3. Students will leave grades 4, 8, and 12 having demonstrated competency in challenging subject matter in the five core subjects (English, math, science, history, and geography).

4. U.S. students will be first in the world in science and math achievement.
5. Every adult American will be literate and will have knowledge/skills to compete in a global economy.
6. Every school in America will be free of drugs and violence and will offer a disciplined environment conducive to learning (U.S. DOE, 1991).

The language in the six goals of *America 2000* referred to "all" children and "every" American. Yet, as noted by Hocutt et al. (1991), "the silence about the needs of, or outcomes for, handicapped children in the current [general education] reform movement is deafening" (p. 24). None of the various critiques of general education (including America 2000) contained any specific reference to students with disabilities or to special education (Pugach & Sapon-Shevin, 1987; Lilly, 1987). Kauffman and Hallahan (1993), in discussing the "varied meanings of ALL," stated that *"all* usually represents only an approximation . . . of every individual. *All*, then, is frequently understood to exclude certain individuals, sometimes for reasons that are justifiable and sometimes for reasons that are not. The varied meanings of *all* are therefore of considerable consequence to those who may be tacitly excluded" (p. 74). This reality led the National Association of State Directors of Special Education (NASDSE) to issue a position paper stating that America 2000 applies to ALL students (NASDSE, 1992). In effect, NASDSE's position was that "all" must mean ALL.

Another irony of the REI was that it called for greater integration of general and special education at a time when most reports were emphasizing the necessity of a commitment to excellence in general education—typically interpreted as higher standards, more courses, and more homework (Ysseldyke, Algozzine, & Thurlow, 1992). Under attack from the public because American children were demonstrably behind children from other countries in academic achievement, a number of educators called for more emphasis on higher order thinking skills and accountability for higher student performance on achievement tests of various kinds (Hocutt, Martin, & McKinney, 1991). Associated issues included violence in the schools, discipline and behavior problems which limited academic instruction, and the perception that many teachers were poorly trained. These circumstances led Keogh (1988b) to question whether general education had a "reasonable probability" of meeting the needs of exceptional students (Keogh, 1988b, p. 4).

A third irony of the REI was that, in spite of its somewhat misleading name, it was never an initiative that came from the regular education community. It emerged from the special education community and was discussed by special educators, without any significant input from regular educators (McKinney & Hocutt, 1988a; Hocutt, Martin, & McKinney, 1991). "There are no clamoring masses anxious to teach students with unique abilities and special learning needs, especially those with serious behavior problems" (Ysseldyke, Algozzine, & Thurlow, 1992, p. 127). Indeed, there is empirical evidence showing that general education teachers have low tolerance for maladaptive classroom behavior (Gersten, Walker, & Darch, 1988) and that teacher behaviors effective for teaching lower order cognitive skills in special class settings may not be the most effective means of teaching higher order thinking skills in general classes (Morsink, Soar, Soar, & Thomas, 1986).

The Transition from the REI to Inclusion

Toward the end of the 1980s and early in the 1990s, the REI debate became framed in terms of the cascade of services model (Deno, 1970) which represents the current continuum of special to general education placements. The central question became one of whether or not the cascade of services should be abolished (Fuchs & Fuchs, 1991; Fuchs, Fuchs, 1994). In analyzing the debate around this question, Fuchs & Fuchs (1991) separated the major players into Abolitionists (those who argue for elimination of the cascade and therefore for the REI) and Conservationists (who argue for preservation of the cascade). Specifically, Fuchs & Fuchs (1991) characterized the Abolitionists as future-oriented, nonempirical (i.e., research is not regarded critically), credulous (optimistic, perhaps naive, about change), advocates (rather than analysts), heavy on the subjunctive (express wishes), and idealists. They then characterized the Conservationists as pragmatic, dubious about general education's ability to accommodate students with disabilities to a much greater extent, analysts (rather than advocates), and empirical (with a tendency to look critically at research). Fuchs & Fuchs (1991) further noted that Abolitionists and Conservationists typically advocate for different populations of students (Abolitionists tend to be members of The Association for the Severely Handicapped, or TASH, while Conservationists tend to have worked with mildly handicapped populations) and have different goals for those students (social/attitudinal goals for the Abolitionists and academic goals for the Conservationists).

INCLUSION: SUCCESSOR TO THE REI

In any event, perhaps because the nature of the debate was viewed as unproductive and/or the research underpinnings of the REI had been effectively challenged, the term *Regular Education Initiative* fell into disuse and was replaced by the term *Inclusion*, which referred to the integration of students with disabilities into general education classrooms. The Inclusion movement is clearly related to the REI, for the two initiatives have in common the ideal of serving more students with disabilities in the general education system. However, in our view, there are also some notable differences.

At the 1993 convention of the Council for Exceptional Children (CEC), there was (yet again) considerable debate over the wording of a CEC Policy Statement on Inclusive Schools and Community Settings (CEC, 1993a). The final statement adopted by the CEC delegate assembly may be characterized as having:

- an emphasis on outcomes not only during but following completion of schooling;
- support for the cascade/continuum of services and a rich variety of early intervention, educational, and vocational programs and options for disabled students;
- support for access to these services to be based on the educational needs of, and desired outcomes for, the individual student;

- support for the concept of inclusion and the provision of educational services whenever possible in neighborhood schools and community settings;
- practical policy implications, e.g., adequate support and technical assistance, high quality preservice and inservice training to prepare general educators to work effectively with students having a wide range of abilities and disabilities, greater autonomy for professionals in individual schools, funding of critical support programs, interagency collaboration, school-community collaboration, the establishment of ambitious goals for students, and monitoring/accountability for the progress of students toward those goals.

One of the most interesting aspects of the CEC position paper was language that ultimately was not included. One draft of the paper stated that "inclusion is not a program model to be proven or disproven by research, but a philosophy or belief about the education of children and youth with their nondisabled peers. This philosophy is supported by legal and legislative intent" (CEC, 1993b). In our opinion, by omitting this language in the final position paper, the CEC delegate assembly accepted the concept that sound empirical evidence with regard to student outcomes is a critical component of the Inclusion movement and therefore implicitly rejected any approach to special education reform characterized primarily by ideology rather than analysis. (Ideological issues are the focus of other chapters in this volume, especially chapters one and eleven).

Later Efforts of the Office of Special Education Programs

Empirical evidence with regard to student outcomes and school restructuring is a hallmark of much of the research undertaken by OSEP in the late 1980s and early 1990s. In 1987, OSEP contracted with SRI International to conduct a national longitudinal transition study of special education students. This study was designed to provide information not only about the educational programs received by youths with disabilities in secondary school, but also to examine their social integration, educational achievements, and employment experiences (Wagner, 1989). The findings were inconclusive, but on the whole the outcomes were disappointing. In comparison to nondisabled youth, the students with disabilities were less likely to graduate from high school, move on to some form of postsecondary education, or become employed. Perhaps the most disheartening statistic was that fewer than 70% of youths with disabilities who had been out of high school more than one year were engaged in any productive activity (Wagner, 1989).

Students with LD (who spent an average of 64% of their time in general education classrooms) achieved a gradepoint average (GPA) of 1.94 in general education classes for the most recent school year, considerably below the GPA of 2.18 for their nondisabled peers. Further, there was a negative relationship between course failure and/or grade failure and the extent to which the students with LD were mainstreamed. However, in presenting these results, Wagner (1989) also stated that while the students with LD participating in the study were held to the same standards as their nondisabled peers, neither they nor their teachers received assistance in the general education settings to improve outcomes or instruction.

The National Center on Educational Outcomes (NCEO) was also funded by OSEP to work with states and other policy groups to develop a model of educational outcomes for students with disabilities and to generate a list of indicators of these outcomes (Ysseldyke et al., 1992). The Center's work is based on the premise that "if students receiving special education services are not being evaluated on the same or a complementary set of outcomes [as general education students], then educators and the general public may not see the value of the participation of these students in general education settings" (Ysseldyke et al., 1992, p. 4).

NCEO showed clearly the lack of attention in national and state data collection/accountability efforts to outcomes for students with disabilities. NCEO staff examined the extent to which individuals with disabilities have been included in major national data collection efforts involving student outcomes (McGrew et al., 1992). Included in the NCEO's review were the National Assessment of Educational Progress (NAEP), the National Longitudinal Study (NLS), High School and Beyond (HSB), and the National Education Longitudinal Study (NELS). Some conclusions from this review were that:

- At the national level, it is estimated that approximately 40 to 50% of school-age students with disabilities are excluded from prominent national data collection programs;
- Exclusion of students with disabilities from national and state data collection programs occurs at many different points, from the development of assessment instruments to the reporting of results;
- A sizable portion of excluded students should not have been excluded from these data collection programs since they were capable of participating (some with testing accommodations, others without) in such data collection programs;
- Exclusion criteria typically are developed by local school personnel who understandably are most concerned about their immediate setting and who may not appreciate the potential usefulness of such information for school improvement and the development of educational policy (McGrew et al., 1992).

In addition to this review, NCEO developed a conceptual model of educational outcomes for children and youth with disabilities with the assistance of a number of prominent educators and input from all stakeholder groups concerned with the issue of outcome assessment and educational reform. Essentially, this model shows that enabling outcomes (e.g., presence/participation and accommodation/adaptation) facilitate the achievement of educational outcomes in the domains of physical health, responsibility and independence, contribution and citizenship, academic and functional literacy, personal and social adjustment, and satisfaction. As stated by Ysseldyke et al. (1992), these outcomes are those which:

- are valued by society;
- reflect the extent to which essential cultural expectations have been achieved by individuals with disabilities;
- include direct and indirect results;
- are relevant for all individuals; and
- are the product of learning and experience (what has been learned rather than how it has been learned).

OSEP also funded a number of model demonstration projects designed to examine the systemic changes needed in schools to both increase the inclusion of disabled students in mainstream settings and to foster improved outcomes for all students. (A number of the chapters in the book relate to information derived from partnerships between University of South Florida faculty and the schools participating in one of these projects). This research priority was designed to build on research projects mentioned earlier in this chapter, e.g., those projects designed to enhance instructional program options, increase teaching/learning efficiency, educate students with mild disabilities in general education classrooms, and implement school building models for educating students with disabilities in general education settings. While individual practices used in the earlier studies (e.g., direct instruction, curriculum-based assessment, learning strategies, and cooperative learning) had proven to be effective in many of the projects, they were limited in their impact for a number of reasons. First, they were research projects carried out primarily by special educators in general education settings. Second, they were projects driven by special education models of effective practices that were externally imposed upon general education. Third, very little in general education really changed. General educators no doubt were grateful for the extra assistance from the special educators; however, we know of no fundamental changes in school policies, organization, administration, procedures, or even instruction that incorporated these effective practices into the daily practice of general education. Consequently, OSEP funded a priority to determine what *systemic* changes were necessary to make in schools already restructuring to foster increased inclusion and improved student outcomes.

Thus, a great number of the projects funded by OSEP in recent years have focused on student outcomes and systemic (as opposed to instructional or curricular) changes necessary to promote both increased inclusion and improved outcomes for students with disabilities. Additionally, by requiring the model demonstration projects to be implemented in schools already in the process of restructuring, OSEP attempted to forge links between the general and special education reform movement at the levels of planning and implementation. However, it is too early to determine whether, and the extent to which, systemic changes designed to foster inclusion and institutionalize needed changes will—or can be—made in general education, and whether the student outcomes associated with those changes will be positive for both general and special education students.

The Changing Context of the Inclusion Initiative

It seems to us that during the early 1990s, the reform focus appears to have shifted toward more structural, as opposed to pedagogical, change. The Center for Policy Research of the National Governors' Association (David et al., 1990) published *State Actions to Restructure Schools: First Steps*, a document suggesting specific actions that could be implemented by states to stimulate school reform. Specific examples of possible reforms include state-level waivers for such things as class-size limits (to allow for unusually large groups for some activities and very small groups for others), grade-level restrictions for teacher assistants, and definitions of high school credits.

At the individual school level, site-based management and shared decision making have become reasonably common efforts. Sailor (1991) noted that recent school restructuring models have in common at least three of the following four characteristics: organizational autonomy for individual schools, site-based management and shared decision making, coordination of categorical resources, and community involvement. (It is interesting to note that there is one level—the school system—which has received relatively little attention in the reform literature. Its primary function appears to be to give more autonomy to individual schools).

In any event, there have been a number of calls for reforming/restructuring/transforming schooling as it currently exists (Kauffman & Hallahan, 1993). In Florida, these calls have resulted in *Blueprint 2000: A System of School Improvement and Accountability* (1992) developed by the Florida Commission on Education Reform and Accountability and based on legislation enacted in 1991. Since that time, every school in the state has been responsible for developing a school improvement plan (with the assistance of an advisory council that is representative of the community). The plans are sent to the school district for review and approval. The goals set by individual schools must relate to the goals of *Blueprint 2000* (1992), which contains goals that reflect the national goals of America 2000/Goals 2000.

This major redesign initiative being implemented throughout the state of Florida is but one example of similar activities in other states. Our point is that such initiatives were not being implemented—particularly on a statewide basis—during the 1980s. However, it is far too soon to determine the extent to which such initiatives will result in improved schools in terms of restructuring (e.g., effective use of resources), better student outcomes across the board, or better outcomes for students with disabilities.

Another way in which the context has changed is a step towards the development of public policy which recognizes the place of students with disabilities in the reform effort. Legislation entitled Goals 2000: Educate America Act was introduced in Congress by the new Clinton administration in early 1993. *The Senate Report on the Goals 2000 Legislation* (Senate Report 103-85 to accompany S. 1150) is the first legislative document that directly addresses the needs of disabled students in the context of the six national goals first established by America 2000. This report states unequivocally that Goals 2000: Educate America Act is consistent with the Americans with Disabilities Act, Part B of the Individuals with Disabilities Education Act (IDEA), and section 504 of the Rehabilitation Act of 1973. It further specifies exactly how specific provisions of Goals 2000 apply to students with disabilities and discusses the work of the National Education Goals Panel and the National Education Standards and Improvement Council vis-a-vis students with disabilities.

One portion of the Senate Report applies to the six national educational goals and discusses the application of these goals to students with disabilities. With regard to goal 1 (school readiness), the Senate Committee on Labor and Human Resources (the committee with responsibility for general, special, and remedial education legislation) encourages all states to fully implement Part H of IDEA having to do with early family-centered intervention. With regard to goal 2 (school completion), the Committee notes the need to reduce the dropout rate for disabled students. With regard to goal 3 (student achievement and citizenship), the Committee states that the work of the National Center on Educational Outcomes at the University of Minnesota will "increase the likelihood of making valid, reliable, fair and nondiscriminatory assessments about the extent to which education works for all students, including students with disabilities" (p. 25). With regard to goal 4 (math, science, and technology), the Committee states that it expects the number of disabled students entering the fields of math, science, and engineering to increase. With regard to goal 5 (adult literacy/lifelong learning), the Committee urges equal access to postsecondary education programs for students with disabilities and notes that recent amendments to Part B of IDEA and Title I of the Rehabilitation Act of 1973 focus on the transition from school to work and postsecondary education. Finally, with regard to goal 6 (safe schools), the Committee states its intent that students educated in a safe school must include students with disabilities.

Another portion of the Senate Report deals with the National Education Goals Panel, whose purpose is to review the national goals and objectives and recommend any adjustments needed in them to guarantee education reform. The Report states that the Senate Committee authorizes the Panel to recommend adjustments to national goals and objectives (including voluntary standards set locally) so they are more responsible to the educational needs of all students. Most important, the Report clearly indicates that assessment data relevant to these national goals include information on the performance of all students (including students with disabilities),and that data applicable only to students with disabilities be separated to the extent that separate data is reported for other groups with specific characteristics.

The Senate Report also addresses the work of the National Education Standards and Improvement Council, whose job it is to certify voluntary content, performance, and opportunity-to-learn standards and certify acceptable content and performance standards submitted by the states. Essentially, the Report states that: a) the Council should include persons with knowledge of and experience in educating students with disabilities; b) the Council must certify standards that will give a "fair opportunity" to all students to achieve the requisite knowledge and skills; c) the IEP is a mechanism for establishing appropriate goals and objectives for students with disabilities; d) the standards should include provisions for adaptations and accommodations necessary to enable students with disabilities to meet requisite skills and IEP goals; and e) the assessment system tied to the standards must encourage, not discourage, local educators to include students with disabilities who are receiving their education in general education classrooms in the assessment process.

Finally, with regard to state and local reform efforts, the Report states that such efforts must include students with disabilities. Both state and local improvement plans must include specific strategies for meeting the national education goals, and the Senate Report discussion regarding the development of standards and assessment with respect to students with disabilities is applicable to these plans.

CONCLUSION

The title of this chapter contains the phrase "Moving Beyond the Regular Education Initiative." In some ways, this phrase is inaccurate because the current Inclusion Initiative is an extension of the REI. Both concern the relationship between general and special education and the education of disabled students in general education settings. Indeed, we are concerned about some of the similarities.

One similarity is that the Inclusion Initiative comes primarily from the special education community. To our knowledge, inclusion is not a topic much discussed by the general education community. Like Ysseldyke, Algozzine, & Thurlow (1993), we have not noticed general educators clamoring to teach disabled students, especially if the students have behavioral problems.

Another similarity is the insistence by some special educators (i.e., the "Abolitionists") that greater inclusion is a goal in and of itself, quite apart from student outcomes. In our view, placement decisions always should be made on an individualized basis as a means of achieving improved student outcomes. The mere presence of special education students in general education classrooms ensures neither their full participation in general education nor improved outcomes. While inclusion itself may be attainable, achievement of inclusion *with* improved outcomes for students with disabilities may be more elusive.

Yet another similarity between the REI and Inclusion appears to be the desire on the part of some to have a unitary, rather than a comprehensive, educational system. We fully agree with Kauffman and Hallahan (1993) that "no single curriculum, instructional approach, grouping plan, or learning environment is appropriate for all students" (p. 89).

However, in other very important ways, we believe that the Inclusion Initiative has moved beyond the REI. One difference is the context in which the Inclusion movement is taking place. In 1988 we wrote that "until and unless [the general education reform movement] is accompanied by fundamental changes in the organization of schools, especially at the secondary level, as well as by effective staff development, it will be extremely difficult for even the ablest exceptional students to measure up to expectations fostered by the school reform movement" (p. 25). It certainly is possible that fundamental changes in schooling will enable general educators to be more accommodating and successful with regard to meeting diverse educational needs of students.

In effect, we have seen some movement away from "more of the same," e.g., requiring additional math and science courses and higher standards for graduation, toward an understanding that the educational system must be changed. We are beginning to see greater attention to the roles and responsibilities of different types of educators, the extent to which general and special educators consult and cooperate with each other, and the extent to which teacher training efforts prepare teachers for more sharing, cooperative roles. We are beginning to gather information about conditions that facilitate the adoption and maintenance of effective practices. (Discussions of some of these changes are found in other chapters in this book.) Such changes—particularly if they are viewed as progress toward improved outcomes for all students, and not an end themselves—may enable schools to serve all students more effectively.

However, in our opinion, the major way in which the Inclusion Initiative appears different from the Regular Education Initiative is its greater focus on student outcomes. Given the discouraging data on outcomes from the National Longitudinal Transition Study, it appears that neither general nor special education as currently constituted have been particularly effective in promoting success for students with disabilities in school—particularly in general education classrooms—or in life after the students have left school. The work of the National Center on Educational Outcomes will be an effective vehicle for keeping this outcome focus.

In the past we have argued for more analysis as opposed to more advocacy (McKinney & Hocutt, 1988a), and we remain committed to that position. If the focus of the Inclusion Initiative is kept on student outcomes, and if reason and solid evidence as well as values are used to select the best policy solution (the "best" being the solution(s) most likely to lead to optimal student outcomes), we will in fact be better able to meet the needs of diverse students with disabilities and thus promote better outcomes.

REFERENCES

Alberg, J. (1991). Models for integration. In J. W. Lloyd, N. N. Singh, & A. C. Repp (Eds.), *The regular education initiative: Alternative perspectives on concepts, issues, and models* (pp. 211–221). Sycamore, IL: Sycamore.

Biklen, D., & Zollers, N. (1986). The focus of advocacy in the LD field. *Journal of Learning Disabilities, 19,* 579–586.

Blatt, B., & Kaplan, F. (1966). *Christmas in purgatory: A photographic essay on mental retardation.* Boston: Allyn & Bacon.

Boyer, E. L. (1983). *High school: A report on secondary education in America.* Princeton, NJ: Carnegie Foundation for the Advancement of Teaching.

Bryan, T., Bay, M., & Donahue, M. (1988). Implications of the learning disabilities definition for the regular education initiative. *Journal of Learning Disabilities, 21* (1), 23–28.

Bryan, J., & Bryan, T. (1988). Where's the beef? A review of published research on the adaptive learning environments model. *Learning Disabilities Focus, 4* (1), 15–23.

Budoff, M. (1972). Providing special education without special classes. *Journal of School Psychology, 10,* 199–205.

Carlberg, C., & Kavale, K. (1980). The efficacy of special class versus regular class placement for exceptional children: A meta-analysis. *Journal of Special Education, 14,* 295–309.

Carnegie Forum on Education and the Economy. (1986). *A nation prepared: Teachers for the
twenty-first century.* New York: Author.

Cooper, D. H., & Speece, D. L. (1990). Maintaining at-risk children in regular education settings: Initial effects of individual differences and classroom environments. *Exceptional Children, 57* (2), 117–126.

Council for Exceptional Children (1993a). *CEC Policy on Inclusive Schools and Community
Settings.* Reston, VA: Author.

Council for Exceptional Children (1993b). *Proposed CEC Policy on Inclusive Schools and Community Settings:* Language submitted to the CEC delegate assembly for approval at the
1993 CEC Convention, San Antonio, TX.

David, J. L., Cohen, M., Honetschlager, D., & Traiman, S. (1990). *State actions to restructure schools: First steps.* Washington, DC: National Governors' Association.

Deno, E. (1970). Special education as developmental capital. *Exceptional Children, 37,*
229–240.

Deno, S., Maruyama, G., Espin, C., & Cohen, C. (1990). Educating students with mild disabilities in general education classrooms: Minnesota alternatives. *Exceptional Children, 57*
(2), 150–161.

Dunn, L. M. (1968). Special education for the mildly handicapped—Is much of it justifiable?
Exceptional Children, 35, 5–22.

Florida Commission on Education Reform and Accountability (1992). Blueprint 2000: A system of school improvement and accountability. Tallahassee, FL: Author.

Fuchs, D., & Fuchs, L. S. (1988). Evaluation of the Adaptive Learning Environments Model.
Exceptional Children, 55, 115–127.

Fuchs, D., & Fuchs, L. S. (1989). Exploring effective and efficient prereferral interventions:
A component analysis of behavioral consultation. *School Psychology Review, 18,* 260–283.

Fuchs, D., & Fuchs, L. S. (1990). Making educational research more important. *Exceptional
Children, 57* (2), 102–107.

Fuchs, D., Fuchs, L. S., & Bahr, M. W. (1990). Mainstream assistance teams: A scientific basis
for the art of consultation. *Exceptional Children, 57* (2), 128–139.

Fuchs, D., & Fuchs, L.S. (1991). Framing the REI debate: Abolitionists vs. conservationists.
In J. W. Lloyd, A. C. Repp, & N. N. Singh (Eds.), *Perspectives on the integration of atypical learners in regular educational settings* (pp. 241–255). Sycamore, IL: Sycamore.

Fuchs, L. S., & Deno, S. L. (1992). Effects of curriculum within curriculum-based measurement. *Exceptional Children, 58* (3), 232–241.

Fuchs, L. S., Fuchs, D., & Bishop, N. (1992). Teacher planning for students with learning disabilities: Differences between general and special educators. *Learning Disabilities Research
and Practice, 7* (3), 120–128.

Fuchs, L. S., Fuchs, D., Hamlett, C. L., & Ferguson, C. (1992). Effects of expert system
consultation within curriculum-based measurement, using a reading maze task. *Exceptional Children, 58* (5), 436–450.

Fuchs, D., & Fuchs, L. S. (1994). Inclusive schools movement and the radicalization of special education reform. *Exceptional Children, 60* (4), 294–309.

Gersten, R., Walker, H., & Darch, C. (1988). Relationships between teachers' effectiveness
and their tolerance for handicapped students: An exploratory study. *Exceptional Children, 54,* 433–438.

Gersten, R., & Taylor, R. (in press). Direct instruction and diversity. In L. Myers and C. Utley
(Eds.), *The school reform movement: Implementing effective schooling practices and intervention strategies for multicultural students with mild disabilities.* Baltimore: Paul Brookes.

Goodlad, J. I. (1984). *A place called school: Prospects for the future.* New York: McGraw-Hill.

Hallahan, D., Keller, C., McKinney, J., Lloyd, J., & Bryan, T. (1988). Examining the research base of the regular education initiative: Efficacy studies and the adaptive learning environments model. *Journal of Learning Disabilities, 21,* 12–18.

Hallahan, D. P., McNergney, R. J., & McKinney, J. D. (1986). *Improving teacher effectiveness with learning-disabled mainstreamed students.* (OSERS Project, U.S. Department of Education). Charlottesville, VA: University of Virginia.

Hocutt, A. M., Martin, E. W., & McKinney, J. D. (1991). Historical and legal context of mainstreaming. In J. W. Lloyd, N. N. Singh, & A. C. Repp (Eds.), *The regular education initiative: Alternative perspectives on concepts, issues, and models* (pp. 17–28). Sycamore, IL: Sycamore.

Jenkins, J. R., & Leicester, N. (1992). Specialized instruction within general education: A case study of one elementary school. *Exceptional Children, 58* (6), 555–563.

Kauffman, J. M. (1991). Restructuring in sociopolitical context: Reservations about the effects of current reform proposals on students with disabilities. In J. W. Lloyd, N. N. Singh, & A. C. Repp (Eds.), *The regular education initiative: Perspectives on concepts, issues, and models* (pp. 57–66). Sycamore, IL: Sycamore.

Kauffman, J. M., Gerber, M. M., & Semmel, M. I. (1988). Arguable assumptions underlying the regular education initiative. *Journal of Learning Disabilities, 21,* 6–12.

Kauffman, J. M., & Hallahan, D. P. (1993). Toward a comprehensive delivery system for special education. In J. I. Goodlad & T. C. Lovitt (Eds.), *Integrating general and special education* (pp. 73–102). New York: Merrill.

Kaufman, M. J., Kameenui, E. J., Birman, B. & Danielson, L. (1990). Special education and the process of change: Victim or master of educational reform? *Exceptional Children, 57* (2), 109–115.

Keogh, B. K. (1988a). Improving services for problem learners: Rethinking and restructuring. *Journal of Learning Disabilities, 21,* 19–22.

Keogh, B. K. (1988b). Perspectives on the regular education initiative. *Learning Disabilities Focus, 4* (1), 3–5.

Kraft, A. (1972). Down with (most) special education classes. *Academic Therapy, 8,* 207–216.

Lilly, M. S. (1987). Lack of focus on special education in literature on educational reform. *Exceptional Children, 53,* 325–326.

Lipsky, D. K., & Gartner, A. (1991). Restructuring for quality. In J. W. Lloyd, N. N. Singh, & A. C. Repp (Eds.), *The regular education initiative: Alternative perspectives on concepts, issues, and models* (pp. 43–56). Sycamore, IL: Sycamore.

Lloyd, J. W., & Gambatese, C. (1991). Reforming the relationship between regular and special education: Background and issues. In J. W. Lloyd, N. N. Singh, & A. C. Repp (Eds.), *The regular education initiative: Alternative perspectives on concepts, issues, and models* (pp. 3–13). Sycamore, IL: Sycamore.

Madden, N., & Slavin, R. (1983). Mainstreaming students with mild handicaps: Academic and social outcomes. *Review of Educational Research, 53,* 519–569.

McGrew, K. S., Thurlow, M. L., Shriver, J. G., & Spiegel, A. N. (1992). *Inclusion of students with disabilities in national and state data collection programs* (Technical Report 2). Minneapolis, MN: University of Minnesota, National Center on Educational Outcomes.

McKinney, J. D., & Hocutt, A. M. (1988a). The need for policy analysis in evaluating the regular education initiative. *Journal of Learning Disabilities, 21,* 12–18.

McKinney, J. D. & Hocutt, A. M. (1988b). Policy issues in the evaluation of the regular education initiative. *Learning Disabilities Focus, 4,* 15–23.

Morsink, C., Soar, S., Soar, R., & Thomas, R. (1986). Research on teaching: Opening the door to special education classrooms. *Exceptional Children, 53*, 32–40.

National Association of State Directors of Special Education. (1992). *NASDSE's commitment to America 2000 educational goals.* Washington, DC: Author.

National Center on Educational Outcomes. (1993). *Educational outcomes and indicators for students completing school.* Minneapolis, MN: Author, University of Minnesota.

National Commission on Excellence in Education. (1983). *A nation at risk: The imperative for educational reform.* Washington, DC: U.S. Government Printing Office.

Nirje, B. (1969). The normalization principle and its human management implication. In R. B. Kugel & W. Wolfensberger (Eds.), *Changing patterns in residential services for the mentally retarded* (pp. 179–195). Washington, DC: President's Commission on Mental Retardation.

Nowacek, E. J., McKinney, J. D., & Hallahan, D. P. (1990). Instructional behaviors of more and less effective beginning regular and special educators. *Exceptional Children, 57* (2), 140–149.

Pugach, M., & Sapon-Shevin, M. (1987). New agendas for special education policy: What the national reports haven't said. *Exceptional Children, 53* (4), 295–299.

Reynolds, M. C. (1991). Classification and labeling. In J. W. Lloyd, N. N. Singh, & A. C. Repp (Eds.), *The regular education initiative: Alternative perspectives on concepts, issues, and models* (pp. 29–41). Sycamore, IL: Sycamore.

Reynolds, M. C., Brand, J., & Copeland, W. C. (1983). Symposium on public policy and educating handicapped persons. *Policy Studies Review, 2* (1), 12–19.

Reynolds, M., & Wang, M. C. (1983). Restructuring "special" school programs: A position paper. *Policy Studies Review, 2*, 189–212.

Reynolds, M. C., Wang, M. C. & Walberg, H. J. (1987). The necessary restructuring of special and regular education. *Exceptional Children, 53*, 391–398.

Rivera, G. (1972). *Willowbrook.* New York: Random House.

Sailor, W. (1991). Special education in the restructured school. *Remedial and Special Education, 12* (6), 8–22.

Schulte, A. C., Osborne, S. S., & McKinney, J. D. (1990). Academic outcomes for students with learning disabilities in consultation and resource programs. *Exceptional Children, 57* (2), 162–172.

Schumaker, J., & Deshler, D. (1988). Implementing the regular education initiative in secondary schools: A different ball game. *Journal of Learning Disabilities, 21* (1), 36–42.

Schumm, J. S., & Vaughn, S. (1992). Planning for mainstreamed special education students: Perceptions of general classroom teachers. *Exceptionality, 3*, 81–98.

Semmel, M. I., Abernathy, T. V., Butera, G., & Tesar, S. (1990). Teacher perceptions of special education reform: An empirical study of the regular education initiative. Unpublished manuscript, University of California at Santa Barbara.

Sizer, T. (1984). *Horace's compromise: The dilemma of the American high school.* Boston: Houghton Mifflin.

Teacher Education Division. (1986). *Message to all TED members concerning the national inquiry into the future of education for students with special needs.* Reston, VA: Author.

U.S. Department of Education. (1991). *America 2000: An education strategy sourcebook.* Washington, DC: Author.

U.S. Department of Education. (1993). *Goals 2000: Educate America act fact sheet.* Washington, DC: Author.

U.S. Senate. (1993). *Senate report 103-85 to accompany S. 1150.* Washington, DC: U.S. Government Printing Office.

Vaughn, S., Zaragoza, N., Hogan, A., & Walker, J. (1992). A four-year longitudinal investigation of the social skills and behavior problems of students with learning disabilities. *Journal of Learning Disabilities, 26* (6), 404–412.

Wagner, M. (1989). *The transition experiences of youth with disabilities: A report from the national longitudinal transition study.* Menlo Park, CA: SRI.

Walker, H., & Bullis, M. (1991). Behavior disorders and the social context of regular class integration: A conceptual dilemma? In J. W. Lloyd, N. N. Singh, & A. C. Repp (Eds.), *The regular education initiative: Alternative perspectives on concepts, issues, and models* (pp. 75–93). Sycamore, IL: Sycamore.

Wang, M. C., & Birch, J. W. (1984). Comparison of a full-time mainstreaming program and a resource room approach. *Exceptional Children, 51,* 33–40.

Wang, M. C., Peverly, S., & Randolph, R. (1984). An investigation of the implementation and effects of a full-time mainstreaming program. *Remedial and Special Education, 5* (6), 21–32.

Wang, M. C., Reynolds, M. C., & Walberg, H.J . (1986). Rethinking special education. *Educational Leadership, 44* (1), 2–31.

Weintraub, F. J. (1991). The REI debate: What if everybody is right? In J. W. Lloyd, N. N. Singh, & A. C. Repp (Eds.) *The regular education initiative: Alternative perspectives on concepts, issues, and models* (pp. 67–71). Sycamore, IL: Sycamore.

Whinery, K. W., & Fuchs, L. S. (1992). Implementing effective teaching strategies with learning disabled students through curriculum-based measurement. *Learning Disabilities Research and Practice, 7,* 25–30.

Will, M. (1986). Educating children with learning problems: A shared responsibility. *Exceptional Children, 52,* 411–416.

Wolfensberger, W. (1972). *Normalization: The principle of normalization in human services.* Toronto: National Institute on Mental Retardation.

Ysseldyke, J. E., Algozzine, B., Shinn, M., & McGrue, M. (1982). Similarities and differences between underachievers and students classified learning disabled. *Journal of Special Education, 16,* 73–85.

Ysseldyke, J. E., Algozzine, B., & Epps, S. (1983). A logical and empirical analysis of current practice in classifying students as handicapped. *Exceptional Children, 50,* 160–166.

Ysseldyke, J. E., & Algozzine, B. (1990). *Introduction to special education.* 2nd ed. Boston: Houghton Mifflin.

Ysseldyke, J. E., Algozzine, B., & Thurlow, M. L. (1992). *Critical issues in special education.* 2nd ed. Boston: Houghton Mifflin.

Ysseldyke, J. E., Thurlow, M. L., Bruininks, R. H., Gilman, C. J., Deno, S. L., McGrew, K. S. & Shiner, J. G. (1992). *A conceptual model of educational outcomes for children and youth with disabilities: Working Paper 2.* Minneapolis, MN: University of Minnesota, National Center on Educational Outcomes.

Ysseldyke, J. E., Christenson, S. L., & Thurlow, M. L. (1993). *Student learning in context model project: Final report.* Minneapolis, MN: University of Minnesota College of Education.

Zigmond, N., & Baker, J. (1990). Mainstream experiences for learning disabled students (Project MELD): Preliminary report. *Exceptional Children, 57* (2), 176–185.

4

THE LAW AND SPECIAL EDUCATION
Reconstructing the Legal Case for Care and Reform

PHILIP R. JONES

INTRODUCTION

THE summer and fall of 1975 saw congressional action that has had tremendous impact on the lives of disabled children and youth as they have pursued educational opportunities in the elementary and secondary schools of the United States. The conference report on Senate Bill 6 (S.6) was accepted by the House on November 18 with Senate approval following the next day. It is significant that only seven negative votes were recorded in each chamber as the conference report was approved (Weintraub, et al., 1976).

Ten days later, on November 29, 1975, President Gerald R. Ford signed S.6 and the Education for All Handicapped Children Act of 1975 (Public Law 94-142) was created. Culminating four years of hearings and introduction of several bills, a national mandate for special education was in place, even though such policy had been criticized by a variety of individuals and organizations.

The President expressed concerns in the following statement released at the time he signed the conference bill which had passed both the House and the Senate:

> I have approved S.6, the "Education for All Handicapped Children Act of 1975." Unfortunately, this bill promises more than the Federal Government can deliver and its good intentions could be thwarted by the many unwise provisions it contains. Everyone can agree with the objective stated in the title of this bill—educating all handicapped children in our nation. The key question is whether the bill will really accomplish that objective.
>
> Even the strongest supporters of this measure know as well as I that they are falsely raising the expectations of the groups affected by claiming authorization levels which are excessive and unrealistic.

Despite my strong support for full educational opportunities for our handicapped children, the funding levels proposed in this bill will simply not be possible if Federal expenditures are to be brought under control and a balanced budget achieved over the next few years.

There are other features in the bill which I believe to be objectionable, and which should be changed. It contains a vast array of detailed, complex and costly administrative requirements which would unnecessarily assert Federal control over traditional State and local Government functions. It establishes complex requirements under which tax dollars would be used to support administrative paperwork and not educational programs. Unfortunately, these requirements will remain in effect even though the Congress appropriates far less than the amounts contemplated in S.6.

Fortunately, since the provisions of this bill will not become fully effective until fiscal year 1978, there is time to revise the legislation and come up with a program that is effective and realistic. I will work with the Congress to use this time to design a program which will recognize the proper Federal role in helping States and localities fulfill their responsibilities in educating handicapped children. The Administration will send amendments to the Congress that will accomplish this purpose. (Office of the White House Press Secretary, 1975)

A veto of the bill, like previous Ford vetoes on popular programs such as day care for young children and school lunch, would have probably been reversed by Congress given the margin of passage.

DEVELOPMENT OF STATE RESPONSIBILITY

Prior to the education of children and youth with disabilities becoming national policy, there was an initial period of benevolence which led to permissive state legislation and subsequent state mandation and litigation. During the benevolence period, which extended into the 1930s, churches and charitable organizations provided some educational services (primarily in larger communities) to supplement the limited services provided by parents. Parents had very limited options for programs in most communities. If local programs did not exist, state residential and private residential facilities were the primary options next to keeping the disabled child at home. State legislatures began to acknowledge limited public responsibility for educating learners with disabilities through the passage of measures that allowed local education agencies (LEA) to claim state aid if they elected to operate special education programs meeting limited guidelines. In essence LEAs were given permission to operate programs and receive limited financial assistance if they actually established special education classes.

As might be expected, some localities developed programs while others didn't. Even LEAs that offered services usually did not provide programs for all categories of children with disabilities. Parents began to question why, as taxpayers who were entitled to public school education for their nondisabled children, they could not do the same for their disabled children. Parents began exerting pressure on state legislators and through the courts when local school boards failed to offer programs under permissive legislation. Beginning in the 1940s and continuing into the 1970s, state legislatures gradually passed partial and full program special education mandates. State court decrees also resulted in program mandates, usually confined to one category of disability such as educable mentally retarded.

During this same period, parents banded together to form organizations to assist in conveying their concerns to policy makers. The National Association for Retarded Children was chartered in 1950 (Jones, 1981). This group now known as The ARC became the largest parent organization with a system of state and local units. Professional organizations such as The Council for Exceptional Children also became active in the public policy arena at the state and federal level.

IMPACT OF FEDERAL COURTS

The 1954 landmark Supreme Court decision in *Brown* v. *Board of Education*, a case concerning racial discrimination, provided a basis for the rights of the disabled to become an issue in federal courts at a later date. The Brown decision stated in part:

> In these days it is doubtful that any child may reasonably be expected to succeed in life if he is denied the opportunity of an education. Such an opportunity, where the state has undertaken to provide it, is a right which must be available to all on equal terms.

The Pennsylvania Association for Retarded Citizens (PARC) filed a class action suit in federal district court against the Commonwealth of Pennsylvania on January 7, 1971, the case was on behalf of all mentally retarded persons, residents of the Commonwealth of Pennsylvania, who have been, are being, or may be denied access to a free public program of education and training while they are, or were, less than twenty-one years of age (PARC, 1971). The resulting consent decree clearly established the right to education and training of Pennsylvania's mentally retarded children in local schools and public residential facilities.

Where the PARC case concerned only the mentally retarded, the 1972 decision in *Mills* v. *Board of Education* of the District of Columbia extended the right to education for all categories of children and youth with disabilities. Mills (1972) also denied the district school's argument that a lack of fiscal resources prevented the provision of special education and related services by stating: "available funds must be expended equitably in such a manner that no child is entirely excluded from a publicly-supported education consistent with his needs and ability to benefit therefrom."

The two federal cases, PARC and Mills, also addressed the issues of nondiscriminatory evaluation, least restrictive environment, timely notice, free public education and related services for the plaintiff classes. These rights were subsequently included in the federal mandate (P.L. 94-142, 1975).

Only the states of Ohio and Mississippi did not have some form of special education mandate by the date P.L. 94-142 was signed. State statutes or court decrees existed in the other 48 states (Abeson & Ballard, 1976). Lack of enforcement of the state mandates, limited coverage of age groups, and limited age ranges served continued to result in the lack of services in communities throughout the nation. The Michigan statutory mandate, passed in 1971, provided for comprehensive services for all children with disabilities from birth through age 25. Many of the state mandates restricted the age range from 5 to 18.

Unique features of P.L. 94-142, which revised only Part B of the Education of the Handicapped Act containing the state grant program, included the following:

- it was permanent legislation and did not require periodic reauthorization as did other parts of the EHA
- it was based primarily on existing state and federal statutes and case law
- it had a funding formula which permitted every state, congressional district, and LEA to qualify for funds.

The latter factor, having strong political appeal, is probably the reason that the margin of passage was so great. The development of the formula had come a few months before passage of the act culminated four years of debate.

While P.L. 94-142 language called for education and related services for eligible children and youth ages 3 through 21, statutory language also included the statement "unless inconsistent with state law or policy." Thus many states with mandates for narrower age ranges were *still* not required to meet the 3–21 policy. The true mandated ages were 6–18. In practice, the family with a 3-year-old preschooler with disabilities receiving an educational program in Michigan would have no program if they moved to a state such as West Virginia where state mandates began at age 6.

Major Amendments to Statutes

While Congress made relatively minor changes in the Education for All Handicapped Children Act for an 11-year period, clearly the need to address the narrow age ranges of approximately half the states was a major factor in P.L. 99-457, which amended the act. In essence all states were required to serve preschool children within a four-year period. Additional incentive funds were authorized and appropriated by Congress to assist states in implementing special education for ages 3 through 5. The 1986 amendments also created the infants and toddlers program (Part H, Education of the Handicapped Act). Part H provided additional funding to states to plan for and initiate limited services for eligible children birth through 2 years of age. States are still not required to serve students with disabilities aged 19, 20, or 21, if their state mandate ends at age 18.

The 1990 Education of the Handicapped Act Amendments, P.L. 101-476, was signed October 30, 1990. The most obvious amendment was the renaming of the Education of the Handicapped Act to the Individuals with Disabilities Education

Act (IDEA) with technical amendments to change terminology from "handicapped children" to "children and youth with disabilities." The IDEA also contained several other additions and changes including:

- adding autism and traumatic brain injury to the list of disabilities which may result in the need for special education
- adding rehabilitation counseling and social work services to the listed related services
- defining transition services to promote movement from secondary school to postsecondary education, training, employment, or other adult or community programs and services
- requiring the IEP to include a statement on transition services by age 16 or younger when appropriate
- defining assistive technology devices and services
- clearly stating that no state is immune to federal suit for violations.

Other changes having less direct impact on the education of disabled children and youth dealt with administration of discretionary grants, regional resource centers, personnel training, and research.

In the 15-year period from 1975 through 1990, special education mandates were not only passed at the federal level, two major amendments were enacted. Each of the major amendments significantly expanded the scope of the 1975 statute.

Related Statutes

The discussion up to this point has focused on special education law as it developed in the twentieth century. In reality the federal government had been involved in the education and care of disabled citizens since the passage of P.L. 19-8 in 1827 . . . "to complete the location of the grant to the Deaf and Dumb Asylum of Kentucky" (La Vor, 1976). Over the next 100 years, 28 federal acts relating to citizens with disabilities were passed by Congress. The period 1927 to 1949 saw 32 such acts followed by 1950 to 1959, 18 acts; 1960 to 1969, 54 acts; and 1970 to 1975, 75 acts.

The most significant related federal statute passed by Congress in the period immediately prior to P.L. 94-142 was P.L. 93-112, The Rehabilitation Act of 1973. Section 504 of that act has far-reaching implications for individuals with disabilities in all aspects of their lives. Section 504 guarantees the civil rights of and prohibits discrimination against individuals with disabilities in education, employment, and all activities. The actual language of Section 504 is brief:

> no otherwise qualified individual with a disability in the United States, . . . shall, solely by reason of his disability, be excluded from the participation in, be denied the benefit of, or be subjected to discrimination under any program or activity receiving federal financial assistance. (Note: original terminology of *handicapped* replaced with the current preferred terminology of *disabled*)

Public education is a covered program since a host of federal programs provide funding for school lunch, Chapter 1, special education, and other activities. There are, in reality, few activities that do not receive federal financial assistance. A grocery store, for example, receives food stamps which are a form of federal financial assistance.

While Section 504 predated P.L. 94-142 by two years, parents and advocates focused their attention primarily on P.L. 94-142 compliance issues and litigation through the late 1980s. Only then did Section 504 complaints become common in public education. An individual with a disability may not need special education and therefore would not qualify for special education services under IDEA. The individual would be covered under Section 504 if otherwise qualified to participate in the activity. Modifications to the activity or procedure may be required to allow for participation and, in the schools, a Section 504 plan would be developed. Modifications might include such things as allowing additional time to complete a test or seating in a quiet room to complete a test if the individual was diagnosed to have attention deficit hyperactivity disorder (ADHD). If the condition is severe, ADHD could result in the need for special education and related services generally under categorical determinations of learning disabled, emotionally disturbed, or other health impaired. In such cases the full protections of the IDEA would apply and an IEP would be developed by the required team. A Section 504 plan is not as formal in terms of content or required participants in its development as is an IEP.

The most recent major act passed by Congress was the Americans with Disabilities Act (ADA), P.L. 101-336. This act basically extended the Section 504 protections to all programs and activities, not just those receiving federal financial assistance. ADA, passed in the same session as IDEA, has had less impact on students with disabilities in the schools because Section 504 had been in effect since 1973.

MAJOR PROVISIONS OF FEDERAL SPECIAL EDUCATION LAW

Major Provisions of Part B of the Individuals with Disabilities Education Act include the right to a free appropriate education, delivery of services in the least restrictive setting possible, nondiscriminatory testing and evaluation, and procedural safeguards. The statute and implementing regulations are highly procedural and describe step-by-step sequences of events to be followed when a child is referred, evaluated, eligibility is determined, an individualized education program is developed, and placement is determined.

Free Appropriate Public Education

Each eligible child with a disability must be provided a free appropriate public education. Among the many definitions contained in Section 602 of IDEA may be found:

> The term free appropriate public education means special education and related services that (A) have been provided at public expense, under public

supervision and direction, and without charge, (B) meet the standards of the State educational agency, (C) include an appropriate preschool, elementary, or secondary school education in the State involved, and (D) are provided in conformity with the individualized education program required under section 614(a)(5) of this title.

The terms *special education, related services,* and *individualized education program,* also defined in this section, become important since they are mentioned above. These definitions state:

The term *special education* means specially designed instruction, at no cost to parents or guardians, to meet the unique needs of a child with a disability, including (A) instruction conducted in the classroom, in the home, in hospitals and institutions, and in other settings; and (B) instruction in physical education. The term *related services* means transportation, and such developmental, corrective, and other supportive services (including speech pathology and audiology, psychological services, physical and occupational therapy, recreation, including therapeutic recreation, social work services, counseling services, including rehabilitation counseling, and medical services, except that such medical services shall be for diagnostic and evaluation purposes only) as may be required to assist a child with a disability to benefit from special education, and includes the early identification and assessment of disabling conditions in children.

The term *individualized education program* means a written statement for each child with a disability developed in any meeting by a representative of the local educational agency or an intermediate educational unit who shall be qualified to provide, or supervise the provision of, specially designed instruction to meet the unique needs of children with disabilities, the teacher, the parents or guardian of such child, and whenever appropriate, such child, which statement shall include: A) a statement of the present levels of educational performance of such child; B) a statement of annual goals, including short-term instructional objectives; C) a statement of the specific educational services to be provided to such child, and the extent to which the child will be able to participate in regular educational programs; D) a statement of the needed transition services for students beginning no later than age 16 and annually thereafter (and, when determined appropriate for the individual, beginning at age 14 or younger), including when appropriate, a statement of the interagency responsibilities or linkages (or both) before the student leaves the school setting; E) the projected date for initiation and anticipated duration of such services; and F) appropriate objective criteria and evaluation procedures and schedules for determining, on at least an annual basis, whether instructional objectives are being achieved. In the case where a participating agency, other than the educational agency, fails to provide the agreed upon services, the educational agency shall reconvene the IEP team to identify alternative strategies to meet the transition objectives.

The Supreme Court first addressed special education in 1982. The decision in *Board of Education* v. *Rowley* did not support the assignment of a sign language interpreter for Amy Rowley since the Hendrick Hudson School District had followed procedures, provided the program and services specified in the IEP, and Amy was receiving passing grades which allowed her to progress from grade to grade. In Amy's case, the provision of a sign language interpreter would have approximated an ideal or most appropriate program. The Court made it clear that the statute requires the program to be appropriate, but not ideal. The decision, while resolving the issue of the interpreter only for this child at this time, had more importance in that the Court reaffirmed the procedural requirements of IDEA and provided a test to determine if a program is appropriate. Addressing procedures, the Court stated:

> When the elaborate and highly specific procedural safeguards embodied in Section 1415 are contrasted with the general and somewhat imprecise substantive admonitions contained in the Act, we think that the importance Congress attached to these procedural safeguards cannot be gainsaid (458 U.S. 176, 204).

Subsequently, the Court elaborated on procedures as it established a test to determine appropriateness of program in stating:

> First, has the state complied with the procedures set forth in the Act? And second, is the individualized educational program developed through the Acts procedures reasonably calculated to enable the child to receive educational benefits? (458 U.S. 176, 206-207)

A negative answer to the first question can negate even considering the second question. In other words, procedural violations alone can result in a court's decision that a disabled child has been denied a free, appropriate public education. Had the Hendrick Hudson School District not followed the mandated procedures, it is possible the Court would have required the provision of the interpreter. In *Spielberg* v. *Henrico County School Board* (1987), the judge concluded that school officials had determined that the Spielberg child would be returned from an out-of-state private residential school placement and placed in a local day school program before an IEP was developed with the Spielbergs. This was a clear procedural violation so the court did not even review the quality of the program available locally and required the school district to continue paying tuition to the private facility. Procedural violations had been previously found to deny a free, appropriate public education in the appellate court decisions of *Hall* v. *Vance County* (1985) and *Jackson* v. *Franklin County* (1985). Even the best IEP may be deemed worthless if the required participants were not in the meeting and merely asked to sign the document later!

The Supreme Court has also addressed related services in the case of Amber Tatro (1984), a child with a disability who required clean intermittent catheterization

(CIC). Two issues were addressed by the court. First, was CIC a service that was required to assist Amber in benefitting from special education, and second, was CIC a medical service beyond those required for diagnosis or evaluation? The decision clearly indicated that Amber would be unable to attend school, and even receive special education, if CIC was not provided as needed during the school day. CIC was ruled to be a required related service that could be performed in a few minutes by a layperson with less than an hour's training and therefore was not a medical service. Courts have tended to determine if a service is medical by determining whether or not the individual providing the service must be a physician. Many related services that are medically related (and even prescribed in cases such as administration of medication or physical therapy) may be performed by a teacher, an aide, a counselor or social worker, a qualified therapist, or other personnel.

Least Restrictive Setting

The older terms of *integration* and *mainstreaming* coupled with more recent terms coming from reform movements such as *regular education initiative* and *inclusion* all are related to the concept of *least restrictive environment* (LRE) which is based on the statutory language of IDEA. Section 612 states:

> The State has established . . . procedures to assure that to the maximum extent appropriate, children with disabilities, including children in public or private institutions or other care facilities, are educated with children who are not disabled, and that special classes, separate schooling, or other removal of children with disabilities from the regular educational environment occurs only when the nature or severity of the disability is such that education in regular classes with the use of supplementary aids and services cannot be achieved satisfactorily. . . .

Implementing regulations translate this requirement to each public agency which includes all LEAs. Section 300.551 provides elaboration on what is required:

> a) Each public agency shall ensure that a continuum of alternative placements is available to meet the needs of children with disabilities for special education and related services. b) The continuum must—1) Include the alternative placements listed in the definition of special education under Sec. 300.17 (instruction in regular classes, special classes, special schools, home instruction, and instruction in hospitals and institutions); and 2) Make provision for supplementary services (such as resource room or itinerant instruction) to be provided in conjunction with regular class placement.

Section 300.552 continues and describes the procedural steps to be taken by LEA officials in deciding placement:

Each public agency shall ensure that: a) The educational placement of each child with a disability—1) Is determined at least annually; 2) Is based on his or her IEP; and 3) Is as close as possible to the child's home. b) The various alternative placements included at Sec. 300.551 are available to the extent necessary to implement the IEP for each child with a disability. c) Unless the IEP of a child with a disability requires some other arrangement, the child is educated in the school that he or she would attend if nondisabled. d) In selecting the LRE, consideration is given to any potential harmful effect on the child or on the quality of services that he or she needs.

Both in the statute and regulations, it appears a clear preference exists for providing special education and related services when possible with children without disabilities, given the language "to the maximum extent appropriate" and "provided in conjunction with regular class placement." However, the language suggests that not every child with disability can be accommodated in the regular classroom by stating a continuum of alternative placements must be available.

As special education programs and services have developed since the passage of P.L. 94-142, the greatest percentage of children identified could be considered to have mild disabilities. This is particularly true for children with learning disabilities, educable mental retardation, and emotional disturbance. Over half of the 4.7 million children served under IDEA in 1991–92 were classified as learning disabled. So-called pull-out programs—special classes, resource rooms, and therapy sessions have required the child to leave the regular classroom for short or extended periods of time. While special educators may have supported such programs, often regular educators did not want to adapt their programs to accommodate the learner with mild disabilities and sought the full or partial removal of the child from the regular class. Children with moderate or severe disabilities were usually segregated into special classes and separate schools. As a result, special education was often accused of being separate from regular education. The actual degree of separateness varied greatly depending on the various LEAs.

Madeline Will (1986) explored these issues in an article entitled "Educating Children with Learning Problems: A Shared Responsibility." This article is often cited as the stimulus for the Regular Education Initiative. A merger of regular and special education was proposed. As the nation entered yet another period of educational reform in the late 1980s, some special educators have tended to line up behind the call for inclusion of special education students in regular classrooms or full inclusion of all children with disabilities in regular education. At the same time, other special educators are calling for a maintenance of the continuum of services. In its 1993 international convention, the Council for Exceptional Children adopted a policy statement on inclusion. The Council membership had been studying the issue for several years. The adopted statement basically calls for an individual decision based on the needs of each child and suggests that inclusion is one aspect of the mandated continuum of services. As professionals have grappled with the issue, so have the courts.

While no cases have yet reached the Supreme Court solely on the LRE issue, it appears to be only a matter of time. Circuit courts have issued apparently conflicting opinions. Recognizing the congressional preference for regular education placement with supplementary aids and services and placement as close to the child's home as possible, the circuit decisions up to the 1990s supported the need for the continuum and called for the individual determination in every case as opposed to having a separate school for all children with like disabilities. If, for example, an LEA placed all children with trainable mental retardation in a separate school, they did not have the needed continuum. It also appeared the reverse would be true. Advocates of inclusion hailed the decision in the Oberti case (1992). This case, upheld by the Third Circuit in May 1993, required the placement of a child with Down syndrome in a regular classroom. The Clementon School District did not provide a local program for children with trainable mental retardation and had placed the child in a segregated school outside of district boundaries. Clementon provided no opportunity for services to such children *with* children without disabilities, which led the court to decide in favor of the regular classroom placement.

Another case involving a child with moderately mentally retardation was decided in 1992. In *Board of Sacramento City Unified School District* v. *Holland* (1992), the school district had been serving Rachel Holland in special education classes with part-time placement with children without disabilities (approximately one hour per day) and had proposed half-time placement in regular classes and half-time placement in special education classes. The parents sought full-time placement in the regular program with supportive services. When the parents prevailed at the due process hearing level, the school district appealed to the court. After reviewing the educational benefits and nonacademic benefits to Rachel, the effect on the teacher and other children, and cost factors, the court ordered placement in a regular second grade classroom with supplemental services from a special educator and an aide. The Holland decision has been upheld by the Ninth Circuit Court of Appeals. Where the Clementon schools provided no opportunity for services with children without disabilities, Sacramento did.

Litigation will continue on inclusion and LRE issues. As noted earlier, the Supreme Court will soon be required to decide one of these types of cases due to apparent conflicts in decisions of the various circuits. It appears the Sacramento case will be appealed and the Supreme Court must then decide whether or not review is warranted.

Nondiscriminatory Testing and Evaluation

Special education classes prior to the passage of the federal mandate served a disproportionate number of children and youth from minority groups. This was particularly true for black children and, in border states, Mexican-American children. Section 612 of IDEA contains the following language to address this problem:

5) The State has established . . . C) procedures to assure that testing and evaluation materials and procedures utilized for the purposes of evaluation and placement of children with disabilities will be selected and administered so as not to be racially or culturally discriminatory. Such materials or procedures shall be provided and administered in the child's native language or mode of communication, unless it clearly is not feasible to do so, and no single procedure shall be the sole criterion for determining an appropriate educational program for a child.

Section 300.532 of the regulations provides additional guidance on the implementation of the requirement. The section, entitled "Evaluation Procedures," states:

State educational agencies and LEAs shall ensure, at a minimum, that: a) Tests and other evaluation materials—1) Are provided and administered in the child's native language or other mode of communication, unless it is clearly not feasible to do so; 2) Have been validated for the specific purpose for which they are used; and 3) Are administered by trained personnel in conformance with the instructions provided by their producer. b) Tests and other evaluation materials include those tailored to assess specific areas of educational need and not merely those that are designed to provide a single general intelligence quotient. c) Tests are selected and administered so as best to ensure that when a test is administered to a child with impaired sensory, manual, or speaking skills, the test results accurately reflect the child's aptitude or achievement level or whatever other factors the test purports to measure, rather than reflecting the child's impaired sensory, manual, or speaking skills (except where those skills are the factors that the test purports to measure). d) No single procedure is used as the sole criterion for determining an appropriate educational program for a child. e) The evaluation is made by a multidisciplinary team or group of persons, including at least one teacher or other specialist with knowledge in the area of suspected disability. f) The child is assessed in all areas related to the suspected disability, including, if appropriate, health, vision, hearing, social and emotional status, general intelligence, academic performance, communicative status, and motor abilities.

The regulations are fairly detailed, as is the case throughout. Little current litigation has been observed in this area. This does not mean that the problem is solved but it may be that the detail of the regulation has resulted in resolution of disputes at the due process hearing level. In the early to mid 1980s, cases in California (Larry P.) and Illinois (PASE) resulted in conflicting decisions. In California, standardized I.Q. tests were found to be racially discriminatory toward black children, and the court enjoined the state from using such tests in the placement of black children in classes for the educable mentally retarded. In Illinois, such tests, when used with other criteria, were ruled not to discriminate against black students in the special education eligibility determination for educable mentally handicapped. As suggested by the regulations, the use of multiple measures seemed to be the key factor in the Illinois case.

Procedural Safeguards

The extensive procedural safeguards afforded parents and their disabled children are covered in Section 615 of IDEA and Sections 300.500–515 of the regulations. (The complete text of these sections has not been included due to limitations on space. The interested reader is encouraged to review the full text of these sections if they have not already done so.) The entire special education process is built on a system of input and discussion between parents and professionals. As stated by Jones (1981):

> While the procedures are of great significance, in reality they merely call for fair play and parental involvement in decisions regarding a handicapped child. Active and open communication with parents can resolve many disputes and reduce the number of potential due process hearings.

The parents of a child with a disability have the right to review all of the education records of their child. This is a right during the time of referral, evaluation, placement, or provision of special education to the child.

If the parents disagree with the evaluation of their child, they are entitled to an independent educational evaluation at public expense unless the school district initiates a hearing to show that its evaluation is appropriate. Independent evaluations are to be completed by qualified examiners not employed by the school district. Parents may obtain independent evaluations at their own expense at any time, and the schools must consider the results of such evaluation in planning the child's program.

Parental consent must be secured before the schools conduct a preplacement evaluation. If the child is found eligible for special education, parental consent must again be obtained before the initial placement. Consent is defined as informed consent in which the parent is fully informed of the activity, and the consent must be given in writing. The parent must also be informed that consent may be revoked at any time. If the parents refuse consent, the schools may initiate a hearing to attempt to gain approval to proceed. Unfortunately, many LEAs do not pursue the hearing route when the child is suffering educationally, even though they have a moral obligation to proceed to a hearing.

Written notice must be provided to the parents in a reasonable time before the LEA proposes to initiate or change the identification, evaluation, or educational placement of the child or provision of free appropriate education of the child. Such notice must also be made when the LEA refuses a parental request in the above procedures. The notice must inform the parents of all their rights, contain a description of the action proposed and why the agency plans to take the action, and a description of other options considered. The notice must also describe each evaluation procedure, test, record, or report the LEA used as a basis for the proposal and any other relevant information. The language used in the notice must be understandable to the general public and provided in the native language of the home or other mode of communication.

If a dispute arises, hopefully the LEA and the parent may reach an agreement through informal discussion or mediation techniques, in those communities where such are available. The parent or LEA may initiate a due process hearing to resolve a dispute. Discussion and mediation cannot be used to delay a request for a hearing. When a hearing is requested by either party or when the parent requests the information, the LEA must inform the parent of any free or low-cost legal or other relevant services available in the area. The parents must also be informed that if they prevail in the hearing or subsequent litigation, the courts may award them reasonable attorneys' fees.

An impartial hearing officer is appointed based on the procedures of the state. States are required to provide initial and periodic updated training for hearing officers. The hearing officer must conduct the hearing and render a decision within 45 days of the request for the hearing. During the hearing either party has the right to be represented by attorneys or individuals with special knowledge of the problems of children with disabilities. They may present evidence and confront, cross-examine, and subpoena witnesses. The parties must disclose the evidence and list of witnesses they plan to use at least five days before the hearing and any additional evidence may be prohibited. The parties are entitled to a record of the hearing and a copy of the findings of facts and decisions of the hearing officer. Only the parents have the right to have the child present at the hearing and to open the hearing to the public.

After a decision is reached, any party may appeal the decision. In approximately half the states, this appeal goes to the state education agency for review and seeking of additional evidence, if necessary. A decision must be made by the state review officer not later than 30 days after the appeal. The state review officer's decision may be appealed to state or federal court. In the states not having the state education agency review, the initial hearing is actually considered a state hearing and any appeal of the decision goes to the courts as above.

Hearings must be conducted at times and places convenient to the parents and child involved. It should also be noted that the hearing officer may grant specific extensions of the timelines at the request of either party.

During any dispute resolution activity, including mediation, hearing, or judicial proceeding, the child must remain in his or her current placement unless the parents and the school can agree on a change. Since a court case can take years, it seems logical that the parties could agree on changes to allow the child to be placed in age-appropriate situations.

When a parent is unknown or otherwise unavailable, a surrogate parent must be appointed to protect the rights of the child. The surrogate must have no conflict of interest and must have the knowledge and skills to represent the child.

While a number of cases have been heard on whether or not these safeguards have been violated, possibly the provision that the child remains in the current placement during the dispute resolution process has received the most attention by LEA staff. Discipline procedures for children with disabilities are not addressed in IDEA or the regulations. The required free appropriate education has, however, become an issue when an LEA wishes to suspend or expel a child with disabilities. Such action is a change of program and is subject to the requirements of providing notice to the parents. The parents in turn may request a due process hearing if they feel the suspension or expulsion will deprive their child of free appropriate public education. The child must then be maintained in the current placement until the dispute is resolved. Again it should be noted that appeals to the courts can take years before a decision is reached. The Supreme Court ruled that the expulsion of children with disabilities is a change of placement and invokes the procedural safeguards of the statute in the case of *Honig* v. *Doe* (1988). This case clearly established that children with disabilities while subject to the discipline procedures utilized with students without disabilities, also have their additional rights under IDEA. The Honig case does allow the schools to seek a judicial temporary restraining order to remove a child with disabilities who is considered dangerous from the school setting.

Technically a school board may formally expel a child with a disability, but the schools are still obligated to provide a free appropriate public education for the child. It may well be that only the location of program delivery is changed by such action.

A CLOSING NOTE

Dress codes and hair styles along with discipline were the major topics of hearings and court cases involving elementary and secondary education in the 1950s and 1960s. Such issues have been replaced by special education as the primary topic today. Since the passage of P.L. 94-142, thousands of due process hearings and hundreds of court cases have been decided. The body of special education case law continues to evolve and will do so for the foreseeable future. Congress has amended the statute twice in response to Supreme Court decisions. When the Supreme Court decided parents were not eligible for reimbursement of attorneys' fees in *Smith* v. *Robinson* (1984) and decided states were immune from suit under the eleventh amendment to the constitution in *Dellmuth* v. *Muth*, (1989), the Court suggested that Congress might wish to revisit the statute if they had a different interpretation. Congress did just that by clearly allowing attorneys' fees and removing state immunity through amendments.

Special education law is a fascinating area of inquiry. This chapter, at best, is only an introduction. The bottom line is that the federal law is still clearly written and interpreted as was intended. The law is not written to benefit the parents, the teacher, school administrators, or state officials. The law is written for the individual child with disabilities, and special education continues to be delivered under the individualized education program approach.

REFERENCES

Abeson, A., & Ballard, J. (1976). State and federal policy for exceptional children. In F. J. Weintraub, A. Abeson, J. Ballard, and M. L. Lavor (Eds.) (1975). *Public policy and the education of exceptional children*. Reston, VA: The Council for Exceptional Children.

Code of federal regulations, Chapter 34, Part 300, Washington, DC, 1992.

Jones, P. R. (1981). *A practical guide to federal special education law*. New York: Holt, Rinehart and Winston.

La Vor, M. L. (1976). Federal legislation for exceptional persons: A history. In F.J. Weintraub, A. Abeson, J. Ballard, and M. L. La Vor (Eds.) (1975).

Office of the White House Press Secretary (1975). Statement by the President. Washington, DC, December 2.

Weintraub, F. J., Abeson, A., Ballard, J., and La Vor, M. L., (Eds.) (1976). *Public policy and the education of exceptional children*. Reston, VA: The Council for Exceptional Children.

Will, M. (1986). Educating children with learning problems: A shared responsibility. *Exceptional Children, 52* (5), 411–415.

TABLE OF CASES

Board of Education v. Rowley, 458 U.S. 176, 102 S. Ct. 3034, 73 L. Ed., 2d 690 (1982).

Board of Sacramento City Unified School District v. Holland, 786 F. Supp. 874 (E.D. Ca., 1992).

Brown v. Board of Education, 347 U.S. 483 (1954).

Dellmuth v. Muth, 491 U.S. 223 (1989).

Hall v. Vance County Board of Education, 774 F.2d 629 (4th Cir. 1985).

Honig v. Doe, 484 U.S. 305, 108 S. Ct. 592, 98 L. Ed. 2d 686 (1988).

Jackson v. Franklin County School Board, 606 F. Supp. 152 (S.D. Miss. 1985).

Larry P. v. Riles, 343 F. Supp. 1306, *aff'd.*, 502 F. 2d 963, *further proceedings*, 495 F. Supp. 926, aff'd., 502 F. 2d 693 (9th Cir. 1984).

Mills v. D.C. Board of Education, 348 F. Supp. 866 (D.D.C 1972).

Oberti v. Board of Education of Borough of Clementon School District, 789 F. Supp 1322 (D.N.J. 1992).

PASE (Parents in Action in Special Education) v. Hannon, 506 F. Supp. 831 (N.D. Ill. 1980).

Pennsylvania Association for Retarded Citizens (PARC) v. Commonwealth of Pennsylvania, 334 F. Supp. 1257, 343 F. Supp. 279 (E.D. Pa. 1971, 1972).

Smith v. Robinson, 468 U.S. 992, 104 S. Ct. 3457, 82 L. Ed. 2d 746 (1984).

Spielberg v. Henrico County Public Schools, EHLR 558:202 (E.D. Va. 1987).

Tatro v. Sate of Texas, 481 F. Supp. 1224 (N.D. Tex. 1979), *rev'd.*, 625 F. 2d 557 (5th Cir. 1980), *on remand*, 516 F. Supp. 968, *rev'd.*, 703 F.2d 823 (5th Cir. 1983), *aff'd.*, 468 U.S. 883, 104 S. Ct. 3371, 82 L. Ed. 2d 664 (1984).

5

EARLY INTERVENTION IN THE CONTEXT OF SCHOOL REFORM AND INCLUSION

LYNN LAVELY & JAN McCARTHY

INTRODUCTION

CHAPTERS two and three focus on substantive changes currently underway that should impact on programs and services for school-aged children. This chapter will discuss the philosophical, programmatic, professional education, and policy issues and concerns associated with early intervention/early education in the context of educational reform.

SCHOOL REFORM

In 1981 the Secretary of Education, Terrel Bell, established the National Commission on Excellence in Education to study the condition of education in America. The report of the Commission, *A Nation at Risk*, which was released in April 1983, warned us that our country is at serious risk educationally. The now-familiar language describes our educational system as "a rising tide of mediocrity" and told us, "If an unfriendly foreign power had attempted to impose on America the mediocre educational performance that exists today, we might well have viewed it as an act of war" (National Commission on Excellence in Education, 1983, p. 5).

A Nation at Risk got the attention of the American people. The result was a dramatic response from the states in the form of legislation related to school reform. These related reforms came in two waves. The first wave focused on mandates related to external factors designed to increase excellence—more rigorous graduation requirements, increased per-pupil spending, changes in curriculum, particularly related to math and science, more stringent teacher certification requirements, differential salary schedules, and competency testing for teachers and students. The second wave focused on schools and the role of adults.

> Increasingly realizing the top-down policies and mandates were having little impact on schools, many policy makers joined some grassroots reformers in proposing greater decentralization of district authority to individual sites. The school as the center of change and the empowerment of principals and teachers to effect improvement were central to the rhetoric of reconstruction by the beginning of the 1990s. (Goodlad, 1992, p. 1)

Indicative of the second wave of school reforms were such initiatives as site-based management, school choice, business partnerships, and continued emphasis on excellence.

Blatantly missing in both waves of school reform was any emphasis on equity issues or the education of children with handicaps. "The silence about the needs of or outcomes for handicapped children in the current reform movement is deafening" (Hocutt, Martin, & McKinney, 1991, p. 24).

Historically, excellence and equity, goals of national concern, have erroneously been viewed as mutually exclusive and incompatible. "Maintaining a free and open democracy demands that we actively pursue equity along with educational excellence for children who are handicapped because of race, sex, socioeconomic status or physical disability" (Committee on Economic Development, 1985, pp. 23–24). No major report on educational reform recognized or addressed the importance of children with special needs and/or early intervention until *Investing in Our Children* was published in 1985. This report recommended preschool programs for the disadvantaged as part of the 10 imperatives necessary for school reform (Committee on Economic Development, 1985, p. 3). In 1987, another report, *Children in Need*, made an even stronger statement. "Now we call on the nation to embark upon a third wave of reform that gives the highest priority to early and sustained intervention in the lives of disadvantaged children" (Committee on Economic Development, 1987, p. 3).

We are now in the midst of the third wave of school reform, which recognizes the needs of special populations and their families and/or caregivers and early intervention for all children. The focus on families and early intervention is a different policy territory for public schools. This presents new challenges, such as the concepts presented in the Regular Education Initiative and/or Inclusion. These changes have created a context that has influenced the way in which traditional education and teacher educators are having to rethink their work.

EARLY INTERVENTION

As reflected in the following statement, there is a growing national policy commitment to young children and awareness that early education programs are needed:

Our nation is in the midst of a major education reform movement and a major effort to build a new system for serving preschool children and their parents. Our public education system is searching for models and strategies to improve the quality of teaching and learning in classrooms, and to enhance the contribution of education to our economic growth and social welfare. At the same time, the early childhood community has developed a comprehensive vision of the components of effective services for young children and their families. They are working to construct a funding and delivery system to carry out this vision. (National Association of State School Boards of Education [NASSBE] Task Force on Early Childhood Education, 1988, p. vii)

Three assumptions underlie early intervention for young children: a) reduction of academic failure; b) self-realization and self-sufficiency; and c) economic or cost-effectiveness. The efficacy of early education for young handicapped or at-risk children and their families is no longer an issue. There is sufficient evidence and documentation and a growing body of literature that demonstrate intervention programs for young handicapped and at-risk children can benefit from quality preschool programs (Berrueta-Clement, Schweinhart, Barnett, Epstein, & Weikart, 1984; Lazar, 1988; Lazar & Darlington, 1982; Schweinhart & Wiekart, 1980).

Quality preschool programs clearly provide one of the most cost-effective strategies for lowering the dropout rate and helping at-risk children to become more effective learners and productive citizens. It has been shown that for every $1 spent on a comprehensive and intensive preschool program for the disadvantaged, society saves up to $6 in the long-term costs of welfare, remedial education, teen pregnancy, and crime. (Committee on Economic Development, 1991, p. 28)

It would be hard to imagine that society could find a higher yield for one dollar of investment than that found in preschool programs for at-risk children (Committee on Economic Development, 1985).

The rationale for early education of handicapped and at-risk children can be built on eight major premises. Collectively these premises produce a cohesive argument as to why early intervention programs are needed to help handicapped children develop as normally as possible in spite of their limitations. When a young child is found to have a handicap or to be at-risk for developmental disabilities, intervention should be initiated as early as possible because:

1. During the early years the initial patterns of learning and behavior that set the pace for and influence the nature of all subsequent development are established.

2. Research suggests the presence of certain critical periods, particularly during the early years, when a child is most susceptible and responsive to learning experiences.
3. Intelligence and other human capacities are not fixed at birth but, rather, are shaped to some extent by environmental influences and through learning.
4. Handicapping conditions and other factors that render a child at risk for developmental disabilities can interfere with development and learning so that the original disabilities become more severe and secondary handicaps will appear.
5. A child's environment and early experiences, particularly the degree to which these are nurturing or depriving, have a major effect upon development and learning; both greatly influence the degree to which a child reaches his or her full potential.
6. Early intervention programs can make a significant difference in the developmental status of young children and can do so more rapidly than later remedial efforts after a child has entered elementary school.
7. Parents need special assistance in establishing constructive patterns of parenting with a young handicapped or at-risk child and in providing adequate care, stimulation, and training for their child during the critical years when basic developmental skills should be acquired.
8. Early intervention implies some economic–social benefits in that prevention or early treatment of developmental problems in young children may reduce more serious, burdensome problems for society to cope with later, including their accompanying costs. (Peterson, 1989, pp. 5–6)

Early education for all our young children is a necessary condition for the economic growth and social welfare of our nation. Other modern nations give far more attention to the preschool child than the United States does. In 1985 there were only 400,000 children actually in Head Start while at least 3 million were eligible (Hodgkinson, 1985).

A persistent problem and concern to us is that children who have the greatest need for early childhood services are the least likely to receive those services.

> The combination of state, federal, and local programs falls far short of meeting needs of at-risk children for preschool, working parents for child care, or new parents for education and support. Under present arrangements, children of low-income parents (who derive the most dramatic benefits from high-quality preschool experiences) are less likely to be enrolled than children from middle- and upper-income homes. (Fewer than 33% of four-year-olds whose families had incomes of less than $10,000 in 1985 were enrolled in a preschool program. In contrast, 67% of four-year-olds whose families earned $35,000 a year or more attended preschool. (NASSBE Task Force on Early Childhood Education Report, 1988, p. 6)

Fortunately, a growing awareness of the need for early education and a national policy that gradually is strengthening the commitment to young children have resulted in an escalation of services for preschool children and a new sense of urgency. Early education is beginning to be viewed as a critical component for meeting the educational, social, and economic goals of our country.

> Several facts illustrate the increasing activity and financial commitment in this area. In 1984, for example, eight states appropriated approximately $160 million to fund early childhood programs aimed especially at children living in poverty. In 1986, by contrast, 22 states spent $330 million for similar programs. These programs currently provide some 150,000 families with early childhood education and day care or with parent education.
>
> The momentum for early childhood programs remains strong. State legislatures and other policy-making bodies in the United States seem more willing than ever to consider investing in high-quality early childhood programs. A growing constituency, which includes chief executive officers as well as welfare mothers, considers public spending for such programs worthwhile. (Schweinhart, Koshel, & Bridgman, 1987, p. 524)

NATIONAL POLICY

Public policy commits the government to certain goals, determines whose interests and values will prevail, and regulates and distributes resources (Seekins & Fawcett, 1986). Local, state, and federal laws, regulations, executive orders, guidelines, ordinances, and judicial rulings are all forms of public policy.

NATIONAL GOALS

In September 1989, a precedent-setting educational summit was held in Charlottesville, Virginia. President Bush and the governors of 50 states agreed on six national goals for education and their associated objectives. The goals focused on: 1) school readiness; 2) high school completion; 3) student achievement; 4) mathematics and science; 5) adult literacy—lifelong learning; 6) citizenship; and 7) safe, disciplined, and drug-free schools.

The first national goal, school readiness, focuses on young children and has three associated objectives.

Goal 1: By the year 2000, all children in America will start school ready to learn. The associated objectives are:

- All disadvantaged children will have access to high-quality and developmentally appropriate preschool programs that help prepare children for school.

- Every parent in America will be a child's first teacher and devote time each day to helping his or her preschool child learn; parents will have access to the training and support they need.
- Children will receive the nutrition and health care needed to arrive at school with healthy minds and bodies, and the number of low birth-weight babies will be significantly reduced through enforced prenatal health systems. (White House, 1990, p. 3)

The school-readiness goal is a strong policy statement recognizing the need and importance of early childhood experiences. However, specific reference to children with special needs is not addressed.

FEDERAL LEGISLATION

Early intervention public policy is considered a relatively new phenomenon. Contrary to many social developments, early intervention policy has progressed from being virtually nonexistent, with the exception of the establishment of Head Start in 1964, to the establishment of legal mandates for services in many states and an expanded federal commitment to provide high-quality early intervention services to handicapped and at-risk children and their families (Smith, 1988).

Federal policy in early intervention began to evolve in the 1960s with the advent of Head Start and has been the impetus for early intervention/early childhood education policy. Although many of the early laws were not exclusively focused on young children with disabilities, they derived very direct and indirect benefits from provisions that impacted on the quality of programs and services. Programs and policies have been established that most states would not have initiated had it not been for federal support (see Table 5.1).

EVOLUTION AND CHRONOLOGY OF EARLY INTERVENTION FEDERAL POLICY INITIATIVES

The first federal legislation on behalf of young children was related to health-care services. In 1963, P.L. 88-156 was passed, which expanded maternal and child health services to low-income expectant mothers. The intent was to prevent mental retardation and to promote optimal development.

Project Head Start, which was part of the Economic Opportunity Act, became law in 1964. Project Head Start was the first national effort to counteract the negative effects of poverty on young children through a variety of services—educational, medical, nutritional, and parent training. The goal of the program was to improve the development of economically disadvantaged children through early intervention.

P.L. 89-313 was an amendment to Title I of the Elementary and Secondary Education Act (ESEA), which passed in 1965. In some ways, this was landmark legislation for preschool children with handicaps as it included funds for children

TABLE 5.1
Chronology of Federal Progams in Early Childhood Special Education

Date	Program	Description
1963	P.L. 88-156	Expanded maternal and child health services to expectant mothers from low-income areas to prevent mental retardation.
1964	Head Start	The Economic Opportunity Act provided funding for educational programs for economically disadvantaged preschool children and was designed to reverse the negative effects of poverty on their development.
1965	P.L. 89-313	Provided funds for state-operated and state-supported programs that allowed for experimental early intervention services.
1967	P.L. 90-248	Early and Periodic Screening, Diagnosis, and Treatment Program (EPSDT), which is a part of Medicaid, focuses on early identification and treatment in an attempt to minimize and prevent developmental and medical problems.
1968	P.L. 90-538	Established the Handicapped Children's Early Education Program (HCEEP). Provides development of effective model programs, methods, and state policies in early intervention and preschool services for handicapped children and their families.
1972	P.L. 92-424	Head Start provided that not less than 10 percent of national enrollment be designated for handicapped children.
1974	P.L. 93-380	Introduced new requirements for special education for preschool, elementary, and secondary students. Requires states to submit plans and timetables serving all handicapped children and youth from birth through age 21. Also mandates Child Find.
1975	P.L. 94-142	The Education for All Handicapped Children Act.
1986	P.L. 99-457	Created the Preschool and Infants and Toddlers Program.
1991	P.L. 101-476	Individuals with Disabilities Education Act (IDEA)— amends P.L. 94-142.

with handicaps at birth through age 21 in state-operated and state-supported schools. It allowed states to develop experimental early education services. This was an important beginning for development of early childhood services for young children with handicaps.

A component of Medicaid, the Early and Periodic Screening, Diagnosis, and Treatment Program (EPSDT), P.L. 90-248, passed in 1967. The goal of this law was to provide early identification and treatment to prevent developmental or medical problems.

The Handicapped Children's Early Education Program (HCEEP), P.L. 90-538, passed in 1968. P.L. 90-538 authorized and awarded funds for the establishment of experimental preschool and early education programs for children with handicaps and their families. This was the first federal program developed specifically for young children with handicaps. It was also intended to expand the knowledge base related to the efficacy of each intervention.

Provisions in the Head Start program were expanded to mandate that at least 10 percent of the national enrollment must be children with handicaps. This provision was passed in 1972 (P.L. 92-424).

The Education for All Handicapped Children Act, P.L. 94-142, became law in 1975. It mandated a free and appropriate education in the least restrictive environment for all handicapped children. In addition the act outlined rights of handicapped children and their families, including due process, program placement, nondiscriminatory testing, use of records, and so forth. The act did not mandate services for preschool children, but it did provide funding for children ages 3 through 5 with handicaps and for preschool incentive grants.

P.L. 99-457, which passed in 1986, mandated services for 3- to 5-year-old handicapped children by 1992. All states that participated in the program as stipulated in P.L. 99-457 were required to develop a plan and implement a statewide system of early intervention services for handicapped infants and toddlers. They were also required to designate a lead agency and to establish an interagency coordinating council. States that elect to participate in the fifth year of the program must provide entitlement for handicapped high-risk infants and toddlers (birth through age 2).

In 1991, the Individual with Disabilities Act (IDEA), P.L. 101-476, amended P.L. 94-142 and changed the name of the act. Demonstration and outreach programs were added priorities in the area of early childhood. Also, social work services were added, as were specified requirements related to dissemination and training.

It should be noted that it required extensive government intervention to initiate and preserve social justice and civil rights. However "reviewing the legislative history in early childhood also reveals the limits of federal policy in achieving a national goal" (Hebbeler, Smith, & Black, 1991, p. 111). Despite years of legislative activity, universally available early childhood services have not yet been achieved.

INCLUSION

It is not within the scope of this chapter to present an exhaustive review of the debate on the feasibility of full inclusion as a national policy. Although there are differences and inconsistencies in the defining of inclusiveness, the term generally applies to the advocacy of regular education assuming some to full responsibility for children with special needs and/or disabilities. Perhaps an oversimplification, inclusion can be viewed as a continuum of possible placement options for children with handicaps, with special schools and self-contained special classes at one end of the continuum (exclusion) and full-time regular classes (full inclusion) at the other end of the continuum. The assurance of appropriate educational programs for individual children should not be assumed to be a subsequent result of any particular placement.

Schrag (1993) discusses three models that have emerged:

> The first model is the more traditional in nature that maintains special education as a separate program but with a continuum of options. The second model of inclusive schools keeps a separate division within schools devoted to special education but maintains that all students with disabilities should be educated within their neighborhood schools or other comprehensive schools and to the maximum extent possible with nondisabled age peers. The third model would then reflect a unified system that merges all programs and personnel resources. It would provide services to any student at risk of school failure and maximize the schools' flexibility in designing programs. (p. 11)

The Controversy

In 1975 one of the most comprehensive laws ever to pass, P.L. 94-142, the Education for All Handicapped Children Act (EHA), merged various successful features of both federal and state legislation into one national public policy. This law mandated that a free appropriate public education within the least restrictive environment be made available to all students with handicaps between the ages of 3 and 21. "Although the mission of enculturating all is at the core a moral one, it is now defined in fact by legal terms" (Goodlad, 1993, p. v). P.L. 94-142 is a classic example of seeking to incorporate into law human rights and social justice and attempting to rid our schools of inequities and malpractice. As a result of this law, extensive state and local educational practices have been revised. Hailed as a "Bill of Rights" for children with handicaps, the law outlined a process whereby all children, regardless of the severity of their handicaps, were to be guaranteed the same educational rights and privileges accorded to their nonhandicapped peers: "a free appropriate public education" (Singer, 1988, p. 409). EHA requirements stipulate that students be removed from regular education programs only where the nature or severity of their exceptionality is such that education in a regular classroom, even with the use of supplementary aids or services, cannot be conducted satisfactorily (Office of the Federal Register, 1987). In 1986 P.L. 99-457 amended the EHA and extended full services to 3-year-olds by 1992 and established a new program (full service) for infants, toddlers, and families requiring a state's fifth year of participation to include entitlement.

We are now in the middle of a major controversy related to the mandates of P.L. 94-142. Professionals disagree on the interpretation of these mandates. Some professionals feel that full inclusion in the regular class is a civil rights issue guaranteed by law. They feel that education outside the regular classroom reduces curricula options for children with exceptionalities, has led to discontinuity of instruction, and has provided education with a limited scope that prevents children from gaining skills that would facilitate their full-time reentry into the regular classroom. They state that the current system of educating children with handicaps has created a dysfunctional and dual educational system (Dunn, 1968; Gartner & Lipsky, 1989; Lilly, 1986; Stainback & Stainback, 1992; Wang, Reynolds, & Walberg, 1986).

> The current system of special education needs to be changed for a basic reason: It does not work. That is it fails to serve well the students. Although particular practices are faulty, the cause is not in practice but in basic conception. (Lipsky & Gartner, 1991, p. 43)

Others argue that a range of service options and a full continuum of services must be presented as required by law and that the Regular Education Initiative (REI), the increased practice of mainstreaming, is a deeply flawed, totally misconstrued proposal. "Specific exclusions from any level of a full continuum of services constitutes functional exclusion as much in the 1990s as it did in the 1950s and 1960s" (Veragson & Anderegg, 1992, p. 53).

Some would suggest "it is strange logic that calls for the regular system to take over responsibility for pupils it has already demonstrated it has failed" (Keogh, 1988, p. 20).

> Special education is accurately portrayed as justified in part by two ideologies: civil rights and normalization. Both ideologies have been of considerable value to special legislation, but both have been invoked inappropriately in attempts to justify proposals that undermine its conceptual foundations. In our view they are dangerous exaggerations that distort perceptions to create a climate in which research data are devalued in favor of ideology that, although otherwise defensible, have been twisted into parodies. (Kauffman & Hallahan, 1993, p. 79)

Although there is a considerable range of points of view on the issues of full inclusion, also known as the Regular Education Initiative and to some extent mainstreaming, which could be considered partial inclusion, most would agree that regular and special education should be brought closer together. Many of the differences, beliefs, personal investments, and "literature that is steeped in rhetoric and overgeneralizations and is affectively loaded," have lead to polarization between regular and special educators resulting in adversarial positions (Keogh, 1988, p. 19).

Kauffman and Hallahan (1993) strongly support a comprehensive delivery system for special education.

> The capacity of American public education to respond humanly and effectively to variance among students should be expanded, but this can be accomplished only by mainstreaming and strengthening the essential structure on which a comprehensive delivery system is based. Although general and special education are now distinctive parts of an integrated system their interface needs more attention. (p. 97)

Davis (1989) makes the interesting observation that most of the debate on full inclusion is primarily among researchers and scholars from colleges and universities affiliated with special education departments. It appears a bit arrogant, naive, and remiss not to include the other major stakeholders—regular educators, students, parents, and practitioners—in the debate.

The debate clearly has no potential for simple and definitive solutions. However, based on the literature, it appears that changes are needed in both regular and special education. The two must be brought closer together, the extent to which remains a debatable point in the center of this major controversy.

This was evidenced at the national convention of the Council for Exceptional Children (CEC) in April 1993, where a policy statement mildly endorsing the concept of full inclusion was adopted by the general assembly. At the same meeting, the Division for Early Childhood (DEC) adopted a much stronger endorsement of full inclusion. We must remember that disagreements can be positive in the pursuit of good education. Debate has the potential to assist in clarifying critical issues. Goodlad so eloquently reminds us that we have a moral mission to educate all children, but perhaps there is no single fixed route to fulfilling this mission (Goodlad, 1993).

Early Childhood Education and Inclusion

Regardless of where one stands on the issue of full inclusion, there can be little disagreement that it is logical and feasible to assume that preschool programs should be able to develop models for successful full-inclusive programs, if for no other reasons than the ages of children when developmental differences are not yet so apparent and the philosophic similarities among regular and special education early childhood professionals. However, as a general policy, informed decisions should be based on careful consideration of the quality and appropriateness of programs and the individual needs of children and their families. The DEC's position on full inclusion is in accord with these beliefs. The characteristics of high-quality early childhood programs described in the NASSBE Task Force on Early Childhood Education report (1988) make no distinction between regular and special education of young children and their families. The report describes:

- A curriculum and classroom environment that responds to learning patterns of children within a given age range, to individual differences among children, and to cultural and linguistic diversity among children.
- A program that actively involves and supports parents as partners in the development of their children.
- A program that responds to the comprehensive needs of children for health, nutrition, child care, social and emotional support, and language development, as well as cognitive development.
- A program that draws on the resources and expertise of all agencies and informal networks in the community to provide continuity for children in their daily schedules and as they grow and develop.

There is already some evidence of programs successfully mainstreaming young children with mild-to-profound handicaps in preschool settings (Hanline, 1990; Gural, 1990; McLean & Hanline, 1990; Templeman, Fredericks, & Udell, 1989).

In 1987 the National Association for the Education of Young Children (NAEYC) produced guidelines for developmentally appropriate practices in early childhood (Bredekamp, 1987). These guidelines are compatible with the literature and recommended practices for early childhood special education. Salisbury (1991) has made these observations:

- Recommended practices in early childhood education appear to be generally consistent with many of the indicators from regular education. While the practices related to positive child outcomes underlying these two research bases may be enacted differently, their intent may well be similar.
- Despite differing theoretical foundations, there may be greater consonance in actual practice, and a consensus of desired outcomes provides a sufficient basis for the resolution of pedagogical differences.
- There are numerous areas of consistency between early childhood intervention and general early childhood practices.

Given that similarities exist related to practices, goals, and philosophy, there appears to be an excellent foundation for the merger of regular and special education for early childhood in practice.

EARLY CHILDHOOD SPECIAL EDUCATION AND EARLY CHILDHOOD EDUCATION: UNITING THE FIELDS

The uniting of early childhood education and early childhood special education holds promise for a perfect union. Three features stand out in support of uniting programs that serve children during the early years: 1) the degree of differentness among children is less; 2) the expectations of institutions that serve them are not limiting their measures of success to cognitive functioning; and 3) family involvement is a hallmark of both groups. As those who work with young children know, whether the children are typical or atypical, this union will not be as easily accomplished as one might expect. To truly integrate the two fields and develop inclusive classrooms, several understandings and challenges must be openly acknowledged and discussed in a nonaccusatory forum in order to promote a unification that serves all children, their families, and their teachers in an effective and supportive manner.

Among the understandings and challenges, it seems appropriate to focus on three areas, namely: 1) What do we know about young children—typical or atypical—and how they learn? 2) What do we need to know about the major forces that have driven program development for early childhood education and early childhood special education? 3) What attitudes or barriers do we need to address?

WHAT DO WE KNOW ABOUT YOUNG CHILDREN—TYPICAL OR ATYPICAL—AND HOW THEY LEARN?

As public scrutiny of our nation's education system intensified during the 1980s, the field of early childhood education began a serious examination of practices for young children. Even though the national interest was focused toward older children and postsecondary education, the increased emphasis on formal instruction and academic skills began to be reflected in programs for younger children. Elkind (1986) points out that this occurrence was based on misconceptions about early learning, with no evidence to support change in what young children need for optimal development or how they learn. Actually the documentation that affirmed the position statement on developmentally appropriate practices developed by the NAEYC showed that children learn most effectively through a concrete, interactive, play-oriented approach to early childhood education (NAEYC, 1986).

From the consensus within the field that guided the development of the position statement, one could draw the following conclusions regarding young children and how they learn.

- Each individual is unique.
- Only individuals learn, not groups.
- Young children learn from each other.
- Young children learn through interactions with people and things.
- All children with the same exceptionality do not respond to learning experiences in the same way.
- Most developmentally appropriate learning experiences and classroom management techniques are effective for both atypical and typical children.
- Sharing common learning experiences with those different from themselves is valuable to all children.
- All young children learn through concrete play-oriented experiences.

WHAT DO WE NEED TO KNOW ABOUT THE MAJOR FORCES THAT HAVE DRIVEN PROGRAM DEVELOPMENT IN EARLY CHILDHOOD EDUCATION AND IN EARLY CHILDHOOD SPECIAL EDUCATION?

As atypical children are integrated in early childhood programs, and as early childhood special educators and early childhood educators are expected to co-act, a harmonious union is unlikely without an understanding of the philosophical and psychological theories and instructional practices that have guided development within each field of specialization. Numerous approaches associated with different theories of child development reflect early childhood educators' views about educational experiences for young children (Weber, 1984). These perspectives tend to fall into three major clusters as now practiced: constructivists, behaviorists, and maturationists.

The constructivist perspective, strongly influenced by the work of Piaget, is the most widely accepted position by the early childhood profession and is exemplified in the profession's consensus definition of developmentally appropriate practices published by the NAEYC (Bredekamp, 1987). The distinguishing feature of the constructivist approach is the interactional view of development. The child constructs knowledge from experiences with the social and physical environment (Kamii & DeVries, 1978). Programs depicting a Piagetian perspective have been implemented in varying ways; therefore, few assumptions that are generalizable can be made about programs even though they are identified as a specific model (DeVries & Kohlberg, 1987; Lavatelli, 1968; Kamii & Radin, 1970).

The maturational view involves the child's readiness for an experience based on intrinsic biological influences. This contrasts with the behaviorist view that external environmental influences are the determinants of readiness. In practice, few programs adhere to the extremes in either the maturational or behavioral positions, but those that do differ in their emphasis on the relationship between development and environmental interactions (Kennedy, 1978).

Historically, philosophy and practice in special education have been influenced by the medical model and the educational model, with individualized teaching being the current guiding principle (Strain, 1988). Strain emphasizes that individualized teaching involves a combination of compensation and secondary prevention of problems for which a disability places one at risk, rather than remediation or cure. From this perspective, several issues should be raised by special educators regarding the impact that some early childhood programs have on the atypical child's development.

Safford (1989) raises a concern regarding the developmental curriculum orientation of some early childhood programs inasmuch as the developmental orientation is based on four related areas: 1) the assumption of normality; 2) the issue of age-appropriateness; 3) the issue of functionality; and 4) the problem of readiness. He believes that the assumption of normality reflects the fact that the normative measure is standardized with nonhandicapped, rather than with handicapped children, which does not account for possible qualitative differences in how children with specific disabilities accomplish developmental milestones. Furthermore, he points out that this may lead to erroneous and limiting descriptions of a child's current status and future accomplishments.

The issues associated with age-appropriateness center around chronologically older children being given unmotivating, unrewarding, and stigmatizing tasks because they are assumed to function at a younger level when, in reality, they are capable of performing a task more appropriate for their chronological age. For programs that consider early childhood as birth through age 8, this would be of concern for primary-age children.

Additionally, Safford states that the dominant view in special education advocates for teaching functional skills rather than skills that in themselves have no demonstrable function. He believes this may not be the context within which many regular early childhood teachers are accustomed to operating. He also expresses concern about programs that reflect a maturational point of view rather than interactional. Delaying instruction until children are "ready" would only further delay some children's progress.

Peterson (1987) expresses the perspective that programs serving atypical young children should be a blend of special education, early childhood education, compensatory education, and the values that are derived from these fields. The focus on the optimal development of the individual is emphasized in these fields; however, the programs designed to meet the goals are often quite different for the children. Kaufman (1980) suggests a basic incompatibility between early childhood and special education. He states that teachers report frequent differences in perspective and in terminology, which is understandable based on the historical roots of the two fields. Another difference that is cited is how teaching is conceptualized. Precision and systematic instruction and manipulation of environmental variables under the teachers' control are more observable in special education classrooms.

Likewise, differences are observed in the physical classroom environment. Bailey, Clifford, and Harms (1982) made a comparison of early intervention and typical preschool environments and found similarities as well as several standard elements lacking in the special programs. Even though this was not the case in every classroom, they noted a lack of sand and water play, areas for free play, space for children to be alone, dramatic play areas, and displays for children's work.

The uniting of early childhood education and special education holds great promise. Both fields strongly advocate for young children and recognize the importance of the individual. The ingredients for success will be based on a willingness to minimize extreme points of view and a willingness to submit all programs to careful scrutiny to determine their capability to meet the needs of all children, with both early childhood educators and special educators demonstrating a willingness to collaborate.

WHAT BARRIERS OR ATTITUDES DO WE NEED TO ADDRESS?

The compliance of program administrators with the requirements set forth in the Individuals with Disabilities Education Act (IDEA) specifying that children with disabilities be placed in the Least Restrictive Environment (LRE) in which they will learn has been challenging for several reasons. These challenges tend to fall in two categories: 1) those related to the availability of programs for children younger than kindergarten and 2) others related to attitudes regarding the inclusion of young children with special needs in "regular educational environments."

Program Availability

Local Education Authorities (LEA) have exercised various options to meet both the spirit and intent as well as the legal requirements of the LRE. LEAs that operate prekindergarten programs have included children with special needs; however, many of these programs are designed to serve children identified as "at risk," which raises a question regarding whether they are indeed serving typically developing children.

Other LEAs not providing services to prekindergarten children have developed collaborative arrangements with community-based programs, such as Head Start and child-care centers. The nature of these arrangements has been questioned inasmuch as the quality of child care varies greatly from state to state and from program to program within states. The lack of professionally prepared personnel mitigates against appropriate experiences that are the intent of placing special-needs children in a learning environment with typically developing children.

Additionally, the shortage of programs for typically developing infants and toddlers has created another dilemma. How can we provide an inclusive environment for special-needs infants and toddlers, and how do we resolve the concerns of parents who need affordable care for typically developing infants and toddlers but find no support available to them?

Attitudes

Rose and Smith (1993) reported a recent national survey, conducted by Allegheny-Singer Research Institute, of special education program and policy officials; program directors of child-care centers, Head Start, and special education services; and parents to collect information about barriers to preschool special-needs services. Sixty percent of the respondents cited attitudes as a major barrier. There was a variation in responses by position. All parents cited attitudes as a major barrier, but only one-third of the child-care directors shared this view.

This study reported the attitudes in five categories as follows: 1) turf; 2) teacher preparedness; 3) awareness; 4) "someone will lose;" and 5) communication/collaboration/respect.

Turf. Tradition sets the direction and leads to turf building. The special education community has great pride in its provision of services to children with special needs and is holding on to this rightfully earned reputation. Adherence to a system as it existed and worked is not easily relinquished. To some, this may appear to be turf guarding; to others, the concern is related to quality of services.

Support for quality early childhood programs is fragmented and disparate. Programs may be school based, community based, or provided by the private sector. As more children with special needs are placed in programs outside the direct purview of the public school system, special educators report concern about how "their" children are being educated. Respondents also expressed concern that intensive services cannot be provided in the nonpublic sector.

Teacher preparedness issues. In most cases, public school personnel must meet higher standards of professional preparation than personnel working in community-based programs serving young children. Respondents reported concern about having children with disabilities placed in community-based programs when the level of professional expertise is questionable, the resources are limited, and support personnel are unavailable.

Community-based service providers likewise expressed concerns about their ability to meet the challenges of medically fragile children; however, child-care teachers reported that special educators lack basic child development knowledge that child-care teachers believe they have. Respondents also reported that they have some concerns about the appropriateness of the prekindergarten and kindergarten programs that have an academic focus, programs that often ignore the individual progress of children and fail to recognize the variation in levels of performance among children within the same age range.

Awareness issues. Respondents reported a lack of information sharing among special educators, early childhood educators, parents, and administrators with respect to children with special needs. Furthermore, each group had little understanding of the role and function of the other groups in such matters as early childhood programming and services, curricula and methods, integration efforts, and medical needs.

"Someone will lose" issues. Respondents expressed concern that integrated placement would have a negative effect on the early educational experiences of both typically and atypically developing children. The concerns for typically developing children centered on diminishing the quality of the educational experience because the children with disabilities would require an inordinate amount of time and attention from the teacher. They also fear that a child with a disability would be too disruptive in the classroom. For atypically developing children, the concerns focused on the quality of community-based programs and the lack of professionally credentialed teachers. Some parents questioned whether better special services would be provided in special education settings.

Communication/collaboration/respect issues. Attitude barriers to communication, collaboration, and respect all appear to stem from a lack of information sharing that is reported to occur at the local, state, and federal levels. Public school personnel view the community providers as not being receptive to technical assistance from the special education community. Parents indicated that people make decisions about their children without knowing the issues related to having children with special needs. All groups reported that information about specific programs such as Head Start, infant/toddler care, and other community-based efforts were not effectively communicated.

THE NEED FOR TEACHER EDUCATION REFORM

Many of the school reform reports allude to the quality of teachers and teacher education as a factor in our "failing schools." "Schools [programs], can be no better than the teachers who staff them. Our success in restructuring the nation's schools will depend largely on our ability to attract highly qualified people to the profession of teaching, keep them in it, and improve their overall effectiveness" (Committee on Economic Development, 1991, p. 61). In *Investing in Our Children*, it was suggested that nothing less than a revolution in the role of the teacher and the management of the schools could bring about significant reform (Committee on Economic Development, 1985). "The search for the excellence [and equity] in schools is the search for the excellence [and equity] in people" (Clark, Lotto, & Astuto, 1984).

Over the past several years, a great deal of attention has been given to the preparation of quality teachers. Goodlad and others feel there are serious flaws in how colleges and universities undertake the mission of preparing teachers and describe a significant disconnection between the schools and universities that prepare teachers. "In effect, the preparation of teachers is without economic, social, political, or professional mission" (Goodlad, 1993, p. 5). Goodlad points out to us that teacher education programs tend to perpetuate rather than challenge long-standing practices in the schools (Goodlad, 1984). One of these practices is the degree to which regular and special education exist in school districts as two largely separate systems. This separation begins in the colleges and universities where teachers are educated, resulting in an undesirable paradigm (Pugach & Warger, 1993).

One of the major areas in the preparation of teachers needing attention is the current practice of separateness between students, professors, and programs in both regular and special education. This practice perpetuates and contributes to further the concept of a dual educational system that only serves to be detrimental to all children. "Isolating concern for handicapped students in departments and programs of special education mislocates the energy of those who wish to promote inclusive schooling. If there is to be a counterpart in teacher education to the dual goal of accepting diversity and preventing failure in the schools, unification at the level of higher education is a requisite condition" (Pugach, 1992, pp. 255–256).

Pugach makes it clear that her remarks should not be misinterpreted to mean that departments of special education and regular education should be merged, but rather a reconceptualization should take place, with children and youth kept at the forefront of the dialogue for the redesign of teacher education (Pugach, 1992).

There is no question that there is a need for teacher education reform and the subsequent strengthening of professional roles of teachers, school management, and leadership. We must also develop new roles for teachers and reorganize the process of teaching so that experienced teachers can become managers of the educational process (Committee on Economic Development, 1991). In order to accomplish the mission of teacher education reform, we will have to overcome the neglect by college and university leaders of the mission of preparing teachers and the "legacies of chronic prestige deprivation surrounding school teaching in our society and in higher education" (Goodlad & Field, 1993, p. 233). We are at a crossroad in the teacher education reform movement. There do appear to be optimistic signs and examples of higher-education institutions relating and responding to the communities they serve and attempts to better connect and collaborate with the schools. One example would be the involvement and participation in professional development schools, which is a joint venture between the higher-education faculties and school faculties to work together on staff development activities and the goals of a particular school. However, there does seem to be some indifference to this agenda. "Much of the optimism is based on isolated and ad hoc efforts by bold leaders, not a sea of change in the way higher education defines its role" (Finney, 1992, p. 21).

The education of teachers for general and special education for preschool children holds great promise for collaboration, integration, and unification. There is already evidence to suggest that this is an accomplishable mission.

In July 1993 the governing board of the NAEYC endorsed the Council for Exceptional Children, Division of Early Childhood's (DEC) position on inclusion, which calls for full inclusion with the necessary support mechanisms. In their July 1993 minutes, the NAEYC Governing Board also stated that they would publish this endorsement in their journal with an introduction that reminds their members that the NAEYC has set standards for high-quality programs for all children and that inclusion should take place in the context of programs that meet high standards (NAEYC Governing Board, 1993).

A joint position statement on early childhood teacher certification adopted by the Association of Teacher Educators (ATE) and the NAEYC in August 1991 included a statement that addresses the unique developmental characteristics of young children and the implications for curriculum and instruction.

> Furthermore, this knowledge must embody an understanding of variations due to cultural differences and/or the presence of a handicapping condition. These are not separate aspects of a young child's life and therefore should be merged in teacher education programs. (ATE & NAEYC, 1991)

Another example is the recent development of early childhood teacher certification in Florida. As a part of the process in the certification development of two certification areas, birth through age 4 and age 3 through grade 3, a survey of 64 and 65 competencies respectively was sent to 4,500 Florida professionals who are involved in experiences with young children, including child-care workers, special education teachers, general education teachers, university and college teacher educators, parents, administrators, and so on. Respondents were asked to rate the competencies on a four-point Likert scale. The results indicated no significant differences among those who work in regular education from those who work in special education regarding the competencies teachers need to teach young children (Lavely, McCarthy, Huggins, & Bryant, 1993).

Children in Head Start programs, with the exception of those who are handicapped, must qualify on an economic criterion; therefore, they are not a representative sample of all 4- and 5-year-olds. However, limited and modest claims can be made for the successful demonstration of fully inclusive programs for preschool, which include children with handicaps.

These examples and others give us cause for optimism for the development of a collaborative teacher education program for preschool children regardless of their social, emotional, physical, and/or intellectual abilities.

ADDRESSING THE CHALLENGES OF SERVING YOUNG CHILDREN WITH SPECIAL NEEDS

Building a constituency is the most powerful step in addressing the challenges associated with comprehensive program development and service delivery for atypically developing young children. The spectrum of needs demands a broad base of support from political leaders, parents, special educators, early childhood educators, teacher educators, program administrators, and representatives from related disciplines such as social services, medicine, health, and mental health. To gain and maintain commitment, it is imperative to actively engage these leaders in reform efforts at local, state, and national levels.

Broad-Based Involvement

With broad-based involvement, many of the negative perceptions cited in the survey reported by Rose and Smith (1993) would no longer exist. The constituents would have:

1. studied the demographics related to young children and their needs;
2. engaged in diagnosing the problems without placing blame;
3. determined the desirable outcomes;
4. assessed the range of available programs;
5. developed a vision of what a functioning system should be;
6. examined policies that bear on the issues;

7. maintained communication and dialogue with counterparts at all levels: national, state, and local; and
8. acted to change policies that hinder goal attainment.

As a nation we will fail to support our youngest and most vulnerable population unless we engage in constituent building at the national and state levels as well as at the local levels. Although the national goal that all children will start school ready to learn is a major first step, a commitment to supporting reform at the state and local levels must be demonstrated. People leading institutions/agencies have little inclination for change unless there is an incentive or compelling reason to do so. The most promising programs that demonstrate concern for the well-being of young children are coming from community-based commitments with only a handful of states taking action (Committee on Economic Development, 1991).

Personnel

The success of programs serving young children with special needs, especially infants and toddlers, will be greatly influenced by the preparation of the teachers in programs. This calls for rethinking teacher education at several levels: 1) speciality organizations that develop guidelines for teacher education; 2) state departments of education that develop licensure standards; and 3) institutions of higher education that offer teacher education programs.

A few states have developed licensure standards for early childhood special education teachers (McCarthy, 1988). Inasmuch as state standards tend to drive teacher education programs, regular early childhood teachers have been prepared for inclusion of atypical children only with information regarding legal requirements and characteristics of disabling conditions (Ayers & Meyer, 1992). This limited preparation fails to provide teachers with the knowledge for planning learning experiences that accommodate the needs of atypically developing children or to work effectively as members of an implementation team. One example of a state that is developing an integrated early childhood and special education certification is exemplified in the Florida model; two early childhood licensure patterns (birth through age 4 and age 3 through grade 3) that will soon be implemented include all competencies required for an endorsement in early childhood special education.

A crucial component of a teacher preparation program should include teaming competencies. Three patterns of teaming exist: 1) multidisciplinary; 2) interdisciplinary; and 3) transdisciplinary. The success of a team in accommodating the needs of a child and family greatly depends on how each member understands their role and function, interacts with professionals from other disciplines, recognizes and accepts differences among team members, and is willing to engage in role enrichment, role exchange, role expansion, and role release. Without knowledge and experiences with these processes, novice teachers may be reticent to participate in team meetings.

DELIVERY SYSTEM(S) AND THE LEAD AGENCY FOR THE PREKINDERGARTEN POPULATION

A system for reaching prekindergarten children under age 3 who are eligible for special services is a fragmented process. Few states have entitlements for services to the birth through age 3 population, which also impedes development of comprehensive collaborative delivery of services within a functioning structure. Currently, local leadership is the main thrust for initiatives for this segment of the population. The cost of services for this age group is very high, and funding is scarce; therefore, programs for this age group are somewhat tenuous. Meeting the needs of this population is further hindered by the lack of competent personnel and confusion regarding which agency or group should assume the leadership role.

Communication

Broad-based planning should dispel some of the misunderstanding that comes from misinformation or lack of information; however, procedures must be established that will assure that lines of communication are working. Local constituents, especially parents, often cite program or legislative changes that have occurred but were not communicated to them. These occurrences then lead to turf guarding and mistrust, as well as to diminishing collaborative efforts.

SUMMARY

Many milestones have occurred in the process of fulfilling our obligation as a nation to a long-neglected segment of our population. The initiative is not yet complete. Yet to be determined is whether or not policy makers are informed by research that verifies the cost-effectiveness of preventive measures and also choose to support the spirit and intent of legislative actions with resources for fulfilling our obligations.

Programs serving both typically and atypically developing young children from birth through age 8 are delivered in a variety of ways under the supervision of several different agencies. For the upper end of the early childhood continuum, kindergarten through grade 3, an existing functioning structure—the public education system—provides the mechanism for bringing together the personnel with special expertise essential for the development of comprehensive seamless services for children with special needs and their families. The state education unit provides the leadership for planning and assists local education units in identifying needs, planning and delivery services, monitoring programs, and maintaining compliance with state and federal regulations.

For prekindergarten children, the system and quality of services are less predictable. The state agency or agencies responsible for early childhood special-needs programs vary from state to state, with more than one agency being responsible for services in some states. For example, programs for infants and toddlers with special needs may be under the aegis of one state agency while programs for nursery-school-age children (3s and 4s) may be guided by a different agency. Program administrators engaged in providing services to both age groups have reported difficulties in complying with mandates from two agencies, especially when a different philosophical orientation prevailed. Additionally, continuity of services and weakened program articulation were cited as concerns. Even though a transition plan is developed for a child and the child's family in a move from one program to the next, accommodations sometimes inhibit a comfortable and positive change (Hazel & Fowler, 1992).

Outside of the public school system, there is a tremendous variation in programs for young children. The agency responsible for monitoring child care may not be the same agency that monitors prekindergarten at-risk programs. Therefore, several delivery systems and varied working relationships need to be developed. Unlike the public schools, early childhood programs will vary in 1) types and qualification of personnel employed; 2) purpose and philosophy of program; 3) amount and source of financial support; 4) where they are located (churches, community centers, child-care centers, hospitals, elementary schools, etc.); 5) who is sponsoring the program, (private, church, university, governmental agency, etc.); 6) length of day and length of program year; 7) population served; and 8) staff compensation.

Conditions in early childhood programs vary not only from state to state but from community to community and from site to site. This creates circumstances that have the potential for either being problematic or for encouraging new ways to respond with more flexibility and without the restrictions of an existing structure. Effective programming for children younger than school age will require extensive collaboration and supportive interactions among all agencies and institutions.

REFERENCES

Association of Teacher Educators and the National Association for the Education of Young Children (1991, August). *Position statement on early childhood teacher certification*, 16–21.

Ayers, B., & Meyer, L. H. (1992, February). Helping teachers manage the inclusive classroom: Staff development and teaming star among management strategies. *The School Administrator*, 30–37.

Bailey, D. B., Clifford, R. M., & Harms, T. (1982). Comparison of preschool environments for handicapped and nonhandicapped children. *Topics in Early Childhood Special Education, 2*, 9–20.

Berrueta-Clement, J., Schweinhart, L., Barnett, W. S., Epstein, A., & Wiekart, D. (1984). *Changed lives: The effects of the Perry Preschool Program on youths through age 19.* Ypsilanti, MI: High/Scope Press.

Bredekamp, S., (Ed.), (1987). *Developmentally appropriate practices in early childhood programs serving children from birth through age 8.* Expanded edition. Washington, DC: National Association for the Education of Young Children.

Clark, D., Lotto, L., & Astuto, T. (1984). Effective schools and school improvement: A comparative analysis of two lines of inquiry. *Education Administrative Inquiry Quarterly, 20* (3), 41–68.

Committee on Economic Development (1985). *Investing in our children.* New York: Author.

Committee on Economic Development (1987). *Children in need.* New York: Author.

Committee on Economic Development (1991). *The unfinished agenda: A new vision for child development and education.* New York: Committee for Economic Development.

Davis, W. (1989, February). The regular education initiative debate: Its promises and problems. *Exceptional Children, 55* (5), 440–446.

DeVries, R., & Kohlberg, L. (1987). *Constructivist early education: Overview and comparison with other programs.* Washington, DC: National Association for the Education of Young Children.

Dunn, L. (1968). Special education for the mildly retarded: Is much of it justifiable? *Exceptional Children, 35,* 5–22.

Elkind, D. (1986, May). Formal education and early childhood adduction: An essential difference. *Phi Delta Kappan,* 631–636.

Finney, J. (1992). *At the crossroads: Linking teacher education to school reform.* Denver: Education Commission of the States.

Gartner, A., & Lipsky, D. (Eds.), (1989). *Beyond separate education: Quality education for all.* Baltimore: Paul H. Brookes.

Goodlad, J. (1984). *A place called school.* New York: McGraw-Hill.

Goodlad, J. (1992). Access to knowledge. In J. Goodlad & T. Lovitt (Eds.), *Integrating general and special education.* New York: Macmillan.

Goodlad, J., & Field, S. (1993). Teaching for renewing schools. In J. Goodlad & T. Lovitt (Eds.), *Integrating general and special education.* New York: Macmillan.

Gural, M. J. (1990). Major accomplishments and future directions in early childhood mainstreaming. *Topics in Early Childhood Special Education, 10* (2), 1–17.

Hanline, M. F. (1990). A consulting model for providing opportunities for preschool children with disabilities. *Journal of Early Intervention, 14* (4), 360–366.

Hazel, R., & Fowler, S. (1992). In K. E. Allen (Ed.), *The exceptional child: Mainstreaming in early childhood education.* Albany, NY: Delmar.

Hebbeler, K., Smith, B., & Black, T. (1991). Federal early childhood special education policy: A model for the improvement of services for children with disabilities. *Exceptional Children, 58* (2), 104–112.

Hocutt, A., Martin, E., & McKinney, J. (1991). Historical and legal context of mainstreaming. In J. Lloyd, N. Singh, & A. Repp (Eds.), *The regular education initiative.* Sycamore, IL: Sycamore.

Hodgkinson, H. (1985). *All one system.* Washington, DC: The Institute for Educational Leadership, Inc.

Kamii, C., & Radin, N. A. (1970). A framework for preschool curriculum based on Piagetian concepts. In I. J. Atyhey & O.D. Rubaduau (Eds.), *Education implications of Piaget's theory* (pp. 89–100). Waltham, MA: Ginn-Blaisdill.

Kamii, C., & DeVries, R. (1978). *Physical knowledge in preschool education: Implications of Piaget's theory.* Englewood Cliffs, NJ: Prentice-Hall.

Kaufman, B. A. (1980). Early childhood education and special education: A study in conflict. *Volta Review, 82,* 15–24.

Kauffman, J., & Hallahan, D. (1993). Toward a comprehensive delivery system for special education. In J. Goodlad & T. Lovitt (Eds.), *Integrating general and special education.* New York: Macmillan.

Kennedy, M. (1978). Findings from the follow through planned variation study. *Educational Researcher, 1,* 3–11.

Keogh, B. K. (1988). Improving services for problem learners: Rethinking and restructuring. *Journal of Learning Disabilities, 21,* 19–22.

Lavatelli, C. S. (1968). A Piaget-derived model for compensatory preschool education. In J. L. Frost (Ed.), *Early childhood education rediscovered* (pp. 530–544). New York: Holt, Rinehart & Winston.

Lavely, C., McCarthy, J., Huggins, A., & Bryant, M. (1993). *Competencies needed for early childhood education teachers.* Tallahassee: Florida Department of Education (in press).

Lazar, I., & Darlington, R. (1982). Lasting effects of early education: A report from the consortium for longitudinal studies. *Monographs of the Society for Research in Child Development, 47* (nos. 2–3).

Lazar, I. (1988). Measuring the effects of early childhood programs. *Community Education Journal, 18,* 8–11.

Lilly, S. (1986). The relationship between general and special education: A new face on an old issue. *Counterpoint, 4* (1), 10.

Lipsky, D., & Gartner, A. (1991). Restructuring for quality. In J. Lloyd, N. Singh, & A. Repp (Eds.), *The regular education initiative.* Sycamore, IL: Sycamore.

McCarthy, J. (1988). *State certification of early childhood teachers: An analysis of 50 states and the District of Columbia.* Washington, DC: National Association for the Education of Young Children.

McLean, M. B., & Hanline, M. F. (1990). Providing early intervention services in integrated environments: Challenges and opportunities for the future. *Topics in Early Childhood Special Education, 10* (2), 62–77.

National Association for the Education of Young Children. (1986). Position statement on developmentally appropriate practice in early childhood programs serving children from birth through age 8. In S. Bredekamp (Ed.), *Developmentally appropriate practice in early childhood programs serving children from birth through age 8.* Washington, DC: National Association for the Education of Young Children.

National Association for the Education of Young Children Governing Board. (1993, August). Personal correspondence, Barbara Willer. Washington, DC.

National Association of State School Boards of Education Task Force on Early Childhood Education Report. (1988). Alexandria, VA: Author.

National Commission on Excellence in Education. (1983). *A nation at risk: The imperative of educational reform.* Washington, DC: U.S. Government Printing Office.

Office of the Federal Register, National Archives and Records Administration. (1987). *Code of federal regulations: Education.* Washington, DC: U.S. Government Printing Office.

Peterson, N. (1987). *Early intervention for handicapped and at-risk children.* Denver: Love.

Pugach, M. (1992). Unifying the preservice preparation of teachers. In W. Stainback & S. Stainback (Eds.), *Controversial issues confronting special education.* Boston: Allyn & Bacon.

Pugach, M., & Warger, C. (1993). Curriculum considerations. In J. Goodlad & J. Lovitt (Eds.), *Integrating general and special education.* New York: Macmillan.

Rose, F. D., & Smith, B. J. (1993). Preschool mainstreaming: Attitude barriers and strategies for addressing them. *Young Children, 48* (4), 59–62.

Safford, P. L. (1989). *Integrated teaching in early childhood: Starting in the mainstream.* White Plains, NY: Longman.

Salisbury, C. L. (1991). Mainstreaming during the early childhood years. *Exceptional Children, 58* (2), 146–154.

Schrag, J. (1993). Interview: Special education at a crossroads within the whole context of educational reform. *MR Express, 3* (2), 11.

Schweinhart, L., Koshel, J., & Bridgman, A. (1987). Policy options for preschool programs. *Phi Delta Kappan, 68* (7), 524–529.

Schweinhart, L., & Weikart, D. (1980). *Young children grow up: The effects of the Perry Preschool Program on youths through age 15.* Ypsilanti, MI: High/Scope Press.

Seekins, T., & Fawcett, S. (1986). Public policy making and research information. *The Behavior Analyst, 9,* 35–45.

Singer, J. (1988). Should special education merge with regular education? *Education Policy, 2* (4), 409–424.

Smith, B. (1988). Early intervention public policy: Past, present and future. In J. Jordan, J. Gallagher, P. Huntinger, & M. Karnes (Eds.), *Early childhood special education.* Reston, VA: Council for Exceptional Education and the Division for Early Childhood.

Stainback, W., & Stainback, S. (Eds.), (1992). *Controversial issues confronting special education.* Boston: Allyn & Bacon.

Strain, P.S. (1988). The evaluation of early intervention research: Separating the winners from the losers. *Journal of the Division for Early Childhood, 12,* 82–190.

Templeman, T.P., Fredericks, H.D., & Udell, T. (1989). Integration of children with moderate and severe handicaps into a day-care center. *Journal of Early Intervention, 13* (4), 315–328.

Veragson, G., & Anderegg, M.L. (1992). Preserving the least restrictive environment. In W. Stainback & S. Stainback (Eds.), *Controversial issues confronting special education.* Boston: Allyn & Bacon.

Wang, M., Reynolds, M., & Walberg, H. (1986). Rethinking special education. *Education Leadership, 44,* 26–31.

Weber, E. (1984). *Ideas influencing early childhood education: A theoretical analysis.* New York: Teachers College Press.

White House (1990). *National Goals for Education (press release).* Washington, DC: Author.

6

RETHINKING THE PARTICIPATION OF FAMILIES IN THE EDUCATION OF CHILDREN
CLINICAL AND POLICY ISSUES

ALBERT DUCHNOWSKI, GLEN DUNLAP,
KATHLEEN BERG, & MARIA ADIEGBOLA

INTRODUCTION

PARENTS and families of children who have disabilities have always played an important role in the education of their children. When the first compulsory education laws were enacted in this country around 1920, parents found that the laws did not apply to their children with disabilities. They had to petition schools and the legislature on behalf of these children. Through years of struggle they learned that there was more power in uniting for a common purpose. In 1950 the National Association of Parents and Friends of Mentally Retarded Children was formed and eventually became the National Association of Retarded Citizens (NARC) with state-level organizations and grass roots community-level chapters.

The accomplishments of the ARCs include intensive efforts on some of the major pieces of legislation that have ensured rights and services for people with disabilities. For example, in one of the best-known of these efforts, the Pennsylvania ARC obtained a consent decree in 1971 that established far-reaching changes in that state's education policy as it related to children with disabilities. A few years later, this decree became a major part of the foundation upon which the federal Education of All Handicapped Act (P.L.94-142) was established. The ARC's have been joined by other family-driven organizations over the last two decades to continue establishing and refining legislation that benefits persons with disabilities. The passage of the Americans with Disabilities Act in July of 1992 is the most recent example of the role of families as advocates.

Over the years several different roles have emerged for families of children who have disabilities, and not all of these are positive. Some of the most comprehensive work in identifying and describing these roles has been done by the Turnbulls (see, for example, Turnbull & Turnbull, 1986). They have identified several major roles that have emerged, beginning with "source of the problem," and "passive recipient of professional decisions," but also including "teacher," "organizational member," and "decision maker." The fact that the majority of the educational establishment perceives families in the first two more negative roles has been well documented (Bailey, Buysse, Edmonson, & Smith, 1992; Duchnowski, Berg, & Kutash, in press; Friesen & Koroloff, 1990). However, since the end of the 1980s, there is some evidence of the beginning of a positive change in how professionals view and work with families and consequently reason for hope in the future (Duchnowski & Kutash, 1993).

In this chapter we present the case that school restructuring is an opportunity to reconceptualize the roles of families, especially those who have a child with a disability, in the overall education of their children as well as in the general improvement of schools. We have attempted to use empirical evidence as much as possible, but this is an emerging area and the methodologies for even collecting the data are still being developed (Winton & Bailey, 1993). Consequently, we have used a blend of anecdotal reports, empirical data, and sometimes the impressions of advocates. We begin with a discussion of how schools need to understand the expanded needs of families. Then, to meet these needs, we explore the role of parents as partners and parents as decision/policy makers. We have included a separate discussion of the barriers to partnership faced by families that are culturally and ethnically diverse.

SCHOOLS AS A RESOURCE FOR MULTIFACETED SERVICES AND SUPPORT

As schools are restructured to meet the idiosyncratic needs of diverse student populations, they must also work to address the complex challenges that are faced by the families of these populations. Schools must be reshaped, in partnership with families, to become the central community resource for strengthening family systems and creating a broad-based milieu of comprehensive caring and sustenance. The importance of this movement is evident for all families, but it is especially salient when families include a child whose development is atypical and who has needs for specialized and extensive assistance. In these circumstances, families often experience a range of needs. The school is the logical single source from which these needs can be addressed. In order to do so, however, restructured schools must create a means for delivering an array of services that are required for comprehensive family support.

When a child experiences a disability, or any kind of special need, the family encounters challenges of various kinds. The extent to which these challenges become needs for external assistance depends upon the intrinsic strengths and resources of the family system and on the severity of the child's disability. All families that include a member with a disability have special needs at some time in the course of the child's and family's development (e.g., Dunlap, Robbins, & Darrow, in press).

Although it is not possible to delineate all of the supports that families may need and that restructured schools can provide or expedite, it is worthwhile to describe some of the more prevalent types of assistance that can be made available.

Information

Families have tremendous needs for information about aspects of their child's strengths and deficiencies, the nature of their child's disability, appropriate services and educational programs, civil and legal rights, and numerous other topics. Frequently, it is extremely difficult for families to obtain this information. Many different sources need to be tapped and families often conduct considerable independent research in libraries and resource centers. This process can be time consuming and energy depleting. Information services that are specific and comprehensive are extremely important and should be accessible through public school campuses.

Of the various family support options that we are suggesting, this is one that has been the object of some very positive activity. Increasingly, information is becoming available through easily accessed sources, such as the Parent Training and Information Centers (PTIs) that are established in every state through funding from the U.S. Department of Education. An additional step could be to locate this information at every school campus, perhaps in partnership with the PTIs and related community-based efforts.

Training

In addition to information, many families can benefit from training in such areas as child development, parenting, positive behavior management, and advocacy. Indeed, specific skill training is perhaps the best documented component of family support that can be found in the literature (Dangel & Polster, 1984). Numerous studies have shown that parents, and occasionally siblings, can learn to use interaction strategies that facilitate language development, positive social interactions, acquisition of self-care skills, and reduction of problem behaviors. The extent and intensity of training vary a great deal across these studies, and it seems logical that the format and duration should be gauged to the family's objectives and the severity of the child's disability.

Practical instruction in interaction strategies can be extremely useful, but so too can more general training in child development and parenting. When a child is born with or develops a disability, it is possible for families to lose sight of typical expectations and normal stages of growth. Knowledge in these areas can be helpful as parents evaluate and promote their own children's behavioral maturation.

Another important target for training is advocacy and negotiation skills. Families are their children's most important and most enduring advocates. As children progress through the support systems of the school years and on through adulthood, parents have occasion to engage in negotiations regarding placements, support programs, curricula, and other features that affect their children's lives. Too frequently, these negotiations are confrontational and adversarial. It can be very helpful for families to have information and specific skill training on effective bargaining within the human service systems.

Planning and Assistance

Many families that include a child with special needs have little opportunity or resources with which to develop sensible plans for their child's future. However, the lack of such plans can be associated with tremendous, often subliminal, anxiety. Therefore, a most valuable type of family support can be an explicit process of planning for the future. This is especially beneficial when the planning is specific and when the steps are operationalized and accompanied by tangible assistance.

Planning can focus on any issues that might be of concern to the family. For example, planning can address specific events within the child's foreseeable future. Such events might include a transition to another school, in which case planning considerations might include transportation, recreation, and the availability and development of friends and supportive social networks. Alternatively, and very importantly, planning can be approached as a significant longitudinal process that incorporates broad visions for the child's development over a three- to five-year period, or perhaps even longer. This process is referred to as personal futures planning, and it ideally includes all people who know the child well and who are involved in the child's care and support. Personal futures planning is best viewed as a process that addresses all dimensions of a child's life and development, in the context of the child's family, school, and community life. An objective of the process is to bring all relevant participants and resources together in a coordinated effort on behalf of the child's optimal growth and adaptation. There is little that can be as supportive for a family as this kind of strategizing, organizing, and collective encouragement.

The planning process might also include financial considerations. When a child has a severe disability of any kind, there are always financial matters that need to be addressed at some point. If they are not addressed explicitly, they can contribute to uneasiness and, in some cases, a sense of dread and foreboding. It is important for families to have clear information and to have access to resources for short- and long-term planning. Restructured schools should have these resources readily available for all families.

Case Management

Children with special needs usually require services and supports from a variety of agencies and disciplines. Traditionally, the monumental task of identifying and coordinating these services has been left to the family. This is an onerous responsibility that unnecessarily exhausts the energy and creativity of the family. Ideally, the various needs that a child experiences should be matched with appropriate services that are brought to the child and family in an efficient and informed manner. It is reasonable that this management could be provided from the school, which is by far the most pervasive and enduring service facility that the child will experience.

Social/Emotional Support

A sizable domain of family need is in the general area of social and emotional support. Family members can experience a range of feelings associated with their child with special needs. As is true for all families, these feelings vary from positive to negative, but there are some social and emotional experiences that pertain specifically to the raising of a child with disabilities. Many families have the need to share these experiences and to receive empathy and support that responds directly to these distinctive challenges. For some families, the presence of a child with distinctive characteristics can alienate the family members from their social networks. Such alienation, and social deprivation, can be a deleterious influence on parent-child interactions (e.g., Wahler, 1980), and it can, of course, be detrimental to a family's ability to cope and to derive optimal enjoyment from family and community life.

Families have different needs for social and emotional support. Some parents seek counseling, while others are fulfilled by the opportunity to share stories with other families of children with a similar disability. For some families, sibling support may be a particular priority. For others, the most important source of strength that can be provided is the opportunity to forge friendships with people who understand, are sympathetic, are nonjudgmental, and, perhaps, can help in practical ways through the relating of their own experiences.

Schools can serve as important facilitators of social and emotional support programs. They can work to create a sense of community; they can sponsor support groups; they can offer tangible assistance for parent-initiated efforts,such as Parent-to-Parent; and they can develop an open atmosphere that is inviting to and accepting of families. Importantly, schools can recognize that families have individual strengths and needs, and that the mission of the school should include efforts to strengthen families, just as it strives to strengthen children.

Summary

The above synopsis of support options that restructured schools can harbor is by no means complete. Families can be supported and strengthened in innumerable ways, many of which have not been delineated. For example, one major component of many family support programs is respite care. For family systems that are overworked and overstressed, respite programs may be the most crucial of all resources (e.g., Robbins, Dunlap, & Plienis, 1991).

The essential message of this discussion is that families are the most fundamental and enduring resource that influences a child's development and that schools must do more to work with and enhance family functioning. This must be done through developing partnerships with families and, increasingly, working to establish a collaborative and responsive milieu in which families and schools together can flourish for the optimal benefit of children.

PARENTS AS PARTNERS

The assumption that no two families are exactly alike is an important value in the family movement. Their differences lie in areas such as culture, socioeconomic status, and living environment, as well as in their individual strengths, challenges, and needs. Families would like the recognition of their uniqueness to be a primary goal of every professional in caregiving systems. Families hope that through training and experience, professionals will learn to recognize and understand the unique strengths, resilience, and ability that each individual member brings to create their own distinctive family.

A second value important to families is that a family's strengths are developed through its challenges. This value has produced much of the strain between families and special educators because of special education's emphasis on a deficit-oriented approach, rather than one that builds on strengths. Many families successfully cope on a day-to-day basis with the difficult behaviors and needs of their child and maintain some sense of "normalcy" in their family and community. Parent's efforts to help their child and family are often further burdened by the perception, by many professionals and society at large, that parents themselves have caused, or are in some way responsible, for their child's disability (Friesen & Koroloff, 1990).

The conflict between parents and professionals is illustrated by an example of what may happen when a family tries to access the fragmented system of care that is currently in place to help them and their child. Many families do not seek assistance until they have exhausted all of their own resources. At this point they begin traversing the very complicated, uncoordinated system set up to supply services for their child (Knitzer, 1982). Then, for a variety of reasons, such as a lack of clear communication or not understanding the demands and stresses experienced by the family, many professionals misinterpret a family's pattern of behaviors. They may believe families are "shopping around," not following through on recommendations, or living in a state of denial despite evidence that such behavior may simply be the family's inability to find the services they believe their child needs (Olson, et al. 1983).

Partnership of Experts

Families work, play, laugh, cry, fight, love, and grow whether they have only "typical" children or a child with a disability. The noticeable diversities come with some of the additional lessons families learn when they have a child with special needs, lessons that "typical" families may never have a reason to learn. They learn about commitment, sacrifice, perseverance, and dignity. They become experts in areas they never dreamed of, such as education, mental health, developmental disabilities, speech therapy, occupational therapy, physical therapy, neurology, and psychopharmacology. It is not accurate to call these families consumers because they are really educators, case managers, policy makers, and legislative advocates. Having a child with special needs changes a family but certainly not in the direction of dysfunction. This newly acquired expertise can serve as a common ground for building the parent-professional partnership.

Over the past decade, the concept of partnerships between parents and professionals has gained increased credibility and support among both parents and the professionals serving their children. More and more, families are recognized as the experts on their children (Duchnowski, Berg, & Kutash, in press; Friesen & Koroloff, 1990), with professionals acknowledged as the experts in the general fields of special education, mental health, developmental disabilities, and so on. Acceptance of this philosophy of shared responsibility in the development and implementation of services for children is reflected in a growing body of professional literature and in the activities of parent self-help and advocacy groups (Turnbull & Turnbull, 1985).

A guiding principle for this newfound belief in partnerships is that the development of any services should reflect the needs of the child and family, and that families must be full participants in all aspects of planning and delivering services (Friesen, Griesbach, Jacobs, Katz-Leavy, & Olson, 1988; Stroul & Friedman, 1986). There are several proven strategies families and professionals should consider while developing a working relationship. Professionals need to recognize their own abilities and limitations and realize that in recognizing and acting upon the expertise of families in regard to their own children, they are joining in a very effective collaboration. This is a collaboration that will make their job so much easier; a partnership that can only be to a child's advantage. Using specialized skills obtained through training and experience, professionals offer families opportunities to gain new knowledge about their children's diagnosis/disability. They offer avenues to explore and new methods for adapting or changing behaviors to make families more successful. For their part, families need to understand the dedication, commitment, and content expertise of professionals. Successful partnerships occur only when families and professionals blend skills and knowledge, and recognize the unique contributions each brings to the relationship (Vosler-Hunter, & Exo 1989).

In summary, families, as truly individual social systems, are the unique experts and essential resources necessary for collaborative partnerships in every aspect of care and education for their children.

Cultural Diversity: A Barrier to Partnerships

While there have been strides made in developing partnerships between families and schools, the progress has been uneven. For the most part it is families of the majority culture, i.e., white, middle-class, that enjoy the most acceptance. For families of color, the situation is all too often as Beth Harry has described it: difference, deficit, dysfunction (Harry, 1992, p. 90). Families who are culturally diverse and have a child with a disability experience guilt, confusion, and lack of participation that is magnified by an overall impression that the system is not sensitive to their ethnic and cultural traditions and values (National Mental Health Association, 1989). Patterns of both over- and under-identification and ineffective service for children of color in special education have been well documented (see, for example, Cross, Bazron, Dennis, & Isaacs, 1989; Harry, 1992; National Mental Health Association, 1989). Cross and his colleagues, for example, investigated children of color with emotional disabilities and concluded that these children and their families are the poorest served because they are either placed in the most restrictive settings, or they are not served at all. Similar findings have been reported for all categories of disability in relation to children of color (Harry, 1992).

The situation is further exacerbated by the correlation and confounding of two variables; race and socioeconomic level. While there is an overlap between poverty and racial minority status, the implications, interpretations, and practical considerations associated with this relationship are complex. The social theories of the 1960s presented negative views of poor families, and these were closely related to the deficit theories of minority ethnic cultures. Examples of these views are concepts such as "culturally deprived" (Reissman, 1962), "tangle of pathology" used by Moynihan to describe poor African-American families (U.S. Department of Labor, 1965), and "socially disadvantaged" (Deutsch, 1967). These theories have left their imprint on a generation of teachers, administrators, social workers, and counselors, as well as the academicians who have trained them.

Over two decades later, more recent research offers a different view of poor and ethnic families. Lareau (1989) compared upper-middle-class families with lower-class families and found that parents in both groups valued education. However, social class afforded resources and differential treatment that critically affected the involvement of parents in the education of their children. Although the poor families wanted to be involved with their children's schools and see their children do well, they felt school was "an alien world" for them and not in their domain of influence. On the other hand, upper-class parents received a warmer welcome from school personnel and were able to achieve what Lareau called a "customized and individualized" education for their children. Lower-class families were only able to obtain a "generic" program for their children (Lareau, 1989). Warren (1988) compared families in a typical Anglo middle-class school district in northern California with a bilingual school district serving poor Mexican-American families in southern California. He found that both groups shared common norms and values toward education but that the way in which relationships in school developed were complex and stressful. He concluded that sharing common values is not enough for some families to overcome some of the basic conflicts between parents and teachers.

Recently, Harry reviewed the results of several projects that were developed to assist poor families, who were also ethnic minorities, to become more involved in their children's schools (Harry, 1992, pp. 93–94). She reports that even in cases where the families spoke a language other than English, they could acquire the skills and strategies to help their children. Their sense of isolation and powerlessness could be changed to a feeling of empowerment. These data, though slim, offer hope that given the appropriate climate and training, parents from culturally diverse backgrounds can serve as effective partners in matters relating to the education of their children.

Parents as Decision/Policy Makers

The current movement to reform schools, especially through the broad class of activities that have been referred to as restructuring, offers an opportunity to increase the effective involvement of parents and families in the education of their children. This can be accomplished through changing and enhancing the roles parents play in the schools and building on the successes that have occurred in the past.

Keesling and Melaragno (1983) studied specific functions that parents serve in schools. They identified several roles that included decision making, educating (as paraprofessionals), and facilitating school-community relations. These roles are very consistent with the vision of school reform at the federal, state, and local levels. In their study, Keesling and Melaragno focused on families that had a child in a federally mandated program. They found differences in roles as a function of which program served their child. Compared to families with children in special education, more governance and policy making functions were found in families with children in Head Start or programs funded through the Elementary and Secondary Education Act (ESEA). Examples of the latter were Title I (Compensatory Education) and Title VII (Bilingual Education Act). Keesling and Melaragno explain these results in terms of the mandates and guidelines of these programs. Head Start and ESEA have their roots in the antipoverty programs of the 1960s, programs that required strong participation at all levels by those who were served. On the other hand, the special education legislation (P.L. 94-142) has cast parents in the role of passive recipients of service. While it is true that there are provisions for parent consent and participation in planning, the lack of overall parental involvement has been well documented (see, for example, Duchnowski, Berg, & Kutash, in press). The results of the Keesling and Melaragno study indicate that, given the appropriate mandates and attitudes, families can engage in quality governance and policy making in their children's schools. Again, the evidence is slim but there are indications that, given adequate support, families can play a major role in developing policy in the restructured school.

Current Status; Future Vision

It is clear from the discussion above that the current level of family involvement in the education of their children is generally poor and probably even worse for families of children with disabilities. However, it should also be clear that there are mechanisms, models, and programs that currently exist that do foster effective family involvement in the education of their children. As schools enter into what many think will be an era of major reform through restructuring, the role of families can be enhanced through some specific steps.

Outreach. If family members will be expected to attend meetings in school, the school will have to engage in aggressive outreach and support to ensure family representation. This is particularly true if the schools want a representative mix of families that mirror the demographics of the school. Upper-middle-class families can be involved relatively easily. Single mothers who are poor have formidable obstacles to overcome and need support to be full participants. These obstacles are not insurmountable and can be overcome with creative responses to such everyday issues as transportation, child care, and time of meetings.

An axiom that has developed in the family movement is that no committee or panel should include just one token parent. Schools need to build relations with a pool of potential family participants so that there can be several family members serving on the various committees charged with school reform. The dynamics of parent-professional meetings are such that most parents do not feel valued (Duchnowski, Berg, & Kutash, in press). With some encouragement from each other, parents are more likely to be contributing members to meetings, rather than passive participants.

Training for partnerships. Professionals typically receive an undergraduate degree and then several years of graduate training. They have professional journals available and receive continuous in-service training to keep up with the latest information. This investment in the training of professionals has resulted in their effective participation in the new wave of site-based management approaches to school reform. Unfortunately, few family members have received comparable training. Family members do not need the content training given professionals but rather the process experience to understand the vision and be able to articulate their unique perspective on the education of their children.

Change will require an even greater investment and commitment by parents. This is a time for creativity and innovations, such as flex time for school personnel to allow for more evening and Saturday meetings, partnerships with universities to facilitate such training, different uses of welfare and unemployment payments for eligible parents to assist and enhance their participation on standing committees.

When parents are adequately prepared, they can become a powerful force for needed change in the system. An example of this process is the accomplishments of the Parent Involved Network (PIN) of Southeastern Pennsylvania (Fine & Borden, 1989). A parent-run organization, PIN has advanced to the point where their members are part of national, state, and local task forces, panels, and standing committees concerned with reform in special education. They exemplify another source of parent training, i.e., self-help. They have learned how to maximize their own skills as well as how to obtain what they feel they need.

In planning for school reform, schools need to rethink their concept of parent training. Parents feel they know what to do with their children. What they need is support to implement good child-rearing practices (Friesen & Koroloff, 1990). The training they want is skill development to enable them to articulate their views as equal partners in the education of their children.

Participatory research and evaluation. The database describing school reform, and particularly the role of families, is virtually nonexistent. Our review of the literature revealed only a few studies, most of which were mentioned above. In order to effectively explicate the role of families, a systematic program of research needs to be undertaken. To achieve the most useful results, this research should be participatory. Families should be included at every step of the process in order to ensure that the right questions are asked, the methodology is family friendly, and that results are disseminated in a usable manner.

Families can also play a participatory role in program evaluation (Fine & Borden, 1989). An obvious advantage of this approach is that families will buy into the evaluation and support the implications of the results. This gives a broader base of support when policy makers are approached to make changes based on these data. The concept of participatory research, though relatively new, is receiving much attention, and the expectation is that there will be several such initiatives in the near future.

Focus on neighborhoods. While problems exist throughout the country, urban centers are particularly hard pressed and are producing some of the poorest educational outcomes at the present time. The positive effects of an increased family role in the education of their children can be enhanced by a renewed focus on neighborhoods. Some of the most effective leadership in this area is being supplied by the Annie E. Casey Foundation in their children's mental health initiative (Duchnowski & Kutash, 1993; Kutash, Duchnowski, Meyers, & King, in press). In this program, the focus is on the neighborhood, which is composed of families, schools, social service agencies, churches, and businesses. All of these components are employed to improve outcomes for children and their families. This marshalling of stakeholders is very consistent with the vision expressed in America 2000, the document that has given impetus to the current reform movement in education.

The Casey initiative has adopted the participatory model. Families play a primary role in every aspect of the program including determining needs, developing an implementation plan, fiscal management, and evaluation. This recognition of the strengths and competencies of families can serve as an exemplar for other reform efforts in which families are key players.

Training professionals. The final link in the recognition of new roles for families is the training curriculum for professionals who serve children and families. The current generation of practitioners in education, mental health, and social services has been influenced, to a great degree, by the psychodynamic-oriented, medical, deficit model of their training. This is an approach that does not recognize the expertise of families, and, at its worst, is family blaming (Duchnowski, Berg, & Kutash, in press; Schreibman, 1988). The more recent models of service for children with disabilities are described as being family focused and child centered (Friesen & Koroloff, 1990). These models are based on strengths, accept families as equal partners in the education and treatment of their children, and advocate an expanded role for families in the development of research, evaluation, and policy.

The challenge for the field is to incorporate these values and competencies into training programs for all appropriate professionals. The fields of developmental disabilities (Turnbull & Turnbull, 1986), mental health (Magrab & Wohlford, 1990), and child welfare (Zlotnik, 1993) have taken the lead in raising awareness and actually developing curriculum materials to prepare professionals to join with families in their expanded roles. Regular and special educators need to revise their undergraduate and graduate programs in order to develop the attitude of collaboration in future teachers and administrators. (Recently, the U.S. Office of Special Education Programs has funded two training grants with such a focus.) Appropriate in-service programs can also help to better prepare current practitioners to form effective partnerships with families.

CONCLUSION

The current movement to reform schools through restructuring offers another opportunity to realize the potential contribution of families to the education of their children. The history of education reveals many instances of effective contributions of families. Unfortunately, that same history also reveals a perception by professionals that families are apathetic, uninformed, and too dysfunctional to be effective partners in the various roles needed to improve outcomes for their children. This chapter has presented some indications that there is no basis for such generalizations. While families may seek their own level of involvement, there are indications that many families are ready to assume a more active role. Outreach, training, and accommodations may be needed, but the costs-benefit analysis will almost certainly reveal that the efforts are worth it for tomorrow's children.

REFERENCES

Bailey, D. B., Buysse, V., Edmonson, R., & Smith, T. (1992). Creating family-centered services in early intervention: Perceptions of professionals in four states. *Exceptional Children, 58*(4), 298–304.

Cross, T. L., Bazron, B. J., Dennis, K. W., & Isaacs, M.R. (1989). *Towards a culturally competent system of care.* Washington, DC: Georgetown University Child Development Center, CASSP Technical Assistance Center.

Dangel, R. F., & Polster, R. A. (Eds.). (1984). *Behavioral parent training: Issues in research and practice.* New York: Guilford Press.

Deutsch, M. (1967). The disadvantaged child and the learning process. In M. Deutsch (Ed.), *The disadvantaged child*. New York: Basic Books.

Duchnowski, A.J., & Kutash, K. (1993, September). *Developing comprehensive systems for troubled youth: Issues in mental health*. Paper presented at the Shakertown Symposium: Developing comprehensive systems for troubled youth, Shakertown, KY.

Duchnowski, A. J., Berg, K., & Kutash, K. (in press). Parent participation in and perception of placement decisions. In J. M. Kauffman, J. W. Lloyd, T. A. Astutu, & D. P. Hallahan (Eds.), *Issues in the educational placement of pupils with emotional or behavioral disorders*. Hillsdale, NJ: Lawrence Erlbaum Associates.

Dunlap, G., Robbins, F. R., & Darrow, M. A. (in press). Parents' reports of their children's challenging behaviors: Results of a statewide survey. *Mental Retardation*.

Fine, G., & Borden, J. R. (1989). Parents involved network project. In Friedman, R., Duchnowski, A., & Henderson, E. (Eds.), *Advocacy on behalf of children with serious emotional problems*. Springfield, IL: Charles C. Thomas.

Friesen, B. J., Griesbach, J., Jacobs, J. H., Katz-Leavy, J., & Olson R. (1988). Improving services for families. *Children Today, 17*(4), 18–22.

Friesen, B., & Koroloff, M. (1990). Family-centered services: Implications for mental health administration and research. *Journal of Mental Health Administration, 17*, 13–25.

Harry, B. (1992). *Cultural diversity, families, and the special education system*. New York: Teachers College Press, Columbia University.

Keesling, J. W., & Melaragno, R. J. (1983). Parent participation in federal education programs: Findings from the federal programs survey phase of the study of parental involvement. In R. Haskins & D. Adams (Eds.), *Parent education and public policy* (pp. 230–256). Norwood, NJ: Ablex.

Knitzer, J. (1982). *Unclaimed children: The failure of public responsibility to children and adolescents in need of mental health services*. Washington, DC: The Children's Defense Fund.

Kutash, K., Duchnowski, A. J., Meyers, J., & King, B. (in press). Community and neighborhood based services for youth. In S. Henggler & A. B. Santos (Eds.). *Innovative models of mental health treatment for "difficult to treat" clinical populations*. Washington, DC: American Psychiatric Press.

Lareau, A. (1989). *Home advantage: Social class and parental intervention in elementary education*. New York: Falmer.

Magrab, P. R., & Wohlford, P. (Eds.). (1990). *Improving psychological services for children and adolescents with severe mental disorders: Clinical training in psychology*. Washington, DC: American Psychological Association.

National Mental Health Association (1989). *Children in need of mental health care*. Draft proposal from the National Mental Health Association, Alexandria, VA.

Olson, D., McCubbin, H., Varnes, J., Larsen, A., Muxen, M., & Wilson, M. (1983). *Families: What makes them work*. Beverly Hills, CA: Sage Publications.

Reissman, F. (1962). *The culturally deprived child*. New York: Harper & Row.

Robbins, F. R., Dunlap, G., & Plienis, A. J. (1991). Family characteristics, family training, and the progress of young children with autism. *Journal of Early Intervention, 15*, 173–184.

Schreibman, L. (1988). *Autism*. Newbury Park, CA: Sage.

Stroul, B. A., & Friedman, R. (1986). *A system of care for severely emotionally disturbed children and youth*. Washington, DC: Georgetown University Child Development Center, CASSP Technical Assistance Center.

Turnbull, A., & Turnbull, R. (1986). *Parents speak out: Then & now* (2nd ed.). New York: Macmillan.

U.S. Department of Labor. (1965). *The Negro family: The case for national action*. Washington, DC: U.S. Government Printing Office.

Vosler-Hunter, R. W., & Exo, K. (1989). *Working together: A training handbook for parent-professional collaboration*. Portland, OR: Research and Training Center of Family Support and Children's Mental Health. Regional Research Institute, Portland State University.

Wahler, R. G. (1980). The insular mother: Her problems in parent-child treatment. *Journal of Applied Behavior Analysis, 8*, 207–219.

Warren, R.L. (1988). Cooperation and conflict between parents and teachers: A comparative study of three elementary schools. In H. Trueba & C. Delgado-Gaitan (Eds.), *School and society: Learning content through culture* (pp. 137–162). New York: Praeger.

Winton, P. J., & Bailey, D. B. (1993). Communicating with families: Examining practices and facilitating change. In J. L. Paul & R. J. Simeonsson (Eds.), *Children with special needs: Family, culture, and society* (pp. 210–230). Fort Worth, TX: Harcourt Brace Jovanovich.

Zlotnik, J. (1993). *Social work education and public human services: Developing partnerships*. Alexandria, VA: Council on Social Work Education.

7

ETHICAL DILEMMAS IN THE RESTRUCTURING OF SPECIAL EDUCATION

Lynne H. Cook, Frederick J. Weintraub, & William C. Morse

INTRODUCTION

THE purpose of this chapter is to discuss some of the ethical issues special educators face as their roles and responsibilities change with school restructuring. The chapters in this book emerge from divergent philosophical positions, many with a postmodern basis (Danforth, chapter 11 and Paul, chapter 1). In contrast, this chapter is written from a pragmatic stance.

First, we highlight aspects of the restructuring movements in general education and special education that we believe will have significant impact on the roles and responsibilities of education professionals. Based on this discussion, we argue for a redefinition of the special educator's role to include that of teacher leader in ethical deliberation and collaborative decision making. Next, we consider a framework for ethical decision making that includes policy, values and facts, and standards of professional practice. This is followed by a discussion of several issues and dilemmas illustrative of those that will confront professionals who serve students with disabilities and other special needs in restructured schools. Finally, we present challenges emphasizing anew the study of ethics and the development of skills in ethical decision making in professional preparation and continuing education programs.

Our discussion is framed, first, within the context of all educational professionals operating in restructured schools; we include administrators, consultants, teachers, and related services providers in our referent to professionals. We also use a second, more focused frame which is that of the educational professional who is serving students with disabilities or other special needs.

RESTRUCTURING AND PROFESSIONAL ROLES

Reforms proposed for American schools touch nearly all aspects of education; they represent a wide array of options and directions for general education as well as for special education. Others have argued that special education has received inadequate attention in the overall school reform recommendations (Pugach & Sapon-Shevin, 1987), yet it is clear that services for students with disabilities currently are the target of many proposed reforms (e.g., see chapter three). Although recommendations for overall school reform may be advanced in different literature or contexts than those in which special education reform issues are discussed, proposed reforms in both areas have caught the attention of the nation. Considerable controversy exists regarding the roles and responsibilities of teachers in enacting and maintaining the reforms. In this section, we first consider some key issues in school reform and restructuring and then attend to special education reform including issues in restructuring the relationship between special and general education. The topics we discuss relative to both areas of reform are among those that we believe will have significant implications for changing the roles of special educators and influencing their ethical responsibilities.

School Restructuring

School reform efforts of the last decade are generally viewed as occurring in two distinctive phases. The first is described as a "top-down" movement of externally imposed strategies designed to improve education and the status of teachers by increasing public control and instituting higher standards (Conley & Bacharach, 1990; Midgley & Wood, 1993). Career ladders, merit pay, and rigorous academic standards for teachers and students are among the approaches associated with the first wave of reform. The second wave emphasizes "bottom-up" strategies of empowerment, collaboration and professionalization of teaching (Darling-Hammond, 1988; Maeroff, 1988).

Restructuring is an often overused term that has been associated with all aspects of reform and used to refer to widely divergent approaches to making significant changes in the fundamental core of schooling. The strategies associated with restructuring include, but are not limited to, redesigning curriculum and instruction, redefining teaching and learning, providing a supportive environment for teachers, modifying how schools are organized and governed, increasing the involvement of parents and the community in all aspects of schooling, and building networks and partnerships (Bacharach, 1990; Lieberman, 1988; Prestine & Bowen, 1993; Sergiovanni & Moore, 1989).

It is not our intention to review the literature on school restructuring (see chapters two and three), but to clarify our use of the term. We understand *restructuring* to refer to the full range of fundamental school reforms, noted above, that are designed to bring about significant improvements in student learning and educational outcomes. Further, we note that restructuring is commonly discussed as part of the participatory governance and school-based management strategies that characterize the second phase of the current education reform proposals.

Although we acknowledge the breadth of approaches associated with restructuring, our central focus in this examination is on the second wave vision of "empowered and deregulated professional teachers entrusted with greater autonomy in school-based management" (Sockett, 1990, p. 224). This vision expands and adds new professional responsibilities to the already multifaceted role of the teacher. It is a vision of teachers as effective participants and leaders of collegial problem solving and decision making groups. We have selected for consideration and illustration three topics related to school restructuring that have significant implications for teachers' roles and responsibilities. These elements are: a) professionalization of teaching; b) empowerment; and c) collegiality. We note at the outset that the topics are highly related and often overlapping; the distinctions we draw among them are for the convenience of discussion.

Professionalization of teaching. Most analyses of the question conclude that teaching is only marginally a profession, or a "semi-profession," because it fails to meet several criteria that characterize recognized professions such as dentist, engineer, lawyer, minister, physician, and psychologist (Heller, 1983; Lieberman, M., 1956; Van Scotter, Haas, Kraft, & Schott, 1991, Sockett, 1990). While recognizing the need to improve the status of the teaching profession, Darling-Hammond and Berry (1988) offer a more dynamic framework for evaluating professionalism when they assert that it

> is not a dichotomous event or state of grace into which an occupation clearly falls or does not. Rather, it describes points along a continuum representing the extent to which members of an occupation share a common body of knowledge and use shared standards of practice in exercising that knowledge on behalf of clients. It incorporates conditions of specialized knowledge, self-regulation, special attention to the unique needs of clients, autonomous performance, and a large dose of responsibility for client welfare. (p. 8)

A number of second wave reform reports have pointed to the need to enhance the status of teaching as a profession (e.g., Carnegie Task Force on Teaching as a Profession, 1986; Holmes Group, 1986). In essence, these reports call for the transformation of teaching from an occupation to a profession. The recommendations focus on improving the quality of education by improving the competence of teachers through more rigorous preparation, certification, and selection. Strategies include identification of the knowledge base of teaching, increasing the arts and sciences requirements of preservice programs, and implementing a national board of professional teaching standards to ensure the articulation of standards from the profession (Shulman, 1987). Ideally, teacher competence "will be guaranteed in exchange for the privilege of professional control over work structure and standards of practice" (Darling-Hammond, 1988, p. 59).

Empowerment. The professional control to be realized through professionalization is closely related to the concept of empowerment. Teacher empowerment refers to conditions and structures designed to enable educators to increase their participation in educational decision making so that they are more respected and able to exercise their autonomy (Maeroff, 1988; Friend & Cook, 1990). Empowerment has as its aims increased morale and job satisfaction leading to higher quality performance (Meek, 1988), and it calls for significant changes in the roles and responsibilities of teachers.

As schools are restructured to allow professionals and community members to collaboratively design and implement programs to achieve better outcomes for students, the locus of decision making will shift from centralized bureaucracies (e.g., state or federal levels) to more local (district and school) levels. Teachers, other educational professionals, and parents will have central roles and unprecedented autonomy in the new decision making processes.

Collegiality Themes of collaboration, community, mutuality, and team participation run through the second wave reform and related change movements (Cook & Friend, 1991a; Donaldson, 1993; Little, 1993; Maeroff, 1993). Many reports and studies contend that teacher isolation and other detrimental aspects of school culture contribute to poor morale, a depressed teacher retention rate, and inadequate performance of many teachers (Barth, 1990; Goodlad, 1984). The Carnegie Task Force on Teaching as a Profession (1986) proposed that teachers should "work together in a school, not separately in isolated classrooms; they [should] take mutual responsibility for the curriculum and instruction on the basis of thinking together" (p. 58). In response to reform reports and related studies, there has developed a strong movement to raise the status of the profession and the quality of schooling by collective, collaborative effort (Fullan & Miles, 1992; Prestine & Bowen, 1993; Ruck, 1986).

Collegiality is one of the terms most frequently used to describe the types of relationships recommended for professionals within restructured schools. A widely accepted definition refers to "specific support for discussions of classroom practice, mutual observation and critique, shared efforts to design and prepare curriculum, and shared participation in the business of instructional improvement" (Little, 1982, pp. 331–332). Collegiality exists as a specific kind of collaboration, a condition in which professionals engage in goal-driven activities based on voluntary relationships that stress parity, shared responsibility for decisions, and shared accountability for outcomes (Cook & Friend, 1991b). These definitional elements create unique questions and conditions relative to restructuring. We will consider some of these in a subsequent section that addresses challenges and deliberation.

Special Education Reform

Special education has traditionally focused on providing access to services for the millions of infants, toddlers, children, and youth with disabilities whose developmental and educational needs are not otherwise being met. The "right to education" court decisions of the early 1970s and the passage of P.L. 94-142 in 1975 embodied the values of special educators in mandating access to special education and related services, and fair procedural safeguards in decisions about services to be provided. P.L. 99-457, enacted in 1986, extended these opportunities to all students from birth through age 21.

By the 1990s special education had reasonably well met its original goal of serving most students deemed to need and be eligible for such services, except for the infants and toddlers covered under the newer requirements. Today, students are no longer excluded from education because of their disabilities, and children with disabilities who are not thriving in general education are not denied the special education they need because of limited services. Procedural safeguards enable parents and professionals to advocate not only for available services but for appropriate services regardless of administrative convenience or resource availability. The courts have been clear in supporting parents in obtaining FAPE (Free Appropriate Public Education) through applications of both P.L. 94-142 and Section 504 of the Vocational Rehabilitation Act. In simple terms, special education has met the primary goals established by public policy to serve all eligible students and to do so in a manner that protects the rights of students and their families.

However, the original goal of special education availability is no longer adequate. Due to past accomplishments, emerging knowledge, and new technologies, the next major goal is quality of programs as evidenced by outcomes. Parents and advocates of students with disabilities take for granted that schools are obligated to serve their children and now concentrate more on the nature and quality of the services they seek and on the outcomes they expect. Similarly, the majority of current special educators entered the profession after the "access era" of the 1970s and now recognize the need for new, more progressive goals. They are articulating their own goals for the students they serve and for their profession. A new generation of policy makers and disability advocates has expanded disability rights to all aspects of society; they now examine the degree to which special education prepares students to participate in a society affording adults with disabilities greater opportunities than ever in our history. In sum, the issue is no longer about what special education has achieved, but what will be achieved in the future.

These advances have occurred simultaneously with the overall school reform movement of the 1980s and 1990s. A critical analysis of the special education reform proposals is presented in chapter three where Hocutt and McKinney trace the evolution of the Regular Education Initiative (REI) and its extension into the current Inclusion Initiative. While the recommendations for special education reform have not been closely integrated with those for education in general, they share at least two predominant themes through which the reform movements merge: Both focus on enhancing the expected outcomes for students and on restructuring the way education is delivered in order to attain such outcomes. Special education initiatives concern creating a partnership between general and special education with the goal of increasing the participation of students with disabilities in general education and providing more assistance to students with learning problems too mild to qualify for special education (Hocutt, Martin, & McKinney, 1991; Will, 1986). This emphasis essentially requires a restructuring of the relationship between special and general education and is consistent with general education's call for coordination of categorical resources (Sailor, 1991). Critics and proponents of special education have all expressed concern about the educational outcomes for students receiving special education services. Both argue for a new emphasis on outcomes rather than on program access or program completion.

Leadership and Decision Making Roles

Even the briefest review of these topics reveals the profound changes likely to occur in teachers' roles and responsibilities as the various forms of restructuring proceed. Professionalization calls for teachers to regulate their profession and to help identify and promote a common body of knowledge to inform practice. Empowerment requires teachers to engage routinely in reflective problem solving and decision making in matters they believe to be of critical importance to schools. Collegiality requires schoolpeople to work together—sharing goals, responsibilities and accountability—as they engage in reflective, collaborative decision making at the local level. These and similar restructuring issues add many new demands and opportunities to the teaching role. This emerging, yet ambiguous role may be expanded even further by the challenges and uncertainties that accompany the decision to increase the inclusion of students with disabilities in general education programming. In addition to the role changes for all teachers, special educators and others with major professional responsibilities for students with disabilities will have to assume new levels of disability advocacy because they may be the only members of site-based teams with the knowledge and values needed to effectively fill these roles.

Teacher decision making and empowerment are the restructuring principles with the greatest relevance to teachers' roles and to this chapter. They are operationalized in a variety of ways, often referred to as site-based management, which are in no way ends in themselves. Site-based management, or site-based decision making (SDM) as we prefer to call it, takes many different forms depending on the situation and constituencies involved. In some situations, parents, community members, other educational and related professionals and students may be included in the process. In other cases, SDM may involve only faculty committees. The range of problems and issues addressed and the impact of decisions made by such groups also vary greatly. Some groups may simply serve in an advisory capacity, sharing their reactions to proposals with school administrators; others may be responsible for solving problems, including generating and implementing solutions.

SDM, specifically site-based management, is often criticized as being "piecemeal," composed of seemingly unrelated and trivial issues (Lieberman & Miller, 1990; Midgley & Wood, 1993). The tie between SDM and instructional improvement or student outcomes is frequently elusive. The more superficial examples of this approach appear to be driven by the naive hope that if teachers are given more decision making control, their instruction and its outcomes will automatically improve.

In the past, educators—particularly special educators—have participated in many key decisions regarding students and curriculum, but these decisions have typically been limited by district, state, and federal policies. That is, "decision making" has traditionally taken the form of "choice making" as educators have selected among alternatives prescribed by the bureaucracy in which they function. In restructured schools, teams of educators will be expected to act with unprecedented leadership and autonomy in making and implementing significant decisions about their schools and the students they serve. They will be expected to make decisions and design alternative programs that have not been imposed by the larger system. As Jim Paul points out, the "geography" of decision making will change in restructured schools.

Under these conditions, educators will not look to centralized bureaucracies or to externally imposed policies for guidance in making decisions. They will have to look to their collective knowledge, skills, and ethics for that guidance. They will have to become effective participants in collaborative decision making groups and assume leadership of these groups when appropriate. We contend, therefore, that the role of special educator must be redefined to include that of "teacher leader" in collaborative decision making groups. The profession has developed and adopted professional standards of practice, and the knowledge base is developing. Yet there is a conspicuous absence of a conceptual framework as a basis for decision making in the debates about restructuring and reform in general education as well as in special education. Underlying much of the argument is the matter of equity versus excellence, given finite resources, with special education valuing equity.

ETHICAL DELIBERATION: A FRAMEWORK

> Education is rife with ethical problems—problems concerning how to treat individual students, how to ensure equal educational opportunity for all, how to respect the views of parents, how to deal with colleagues, and how to do all these things while maintaining one's personal integrity and allegiance to the practice of education. (Howe & Miramontes, 1992, p.1)

The ethical problems of education are often intensified in special education, a situation which Howe and Miramontes (1991) attribute to two primary causes. First, they note that special education as a field evolved from an ethical conviction that all individuals are entitled to a decent public education regardless of their abilities or potential for school performance. As a second reason, they offer the argument that special education is a relatively new field and one that challenges the knowledge and skills of teachers as well as the resources and traditional structure of schools. We agree with this analysis and believe that the restructuring topics discussed and illustrated in this chapter represent a special strand of ethical concerns and issues emerging from the ongoing school reform movements.

Benjamin and Curtis (1981) tell us that ethical deliberation aims to answer the question: "What ought to be done in these particular circumstances, when all things are considered?" To answer this question, scholars in special education or ethical theory suggest that professionals must take into consideration a nearly unending array of concerns including law, ethics, values, conceptions of "the good life," as well as personal feelings and beliefs. It is consideration of these multiple, often conflicting, concerns that often render ethical deliberations complex, uncertain, subjective, and personal (Howe & Miramontes, 1992; Kauffman, 1992; Lenz & Deshler, in press). If professional educators are to be entrusted with greater autonomy in collaborative SDM, they must embrace a set of principles to guide their involvement in matters that require ethical deliberation. In this section, we outline a general framework to guide ethical deliberation and decision making. This framework attempts to ensure that many major influences are considered during ethical deliberation. It offers a way to identify and "sort" different sources of influence in decision making including values, law and policy, the professional knowledge base, and professional standards. Recognizing and examining these sources is necessary if teachers are to gain the perspective needed to view the complex interactions of factors that affect their decisions. For two reasons the framework stops short of offering a step-by-step process for ethical deliberation. First, others have done so, and their useful approaches are well documented in the literature (Paul, Gallagher, Kendrick, Thomas, & Young, 1992). Second, we have found that the framework fits nicely with most general problem solving or decision making processes and do not feel the space required for this examination is warranted here.

Although we used this framework ourselves in an experimental course which we co-taught to practicing teachers, we are the first to admit that it does not lead to simple resolutions. As is no doubt obvious, there are few simple answers to complex ethical questions; often there are only more questions. This may be one reason that inadequate attention is given to the study of ethical concerns in preparation programs and in the literature. In their analysis of practitioners' search for solutions to multiple service delivery problems they confront, Ysseldyke and Algozzine (1982) noted, "The critical issue . . . seems to be the demand for instant, simple solutions to incredibly complex problems. . . . the demand for simple solutions has been so strong that it has created a receptive natural environment for those people who believe that they do have those answers" (p. 256).

Law and Policy

From its inception, special education has had a strong base in ethics and values. But, as noted earlier, the majority of today's special educators completed preparation programs in the 1980s or later when the predominant emphasis was on meeting the initial public policy goal of providing access to special education for the millions of children and youth who required it. During this period, the federal and state laws and regulations became a central mechanism in special education, i.e., meeting the legal mandates. Litigation and legislation characterized the field and were used to ensure that state and local education agencies promulgated and enforced regulations and other policy guidance to implement the laws appropriately. It appeared to many that the laws and regulations were separate from, and possibly more important than, the professional practice and ethical foundations of the field (Cook & Cavallaro, 1983). But one has only to read the original text of P.L. 94-142, and the congressional testimony that laid its foundation, to realize that constitutional principles, the highest ethical standards, and the best of the available knowledge about practice are embodied in that legislation.

The relationship between law and ethics is intricate, to be sure. First, laws are at some level a reflection of the predominant social values and mores and, thus, represent the ethics of a society. Second, laws are usually imprecise and require interpretation that will most likely have ethical content. Next, Howe and Miramontes (1992) note two additional relationships: 1) laws may be criticized for failure to comply with ethical principles that are external to the law in question; and 2) because they are very general in nature, laws neither capture ethics with precision nor eliminate the need for deliberation. The interdependent characteristics of laws and ethics serve to illustrate the overlapping nature of the various elements of the framework. Just as law and ethics cannot be separated, ethics cannot be separated from the other components of the framework, nor can they be separated from one another.

Facts

The second element of the framework is facts or knowledge. Facts have several aspects with noteworthy relevance to this chapter. First, they are closely tied to values, as is discussed below. In this sense, facts are used simply as tools to lend an air of rationality to what would otherwise be an emotional, value-laden debate. In other words, policy makers and others often hide behind seemingly rational facts or data in order to champion the same value-driven position they would have taken anyway. A second aspect of facts is that a shared, specialized knowledge base is an essential component of a profession. The facts that are agreed upon as unifying truths to be supported by all members of a profession are key to the knowledge base that underlies the profession. Third, facts may be the most controversial of the components of the framework—especially within the context of the new paradigms and new ways of knowing that are central constructs in some of the predominant arguments for special education reform. Readers are referred to other chapters (chapters 1, 11) for discussions of the underlying assumptions of the field and alternative approaches to defining them.

Values

Values play an essential role in ethical deliberations. Each of us has a unique personal, professional, and/or political value orientation. These values influence how we view the facts and information relative to a particular question or set of questions. In fact, major organizations have recommended that broad principles, or commonly held values, should be applied to clarify the issues and resolve ethical dilemmas in service, research, and public policy (e.g., Lenz & Deshler, in press; National Commission for the Protection of Human Subjects of Biomedical and Behavioral Research, 1978). Among the values most frequently espoused and advocated are: *beneficence* (avoidance of unnecessary suffering or harm, and the maximization of good outcomes), *justice* (equitable distribution of social benefits and costs), and *respect* (a concern for the autonomy and dignity of persons).

Human services professionals may concur on broad principles such as these, but the exercise of applying them to ethical deliberation is much less likely to be met with consensus. For example, the principle of beneficence dictates that we maximize positive outcomes while avoiding unnecessary suffering or harm. How does one assess the positives and negatives to determine if the benefits of receiving individualized instruction using specialized, laboratory-bound technology outweigh the costs of removing a student from a successful general education classroom for one period each day? We have found the number and diversity of the answers to this question to be as great the number and diversity of the teachers of whom we ask it. Teachers answer such questions in terms of the facts as they interpret them, and their interpretations are generally value-bound. The importance of each individual's personal code of ethics, values, and philosophy is emphasized in Lippitt's (1969) statement:

> Both research and practical experience underscore the fact that the single most important factor in the practice of ethical behavior is the individual's personal code and standards. Each person represents in his own life the influence of his environment and his experience, and this contributes to the criteria he uses to appraise the ethical implications of particular situations. (p. 178)

Ethical deliberation requires an understanding of the relationship between values and facts, particularly in light of the great influence values have in decision making. Howe and Miramontes (1991) warn of the danger of too sharply distinguishing between facts and values, since they are related in several ways. First, facts are necessary to determine if established ethical principles apply to a particular case. Second, when ethical principles are not well established, facts are necessary to determine if any discernible link can be made between the facts and the ethical principle in question. Finally, because many fundamental educational concepts "derive their meaning within a complex, socially constructed web of meanings that is permeated with value commitments" (1991, p. 12), interpretation of facts is often camouflage for an expression of values.

Professional Standards

In the earlier overview of professionalism, we stated that one characteristic of a profession is its code of ethics and standards of practice that are developed, adopted, and enforced by members of the profession. Professional codes of behavior are essential for self-discipline and professional regulation (Gallessich, 1982; Sockett, 1990). Reliance on individual values and standards is insufficient for public protection, one of the primary purposes for regulation of professional practice. Professional associations are the vehicles for advocacy of ethics and standards.

Throughout this chapter we have referred to teachers, special education teachers and professionals without making or clarifying distinctions. Now we must attempt to do that. First, the empowered and ethical teacher leaders of collegial decision making groups are professionals. They belong to a bonafide profession that meets the standards referenced by Darling-Hammond and Berry (1988) and others—i.e., they share a common body of knowledge and use shared standards of practice in applying that knowledge to their work with clients. They are committed to client welfare, autonomous performance, self-regulation, specialized knowledge, and special attention to the unique needs of their clients. The status of the teaching profession was reviewed and some suggestions for improving it examined earlier in this chapter. It is clear that professional associations play a critical role in advancing the status of a profession. There are three associations of particular import for special educators: the American Federation of Teachers (AFT), the Council for Exceptional Children (CEC), and the National Education Association (NEA). NEA and AFT are the two international professional associations for teachers, and CEC is the international professional association for special educators.

Whether special education is a separate profession or a specialized area within the education profession can be debated. For purposes of this discussion, we will treat special education as a distinct profession and look to CEC and its standards. We do this with the full understanding that the standards of the three relevant organizations are highly compatible with one another and that potential realignments (e.g., merger of NEA and AFT; structural integration of special education with the broader field of education, and other forms of restructuring) may well lead to a more fully articulated and comprehensive set of standards in the future. We hasten to point out, however, that with "conditions of specialized knowledge" incorporated in the criteria for a profession, it is likely that many special educators would elect to affiliate with one of the primary education associations and with CEC, the special education professional association.

The 1983 CEC Delegate Assembly unanimously adopted three documents that established standards relating to professional preparation, performance, practice, and behavior: a Code of Ethics, Standards for Professional Practice, and Standards for the Preparation of Special Education Personnel (CEC, 1993). The first two have particular significance for this chapter. Although ethics and standards of practice are often incorporated into a single document, CEC elected to distinguish between a belief statement (ethic) that remains constant over time and a standard of practice which may well change as knowledge advances (Heller, 1983). CEC further articulates standards of practice in its policy statements adopted and revised during annual meetings of the Delegate Assembly. Together, CEC's code of ethics, standards of practice, and policy statements address professional rights and responsibilities, qualifications, and appropriate standards and conditions for professional practice.

Subsections of the Standards for Professional Practice address the rights and responsibilities of special education professionals in three distinct categories: in relation to persons with exceptionalities and their families, in relation to their professional employment, and in relation to the profession and other professionals. These standards provide a yardstick against which to judge the performance of all professional special educators in a variety of existing and evolving roles.

Applying the Framework

We stated at the outset that the framework exists as a set of guiding principles for deliberation, not for finding simple resolutions to complex matters. In applying the framework, professionals analyze a situation by determining what guidance about the matter can be derived from each of the major components: law/policy, facts, values, and professional standards. This examination requires adequate reflection to encourage honesty and integrity in the analysis. Such an analysis aims at preventing the unwitting use of one element of the framework to the exclusion of the others. Space does not permit the exercise here, but each of the components of the framework can be applied in the situations described below, and each leads to different conclusions.

ETHICAL ISSUES AND DILEMMAS

Having had the provocative experience of co-teaching a prototype, experimental course at California State University, Northridge, using the framework we describe, the three authors are acutely aware of the seemingly infinite number of ethical questions that confront special educators daily. We include the most limited sampling here for purposes of example. First we discuss accountability—one of several overarching ethical issues that derives from the reform-related trends and cuts across most of the more specific questions and dilemmas emerging in the reform movements. Then we illustrate such ethical dilemmas. We have found, as have others, that using case material is the most effective means of developing skill in ethical deliberation. Whereas case material for the purpose of skill development should be specific and detailed, we use brief and skeletal, illustrative case descriptions here as a small sampler of the wide range of dilemmas that may arise. The reader is referred to Howe & Miramontes (1992) chapters 3, 4, 5 for more detailed cases. The mini-case we present in Table 7.1 and reference throughout the discussion has been designed to incorporate some of the newer dilemmas that are beginning to emerge with increased efforts to more fully include students with disabilities in general education. Readers are referred to the several recently published discussions of ethical practice in special education for more case material (e.g., Friend & Cook, 1992a; Gable, Arllen, & Cook, 1993; Howe & Miramontes, 1992; Paul, et al., 1992).

TABLE 7.1
Co-teaching Case

A site-based program team at the local middle school has decided that two of its members, the special education teacher and the science teacher, will work together to include three students with disabilities in an advanced science class and has left the program design to the teachers. The teachers believe it will be best to fully include the students by not distinguishing them as "special" in any way. As part of the strategy, the site-based team has agreed that the special education teacher will consult twice a week and co-teach with the classroom teacher three periods during the week.

As they plan for the class, the teachers agree that the science teacher will provide most of the direct instruction and large group presentation because the special educator does not have adequate content knowledge. In keeping with the plan to avoid singling the students out and to minimize the teacher's content limitations, they agreed that the special education teacher will only provide direct instruction to the three students when they are in different small groups with other students.

Accountability: An Overarching Issue

Accountability is one of the major areas of concern that surfaces as we consider some of the structural and relationship changes occurring in the name of restructuring. Specifically, who is accountable, to whom, and for what are they accountable? These are not mutually exclusive questions. All three areas are highly correlated with one another, and they correspond to the selected themes and standards we address in subsequent discussion.

Who is accountable? The work of teachers in traditionally structured schools is described as isolated and separate (Barth, 1990; Goodlad, 1984). As schools restructure, teachers are expected to develop more collaborative relationships with colleagues. Characteristics of collaboration with colleagues include shared responsibility and shared accountability (Friend & Cook, 1992a). This represents a serious departure from traditional systems of accountability where professionals are held individually accountable for their actions and their performance. Systems for regulating the performance and ethical behaviors of members of the profession (e.g., boards with broad authority in the areas of ethics, certification, and licensure) are universally built on principles of individual accountability. What strategies will we employ and how will we resolve the conflicts inherent in responding to those recommendations for professionalization that are based on rigorous evaluation of individuals while we move to a collaborative, community structure for schooling? This is perhaps the most pressing of the problems to be faced in determining *who* is accountable.

Using the material in the middle school case, who is accountable for the success of the students in the program? Is it all the members of the team, the two co-teachers, or an individual teacher? The emphasis on shared accountability and shared responsibility, as well as other themes of reform, lead to role ambiguity for all educational professionals. Role ambiguity is associated with teacher dissatisfaction and stress (Billingsley, 1993; Cook, 1978), which is probably why efforts to avoid it are addressed directly in the CEC standards of practice:

> Professionals should receive clear written communication of all duties and responsibilities, including those which are prescribed as conditions of their employment. (CEC, 1993, Standard 3.2c1, p.6)

To whom are special educators accountable? This question has two parts. The simple answer is, "Professionals are responsible to their client(s)." Thus, we must also ask, "Who are the clients of special educators?" Teachers have many different roles and, hence, many different constituencies to whom they are accountable. The codes of ethics and standards of practice for the education professions all identify students, parents, and colleagues as the persons to whom teachers are accountable (AFT, 1946; CEC, 1993; NEA, 1993). Typically formal standards clarify teachers' responsibilities for promoting the education and welfare of their students, responding to the rights and informational needs of parents, and respecting and supporting colleagues. But teachers are also accountable to the public, their supervisors, and sometimes to the students of their colleagues, and to other members of the school community. They hold multiple roles and related responsibilities that increase in number and complexity as school restructuring proceeds. The individual or collective professional standards do not stress themes of the current reforms, such as teachers' responsibilities to assist colleagues in improving their instructional skills, work collaboratively with others in school budget management, develop a broad-based vision statement that reflects the educational goals of the entire community, or work to ensure that graduates have the skills needed by local businesses. One CEC standard indirectly addresses the question, "to whom is the special educator accountable?" in ways that are consonant with the new and emerging roles characterizing reform. This standard is cited and examined in the context of the third question regarding accountability.

In the middle school example, the special educator is only accountable to the students with disabilities. Or is he? Given the team decision that the special educator will consult and co-teach with the science teacher and not provide direct instruction except when the students are members of small groups with their nondisabled peers, is the special educator accountable to the students with disabilities? Is he accountable in any way to the general education students (or their parents?) who are in the small group follow-up lessons he teaches? What about his accountability to the science teacher? Presumably, he is accountable for the way he participates and completes his tasks in the implementation of the team decision.

There is little doubt that in restructured schools teachers will continue to be accountable to their primary clients (students, parents, and colleagues), but now they will have additional clients and increased accountability to some constituents. How will teachers balance their accountability to multiple stakeholders? What is the special educator to do when the needs and best interests of two or more clients conflict with those of another?

For what is the special educator accountable? Teachers have typically been accountable for their individual teaching performance (consider the nature of traditional teacher evaluation). In restructured schools teachers will be asked to work together for the betterment of the school, all students within the school, and their colleagues (National Education Goals Panel, 1991; Ysseldyke, Thurlow, & Shriner, 1992). One CEC standard was particularly forward-looking when it specified that

> Professionals promote educational quality, and intra- and interprofessional cooperation through active participation in the planning, policy development, management, and evaluation of the special education program and the education program at large so that programs remain responsive to the changing needs of persons with exceptionalities. (CEC, 1993, Standard 3.2c2, p.6)

Another dimension to consider in determining to whom the special educator is accountable is the current emphasis on student outcomes. From this frame of reference, teachers' academic credentials and teaching behaviors are only as valuable as their effectiveness in teaching students. Student outcomes are being operationalized in many schools to rely primarily on measures of achievement for entire classrooms or schools. In some settings, the school is the unit of assessment, and all professional staff have responsibility for the performance of all students. The Kentucky Reform Initiative is an example of this arrangement. If, over time, a school does not increase the percentage of students with which it has success, assistance is given to that school. For an extended period (up to one year), assistance may take such forms as consultation, management, support, and in-service training as needed to improve the performance of the instructional unit. Under this scenario, the special educator and all other educators in a building are collectively accountable for the success of all students in that building. If this becomes the direction or model of the future, what special preparation and skills will special educators require to become accountable for the performance of students who are not in their classes? What kinds of protections will be afforded truly excellent teachers with the misfortune of being assigned to a failing school? How will such collective accountability affect collegial relationships among teachers?

The fictitious middle school situation offers another perspective regarding to whom the special educator is accountable. In this case the teachers decided that the science teacher would be responsible for the primary instructional delivery. What then is the special educator's accountability for the progress of the students with disabilities? What is his accountability for the quality of instruction in science? What level of accountability, if any, does the special educator have for the nature of the behavior management strategies the science teacher uses? Who will be responsible for evaluation? Will the special students be evaluated in the same manner as the regular students? Will they take the standardized achievement tests and be counted in for school norms?

Dilemmas: Some Illustrations for Consideration

For this discussion we have selected, based on CEC standards, three areas of responsibility in which professionals may face ethical dilemmas as they participate in school restructuring or as they practice in restructured schools that aim at increasing the participation of students with disabilities in general education. They include: 1) responsibilities to individual children and their parents; 2) responsibilities to fellow professionals; and 3) responsibilities to attain and maintain appropriate qualifications. These areas are used simply to illustrate a few of the critical issues that the profession must face; we expect that readers will be able to generate substantial lists of additional dilemmas. It is not our intention to offer resolutions to any of the situations we highlight, rather we hope to demonstrate the need to devote more attention and resources to understanding the implications of school restructuring and the concomitant relationship changes for the professionals who serve children with exceptionalities. Further, we believe that discussion of these illustrations provides a rationale for increasing the emphasis on the study and application of ethics and standards in professional preparation and continuing education programs.

Responsibilities to individual children and their parents. The first statement in the CEC Code of Ethics and one of the central ethical principles of the profession, emphasizes the responsibilities of professionals to the individuals they serve.

> Special education professionals are committed to developing the highest educational and quality of life potential of individuals with exceptionalities. (CEC, 1993, Principle A, p. 4)

The principle of responsibility for individuals is reflected in many of the CEC standards of practice. The rights, needs, and treatment of individuals with exceptionalities are key to these standards. For example, several standards stress "meeting the individual needs of individuals with exceptionalities" and one specifies that grading, promotion, and graduation must be based on the unique goals and objectives for individuals with exceptionalities. An entire subsection of the standards is devoted to codifying professional responsibilities to parents of individuals with exceptionalities. Seven standards are set forth to guide professional behavior in developing relationships with parents; they are based on mutual respect for their roles in achieving benefits for the individual with exceptionalities.

One of the primary changes that is occurring in the current wave of school reform, and one that will surely characterize restructured schools, is the definitive emphasis on outcomes. Often those outcomes are measured and evaluated on a classwide or schoolwide basis. This shift represents a change in approach for both general and special educators, but the ethical dilemma for the special educator will undoubtedly be greater as class and school outcomes represent a refocusing on the performance of the group rather than on individual progress. How will special educators continue to meet their responsibilities to respond to each individual's unique needs while assuming responsibility for the performance of entire groups?

The arguments associated with the case example are similar to those advanced in the discussion of to whom the special educator is accountable. However, the crux of this dilemma is more focused on the conflict that exists between accountability and/or responsibility to individual students and their families or to general education students placed in the small groups with which the special educator conducts follow-up activities. Traditionally, and in accordance with the standards of the profession, the special educator's central responsibility is to the student with exceptionalities and his/her parents. In a true co-teaching situation where accountability for the entire project is shared among the participants, the special educator's responsibility to the general education students becomes much more pronounced, and the ethical questions surrounding the issue are far less easily resolved.

Responsibilities to fellow professionals. Special educators, perhaps because of the collaborative and interdisciplinary nature of their practice, have long recognized their responsibilities to other professionals. One full subsection of the CEC standards is devoted to describing elements of desired professional relationships. Underlying the standards for professional relationships is the belief that special educators should operate in explicitly defined roles and within clear lines of accountability. Moreover, there is an expectation that special educators will characteristically display such behaviors as "strive to develop positive attitudes among others," "cooperate," "provide consultation and assistance," and "helping . . . develop and maintain positive and accurate perceptions."

In restructured schools, teachers will be expected to collaborate with others while their roles and the roles of their colleagues are continually reshaped and redefined. Without the security of well-defined roles and clear lines of accountability, the helping role of the special educator may become less legitimate. Collaboration requires reciprocity, parity, and mutual respect (Cook & Friend, 1991a). The assumption is that all parties in the collaboration come to the table with equally valued expertise—and that all will make equally valued contributions. Consider the case example where each participant's role is defined within the context of the collaboration. Each teacher has responsibilities to the other. The science teacher must plan well-designed group lessons that accommodate the learning needs of all students. The special education teacher must learn the content well enough to design and implement meaningful follow-up activities. The co-teaching arrangement will not be successful unless each teacher meets his or her responsibilities to the other.

Responsibilities to attain and maintain appropriate qualifications. Specialization of qualifications is one of the most significant characteristics of a profession (Darling-Hammond, 1988; Heller, 1982) and one of the least practiced in education—especially in special education. There is no area of education with as severe shortages of fully qualified professionals as special education (Boe, Cook, Kaufman, & Danielson, 1993; Boe, Bobbitt, & Cook, 1993). There are several promising developments in the field that provide a structure for establishing, enforcing, and promoting appropriate qualifications for special educators. Among these are the CEC-approved statement of knowledge and skills deemed essential for all entering special education teachers (CEC, 1992), the CEC Standards for the Preparation of Special Education Personnel (CEC, 1993; Heller, 1983), the revitalization of the National Council for the Accreditation of Teacher Education (NCATE, 1992), and the establishment of the National Board for Professional Teaching Standards. Each of these mechanisms offers an avenue for the profession to set and enforce professional qualifications of its members.

Equally as important, professionals are charged with striving "to advance their knowledge and skills regarding the education of individuals with exceptionalities" by their Code of Ethics (CEC, 1993, Principle E, p.4). Several standards require special educators to attain appropriate certification and participate in ongoing continuing education. One specific standard with express meaning to the case being scrutinized in this text is:

> Professionals practice only in areas of exceptionality, at age levels, and in program models for which they are prepared by their training and/or experience. (CEC, 1993, Standard 3.2c2, p.6)

In the co-teaching case described in Table 6.1, there is no significant ethical issue regarding the qualifications of the professionals for the roles they are filling. The science teacher has primary responsibility for the science content and delivery. The special educator, who has been determined to lack appropriate qualifications for science teaching, will support the classroom teacher while fulfilling a role similar to that of a student teacher. This role is within the limits of the special educator's competence and will be executed under the guidance of the science teacher. Where the ethical questions enter the picture is in other consultation, collaboration, or co-teaching situations that require the special educator to practice in areas for which she is not appropriately prepared through experience or training. As restructuring leads to greater flexibility and a decreased emphasis on categorical programming, such situations are likely to be frequently encountered.

SUMMARY

Perhaps more than ever before in the history of special education, ability and skill in ethical deliberation are critically needed by special education teachers. Reform is rapidly changing the face of special education to include greater teacher participation in decision making. New conceptualizations of the roles of special educators are needed to include the role of teacher leader with knowledge and skills to participate and lead colleagues in their efforts to make effective and ethical decisions regarding students. Along with the role change, a framework for ethical deliberation and decision making is essential and should include attention to policy/law, facts, values, and professional standards. Only when special educators are fully prepared to participate with and lead colleagues in making ethical decisions regarding students will we have effective special education reform. It is in the collegial decision making that school reform and special education reform merge. And it is at this juncture that the most serious ethical questions arise about increasing the participation of students with disabilities in general education programs.

REFERENCES

American Federation of Teachers (1946). *AFT code of ethics*. Washington, DC: Author.

Bacharach, S. B. (Ed.). (1990). *Educational reform: Making sense of it all*. Boston: Allyn & Bacon.

Barth, R. S. (1990). *Improving schools from within*. San Francisco, CA: Jossey-Bass.

Benjamin, M., & Curtis, J. (1981). *Ethics in nursing*. New York: Oxford University Press.

Billingsley, B. S. (1993). Teacher retention and attrition in special and general education: A critical review of the literature. *The Journal of Special Education, 24*, 137–174.

Boe, E. E., Bobbit, S. A., & Cook, L. H. (1993). *Whither didst thou go? Retention, reassignment, migration, and attrition of special education teachers in national perspective* (Research Rep. 1993-TSD2). Philadelphia: University of Pennsylvania, Graduate School of Education, Center for Research and Evaluation in Social Policy.

Boe, E. E., Cook, L. H., Kaufman, M. J., & Danielson, L. (1993). *From whither didst thou come? Sources of special and general education teachers in national perspective* (Research Rep. 1993-TSD1). Philadelphia: University of Pennsylvania, Graduate School of Education, Center for Research and Evaluation in Social Policy.

Carnegie Task Force on Teaching as a Profession. (1986). *A nation prepared: Teachers for the 21st century*. New York: Carnegie Forum on Education and the Economy.

Conley, S. C., & Bacharach, S. B. (1990). From school-site management to participatory school-site management. *Phi Delta Kappan, 75*(3), 539–544.

Cook, L. (1978). The relationship of teachers' training to perceptions of student behavior problems, teaching competence, and the utility of support roles (Doctoral dissertation, University of Michigan, 1979). *Dissertation Abstracts International,* 6059A.

Cook, L., & Cavallaro, C.C. (1983). *Experimental internships in teaching students with serious emotional disturbances* (Grant No. GOO8301304). Washington, DC: U.S. Department of Education.

Cook, L., & Friend, M. (1991a). Collaboration in special education: Coming of age in the 1990s. *Preventing School Failure, 35*(2), 24–27.

Cook, L., & Friend, M. (1991b). Principles for the practice of collaboration in schools. *Preventing School Failure, 35*, 6–9.

Council for Exceptional Children. (1983). Code of ethics and standards for professional practice. *Exceptional Children, 50*, 205–209.

Council for Exceptional Children. (1992). CEC common core knowledge and skills essential for all beginning special education teachers. Reston, VA: Author.

Council for Exceptional Children. (1993). Professional standards and practice. *Policy Manual,* (Section Three, Part 2, pp. 1–7). Reston, VA: Author.

Darling-Hammond, L. (1988). Policy and professionalism. In A. Lieberman (Ed.), *Building a professional culture in schools*. New York: Teachers College Press.

Darling-Hammond, L., & Berry, B. (1988). *The evolution of teacher policy*. Santa Monica, CA: Rand Corp.

Donaldson, G. A. (1993). Working smarter together. *Educational Leadership, 51*(2), 12–16.

Friend, M., & Cook, L. (1990). Collaboration as a predictor for success in school reform. *Journal of Educational and Psychological Consultation, 1*(1), 69–86.

Friend, M., & Cook, L. (1992a). *Interactions: Collaboration skills for school professionals.* White Plains, NY: Longman.

Friend, M., & Cook, L. (1992b). It's my turn: The ethics of collaboration. *Journal of Educational and Psychological Consultation, 3,* 181–184.

Fullan, M. G., & Miles, M. B. (1992). Getting reform right: What works and what doesn't. *Phi Delta Kappan, 73*(10), 745–752.

Gable, R. A., Arllen, N. L., & Cook, L. (1993). But let's not overlook the ethics of collaboration. *Preventing School Failure, 37*(4), 32–36.

Gallessich, J. (1982). *The profession and practice of consultation.* San Francisco, CA: Jossey-Bass.

Goodlad, J. (1984). *A place called school.* New York: McGraw-Hill.

Heller, H. W. (1983). Special education professional standards: Need, value, and use. *Exceptional Children, 50*(3), 2–7.

Hocutt, A. M., Martin, E. W., & McKinney, J. D. (1991). Historical and legal context of mainstreaming. In J. W. Lloyd, N. N. Singh, & A. C. Repp (Eds.), *The regular education initiative: Alternative perspectives on concepts, issues and models* (pp. 17–28). Sycamore, IL: Sycamore.

Holmes Group (1986). *Tomorrow's teachers.* East Lansing, MI: Author.

Howe, K. R., & Miramontes, O. B. (1991). A framework for ethical deliberation in special education. *Journal of Special Education, 25*(1), 7–25.

Howe, K. R., & Miramontes, O. B. (1992). *The ethics of special education.* New York: Teachers College Press.

Kauffman, J. M. (1992). Foreword in Howe & Miramontes, *The ethics of special education* (pp. xi–xvii), New York: Teachers College Press.

Lenz, B. K., & Deshler, D. D. (in press). Ethical issues related to translating research in learning disabilities into practice. In S. Vaughn & C. Bos (Eds.), *Research issues in learning disabilities: Theory, methodology, assessment, and ethics.* Boston: Springer-Verlag.

Lieberman, A. (Ed.). (1988). *Building a professional culture in schools.* New York: Teachers College Press.

Lieberman, A., & Miller, L. (1990). Restructuring schools: What matters and what works. *Phi Delta Kappan,* 759–764.

Lieberman, M. (1956). *Education as a profession.* Englewood Cliffs, NJ: Prentice-Hall.

Lippitt, G. L. (1969). *Organizational renewal.* Englewood Cliffs, NJ: Prentice-Hall.

Little, J. W. (1982). Norms of collegiality and experimentation: Workplace conditions of school success. *American Educational Research Journal, 19,* 325–340.

Little, J. W. (1993). Teachers' professional development in a climate of educational reform. *Educational Evaluation and Policy Analysis, 15*(2), 129–151.

Maeroff, G. I. (1988). Blueprint for empowering teachers. *Phi Delta Kappan, 69*(7), 472–477.

Maeroff, G. I. (1993). Building teams to rebuild schools. *Phi Delta Kappan, 74*(7), 512–519.

Meek, A. (1988). On teaching as a profession: A conversation with Linda Darling-Hammond. *Educational Leadership, 46*(3), 11–17.

Midgley, C., & Wood, S. (1993). Beyond site-based management: Empowering teachers to reform schools. *Phi Delta Kappan, 75*(3), 245–252.

National Commission for the Protection of Human Subjects of Biomedical and Behavioral Research. (1978). *The Belmont report: Ethical principles and guidelines for the protection of human subjects of research* (DHEW Publication No. OS 78-0012). Washington, DC: U.S. Government Printing Office.

National Council for the Accreditation of Teacher Education. (1992). *Standards, procedures, and policies for the accreditation of professional education units*. Washington, DC: Author.

National Education Association. (1993). Code of ethics of the education profession. *1993–94 NEA Handbook* (pp. 376–377). Washington, DC: Author.

National Education Goals Panel. (1991). *The national education goals report: Building a nation of learners*. Washington, DC: U.S. Government Printing Office.

Paul, J. L., Gallagher, J. J., Kendrick, S. B., Thomas, D. D., & Young, J. F. (1992). *Handbook for ethical policy making*. Chapel Hill: North Carolina Policy Institute, University of North Carolina.

Prestine, N. A., & Bowen, C. (1993). Benchmarks of change: Assessing essential school restructuring. *Educational Evaluation and Policy Analysis, 15*(3), 298–319.

Pugach, M., & Sapon-Shevin, M. (1987). New agendas for special education policy: What the national reports haven't said. *Exceptional Children, 53*, 265–299.

Ruck, C. L. (1986). Creating a school context for collegial supervision: The principal's role as contractor. *Oregon School Study Council Bulletin, 30*(3).

Sailor, W. (1991). Special education and the restructured school. *Remedial and Special Education, 12*(6), 8–22.

Sergiovanni, T. J., & Moore, J. H. (Eds.). (1989). *Schooling for tomorrow: Directing reform to issues that count*. Boston: Allyn & Bacon.

Shulman, L. (1987). Knowledge and teaching: Foundations of the new reform. *Harvard Educational Review, 57*(1), 1–22.

Sockett, H. (1990). Accountability, trust, and ethical codes of practice. In J. I. Goodlad, R. Soder, & K. A. Sirotnik (Eds.), *The moral dimensions of teaching*, (pp.224–250). San Francisco, CA: Jossey-Bass.

Van Scotter, R. D., Haas, J. D., Kraft, R. K., & Schott, J. D. (1991). *Social foundations of education*. Englewood Cliffs, NJ: Prentice-Hall.

Will, M. C. (1986). Educating children with learning problems: A shared responsibility. *Exceptional Children, 52*, 411–415.

Ysseldyke, J. E., & Algozzine, B. (1982). *Critical issues in special and remedial education*. Boston: Houghton Mifflin.

Ysseldyke, J. E., Thurlow, M. L., & Shriner, J. G. (1992). Outcomes are for special educators too. *Teaching Exceptional Children, 25*, 36–50.

8

REFORMING TEACHER EDUCATION
Challenging the Philosophy and Practices of Educating Regular and Special Educators

PAUL SINDELAR, MARLEEN PUGACH,
CYNTHIA GRIFFIN, & BARBARA SEIDL

INTRODUCTION

IN this chapter, we argue for a reconceptualization of teacher education in which programs for classroom teachers and teachers of students with mild disabilities are fully integrated. We also recognize and argue the need to maintain distinct programs in certain areas in which specialized skills are required for effective teaching, including severe emotional disturbance (SED), severe and profound disabilities, visual disabilities, and hearing impairments. In all cases, the process of teacher education should occur in the context of inclusive education.

We begin this chapter by considering the characteristics of traditional special education teacher education, the context in which it now exists, and how these factors affect the probability of serious reform. We describe several forces that have exerted considerable influence on contemporary teacher education, including changing conceptions of teaching and learning to teach, education and special education reform, and marketplace and demographic realities. On the basis of this analysis and some speculation about the work of teachers in the schools of the future, we argue for the union we have described. We present what we believe to be elements essential to the success of integrated teacher education and conclude by discussing what special education teacher education programs still would be required, by virtue of the specialized skills they comprise.

CONTEMPORARY SPECIAL EDUCATION TEACHER EDUCATION

The distinctive character of special education teacher education has set it apart from general teacher education. For one thing, the idea that special education begins where general education ends has been pervasive and has shaped school practice and teacher education. Special education teacher education also seems to have clung to a competency-based orientation and has been, in general, more technological and positivistic. The nature of the students it has served is diverse, and this diversity has made it and kept it categorical. Unlike general teacher education, it is federally subsidized, but in spite of substantial state and federal investment since 1958, critical shortages are chronic and severe. In the sections that follow, we elaborate each of these points for the purpose of contrasting the character of general and special education teacher education.

The Effect of Teacher Education on School Practice

One of us (Pugach, 1988) has argued that the reform of general teacher education has been slowed by the existence of special education and the dependency it has created in classroom teachers who rely on its assistance for handling problems. By teaching classroom teachers to refer students who pose problems, teacher educators have limited the number and nature of the problems that may be accommodated in classrooms. By teaching classroom teachers to relinquish responsibility for students with problems, teacher educators of both stripes have worked to perpetuate the distinction between special and general education.

For our purposes in this chapter, we need to emphasize only that our traditional concepts of general and special education practice have influenced teacher education. Because classroom teachers refer problems, the work of teacher educators has not encompassed in any serious manner strategies for accommodating students with problems. Because special education has served as the repository for students with problems, its work has focused on preparing teachers for work with students with disabilities in a manner independent from the general education enterprise. Although we have recognized the problem, we have only begun to explore the issues of integration (Gartner & Lipsky, 1987; Gersten & Woodward, 1990).

Competency-Based Teacher Education

Competency-based teacher education (CBTE) emerged in special education in the early 1970s (Shores, Cegelka, & Nelson, 1973), simultaneous with its emergence in teacher education (Freiberg & Waxman, 1990). Although interest in CBTE peaked in the late 1970s, elements of it have lived on to become part of the fabric of special education teacher education. One reason for this persistence is the requirement for competencies in applications for Office of Special Education Programs (OSEP) personnel preparation grants. Among the criteria with which such grants are evaluated is "the extent to which the application includes a delineation of competencies that program graduates will acquire" (U. S. Department of Education, 1993, p. 38). However, in addition to OSEP reviews, state department and accreditation reviews often require the delineation of competencies as well (Gable, 1991).

Positivism. Special education is an offspring of psychology and was influenced strongly by behavioral psychology. One legacy of these historical roots is a strong, pervasive positivistic orientation (Frudden & Healy, 1986). We have believed that our actions as teachers have predictable and measurable effects on our students. We have believed that we can break down complex behaviors into components that may be taught in isolation and put back together. To the extent that task-analytic, skill-based instruction governs contemporary special education practice, we are distanced from our general education colleagues, for whom phenomenological and wholistic instruction prevails, as we note later in this chapter.

Disability Categories

Disability categories are the infrastructure of special education and have been since the passage of P. L. 101–476, the Individuals with Disabilities Education Act (IDEA) (1975). The implementation of IDEA requires the categorical classification of students. Brady, Conroy, and Langford (1984) and Hagerty and Abramson (1987) both commented that categorical identification spurred by IDEA begat categorical service delivery, which in turn begat categorical licensure and teacher education. Thus, that special education licensure has been (and remains largely) categorical has deep roots in the ways schools are funded for special education programs.

A more basic concern about special education classifications is Reynolds's (1979) argument about the aptitude-treatment interaction (ATI) assumption that undergirds special education practice. He contended that this assumption has buttressed our belief in categorical classifications. We believed we would find educational approaches that worked differentially well for individuals with particular kinds of disabilities, as learning braille works uniquely well for students who are blind. With this rationale for identification and classification by disability, categorical service delivery, categorical licensure, and categorical teacher education were natural consequences. Unlike the ongoing impact of legislation, however, our faith in the assumption of aptitude-treatment interactions has lapsed. In arguments about categorical versus noncategorical practice, ATI is seldom evoked to defend current practice.

Argumentation may be too strong a characterization for the nature of the discourse on noncategorical teacher education. Beginning with Reynolds's (1979) call for noncategorical teacher education, the debate seems somewhat one-sided, with calls for noncategorical special education practice predominating. What's more, the small body of empirical work on the validity of categorical teacher education

(Gable, Hendrickson, Shores, & Young, 1983; Marston, 1987; O'Sullivan, Marston, & Magnusson, 1987) has provided consistent support for a noncategorical approach. Gable et al. demonstrated that teachers did not plan or behave differently as a function of the classification of their students, all of whom were classified in mild disability categories. Marston and his colleagues documented that teachers trained and licensed to work with students with a particular disability were no more (or less) effective in working with them than teachers who were trained and licensed to work with a different classification of students.

Nonetheless, this strong and widespread sentiment for noncategorical teacher education and licensure has had little effect on the way states license teachers. Three related studies are pertinent to this point. Belch (1979) reported that 22% of the states (and the District of Columbia) described themselves as having an equivalent to Pennsylvania's comprehensive special education license. (At the time of this survey, the Pennsylvania license covered all disabilities except sensory impairments, on a K–12 basis. For the purpose of comparisons with the studies that followed, we would judge these to be truly noncategorical.) In a later survey (Chapey, Pyszkoski, & Trimarco, 1985), 49% of the states described themselves as having exclusively noncategorical or a combination of categorical and noncategorical special education licensure. However, only 29% were truly noncategorical (although 70% expressed a desire to become so). In a third replication of this survey, Cranston-Gingras and Mauser (1992) reported that 65% of state special education directors characterized their licensure as noncategorical or a combination. However, only 27% reported themselves as being strictly noncategorical.

Although these data are open to interpretation, there are two points that jump out of them at us: First, there has been little change over 14 years separating the first and last of these surveys in the number of states that characterize themselves as having strictly noncategorical certification. Second, after two decades of serious discussion about the validity of categorical teacher education, nearly three-fourths of the states maintain some kind of categorical licensure (Cranston-Gingras & Mauser, 1992). Clearly, categorical teacher education and licensure are alive and well.

Federal Subsidization

Federal support for the preparation of personnel to work with individuals with disabilities dates from 1958 (Sutherland & Castleberry, 1985). For FY 1994, the Clinton administration requested $90,122,000 for personnel preparation (U. S. Department of Education, 1993) of which $20 million has been earmarked for new projects (U. S. Department of Education, 1993). In FY 1990, the last year for which such data are available, federal support under Part D for persons preparing for careers in special education and related fields reached 7,410 students (U. S. Department of Education, 1992), with 1,925 funding recipients receiving degrees. An additional 2,792 students were supported through the Part H Infant and Toddler program.

Unmet Demand for Teachers and Other Professionals

In 1989–90, over 290,000 special education teachers were employed in our nation's schools. An additional 26,310 were needed, however, to fill vacancies and positions occupied by unlicensed staff (U.S. Department of Education, 1992). As large as this shortfall is, it represents a 6% reduction from 1988–89. Furthermore, recent research has illuminated our understanding of teacher shortages. We now know that shortages are not universal, for example, and that the problem does not result exclusively from undercapacity. Further, particularly in urban areas, shortages may be due in part to the overidentification of minority students as having disabilities (Pugach, 1993).

The U. S. Department of Education annually reports to Congress teacher shortages by state and disability category, and the variability in these data make clear that shortages are neither universal nor uniform. In 1989–90, for example, overall shortfalls (as a percentage of total teachers employed) ranged from less than ½% in Connecticut to nearly 29% in Montana. In three states, shortfalls were more than one standard deviation below the national mean; in eight others, they were more than one standard deviation above it. Although it would be hard to characterize these two groups of outlying states demographically, recent research (Lauritzen & Friedman, in press; Smith-Davis & Billingsley, in press) suggests that the state may not be the appropriate unit of analysis. Shortages constitute a particular problem in rural and inner city schools, while none may exist for teachers of students with mild disabilities in suburban schools.

Shortages by disability category range from 22% in deaf-blind and 14% in emotional disturbance and other health impairments, to 7% in mental retardation and 7½% in specific learning disabilities (U.S. Department of Education, 1992). In this sense, classifications are like states in that teacher shortages are not uniform across them.

Research on teacher retention and attrition, reviewed recently by Brownell and Smith (1992) and Billingsley (1993), has added to our understanding of teacher shortages. It is clear that attrition exacerbates undersupply and that students who populate traditional teacher education programs—young, white females from middle-class backgrounds—are at greatest risk to leave teaching within five years of entering the profession. Although less is known about successful retention strategies, OSEP has invested substantially in studies of attrition and retention. This research program has the potential to offer schools strategies for promoting retention.

Summary

We have argued that, in the traditional model of school practice, special education begins where general education ends, and the two are not well integrated. In a similar sense, traditional special education teacher education may be conceptualized as being complementary to traditional teacher education, but not integrated with it.

It has been and continues to be competency-based, positivistic, categorical, and subsidized by the federal government, whereas general education is not. If we special educators agree that our job is to provide qualified teachers for all students with disabilities, then we are not doing it well.

These defining characteristics put special education in opposition to general education, which has taken on a more wholistic, phenomenological character and which receives little, if any, support from the federal government. Thus, the union of special and general teacher education will not come easily, as conflicting philosophical beliefs must be reconciled. However difficult to achieve, union still makes sense. The development of a cadre of classroom teachers capable of working effectively with a wide range of students should prevent overlabeling and reduce referrals, thereby slackening the demand for special education placement and consequently special education teachers. At the same time, the promise in IDEA of maintaining students with disabilities in least restrictive placements may be more nearly fulfilled.

FORCES OPERATING ON TEACHER EDUCATION

In this section, we consider the diverse array of forces that provide the context for the reform of teacher education. They include: a) an expanded view of the complexities of learning to teach; b) educational reform reports that delineate problems faced by teachers and outline recommendations for teacher education; c) reform occurring in special education around issues of inclusion; and d) marketplace and demographic realities. Some of these forces militate against change; some work to facilitate it.

Expanding View of Learning to Teach

Contributing toward an increased understanding of the complexities of learning and learning to teach are advances in cognitive psychology and research on teacher thinking and teacher beliefs. Recent developments in cognitive psychology have altered the concept of learning from a mechanical model of knowledge transmission to a process of active construction on the part of the learner in a social environment (Leinhardt, 1992; Prawat, 1992). Theoretical constructs such as cognitive apprenticeship (Rogoff, 1990; Collins, Brown, & Newman, 1990), authentic activity, and situated cognition (Brown, Collins, & Duguid, 1989) have thrown the terminology of scaffolding, mediated activity, zone of proximal development, and intersubjectivity into the laps, and roles, of teachers. The complexity of these constructs illuminates as never before the difficult nature of teaching. These efforts to construct a new understanding of how children learn recasts the nature of teaching as a far more complex and demanding task and compels the field of teacher education to design programs that prepare teachers for this complex role.

Work in the area of teacher thinking (Feiman-Nemser, 1980; Kleinfeld & Noordhoff, 1988) has contributed to a new understanding of the complexity of the knowledge teachers possess and use in their daily work. By identifying teachers' work as occurring in an ill-structured domain, these researchers have redefined the job of teaching from a narrow transmission of information to a process of decision-making in a constantly changing environment (Merseth, 1992). It is difficult to define or delineate all of the knowledge that teachers bring to bear upon these decisions. This difficulty has led to the definition of "craft knowledge" as a "particular form of morally appropriate, intelligent, and sensible know-how" (Grimmett & MacKinnon, 1992, p. 396) in which experience and work provide the context through which teachers construct an understanding of issues concerning content-related and learner-focused pedagogy. This work is supported by Doyle's (1986) assertion that teachers making complicated decisions under conditions of inherent uncertainty are required to engage in practical thinking that leads to action appropriate for a particular set of circumstances. The knowledge teachers must use in dealing with this complexity is experiential and is achieved through "reflection-in-action" (Schon, 1983).

Research in the area of teacher beliefs (Hollingsworth, 1989; Ross & Smith, 1992) has drawn attention to the durability and influence of the beliefs that teacher education students bring with them. Preservice teachers construct new learning through the lens of experience, just as children do. The 12 years of experience in classrooms, the "apprenticeship of observation" (Lortie, 1975) in which all incoming teacher education students have participated, results in rigidly held beliefs about education and the role of the teacher that prove very difficult to overcome (Goodlad, 1984; Hollingsworth, 1989; Lortie, 1975). In her work, Johnston (1992) found that the images that student teachers have concerning the right way to teach were strong and consistent across time. These images act as filters through which preservice teachers screen and construct information presented during their preparation. Further, work in teacher socialization (Little, 1982; Rosenholtz, 1989) has shown that the culture of schools, instead of facilitating broader understandings, acts as a powerful contributor to perpetuate the naive, and often narrow, beliefs that novice teachers bring with them.

It is evident that teachers think and make decisions in a much more sophisticated manner than teacher educators typically have presumed. Further, their beliefs are filters that shape and screen much of what they are exposed to in their programs. Students bring strong beliefs concerning diversity (Ross & Smith, 1992) and what constitutes good teaching that need to be sufficiently challenged to change. Teacher education must be responsive to this fact and provide many opportunities for students to understand the values, attitudes, and beliefs they bring to their work (Johnston, 1992).

These conceptions of teaching differ dramatically from the positivistic conception of special education practice we described earlier. The gulf that separates these two conceptions of teaching must be bridged before general and special education teacher educators can begin to move forward together on a common agenda of reform. Strongly held beliefs are not easily changed, and reconciling diverse and conflicting viewpoints certainly will slow the process of teacher education reform. However, no reform can succeed without first resolving this issue.

Educational Reform

The reform agenda of the 1980s has also exerted considerable influence on teacher education. Beginning with *A Nation at Risk* (National Commission on Excellence in Education, 1983), criticisms of the quality of education in our schools have focused attention on what was perceived as poor teacher preparation and lack of standards (Education Commission of the States, 1983; National Science Foundation, 1983).

These reports carried special significance for the field of special education. In many of them, special education was noticeably absent from the larger picture of reform, an omission that prompted a variety of reactions from special educators. Some questioned whether pressure to teach children who were considered the best and the brightest put excellence before equity in public education (Sapon-Shevin, 1987). This concern appeared to be supported by less publicized reports, such as the Heritage Foundation Report (1984), which criticized what they viewed as excessive spending on the education of students with disabilities to the detriment of children in general education. Others posited that, unless integration between special education and general education occurred, pressure on general education to achieve excellence would even further widen the schism between the two (Shepard, 1987). Further, insistence on separate preparation programs predicated on different areas of expertise perpetuated the manner in which general education used special education placements to manage children who fail to meet standards of excellence (Pugach, 1987).

The conversations that ensued forced faculty in teacher education programs to begin to ask important questions concerning the nature of teaching, the process of preparing teachers to meet the needs of a diverse population, the culture of schools, and the lack of status and limited career opportunities in teaching. Consequently, the second wave of reform reports focused on teacher preparation (Sikula, 1990). In the call for an overhaul of the teaching profession, both the Carnegie Forum on Education and the Economy (1986) and the Holmes Group (1986) focused on restructuring the manner in which teachers are prepared and provided a framework for the professionalization of teaching. To this end, both reports proposed differentiated career opportunities and recommended restructuring school environments to support teachers as leaders and to provide for improved clinical experiences for teacher education students. Goodlad (1990), in his analysis of schools and teaching, supported the notion that teachers must be prepared to be leaders; he concluded that "the problem is one of preparing teachers to confront and deal with the daily circumstances of schooling while redesigning their schools" (p. 4). Simply preparing teachers to function well within existing educational structures is insufficient. The reform agenda clearly outlined the need to prepare teachers capable of challenging the status quo, thus improving the conditions of schools.

To the extent that special education and students with disabilities are now part of the conversation about education reform and restructuring, the job of reforming teacher education is made easier. The question of how best to accommodate students with disabilities is subsumed under the broader issue of accommodating diversity, and the success of efforts to accommodate diversity in classrooms hinges on the effectiveness and motivation of teachers. If we accept the premise that all teachers must work more effectively with hard-to-teach students, then the overlap between general and special education teacher education is made clear.

Special Education Reform

Special education has been deeply involved in reform of its own. Although Madeline Will was not the first to express concern over the segregated nature of special education, her paper on the Regular Education Initiative (1986) brought these dissatisfactions to the forefront. Others have argued for the merger of regular education and special education (Stainback & Stainback, 1984), insisting that a vision of quality education for all could be more readily produced within it (Gartner & Lipsky, 1987). Those who support inclusive education claim that special education has become a dumping ground for difficult-to-teach students, in particular, students from culturally and linguistically diverse backgrounds; that programs are fragmented and lack coherence (Allington & McGill-Franzen, 1989); and that there is seldom an effort to coordinate the teaching that takes place in general and special education classrooms (Gersten & Woodward, 1990). Therefore, much of special education reform has been centered on reducing the use of pull-out programs and instead educating students in general education classrooms (Sailor, 1991).

Realizing this agenda would also necessitate reform in teacher education along the lines we have described. The success of reintegrating students with disabilities, minimizing unnecessary referrals, and preventing inappropriate labelling hinges on the ability of classroom teachers to create and sustain effective classroom environments and, with specialist teachers, to collaborate in planning, implementing, and evaluating instruction.

Professional Interaction

One of the cornerstones of reform in teacher education and special education alike is collaborative professional interaction. As teacher education responds to the demands of teaching in a diverse society, preparing students for increased professional interaction becomes a must. Issues such as the fundamentally complex and difficult nature of teaching, increasing numbers of students at risk, dissatisfaction with the effectiveness of special education delivery models, and new administrative responses to reform add even more to the need for teachers who are capable of interacting professionally in solving problems and creating solutions.

Teaching is a demanding and complex task made even more difficult when performed in isolation and without the benefit of support from others. Professional isolation undermines teachers' abilities to remain committed to improving their work. Research concerning the role of collegiality and collaborative work in creating successful learning environments for teachers and students (Goodlad, 1984; Little, 1982; Rosenholtz, 1989) has demonstrated the importance of professional interaction to success in the workplace. Not only are teachers more satisfied, but their professional growth and ability to meet the needs of students are greatly enhanced.

Contemporary reform efforts are predicated on the assumption that traditional methods and instructional arrangements are not serving the current population of students well. To create effective schools, it is essential that professionals collaborate on such issues as: a) what needs to be done to increase the educational opportunities of our students; b) how to build upon our students' backgrounds and cultural experiences; and c) how to provide a cohesive network of education for all students.

In special education, beginning in the early 1970s, consultation was seen as a natural extension of the service delivery continuum and was considered an indirect service in which special education teachers provided training to classroom teachers (Lilly, 1971). As the importance of parity in effective collaboration and the expertise that classroom teachers brought to problem solving were recognized, professional interaction evolved into a collaborative process in which participants now eschew the expert role (Idol, Paolucci-Whitcomb, & Nevin, 1986; Pugach & Johnson, 1988).

Collaborative work has received even more attention because of recent special education reform, which has focused on inclusion (Sailor, 1991) and has consisted of creating integrated placements for students (Pugach & Warger, 1993; Sailor, 1989; Wang, 1989). These new instructional configurations have propelled collaborative skills for special educators to new heights of importance. Many put special educators to work in classrooms, with classroom teachers, designing and implementing instructional arrangements.

Collaboration also is an important issue in general education reform. The proliferation of site-based management models characterized by shared decision making and teacher empowerment (David, 1989; Harrison, Killon, & Mitchell, 1989) have changed the roles of all of those involved in education and forced the need for increased professional interaction.

The configurations and relationships that bring professionals together to plan collectively and problem solve (Johnson & Pugach, 1992) shape professional interaction. To a large degree, how effectively professionals collaborate in different situations will depend on the quality of their preparation, which hinges on the manner in which teacher education programs are able to merge and share knowledge and responsibilities across disciplines. Instead of contributing to the norms of isolation and autonomy that plague the schools (Su, 1990), teacher education programs must be the initiation point for socializing teachers into a profession in which interaction and collaboration are the norms. Teacher educators must model and provide opportunities for shared problem solving, support students in the attainment of collaborative skills, and foster an ethos in which a community of learners share the responsibility for educating all students—an ethic that makes interaction a must.

Realities of the Marketplace

In this section of our chapter, we examine a number of political, economic, and societal forces operating on reform in teacher education, including the growing diversity of the student population in schools today and the potential for diversity to be commonplace in the schools of tomorrow. In addition, teacher shortages, fiscal exigency, and state licensure requirements are examined for the potential they have to promote or impede reform. Finally, the implications for special education teacher education are discussed.

Changing demographics. The Center for Research on Elementary and Middle Schools (1990) has projected that by the year 2000: a) Hispanics will constitute more than 25% of the birth to 17 population; b) the number of African-American youth will increase by 22%; and c) the number of children whose primary language is not English will increase by 75%. Although the diversity in schools of the future demands the attention of all educators, the diverse group of students who attend public schools today present immediate challenges—challenges influenced by the realities of their worlds.

Some of these realities were made stark in a recent article by Hodgkinson (1991):

- Since 1987, one fourth of all preschool children in the U.S. have been living in poverty.
- Every year, about 350,000 children are born to mothers who were addicted to cocaine during pregnancy.
- Twenty percent of America's preschool children have not been vaccinated against polio.
- The "Norman Rockwell" family—a working father, a housewife mother, and two children of school age—constitutes only 6% of U.S. households today.
- At least two million school-age children have no adult supervision at all after school.
- About one third of preschool children are destined for school failure because of poverty, neglect, sickness, handicapping conditions, and lack of adult protection and nurturance. (p. 10)

These unhappy truths point out "spectacular changes that have occurred in the nature of the children who come to school" (Hodgkinson, 1991, p. 10). Hodgkinson's (1991) demographic analysis is reinforced by additional reports in the popular press documenting the condition of children who attend U.S. public schools. For example:

The child poverty rate rose by more than 11% during the 1980s, reaching 17.9% in 1989. Black children were the most likely to fall into this group. In 1989, a black child had a 39.8% chance of living in poverty, a Native American child a 38.8% chance and a Hispanic child a 32.2% chance. The figure for Asian children was 17.1% and for white children 12.5%. ("Poverty Rates Rise," 1992)

Recently, the conditions at an elementary school attended by immigrant children living near downtown Los Angeles were highlighted:

The student body is more than 93 percent Latino . . . A third of the students were born outside of the United States, and well over half are not proficient in English . . . In the school library there are books in Tagalog, Korean, Vietnamese, Spanish and English. But not even a third of the faculty can speak Spanish . . . Most of the newest immigrants come from Central America, and many bring with them the trauma of war. ("Immigrant Schools: The Wrong Lessons," 1993)

Hodgkinson (1991) concluded his analysis by asking, "What can educators do that they are not already doing to reduce the number of children 'at-risk' in America and to get them achieving well in school settings?" and asserting that "There is no time to waste in fixing blame; we need to act" (p. 10). Despite the urgency in Hodgkinson's message, action is not always easy to accomplish, and the challenge is multidimensional. Part of the challenge lies in the need for teachers to make a distinction between what constitutes a problem and what may be thought of as a resource, as in the case of educating children whose first language is not English. A second dimension pertains to teachers' perceptions of their efficacy. In a study of classroom teachers' teaching efficacy (i.e., the belief that a single teacher can make a difference), Smylie (1988) observed that the lower the achievement levels of students in their classes, the less likely were teachers to believe they could affect student learning. This finding applied to both teachers who did and did not communicate confidence in their ability to teach. Therefore, when teachers with a low sense of efficacy are confronted with a diverse group of students, a kind of professional paralysis may set in, and the effects on both teachers and students may be dramatic.

There are teachers in difficult classroom situations who believe they cannot possibly affect the learning of low-performing students. There are also teachers who are unlikely to modify their instructional practices if they believe that factors outside their control (e.g., poverty and homelessness) are the major influences on student learning (Ashton & Webb, 1986). Yet, the instructional and classroom management challenges facing teachers today probably will not diminish any time soon. With increasing numbers of at-risk children attending public schools and the startling 170% increase in the identification of students with learning disabilities from 1976–77 to 1990–91 (U.S. Department of Education, 1992), teachers are certain to be challenged into the twenty-first century. The challenge for teacher educators is to find ways of preparing teachers to meet such realities.

Teacher shortages. Smith-Davis and Billingsley (in press) described teacher supply and demand as "a puzzle" (p. 1), influenced by many competing variables, but best conceptualized and addressed at the local level. These authors concur with Rudner's (1987) recommendation that teacher supply and demand are "best understood with local data concerning local schools and different teaching areas, not data at the state and national level describing averages" (p. 8). Across the country, supply and demand varies; consequently, the design of intervention strategies should reflect the specific needs of each community.

Establishing the need to examine supply and demand within each community does not negate the importance of considering broad-based, longitudinal data on the supply of and demand for special education teachers. Reports from the Association for School, College, and University Staffing reveal that the demand for special educators has been well documented (Smith-Davis & Billingsley, in press). In these reports, several special education categories rank high on the national teacher shortage list and have been for several years. It would not be surprising then to find that the supply of new special education graduates has historically fallen short of the need for special educators. Using the *Annual Report to Congress* (U.S. Department of Education, 1992) to estimate the demand for teachers and the *Digest of Education Statistics* (National Center for Education Statistics, 1992) to estimate the number of new teachers entering the field, we made comparisons across three academic years, 1986–1989, and found that the percentage of need met by new graduates ranged from 55.8% to 59.4%. Consequently, more than 40% of the need for special education teachers each year was met with other personnel (e.g., returning special educators who had been on leave, teachers teaching out-of-field, and less than fully certified teachers), or was not met at all.

Teacher shortages present a significant barrier to the reform of teacher education. With SEAs, OSEP compliance monitors, and parents pressing districts to hire certified teachers, districts have leaned on teacher education programs to produce more teachers faster. Given strong political pressure to meet district needs for teachers (and current high enrollments), special education teacher educators may be too engrossed in maintaining the status quo to undertake a program of serious and basic reform.

Financial exigency. Special education is an expensive system, which, in times of financial need, becomes vulnerable to funding reductions. That hard financial times currently coincide with a period of movement to more inclusive programs presents problems, most notably the potential for the integration of students with disabilities to be undertaken without an adequate investment in the capacity to do so. In Florida, for example, the "basic mainstream" cost factor was designed to support inclusion by doubling the basic program cost factor for the time special education students spend in integrated programs (Florida Department of Education, 1992–93). However, there is no guarantee that money generated by such "double basic funding" will be used to support students who have been reintegrated. Consequently, special educators have moved slowly to embrace inclusive education, and the process of teacher education reform also has been slowed.

State licensure requirements. The issue here is that reform in teacher educa-tion is often constrained by state requirements for licensure and regulations for program approval (Pugach & Lilly, 1984). Teacher educators are preparing their students for jobs in schools and must be sensitive to market conditions. It would be difficult to justify the preparation of teachers for school positions that do not exist, no matter how sensitive the training program is to future directions. In sum, state regulations tend to reflect current or past practice and can inhibit the design of progressive teacher education programs.

Implications for Teacher Education

Taken together, forces that promote teacher education reform—changing demo-graphics and the convergence of the general and special education reform agendas on issues of equity and accommodation—may very nearly balance out the forces that impede it—conflicting conceptions of teaching, the press in special education to increase the output of teachers, financial exigency, and state licensure and pro-gram approval requirements. We would also suppose that the importance of these factors varies from place to place and time to time, so that the suitability of a con-text for teacher education reform cannot be known with any degree of certainty. However, uncertainty is no excuse for lack of action, and, although we may not feel confident in recommending a preferred course, we do recognize the need for action.

Unanswered to this point in our discussion is the nature of the job for which teachers will be prepared in the future. Like describing a path for reform, advocat-ing a single concept of future practice makes us somewhat uneasy. But in the sec-tions to follow, we do offer an educated guess and use it to describe the implications of future practice for contemporary teacher education.

WHAT TEACHER EDUCATION OUGHT TO LOOK LIKE

Teaching in Restructured Schools

To make decisions regarding what teacher education ought to look like were it to respond to these various forces, a consideration of what teaching and learning itself might look like in restructured schools is warranted. In such schools, what is fore-most for those who have traditionally been concerned with special education is that all teachers would ideally accept professional responsibility for working with students who represent the full range of diversity that characterizes classrooms in nearly all schools nationwide. With this commitment as a foundation, they will need to work from a general curriculum and accompanying programs of instruction that maximize the potential for all students to be successful in school. This is not a goal that has evolved solely because of increased inclusion of students with disabilities in general education classrooms. On the contrary, only fairly recently has special education begun to extend its conception of teaching and learning to include, for example, the constructivist paradigm (McGill-Franzen & Allington, 1991). Instead, what seems to be developing is the recognition that neither the basal text approach favored for so long by general education nor the behavioral approaches favored by special education are likely to be the best available methods.

Current thinking favors a curriculum focused on the development of all students, including the large proportion of students with mild disabilities, into independent, curious, self-motivating learners (see for example, Means, Chelemer, & Knapp, 1991). Fundamental to the success of education of this type is the development of a strong sense of community in classrooms and schools, in which students are actively involved. Operating from the perspective that all students are equal members of their learning communities, teachers will need to structure their classrooms such that all students for whom they have responsibility experience this sense of belonging as a motivating force in their education.

With this in mind, a critical issue with respect to the preparation of teachers is whether there is a single, unified knowledge base to guide their preparation, or whether the segregated preparation that now characterizes special and general teacher education is defensible. Past practice would suggest that the segregated preparation of teachers, like the segregated education of students with disabilities, has served to limit what special education teachers know about the most current approaches to general curriculums and classroom methodology. Likewise, the isolated preparation of general education teachers has narrowed their conceptions of what it means to be responsible for working with a wide range of students—precisely at a time when all classrooms are becoming increasingly diverse and challenging. Finally, there is growing open-mindedness about new methodologies that have the potential to facilitate inclusion, prevent overidentification, and work powerfully for all children.

When we talk about the notion of a unified knowledge base for teachers, it is important to understand that the knowledge base must be one within which it is possible to structure educational programs that embrace student diversity in learning. Teachers need to know how to structure their classrooms such that students are actively involved with their peers in challenging and interesting work. They also need to know how to create flexible grouping patterns that allow students to receive specific assistance when it is needed (Mason & Good, 1993; Pugach & Wesson, in press). Fulfilling these needs requires a major shift in the preparation of all teachers. It also means that teacher educators from special and general education need to rethink what it means to prepare teachers to work with diverse populations in which disability is one factor among many that lead to individual differences.

At an intuitive level, unifying the knowledge base for the preparation of teachers seems to be the right direction to take. It makes sense to operate from the perspective that all children learn in similar ways and that all children, too, bring differences that must be accommodated in all classrooms in all schools. But having institutionalized a conflicting set of beliefs based on the differences between children, teacher educators now must reconcile these differences as programs are redesigned and restructured (Lilly, 1989).

It is extremely important to emphasize that a commitment to unifying the preparation of teachers does not mean that teachers work alone, isolated in their classrooms with increasingly diverse groups of students. Rather, evolving roles for teachers themselves and for how teacher education is related to the work of practicing teachers can support the shift toward an educational philosophy that enables student diversity to be embraced. Modeling the philosophy of working within a community of learners for children, teachers need to recognize the power of their own professional community as a source of support for educating a more diverse student population. Within special education, one example of such role changes is the shift toward greater collaboration. However, in the context of unified teacher preparation, learning how to work collaboratively becomes a responsibility for all teachers, not merely as a means of supporting students with disabilities, but rather as a general way of conducting the day-to-day business of teaching.

Nor does unification mean that prospective teachers are prepared to work in schools where such collaboration and exemplary methodologies do not occur in practice. Instead, an evolving role for teacher educators is working hand-in-hand with practicing teachers to improve the quality of teaching for all students, including those with disabilities. To accomplish this goal, it will be necessary for us to work closely with practicing teachers in school-university partnerships in which teacher education faculty, teachers, and teacher education students work together to develop programs in which inclusive methodologies are practiced. Therefore, as basic conceptions of teacher education change with respect to the knowledge base and the relationship between special and general education, so too do the relationships between teacher educators and teachers with respect to the improvement of practice in the schools.

Integrating the Preparation of Special and General Education Teachers

To achieve the goal of unifying the preparation of special and general education teachers, it first will be necessary to recognize the degree to which our existing paradigms drive our current thinking. If we are to embrace a totally new vision of teaching, and thus of teacher education, then even the language we use to describe our goals does not adequately capture the outcome we wish to achieve. That outcome is the creation of a system of education in which it is possible for teachers to create learning environments in which the natural diversity of children in schools is treated as a natural phenomenon and accommodated as a matter of course. If this accommodation is to be successful, our conceptions of education eventually need to change; it is no longer simply a matter of fitting together pieces that now exist, but rather rethinking entirely what it means to teach in a diverse, multicultural society.

Getting there, however, is another matter entirely. Various institutions of higher education have begun the task of redefining what it means to prepare teachers; the examples we offer here represent various points of departure for this task. In addition to the work going on at the University of South Florida, which is the basis for this book, the University of Cincinnati, as part of its complete reconceptualization of teacher education, has elected to disband its undergraduate program but to continue to play a major role in preparing all teachers in the areas of diversity and collaboration. As a result, special education faculty will be integrally involved in all aspects of undergraduate teacher education. These changes were preceded by several years of intensive dialogue and redesign that placed faculty together to determine their true commitments to teacher education.

At the University of Florida (UF), a collaborative program in which the preparation of students in elementary education and learning disabilities is integrated involves students in practicum settings supported by teacher education faculty from special and elementary education. These practice settings are places where teachers are working to foster the inclusion of children with disabilities, thereby enabling prospective teachers to work in settings that more closely approximate the professional cultures for which they are being prepared. Another program at the University of Florida is integrating the preparation of early childhood personnel in what is known as the "Unified Program" (Kemple, Hartle, Correa, & Fox, in press).

In both of these UF programs, small groups of faculty members from special and general education have worked closely together to effect change. One of the most important understandings to emerge from these efforts is the degree to which trust and mutual understanding need to be built between special and general education faculty (Bondy, Griffin, Ross, & Sindelar, 1993). How these efforts will influence the broader teacher education programs is yet to be determined. Extending the influence of these programs will depend largely on the degree to which the dialogue can be broadened, as has been achieved at Syracuse University, for example. All undergraduate students there are certified in both special education for mild disabilities and general education.

At the University of Wisconsin–Milwaukee, an interdisciplinary Center for Teacher Education is the structure through which special and general teacher education faculty work toward program reform (Pasch, Pugach, & Fox, 1991). Faculty share full responsibility for program development, the establishment of professional development sites in the schools, and the overall conceptualization of the program. One of the underlying principles of the reform design at the University of Wisconsin–Milwaukee is that faculty need ample time to participate in focused dialogue on how reform should progress as a means of ensuring full understanding of each other's concerns.

What these efforts illustrate, and there are others to be sure, is that to redesign teacher education, faculty themselves must engage in extended, honest, and open dialogue designed to reach a set of common commitments to what it means to teach diverse learners. In this way, a common understanding regarding how teachers need to be prepared can be accomplished with a sense of dedication and clear purpose.

To this point, we have argued that teacher education must be based on a conception of what teaching will be like in the schools of the future and that a focus on accommodating diversity—one that we believe to be a high priority—necessitates unified teacher education. However, it also is important in a more general sense that teacher education programs reflect programmatic integrity.

Thematic Focus in Teacher Education

Historically, teacher education programs have included a collection of courses, taken across departments and constructed in the absence of programmatic unity (Pugach, 1992). The lack of linkages across courses has been criticized repeatedly (Association of Teacher Educators, 1991; Carnegie Forum on Education and the Economy, 1986; Holmes Group, 1986).

Some have suggested that the task of developing a coherent teacher education program can be accomplished when a professional knowledge schema for teachers is linked with a programmatic theme (Barnes, 1987; Howey & Zimpher, 1989; Katz & Raths, 1992; Kennedy, 1990; Pugach, 1992). Developing thematic integrity in teacher education also provides a coherent conceptual framework with which students can organize and understand content of the program. Examples of themes in teacher education programs include the Academic Learning Program at Michigan State University, which focuses on fostering conceptual understanding across courses (Feiman-Nemser, 1990) and the theme of developing reflective practitioners in the elementary PROTEACH program at the University of Florida (Ross & Krogh, 1988).

Selecting a program theme must be accomplished carefully so that it brings together important features of the program and is understood by both faculty and students (Pugach, 1992). Faculty interested in joining programs preparing special educators and classroom teachers might develop themes that derive from the changing demographic situation in schools. Future teachers will need to appreciate heterogeneity and human variance (Stainback & Stainback, 1987) and to accommodate a wider range of it in their classrooms.

Examples in the literature of programmatic themes aimed at integrating special and regular education are few. In one such program at La Salle University, developmental theory is used as the unifying theme (Feden & Clabaugh, 1986). The program at La Salle was designed to prepare teachers who: a) make students the focus of education by understanding them as individuals rather than relying on stereotypes to inform practice; b) individualize instruction effectively; c) value life-long service to the profession; and d) use technology to enhance student learning. The Unified Program at UF (Kemple et al., in press) is designed to prepare teachers to: a) serve all children from birth through age 8; (b) provide a family-focused approach; c) be sensitive to multicultural issues; d) implement a model of full inclusion; e) collaborate with other professionals; and f) understand and use developmentally appropriate practices. Specifically, the program serves to "integrate the fields of early childhood education and early childhood special education within a culturally sensitive child development and family focus framework" (p. 29). Finally, in the elementary/special education collaboration at the University of Florida, the programmatic theme of prevention and accommodation emerged after many hours of collaborative team building among faculty from two historically isolated departments (Bondy et al., 1993). In short, overcoming the "dysfunctional divisions that now exist among departments" (Pugach, 1992, p. 256) is essential if teacher education programs are to develop inclusive themes.

Professional Development Schools: Creating Environments for Teacher Education

To the extent that a teacher education program is forward looking, existing classrooms that realize its vision may be few and far between. Thus, unified programs must find or help create environments for field placements and internships, and faculty must work collaboratively with school professionals in shaping school practice and creating settings for field placements. One process for doing so, professional development schools, has been well described.

Professional Development Schools (Holmes Group, 1986, 1990) or Professional Practice Schools (Levine, 1992) are organizational structures proposed to achieve the twin goals of school and teacher education reform. In forging a new relationship between schools and universities and "providing a common ground in which teacher education and school reform can come together to achieve the end result of improving learning" (Levine, 1992, p. 1), professional development schools represent a new order of professional activity.

Professional Development Schools (PDSs) were intended to be places where collaborative work would support the development of the novice professional, the continued development of experienced professionals, and the research and development needs of the teaching profession (Holmes Group, 1990). Conceived as school-university partnerships, they would support innovations toward change, be grounded in learning as "meaning making" (Pechman, 1992), experiment with new mixtures of institutional authority (Neufield, 1992), and promote professional practice in teaching (Darling-Hammond, 1992). Universities across the nation have begun experimenting with the PDS model (Jett-Simpson, Pugach, & Whipp, 1992; Rushcamp & Roehler, 1992). PDSs offer the opportunity for the faculties of schools of education to practice many of the principles they preach: continued and ongoing professional development across a teacher's career, the marriage of theory and practice at the intersection of experience, and the education of all of our nation's children.

The whole school design of PDSs that, as Goodlad (1990) put it, would "prepare future teachers to be stewards of entire schools" (p. 281), offers an opportunity to conceptualize new organizational responsibilities. It also provides a means for including special education in the agenda of change. These models not only offer a chance to forge stronger relationships between universities and schools, but also create a new collaborative space in which general and special education faculty can explore ways to strengthen the education of all students and the preparation of all teachers. Faculty in special education departments have accepted this invitation to change, exploring the benefits of this relationship (Rosselli, Perez, Piersall, & Pantridge, 1993) and experimenting with merging general and special education teacher preparation within their supportive structures (Stewart, Peters, & Patriarca, 1988).

In the preceding discussions, we have talked about integrating teacher education programs that now separately prepare classroom teachers and teachers of students with mild disabilities to support the diversity in today's school populations.

Nevertheless, we believe that there will still be a need for teachers with specialized skills for particular disabilities. It is to this issue that we now turn.

SPECIAL EDUCATION TEACHER EDUCATION

We agree with Shores and Nelson, who asserted in an interview with Gable (1991) that "special education could become more special" (p. 181), and believe that inclusion does not eliminate the need for special skills. We maintain that there are three areas—sensory impairments, severe disabilities, and severe emotional disturbance (SED)—in which the degree of specialization and the low incidence of the disability make it impractical and inefficient to insist that all teachers master the skills necessary to work alone with students with these disabilities.

Sensory impairments include hearing impairment and deafness, visual disabilities, and speech and language disorders. Effective work with students with hearing impairments, for example, requires mastery of knowledge and skills related to the uses of residual hearing, amplification, and manual communication, among others (Luckner, 1991). Competent work with students with severe disabilities demands specialized knowledge and skill in physical management, health and medical issues, and teaching a nontraditional curriculum comprising self-care, alternative and augmentative communication, and recreation and leisure skills (Fox & Williams, 1992; Whitten & Westling, 1985).

Acting out and oppositional students, be they SED or not, continue to present a formidable challenge for teachers and schools. In our decade-long conversation about inclusive education, the inclusion of SED students has defied solution. The difficult nature of working with SED students leaves even noncategorically licensed special education teachers expressing feelings of being inadequately prepared (Cobb, Elliott, Powers, & Voltz, 1989). To deal effectively with the most difficult-to-manage students, teachers must master skills beyond classroom and behavior management including implementation of levels systems, crisis management, and facilitative communication, to name a few (Fink & Janssen, 1993).

It is important to point out that just as the need for specialized skills should not be construed as advocacy for distinct programs, neither should it be seen as support for distinct and separate teacher education programs. We believe that the manner in which specialists should be prepared must mirror the capacity in which they will be working with classroom teachers in providing, to the extent possible, education in inclusive classrooms. Because classroom teachers and specialists must work together to provide inclusive education, the preparation they receive must be grounded in the collaborative nature of their work.

Collaboration can be seen as the foundation on which effective and inclusive education for diverse learners may be built. Therefore, preparation for specialists must become an integrated part of general teacher education programs. Specialist programs must provide classroom teachers and specialists in-training with many opportunities to work together, thereby establishing the expectation that they will. Although the preparation of specialists may diverge at certain points to encompass specialized skills, it must always be conducted in the context of collaboration—the same context in which classroom teachers learn to work collaboratively in accommodating students whose disabilities require close, ongoing contact with other professionals.

SUMMARY

Contemporary teacher education currently exists in a complex context in which reform is helped and hindered in equal measure. For every demographic reality that would motivate us to rethink what we do, there is a demand on our time—to graduate more students faster, for example—that steals the opportunity away. We know that reform is seldom easily achieved and are compelled to move ahead by the moral imperative we see in changing demographics and the need to include special education in the discussion of school reform.

To achieve the goal of equity in education, we see the need for greater accommodation of diversity, including that which may be attributed to disability. Of course, accommodating diversity is no simple matter, and it has serious implications for teacher education. Classroom teachers must have the skills that the accommodation of diversity requires, and they and specialists must develop the skills required for collaboration. To achieve that goal, we have advocated in this chapter for the unified preparation of classroom teachers, teachers who work with students with mild disabilities, and specialists who work with students with sensory impairments, severe disabilities, and severe emotional disturbances.

Although we believe the principles for reform that we have suggested apply equally to early childhood, elementary, and secondary education, our focus here has been on elementary education, about which numerous examples exist. We discussed early childhood education at less length, even though the best thinking in that discipline parallels ours in seeking to prepare all teachers to work with typically developing students and students with disabilities (Burton, Hains, Hanline, Mac-Clean, & McCormick, 1992; Kemple et al., in press). We have not discussed secondary teacher education programs, in part because the reluctance of states to promulgate separate secondary licensure has slowed the development of distinct teacher education programs (Bagwell, 1982; Bursuck & Epstein, 1986). With some notable exceptions (Miller, 1991), few integrated programs exist.

Our recommendations are based on a vision of school practice, a theme—accommodation—derived from it, and contemporary best practice in teacher education (e.g., professional development schools) that allows us to develop places where our concept of best practice may be realized.

REFERENCES

Allington, R. L., & McGill-Franzen, A. (1989). Different programs, indifferent instruction. In D. K. Lipsky & A. Gartner (Eds.), *Beyond separate education: Quality education for all* (pp. 75–97). Baltimore, MD: Brookes.

Ashton, P. T., & Webb, R. B. (1986). *Making a difference: Teacher's sense of efficacy and student achievement.* New York: Longman.

Association of Teacher Educators. (1991). *Restructuring the education of teachers.* Reston, VA: Author.

Bagwell, I. (1982). Certification requirements for secondary learning disabilities teachers. *Teacher Education and Special Education, 5*(4), 56–60.

Barnes, H. L. (1987). The conceptual basis for thematic teacher education programs. *Journal of Teacher Education, 38*(4), 13–18.

Belch, P. (1979). Toward noncategorical teacher certification in special education: Myth or reality? *Exceptional Children, 46,* 129–131.

Billingsley, B. S. (1993). Teacher retention and attrition in special and general education: A critical review of the literature. *Journal of Special Education, 27,* 137–174.

Bondy, E., Griffin, C. C., Ross, D. D., & Sindelar, P. T. (1993). *Planning to prepare teachers for inclusive education: The purposes and processes of team building.* Manuscript submitted for publication.

Brady, M. P., Conroy, M., & Langford, C. A. (1984). Current issues and practices affecting the development of non-categorical programs for students and teachers. *Teacher Education and Special Education, 7,* 20–26.

Brown, J. S., Collins, A., & Duguid, P. (1989). Situated cognition and the culture of learning. *Educational Researcher, 18*(1), 32–42.

Brownell, M. T., & Smith, S. W. (1992). Attrition/retention of special education teachers: Critique of current research and recommendations for retention efforts. *Teacher Education and Special Education, 15,* 229–248.

Bursuck, W. D., & Epstein, M. H. (1986). A survey of training programs for teachers of mildly handicapped adolescents. *Teacher Education and Special Education, 9,* 3–8.

Burton, C. B., Hains, A. H., Hanline, M. F., MacClean, M., & McCormick, K. (1992). Early childhood intervention and education: The urgency of professional unification. *Topics in Early Childhood Special Education, 11,* 53–69.

Carnegie Forum on Education and the Economy, Task Force on Teaching as a Profession. (1986). *A nation prepared: Teachers for the 21st century.* New York: Author.

Center for Research on Elementary and Middle Schools. (1990). *The changing nature of the disadvantaged population: Current dimensions and future trends.* Baltimore, MD: Johns Hopkins University.

Chapey, G. D., Pyszkoski, I. S., Trimarco, T. A. (1985). National trends for certification and training of special education teachers. *Teacher Education and Special Education, 8,* 203–208.

Cobb, H. B., Elliott, R. N., Powers, A. R., & Voltz, D. (1989). Generic versus categorical special education teacher preparation. *Teacher Education and Special Education, 12,* 19–26.

Collins, A., Brown, J. S., & Newman, S. E. (1990). Cognitive apprenticeship: Teaching the crafts of reading, writing, and mathematics. In L. Resnick (Ed.), *Knowing, learning, and teaching: Essays in honor of Robert Glaser* (pp. 453–494). Hillsdale, NJ: Erlbaum.

Cranston-Gingras, A., & Mauser, A. J. (1992). Categorical and noncategorical teacher certification in special education: How wide is the gap? *Remedial and Special Education, 13*(4), 6–9.

Darling-Hammond, L. (1992). Accountability for professional practice. In M. Levine (Ed.), *Professional practice schools* (pp. 81–104). New York: Teachers College Press.

David, J. L. (1989). Synthesis of research on school-based management. *Educational Leadership, 46*(8), 55–58.

Doyle, W. (1986). Classroom organization and management. In M.C. Wilttrock (Ed.), *Handbook of Research on Teaching* (3rd ed., pp. 392–431). New York: Macmillan.

Education Commission of the States, Task Force on Education for Economic Growth. (1983). *Action for excellence: Comprehensive plan to improve our nation's schools*. Denver: Author.

Feden, P. D., & Clabaugh, G. K. (1986). The "new breed" educator: A rationale and program for combining elementary and special education teacher preparation. *Teacher Education and Special Education, 9*, 180–189.

Feiman-Nemser, S. (1980). Growth and reflection as aims in teacher education: Directions for research. In E. G. Hall, S. M. Lord, & G. Brown (Eds.), *Exploring issues in teacher education: Questions for future research*. Austin, TX: Research and Development Center for Teacher Education.

Feiman-Nemser, S. (1990). Teacher preparation: Structural and conceptual alternatives. In W.R. Houston (Ed.), *Handbook for research on teacher education* (pp. 212–233). New York: Macmillan.

Fink, A. H., & Janssen, K. N. (1993). Competencies for teaching students with emotional-behavioral disorders. *Preventing School Failure, 37*(2), 11–15.

Florida Department of Education. (1992–93). *Florida education finance program: Statistical report*. Tallahassee, FL: State Government Printing Office.

Fox, L., & Williams, D. G. (1992). Preparing teachers of students with severe disabilities. *Teacher Education and Special Education, 15*, 97–107.

Freiberg, H. J., & Waxman, H. C. (1990). Changing teacher education. In W. R. Houston (Ed.), *Handbook of research on teacher education* (pp. 617–635). New York: Macmillan.

Frudden, S.J., & Healy, H. A. (1986). Effective teaching research: Its applications to special education teacher training. *Contemporary Education, 57*, 150–153.

Gable, R. A. (1991). Competency-based teacher education revisited: A conversation with Drs. Richard E. Shores and C. Michael Nelson. *Teacher Education and Special Education, 14*, 177–182.

Gable, R. A., Hendrickson, J. M., Shores, R. E., & Young, C. C. (1983). Teacher-handicapped child classroom interactions. *Teacher Education and Special Education, 6*, 88–95.

Gartner, A., & Lipsky, D. (1987). Beyond special education: Toward a quality system for all. *Harvard Educational Review, 57*, 367–395.

Gersten, R., & Woodward, J. (1990). Rethinking the regular education initiative. *Remedial and Special Education, 11*(3), 7–16.

Goodlad, J. (1984). *A place called school*. New York: McGraw-Hill.

Goodlad, J. (1990). *Teachers for our nation's schools*. San Francisco: Jossey-Bass.

Grimmett, P. P., & MacKinnon, A. M. (1992). Craft knowledge and the education of teachers. In G. Grant (Ed.), *Review of Research in Education* (Vol. 18, pp. 385–456). Washington, DC: American Educational Research Association.

Hagerty, G. J., & Abramson, M. (1987). Impediments to implementing national policy change for mildly handicapped students. *Exceptional Children, 53*, 315–323.

Harrison, C. R., Killon, J. P., & Mitchell, J. G. (1989). Site-based management: The realities of implementation. *Educational Leadership, 46*(8), 55–58.

Heritage Foundation. (1984, May 11). The crisis: Washington shares the blame. *The Heritage Foundation Backgrounder*. Washington, DC: Author.

Hodgkinson, H. (1991). Reform versus reality. *Phi Delta Kappan, 73*, 9–16.

Hollingsworth, S. (1989). Prior beliefs and cognitive change in learning to teach. *American Educational Research Journal, 26*, 160–189.

Holmes Group. (1986). *Tomorrow's teachers*. East Lansing, MI: Author.

Holmes Group. (1990). *Tomorrow's schools*. East Lansing, MI: Author.

Howey, K. R., & Zimpher, N. L. (1989). *Profiles of preservice teacher education: Inquiry into the nature of programs*. Albany, NY: State University of New York Press.

Idol, L., Paolucci-Whitcomb, P., & Nevin, A. (1986). *Collaborative consultation.* Austin, TX: Pro-Ed.

Immigrant schools: The wrong lessons. (1993, August). *Newsweek*, p. 23.

Individuals with Disabilities Education Act, 20 U. S. C. § 1400 et seq. (1975).

Jett-Simpson, M., Pugach, M. C., & Whipp, J. (1992, April). *Portrait of an urban professional development school.* Paper presented at the Annual Meeting of the American Educational Research Association, San Francisco.

Johnson, L. J., & Pugach, M. C. (1992). Continuing the dialogue: Embracing a more expansive understanding of collaborative relationships. In W. Stainback & S. Stainback (Eds.), *Controversial issues confronting special education* (pp. 215–222). Boston: Allyn & Bacon.

Johnston, S. (1992). Images: A way of understanding the practical knowledge of student teachers. *Teaching & Teacher Education, 8,* 123–136.

Katz, L. G., & Raths, J. (1992). Six dilemmas in teacher education. *Journal of Teacher Education, 43,* 376–385.

Kemple, K. M., Hartle, L. C., Correa, V. I., & Fox, L. (in press). Preparing teachers for inclusive education: The development of a unified teacher education program in early childhood and early childhood special education. *Teacher Education and Special Education.*

Kennedy, M. M. (1990). Choosing a goal for professional education. In W.R. Houston (Ed.), *Handbook for research on teacher education* (pp. 813–825). New York: Macmillan.

Kleinfeld, J., & Noordhoff, K. (1988, April). *Re-thinking teacher education programs : What are the right questions?* Paper presented at the western meeting of the Holmes Group, Boulder, CO.

Lauritzen, P., & Friedman, S. J. (in press). Meeting the supply/demand requirements of the Individuals with Disabilities Education Act. *Teacher Education and Special Education.*

Leinhardt, G. (1992). What research on learning tells us about teaching. *Educational Leadership,* 20–25.

Levine, M. (Ed.). (1992). *Professional practice schools.* New York: Teachers College Press.

Lilly, M. S. (1971). A training based model for special education. *Exceptional Children, 37,* 745–749.

Lilly, M. S. (1989). Teacher preparation. In D. K. Lipsky & A. Gartner (Eds.), *Beyond separate education* (pp. 143–157). Baltimore, MD: Brookes.

Little, J. W. (1982). Norms of collegiality and experimentation: Workplace conditions of school success. *American Educational Research Journal, 19,* 325–340.

Lortie, D. (1975). *Schoolteacher.* Chicago: University of Chicago Press.

Luckner, J. L. (1991). Competencies critical to teachers of students with hearing impairments. *Teacher Education and Special Education, 14,* 135–139.

Mason, D. A., & Good, T. L. (1993). Effects of two-group and whole-class teaching on regrouped elementary students' mathematical achievement. *American Educational Research Journal, 30,* 328–360.

Marston, D. (1987). Does categorical teacher certification benefit the mildly handicapped child? *Exceptional Children, 53,* 423–431.

McGill-Franzen, A., & Allington, R. L. (1991). The gridlock of low reading achievement: Perspectives on policy and practice. *Remedial and Special Education, 12*(3), 20–30.

Means, B., Chelemer, C., & Knapp, M. S. (1991). *Teaching advanced skills to at-risk students: Views from research and practice.* San Francisco: Jossey-Bass.

Merseth, K. K. (1992). Cases for decision making in teacher education. In J. H. Shulman (Ed.), *Case methods in teacher education* (pp. 50–63). New York: Teachers College Press.

Miller, D. (1991). Merging regular and special education teacher preparation programs: The integrated special education-English project (ISEP). *Teaching and Teacher Education, 7,* 19–23.

National Center for Educational Statistics. (1992). *Digest of education statistics 1992.* Washington, DC: Author.

National Commission on Excellence in Education. (1983). *A nation at risk: The imperative for educational reform.* Washington, DC: U.S. Government Printing Office.

National Science Foundation. (1983). *Educating Americans for the 21st Century: A report to the American people and the National Science Board.* Washington, DC: Author.

Neufield, B. (1992). Professional practice schools in context: New mixtures of institutional authority. In M. Levine (Ed.), *Professional practice schools* (pp. 133–168). New York: Teachers College Press.

O'Sullivan, P. J., Marston, D., & Magnusson, D. (1987). Categorical special education teacher certification: Does it affect instruction of mildly handicapped pupils? *Remedial and Special Education, 8*(5), 13–18.

Pasch, S. H., Pugach, M. C., & Fox, R. G. (1991). A collaborative structure for institutional change in teacher education. In M. C. Pugach, H. Barnes, & L. Beckum (Eds.), *Changing the practice of teacher education: The role of the knowledge base* (pp. 109–138). Washington, DC: AACTE.

Pechman, E. M. (1992). Child as a meaning maker: The organizing theme for professional practice schools. In. M. Levine (Ed.), *Professional practice schools* (pp. 25–62). New York: Teachers College Press.

Poverty rates rise. (1992, July). *Time,* p. 15.

Prawat, R. S. (1992). From individual differences to learning communities—our changing focus. *Educational Leadership, 49*(7), 9–13.

Pugach, M. C. (1987). The national education reports and special education: Implications for teacher preparation. *Exceptional Children,*

Pugach, M. (1988). Special education as a constraint on teacher education reform. *Journal of Teacher Education, 39*(3), 52–59.

Pugach, M. C. (1992). Unifying the preservice preparation of teachers. In W. Stainback & S. Stainback (Eds.), *Controversial issues confronting special education: Divergent perspectives* (pp 255–270). Needham Heights, MA: Allyn & Bacon. 53, 308–314.

Pugach, M. C. (1993, October). *Twice victims: The struggle to educate children in urban schools and the reform of special education and Chapter One.* Paper presented at the National Center on Education in Inner Cities, Invitational Conference on Making a Difference for Students At-Risk, Princeton, NJ.

Pugach, M. C., & Johnson, L. J. (1988). Rethinking the relationship between consultation and collaborative problem solving. *Focus on Exceptional Children, 21*(4), 1–8.

Pugach, M., & Lilly, M. S. (1984). Reconceptualizing support services for classroom teachers: Implications for teacher education. *Journal of Teacher Education, 35*(5), 48–55.

Pugach, M. C., & Warger, C. (1993). Integration as an educational goal: Curriculum considerations. In J. I. Goodlad & T. C. Lovitt (Eds.), *Integrating general and special education* (pp. 125–148). New York: Macmillan.

Pugach, M. C., & Wesson, C. L. (in press). Teachers' and students' views of team teaching of general education and learning disabled students in two 5th-grade classes. *Elementary School Journal.*

Reynolds, M. C. (1979). Categorical vs. noncategorical teacher training. *Teacher Education and Special Education, 2*(3), 5–8.

Rogoff, B. (1990). *Apprenticeship in thinking: Cognitive development in social context.* New York: Oxford University Press.

Rosenholtz, S. J. (1989). *Teachers' workplace: The social organization of schools.* New York: Longman.

Ross, D. D., & Krogh, S. L. (1988, Winter). From paper to program: A story of elementary PROTEACH. *Peabody Journal of Education, 65*(3), 19–34.

Ross, D. D., & Smith, W. (1992). Understanding preservice teachers' perspectives on diversity. *Journal of Teacher Education, 43*(2), 94–103.

Rosselli, H., Perez, S., Piersall, K., & Pantridge, O. (1993). Evolution of a professional development school: The story of a partnership. *Teacher Education and Special Education, 16,* 124–136.

Rushcamp, S., & Roehler, L. R. (1992). Characteristics supporting change in a professional development school. *Journal of Teacher Education, 43*(1), 19–27.

Rudner, L. M. (1987). *What's happening in teacher testing: An analysis of state teacher testing practices.* Washington, DC: U.S. Department of Education, Office of Educational Research and Development.

Sailor, W. (1989). The educational, social, and vocational integration of students with the most severe disabilities. In A. Gartner & D. Lipsky (eds.), *Beyond separate education: Quality education for all* (pp. 53–74). Baltimore, MD: Brookes.

Sailor, W. (1991). Special education and the restructured school. *Remedial and Special Education, 12*(6), 8–22.

Sapon-Shevin, M. (1987). The national education reports and special education: Implications for students. *Exceptional Children, 53,* 300–307.

Schon, D. (1983). *The reflective practitioner: How professionals think in action.* New York: Basic Books.

Shepard, L. A. (1987). The new push for excellence: Widening the schism between regular and special education. *Exceptional Children, 53,* 327–329.

Shores, R. E., Cegelka, P. A., & Nelson, C. M. (1973). Competency-based special education teacher training. *Exceptional Children, 40,* 192–197.

Sikula, J. (1990). National commission reports of the 1980's. In W. R. Houston (Ed.), *Handbook of research on teacher education* (pp. 72–82). New York: Macmillan.

Smith-Davis, J., & Billingsley, B. S. (in press). The supply/demand puzzle. *Teacher Education and Special Education.*

Smylie, M. A. (1988). The enhancement function of staff development: Organizational and psychological antecedents to individual teacher change. *American Educational Research Journal, 25,* 1–30.

Stainback, W., & Stainback, S. (1984). A rationale for the merger of special and regular education. *Exceptional Children, 51,* 102–111.

Stainback, S., & Stainback, W. (1987). Facilitating merger through personnel preparation. *Teacher Education and Special Education, 10,* 185–190.

Stewart, D. A., Peters, S., & Patriarca, L. (1988). A model professional development school: Merging special education and general education in the work place. *B.C. Journal of Special Education, 12,* 215–226.

Su, Z. (1990). The function of the peer group in teacher socialization. *Phi Delta Kappan.*

Sutherland, D. J., & Castleberry, M. S. (1985). Assessing quality in federal grants that support special education teacher-training programs. *Teacher Education and Special Education, 8,* 209–218.

U. S. Department of Education. (1992). *Fourteenth annual report to Congress on the implementation of the Individuals with Disabilities Education Act.* Washington, DC: Author.

U. S. Department of Education. (1993). *New FY 94 application for grants under training personnel for the education of the handicapped.* Washington, DC: Author.

Wang, M. (1989). Adaptive instruction: An alternative for accommodating student diversity through the curriculum. In D. K. Lipsky & A. Gartner (Eds.), *Beyond separate education: Quality education for all* (pp. 99–120). Baltimore, MD: Brookes.

Whitten, T. M., & Westling, D. L. (1985). Competencies for teachers of the severely and profoundly handicapped: A review. *Teacher Education and Special Education, 8,* 104–111.

Will, M. C. (1986). *Educating students with learning problems—A shared responsibility.* Washington, DC: U.S. Department of Education.

9

RE-EXAMINING RESEARCH ON TEACHER EDUCATION
Paradigmatic and Technical Issues

CONSTANCE HINES AND JEFFREY KROMREY

INTRODUCTION

THE radical reforms currently underway in our nation's schools place an unparalleled demand on the educational research enterprise to aid in the generation of new knowledge, in our understanding of increasingly complex phenomena, to guide practice, and to inform policy. Societal concern for the improvement of the educational process and student educational outcomes is the driving force behind the current calls for school reform and the reform of teacher education.

If our efforts in educational reform are to be successful, then our policies, processes and actions must be guided by more than beliefs, historical traditions, or intuition. Knowledge gained from the research enterprise must play a central role in the realization of our goals for improved educational processes and outcomes. This knowledge, as Shulman (1986) notes, "is produced through the inquiries of scholars—empiricists, theorists, practitioners—and is, therefore, a function of the kinds of questions asked, problems posed and issues framed by those who do research" (p. 3). In the field of education, as in any other field, the questions asked and the conceptions of problems and methods are governed by the research paradigm or orientation that is shared by the scientific community of which the researcher is a member.

THE ROLE OF PARADIGMS IN RESEARCH

Paradigms are fundamental to the research enterprise because they provide the framework within which we structure our inquiry. They govern our thinking about the appropriate processes of inquiry, the nature of the questions that are asked and how they are framed, the aspects of phenomena that are emphasized, the processes and procedures that are employed to gather information, and the interpretations that are applied to data. Patton (1975), who built on the conceptualizations of Kuhn (1970), defines a paradigm as:

> a world view, a general perspective, a way of breaking down the complexity of the real world. As such paradigms are deeply embedded in the socialization of adherents and practitioners telling them what is important, what is legitimate, what is reasonable. Paradigms are normative, they tell the practitioner what to do, without the necessity of long existential or epistemological consideration. (p. 9)

Thus, as Rist (1977) suggests,

> adherents of one paradigm as opposed to another are predisposed to viewing the world and the events within them in profoundly different ways. . . . The power and pull of a paradigm is more than simply a methodological orientation; it is a means by which to grasp reality and give it meaning and predictability. (p. 43)

Since the 1960s the field of education has witnessed an ongoing debate between proponents of two main research paradigms—one rooted in the natural sciences (empirical positivism) with an emphasis on empirical quantifiable observations and the explanation and prediction of phenomena; the other derived from the humanities with an emphasis on holistic, qualitative information and interpretive understanding. It is our belief that in this debate a credible case has been made for the value of both quantitative and qualitative research traditions in the field of education. Thus, we view educational research as multiparadigmatic. No one research paradigm can provide the answers to all the important questions we need to investigate. Several broad research traditions (e.g., quantitative, qualitative, interpretive) can legitimately coexist, each contributing meaningfully to the accumulation of knowledge in the field. Within each of these traditions, there are research communities in which research activities are pursued within a context of shared assumptions, goals, methods of inquiry, and interpretive conceptions for investigations (see Shulman, 1986).

The current reform movement, with its emphasis on school restructuring, places schools and the education of our nation's youth at the center of the reform efforts. Reform recommendations have focused on the improvement of teaching and learning for K–12 students, the education of prospective and practicing teachers and other school professionals, and the organization and management of schools (Patriarca & Cegelka, 1992). Teachers are viewed as the critical agents in the realization of the goals of reform. The nature of the current reform efforts, therefore, have implications for the work of colleges of education and the educational research community. Their work and research efforts must have a major focus on schools and school-based practices. This requires the development of new partnerships between and among classroom teachers, prospective teachers, teacher educators, and researchers. For example, classroom teachers, teachers-in-training, teacher educators, and other educational researchers must become actively engaged as collaborators in the development of new knowledge about teaching and learning through systematic inquiry. In this chapter, we will focus on the implications of current reform for research in teacher education and some methodological and ethical issues that are pertinent to our research endeavors.

A FRAMEWORK FOR RESEARCH ON TEACHER EDUCATION

As would be expected, there is not consensus on a single framework which is adequate to guide our research endeavors on teacher education. We have chosen to use a particular framework to provide a structure from which emerges some compelling questions that must be addressed within the context of reform in teacher education. We consider this framework to be flexible enough to yield questions and issues that can be investigated through a variety of research perspectives.

For purposes of our discussion, we will employ the framework proposed by Yarger and Smith (1990). They defined teacher education as "the context and process of educating individuals to become effective teachers or better teachers" (p. 26). This definition includes those variables and activities that bear some influence on the education of prospective and practicing teachers. The framework includes three components (antecedent conditions, process, and outcomes) and the linkages or interplay between and among them. Most teacher education research is seen as focusing on one or more of the components and their linkages (Yarger and Smith, 1990).

Antecedent conditions are described as those environmental conditions that set the context for teacher education and which, in some major way, shape, direct, or dictate the nature of the teacher education process and, most likely, its outcomes. These conditions include student and faculty characteristics, institutional characteristics, physical environments, fiscal conditions, and the social/political context.

Process is described as any factor(s) associated with the intervention of a teacher education program or the practices used to educate prospective and practicing teachers. Thus, process includes "the actual structure of a teacher education program, the components of the structure, the extent of implementation of various parts and the methods used for implementation" (p. 28). Process refers to the essential aspects that are associated with the delivery of a teacher education experience.

Outcomes are considered to be those learned or provoked behaviors which are exhibited by teachers following their participation in an education intervention. Included in this domain are both teacher behaviors and student reactions to these behaviors. Thus, teacher effectiveness and student performance are elements of this domain.

Much of the research on teacher education has been done within the three domains articulated above. However, if research on teacher education is to contribute meaningfully to the generation of knowledge in the field, our research endeavors must not only include studies within each of the domains but also studies that reflect the interplay or linkage between and among domains. Yarger and Smith (1990) posit that the links between and among domains are the basic foundation for research in teacher education. Few linking studies of the type proposed in the framework have been done. Those that have been conducted are primarily of the process-outcome genre (see for example Good & Grouws, 1981; Zeichner & Tabachnick, 1982).

In the next section of this chapter we will provide a brief overview of the nature of the research that has been conducted in each domain and propose what we consider to be critical areas for inquiry. We will use the Yarger and Smith (1990) model as an organizing framework for our discussions. We will also address implications for areas of teacher education research within the current context of reform in special education.

Domains of the Research Framework

Antecedent conditions. Numerous studies have been conducted within this domain over the past three decades. Typically the focus has been on the characteristics of teacher education faculty and students (see for example, Ryans, 1960; Getzels & Jackson, 1963; Prichard, Fen, & Buxton, 1971; Weaver, 1979; Ducharme & Agne, 1982; Vance & Schlechty, 1982). The greatest concentration of research studies in the area has been on the students of teaching (both prospective teachers and practicing teachers who are participants in continuing teacher education). For the most part, this line of inquiry has focused on the students' personality and personal qualities and their academic abilities. Although the descriptions of teacher education students that have emerged from research in this area have been informative, the knowledge yield and its impact on the teacher education process have been limited.

Much of the research on the personal qualities and abilities of students of teaching has been overly simplistic in its conceptualization. In addition, variables of interest are often not clearly operationalized, and treatments of data have been less than adequate. Lanier and Little (1986) characterized the research conducted in this area in the mid-70s to 80s as tending to be "desultory in nature, poorly synthesized and weakly criticized" (p. 535).

Within the past decade, however, there has been a shift in research toward a focus on the study of teachers' intellectual competencies, factors that influence their thinking abilities and the processing of their thoughts and judgments (Lanier & Little, 1986). This growing body of research on the cognitive functioning of prospective and practicing teachers seems more fruitful, especially when examined within the context of process variables. It is also most timely in a period of school reform where the emphasis is on the improved intellectual performance of both students and their teachers.

Traditionally, very little consideration has been given in teacher education research to the environmental or social/political context within which teacher education takes place and which has such a powerful influence on the way we do business. Yarger and Smith (1990) point out, for example, that little attention has been placed on antecedent variables such as the physical environment of the teacher education setting, the structure of the school or college within which teacher education occurs, the legislative context, the autonomy of institutions from external influences, state and federal mandates and accreditation requirements. Without doubt, such factors do influence and give shape to the teacher education process. Our understandings of the ways in which they impact this process is most critical. This is particularly the case within the national and local context of school reform in the 1990s. The current reform climate brings with it pressures on colleges and schools of education to link teacher preparation more closely to the realities of the classroom and the social/political context within which teachers function. The concentrated emphasis on the establishment of professional development schools is due, to a large extent, to a response to such pressures (see for example, the Holmes Group report, *Tomorrow's Schools*, 1990; and the 1986 report of the Carnegie Forum on Education and the Economy, *A Nation Prepared: Teachers for the 21st Century*). With the emergence of professional development schools and other university-school collaborative relationships, comes a shift in the nature of the setting or environment in which teacher education takes place. For example, prospective teachers are much more likely to spend a greater portion of their teacher preparation program time in formalized field settings (e.g., PDS sites), as compared to university classrooms and laboratory settings, than was previously the case. One question we need to address is whether more time spent in field settings such as PDS sites does indeed result in a more desirable outcome, i.e., a better-prepared teacher.

The goal of professional development schools is to develop partnerships in which classroom teachers, administrators, and university faculty work together to restructure the preparation and induction of teachers into the profession (Stallings & Kowalski, 1990). With the movement of teacher education toward the professional development school models, comes the need for more systematic study of these models and the university-school collaborative partnerships. There is need, for example, for in-depth study of the physical, fiscal, and professional environments in which various PDS models are evolving. There is also need for thoughtful analyses of the structure of these models to better inform our practice and decision making. We also need to examine the nature of the partnerships between the universities and schools and school districts and decision-making processes between them.

In addition to describing the nature and structure of the environment relative to professional development schools, we need to undertake studies that will link the antecedent conditions of physical and fiscal environment to teacher education process and outcome conditions. For example, we need answers to questions such as:

1. What are the roles and responsibilities of university and school professionals in the preparation of prospective teachers within a PDS partnership? How do they differ from a non-PDS setting?
2. In what ways does the university-PDS experience influence or impact the teacher education process?

3. How do prospective teachers trained in PDS settings differ from those trained in the regular teacher education program setting (e.g., in terms of their beliefs and attitudes toward teaching, learning, working with children and their families and the profession; their understandings of the professional knowledge base, and the quality of their professional practice?)
4. What elements or configuration of elements need be present in a given PDS-university teacher preparation model to yield a better prepared teacher?

In-depth discussions of issues pertinent to some of these questions are addressed later in Section II, Part Two of this book.

Another example of the influence of antecedent conditions on the teacher education process is evidenced in the social/political context that is driving changes in the education of children with special needs. This social/political context, coupled with the reduction in fiscal resources, is leading us to reexamine the practice of separate education environments for children with special needs. The full inclusion movement is a direct outgrowth of such factors. The realities of the full inclusion model have serious implications for how we prepare teachers for the integrated classrooms of tomorrow. The relevance of the traditional teacher preparation model in which prospective general education and special education teachers are prepared in separate programs is currently the subject of serious criticisms. This model is viewed as contradictory to the realities of the integrated classrooms in which graduates of such programs will teach. As was advocated in the previous chapter by Sindelar, et. al, new teacher preparation models must see a blurring of lines between programs for general and special education teachers. It is proposed that all teachers should be trained to work collaboratively with other professionals within the context of heterogenous classrooms rather than to work "solo" within the context of classrooms assumed to be homogeneous. Systematic study of the contexts within which new and alternate teacher preparation models are being implemented is critical to the success of the inclusion initiatives.

Careful descriptions of the social/political context and the factors present within it are useful to help us understand the external influences at work. The more critical questions we ask are addressed, however, in research studies that examine antecedent conditions in conjunction with process or outcome variables. Examples of such questions are as follows:

1. What social, political, and/or fiscal conditions have influenced the changes in the education of children with special needs?
2. In what way(s) are the new directions for the education of children with special needs influencing the teacher education curriculum? Can *all* teachers be prepared to work effectively with *all* types of students in the integrated classrooms that would result from the implementation of the inclusion model?
3. What is the nature of the teacher preparation model or models that will most effectively prepare teachers for integrated classrooms?

Answers to these questions do not come easily. They need to be derived from carefully conceived and executed research studies, using both qualitative and quantitative methods of inquiry. We also need thoughtful interpretive studies that will help us understand the social, moral, political complexities of the context in which we work.

Studies that investigate antecedent conditions are primarily descriptive in nature. They typically take the form of narratives, case studies or descriptive surveys. Though quite informative, their potential for contributing significantly to the accumulation of knowledge on the teacher education process is greatly minimized when antecedent conditions are studied in isolation of other teacher education process or outcome conditions. For example, a richly detailed description of the professional development school as the setting in which prospective teachers are placed for their field experiences or a detailed analysis of the social/political context within which full inclusion is being advocated provides us with useful contextual information, but fails to realize its full potential to impact the field of teacher education if not linked to the implementation of the teacher education process or to teacher outcomes. This is not to suggest that studies of antecedent conditions are not an important component of research on teacher education. On the contrary, they are essential to our understanding of the context within which the teacher education process occurs. But, the more powerful yield for the study of antecedent conditions lies with the linkages of these conditions to the processes and outcomes of teacher education. More specifically, detailed descriptions and analyses of antecedent conditions that constitute the context within which the teacher education phenomenon of interest occurs will provide for a better understanding of the phenomenon under study. Also, they will provide the basis for synthesis and accumulation of knowledge across local settings or contexts.

Process. Process, as Yarger and Smith (1990) define it, refers to those activities that are associated with the actual delivery of the teacher education program or, more generally, aspects of how teachers are educated or develop as teachers (p. 36). Thus, the teacher education curriculum, methods, and any other program activities that are used to educate the teacher-in-training, are considered process variables. We, therefore, consider the process component to be at the heart of the research model on teacher education.

Research within this domain has typically focused on a particular aspect (or aspects) of the teacher education program. For the most part, studies conducted in this area are qualitative in nature and often take the form of narrative reports that focus on descriptions of overall programs or innovative components or processes within programs. Quantitative studies that investigate the effectiveness of a given program component or intervention or that compare effectiveness across competing programs or interventions also fall in this domain. Of concern in these quantitative studies is what constitutes the dependent variable of interest or effectiveness criterion. Yarger and Smith (1990) are careful in delineating what they consider as appropriate outcome measures within this domain. They make the distinction between summative outcomes associated with the act of teaching and interim outcomes which are considered to be "related to teaching behavior in some fashion, but for which no verified relationship has been established" (p. 34). They consider interim outcomes to be the appropriate outcome measures within this domain. Examples of interim outcomes are student knowledge of teaching facts and teacher behaviors in a laboratory setting.

Due to the specific nature of most teacher education programs or interventions, individual process studies that are limited to descriptions of programs or interventions, though valuable at the local level, contribute little to the overall construction of a general theory for teacher education or general principles for practice (Yarger & Smith, 1990). However, well-executed syntheses of process studies that contain similar elements and provide detailed descriptions of the local context could be undertaken across several multiple sites to yield generalizable knowledge about teacher education programs. Such studies would also provide us exemplars of teacher education programs.

There is a need for expansion of our research initiatives in areas that help us gain a better understanding of the process and interactions that occur within the teacher education learning environment. For example, ethnographies or case studies of university classroom experiences, or field experiences designed to shed light on how the prospective teacher constructs knowledge about teaching and how children learn, or how the prospective teacher learns to link theory with practice, or how he/she learns to teach are most critical. Studies that probe the understandings that prospective teachers have of the tasks and thought processes in which their students need to engage to attain desired outcomes will also contribute much to the development of a practical professional knowledge base.

Drawing on the line of research on teachers' thought processes (see for example, Clark and Peterson, 1986), we propose a line of inquiry within the process domain relating to the thought processes of teachers-in-training as they experience the teacher education curriculum. What should be explored in research studies of this ilk are the ways in which teachers-in-training interact with and process the teacher education curriculum to make sense of it first as students and then in anticipation of their work as classroom teachers. The strong influence of the beliefs that prospective teachers bring with them to their teacher preparation program was discussed earlier in chapter eight. It was noted that these beliefs are filters that shape and screen much of what the novice teachers are exposed to in their programs. Our understanding of the nature of these beliefs and how they are influenced over time as the novice teacher interacts with the curriculum is critical to the outcomes of the teacher education process. Examples of questions that need to be addressed in this line of inquiry are as follows:

1. How do prospective teachers' theories and beliefs about students (e.g., their attributions for student performance), their theories and beliefs about teaching and how children learn, their motivations and expectations relative to students and themselves as future professionals develop and/or change as they experience the teacher education curriculum?

2. How do professional judgment and decision-making abilities of prospective teachers develop as they progress through the teacher preparation program? What are the most influential factors in this developmental process?
3. What influences/experiences help prospective teachers integrate their learnings from foundational areas such as educational psychology, social foundations, curriculum and instruction to structure and organize subject matter content in order to make it comprehensible to them and the students whom they will teach? How do they think about the teaching of subject matter content as they experience these foundational areas?
4. How do prospective teachers think about the social, cultural, and political contexts within which they will teach in tomorrow's schools?

Though answers to these questions are critical to the preparation of prospective teachers in general education programs, they become much more critical for teachers being prepared to enter classrooms within the current context of school reform. Within this context, decision making is becoming more localized, and initiatives in special education such as the Regular Education Initiative (see Will, 1986) and the full inclusion model render the classrooms more diverse in terms of student abilities, needs, types of disability and social development. Teachers' professional judgments, decision making, their expectations for student performance, their attributions for student success and failure, and their theories and beliefs about how students learn are among the most potent factors that will influence interactions and the quality of the learning environments in these classrooms, yet they constitute an area of research that is seriously understudied in teacher education.

As was the case with the antecedent conditions, studies that link process variables with antecedent and/or outcome variables will provide a much greater yield in the generation of knowledge in the field of teacher education. Studies that focus on the teacher education curriculum or program intervention and the context within which it is being implemented, or the teacher education curriculum and resultant teacher behaviors such as teaching in the classroom and skill in working collaboratively with other professionals in an inclusive classroom context are examples of such linkages. Studies that include, in addition, detailed descriptions of given characteristics of prospective teachers or the social/political context within which the teacher education process is occurring are of the antecedent-process-outcome genre.

The need for well-conceived studies that examine process variables along with antecedent conditions and teacher outcome variables is critical. For example, studies that examine the cognitive functioning of teacher education students in conjunction with how they gain understanding of subject-matter knowledge and pedagogy, how they make sense of other teacher education program experiences and the social milieu in which they must teach, and how they organize the various types of learning experiences in the program for subsequent teaching are areas in need of systematic study.

Outcomes. Within the research framework proposed, Yarger and Smith (1990) view outcomes as summative in nature. Outcomes refer to any "actual teacher behavior in the classroom that is used as a criterion for performance." Studies that are usually conducted with outcome variables typically link process and outcomes. Most of these studies are correlational or experimental in nature.

Much of the criticism of research in this area lies with the measurement of the variables used as the outcome variables. Teacher performance in the classroom is hard to measure. Other outcome variables that are less problematic to measure (e.g., SAT, GRE scores) are often seen as irrelevant outcomes of the teacher education process.

As was discussed earlier, studies of the antecedent-process-outcome genre, if well-conceived and executed, will add much to the teacher education research base. Studies of this type will be primarily quantitative in nature. Although more complex than the two-factor linking studies, relationships between and among variables can nonetheless be examined using such techniques as path analysis and structural equation modeling. Statistical models that incorporate mediating process variables in an attempt to explain the relationships between antecedent and outcome conditions may be particularly useful.

The framework we have discussed provides a backdrop against which research questions on teacher education can be conceptualized and framed. The questions vary in nature and complexity. No one research tradition or method will provide the answers to the variety of questions that may be asked. We propose the use of multiple methods of inquiry (e.g., quantitative, qualitative, interpretive) to help us find answers to these questions. We will now turn our attention to the discussion of some broad methodological and ethical issues that are pertinent to our conduct of research in the field of teacher education.

METHODOLOGICAL ISSUES IN THE CONDUCT OF RESEARCH ON TEACHER EDUCATION

Issues of research method go beyond specific topics such as the selection of samples, the coding of interview transcripts, and the computation of statistics for hypothesis testing. In a broader sense, method links the questions researchers ask with the answers they eventually assert and defend. Indeed, Shulman (1981) suggested that method is that which distinguishes research from speculation. As products of philosophical bases, however, methodological choices influence not only how answers are pursued but also the kinds of questions researchers will ask. To maintain the necessary breadth in discussion of methodology, issues related to improving the methods of research in teacher education can be organized by addressing three broad, interrelated questions:

- Are we conducting the right study?
- Are we conducting it well?
- Are we interpreting and communicating the results well?

Conducting the Right Study

The assertion that we should seek answers to only important questions should be self-evident. If the purpose of teacher education is to provide society with teachers who comprehend and apply principles of pedagogy, who are knowledgeable about the content they teach, who analyze and utilize the contexts within which they teach, and who both understand how children learn and use this understanding to bring about student learning, researchers need to explicitly elucidate the connections between current research questions and this purpose. This is the commonly encountered "so what?" question, the answer to which identifies and describes the value of our research for educational practice. If the answer to this "so what?" question is awkward or tangential, perhaps the research we are doing is not especially important for the field of teacher education.

Ideally, the research questions should drive the data collection and analysis plans rather than vice versa. Mills (1959) warned against researchers whose attachment to a particular research method results in the method becoming an end in itself. Similarly, we have all known doctoral students who select a particular research method or statistical technique,then cast about in search of an acceptable question to fit the method. Occasionally, the question so chosen fits the method well, but typically the result is a marginally acceptable effort at best. A more sensible relationship between question and method is to first identify the most important question or questions to be addressed, and then to consider how to best approach these questions methodologically. The result will likely be not a single best method, but a list of potential methods, each with its strengths and limitations.

This unidirectional relationship between research questions and method questions is both overly simplistic and overly optimistic. The training we receive in research methods and our previous research experiences influence and usually limit both the questions we ask and the ways in which we ask them. New arenas of research are fitted to the procrustean beds of the methods in which we already are comfortable (Howe & Eisenhart, 1990). This human tendency may be turned to our advantage, however, if we consciously seek to become comfortable with a broader variety of methods. In short, expanding our experiences with data collection and analysis techniques will help us to ask better questions.

The best path to expanding our research "comfort zones" is to collaborate with other researchers engaged in a variety of techniques. The research community must include representatives from a variety of research traditions. Building a community of quantitative researchers or a community of ethnographers will do little in this regard. As a field, education provides unique opportunities for such interdisciplinary collaboration. Shulman (1988) suggested that education is a field of study rather than a discipline. As such, the breadth of methodologies from a variety of disciplines (e.g., psychology, anthropology, linguistics, and sociology) can be successfully brought to the field of education and to teacher education in particular.

Finally, the questions to be addressed through our research need to be conceptualized within an ecological perspective. The teacher education process is not conducted in a controlled environment. The best questions must take into account factors in the environment that potentially mediate or moderate the relationships of primary interest. Social/political and other antecedent factors interact with process factors (e.g., the teacher education curriculum and instructional procedures) to influence the outcomes of the teacher education process. Although in the initial stages of question development, simplicity may be virtuous (if X happens, what is the result?), the level of complexity soon must be raised to reflect the ecology of the teacher education institution, or field site (if X happens while Y and Z are present, but V and W have been removed, how is this different than when V and W are also present?).

Conducting the Study Well

Once researchers have identified the most important questions to be addressed, a variety of methodological choices present themselves. Rather than review specific aspects of technique that are unique to each method, this section will present those general issues of the research craft that are shared by a variety of methods of disciplined inquiry.

At the forefront, we need to distinguish between exploratory and confirmatory research (a distinction described by Brush [1974] as the context of discovery versus the context of verification). The fundamental difference is between the assertion of hypotheses being subject to verification, and a broader general inquiry from which specific hypotheses may emerge. Both aspects of research are necessary and in most research endeavors, both aspects are present (Tukey, 1980). However, the distinction between these two types of research is important because the meaning of data derived from exploratory research is not the same as the meaning of those obtained in confirmatory investigations. Hypotheses that originate in exploratory studies and analyses must be subjected to independent, confirmatory inquiry.

Secondly, an attitude of adherence to methodological rigor needs to become habit. If we have taken the time to identify important questions toward which to direct our research resources, then we owe it to ourselves to design and conduct the resulting research in such a manner that questions of methodological integrity do not confound the answers we advance. In our efforts to comprehensively investigate questions, we will find the need for a variety of research methods, be they case study, ethnography, survey, correlational study, experimentation, or quasi-experimentation. Any method of inquiry may be applied either carefully and rigorously or desultorily and haphazardly.

A useful technique to prod ourselves into careful scrutiny of our research plans is to ask "what if" questions of the design. During our planning, we may ask "if the results are contrary to all of our expectations, what reasons can we give?" The answers to this question are likely to be encouragingly specific (e.g., maybe the sample was too small, we did not allow sufficient time for the treatment to affect the variables of interest, we did not consider that some instructors are better able to use a particular procedure than others, or that a particular teaching strategy is beneficial to the achievement of some students but detrimental to that of others). All the reasons that are given as answers to this question—reasons related to how the study was conducted—point directly to weaknesses in the methodology. The challenge for researchers is to identify these weaknesses prior to conducting the study or at least during the early stages of the study, and then to correct for them to the extent possible.

The collection of data subsumes a variety of issues related to methodological rigor. Sampling considerations must be given to the selection of variables and their values as well as to college sites, college instructors, teachers-in-training, schools, classrooms, and students. A lack of forethought in the selection of a sample unnecessarily limits the generalizability of conclusions and may confound conclusions because of unrecognized extraneous variables. Researchers must carefully document, with rich, "thick" description, the characteristics of the teacher education settings, activities, and participants in the research. Similarly, adherence to sound principles of measurement are of critical importance for data collection. Applications of measurement principles are needed in strategies ranging from interviewing and observing to administering questionnaires and standardized assessment instruments. The influence of the researcher on the data being collected presents more challenges in designs involving open-ended interviewing and many observational strategies, rather than those involving questionnaires and standardized tests (Babbie, 1992).

Processes of data analysis, or the use of tools for making sense of research data, are important for qualitative as well as quantitative research. The general ideas of data reduction and data display are common to most approaches to research. Whether we are doing multiple regression analysis or semantic domain analysis, general methods have been developed, common pitfalls have been identified, and specific procedures have been recommended (see for example, Denzin, 1978; Burgess, 1984; Miles & Huberman, 1984a; Chatfield, 1988; Stevens, 1992). The fundamental issue is whether another researcher, attempting to make sense of the same data would reach conclusions that are similar to those we have reached.

Researchers who are experienced in quantitative methods feel comfortable with confidence intervals, decision rules, computational algorithms, and error estimates. The discomfort comes in extrapolating decisions to real-world recommendations and advice, given the almost omnipresent violations of statistical assumptions and the uncertainty of our level of uncertainty (Mosteller & Tukey, 1977). Conversely, those experienced in qualitative research traditions feel comfortable with interpretations and extrapolations, but may experience discomfort about the process by which they reached their conclusions. Clear, explicit exposition of the methods used to aggregate, partition, reduce, analyze, and interpret research data are needed. Miles and Huberman (1984b) pointed out two reasons such an exposition is needed. First, the detail of techniques used in data analysis will provide a verification device by which readers can follow the process the researcher used to move from raw data to research conclusions. Secondly, the reported details can be used by secondary data analysts who may apply additional techniques or seek to integrate findings with the results from other studies. The charts and matrices suggested by

Miles and Huberman (1984a) will go a long way toward bridging the gap between field notes and research conclusions.

In seeking improved methods, quantitative researchers should direct their attention both to an increased level of complexity and to the fundamentals of statistical inference. In terms of complexity, quantitative researchers should develop facility with methods that provide for the analysis of multiple variables and their interactions. Recent advances in statistical modeling involving covariance structure analysis (Joreskog & Sorbom, 1979; Loehlin, 1987; Bollen, 1989) and hierarchical linear models (Bryk & Raudenbush, 1992) hold promise for the analysis of multilevel data related to research questions presented at a level of complexity closer to that of the environment of schools. These levels move beyond the single link between two variables, into issues of multiple explanatory variables, mediation and moderation that are closer to the complex ecology of the teacher preparation college or site and schools. For examples of applications of these recent approaches to quantitative analysis, see Marsh and Grayson (1990), and Raudenbush, Rowan, and Kang (1991).

However, in pursuit of such complex models, renewed attention to the fundamentals of inference is needed. Two examples of such fundamentals should suffice. First, the assumption of independence of observations which underlies virtually all inferential statistics (the unit of analysis problem) is often overlooked in educational research in general, and teacher education research in particular, even though the degree of dependence of students within classrooms and classrooms within colleges or schools is far from negligible. Violations of this assumption result in extreme distortions of probability statements (Hopkins, 1982; Scariano & Davenport, 1987). Secondly, researchers need to emphasize the distinction between the results of a statistical hypothesis test (typically a probability statement) and the sample effect size (an index of the strength of relationship between variables). Such a distinction is necessary because the probability statements related to hypothesis testing are a function of both the magnitude of relationship between variables and the sample size. Recommendations for discounting the importance of hypothesis testing have been largely ignored, despite cogent arguments dating from the 1970s (Carver, 1978). However, quantitative researchers need to consider the issue of magnitude of effect independently of whether we reject or fail to reject a statistical null hypothesis.

Qualitative research methods offer distinct advantages in regard to the simultaneous consideration of a large number of variables within the complex ecology of colleges of education, field sites, and schools. The inherent flexibility of these methods (allowing modification of the research strategy during the course of the study, with the addition of new variables and new participants) is a major advantage to many types of qualitative research. However, a disadvantage of such flexibility is that researchers may be too ready to modify their strategies based on the initial data obtained. As with the above recommendations for quantitative researchers, a return to fundamental principles will be helpful for qualitative researchers. The importance of triangulation or corroboration has received much attention in the methodological literature. Patton (1980) described triangulation as "a process by which the researcher can guard against the accusation that a study's findings are simply an artifact of a single method, a single data source, or a single investigator's bias" (p. 332). The convergence of findings from multiple methods, sources, and investigators reduces the skepticism regarding those findings (Stainback & Stainback, 1984). Attention to triangulation should be evident from the study's inception, and a prudent researcher will wait for some degree of corroboration of the initial data before altering the overall strategy of fieldwork.

Similarly, in our field research we must remain self-critical of the adequacy of evidence we are collecting. Erickson (1986) delineates five areas in which the adequacy of our evidence may be lacking: a) amount of evidence; b) variety of kinds of evidence; c) interpretive status of evidence; d) disconfirming evidence; and e) discrepant case analysis. Inadequacy in the amount and variety of evidence results from the researcher not gathering data in enough instances (amount) and not providing for triangulation of the data (variety). Inadequacy in the interpretive status of the evidence results from our misunderstanding of important aspects of the data. The final two types of inadequacy concern data which are lacking in the study. An inadequacy of disconfirming evidence occurs when the researcher fails to search for data that might disconfirm a key assertion or fails to subsequently analyze such data. Similarly, inadequacy related to discrepant case analyses results when the researcher fails to compare features of discrepant cases (instances in which key assertions did not hold) with those features of the confirming cases. The explicit search for and analysis of disconfirming evidence and discrepant cases allows a researcher to refine and adjust major assertions that are developed during the research project. A lack of such a search and such analysis of disconfirming evidence leaves us vulnerable to charges of bias in our definitions of admissible data.

Interpretation and Communication of Results

Whether a particular piece of research is qualitative or quantitative, we should learn to communicate with all educational researchers as well as other constituents. Our language and arguments must be comprehensible so that others can intelligently decide to agree or disagree with us, rather than simply be baffled. The problem is more than that of practitioners not understanding researchers (Phillips, 1980), currently researchers are not even understanding one another.

Researchers in the field of teacher education are obligated to discuss the extent to which the results of their own studies fit with those of previous work. No single study will adequately encompass an area of inquiry, nor unambiguously answer a research question. However, a single study well designed, executed, analyzed, and interpreted may add another piece to the puzzle or suggest where previous pieces have been misplaced. Discrepancies noted in the outcomes of related studies should be explored, and the most plausible reasons for the discrepancies (e.g., weaknesses in the underlying substantive theory, methodological problems) should be elucidated. Researchers should recognize that awareness of discrepancies often precedes creativity (Beveridge, 1980). In addition to a discussion of research results in terms of congruence with previous research and theoretical implications, the results obtained in a particular study, as well as what researchers learn during the conduct of a study, should inform the process to be followed for the next research project.

Although the need for replications and extensions in quantitative research has been thoroughly discussed by Neuliep (1991), qualitative researchers disagree about the issue of replicability. For example, Marshall and Rossman (1989) maintain that:

> qualitative research does not pretend to be replicable. The researcher purposefully avoids controlling the research conditions and concentrates on recording the complexity of situational contexts and interrelations as they occur. Moreover, the researcher's goal of discovering this complexity by altering research strategies within a flexible research design cannot be replicated by future researchers, nor should it be attempted. (p.148)

Such adamant dismissal of the applicability of replication for qualitative research suggests that these authors are narrowly defining the term. In its broader use, *replication* is the corroboration of research results by different investigators in different settings. In this broad sense, the issue of replicability is inherent in establishing the extents and limitations of the generalizability of our research findings. The applicability to qualitative research of this broader definition of replication has been recognized by Miles and Huberman (1984b), and by Guba (1981), who prefers the term *transferability* to replicability.

In interpreting the results of research, we must remain cognizant of the limitations of our studies. Maintaining an ecological frame of reference will be helpful in this regard. The context of any study in teacher education was a particular instance or instances of institutional, classroom, or field site ecology, and generalizations beyond this framework must be suggested with great prudence. Explicit detailed descriptions of the pertinent aspects of the environmental context, the participants, the treatments, and the data collection methods and analyses will allow consumers of the research to judge the applicability of our findings to new contexts. Our innate tendencies to overstate the implications of research results, with its subsequent disappointments, contribute to the pendulum characteristic of educational fashions. The importance of special education to all of society makes the field especially susceptible to bandwagons and fads. This susceptibility must be tempered by the rigorous scrutiny of skeptical researchers demanding high standards for evidence. We should all heed the warnings suggested in Kauffman's (1993) description of special education as a field in which "advocacy for new strategies and practices is very far ahead of reliable data" (p. 13).

A final issue related to the communication of research results is what Grudin (1990) described as the "diplomacy of invention," meaning that the worth of research results depends not only upon what has been discovered, invented, or created but also upon how the discovery is presented to the world. In the "Parable of the White Suit," Grudin describes how the invention of an indestructible material nearly brought about the downfall of its chemist creator, just because it was presented to the world as a man dressed in a white suit. Because of its presentation to the world, the invention was interpreted as something that would lead to loss of jobs and the eventual economic collapse of the garment industry. Had the inventor been more diplomatic, presenting the invention perhaps in the form of indestructible uniforms for firefighters, the impact of the invention on both its creator and the world would have been quite different.

Ethics of Research

Woven throughout every topic related to research methods is the issue of research ethics. This overriding issue includes the consequences of research results to society, the rights of research subjects, the establishment of research priorities and academic freedom, the falsification and misinterpretation of results, and the theft of ideas and credit (Robinson & Moulton, 1985). Adherence to ethical principles of research must become as much a part of researchers' craftsmanship as reviewing and analyzing a body of literature. When a single researcher violates ethical standards, the credibility of all researchers is potentially damaged.

Dockrell (1988) identifies researchers' ethical responsibilities to four publics. First are our responsibilities to the participants in the research. Participation in research should be voluntary, and the volunteerism should be based upon complete understanding of what is required of participants. Additionally, the objectives of the research should be disclosed, unless the participants' knowledge of the objectives will potentially bias the resulting data. In such cases, full disclosure should be made in a debriefing following data collection. Finally, the limits of confidentiality should be disclosed to the participants. Confidentiality is easier to maintain in large-scale research involving multiple college or school sites and classrooms. With case studies, the researcher must honestly appraise the potential for maintaining confidentiality and communicate this appraisal to potential participants.

A second public to whom researchers should recognize ethical responsibility is that of the commissioners of the research, the granting agency that is providing funding for the study. As Dockrell (1988) asserts, this ethical responsibility means that "researchers should not promise more than they can deliver and that consequently they should deliver what they have promised" (p. 182). The researcher must clearly communicate to the granting agency the limits of information that will be available. The results of a research project may be direct advice about a teacher preparation model, solutions to a policy issue, a greater theoretical understanding of the issue, or a family of plausible hypotheses to be subjected to further confirmatory inquiry. The important point is that the granting agency be made aware of what the outcomes of the research are likely to be.

A third public is that of our colleagues. As Dockrell points out, research data are not private property but are individual contributions to the community of researchers. In writing reports of research, we must detail our research design and the analyses of our data to allow others to assess both their quality and their implications. The level of detail of such treatment depends upon the nature of the report

(technical reports typically being more detailed than articles for professional journals). As Denzin (1978) pointed out, research is not "an idealized process, immac-
ulately conceived in design and elegantly executed in practice" (p. 309). Rather, the
execution of research reflects a series of compromises between methodological
ideals and those methods which are feasible in the real world. Researchers are obligated to document and report such compromises to their colleagues. In most cases,
the raw data should be made available for secondary analysis. An additional responsibility to our colleagues is that we exercise due care and rigor in evaluating the quality of the evidence we have for developing conclusions and recommendations. The
need for such prudence is reflected in Medawar's (1984) observation:

> The most heinous offense a scientist as a scientist can commit is to declare to
> be true that which is not so; if a scientist cannot interpret the phenomenon
> he is studying, it is a binding obligation upon him to make it possible for
> another to do so. (p. 6)

The final public to which the researcher owes responsibility is that of the community as a whole. We must take due care that our results are not misinterpreted.
The important research questions are those which carry with them direct implications for the education of teachers and the education of children. If the necessary
caveats which are implicit in the evaluation of empirical evidence are easily overlooked by consumers of our research, it is our responsibility to explicate such
caveats and their ramifications, before our results are misinterpreted and their implications overstated. A final responsibility is that of the social consequences of
research. As Dockrell stated, "The researcher has the obligation to ask questions
fearlessly. He or she also has the obligation to be aware of the consequences of
raising certain issues" (p. 184).

The new design of research communities with multidisciplinary teams carries
new challenges in the ethics of research. First, the diffusion of responsibility among
members of the team raises the risk of ethical violations (LaPidus & Mishkin,
1990). It is encumbent upon all participants to guard the moral integrity of the
team. Secondly, the formation of multidisciplinary teams will be accompanied by
a recognition that ethical principles of best practice differ among research traditions. Differences in our orientations to fundamental issues such as the neutrality
of the researcher, the need for deception of research participants, and the disclosure of data that are potentially harmful to the participants suggest the need for
development of new ethical guidelines that will be recognized and supported by all
participants.

CONCLUSIONS

In our discussions of research on teacher education, we have pointed to the need for
a clearly articulated conceptual framework to guide the development of research
questions. Such a framework helps us to determine the critical conditions, the

important variables, and the salient features of phenomena to be investigated. Drawing on the work of Yarger and Smith (1990), we have proposed one such framework and demonstrated how this framework suggests a system of questions to be addressed through inquiry. The Yarger and Smith model was not selected because it represents the single best conceptual approach to research on teacher education. To the contrary, no single framework completely encompasses the field; other frameworks have been proposed in the literature. Further, as our knowledge of teacher education increases, more refined frameworks will be necessary and will, undoubtly, be developed.

We have argued that, after the research questions, the critical conditions and the relevant variables have been identified, research employing a multitude of methods be pursued. The methodological traditions that are commonly classified as quantitative and qualitative both have important roles in disciplined inquiry, and comprehensive research programs must incorporate an integration of ethnographic studies, case studies, controlled experiments, quasi-experiments, and correlational studies.

Whatever methods are employed, we have suggested that the research questions themselves should drive the data collection and analysis process, and we have urged that particular attention be paid to the methodological rigors of the research traditions, the consideration of the ethics of disciplined inquiry, and the clear communication of research results and limitations of such results. In the consideration of conflicts among alternative paradigms, we concur with Howe and Eisenhart (1990) that the labels we apply to the individual methodological traditions are not important. Whether we call a particular study ethnography, case study, or critical inquiry is of little consequence. Rather, the two essential issues are whether important educational questions are being addressed and whether warranted conclusions are being advanced.

REFERENCES

Babbie, E. (1992). *The practice of social research* (6th ed.). Belmont, CA: Wadsworth.

Beveridge, W. I. B. (1980). *Seeds of discovery*. New York: Norton.

Bollen, K. A. (1989). *Structural equations with latent variables*. New York: Wiley.

Brush, S. G. (1974). Should the history of science be rated X? *Science, 183*, 1164–1172.

Bryk, A. S., & Raudenbush, S. W. (1992). *Hierarchical linear models: Applications and data analysis methods*. Newbury Park, CA: Sage.

Burgess, R. G. (1984). *In the field: An introduction to field research*. London: George Allen & Unwin.

Carnegie Forum on Education and the Economy. Task Force on Teaching as a Profession (1986). *A nation prepared: Teachers for the 21st century*. New York: Author.

Carver, R. P. (1978). The case against statistical significance testing. *Harvard Educational Review, 48*, 378–399.

Chatfield, C. (1988). *Problem solving: A statistician's guide*. New York: Chapman and Hall.

Clark, C. M., & Peterson, P. L. (1986). Teachers' thought processes. In M. C. Wittrock (Ed.), *Handbook of research on teaching* (pp. 255–296). New York: Macmillan.

Denzin, N. K. (1978). *The research act*. New York: McGraw-Hill.

Dockrell, W. B. (1988). Ethical considerations in research. In J. P. Keeves (Ed.), *Educational research, methodology, and measurement: An international handbook*. New York: Pergamon Press.

Ducharme, E. R., & Agne, R. M. (1982). The education professoriate: A research-based perspective. *Journal of Teacher Education, 33*(6), 30–36.

Erickson, F. (1986). Qualitative methods in research on teaching. In M. C. Wittrock (Ed.), *Handbook of research on teaching* (3rd ed.). New York: Macmillan.

Getzels, J. W., & Jackson, P. W. (1963). The teacher's personality and characteristics. In N. L. Gage (Ed.), *Handbook of research on teaching* (2nd ed.). Chicago: Rand McNally.

Good, T., & Grouws, D. (1981). *Experimental research in secondary mathematics classrooms. Working with teachers (Final Report)*. Colombia: University of Missouri. (ERIC Document Reproduction Service No. 219 261).

Grudin, R. (1990). *The grace of great things: Creativity and innovation*. New York: Ticknor & Fields.

Guba, E. G. (1981). Criteria for assessing the trustworthiness of naturalistic inquiries. *Educational Communication and Technology Journal, 29*, 75–91.

Holmes Group. (1990). *Tomorrow's schools*. East Lansing, MI: Author

Hopkins, K. D. (1982). The unit of analysis: Group means versus individual observations. *American Educational Research Journal, 19*, 5–18.

Howe, K., & Eisenhart, M. (1990). Standards for qualitative and quantitative research: A prolegomenon. *Educational Researcher, 19*, 2–9.

Joreskog, K. G. & Sorbom, D. (1979). *Advances in factor analysis and structural equation models*. Cambridge, MA: Abt Books.

Kauffman, J. M. (1993). How we might achieve the radical reform of special education. *Exceptional Children, 60*, 6–16.

Kuhn, T. S. (1970). *The structure of scientific revolutions* (2nd ed.). Chicago: University of Chicago Press.

Lanier, J. E., & Little, J. W. (1986). Research on teacher education. In M. C. Wittrock (Ed.), *Handbook of research on teaching* (3rd. ed., pp. 527–569). New York: Macmillan.

LaPidus, J. B. & Mishkin, B. (1990). Values and ethics in the graduate education of scientists. In W. W. May (Ed.), *Ethics and Higher Education*. New York: Macmillan.

Loehlin, J. C. (1987). *Latent variable models: An introduction to factor, path, and structural analysis*. Hillsdale, NJ: Lawrence Erlbaum.

Marsh, H. W., & Grayson, D. (1990). Public/Catholic differences in the high school and beyond data: A multigroup structural equation modeling approach to testing mean differences. *Journal of Educational Statistics, 15*, 199–235.

Marshall, C., & Rossman, G. (1989). *Designing qualitative research*. Beverly Hills, CA: Sage.

Medawar, P. B. (1984). *The limits of science*. Oxford, England: Oxford University Press.

Miles, M. B., & Huberman, A. M. (1984a). *Qualitative data analysis: A sourcebook of new methods*. Beverly Hills, CA: Sage.

Miles, M. B., & Huberman, A. M. (1984b). Drawing valid meaning from qualitative data: Toward a shared craft. *Educational Researcher, 13*(5), 20–30.

Mills, C. W. (1959). *The sociological imagination*. New York: Oxford.

Mosteller, F., & Tukey, J. W. (1977). *Data analysis and regression: A second course in statistics*. Reading, MA: Addison-Wesley.

Neuliep, J. W. (Ed.). (1991). *Replication research in the social sciences*. Newbury Park, CA: Sage.

Patriarca, L. A., & Cegelka, P. T. (1992). *The school as the center of educational reform: Implications of school-based practice for research*. (ERIC Document Reproduction Service No. ED 353 762).

Patton, M. (1975). *Alternative evaluation research paradigm*. Grand Forks: Universities of North Dakota Press.

Patton, M. (1980). *Qualitative evaluation methods*. Beverly Hills, CA: Sage.

Phillips, D. C. (1980). What do the researcher and practitioner have to offer each other? *Educational Researcher, 9*(11), 17–20.

Prichard, K. W., Fen, S. N., & Buxton, J. H. (1971). Social class origins of college teachers of education. *Journal of Teacher Education, 22*(2), 219–228.

Raudenbush, S. W., Rowan, B., & Kang, S. J. (1991). A multilevel, multivariate model for studying school climate with estimation via the EM algorithm and application to U.S. high-school data. *Journal of Educational Statistics, 16*, 295–330.

Rist, R. C. (1977). On the relations among educational research paradigms: From disdain to detente. *Anthropology and Education Quarterly, 7*(2), 42–50

Robinson, G. M., & Moulton, J. (1985). *Ethical problems in higher education*. Englewood Cliffs, NJ: Prentice-Hall.

Ryans, D. G. (1960). *Characteristics of teachers*. Washington, DC: American Council on Education.

Scariano, S. M., & Davenport, J. M. (1987). The effects of violations of independence assumptions in the one-way ANOVA. *The American Statistician, 41*, 123–129.

Shulman, L. S. (1981). Disciplines of inquiry in education: An overview. *Educational Researcher, 10*(6), 5–12.

Shulman, L. S. (1986). Paradigms and research programs in the study of teaching: A contemporary perspective. In M. C. Wittrock (Ed.), *Handbook of research on teaching* (3rd ed., pp. 3–36). New York: Macmillan.

Shulman, L. S. (1988). Disciplines of inquiry in education: An overview. In R. Jaeger (Ed.), *Complementary methods for research in education* (pp. 3–17). Washington, DC: American Educational Research Association.

Stainback, S., & Stainback, W. (1984). Methodological considerations in qualitative research. *Journal of the Association for Persons with Severe Handicaps, 9*, 296–303.

Stallings, J. A., & Kowalski, T. (1990). Research on professional development schools. In W. Robert Houston (Ed.), *Handbook of research on teacher education* (pp. 251–263). New York, Macmillan.

Stevens, J. (1992). *Applied multivariate statistics for the social sciences* (2nd ed.). Hillsdale, NJ: Lawrence Erlbaum.

Tukey, J. W. (1980). We need both exploratory and confirmatory. *American Statistician, 34*, 23–25.

Vance, V. S., & Schlechty, P. C. (1982). The distribution of academic ability in the teaching force: Policy implications. *Phi Delta Kappan, 64*(1), 2–27.

Will, M. (1986). Educating children with learning problems: A shared responsibility. *Exceptional Children, 52*(5), 411–415.

Weaver, W. J. (1979). In search of quality: The need for talent in teaching. *Phi Delta Kappan, 61*(1), 29–46.

Yarger, S. J., & Smith, P. L. (1990). Issues in research on teacher education. In W. Robert Houston (Ed.), *Handbook of research on teacher education* (pp. 25–41). New York: Macmillan.

Zeichner, K., & Tabachnick, B. (1982). The belief systems of university supervisors in the elementary student teaching program. *Journal of Education for Teaching, 8*(1), 34–54.

10

INTEGRATING THE PARALLEL REFORMS IN GENERAL AND SPECIAL EDUCATION

JAMES PAUL & HILDA ROSSELLI

INTRODUCTION

THE reform of public education, underway since 1983, has been filled with energy for changing the conduct of the nation's education business. Hopeful images have been well-crafted with a rhetoric that captures our highest hopes and reflects our deepest values for America's future. The nature and full meaning of the reforms continue to elude the full grasp of our existing philosophies of education and to resist anything approximating consensus on implementation. Multiple discourses are now grounding quite dissimilar understandings of education, schooling, and learning (Katz, 1991; Noddings, 1992; Lystand, 1984; Giroux, 1982: Gilligan, 1982; Henderson, 1992). The traditional policy machinery has lost its familiar hum, which is disconcerting to some and prima facie evidence of progress to others. Wearied by debates over definitions, values, funding, and accountability, we are having difficulty being as hopeful about our research and our inventive capacities as we are adamant in our critiques of the moral and epistemological foundations, admittedly shaky, on which we stand. The national passion for change in public education is matched by the growing intensity of our uncertainty about how to accomplish those changes. An examination of the general political, professional and policy landscape of these educational reforms, now over 10 years in the making, provides a basis for understanding the national research, policy, and programmatic initiatives which aim at the integration of special and general education reforms (Sailor, 1991).

The emergence and problematic convergence of these reforms constitute the critical framework for this book. The philosophical, programmatic, and political complexity of the reforms is challenging the development of a clear national vision and creating considerable difficulty for those in charge of state and local policies for public schools and for teacher preparation programs. This is the context that has framed the collaborative university-school initiatives in west central Florida described in Part Two, which seek to develop a locally valid programmatic agenda that integrates teacher preparation and instruction in general and special education. The purpose of the discussion that follows is to amplify and integrate the basic issues and understandings presented in the previous chapters, in order to create a conceptual platform for Part Two which focuses on reshaping educational applications.

PART OF THE STORY: REFORM OF GENERAL EDUCATION

A Changing Social and Economic Environment

Since the publication of *A Nation at Risk* in 1983 by the National Commission on Excellence in Education, there has been a growing sensitivity to the challenges facing public schools and the need for change. The report focused attention on the relationship between education and the national interest. Commenting on present and future directions in school reform, Passow (1989) noted that "the equation of the failure of America's schools with a declining economy and weakened national security triggered the current reform movement" (p. 13).

The American workplace had to change dramatically in order to remain competitive in world markets. Corporate hierarchies are "flattening out," workers are increasingly put into situations requiring teamwork, and the very nature of required thinking skills has expanded to now address ambiguous situations, anticipatory thinking, and conflict resolution. Kearns (1988), chairman and chief executive officer of Xerox Corporation, and Doyle (1988), envision worker characteristics that include flexibility, adaptability, inventiveness, even playfulness, balanced by discipline and determination. In response to these realities, the Secretary's Commission on Achieving Necessary Skills (SCANS) released *What Work Requires of Schools: A SCANS Report for America 2000* in 1991. This SCANS document, though not comparable in status with previous reform documents, has become one of the cornerstones in many of the subsequent state reform plans focusing on outcome accountability. In brief, the document emphasized the need for people who can put knowledge to work by optimizing their use of resources, acquiring and using information, working with a variety of technology, understanding complex systems, and working with others. It dramatically supported a curriculum focus that places significance on basic skills, as well as thinking skills and personal qualities.

Also of importance to business leaders have been the changing national demographics. The lag between baby booms has produced fewer workers, and the growing majority of the new workforce includes recordbreaking numbers of women, minorities, and immigrants. These are segments of our nation's population who, based on current conditions, are less likely to achieve a high level of success in our current educational system and of whom many are facing additional challenges created by poverty conditions. Some analysts have even hypothesized that this economic reality has played a key role in focusing the nation on the plight of "endangered" or at-risk students.

The public's response to the grim national picture of students' achievement has fueled the continued compilation and publication of statistical data that points to a general inability to read, comprehend, write, cipher, analyze, and identify geographical entities on a map. We also do not fare well in international comparisons with other industrial nations. America's students are last in mathematics and tied with Ireland and two Canadian provinces for last in science, according to one recent international study (Finn, 1991).

Persuaded that the future of the nation's economy and the quality of public schools *are* fundamentally linked, business and political leaders have forged a growing alliance that has propelled the reform movement (Passow, 1989). The central issue has been understood to be the need to supply a competent workforce for industries in the knowledge age. Historically, schools were organized to meet the needs of an agrarian and, later, an industrial society. They have not changed in ways that noticeably meet the education and training needs of workers for the knowledge age. A well-worn example is the still prevalent agrarian calendar. Given an average of 180 days a year, Finn (1991) calculated that only 9% of an 18-year-old high school graduate's life will have been spent "under the schoolhouse roof." Unfortunately, the remaining 91% often works counterproductively to the time spent in school, e.g., time spent watching television.

Additionally there are marked increases in the percentage of families with children that are female-headed and in the percentage of children under 18 years of age who are living in poverty (Hodgkinson, 1985; Lipsky & Gartner, 1989). Also difficult to ignore are the startling statistics and daily reports of violence, substance abuse, suicide, and devastating conditions of poverty that are influencing the lives of schoolchildren.

Consequently the collaborations discussed in chapters 14–18 have intentionally involved schools with demographically diverse student populations. We believed programs developed collaboratively in real schools with those participating in the school lives of children would be most meaningful and most likely to reflect the diverse interests and moral perspectives of those involved. Another belief guiding our work was that, consistent with the teacher empowerment and site-based management philosophy of America 2000, the staff support, teacher education, and program development initiatives had to be school-based and had to emerge from the collaboration. The alternative, we reasoned, was to impose a program that may or may not fit the lived experiences of the children, their families, teachers, and other educators involved in the collaborations. The issue was not simply efficacy of interventions or a particular protocol for reform; rather it was a more complex matter of working collegially in a local context where decisions were made and validated by those most affected by them. Unlike the politics of reform focusing on national policy issues, the meaningful, productive, and generative force of school reform has to be in the school, involving parents, teachers, and other school leaders. We have sought, therefore, to anchor the transformation of our university training and research programs in local schools (see chapters 10–11).

Waves of Reform

Since 1983 there have been two additional "waves" of reform. The initial efforts, or the "first wave" as it has been called, focused attention on major components of the public education system, such as the curriculum, goals, increasing the salaries of teachers, more teaching time, higher standards for students, elimination of tracking, teacher education, technology, and the relationship between schools and business. Cuban (1989) describes these as "first-order changes" that improved efficiency but left the organizational structure basically intact. Over 270 task forces and commissions were appointed and over 700 statutes enacted nationwide (Timar & Kirp, 1987), stiffer graduation requirements were put into place, and some states experimented with merit pay and career ladders. The concept of a "reform" was applied to these efforts, which in retrospect amounted to "tinkerings" promoted by business leaders, governors, and other political leaders. Noticeable progress was evident if you selected the right barometers. Dropout rates among blacks decreased nationally, SAT scores went up slightly, and more students enrolled in more challenging courses (Finn, 1991; Lewis, 1989). This wave not only ignored the mention of students with disabilities but the voices also were exclusive of those traditionally advocating for these populations.

The "second wave" occurred during the latter part of the 1980s. By this time, earlier reform efforts were being evaluated and more drastic measures were being sought. The next "wave" of reports included the publication of the Holmes Group, *Tomorrow's Teachers: A Report of the Holmes Group* (1986) and the report of the Carnegie Forum on Education and the Economy, *A Nation Prepared: Teachers for the 21st Century (1986)*. These reports focused attention on changes in teacher preparation and the conditions of teaching. The voices of those closest to students began to be uncovered and respected: those of teachers, principals, and parents. Roland Barth (1990) describes the relationships among these adults within schools as crucial and powerful sources for school change. "Teacher empowerment" became the new slogan. After investing $30 million into innovative projects, the Ford Foundation determined in their final report, *A Foundation Goes to School*, that "the ultimate innovator in schools was the teacher" (p. 30, in Lewis, 1989). Coupled with the realization that teaching is still a highly decentralized experience is the fact that "progress and change depend on what over two million teachers, working in relative isolation, know and are able to do in their classrooms" (Kennedy, 1991).

Subsequently a National Board for Professional Teaching Standards was developed and recommendations were made to: raise admission requirements for teacher preparation programs, increase recruitment of minorities to teaching careers, eliminate undergraduate degrees in education, institute 5-year degree programs leading to a masters in teaching, raise teacher salaries and career opportunities (vis-à-vis

"Lead Teachers"), connect rewards or incentives to student performance, and free teachers to make decisions while holding them accountable for student progress. Again, however, the implications for special education were vague.

Ysseldyke, Algozzine, & Thurlow (1992) note that a "third wave" has developed that emphasized the needs of at-risk or disadvantaged students and which culminated in the President's education summit in 1989 and a set of national goals.

This third wave reflects a deeper interest in equity issues and, therefore, begins to bring general and special education interests together. While we are far short of integrating the two reforms, and there continues to be a tension between the excellence agenda and equity, strong reform efforts are now evident on three levels: national, state, and local. At the national level, there are serious policy conundrums in, for example, interpreting slogans like "all means all." Parent and professional groups such as TASH, LDA, and CEC, as well as researchers continue to debate the moral imperative, the practicality, and the research on inclusion (Fuchs & Fuchs, 1994). At the state level, bureaucrats are attempting to reconcile the law and statewide responsibilities which tend to move in the direction of "one size fits all" policies with local control. At the local school level, there are many different scenarios ranging from conducting business as usual, while school-based advisory committees engage in long-range planning, to serious policy, programmatic, and curricular reform. It has been within this active backdrop that we have positioned ourselves as partners with school systems and with local schools and participated in a wide range of productive collaborative programs, as described in chapters 14–21. However, we operated in dual systems, that related to the education of students as well as the education of teachers. Thus, a closer look at the influence of reforms on teacher education is critical.

Influence of Reform on Teacher Education

Teacher education has been criticized for its lack of clarity about the theoretical and political commitments underlying current reform proposals (Murphy, 1991; Lewis, 1989; Barth, 1990). This is not surprising given that teacher education programs reflect a variety of conceptual orientations. Even within a college dedicated primarily to one vision of teacher preparation, discussion of terms such as *reflective teaching, action research,* and *empowerment* can elicit numerous individual interpretations based on diverse perspectives.

Some of this confusion results, in part, from the disparate nature of the waves of reform discussed previously and the impact they have had on teacher preparation (Murphy, 1991). The first wave called for raising program entrance and exit requirements. As reported by Lewis (1989), Hammond and Berry, in a study for the RAND Corporation, found that 27 states instituted stiffer entrance requirements and 41 states mandated some form of assessment of competency for a license. The second wave, which supported a more extensive overhaul of the educational system, called for teachers who could function in productive teams and who possess a "richer and more complex understanding of teaching and learning." The impact of both waves has left teacher education programs in flux, trying to respond to sometimes conflicting messages and value systems.

To help clarify some of the important differences and similarities of reform ideas impacting teacher education, Zeichner and Liston (1990) offer a framework of four distinct reform traditions that emerged within teacher education during the twentieth century; these being: a) the academic tradition; b) the social efficiency tradition; c) the developmentalist tradition; and d) the social reconstructionist tradition. The academic tradition has argued that a sound liberal arts education, accompanied by an apprenticeship in a school, was sufficient, and that professional education courses are intellectually superficial and should be replaced by a mastery of subject matter. This tradition has had a major impact on the preparation of secondary-level teachers who often feel overprepared in their content area and underprepared in the fundamentals of teaching and interacting with students. This deficiency is becoming more evident as general education reform calls for increased integration of curriculum and for cooperative learning, and special education reform calls for increased teacher responsibility in meeting the needs of students with disabilities in the regular classroom.

Criticisms of this academic tradition have emanated from cognitive psychology, which has sought to prepare teachers to teach in ways that promote deeper conceptual understanding. Additional criticism has resulted from the acknowledgment of Western, white, middle-class biases found in the liberal arts curriculum (Gay, 1986). However, the current emphasis on alternative routes to certification and isolated reform efforts such as the American Teacher Corps signify the continuing presence of the academic tradition in teacher education.

The minute analysis of the teaching task into its component parts (Charters & Waples, 1929) characterizes the second reform, the social efficiency tradition. The 1960s and 1970s saw the emergence of this tradition in Competency/Performance-Based Teacher Education (C/PBTE) which has been viewed as the single most influential and controversial trend in teacher education in this century. Although only 13% of 618 institutions surveyed by Sandefur and Nicklas (1981) reported full implementation of C/PBTE, this reform sought to establish the intellectual legitimacy of teacher education through a linkage between observable teacher behaviors with student outcomes. From this tradition has emerged behaviorally specified knowledge and skills, specific instructional, observational, and evaluative systems to monitor student outcomes (micro-teaching), and an emphasis on teacher performance rather than completion of coursework. The view of teachers as decision makers also gives rise to the need for analyzing teacher tasks. Criticisms arise from those who view elements of social efficiency as part of a mechanistic worldview in which every situation can be anticipated, interpreted through one lens, and, as a result, solved in a pragmatic manner. Even within the field of special education where behaviorism has assumed a preeminent posture, there are those who view this approach as mechanistic and lacking both a moral perspective of education and a meaningful understanding of learning (Rhodes, 1990; Heshusius, 1989).

The developmentalist tradition, which advanced the view that the natural development of the learner should guide and determine the content of teacher education programs, has promoted teacher education programs that are more student-centered. Perrone (1989) has traced the emergence of three metaphors stemming from the developmentalist tradition: a) teacher as artist; b) teacher as naturalist; and c) teacher as researcher. Programs such as the Art Combs' "humanistic" teacher education program at the University of Florida, the "Developmental Teacher Education Program" at the University of California–Berkeley and the Integrated Day Program at the University of Massachusetts are all examples of this tradition.

The view that schooling and teacher education constitute a critical piece in a social movement towards a more just society resulted in the fourth tradition, the social reconstructionist tradition. Though its proponents have been divided in the extent to which conscious indoctrination versus reflective inquiry should influence the development of a new social order, the early "frontier educators" certainly considered the awakening of social consciousness among teacher educators as critical to this tradition. Manifestations of this perspective guided the founding of New College at Teachers College at Columbia University which provided students with a reality contact with life that would hopefully influence the development of a social welfare outlook. Thus was born the initiation of courses such as Social Foundation of Education, which focused on the interconnections of school, society, and culture. More contemporary attempts to develop reconstructionist teacher education programs can be found in the work of those who have sought to create an agenda for "egalitarian" teacher education and of others, such as Adler and Goodman (1986), who proposed methods courses as a means of helping teachers learn analysis and development skills necessary to participate in more democratic school environments. Kliebard (1986) and Cremin (1988) believe that this tradition has represented more of an academic discussion than a lasting influence on teacher education due to its marginal status among teacher education programs in the United States (Zeichner & Liston, 1990).

Using Zeichner and Liston's framework of reform in teacher education, it becomes easier to analyze the tasks and challenges faced by teacher educators as they respond to current school reform efforts. For example, the reforms suggested by the National Board for Professional Teaching Standards (funded by the Carnegie Corporation) seeks to establish more rigid and rigorous standards for what teachers should know and be able to do. Following this academic and social efficiency tradition, it is easier to predict the next steps which involve assessment measures and certificates.

On the other hand, the agenda proposed for the National Center for Research on Teacher Learning (NCRTL) (Kennedy, 1991) shows an orientation towards cognitive science as it attempts to define teacher learning as a function of both what teachers bring with them to new experiences and the new experiences themselves. Elements of both a developmentalist perspective and an academic tradition influence activities that ask what teachers need to learn about both subject matter and learners. Other NCRTL research agendas merge elements of the developmentalist perspective and the social efficiency tradition by recognizing the disparity between a belief that teaching derives from general principles of good practice and the argument that teacher knowledge is situation-specific.

The university-school partnerships described in chapters 14–18 were created in a context of integrated interests, trust, and collaboration within the university. The partnership within the university described by the dean in chapter 12 and by the collaborating chairs of childhood, secondary, and special education in chapter 13 has turned primarily on values represented in the developmentalist tradition. However, there has not been a single voice in the many discussions and debates of policy and programmatic issues. Within the college and the three departments there are those who ground their arguments more in the academic and social efficiency traditions. Change is difficult, and we have learned that we make most gains in productive and respectful dialogue where there is an institutional commitment to do things differently. In this context, the most significant departure from our traditional mode of operation involves entering into collaborative relationships with schools in ways that reduce our control and require us to reinvent our roles as professors and our work as teacher educators and researchers.

Influence of Reform Traditions on Research in Teacher Education

The direction that reform in teacher education takes has a significant impact on the manner in which research on teacher education is to progress. Teachers today face numerous demands to improve their practice (i.e., changes in the workplace, changes in student demographics, changes in national and international politics, and changes in expectations for learning in academic subjects). Kennedy (1991) notes that these forces suggest a shift away from traditional research on teacher learning that has focused on helping novice teachers or relatively less-proficient teachers become as good as most teachers are. Present teaching practices are not sufficient as norms to meet today's demands on teachers. In some ways this is analogous to changing the wheels on the vehicle while it is moving. Research in teacher education must address the messy problems/dilemmas that confront those attempting to prepare teachers to work in restructured schools (see chapters 8 and 9).

Realities such as these have influenced the conceptions and processes of investigations in teacher education as teacher preparation practices shift towards: a) the use of field experience as a vehicle for critical reflection (Armaline & Hoover, 1989); b) a focus on the ethic of caring in teacher education programs (Rogers & Webb, 1991); c) the use of teaching cases to explore established theories, complex problems for which no theories exist, or cases for personal study and reflection (Merseth, 1991); d) the use of autobiography as a tool of inquiry; and e) a philosophical orientation for the meaning constructs held by teachers (Stone, 1992).

A more pluralistic view of inquiry, leading to a variety of methods to study and learn about collaboration, restructuring, inclusion, and school-based teacher education, is reflected in the descriptions of the collaborations and the lessons learned and reported in chapters 14–18.

Partnerships in Restructuring

If teacher preparation programs are to assume an active role in school restructuring and the reform of special education, a new chapter is needed in the history of university-school relationships. Barth (1990) notes that, historically, when universities and schools interact, the university voice tends to dominate. Goodlad (1990) reminds us that the differences between universities and schools—such as function, structure, clientele, reward systems, rules and regulations, ambiance, and ethos—are sometimes the cause of our inability to collaborate. The assumed roles and responsibilities of both schools and teacher preparation programs have become dichotomized to the extent that some believe theory resides in universities and practice resides in schools (Barth, 1990). This belief system can and has created a status hierarchy valuing ideas over "practical work," a caste system that has severely limited and constrained collaborative work.

Goodlad believes that the mutual satisfaction of self-interests and sufficient selflessness on the part of each partner can and must be created through the intentional resolve of both schools and universities. Professional Development Schools (PDS) offer one venue for collaboration of this nature. PDSs promise a rich context within which to collaboratively renew shared university and school commitments to reform and restructuring. Levine (1992) has identified a triple mission for professional development (practice) schools: a) supporting student learning; b) supporting the professional education of teachers; and c) supporting inquiry directed at the improvement of practice.

The work of Levine (1992); Lieberman (1988, 1992); and Whitford, Schlechty, and Shelor (1987) all share a common understanding that restructuring cannot and should not be confined to the schools alone. Colleges of education must be engaged in restructuring or reinventing teacher education. This process involves a thorough examination of the philosophy, vision, rhetoric, and practice existing in teacher education programs. Beliefs such as: a) the education of teachers takes place on the university campus; b) one university professor serves as primary instructor of each course, the content is determined by published texts or the personal perspective of a professor or by department philosophy; and c) the program consists of a series of segmented courses, are susceptible to scrutiny when teacher preparation programs become seriously involved in restructuring.

Chapters 12–18 describe the restructuring that has occurred in the College of Education at the University of South Florida and the university-school partnerships that were created. It is important to note that the restructuring has been iterative, with university-school partnerships helping inform the university of changes needed and changes within the university impacting the partnerships.

Visions of Reform: The Challenges for Policy Makers

Visionaries are continuing to craft different images of schooling in the twenty-first century, and many of the themes are relatively consistent—emphasis on outcomes rather than process, school-based decision making, community involvement, and parent choice, among others. However, the reports that have helped create and shape reform have not adequately addressed implementation. Perhaps this is because visions are often misapplied in the change process (Fullan, 1993). Fullan argues that visions come later as a result of reflective experience, shared vision building over time, and concomitant skill development. Barth (1990) suggests that visions should be gathered from schoolpeople as well, in order to capitalize on the rich insights and practical knowledge resulting from their 190 days a year spent in a school setting.

The artifacts of reform that are shared with schools are often in the form of lists: conditions of effective schools, teacher/administrator characteristics, standards of excellence, performance objectives, desirable outcomes, measurable performances, and professional competencies, to name just a few. But this type of "list logic," as Barth (1990) describes, can evoke additional hurdles for school restructuring as the players closest to the real action respond with "feelings of tedium, oppression, guilt and anger" (p. 39). By expecting that any one list describing a "desirable" or "effective" school will fit any school needing improvements, reformers have ignored the very essence of the evolution by which "desirable" schools emerge: personal ownership, trial and error, and collaboration, as well as situational problem finding and solving (Barth, 1990).

Operating within this context of change, states are now attempting to develop implementation policies and plans. The challenges range from developing governance systems that empower school-based leaders to the development of valid and reliable measures of educational outcomes. Yet change by mandate may result in short-lived gains since mandates are limited to that which can be easily monitored and which require limited skills (Fullan, 1993). Already, attempts to implement shared school leadership models have been met by teachers and building administrators with responses that include mistrust and anger, as well as celebration. We have certainly found this variability within schools with which we have worked.

One of the lessons of the reform has been the increasing understanding that the issues that must be addressed in making important changes in schools are systemic. In a study conducted by David (1991) for the Center for Policy Research in Education, several common themes emerged from a careful examination of the restructuring process in four school districts successful in restructuring:

- It is not just adding or changing a part of the system. It is fundamental change.
- Access to new knowledge and skills is as important as increasing autonomy and flexibility.
- New coalitions must be built uniting former adversaries who will operate under a shared set of expectations.

Regarding the future, Passow (1989) raises several basic questions about reform. He notes that there continue to be uncertainty and lack of consensus on *what* is to be reformed. "The curricular and instructional agendas for reform are constantly being reviewed and revised" (p. 31). What may also be necessary for successful restructuring is a careful examination of the reciprocal relationship between restructuring and "reculturing" or the establishing of a culture conducive to change (Fullan, 1993). Too often the structure of restructuring "attempts to push cultural change, and mostly fails" (p. 131). Lewis (1989) also points to a "micro" view of change needed for the reform movement to be successful, which she defines as involving those most closely affected by decisions in the decision-making process and the intentional development of a sense of ownership and responsibility in those carrying out the reforms.

In our experience in the university, as reported in chapters 12–13, as we have approached serious changes, such as the teacher education curriculum, or the role of a professor, it has been, and continues to be, necessary to work carefully with all of the policy committees and other gatekeeping forces responsible for maintenance of the culture. Similarly, as partnerships have had systemic impact on schools, it has been necessary to work through the operations, values, norms, and/or interests affected by the change.

ANOTHER PART OF THE STORY: REFORM OF SPECIAL EDUCATION

Another part of the story involves what has been happening in the education of children with disabilities. It is evident that the focus and mission of reform has changed during the past 10 years, as both the nature of the problems facing schools and the difficulties in changing schools have come more into focus. In a survey conducted by Lewis (1989) for the American Association for School Administrators, over 40 major ideas were found among various restructuring plans. According to Lewis, restructuring amounts to "those actions that allow and encourage higher expectations of both teachers and students" (p. 6). While there has been limited interest in balancing issues of excellence and equity, the predominant focus of the reform movement had been on excellence, as evidenced by the virtual absence of the education of children with disabilities in the reform proposals until toward the end of the 1980s (Sapon-Shevin, 1987; Pugach & Sapon-Shevin, 1987; Ysseldyke, Algozzine, & Thurlow, 1992).

On the surface, advocacy groups such as the National Coalition of Advocates for Students included at-risk children in their broader view of education and subsequently noted that current systems of schooling jeopardized the opportunities for many students and that radical change or restructuring needed to be for all. The Education Commission of the States in their review of state leadership in school reform in 1987 admitted that youth-at-risk had been overlooked in the first wave of reforms.

This lack of balance between equity and excellence did not go unnoticed. Lewis (1989) notes that in 1987 at a symposium at Harvard University on Excellence and Equity in Education, Harold Howe II, former Commissioner of Education lamented over the obvious economic argument that was driving the present school reform movement. It demands that schools produce excellence among the children of the poor for the sake of the nation's economic health. It wastes little time with concepts of equity or of our nation's need for independent-minded citizens to make a democracy and complex society workable . . . I am not at all sure where this trend of doing the right things for the wrong reasons will take us. (pp. 32–33)

The National Council on Disability also voiced their concerns in a report to the president entitled *The Education of Students with Disabilities*. Twenty-eight findings substantiated the need for reform clustered around issues that included: equity of access, parent rights, general education reform, role of the federal government, and transition. Although the council's request for the establishment of a national commission on excellence never materialized, a useful set of 20 questions were developed that included several posing shared agendas between general and special education.

The absence of special education policies and practices in the discussion of general education reform (see chapter two) is still obvious as a plethora of publications on educational reform continue to appear. For example, a review of papers given at the Policy Forum on New Roles and Responsibilities in the Public School, sponsored by the Center for Policy Research in Education (Elmore, 1991) never once mentioned students with disabilities and very minimally acknowledged at-risk students. A recently published call and prescription for reform from the conservative ranks, *We Must Take Charge* (Finn, 1991), also failed to even reference mainstreaming, special education, REI, students with disabilities, and so on. Finn's prescription for the other "lost populations" or at-risk students combines: accelerated and intensified efforts with individual students, Escalante-style teachers who truly love and believe in children, expanded learning time, and metacognitive coaching as the critical ingredients for success for "all" children.

Since the mainstreaming reform of the late 1960s when children with mild disabilities, especially those with mild mental retardation, were educated in regular classrooms, there have been major policy debates on how and where children with disabilities can be provided the most appropriate education. In 1975, with the passage of P.L. 94-142, the right to a free appropriate public education in the least restrictive environment was established in law and important principles were introduced including: nondiscriminatory evaluation, individualized educational plans, least restrictive environment, and due process.

Gerber noted that amidst growing numbers of students receiving special education services, particularly those students identified as having specific learning disabilities (Hagerty & Abramson, 1987), a continuing debate has ensued among professional special educators regarding what is "appropriate" and what is "least restrictive." When, in the case of *Board of Education v. Rowley* (1982), the Supreme Court tried to define a "free appropriate public education" in terms of access to specialized instruction and related services, many feared that the heart of P.L. 94-142 had been sacrificed. Subsequent case-by-case analysis has, however, shown that the courts have continued to support parents in their efforts to expand opportunities for their children with disabilities (Gallegos, 1989). However, it could be argued that the criterion of "most reasonable" rather than the "best possible" has influenced most court decisions.

Fueled by the civil rights movement, a deep social consciousness about the right of equal access and litigation has supported the right to due process and remedies for those denied access (see chapter four). The growing disproportionate representation of minorities in special classes, the biased instruments and procedures associated with placement, the negative social stigma associated with labelling and placement, and a poor performance of special education services in comparative efficacy studies, contributed to support for mainstreaming policy. Also fostering the mainstreaming movement was the belief that such integration could help reverse the prejudices that nondisabled children may have about children with disabilities.

A similar policy shift was occurring in mental health and social services with the deinstitutionalization movement for adults with disabilities, which resulted in a national policy on the reduction of institutional dependence. Like mainstreaming, deinstitutionalization was driven by human rights values buffeted by data on the negative effects of segregated placement. The advocacy movement guided by a philosophy of normalization, coupled with strong professional and political efforts, effected basic changes in the caregiving system by promoting community-based alternatives for institutionalized populations and the development and enforcement of standards for congregate care and community-based services.

Since the basic principles of rights to access and to due process were established, and the negative effects of segregated services were broadly accepted, the debates about whom to "include," when to include them, and how and under what circumstances to include them have waxed and waned among and between professionals, political leaders, policy makers, bureaucrats, parents, and advocacy groups. The debates have at times been about the weight of evidence—do children with disabilities fare as well in regular classrooms as they do in pull-out programs? Which children fare best in which settings? For how long? The "regular education initiative"(REI), a policy initiative of the administration of Assistant Secretary Madeline Will, was a national policy directive that focused the debate and suggested that the education of students with disabilities should be the shared responsibility of all educators. Will believed that "the creation of special programs has produced unintended effects, some of which make it unnecessarily cumbersome for educators to teach as effectively as they desire—and children to learn—as much and as well as they can" (Will, 1986, in Ysseldyke, Algozzine, & Thurlow, 1992).

Four areas of concern stemming from current practices were referenced in her report to the U.S. Department of Education: a) students fall through the categorical cracks; b) dual systems contribute to a lack of coordination and accountability; c) students with disabilities suffer from the labelling and separation practices; and d) parent/teacher relationships tend to be adversarial rather than cooperative. This stance was supported by the research conducted by Wang and colleagues who reported that students with learning disabilities were better off in mainstreamed settings than in their traditional resource rooms, self-contained classes, and pull-out programs.

Sailor (1991) and Ysseldyke, Algozzine, and Thurlow (1992) among others, have summarized the diverse theoretical and pragmatic arguments against the REI movement, such as that the movement lacks regular education support (Singer & Butler, 1987), neglects the special needs of certain groups of students with disabilities (Braaten, Kauffman, Braaten, Polsgrove, & Nelson, 1988), ignores the role of specially trained teachers, downplays the need and efficacy of specialized instruction, and places equity in site resources over quality of instruction (Sailor, 1991).

It has been difficult to argue the data because data are available supporting both arguments. Also it has been difficult to win the moral argument since the position one accepts regarding the likely effects of the REI for children determines the position one takes on the welfare and interests of children. The debates have been rich and thick with both empirical (what are the effects and is it practical?) and moral (what is the right thing to do?) arguments.

At issue is the philosophy of education, that is, our basic beliefs about the goals and nature of education. If we focus primarily on outcomes linked to academic achievement, we reach conclusions quite different from those we reach if we see the goals of education primarily in terms of social skills necessary to live in an inclusive, though diverse, society. One could observe that Passow's view (Passow, 1989) of the curricular and instructional agenda in general education which, he argues, is constantly being reviewed and revised, applies equally to special education.

Due to a number of reasons, the Regular Education Initiative, discussed in chapter 3, never became a broad-based general educational reform. Some used the analogy of "parallel play" often observed in young children where minimal interchange occurs but they will say they were playing together (Ysseldyke, Algozzine, & Thurlow, 1992). Special educators were focusing on "their issues" while general educators were busy with theirs, and meaningful exchanges were absent.

One of the challenges in our work has been to create forums in which inclusion and restructuring issues could be discussed and meaningful actions taken. The collaborative relationships between the childhood, secondary, and special education departments, described in chapter 13, were essential in this regard. The positive relationship between these three departments has made it possible to work on serious issues in the university, such as faculty workload, alternative strategies for generating Full Time Equivalent (FTE) in order to make resources available for working with schools, and policies governing the teacher education program. The partnerships with schools, comprised in every instance of general and special education staff, have provided dynamic contexts for discussion and work on integration.

General and Special Education Reform: Ships Passing in the Night?

While special educators have debated full inclusion, the most current philosophical iteration of the least restrictive placement policy, general educators have been invested in broader systemic reforms of schools. Now that it is clear that most of these reforms have not addressed special education, the important question becomes

"Why?" Some analysts suggest that the efficacy and very existence of special education is at the heart of this issue.

Lilly (1987), for example, notes that although neither Sizer (1984), Boyer (1983), nor Goodlad (1984) focused directly on special education, all three pointed to the need for adaptation to individual differences, to the extent that, if implemented, there would not need to be special education programs for children with mild disabilities. Lilly suggests that current practices and policies for this population lack sufficient conceptual soundness and quality to warrant inclusion in the visionary plans for educational reformers such as Sizer, Boyer, and Goodlad; thus, special education is perceived as a problem rather than a solution. Lilly's suggestion for special educators to become integral members of the educational system rather than separate entities is echoed by Stainback & Stainback (1985), Sailor (1991), Shepard (1987), and Pugach (1987).

Sailor (1991), in one of the most insightful analyses of the parallel reforms in general and special education, suggests that: "Sufficient parallels exist between the general and special education reform agendas to suggest that the time may be at hand for a shared educational agenda" (p. 8). However, one of the impediments to reform within special education, as noted by Hagerty and Abramson (1987), stems from the natural tendency to "hold on to what has been won." This response limits and even jeopardizes the capacity of our existing system to restructure significantly enough to respond to the most innovative levels of general education reform suggested. Also, special educators have tended to focus on the settings in which instruction takes place rather than the features of that instruction (Sapon-Shevin, 1987).

Despite the protests of special education, however, a changed destiny for special education is already apparent. One such example stems from the federal report *To Secure Our Future: The Federal Role in Education* (1989). In its attempt to restructure schools for high performance, the National Center on Education and the Economy called for a comprehensive restructuring of the way in which federal categorical programs are operated. Sailor (1991) suggests in his analysis of this recommendation that the rights of children with disabilities must still be maintained under the auspices of the Individuals with Disabilities Act (IDEA) and that "compromising these protections is dangerous, unwise, and unwarranted" (p. 13). However, he favors an integrated programmatic structure that would still utilize IDEA resources to improve outcomes for children with disabilities in ways that have positive impacts on the total school population.

Shepard (1987), in another plan, suggests that, in order to avoid an eventual political backlash, special education consider a quota system. Under this plan, state and federal governments might pay the full cost of educating 4% of students who are most severely disabled with the understanding that the district would match these dollars to serve low-achieving students not included in this pool.

Because special education carries a price tag of over $1.3 billion a year and serves about 4.4 million students, the temptation to stretch the nation's resources to benefit larger numbers of students is one that is likely to remain in the minds of many policy makers and voters.

The challenge for general and special educators is to use the flexibility that is ostensibly provided with a site-based philosophy in designing integrative educational support services for all children. The adhocratic form proposed by Skrtic (1991) is the most appealing to the present authors.

The collaboration within a college of education, described in chapters 12–13, and the partnership initiatives, described in chapters 14–18, were designed to effect the integration of general and special education. The lessons learned from these partnerships were, and continue to be, about systemic issues in integrating restructuring and inclusion agendas within the cultures of local schools.

Integration of General and Special Education: Implications for Teacher Education Reform

Although a number of reform reports (such as Goodlad, Sizer, and *A Nation at Risk*) favor heterogeneous grouping, none of them discusses how teachers will learn to provide instructions in these settings. Pugach (1987) believes that the oversight may be, in part, due to the presence of special education teacher preparation programs, stating: "Special education will continue to serve students who are the indirect casualties of a general teacher education system that has developed a narrow conceptualization of its responsibilities—partly due, no doubt, to its long-standing dependence on special education" (p. 311). (See chapter 7 for an extensive discussion of this issue.) Consequently, the perception is perpetrated that good pedagogical skills for children with disabilities are the property of special education teachers and distinct from good academic teaching.

Goodlad (1984) suggests that replacing specialists with "in-house" consultants would give schools the benefits of specialization without creating permanent hegemonies or hierarchies that separate general and special education. Similarly, Hagerty and Abramson (1987) go as far as recommending comprehensive systems of personnel development (CSPD) which would result in specially trained regular educators. Reforms such as this would obviously impact teacher preparation programs in special education. In fact, Pugach (1987) suggests that this type of approach would substantially remove the need for locating advanced teacher preparation on instructional and management techniques in separate programs of special education. Furthermore, she points out that Sarason and Doris as early as 1979 blamed teacher preparation programs for the formalized separation of roles and labor, e.g., regular education and special education.

A fundamental ethic driving change in our teacher education program is the integration of general and special education. In addition to being informed by our experimental partnership initiatives with schools, we have an active research program in developing teaching cases as an integrative medium that fits both our epistemological preference and our philosophy of education.

In our work we have taken the ethics of care, continuity, and collaboration at the local school level to be essential features of the reform of the structure of service delivery, curriculum, and teaching practices. These are evident in the partnership initiatives described in chapters 14–18 and 20 but they also influenced the reinvention of teacher education (chapters 12 and 13) within our department.

THE REST OF THE STORY: REFORM AND TRANSFORMATION OF EDUCATION AND RESEARCH

During the past few years it has become increasingly clear that the reforms in general and special education are embedded in larger epistemological, social, political, and moral contexts. Shifts in the intellectual currents of human science and society were deeper than had been appreciated earlier. The serious reform of schooling involves rethinking the nature of knowledge, learning, and the learner. It also requires attention to the nature and moral vision of the goals of education. At issue is how we will live together in a connected, interdependent, multiethnic society.

What has been increasingly clear is that our sciences, the knowledge base of our work, are flawed not only with technical inadequacies, but systematically biased in ways that exclude the perspectives and interests of women and non-Western understandings of knowledge and knowing. What passed as unbiased, reflecting the logical empiricist epistemological tradition, turned out to be profoundly biased, not only in reflecting an absolutist and reductionistic view of knowledge and reality, but a distinctly Western philosophy of science.

The traditional logical positivist response to human questions that could not be addressed empirically or logically, was captured by Wittgenstein in his classic *Tractatus Logico-Philosophicus*: "Wovon man nicht sprechen kann darüber muss man schweigen" ("What we cannot speak about we must consign to silence") (from Ayer, 1982; p.112).

In the 1980s it became clear that too much had been consigned to silence. Previously unchallenged assumptions about the nature of knowledge and knowing were now coming into focus. Factual knowledge claims were no longer accepted as independent of value (Polanyi, 1966). Psychologists and special educators, considering the nature of knowledge upon which clinical practice and policy development are based, developed new critiques regarding the inextricable implication of values in knowledge claims (Gallagher, 1990).

Young (1990), in his presentation of a critical theory of education, commented on the nature of "modernity and its discontents:"

> One of the characteristics of current discussions is the re-emergence of eighteenth- and nineteenth-century themes—a going back to and a going over the fundamental assumptions of the democratic state, of the idea of the liberty of the individual, of the role of mass schooling in the education of an enlightened citizenry and the like. The very roots of modernity, from Mill and the French philosophers to the fathers of modern democratic constitutionalism, are being inspected anew. (p. 7)

A significant movement in psychology and education has been the rejection of an understanding of human capacity in terms of measurable linguistic and logical-mathematical aptitude. Gardner's seminal work on multiple intelligences (1983) is the quintessential illustration of what he calls a cognitive revolution. His work reflects a broader movement toward what Geertz (1983) characterized as a blurring of the genres of the sciences and the humanities.

Another perspective leading to new understandings is chaos theory which grows out of systems theory. In a helpful analysis of chaos theory and its implications for special education, Guess and Sailor (1993) point out that "Chaos represents a rapidly growing body of knowledge that has attracted the attention of many diverse fields and disciplines, such as mathematics, physics, meteorology, economics, biology, chemistry, and psychology" (p. 16) (for a more extensive discussion of chaos, self-organization, and psychology, see Barton, 1994).

Both reflecting and helping create the awareness of and respect for diversity in knowledge orientations, a paradigm dialogue (Guba, 1990) began to overshadow earlier debates about theories that had occurred within the paradigm of classic science, i.e., logical empiricism. Ontological as well as epistemological and methodological issues came into focus. The paradigm of construction, which implicates the knower in the creation of knowledge and the meaning made of it, began to challenge the paradigm of discovery, rooted in the Cartesian dualism of the absolutist position of positivism and the relativist position of post-positivism.

The constructivist paradigm turned attention to the knower and the activities of the mind. The growing emphasis on reflection and theorizing in teaching is an example of the fundamental shift that has been occurring away from a positivist paradigm, e.g., behaviorism, to constructivism. Indeed teachers hold an important role as "bridgemasters" for students who approach whatever is being taught from many different ways of knowing. Teachers need to be able to draw upon a rich personal bank of metaphors, illustrations, examples that take into consideration a myriad of student backgrounds, learning styles, and prior experiences. A review of recent research on teacher knowledge by Wilson, Shulman, and Richert (1987) describes an important partner to a teacher's knowledge of subject matter—that being "lesson structure knowledge." This term, coined by Leinhardt and Smith (1985), defines the process by which teachers learn to plan and run a lesson smoothly, explain material, and so on. Unfortunately, at the secondary level where teachers are required to take numerous courses in a particular discipline, minimal attention is paid to connections between the subject matter and the teaching experience of that subject matter. Dewey describes this situation aptly in his 1902 seminal piece, *The Child and the Curriculum*, in which he describes the two aspects of any subject: one for the scientist as a scientist; the other for the teacher as a teacher. He states,

> Hence, what concerns him, as teacher, is the ways in which that subject
> may become a part of experience; what there is in the child's present that is
> usable with reference to it; how such elements are to be used; how his own

knowledge of the subject matter may assist in interpreting the child's needs and doings, and determine the medium in which the child should be placed in order that his growth may be properly directed. He is concerned, not with the subject-matter as such, but with the subject-matter as a related factor in a total and growing experience. Thus to see it is to psychologize it. (1990, p. 201)

In further support of this description of teachers' ways of knowing, Wilson, Shulman, and Richert (1987) found that teachers, in the process of learning to teach, "transform" subject matter by developing alternative representations of the content to initiate understanding on the part of students; thus, multiple representations are necessary to accommodate multiple students. (Perhaps it is at the heart of this transformational process of interpreting, representing, adapting, and tailoring, that teachers can begin to naturally find ways of meeting the needs of atypical students.)

Still another example of the constructivist paradigm's key to the empowerment of teachers and enlightened attitudes towards reform lies in the skill of critical reflectivity (Armaline & Hoover, 1989). In this manner, teachers will more comfortably determine the validity of their own professional judgments and thus acquire the role of "transformative intellectuals" (Aronowitz and Giroux, cited in Armaline & Hoover, 1989).

Critical theorists have contributed basic substance to the debate about knowledge. The focus of their critiques, e.g., feminist theory, has been on the predominantly Western white-male values mediating knowledge (Gay, 1986). Gilligan (1982), for example, challenged Kohlberg's claims about the universal nature of moral development because his conclusions were based solely on studies of boys. Her research with girls led Gilligan to the formulation of a more empathic ethic of care in contrast to Kohlberg's ethic of justice. The rapidly growing literature on care reflects this general orientation that is sensitive to the issues of diversity in the knowledge bases of the human sciences (Noddings, 1992).

Others have gone beyond postmodernity to question the philosophical project, especially epistemology (Rorty, 1982). This is discussed in considerable depth in chapter 11. The question of the *a priori* nature of epistemology, which implies a special status independent from particular values and perspectives, has led to a general challenge to foundationalism and structuralism. Rooted in the French existentialist movement, deconstruction became a literary movement with considerable impact in the human sciences. Within the general narrative genre, text analysis in general and hermeneutics in particular have been useful in focusing attention to nonempirical realities, especially meaning. Derrida's observation that textuality and reality are coextensive illustrates this focus.

Deconstructive method has been useful in examining some of the major issues and policy conundrums in general and special education. The important work of Skrtic (1991) is an excellent example. The process of inventing schools of the future will require a more critical analysis of educational systems, including special education, than has characterized educational philosophy and policy debates in the past. Many of the arguments that typified educational philosophy and policy in the

1960s, 1970s, and 1980s proceeded from a concern with the relative efficacy of different instructional programs and environments. The current discourse on school reform reflects a deeper analysis of cultural, ethical, and epistemological issues.

There is, the authors believe, an increasing sensitivity to the ethical dimension of decisions associated with research, policy development, and with professional practices. Kauffman (1993) has described the ethical dilemmas in debates about special education policy during the past 10 years. Specific work on ethical decision making in special education has been reported in recent publications (Paul, et al., 1992; Howe & Miramontes, 1992). The development and teaching of ethical reasoning applied to special education, in contrast to the familiar logics of research and practice, constitutes a significant new scholarly vista for leadership and teacher education programs as well as for teachers, policy makers and other stakeholders in the education of children with disabilities.

The narrative genre of inquiry has attracted an increasing number of scholars in the social sciences broadly, and education in particular, to the notion of the storied nature of science and of our work in educating children. It has made explicit the participation of the narrator in the construction or deconstruction of the story being told. Interest in the cultural embeddedness of knowledge is one of the major forces driving the current interest in teaching cases. Cases presuppose the moral and cultural complexity of reality and that multiple interpretations of facts and their meanings are possible. The perspective of inquiry, in contrast to quantitative models, emerges from the narrative tradition (Ferguson, Fergusen, & Taylor, 1992).

These movements have created a new discourse about education, knowledge, learning, and children. While that discourse is discussed in some depth in chapters 1 and 11, the entire book reflects the values and perspectives embedded in the discourses on education that have emerged during the past decade and are still being focused and refined.

The policy commitment to reform public education is confounded by these new, dynamic, complex, morally confounded, and, in some cases, disconcerting views. The reform of education must account for the purpose of education and its goals in an environment in which the political visions of consensus, the process of consensus building, and the "one size fits all" view of broad state policies may be in conflict with the moral vision of individual and group interests in knowledge construction. What we believe and what we take to be true and good are now recognized by many as incredibly more private and local than had been assumed when there were widely accepted universal standards and criteria for truth claims. While major philosophical and methodological contributions are being made from sociology, anthropology, and the humanities broadly, there is no accepted philosophy of education at the present time to guide an authentic and culturally valid construction of restructured schools for the twenty-first century.

What we have, rather, is an extraordinarily interesting environment with competing perspectives that draw the participants into the debate about education. What the "experts" know is no longer an unaccountable political force in deciding how and what to teach. This has created a major challenge for teacher educators (see chapter 8). The hegemony of empiricism has been mollified. The personal stories of the participants—students, teachers, parents, administrators, teacher educators, and others—are more relevant to the understandings of educational environments (see chapter 20). There are new ideas and a new sense of power in defining practice. Old partitions such as theory and practice or abstract and concrete are being challenged.

There are new partners in the struggle with old texts and the creation of new stories. These partners or collaborators are from different disciplines and from different kinds of institutions, such as schools, human service agencies, and universities. The productivity of these new partnerships, as described in chapters 14–18, is not yet clear. The perspective changes that are occurring and the new forms of activity following and informing those changes are not reportable in the same ways that our research literature was once reported.

New Questions

Through our collaborative work on restructuring, we have begun to seek out the heretofore muted voices of teachers as collaborators and colleagues rather than as objects of study (see chapter 20). We have embraced more pluralistic "meaning constructs" (see chapter 11) from which to analyze the various possible meanings of general contexts; thus, moving us further away from the natural science paradigm governing the forms of inquiry considered acceptable at a research university (see chapter 1). As a result of this process, "crystallizing moments" have occurred in the site-based collaborative programs (see chapter 20) during which the very nature and structure of teacher education programs can be viewed clearly in their sometimes inadequate and antiquated forms.

This has caused us to begin a long and arduous task of seeking homeostasis while continuing ahead at breakneck speed. As we take seriously the implications of school-university partnerships, the source of input into professional standard-setting processes naturally extends beyond the university walls to include a diverse group of stakeholders: master teachers, novice teachers, second-career teachers, families, administrators, and students. We then are faced with a dual system: one in which faculty associated with school restructuring are redefining their philosophy, vision, knowledge base, practices, and outcomes, while others remain bound by more traditional modes of teacher education.

Our work at connecting with schools, described in chapters 14–20, is bringing new meaning to what was formerly a somewhat innocuous and ambiguous role in school restructuring by posing hard questions that challenge the familiar and well-established foundation upon which we have operated within the university system. These questions encompass the meaning of scholarly activity, the role and authority of "professionals," the empowerment versus training dilemma in teacher education, the roles and responsibilities of faculty involved with school restructuring, and the ethical dilemmas involved in the determination, implementation, and reward of a new research agenda. As colleges of education take seriously the business of restructuring to meet the changing needs of their clients, policies governing hiring qualifications, job descriptions, sabbaticals, productivity, and rewards all represent areas of change that have potential for increasing the effectiveness of teacher educators to collaborate meaningfully with schools in restructuring.

CONCLUSION

In this chapter we have discussed the general issues associated with restructuring and inclusion that form the conceptual platform for the research and educational applications discussed in Part Two. The basic principles and assumptions grounding our work are listed below:

Part of the Story: Reform of General Education

- Consistent with the rapidly changing social and economic context of education and our interest in developing valid knowledge about university-school partnerships that can help guide our teacher education and research programs, we have worked with demographically diverse schools that are in the process of restructuring for inclusion.
- Consistent with the issues addressed in the third wave of reform, we have involved ourselves in partnerships with local school leaders, including the principals and the policy machinery, such as school advisory committees, in which equity-related policy issues could be addressed.
- Consistent with our belief that the reform of teacher education needed to be guided, in part, by valid and meaningful alliances with public schools, the partnership initiatives reflect our commitment to sharing responsibility with local schools for the future course of our teacher education curriculum and delivery mechanisms.
- Consistent with our support for the epistemological pluralism now characterizing educational research broadly, and research on teacher education in particular, we have approached our research agenda as learners and creators of ways to develop useful knowledge about collaboration, restructuring, inclusion, and school-based teacher education.
- Consistent with the vision of reform as requiring deep institutional changes in values and operations, we have focused our work on the culture of change in schools and in the university.

Another Part of the Story: Reform of Special Education

- Consistent with our belief in the systemic nature of many of the barriers to restructuring and inclusion, much of our work has focused on systemic and cultural issues related to inclusion.
- Consistent with our belief in the site-based philosophy of management and our desire to be a part of mutually transformative relationships with schools, we were guided by the ethics of care, continuity, and collaboration.

The Rest of the Story: Reform and Transformation of Education and Research

- Consistent with our interest in and willingness to be guided by paradigmatic shifts in curriculum, teaching, learning, and research, we developed different collaborative research groups dedicated to finding relevant voice and meaningful ways of changing the way we do our business in the university and participating in changes in schools. This has led us into different discourses on reform and different understandings of the depth of changes required in our own thinking about children, education, and ourselves as knowledge workers.

REFERENCES

Adler, S., & Goodman, J. (1986). Critical theory as a foundation for methods courses. *Journal of Teacher Education, 37*(4), 2–8.

Armaline, W. D., & Hoover, R. L. (1989). Field experience as a vehicle for transformation: Ideology, education, and reflective practice. *Journal of Teacher Education, 40*(2), 42–48.

Ayer, A. J. (1982). *Philosophy in the twentieth century.* NY: Vintage Books.

Barth, R. S. (1990). *Improving schools from within.* San Francisco: Jossey-Bass.

Barton, S. (1994). Chaos, self-organization, and psychology. *American Psychologist, 49*(1), 5–15.

Boyer, E. (1983). *High school: A report on secondary education in America.* New York: Harper & Row.

Braaten, S. R., Kauffman, J. M., Braaten, B., Polsgrove, L.& Nelson, C. M. (1988). The regular education initiative: Patent medicine for behavioral disorders. *Exceptional Children, 55*(1), 21–27.

Carnegie Forum on Education and the Economy. (1986). *A nation prepared: Teachers for the 21st century.* New York: Author.

Charters, W., & Waples. D. (1929). *Commonwealth teacher training study.* Chicago: University of Chicago Press.

Cremin, L. (1988). *American education: The metropolitan experience 1876–1980.* New York: Vintage Books.

Cuban, L. (1989). The district superintendent and the restructuring of schools: A realistic appraisal. In T. J. Sergiovanni & J. Moore (Eds.), *Schooling for tomorrow* (pp. 251–272). Needham Heights, MA: Allyn & Bacon.

David, J. (1991). Restructuring in progress: Lessons from pioneering districts. In R. Elmore & Associates (Eds.), *Restructuring schools: The next generation of educational reform.* San Francisco: Jossey-Bass.

Dewey, J. (1990). *The school and society and The child and the curriculum.* Chicago: University of Chicago Press.

Elmore, R. F. (Ed.). (1991). *Restructuring schools: The next generation of educational reform.* San Francisco: Jossey-Bass.

Ferguson, P. M., Fergusen, D. L., & Taylor, S. J. (1992). *Interpreting disability: A qualitative reader.* NY: Teachers College Press.

Finn, C. (1991). *We must take charge: Our schools and our future.* New York: The Free Press.

Fuchs, D., & Fuchs, L. (1994). Inclusive schools movement and the radicalization of special education reform. *Exceptional Children, 60*(4), 294–310.

Fullan, M. (1993). *Change forces: Probing the depth of educational reform.* London: Farmer Press.

Gallagher, J. J. (1990). Emergence of policy studies and policy institutes. *American Psychologist, 45*(12), 1316–1324.

Gallegos, E. M. (1989). Beyond Board of Education v. Rowley: Education benefit for the handicapped. *American Journal of Education, 97*, 258–288.

Gardner, H. (1983). *Frames of mind: The theory of multiple intelligences.* New York: Basic Books.

Gay, G. (1986). Multicultural teacher education. In J. Banks & J. Lynch (Eds.), *Multicultural education in western societies* (pp. 154–177). NY: Praeger.

Geertz, C. (1983). *Local knowledge.* New York: Basic Books.

Gilligan, C. (1982). *In a different voice: Psychological theory and women's development.* Cambridge, MA: Harvard Educational Press.

Giroux, H. (1982). *Theory and resistance in education: A pedagogy for the opposition.* South Hadley, MA: Bergin and Garvey.

Goodlad, J. (1984). *A place called school.* New York: McGraw-Hill.

Goodlad, J. (1990). *Teachers for our nation's schools.* San Francisco: Jossey-Bass.

Guba, E. G. (1990). *The paradigm dialog.* Newbury Park, CA: Sage.

Guess, D., & Sailor, W. (1993). Chaos theory and the study of human behavior: Implications for special education. *Journal of Special Education, 27*(1), 16–34.

Hagerty, G. J., & Abramson, M. (1987). Impediments to implementing national policy change for mildly handicapped students. *Exceptional Children, 53*, 4, 315–323.

Henderson, J. G. (1992). *Reflective teaching: Becoming an inquiring educator.* NY: Macmillan

Heshusius, L. (1989). The Newtonian-mechanistic paradigm, special education, and contours of alternatives. *Journal of Learning Disabilities, 22*(7), 403–415.

Hodgkinson, J. L. (1985). *All one system: Demographics of education—Kindergarten through graduate school.* Washington, DC: Institute for Educational Leadership.

Holmes Group. (1986). *Tomorrow's teachers: A report of the Holmes Group.* East Lansing, MI: Authors.

Howe, K. R., & Miramontes, O. B. (1992). *The Ethics of Special Education.* New York: Teachers College Press.

Katz, R. (1991). *The Straight Path: A story of healing and transformation in Fiji.* Reading, MA: Addison-Wesley.

Kauffman, J. M. (1993). How we might achieve the radical reform of special education. *Exceptional Children, 60*(1), 6–16.

Kearns, D. T., & Doyle, D. P. (1988). *Winning the brain race: A bold plan to make our schools competitive.* San Francisco: Institute for Contemporary Studies Press.

Kennedy, M. M. (1991). *An agenda for research on teacher learning.* East Lansing, MI: National Center for Research on Teacher Learning.

Kliebard, H. (1986). *The struggle for the American curriculum, 1893–1958.* Boston: Routledge & Kegan Paul.

Leinhardt, G., & Smith, D.A. (1985). Expertise in Mathematics instruction: Subject matter Knowledge. *Journal of Educational Psychology, 77*, 247–271.

Levine, M. (Ed.). (1992). *Professional practice schools: Linking teacher education and school reform.* NY: Teachers College Press.

Lewis, A. (1989). *Restructuring America's schools.* Arlington, VA: American Association of School Administrators.

Lieberman, A. (1988). The metropolitan school study council: A living history. In Sirotnik, K., & Goodlad, J. (eds.) *School-University partnerships in action: concepts, cases, and concerns,* (pp. 69–86). New York: Teachers College Press.

Lieberman, A. (1992). School/university collaboration: A view from the inside. *Phi Delta Kappan, 74*(2), 147–156.

Lilly, M. S. (1987). Lack of focus on special education in literature on educational reform. *Exceptional Children, 53,* 325–326.

Lipsky, D. K., & Gartner, A. (1989). *Beyond separate education: Quality education for all.* Baltimore, MD: Brookes.

Lystand, J. F. (1984). *The postmodern condition: a report on knowledge.* Minn: University of Minnesota Press.

Merseth, K. (1991). The early history of case-based instruction: Insights for teacher education today. *Journal of Teacher Education, 42,* 243–249.

Murphy, J. (1991). Helping teachers prepare to work in restructured schools. *Journal of Teacher Education, 41,* 4, 50–56.

National Center on Education and the Economy. (1989). *To secure our future: The federal role in education.* Rochester, NY: National Center on Education and the Economy.

National Commission on Excellence in Education, (1983). *A nation at risk.* Washington DC: U.S. Department of Education.

Noddings, N. (1992). *The challenges to come in schools: An alternative approach to education.* Berkeley: University California Press.

Passow, H. (1989). Present and future directions in school reform. In T. J. Sergiovanni & J. Moore (Eds.), *Schooling for tomorrow* (pp. 13–40). Needham Heights, MA: Allyn & Bacon.

Paul, J. L., Gallagher, J. J., Kendrick, S. B., Thomas, D. D., & Young, J. F. (1992). *Handbook for ethical policy making.* Chapel Hill, NC: North Carolina Institute for Policy Studies.

Perrone, V. (1989). Teacher education and progressivism: A historical perspective. In V. Perrone (Ed.), *Working papers: Reflections on teachers, schools, and communities.* New York: Teachers College Press.

Polanyi, M. (1966). *The tacit dimension.* London: Routledge & Kegan.

Pugach, M. (1987). The national education reports and special education: Implications for teachers preparation. *Exceptional Children, 53*(4), 308–314.

Pugach, M., & Sapon-Shevin, M. (1987). New agendas for special education policy: What the national reports haven't said. *Exceptional Children, 53*(4), 295–299.

Rhodes, W. C. (1990). The new holistic paradigm in special education. In J. Paul & B. Epanchin (Eds.), *Emotional disturbance in children: Theory and practices for teachers.* Columbus, OH: Merrill.

Rogers, D., & Webb, J. (1991). The ethic of caring in teacher education. *Journal of Teacher Education, 42*(3), 173–181.

Rorty, R. (1982). Method, social science and social hope. In R. Rorty (Ed.), *Consequences of pragmatism* (pp. 191–229). Minneapolis, MN: University Press.

Sailor, W. (1991). Special education in the restructured school. *Remedial and Special Education, 12*(6), 8–22.

Sandefur, W. S., & Nicklas, W. L. (1981). Competency-based teacher education in AACTE institutions: An update. *Phi Delta Kappan, 62,* 747–748.

Sapon-Shevin, M. (1987). The national education reports and special education: Implications for students. *Exceptional Children, 53*(4), 300–306.

Secretary's Commission on Achieving Necessary Skills. (1991). *What work requires of schools: A SCANS report for America 2000.* Washington, DC: U.S. Department of Labor.

Shepard, L. A. (1987). The new push for excellence: Widening the schism between regular and special education. *Exceptional Children, 42*(4), 327–329.

Singer, J. D., & Butler, J. A. (1987). The education for all handicapped children act: Schools as agents of social reform. *Harvard Educational Review, 57,* 125–152.

Sizer, T. (2984). *Horace's compromise: The dilemma of the American high school.* Boston: Houghton Mifflin Company.

Skrtic, T. M. (1991). *Beyond special education: A critical analysis of professional culture and school organization.* Denver: Love.

Stainback, S., & Stainback, W. (1985). The merger of special and regular education: Can it be done? *Exceptional Children, 51*, 517–521.

Stone, L. (1992). Philosophy, meaning constructs and teacher theorizing in teacher personal theorizing. In E. W. Ross, J. W. Cornett, & G. McCutcheon (Eds.), *Connecting curriculum practice, theory and research.* New York: State University of New York Press.

Timar, T. B., & Kirp, D. L. (1987). Education reform and institutional competence. *Harvard Educational Review, 57*(3), 308–330.

Whitford, B. L., Schlechty, P.C., & Shelor, L. G. (1987). Sustaining action research through collaboration: Inquires for invention. *Peabody Journal of Education, 64*, 151–169.

Will, M.C. (1986). Educating children with learning problems: A shared responsibility. *Exceptional Children, 52*, 411–415.

Wilson, S. M., Shulman, L. S., & Richert, A. (1987). 150 different ways of knowing: Representations of knowledge in teaching. In J. Calderhead (Ed.), *Exploring teachers' thinking.* London: Cassell.

Young, R. E. (1990). *A Critical Theory of Education.* New York: Teachers College Press.

Ysseldyke, J., Algozzine, B., & Thurlow, M. (1992). *Critical issues in special education.* Boston: Houghton Mifflin.

Zeichner, K. M. & Liston, D. (1990). Traditions of reform in U.S. teacher education. *Journal of Teacher Education, 41*(2), 3–20.

11

INVENTING THE FUTURE
Postmodern Challenges in Educational Reform

Scot Danforth, William Rhodes, & Terry Smith

INTRODUCTION

Richard Gibboney (1991), in his review of what he calls "the killing fields of reform," describes three decades of educational restructuring movements which merely reified and maintained previous standard practices. In his eyes, school reform movements are primarily the same old stuff dressed up in brand new outfits. What remains unaddressed, unchallenged, and unchanged during all these fashion shows is our "technological mind-set," our modernist consciousness of classic science and absolute knowledge, our underlying assumptions about what the world is, what schools are, and what our task of educating children is.

To arrive at radically different ways of schooling children, we must first *change our minds*. In an effort to clarify this crucial but difficult point, we will begin this discussion of postmodern education with an introductory narrative: a concrete, contextual example of self-transformation from Scot Danforth's dissertation. This research is an interpretive biography of "Dave" (pseudonym), a 19-year-old man who was labelled seriously emotionally disturbed (SED) and was involved in numerous educational and mental health programs. The study involved over 10 months of participant observation and informal interviews in order to build a trusting relationship from which to tell the stories of one anguish-filled childhood. The following passage from this research text is written in the first person from the perspective of Scot Danforth, describing one such interview and the researcher's moral reflections upon his own teaching and thinking. The scene is set in a diner in a small Florida town where Dave and the first author share thoughts on spirituality and relationship.

A STORY OF SELF-CHANGE

"Dave, do you believe in God?" I blurted it right out.

Dave began to grin slowly and turned his head to the side. He sat there, hanging still. It was as if I had looked right into his heart. Dave was quiet for a moment. He seemed to be sorting out his feelings about my seeing into him. I was squirming about, knowing that I had hit on just the right question and feeling uncertain about how much I enjoyed viewing into this young man's heart.

While Dave spoke, he continued to grin knowingly. "Why'd you ask me that?"

I don't know," I replied. "It just came to me."

"It's funny you asked me that now. I just got baptized." He then told me about being baptized, a description that probably took him two minutes to explain.

As I listened, I focused on the way he turned to a God that would accept him as he is. I asked him about the theme of acceptance and what that meant to him. He told me that he had not felt accepted by his parents or by the teachers, therapists, and houseparents at Kids' House (a residential psychiatric facility where Dave had lived for three years). He said that all these people had been critical of him, always trying to change him and correct him.

I thought about my own experience teaching in therapeutic facilities similar to Kids' House. I recalled that my colleagues and I assumed that our job was to change the child. "Emotionally disturbed" children came into our program. When a new child would enter our program, most of the staff wouldn't know anything about the child. The question immediately jumped to our minds and perhaps to our lips, "Why's he here?" This may be translated as "What's wrong with him?" or "What did he do wrong?" From that initial story of "wrongness" in the outside world, we, the staff, were to look for areas of weakness and then influence the child to change those areas. Our acceptance of the child was limited: Yes, we accept him as a person, but . . . much of our job involved doubt and suspicion. We cared for the kids, but we seemed to have a self-appointed responsibility of doubting much of what they said and did.

As Dave told of his own feelings of not being accepted and valued at the Kids' House, I felt sad and guilty for the kids I had not accepted in my teaching career. I felt sorry that I had done it "for the good of the the kids."

After Dave had told me about the many adults who had not accepted him, I asked, "Do you feel that I accept you?"

"Yes. I wouldn't be sitting here with you if you didn't. I would have blown you off months ago."

"How do you know I accept you?"

"I can tell. If you didn't, you wouldn't spend all this time listening to me. And you wouldn't be writing a book about how I see things."

I felt pleased to hear this. Perhaps I was learning how to understand and relate in a more equal and caring way.

I had decided months earlier to teach myself to change my way of understanding and speaking, to unlearn the habitual pathology metaphor which I and other mental health and special education professionals take as "reality." To those of you who simply take this modernist metaphor as "reality," this explanation may sound ludicrous. But I'll explain anyway.

As Dave and I worked together on this text, I was teaching undergraduate special education courses at a local university. I found that the textbooks and the very typical university coursework I was offering amounted primarily to an initiation into deficit thinking. In order to become special educators, the university students were to learn to view their students in terms of specific categories of substandard humanness. They were to take on the pathology metaphor without even seeing it as an adopted lens used to view students. Acceptance of that mode of seeing and understanding children was central to becoming a professional special educator.

As both my university teaching and my relationship with Dave moved along side by side, I began to feel an intense, internal conflict about the way I was understanding and describing the persons we special educators seek to help. The metaphor of pathology provides helping professionals with the explanation that some people behave in unexpected or unusual ways because of deficits or abnormalities ascribed to those people. It is a powerful way of retaining a professional knowledge over the mysteries of living.

If I am eating dinner in a fancy restaurant and my fellow diner treats the waiter in what I view as a cruel manner, I may be able to explain that behavior in terms of pathology. If my fellow diner is the dean of my university or a respected friend, I will probably view the cruel behavior as either warranted or excusable. If my fellow diner is Dave, a child diagnosed as emotionally disturbed and classified under a series of DSM-III classifications, then I am allowed to explain his actions as part of his psychopathological condition.

For example, Dave was often late to our weekly meetings. And sometimes he didn't show up at all. My initial understanding of this was created by comparing Dave's actions to my standards of time and responsibility. To me, an appointment was an obligation which I jotted down in my little schedule book. Being on time for that appointment was an important part of my maintaining the trust and respect of my professional colleagues and friends. It became evident to me that Dave did not live by the same concepts of time and obligation. I first thought that I should ask him to adapt to my standards. I would feel much more comfortable and save a fair amount of inconvenience if he could handle appointments as I did.

As a teacher, I would have considered his behavior irresponsible. Emotionally disturbed children often behaved irresponsibly and required much correction and education in how to behave in socially acceptable ways. That's the pathology and remedy story I knew so well.

But what if I didn't seek to change him to suit my needs of timeliness? What if I sought instead to understand and adapt to his understandings of time and responsibility? In this relationship of two people, perhaps my task was not to correct the pathology in my counterpart but to understand him as a person. I didn't view any of my other friends as bearers of pathology. I had that metaphor reserved for certain diagnosed people.

Could I set aside this way of viewing Dave in order to experience him in a new way?

I began my endeavor of teaching myself to set aside my pathology metaphor for a relationship metaphor. While the pathology metaphor allows a professional the comfort of explaining almost everything the child does, I find that the relationship metaphor leaves most of life's activities unexplained. This state of "not knowing" is not always comfortable to me. But it feels important for me to honor the mystery and sacredness which expands far beyond my simple comprehension. My goal in relation to Dave has become one of allowing and valuing the unexplained and unknown, to perhaps rest easy with a sense of trust and appreciation in him as my friend.

From Accurate Pictures to Moral Imaginings

In this brief example, we see one professional shifting from an interpretive frame which seeks a firm truth to explain Dave's behavior and motivation to a relationship metaphor implicating each of the two actors within a moral drama of negotiated reality. Knowledge is not viewed as absolute. There is no correct way of viewing Dave, his habits of time management, or the researcher's need to write appointments down in a little calendar book. Instead of seeking an accurate picture of the reality of Dave, the researcher, through an understanding of the contingency and provisional nature of all knowledge, revises his approach to include a moral imagination for the connection of two persons.

Such an expansion of our traditional educational epistemology beyond the narrow confines of modern objectivity serves as an apt introductory example of the postmodern exploration and embrace of diverse knowledges and devalued persons. That is, postmodernism brings us to reenvision our understandings of children, schools, and our work as educators, allowing for a loss of the fetishized guarantees of absolute knowledge, clearing avenues for a dispersal of epistemic authority. The modernist's single, correct picture of reality is set aside as a misleading representation and an inhibition to personal and professional growth. In the ensuing vacuum, the many pictures of reality and truth are brought forth from the scattered spaces of society, constructing a dialogue of images and social meaning. Such is the contingent conversation of postmodernism, a shift from the single to the multiple, from the familiar to the previously occluded, from the customary to the imaginative.

In the remainder of this chapter we will briefly examine the reenvisioning taking place among postmodern educators who are creating fresh and divergent understandings with implications for theory, research, and pedagogical practice. As we travel through our treatment of three facets of postmodern education, the reader should keep in mind that there is no one postmodernism. There are many postmodernisms, from the growing proliferation of feminism (Lather, 1991; Nicholson, 1990) to Rorty's (1979) pragmatism, the poststructuralist interpretations of language (Poster, 1989), and the many critical postmodern theories (Aronowitz & Giroux, 1991; Foster, 1983 Giroux, 1992; Zavarzadeh & Morton, 1991). We will limit our discussion to three major facets or directions being taken in postmodern thought and inquiry: a) a hermeneutic or interpretive facet; b) a critical-political and deconstructive facet; and c) science revolution facet. In order to bring our theoretical meanderings to earth in a pragmatic way, we will close this discussion with our current vision of what the postmodern teacher looks like.

HERMENEUTICS AND POSTMODERNISM

Exploring Meaning

The educational arena is bustling with dialogue among educators who are giving voice to visions of the future. Some of these visions are firmly embedded in a traditional, mechanistic worldview and reflect the axioms of traditional science that have become ingrained in Western thought. Other visions are based in a postmodern view and reflect assumptions that are fundamentally different from those of traditional education. Not only the future of education, but the present moment holds completely different meanings depending on the worldview that one espouses.

The modern worldview is familiar, almost "second nature" to the Western mind and needs little introduction. However, to appreciate the postmodern view, one must suspend belief in those traditional assumptions for a moment and look at reality through a different system of meaning. Oliver & Gershman (1989) describe the process involved in entertaining postmodern meanings:

> Taking cultural visions and imagination seriously requires a radical new mindset, one that is willing to try on different lenses, to add and subtract them in combination without fear of losing the identity or integrity associated with 'owning' or understanding one particular lens. The universe is then more like the shifting patterns in a kaleidoscope than a complex machine. The prisms of glass shift and vary the frequencies of light which pass through them; while one sees different and changing patterns that dance before the eye, at a single moment there is a unitary pattern which is both inside the mind, inside the eye, and in the world. And there is at that moment the search for what mind and eye and pattern mean as an interrelated unity. (p. 55)

As we stand at a crossroads, faced with the challenge to restructure education into a meaningful system, we would be wise to explore new systems of meaning within which education can be situated.

Meaning Constructs

Modern and postmodern thinkers do not structure experiential, social reality in the same way; they adhere to different views of the world and different conceptualizations of knowledge. One way to think about multiple worlds of meaning is proposed by Linda Stone (1992). She proposes the concept of "meaning construct" to illustrate the underlying mental structures that undergird modern and postmodern thought. She suggests that day to day meanings and personal theories are undergirded by foundational beliefs about reality and knowledge. These "meaning constructs," according to Stone are "founding, ideational, multiple, and fluid structures that when explicated help to make sense of more specific beliefs, ideologies, theories, practices, and institutions" (p. 26).

Stone proposes four meaning constructs. The first two are modern, while the last two are postmodern. The first construct, *the meaning of the spectator,* is based on the traditional and dominant view of knowledge that seeks to represent a world that is independent of the perceiving subject. Spectator meaning undergirds Western culture and has resulted in language that attempts to represent the one "right" world, a language that endeavors to match thought with reality. Spectator meaning results in knowledge as control.

The second meaning construct Stone proposes is that of the *storyteller*. Whereas spectator meaning attempts to "capture" the one objective world, storyteller meaning focuses on the world of the subject. It is meaning derived from senses, emotions, self-awareness, and relationship. It is the art and poetry of experience from the inside. Language is once again used to represent reality, but in this case the subjective world is represented.

The first postmodern construct is the *meaning of the conversationalist.* In this view, the world is a construct in which understanding is achieved through language in an interactive rather than an individual process. Dynamism and diversity are presumed, and the possibility of the reification of knowledge that is assumed in modernist constructs is rejected.

The final meaning construct is the *meaning of the visionary.* Stone suggests this is a new construct that is just emerging and of which we have only seen glimpses. According to Stone, "The visionary constructs meaning with these features: a world as fluid and forming; a centrality and continual dispersion of marginality, difference, particularity, and pluralism; and change as probable and natural" (p. 32). Visionary identity is based on the continual self-critical interaction with particular situations and is involved in an ongoing process in which multiple meanings and multiple worlds exist in continuous flux and transformation.

Stone's constructs both elucidate the way language is used in different systems of meaning, as well as the focus and level of involvement different worlds of meaning require. Modern constructs use language to describe and encode "knowledge," whereas postmodern constructs use language in dialogue to negotiate meaning. Meaning constructs provide an insightful framework through which to view the current transition in education. As we listen to the clamoring voices in the educational arena, as we voice our own visions, and as we enter into dialogue with other voices in attempts to construct new meanings and directions for education, we can examine how language is used as a door to understanding the worlds of meaning that define its use.

Teaching and Learning in the Postmodern Era

As education moves into the postmodern era, new avenues of communication are opening up. Teachers are being encouraged to tell their stories (Ayers, 1992). Researchers are engaging members of the school community in dialogue (Gilligan & Brown, 1992; Poplin 1992). Teachers and students are being encouraged to work collaboratively and cooperatively together (Henderson, 1992). In many respects, education is moving away from the top-down, unidirectional spectator language of control to using language in dialogue to negotiate meaning. Bruner (1986) sums it up beautifully:

> I think it follows from what I have said that the language of education, if it is to be an invitation to reflections and culture creating, cannot be the so-called uncontaminated language of fact and "objectivity." It must express stance and must invite counter-stance and in the process leave place for reflection, for metacognition. It is this that permits one to reach higher ground, this process of objectifying in language or image what one has thought and then turning around on it and reconsidering it. (p. 129)

Knowledge has become contextualized knowing in the postmodern mind; no longer a thing, but a process, a fluid relationship. It can no longer be given, hoarded, withheld, ultimate, or privileged. Each way of knowing has its own integrity. According to Oliver & Gershman (1989), "None is supreme, none is exclusive, none is discounted" (p. 57). This changes the nature of teaching and learning completely. In this view, traditional conceptualizations of "curriculum" make no sense. In postmodern education, student becomes curriculum and curriculum becomes student. There is no Cartesian partition. There is, instead, a constant exchange and transformation, as exemplified in the process of hermeneutic knowing.

Hermeneutic Pedagogy

In hermeneutics, as presented by Hans-Georg Gadamer (1980) and by Richard Bernstein (1971, 1978, 1983), reasoning constitutes a fluid, "circle" of understanding in which the child's reasoning moves "outward" into the "subject matter" being studied and, simultaneously, back again into the child's current personal or "inner" understandings, like a refluent stream. The child explores, compares, and contrasts the particular texts, works of art, traditions, institutions, persons and/or forms of life being presented as the "subject matter" of the curriculum with his or her own understandings, biases, points of view, feelings, and so on. It is a metacognitive or self-reflective way of exploring "subject matter."

But hermeneutics takes reasoning further. It asks the child to try to understand or fathom the reasoning and responsivity of authors involved in the texts, works of art, traditions, personal forms of life being presented in the curriculum. It engages the child in a dialogue with the authors, as well as with the productions themselves. It asks the child to try to put her/himself in the frame of mind of the place and time of such author/s.

Hermeneutics also adds an historical dimension to the child's knowing in which the child learns that knowledge evolves, grows, and differs through time—that knowing is embedded in its own time and place. The meaning of text, work of art, scientific discovery, tradition, person, and/or form of life is attached to the time and place of its occurrence. By taking his/her current understandings and immersing her/himself in the mind frame of the time and place of the meanings emanating from the text or subject matter being studied, the child compares and contrasts not only her/his understandings with those of the authors or producers of the subject matter being studied, but the child amalgamates these and comes out with "different" or broader understandings.

THE POLITICS OF POSTMODERNISM

The first section of this chapter, emphasizing the hermeneutic direction of postmodernism, alluded to the relationship between power and knowledge. Education, in its postmodern version, is moving away from the top-down, unidirectional, spectator language of control to using language in dialogue to negotiate meaning. In the second section below, leaving hermeneutics, this chapter takes an increased hard edge in critical theory and deconstruction. It points out that the "modern" view of reality and knowledge tends to subjugate, hierarchize, and separate or exclude. Modernism preempts reality and knowledge for classic Western thought and adapts a privileged spectator role in the universe. Thus the postmodern critical theory, and deconstruction strategy, reveals how the modern Western-Cartesian worldview politicizes knowledge and institutionalizes its privileged position in social structures such as schools.

Postmodernism, Knowledge, and Politics

Rorty (1979) describes the postmodern knowledge context as a conversation, a dialogue without a self-justifying, teleological destination or the privileging of certain knowledge forms or knowledge producers under assumed criteria of "good knowledge." There are no transcendent criteria for the privileging of some knowledge above others. This is a dramatic change from traditional science which has promoted the development of knowledge-based hierarchies with Western intellectuals and scientific experts standing at the top of the cultural heap. Yet, the question remains: within this postmodern knowledge context, are all participants heard and valued equally? Postmodernists within the critical theory and deconstruction emphasis typically think not.

The postmodern political agenda views schools as examples of institutional forms which play a key role in social processes of domination. The stance is very direct: Western society, for all of its strengths, is not free of social, economic, and political inequality. As a vital institution within a culture of inequality, education plays an important role in the transmission, perpetuation, and contestation of those values (Apple, 1990; Giroux, 1982, 1988; Kanpol, 1992).

Certain critical questions thus must be posed in an examination of institutions, practices, standards, and discourse. How and where are certain forms of knowing and contributors within knowledge work denied equal access to the educational arena? In what ways is this epistemic conversation currently denying fundamental egalitarian, democratic principles of equal access and participation? How are certain types of knowledge—certain voices—excluded or prohibited from full participation? What hegemonic structures are embedded within unexamined cultural values and standards passed on within educational institutions? These questions of inequality are crucial places of focus within postmodern politics.

Following closely in the political tradition of the Frankfurt School, critical theorists and early feminists, postmodern educators (Apple, 1990; Aronowitz & Giroux, 1991; Gilligan, 1982; Giroux, 1982, 1988; Grumet, 1988; Kozol, 1967; 1991; Noddings, 1984, 1992) claim that this cultural dialogue is far from open and equal. For example, in her examination of global, social scientific discourse, Weeks (1990) explains how Third World scholars and research are subordinated under the hegemonic dominance of First World theories. The international academic structures and practices promote the First World representations of Third World nations, thereby silencing Third World scholars' representations of their own cultures and forcing these scholars to depend upon Western knowledge and technology for legitimacy.

Within the more local context of American education, postmodernists continuously advocate for the silent voices—those children and families whose knowledge and life experience are routinely ignored or devalued. These persons are often seen by schools as different from the Eurocentric standards which primarily support the academic and financial "achievers" of past generations: most narrowly defined as Anglo, professional class males studying within a rational-technological knowledge tradition. Given the current pluralization of schools and other American institutions (business, the military, professions) in terms of ethnic background, language, social class, gender, sexual orientation, and disability, postmodernists are concerned with the issues of social equality in an era of growing human difference. As persons of difference increasingly live, work, and study together, the political handling of difference is of priority.

The political ordering of this growing human heterogeneity can contribute to social relationships of domination and subordination. As Boyne (1990, p. 124) says, "Difference, in the West, has come to mean the absence of value." In a cultural context in which homogeneity is valued and "different from" is often seen as "less than," the cultural and personal meanings of those subordinated to lower status positions are often not heard. Postmodernists point to what Maxine Greene (1993, p. 14) calls "long dumb voices . . . absences and silences that are as much a part of our history as the articulate voices." In a dramatic sense, our educational institutions which are often held up as the backbone of American democracy serve to maintain a Eurocentric canon which limits the types of discourse and the participating actors within that discourse (Apple & Weiss, 1983).

Cultural beliefs and standards which perpetuate silent places and disenfranchised voices, which create and continue situations of political domination reside within what may be called "business as usual," our much-relied-on cultural processes, practices, and institutions. What seems at first glance to be "the way it is," upon further critical examination may be understood as a place of social inequality.

Hegemony as Classroom Cultural Biases

While many understand the existence of numerous inequalities and injustices beneath the occluding surface of positive intentions and standard practice, it can be helpful to catch a glimpse of how that underside lives and thrives in the classroom. Alton-Lee, Nuthall, and Patrick (1993) provide poignant insight into the "hidden curriculum" of racist and sexist hegemony in their study of the private world of sixth-grade social studies students in New Zealand. In this unique investigation, small microphones were attached to each of 29 students in order to record their private and public utterances during a 36-minute lesson on the history of New York City. Only four students—two boys and two girls—were actually recorded by the researchers. Their utterances were interpreted as one form of entrée into the private world of children, the interactions and spoken words occurring beyond the teacher's awareness and knowledge. Indeed, the researchers found that 86% of the utterances were private speech acts, words spoken to oneself or to a peer. Most of the discourse and meaning negotiation among the children occurred in the seemingly silent alleys between desks, beyond the borders of the "official" lesson.

Although the greater part of the classroom construction of knowledge and relationship was secretive, those hidden utterances primarily occurred in individual and social interactions with the official subject matter. As the children attempted to make sense of the history lesson, their utterances spoken to self and peers usually revolved around the central stream of curricular knowledge maintained by the teacher and acts of student public participation.

Within this complex web of personal, relational, and public meaning making, the teacher and students perpetuated cultural biases in regard to both race and gender. During the course of this single lesson on the colonization of New York City, 97.6% of the teacher's references to historical figures were to white European men. His few references to women spoke primarily of prostitutes and women of devalued status. In a similar study of 52 hours of classroom teaching on the Middle Ages, less than 4% of the teacher's historical references spoke of women (Alton-Lee, Densem, & Nuthall, 1991; Alton-Lee & Densem, 1992). Additionally, although the class studying New York was split fairly evenly (14 girls, 15 boys), of the total instances in which students were called upon to participate in the discussion, 70% of those public nominations were boys.

This perhaps subtle cultural climate of sexism existed in a more overt and dramatic manner in the boys' public silencing of girls through the use of sexual innuendo and harassment.

> One girl in the class, Sarah, had a high status among the children because she was a class counselor. This status enabled her to respond publicly more frequently than any other girl in the class, thereby breaking the pattern of male dominance. During the brainstorming session, however, when she responded that New York made her think of break-dancing, Joe called out, labeling her "New Zealand Knickers" (referring to her underpants), making her the focus of sexual innuendo and silencing her: she stopped participating after he made that remark. (Alton-Lee, Nuthall, & Patrick, 1993, p. 79)

The climate of sexual bias involved the public silencing of the girls and the tacit approval of the teacher in his enacted curriculum of an exclusively male history.

While sexism ran as a public thread through the classroom, racism existed in a powerfully private form, implicating both the teacher and the children in the interactions of enacted curriculum and private student discussions. As the teacher described the white European colonization over the native Manhattan Indians, his language slipped from a speaking of the colonists as a distant "they" to siding with the colonists as "we." As his description became Eurocentric in its posture, racial tension spread from his biased words to influence student racial conflict. In the following transcription of utterance data, one white student (Joe) feeds off the teacher's words to harass a black peer (Ricky).

TEACHER: Because white people . . .
JOE (talking to Ricky): Honkies.
RICKY (talking to Joe) Shut up!
TEACHER: Europeans, we were. . . .
JOE (talking to Ricky): Nigger!
TEACHER: Watch this way please, Ricky—were often wanting to get things . . .
JOE (talking to Ricky): Black man! Samoan!

(Alton-Lee, Nuthall, & Patrick, 1993, p. 77)

The theme of racial bias reverberates between the teacher's spoken descriptions of history and the private talk of two boys. As the lesson progresses, Ricky, the victim of racial harassment, is repeatedly reprimanded for being disruptive. In fact, he is viewed by the teacher as a disruptive student, serving to only further reify the racial dominance in this classroom.

Postmodernists researching and teaching from a critical/deconstructive stance focus on the centrality of power to the enactment of knowledge in all aspects of professional work. The work of Foucault (1973) on the historical construction of madness stands as one exemplary postmodern engagement of these casual hegemonies in modern Western society. Foucault's (1973; 1977; 1980; 1981) work, by explicating the social development of our common perceptions and approaches to human difference, carries many lessons for special educators. We will briefly examine his work in the area of madness or "emotional disturbance," paying particular attention to the cultural handling of human difference, and talk about it in relationship to "modern" or classic education.

Foucault, Madness, and Human Difference

In his many studies of modern institutions and perception, Foucault created striking historical depictions of unexamined moral terrain of modern Western society, provoking an unsettling of the certainty of common understandings of difference and deviance. He repeatedly exposed the cultural development of institutions which seemed to modern scholars to exist in an ahistorical space, unquestioned and unexamined, merely trusted as "the way it is." (Foucault, 1980; Poster, 1989)

An example of Foucault's strategy that is pertinent to special and general educators alike is *Madness and Civilization* (1973), his examination of the social, historical construction of insanity across the fifteenth through eighteenth centuries in Europe. What may seem to be an objective reality in modern society—the existence of mental illness or "emotional disturbance" located "in" specific persons, and the simultaneous authority of mental health professions to identify and address these instances—Foucault traces as an historical, cultural development across decades of concrete time and space.

In his analysis, Foucault found that the precursor of insanity as the primary form of excluded "Otherness" in modern Western society was physical—the scourge of leprosy. Since Old Testament times, the lepers—the carriers of a physically damaging, deadly disease—were the "Other" which European culture pushed away into confinement. By the end of the Middle Ages, the combined result of the Crusades and the common practice of placing lepers in institutions had all but cleansed Europe of leprosy. The lepers had died off in the confines of leper colonies and lazar houses segregated away from the mainstream population.

As the leper colonies emptied, a new form of "Other" developed on the fringes of the community, and the institutions of Paris and London were reopened to house the new outcasts. These were persons construed as taken by "madness," a lack of reason.

Foucault emphasizes the political and moral constitution of what might otherwise be viewed as objective reality by placing the development of the category "insanity" within the sociocultural, economic, and related historical developments and processes. As the feudal economies of Europe gradually changed into early capitalist societies, a natural outgrowth of the competitive marketplace was unemployment. Simultaneously, the Protestant Reformation brought about the growth of a new Christianity based on the ideas of Luther and Calvin. The meeting of Protestant morality and capitalist opportunities for profit produced the Protestant work ethic, the moral understanding that God's chosen are hardworking, productive, and prosperous. Idle hands, lazy bodies, and the poverty of a man without work within the Calvinist morality of seventeenth century Europe were the sinful symptoms of evil pride. In Foucault's (1973, p. 57) words:

> Between labor and idleness in the classical world ran the demarcation that replaced the exclusion of leprosy. The asylum substituted for the lazar house, in the geography of haunted places as in the landscape of the moral universe. The old rites of excommunication were revived, but in the world of production and commerce. It was in these places of doom and despised illness, in the space invented by society which had derived an ethical transcendence from the law of work, that madness would appear and soon expand until it had annexed them.

Essentially, the designation of "Otherness" was made on the basis of the Protestant values of hard work and efficiency during the concurrent rise of both capitalism and Protestantism. Those lacking these values were stigmatized as mad or insane and confined with moral righteousness.

Such an analysis brings to the forefront the existence of customarily excluded or silent voices—the worlds and knowledge of those deemed insane or, in educational circles, children called emotionally disturbed or behaviorally disordered. Even a cursory examination of current education discourse and practices vis-à-vis these children demonstrates the near-total lack of child and family participation in producing knowledge and meaning about their lives and experiences. These children and their families are seen as the location of psychopathology, a lack of reason requiring institutional control.

Children labelled emotionally disturbed and their families have traditionally played a very small role in constituting their own self-formation, in defining themselves or contributing meaningfully to their own definition within educational arenas. Instead, they have been treated as passive objects of psychometric analysis during assessment and research processes, objects to be constituted, understood, judged, and defined within the totalizing theories of positivism. The way in which a child construes or constructs his own biography has been largely washed away in the various special educational processes.

As Aronowitz and Giroux (1991, p. 163) state:

> The objective of schooling, conscious or not, is among other things to strip away what belongs to the student, to reconstitute his or her formation in terms of boundaries imposed by hegemonic intellectuals acting for the prevailing social order. . . . Those who fail or otherwise rebel must recognize that their own subculture is not the real thing even if they own it.

It is at this point of student failure or rebellion that education often intervenes, too often situating the child's "subculture," home life, and personal experiences as part of the pathology to be corrected. Just as Aronowitz and Giroux (1991) direct us to the devaluing of students within educational processes on the basis of gender, race, and social class, we would encourage the reader to consider the subjugation of "exceptional" students, considered "other," within all phases of identification, assessment, placement, and intervention.

Beyond Hierarchy: Special Education and School Restructuring

Special and categorical education can be understood as an institutional means of dealing with extremes in human difference or variance. It is one aspect of the school's bureaucratized approach based within hierarchical reasoning, a top-down structuring of that human difference. Differences between persons are viewed within schools in terms of value and value-absence. The diversity of human characteristics are scaled along a value continuum from "best" to "worst," the latter sometimes leading to labels of disability and intervention, but more often characterized in various forms of "tracking," "grouping," or federalized categorical programs (e.g. "migrant," "disadvantaged," and so on).

As Boyne (1990) points out, one major significance of Foucault's history of madness is that it explains the social mechanism of the loss of status of whomever seems radically different. This absence of value means that a threat exists, a threat from a place which is not locked within the social hierarchies.

Difference is a threat because it is beyond the comprehension of human hierarchical reasoning and beyond the customary institutional capacities of Western culture which are dominated by hierarchical politics. If allowed to be in its own alien otherness, says Boyne, difference is outside the control mechanisms which are well established for those subjects who are firmly embedded in social hierarchies. There are two logical strategies for dealing with such a threat, according to Derrida (1976, 1981); one is exclusion and the other is neutralization. Foucault's studies suggest that, as a general rule, differences will be neutralized even when incorporated.

SCIENCE AND POSTMODERNISM

The last section talked about the political dimension of knowledge, embedded in the divergent worldviews of modernism and postmodernism. That section picked up the thread of the first section which dealt with the link between power and knowledge in modern thought. It deepened and widened that connection which spoke about the top-down, unidirectional nature of modern thought and presented education as an example of institutionalization of the classic spectator worldview.

The critical analysis of that section became more concrete when it talked about how education structured "differences" or "otherness" into its social system of schools. This third section, using the scientific revolution's contribution to postmodernism, will delve further into the ways in which educational systems neutralize and incorporate differences or "otherness."

Nowhere in education and its systems is prerevolutionary, "modern" science as thoroughly ensconced as it is in federally mandated programs. This is particularly true in programs for "exceptional" children. Nowhere have the hierarchical strategies of neutralization and exclusion that were talked about in the last section been more thoroughly "scientized" in the postrevolutionary perspective than it has in that area called "special" education.

Education and the Science Revolution

At the close of the twentieth century, the revolution in physics, mathematics, chemistry, and biology began showing us that the world is as removed from our current or "modern" science as our current "modern" science is from the occult certainties of the Middle Ages. (Briggs & Peat, 1984). It has moved beyond modern science into the postmodern era. The message the postmodern theorists bring us, according to Briggs and Peat, is actually simple: "The flowing, swirling universe is a mirror" (p. 15).

Like Alice in Lewis Carroll's *Through the Looking Glass*, we have stepped through the mirror and, lo and behold, we have discovered ourselves. Scientists have learned that much of what we find in the "world" is largely what our mind has imprinted there. In the process, we discover that it all depends on how we view the problem as to what it "really" is. The mental framework that we impose on reality helps "make" both our problems and our solutions to them.

This applies to education, where that broadly diversified "problem" of differences in children is neutralized by embedding them within the waning context of "modern" or classical medical and psychological science. This is a view in which the universe does not swirl or flow, does not depend on the mind's movement to actualize it. It is a world solidified in certainty and matter. It is solid, preexistent and external to the viewer experiencing it.

Education, in its special treatment of children, is stuck in that classic or "modern" view, still captured, for instance, in the simple descriptive or explanatory models of medicine and psychology when Public Law 94-142 was enacted in 1975. As a consequence, it is stuck with the prerevolutionary mind-set of classic science at a time in which science itself seems to be moving rapidly into a postmodern era; into a postmodern world that reflects the swirl and flow of a metamorphosing mind.

The "Fact" Problem

Special education sees medical and psychological constructions of exceptionality as "scientific," which, in prerevolutionary science, means "certainty" and "demonstration of physical things." These "things" are grounded in behavioral, physiological, and neurological events "within" the child. But, in postmodern science, these are "facts" only as long as they remain embedded within the prerevolutionary worldview. As Kuhn (1970) showed us in his hermeneutic study *The Study of Scientific Revolutions*, "facts" are not self-contained realities. Facts are made by their containing theories or paradigms. When theories or paradigms change, "facts" change. With the shift from Newtonian to quantum and relativity theory in physics, the "facts" of physical reality changed dramatically. From this changed perspective, the scientific facts of special education lose much of their validity for postmodern education. The self-contained reality of "things" within the child, separate from the flowing, swirling context of their occurrence (the fluid ecological composite of neighborhood, school, community, culture, and so on), are no longer regarded as "facts" in a postmodern scientific worldview. This a view that does not resonate to postmodern thought.

This "modern" or classical view is itself a problem for special or categorical education defenders at a time when education in general seems to be groping its way toward the postmodern mentality of a flowing, swirling universe in which there is no absolute knowledge, no certain knowledge. Knowledge itself becomes, largely, the systematically flowing actions of the evolutionary mind, a mind involved in the reconstructed reality of complementarity, indeterminacy, and relativity. From this emerging vista, education seems to be dimly perceiving the creating or constructing mind as its natural habitat; the only place it can move in the postmodern world. In this world, knowledge, like the universe itself, is not fixed, absolute, or "out there." It is, largely, a living, swirling, moving mental construction. It blends with its evolving historical vista, becoming one with that vista, as it strives to make its reality into its own image. James Burke's (1985) epic hermeneutic study, *The Day the Universe Changed*, shows us how dramatically knowledge structures and meanings change with the periodic mental revolutions which occur during critical, episodic periods in history. Burke (1985) says:

> The knowledge acquired through the use of any structure is selective. There are no standards or beliefs guiding the search for knowledge which are not dependent on the structure. Scientific knowledge, in sum, is not the clearest representation of what reality is; it is the artifact of each structure and its tool. Discovery is invention. Knowledge is man-made.—The universe is what we say it is. The truth is relative. (p. 337)

Making Knowledge

Only when we build our schemas around the rapidly eroding "modern" era or classic views of the world, do traditional medical and sociopsychological theories make sense for education. Only then are we able to compartmentalize children according to behavioral or physical "thingness" which can be said to interfere with their "gaining" knowledge. However, in the emergent era of postmodern thought, children "make" or "construct" knowledge. They do not simply "gain" knowledge.

In the eroding classic or modern idiom, education could build its special or categorical education programs around "certain" and "demonstrated things" that had to be remediated in order for the child to learn. Only in this one-dimensional scientific world could the child be equated with her/his "thingness." In the holographic world of postmodernism, this unidimensional concentration makes no sense for education.

The child becomes a multidimensional potential. For instance, the "multiple intelligence" construct fits with this view. Within such an "intelligence" framework how can "mental retardation" or "intelligence quotient" make sense?

Classic special or categorical education sees "things" in children which have to be made right in order for them to learn. These "things" fit very well within the tapestry of prerevolutionary science. The tapestry itself gives "meaning" to them. However, in the revolutionary tapestry of postmodern science, "modern" classic psychomedical science becomes obsolete or asynchronous with educational processes. In the thinking of postmodernism, teaching/learning to construct knowledge is what education is all about. In this view, as in the first section of this chapter describing visionary teaching, the fluid redesign of knowledge, not simply the absorption of knowledge, is what contributes to mental growth.

In this fluid view of knowledge-making, children project their understandings grounded in the swirling mosaic of their own neighborhoods, their own families, their own cultures, their own time, into their knowledge-construction project. It becomes part of their classroom and their curricula. This is where the school, in the postmodern era, has to begin its influence—with this immediate reality of the child—as education strives to teach the mind to reflect a greater reality. Within this context, the "thingness" of classical medical and psychological theories is alien to the immediate base of children's experience. When we try to impose this theoretical "thingness" upon their own self-concept, which is what special education unconsciously does (in its Pygmalion theories of "learning disabilities," "behavioral disorders," or "mental retardation," and so on), children reject this alien, confusing spectator reality as meaningless and punishing to themselves. It has nothing to do with their experience in their immediate parochial world. Therefore, it encourages distancing rather than engagement of the reality presented them.

Educational Inclusion

The recent movement toward educational "inclusion" in its various guises, assumes that all children are, and can be, knowledge makers. This atmospheric change in the swirling, flowing school reality should encourage children to make knowledge, instead of teaching them to see themselves as knowledge problems. Instead of encouraging them to reflect upon themselves as scientific problem "things," we should teach them to reflect upon themselves as problem solvers in both their parochial settings and their larger world. In this sense we teach the postmodern scientific method, in which they are postmodern scientists, conducting an experiment in which they themselves are the experiment. From this perspective, they are reconstructing their world, which is the same as reconstructing themselves.

This is the way that Wigginton (1985) taught his "Foxfire curriculum" to his Appalachian mountain children. In the Foxfire books, we see these children make their rural lives into an experiment in which they themselves are the experiment, and in their parochial cultural existence become the hermeneutic constructors of their own lives. "Hermeneutic" is used here in the sense that they took the context of their own existence and by reflecting upon it, transformed it into a broader reality. Such transformation is the very stuff of postmodern education—not through class psychotherapy or behavior modification—but through life-experimentation. This self-reflective experimentation, the essence of postmodern science, could be taught to children who come from the inner cities, out of cultures of war and violence, or the disarray of family dissolution on all social levels, and the general social turbulence of our times. In stepping through the looking glass, they come upon an expanded self.

The classic or modern views of exceptionality are isolationist, separatist views. They emphasize exclusion of or hierarchical layering of learners. This, at a time when the postmodern trend in education is focused on detracking, degrouping, destreaming, inclusion, collaboration, and cooperation.

The failing, or inadequate, classic constructions of modernism speak of categorical certainty at a time when education is accepting the uncertainty principle of postmodern science. Classic or modern special education speaks of minds as reflecting nature (for example, in "disabilities" such as mental retardation, behavioral disorders, specific learning disabilities) at a time when physical science itself is saying that mind discovers in nature what mind puts in nature.

The Heisenberg Difference

Early in the twentieth century, physicists began to glimpse a world that transcended the capacities of the Newtonian or modern worldview to explain reality. Heisenberg described the tremendous impact this discovery had on those involved in this critical period of history as they began to grasp that the world they were experiencing could only make sense in a different world of meaning, a different worldview.

> But it was not a solution which one could easily accept. I remember discussions with Bohr which went through many hours till very late at night and ended almost in despair; and when at the end of the discussion I went alone to walk in the neighborhood park I repeated to myself again and again the question: Can nature possibly be so absurd as it seemed to be in these atomic experiments? (Heisenberg, 1962, as cited in Capra, 1988, p. 20)

It may seem just as absurd to say, from the postmodern perspective, that the application of classic or prerevolutionary science to difference in children has not and can not transcend those differences, educationally or otherwise. It may be absurd to say that we must find meaning constructs that transcend "difference" itself. Within the modern worldview, this is not easy to accept, but in postmodernism it follows necessarily.

In the final section, we will utilize Linda Stone's (1991) concept of visionary postmodernism to describe one possibility in postmodern teaching. In offering this single vision of the visionary instructor, we do not intend to imply that there is one postmodern pedagogy. Nor do we believe that postmodern approaches are dreams for the future. There are public school teachers who currently live and breathe post-modern imagination in their daily work with children. In presenting this description of the visionary teacher, we are indebted to those many creative and daring teachers from whom we have learned.

One Postmodern Pedagogy: Visionary Teaching

From the start there is a problem with talking about what a "postmodern" teacher might be like, because the meaning of the term *teacher* would have to be altered in a fundamental way in a postmodern frame. "Teacher" is generally thought of as one side of a dichotomy in which "learner" or "student" occupies an inferior position. In the modern view, teaching implies a certain stance towards the learner, a certain position of authority. This is possible because, in the traditional sense, teacher, student, and knowledge are three separate and distinct entities in which knowledge exists in an absolute sense and is encased in fact and theory and inscribed in language and prescribed. In this view, the knowledge that teachers impart is not their own, but imported from a different time and place, with no one to answer for it. The truths that are taught in school are not intended to be challenged. No one in the school makes knowledge or rules; everyone hands them down. The language this occurs in is descriptive; it is definite, objective and closed. Teaching in this sense is giving, and learning is getting.

In the postmodern view, knowledge, teacher, and learner are not separate entities, but exist in dynamic relationship. Knowledge is a social construction. Education is interaction, the process of negotiation. All people involved in the interactive process both teach and learn. All engage in their own unique way of knowing. All contribute to the ever-changing meanings. Some contribute by their stories, some by their theories, some by their questions, some by their silence, some by their anger, some by their inattention. All enter the dance and influence the ritual of meaning making that takes place in time and space, in community, in culture. Where is the teacher to enter, and what is s/he to contribute? A postmodern thinker might hesitate to say, cautious not to limit the possibilities, not wanting to stifle the curiosity of the moment or the endless creativity of human beings.

"Teacher" no longer seems to be an appropriate term. Perhaps we need to come up with new ways of envisioning an active learning process and the possible roles the participants can play. One possibility for a transformed role of teacher is Linda Stone's (1991) description of the "visionary." Visionary meaning is a postmodern meaning construct that Stone suggests is just beginning to emerge. Although she does not propose "visionary" as a new metaphor for "teacher," I would like to borrow her description of visionary as one viable new image we may want to consider as we recreate education and the possible transfiguration of teaching.

Stone describes visionary meaning as transformative and as constructed by a person seeking change. *Learning, broadly defined, is change.* The visionary identity is continually reformed in engagement with specific contexts. She points out that the visionary is continuously involved in self-critical reasoning, not from a position of power or control, but from ground level, from engaging in the process of meaning making.

The visionary is deeply aware of the constructed nature of knowledge, of the unity between eye, mind, and pattern, of the holographic nature of knowing. The visionary knows that knowledge is constructed in negotiation and dialogue, in relationship with other human beings in community, and as such is willing to undergo continuous personal change as a participant in meaning making. The visionary is willing to let go of knowledge to engage in knowing; to let go of truth in the search of meaning; to relinquish authority to enter into mutually empowering relationships.

Education is viewed as the arena for becoming, engaging, and knowing, as the natural habitat of the evolving adventures of mind. Schools involve learners in a process in which they are encouraged to bring their own meaning, their own culture, their own unique way of seeing and saying.

Language use and culture creating are central to postmodern education. "Classes," rather than being rigidly organized around a certain subject "matter," a certain age grouping, or a certain "exceptionality," might rather be fluid groups formed and reformed around different themes, different languages, different cultural perspectives, different aspects of creativity, different experiences of knowing, and so forth. Rather than focusing on explaining the "facts" to students, visionary-teachers focus on the group dynamics of creation, of examining the process of establishing meaning and criteria for goodness within the group as a holographic representation of meaning making on many dimensions of human experience.

Visionary-teachers bring their "self" into the classroom—whole, human, and open to process. Participating in establishing relationships, forming agreements (not necessarily consensus; the agreements may be to disagree), examining languages and the nature of transactions, the visionary-teacher attempts to understand the worlds of students through constant interchange, through talking and watching, through agreement and disagreement, through interactions with others, through the languages of art, drama, play, poetry, math, science, and so on. Together with a child, or a group, or a class, the visionary-teacher might share her/his view, story, perspective, experience, vision, but always open for revision, for counterviews, for refinement, for evolution. Visionary-teachers work to establish a connection and useful communication with students, not in a prescribed preordained manner, but in responsivity to the lives of students and their unique ways of knowing.

Visionary teaching is fluid and responsive; however, it does not operate on the premise that "anything goes." Rather, in the postmodern view, values can not be "disconnected" from the determination of meaning and, therefore, become central issues addressed in the meaning-making process. Values, ethics, power, culture, beliefs, relationship, context, negotiation, agreement, disagreement are all integrally intertwined in meaning-making processes and constitute important interrelated "dimensions" of study.

Visionary-teachers help students create opportunities for exploration and learning. They work with students to develop different abilities and languages, or help them envision and plan projects. They work to help students network with other students, other teachers, or community members. They might work with students, families, and others to design education plans. Or they might focus their energies in a certain "world" of knowing. But whatever the visionary-teacher does, it isn't static or predetermined, but open to engagement, to possibility.

This is a very different image than that of the traditional teacher. It requires people who delight in adventure and uncertainty, whereas the traditional role often attracted people who sought certainty in a "knowledge" that they perceived as objective and separate from themselves. It requires an honest and complete involvement in the lives of other learners, rather than keeping a "professional distance." It requires confidence in the human spirit and mind, and a delight in diversity and difference. It requires courage, and a willingness to risk, to change, to learn. It requires embracing new dreams and new visions.

SUMMARY

This chapter presented three facets or directions of the postmodern worldview: the hermeneutic or interpretive facet, the critical and deconstructive facet, and the revolutionary science facet. In each, the postmodern worldview was contrasted with the modern or classic worldview, hopefully spurring some understandings of how we might change our minds, how we might reenvision ourselves, our educational institutions, our students, and our work. We have concluded with one description of postmodern pedagogy.

Postmodernism has joined and broadened the restructuring dialogue as educators express their visions for the future. A holographic view of reality and knowledge enters into negotiations with the long-reigning mechanistic view, offering alternative visions not available before. As was said early in the first section of this chapter: "Not only the future of education, but the present moment, holds completely different meanings depending on the worldview that one espouses."

REFERENCES

Alton-Lee, A., & Densem, P. A. (1992). Towards a gender-inclusive school curriculum: Changing educational practice. In S. Middleton & A. Jones (Eds.), *Women and education in Aotearoa* (Vol. 2, pp. 197–220). Wellington, New Zealand: Bridget Williams.

Alton-Lee, A., Densem, P. A., & Nuthall, G. A. (1991). Imperatives of classroom research: Understanding what children learn about gender and race. In J. Morss & T. Linzey (Eds.), *Growing up: Lifespan development and the politics of human learning* (pp. 93–117). Auckland, New Zealand: Longman Paul.

Alton-Lee, A., Nuthall, G., & Patrick, J. (1993). Reframing classroom research: A lesson from the private world of children. *Harvard Educational Review, 63*(1), pp. 50–84.

Apple, M. (1990). *Ideology and curriculum.* New York: Routledge.

Apple, M., & Weiss, L. (Eds.), (1983). *Ideology and public schooling.* Philadelphia: Temple University Press.

Aronowitz, S., & Giroux, H. (1991). *Postmodern education: Politics, culture, and social curriculum.* Minneapolis: University of Minnesota Press.

Ayers, W. (1992). Teachers' stories: Autobiography and inquiry. In E.W. Ross, J. Cornett, and G. McCutcheon (Eds.), *Teacher personal theorizing: Connecting curriculum practice, theory, and research* (pp. 35–49). Albany, NY: State University of New York Press.

Bernstein, R. J. (1971). *Praxis and action: Contemporary philosophies of human activity*. Philadelphia: University of Pennsylvania Press.

Bernstein, R. J. (1978). *The restructuring of social and political theory*. Philadelphia: University of Pennsylvania Press.

Bernstein, R. J. (1983). *Beyond objectivism and relativism: Science, hermeneutics, and praxis*. Philadelphia: University of Pennsylvania Press.

Boyne, R. (1990). *Foucault and Derrida: The other side of reason*. Boston: Unwin Hyman.

Boyne, R., & Rattansi, A. (1990). *Postmodernism and society*. New York: St. Martin's Press.

Briggs, J. P., & Peat, F. D. (1984). *Looking glass universe: Emerging science of wholeness*. New York: Simon and Schuster.

Bruner, J. S. (1986). *Actual minds, possible worlds*. Cambridge: Harvard University Press.

Burke, J. (1985). *The day the universe changed*. Boston: Little, Brown.

Capra, F. (1988). *Uncommon wisdom: Conversations with remarkable people*. New York: Simon and Schuster.

Derrida, J. (1976). *Of grammatology*. Baltimore: Johns Hopkins University Press.

Derrida, J. (1981). *Positions*. Chicago: University of Chicago Press.

Foster, H. (Ed.). (1983). *The anti-aesthetic: Essays on postmodern culture*. Port Townsend, WA: Bay.

Foucault, M. (1973). *Madness and civilization*: A history of insanity in the age of reason. New York: Vintage.

Foucault, M. (1977). *Discipline and punish: The birth of the prison*. New York: Vintage.

Foucault, M. (1980). *Power/Knowledge: Selected interviews & other writings 1972–1977*. New York: Pantheon.

Foucault, M. (1981). *The history of sexuality, Part 1*. New York: Vintage.

Gadamer, H. G. (1980). *Dialogue and dialectic: Eight hermeneutical studies on Plato*. New Haven: Yale University Press.

Gibboney, R. A.(1991, May). The killing fields of reform. *Phi Delta Kappan*, pp. 682–688.

Gilligan, C. (1982). *In a different voice: Psychological theory and women's development*. Cambridge: Harvard University Press.

Gilligan, C. & Brown, L. M. (1992). *Meeting at the crossroads: Women's psychology and girls' development*. Cambridge: Harvard University Press.

Giroux, H. (1982). *Theory and resistance in education: a pedagogy for the opposition*. South Hadley, MA: Bergin and Garvey.

Giroux, H. (1988). *Teachers as intellectuals: Toward a critical pedagogy of learning*. Granby, MA: Bergin and Garvey.

Giroux, H. (1992). *Border crossings: Cultural workers and the politics of education*. New York: Routledge.

Greene, M. (1993). The passions of pluralism: Multiculturalism and the expanding community. *Educational Researcher*, 22(1), 13–18.

Grumet, M. R. (1988). *Bittermilk: Women and teaching*. Amherst, MA: University of Massachusetts Press.

Henderson, J. G. (1992). *Reflective teaching: Becoming an inquiring educator*. New York: Macmillan.

Kanpol, B. (1992). *Towards a Theory and Practice of Teacher Cultural Politics: Continuing the Postmodern Debate*. Norwood, NJ: Ablex.

Kozol, J. (1967). *Death at an early age*. Boston: Houghton Mifflin.

Kozol, J. (1991). *Savage inequalities: Children in America's schools*. New York: Crown.

Kuhn, T. (1970). *The structure of scientific revolutions* (2nd ed.). Chicago: University of Chicago Press.

Lather, P. (1991). *Getting smart: Feminist research and pedagogy with/in the postmodern*. New York: Routledge.

Nicholson, L. (Ed.), (1990). *Feminism/postmodernism*. London: Routledge.

Noddings, N. (1984). *Caring: A feminine approach to ethics and moral education*. Berkeley, CA: University of California Press.

Noddings, N. (1992). *The challenge to care in schools: An alternative approach to education*. Berkeley: University of California Press.

Oliver, D. W., & Gershman, K. W. (1989). *Education, modernity, and fractured meaning: Toward a process theory of teaching and learning*. Albany, NY: State University of New York Press.

Poplin, M. (1992). *Voices from the inside: A report on schooling from inside the classroom*. The Institute for Education in Transformation. Claremont Graduate School, Claremont, CA. Funded by John Kluge Foundation.

Poster, M. (1989). *Critical theory and poststructualism in search of a context*. Ithaca, NY: Cornell University Press.

Rorty, R. (1979). *Philosophy and the mirror of nature*. Princeton, NJ: Princeton University Press.

Stone, L. (1991). *Postmodern social construction: Initiating dissonance*. Paper presented at the annual meeting of the American Educational Research Association, Chicago.

Stone, L. (1992). Philosophy, meaning constructs and teacher theorizing in E. W. Ross, J. Cornett, and G. McCutcheon (Eds.), *Teacher personal theorizing: Connecting curriculum practice, theory, and research* (pp. 19–34). Albany, NY: State University of New York Press.

Weeks, P. (1990). Post-colonial challenges to grand theory. *Human Organization, 49*, 236–244.

Wigginton, E. (1985). *Sometimes a shining moment: The Foxfire experience*. Garden City, NY: Anchor Press/Doubleday.

Zavarzadeh, M., & Morton, D. (1991). *Theory, (post)modernity, opposition*. Washington, DC: Maison-Neuve.

II

RESHAPING EDUCATIONAL PRACTICES

EXPERIENCES IN RESHAPING
THE MISSION AND WORK OF
A COLLEGE OF EDUCATION

JAMES L. PAUL

SECTION One focuses on the environment within one college of education that made possible six different collaborative relationships with school districts for implementing a reform agenda. In order to understand the individual university-school collaborations, it is necessary to appreciate the social, political and academic environment in which they occurred. In the first chapter in this section, Katzenmeyer, dean of the University of South Florida's College of Education, briefly traces the critical history that shaped the moral and technical features of the college's vision of reform in teacher education. He describes the deep social, cultural, and economic changes during the past 50 years that have restructured the rules, roles, and relationships which prevailed when our existing system of schooling was invented. He argues that our historical assumptions about education must be rethought in order for schools to respond effectively to the needs of *all* children and families in our present time. He emphasizes the need for simultaneous restructuring of schools and teacher education.

In this context, Katzenmeyer describes the vision of the College of Education and the six basic principles that guide the current reform initiatives, including those described in Section I. These include: 1) creating greater continuity in the caring relationship between children and adults; 2) reinventing learning environments to create positive interdependence; 3) infusing technology to free up teacher time for work with individuals and small groups; 4) creating high-option environments in schools; 5) reinventing the teaching profession to make it more attractive; and 6) creating a level playing field for the achievement of world-class outcomes. These principles are discussed in three contexts: reinventing schools, reinventing teacher education, and reconceiving special education.

Katzenmeyer describes the Suncoast Alliance for School Improvement, which includes parents, and school, university, legislative, and business representatives, created to implement the restructuring agenda. Specific teaching and research agendas and the strategies being used to implement them in professional development schools in the Suncoast area are discussed. Experience in implementing the principles and implications for special education services are discussed.

In the second chapter, Paul, Johnston, and Raines, chairs of the departments of special, secondary, and childhood education respectively, discuss the restructuring of the teacher education program in the college. They describe ethical, psychological, political, and organizational issues that emerged in their efforts to effect partnerships within the college and between the college and public schools. They point out two major forces impacting their work that broadly affect the reform of teacher education. First, there are centrifugal forces that include the organization of knowledge in the university, entrenched professional guilds, and the politics of certification. Second, there are centripetal forces that include political and economic forces and deep changes in the philosophy of knowledge. The authors describe their experience in the context of a new ethos of teacher education being shaped by the changing paradigms of educational foundations and research.

Within this broad context, the authors discuss the partnership they effected among their departments. This includes an analysis of their own value-driven constructions of a partnership, the ethics that formed the partnership, the role of their own personal stories in coming together as a working team, the organizational context in which they work, and current understandings in elementary, secondary, and special education that helped shape the partnership. Specific examples of partnership initiatives are provided and general conclusions drawn regarding the development of partnerships in teacher education.

12

INVENTING THE FUTURE
OF TEACHER EDUCATION
Philosophical and Strategic Reform in Colleges of Education

WILLIAM KATZENMEYER

INTRODUCTION

THE public schools of America have served the purposes for which they were created extremely well; however, both the outcomes we need and strategies for achieving them have changed. An emerging society that differs dramatically from the society for which the schools were created requires that the schools be reinvented to achieve both traditional and new purposes. Chief among these purposes are nurturing, informing, and empowering children, youth, and adults. The faculty and leadership team of the College of Education at the University of South Florida are committed to collaborating with the faculties and administrators of schools to find the new "right things to do" to ensure that America will once again lead the world in the quality of education and the quality of life of our people.

A CONTEXT FOR TRANSFORMATIONAL LEADERSHIP

Especially in times of change, decisions made by effective leaders involve both knowledge and intuition. Decisions about where we ought to go and how we might get there are most likely to be effective if they are informed by an understanding of where we have been and where we are. Following is a brief synopsis of a few of the significant elements of where we have been and where we are.

CIRCA 1945–1960

Society and Schooling.   The economies and productive capacities of both our enemies and our allies were severely damaged as a result of World War II. The economy and productive capacities of the United States were both expanded. After the war we recruited much of the best scientific and mathematical talent from Germany and other nations. This infusion of new talent contributed substantially to our technological leadership. Major investments were made in the higher education infrastructure of our nation through the GI Bill. We made an increased investment in K–12 education, particularly in mathematics and science, following the launch of Sputnik. Investment in research and development were increasing. Putting our newly developed technological and industrial power to good use, we became provisioners to the world. American business and industry dominated the world economy. We earned large balance-of-trade surpluses and became the world's largest creditor nation. The American worker became the highest paid worker in the world. American management practices were viewed as state-of-the-art.

In 1940, the great majority of children arrived at school ready to learn. Eighty-five percent of American school-age children lived in homes where the father was the breadwinner and the mother a full-time caregiver. Rearing children was the major work activity of American mothers, and this investment of their time added substantial value to children. Families, primarily mothers, provided most of the nurturing. The primary role of schools was informing. It was assumed that nurturing, provided by the home, would combine with knowledge and skills learned at school to empower new adults.

In 1950, the United States had the longest school year in the world (180 days). We celebrated our educational system as the most effective and progressive in the world. Colleges of education prepared teachers to work in the world's best system of schooling. The right things to do were known. Doing things right (management), was the order of the day: classroom management by teachers, school management by principals. College of education faculty, most of whom had experience as teachers in elementary and secondary schools, made decisions about what knowledge and skills the graduates of their programs should have. Teacher education curriculum development was an evolutionary process—at any point in time, the existing curriculum reflected the best combination of the collective wisdom that could be negotiated among the faculty. The organizational model for most schools and classrooms was competitive. Students were grouped homogeneously according to ability or achievement levels, so that most students could participate meaningfully in the competitive environment of the classroom. The majority of students with identified handicapping conditions were in special schools or special classes.

Public Reaction.   The public believed that American education was the best in the world. "The schools" referred to schools for white middle-class America. "Separate but equal" has been declared "inherently unequal." America has been forced to recognize that its "melting pot" has not worked for all its citizens. The nation struggles against itself to bring all its people to full membership in the American dream.

CIRCA 1980–1994

Society and Schooling. American business, at this point, had become accustomed to its position as technological leader and sole supplier of major technological and industrial products. American workers had become comfortable with being the highest paid workers in the world. However, as the economies of both our former enemies and allies recovered, a new economic and political context emerged. American products must now compete with products from other nations both in quality and price. For American business to succeed, American professionals and skilled workers must compete in a world economy, which includes professional and skilled workers from the resurgent and emerging economies of Europe and the Pacific rim. Seeking lower labor costs, manufacturing jobs move overseas. American semi-skilled and unskilled workers now must compete for jobs with workers from Third World nations who are eager to work for lower wages. We are no longer provisioners to the world, nor do we dominate the world economy. Japan and Germany have emerged as major economic powers. A large balance of trade deficit has resulted. The United States has become the world's greatest debtor nation. Investments in support of educational enhancement are reduced. Research and development funds are curtailed. American management practice is viewed as out of step with the times. Restructuring is the order of the day.

Most families require two incomes to maintain an acceptable standard of living. By 1990, fewer than 15 percent of school-aged children lived in homes where the father was the breadwinner and the mother was a full-time caregiver. Most mothers commit the major portion of their time to their outside-the-home work, and adding value to their children was relegated to afterwork hours, weekends, and holidays. A substantially smaller proportion of children arrived at school ready to learn. A greater share of the responsibility for nurturing and empowering had shifted to the schools (Barrett, 1990). Japan has a 240-day school year. Germany has a 230-day school year; Korea 250 days. The United States still has a 180-day school year. Results of international tests in mathematics and science reveal that our students are doing poorly relative to students in other nations.

De jure segregation of schools has been eliminated. *De facto* segregation has been greatly reduced through busing. Substantial immigration of Hispanics from the Caribbean and Asians from southeast Asia has increased our cultural diversity. Several states anticipate school populations in which the majority of students will be members of minority groups.

With the enactment of P.L. 94-142 which guarantees "a free appropriate education," there is a substantial increase in the numbers of students identified with disabilities. The ongoing debate around the definition and efficacy of "appropriate" fuels efforts to promote mainstreaming and inclusion of students with disabilities in mainstream classrooms.

Public Reactions: In the 1980s, the multiple failures of our educational system were bemoaned, and the race was on to fix the blame. Commentators decided that the problem must be in the education establishment: perhaps bad teachers, perhaps poor administrators. Either way, the problem was laid at the feet of colleges of education because they prepared these teachers and administrators whose schools are failing. It is argued that much of the problem lies in the absence of academic rigor in teacher preparation programs. The fix is to replace soft "methods" courses with "rigorous" subject matter courses. Legislators and businesspeople decide they can fix the problem. They pass laws that tell educators what to do and how to do it. "Let business people manage the schools." they said. "Choice" and vouchers are offered as panaceas.

The Secretary's Commission on Achieving Necessary Skills (1991) SCANS report suggests the importance of "the ability to work together cooperatively in groups" as an educational outcome. Given the changes in national and international society and in workplace methods, the appropriateness of a model for education that relies heavily on individual competition is questioned.

By 1990, after a decade of legislating the nature of change, it became apparent to everyone that "you can't fix the problem from the top down." School-based management and shared decision making have become the new marching orders. The idea is to reduce bureaucracy—flatten the organization of schools; let the teachers and principals fix it. We are no longer ready to prescribe what the "right things to do" are. Thus the emphasis has shifted from management to leadership—from "doing things right" to figuring out "the right things to do."

FLORIDA'S RESPONSE—BLUEPRINT 2000, AN EXAMPLE

Florida's initiative, Blueprint 2000, recognizes that substantial change in education will necessarily be led by teachers, community, and school-level administrators. The approach strives to assure that the stakeholders have a voice in change, while leaving close-to-the-students leadership free to address the reinvention of schools. Schools are accountable for results, not for adherence to particular processes. Blueprint 2000 identifies seven goals and provides standards to be used in assessing progress toward these goals.

Goal 1: *Readiness to Start School.* Communities and schools collaborate to prepare children and families for children's success in school.

Goal 2: *Graduation Rate and Readiness for Postsecondary Education and Employment.* Students graduate and are prepared to enter the workforce and postsecondary education.

Goal 3: *Student Performance.* Students successfully compete at the highest levels nationally and internationally and are prepared to make well-reasoned, thoughtful, and healthy lifelong decisions.

Goal 4: *Learning Environment.* School boards provide a learning environment conducive to teaching and learning.

Goal 5: *School Safety and Environment.* Communities provide an environment that is drug-free and that protects students' health, safety, and civil rights.

Goal 6: *Teachers and Staff.* The schools, districts, and state ensure professional teachers and staff.

Goal 7: *Adult Literacy.* Adult Floridians are literate and have the knowledge and skills needed to compete in a global economy and exercise the rights and responsibilities of citizenship.

Blueprint 2000 establishes goals, requires participation of various stakeholders in school change, and sets standards for assessing progress towards the goals. It leaves the invention of right things to do to achieve these goals to the schools and their stakeholders (teachers, administrators, school boards, parents, and other community members).

CHANGE: IMPLICATIONS FOR THE "RIGHT THINGS TO DO"

IN TIMES OF CHANGES, LEARNERS SHALL INHERIT THE EARTH, WHILE THE LEARNED ARE BEAUTIFULLY EQUIPPED FOR A WORLD THAT NO LONGER EXISTS.

—ERIC HOFFER

With respect to education we might ask whether, in recent years, other nations have been the learners while we have left our educational system beautifully equipped for a world that no longer exists? While the public schools of America have served the purposes for which they were created extremely well, our long-successful model of schooling has not changed rapidly enough to keep pace with the expanding needs and expectations of our society in the emerging world economy. Perhaps we have not fully recognized the extent to which our educational system has been responsible for our national success. Other nations have recognized the importance of education to their economic success and have responded by extending their school years. For example, the school years of Japan and Germany (240 and 230 days respectively) are more than 25 percent longer than the U.S. school year. In addition, American high school students spend a larger proportion of their in-school time on non-academic activities than do their Japanese and German counterparts. Meanwhile, our school year remains at 180 days.

Our society has been fundamentally altered by the changing context of the last half century. Substantial changes that can inform our thinking about the reinvention of our educational system have occurred with respect to:

- the nature of the caring relationships we provide for our children and youth
- the academic and personal outcomes that schools are expected to achieve
- the cultural diversity of the student population
- the power of our technology
- the rate of change in our society
- the extent to which the teaching profession can compete with other professions for talent
- the level of infrastructure investment needed to achieve world-class outcomes

There are costs associated with these changes which we have been slow to recognize and reluctant to fund. If present and coming generations of children are to be nurtured, informed, and empowered as well as past generations have been, and as well or better than children of other industrialized nations, our society must make substantially greater investments in child rearing than were needed in the past.

John Goodlad (1990) has observed that we must move forward with the "simultaneous renewal of schooling and of the education of educators." Schools need to change in response to changing needs of children and expectations of society, but it would be a doubtful process for school systems to invent schools which required competencies of teachers and administrators which go well beyond those provided by their education and experience. Similarly, teacher preparation programs cannot prepare teachers for schools which do not exist. Thus, concomitant and collaborative changes in schools and in teacher preparation programs must be orchestrated. This renewal will require shared vision and collaboration among those who lead schools and those who lead the programs that prepare professionals for the schools.

Needed if we are to successfully reinvent our educational system to fully nurture, inform, and empower our children, youth, and adults are:

- a national recommitment to providing free and equal "world class" educational opportunities for all citizens without respect to ethnicity, gender, religion, disability, age, or socioeconomic status;
- an understanding that what we have learned about how children learn and what we have learned about how to help children grow cognitively and emotionally have ethical implications for what the "right things to do" in our educational practice are;
- a set of concepts or "right things to do" to organize our thinking and actions as we set about the reinvention of our educational system;
- and, for special education, learning communities that affirm the moral mission of inclusion while maintaining the technical capacity and will to nurture and facilitate the highest quality of learning by all children.

In collaboration with several of the school districts of southwest Florida, we sought to respond to these needs. The first effort was to identify the set of concepts or "right things to do" that could organize and bring common language to our thinking about the reinvention of schools. We sought "right things to do" which were right enough to create consensus among school district and university leaders and faculty. We wanted them to be specific enough to give direction to the renewal process, while leaving the particulars of implementation to the creativity of leaders and faculty in individual school districts, colleges, and departments.

Creating a vision of the "right things to do" involves drawing together what people already know into a synthesis that creates an "aha" or "of course" reaction. I had served as dean of the College of Education for a decade by 1987 and had been fortunate enough to bring together a leadership team (teacher education department chairs and dean's staff) who were in substantial agreement with respect to values and in their commitment to collaborative change. The collaboration was envisioned as including college-school district collaboration and true collaboration among faculties of departments within the college. I had also benefitted from the collective wisdom of the faculty of the college and of many able school and business leaders. I found myself in an "If not me, who; if not now, when?" situation. Proceeding with substantial doubt, I drafted a working paper *Inventing the Schools of Tomorrow* (1993) which identified five concepts or "right things to do" to organize our thinking and actions as we set about the reinvention of schools and our programs for the preparation of professional educators (a sixth was added later). Early drafts were shared with faculty and school district leaders. Changes were many. After several drafts, copies were distributed to all college faculty. The deans met with the faculty and chairs of each department to discuss the appropriateness of the set of "right things to do" for restructuring and reculturing schools and to explore implications for the programs of the college. What we achieved, while short of consensus, was a substantial agreement about the right things to do to reinvent schools and the university programs that prepare professionals for these schools.

We decided that the reinvention should: 1) Create greater continuity and quality in the caring relationships among children and between children and adults; 2) reinvent learning environments to create positive interdependence among students, and between students and faculty; 3) create active, cooperative learning environments, where knowledge is gained in a manner relevant to the life experiences and concerns of the learners and in which our increasing diversity is celebrated; 4) infuse technology in ways that enable teachers to spend more time working with children individually or in small groups; 5) create high-option environments for students, parents, faculty, and staff; 6) reinvent the teaching profession to make it a more attractive alternative for our best and brightest; 7) create a level playing field in terms of infrastructure support and time-on-task to support the achievement of world-class outcomes.

These "right things to do" were not identified to specify the strategies for reinvention, but rather to serve as process standards against which proposed strategies for reinvention of schools and for the reinvention of the programs that prepare professionals for the schools could be evaluated. While these "right things to do" were not originally conceived to serve the needs of special education, the outcomes for special education have been very positive. For each of the "right things to do," Table 12.1 provides a brief statement of the implications for reinventing schools, reinventing teacher education, and reconceiving special education and its relationships to general education.

Desired was the development of a plan for the coordinated reinvention of schools and of our programs that prepare professionals for the schools. A network of professional development schools, committed to reinvention agendas that included the six organizing concepts, outlined in the table on page 247, in their philosophical value ground, was planned. We believed that the organizing concepts, or "right things to do" that were identified, met the criteria of being right enough to create consensus among a sufficient number of school district and university leaders and faculty, but were not so prescriptive as to limit the creativity of leaders and faculty in individual schools or among college faculty. An alliance of the school districts of the Florida Suncoast was begun.

TABLE 12.1
The "Right Things to Do" for Reinventing Schools, Reinventing Teacher Education, and Reconceiving Special Education.

Reinventing Schools	Reinventing Teacher Education	Reconceiving Special Education
1. *Provide a continuity of caring for children.*	*Create a caring community among faculty, staff, and students.*	*Extend the caring community to include students with disabilities.*
Invent ways for teams of teachers to work with the same children for several years. This will provide teachers and students an opportunity to build long-term, mutually supportive relationships. Define the caring of the school to encompass the child's need for a safe environment after school, and for health, nutritional, and medical care.	A community with shared values whose members work toward achievement of a common agenda. A community, characterized by trust, in which each member knows that the others are committed to achieving the shared agenda at a level which transcends self-interest, and each member feels enriched by a colleague's gain and diminished by a colleague's loss.	Create a supportive culture in regular classrooms. Needed is a culture in which nonexceptional students support the learning of exceptional students and see them as valued members of the classroom community.
2. *Reinvent the learning environment to create positive interdependence among students.*	*Reinvent the learning environments of the college.*	*Provide students with disabilities the skills they need to function in a cooperative learning environment.*
Create "positive interdependence" among students and between students and teachers. Invent a learning environment in which it is both appropriate and expected that students will work together in groups as mutual learners, carers, and sharers. Continuous progress, cooperative learning, and integrated curriculum which celebrates our diversity, are promising elements for the reinvented learning environment.	Create "positive interdependence" among students and between students and faculty. Create learning environments in which it is both appropriate and expected that students and faculty will work together in groups as mutual learners, carers, and sharers. Cooperative, active learning in a context that relates new learning to the work and life experiences of the learner, while celebrating our increasing diversity, will be appropriate.	Inclusion of students with disabilities in competitive learning environments often has negative effects on exceptional and regular students. When positive interdependence exists, all students celebrate the learning of other students.

TABLE 12.1—*Continued*
The "Right Things to Do" for Reinventing Schools, Reinventing Teacher Education, and Reconceiving Special Education.

Reinventing Schools	Reinventing Teacher Education	Reconceiving Special Education
3. Infuse technology.	*Infuse technology.*	*Infuse technology.*
Use technology as the primary medium for the delivery of information. This will free the 60–80% of time teachers spend giving information. This time can be reinvested in the more uniquely human roles of helping students learn to think with information, modeling verbal and critical thinking skills, and providing children with continuity and connection. Universal access for all students to the full range of media is a primary goal.	Model for students in the college the most effective use of technology in instruction. Strive to make technology the primary medium for the delivery of information both on-campus and through distance learning. This will free the time we typically spend giving information. This time can be reinvested in the more uniquely human roles of helping students think with information, modeling verbal and critical thinking skills, and providing continuity and connection.	In addition to the benefits of technology which accrue to all students, technology holds particular promise for mitigating the impact of handicapping conditions.
4. Create a "high-option" environment.	*Create a "high-option" environment.*	*Create a "high-option" environment.*
A high-option environment for teachers, students and parents is needed to support the diversity that will lead to identification of "break the mold" alternatives. By eliminating many of the fears that power resistance to change, a high-option environment will free teachers and administrators to explore promising alternatives and will support the development of schools as self-renewing organizations.	Finding new "right things to do" requires that faculty have the choice to pursue promising alternatives. New "channels of opportunity" are needed through which faculty and students can find the "right things to do." To assure a positive future, we must find ways to nurture and celebrate innovations, whether or not they serve our short-term interests.	Exceptional students can thrive best in a high-option environment of services which allows them to seek out the alternatives for which their capabilities are best suited. Funding then follows the needs of the child rather than driving the system in ways that often limit the options available to the child.

TABLE 12.1—*Continued*
The "Right Things to Do" for Reinventing Schools, Reinventing Teacher Education, and Reconceiving Special Education.

Reinventing Schools	Reinventing Teacher Education	Reconceiving Special Education
5. *Reinvent the teaching profession.*	*Reinvent the role of the university professor—build college-school relationships.*	*Integrate much of the preparation program for students of exceptional education with the regular curriculum.*
Develop new rules, roles, and relationships among teachers, students, administrators, parents, and community which make teaching a more attractive and satisfying alternative for able men and women.	Inventing the schools of tomorrow requires that we simultaneously change schools and the programs that prepare professionals for these schools. If we are to participate meaningfully in this reinvention, we must be involved in the reinvention of both on a daily basis.	Blur the lines between special education and general education. In the future, teachers will need the skills to work with a very diverse group of students. The role of the regular classroom teacher in the education of students with disabilities will be increased.
6. *Create a level playing field.*	*Participate with the school districts, and state and federal legislatures in the effort to create a world-class infrastructure for education.*	*Expand current services available for students with disabilities so that all students can be better served.*
If American schools are to succeed in achieving "world-class" outcomes, we must achieve world-class standards with respect to length of school day, length of school year, preparation of Pre-K children for school, and time-on-task in learning areas.	Prepare professional educators who are committed to world-class outcomes and understand what it takes to achieve them.	The infrastructure that has been created to protect the rights and provide services for students with disabilities is a forerunner of full-service schools that are needed to support world-class standards.

THE SUNCOAST ALLIANCE FOR SCHOOL IMPROVEMENT (SASI)

The planning documents for what is now called the Suncoast Alliance for School Improvement reasoned as follows.

If we are to succeed in the simultaneous reinvention of schools and the programs which prepare professionals for the schools, we must develop an alliance for excellence that includes the school districts and the university, the legislative and business communities, and parents, working together to implement the restructuring agenda. For the university, accepting this shared leadership role implies involvement with schools at a level not normally characteristic of institutions of higher education.

Implied in this notion for the university is:

- sharing control of our programs with school districts;
- giving up the "expert" model;
- blurring the lines of relationship between college faculty and school faculties, and between faculties of various departments within the college. The lines between teacher preparation programs in special education and general education are exemplary;
- changing the nature of our research to make it more directly relevant to the invention of new practice; and
- changing our reward system to place applied research and service in primary positions.

Successful leadership of change requires attention to the comfort level of the participants in school districts and universities, and in general education and special education. The old right things to do rest comfortably in policies, precedents, and habits of the mind. The long-entrenched bureaucracies of our educational system (at both the K–12 and university level) are resistant to change. The disquieting prospect of changing habits of the mind and heart nurtures much of the acknowledged resistance to change. Support of those who lead change is needed if the sources of resistance to change are to give way to the rightness of the change. The membership of the Alliance will include leaders from business, local government, the state legislature, education, parents, and the community. The Alliance will have as its charge to do whatever is needed to identify and implement the educational restructuring agenda. The Alliance will have a membership which, collectively, can gather information, examine alternatives, exert influence, promote changes in laws, and insist that the needed changes in our educational system are implemented.

At both the school district and the university, support will be required for getting roadblocks out of the way, making sure that available resources are used most effectively, providing adequate time for planning, and ensuring that teachers play a key role and are able to work toward achieving the desired end product without being constrained by prescribed and/or traditional processes.

The Alliance will support university, school district, and school-level leaders in clearing the way for change.

The Alliance will support university, district, and school-level leaders who:

- Recognize that supporting and evaluating a diversity of approaches is the best way to find the "right things to do."

- Recognize that while "doing the right things" is compatible with top-down decision making, finding "the right things to do" requires both "site-based" and "shared" decision making.
- Implement policies which support and encourage innovation and risk taking. Affirm diversity and provide resources to support innovation. View less-than-hoped-for results as results from which we can learn and progress. Communicate that it's OK not to have all the answers. Acknowledge that we are moving into uncharted waters and that occasional grounding on an unmarked shoal is to be expected.
- Be willing to change the rules, roles, and relationships among teachers, students, parents, and administrators in the interest of providing a better education.
- Provide opportunities for administrators and teachers to develop knowledge and skills needed to fill new roles and function effectively in changed relationships. Examples of needed skills include team building, cooperative planning, consensus building, and conflict resolution.
- Retrain non-teaching professional staff to fulfill new roles as supporters, linkers and technical assistance providers.
- Emphasize internally and externally that what happens at the school and student-team and teacher-team levels is of greatest importance. Soft-pedal administrative activities.
- View education as an upscale activity—one in which quality of output is more important than obtaining results quickly or doing the job at the lowest cost.
- Implied for special education is participation in the redesign of school and university programs to facilitate inclusion and regular education initiatives. The Alliance will support systemic changes that promote viewing inclusion both as a process in which special education students are included in "regular" classrooms and general education students benefit from inclusion of instructional practices long successful in special education and which are appropriate to the new general education paradigm.

The Alliance will support university leaders in clearing the way for change.

In addition to the criteria stated above, the Alliance will support university-level leaders who:

- Recognize effective participation in the coordinated effort to reinvent schools and the programs which prepare professionals for the schools as fundamental to the mission of the university. Give major weight to these activities in the evaluation of faculty performance and in tenure and promotion decisions.
- Recognize that university faculty and administrators must model the instructional and leadership practices they espouse.

- Legitimize new strategies as outlined below for pursuing the teaching and research missions of the university.
- Provide opportunities for faculty to explore alternative paradigms of inquiry and to develop knowledge and skills needed to function effectively within the new research and teaching agendas.
- Give substantial weight in the hiring of new faculty to their interest in and potential for contributing to the success of the educational restructuring agenda.

The Teaching Agenda

The university will enter into partnerships with school districts for the operation of Professional Development Schools. These schools will become major laboratories for the reinvention of schools and for the preparation of professional educators. Each school will be the primary workplace for one or more members of the university faculty. They will function as members of the faculty of the school, as well as university faculty. The university faculty members will coordinate the instructional programs offered by the university at their site, model effective classroom teaching for students and school faculty, and coordinate the research agenda outlined below. Many of the school faculty will serve as clinical faculty in the teacher preparation program of the university. The teacher education faculty of the university, whether housed in Education, Arts and Sciences, Fine Arts, Business, or Engineering should define a common agenda and should model the teaching practices they espouse. (Five partnerships of this type are discussed in Section One of Part Two.)

The Research Agenda: Alternatives

The university faculty housed at each school will collaborate with the school faculty in the identification, implementation, and evaluation of promising new directions for the improvement of the school. The research agenda is directed toward: 1) identifying promising alternatives for the improvement of schools; 2) implementing and evaluating these alternatives in "live" school settings; and 3) the productive, coordinated restructuring of schools and the university programs which prepare teachers and administrators for the schools.

Centennial Elementary School—An example. Centennial Elementary School in Pasco County was the first elementary school in the SASI network of professional development schools. There had been a long-term mutually supportive relationship between the College of Education and the Pasco County Schools. Training in communications skills, learning styles, cooperative learning, and integrated curricula had been provided to large numbers of teachers, and training in Managing Productive Schools (a program providing facilitation in group problem-solving skills for administrators) to most of the principals. Centennial was identified by the assistant superintendent for instruction as having exceptional promise for moving ahead successfully with the change agenda.

The program that emerged, referred to as Continuous Progress, included 1) ungraded multi-aged groups of 100–110 students working together in a common space, 2) teams of four teachers working with the same group of heterogeneously grouped students for approximately three years, and 3) learning environments that emphasized thematic teaching and cooperative learning. The school is built using the pod concept. Pods are referred to as "houses." Each house includes four classrooms with moveable walls which open onto a large common area. Primary houses include children who, in the graded structure, would have been classified K–2. Intermediate houses include children who would have been classified as grades 3–5. Each house is multiaged, including students at different progress levels throughout the range indicated. The program developed by the Centennial teachers and principal involves five organizing concepts, as follows.

1. *Create a Continuity of Caring for Children.* Teachers who participate in the programs organize into teams of four teachers who work with the same group of children for approximately three years. All four teachers work with all of the children. The walls are open most of the time. Children return to the same team of teachers for three years.

2. *Reinvent the Learning Environment to Create Positive Interdependence.* The objective is to create a cooperative rather than a competitive learning environment. Cooperative learning is a primary medium for instruction. The curriculum is integrated. Each team develops themes around which the full range of the curriculum can be taught. As new themes are developed, they are shared among the teams. Thus instead of individual faculty members working with a group of students, Centennial uses teams of four faculty who work with a larger cohort (100+) students.

3. *Infuse Technology.* This is a major item on the developmental agenda of the school. Centennial is a member school of the Schoolyear 2000 project—a Florida project to more fully utilize technology in instruction, but most of this development is still in the future.

4. *Create a "High Option" Environment.* Throughout the development of the program, options have been provided to teachers, students, and parents. At its inception, teachers elected to become a USF professional development school. At the beginning of the effort teachers were asked to volunteer to be the "paradigm pioneers." Fewer than 20 percent volunteered to participate during the first year. Also, in the first year, the program was described to parents who were given the option of having their children included in the program. Approximately 15 percent of the parents chose to participate. The second year, the choices were offered to both groups again. At that time more than half of the teachers and parents indicated a desire to participate in the program. By the beginning of the third year, almost all teachers and parents were ready to embrace the program. The high-option environment permitted very

substantial change in the school program without generating significant opposition from teachers, parents or community.

5. *Reinvent the Teaching Profession.* The new rules, roles, and relationships that are characteristic of this emerging model go a long way toward positive reinvention of the teaching profession. Below are two "what's wrong with teaching" comments often made by teachers in self-contained graded classrooms.

- Teaching is too lonely. "Much as I love the kids, working as the only adult with them all day long, and then spending two to four hours alone grading papers and planning for the next day leaves me sort of empty and wishing for more adult companionship."

   The team of teachers working together with a larger group of students eliminates this problem. Teachers work with each other every day in the interests of the children.

- Teaching is too confining. "They didn't tell me when I was preparing to teach that a major requirement was a good bladder. Forgive me for that, but it illustrates my point. The way we have teaching set up, teachers are so confined that they cannot take time to meet the basic needs as individuals, or as members of a family in which both parents work."

   A good bladder is no longer a prime requirement for successful teaching. A teacher can leave the classroom in the hands of the other three teachers as needed. If a teacher is ill, she need not worry that her students are in the hands of a substitute who does not have sufficient knowledge of their needs or their progress to use the time of the students well. We have quadrupled the probability that every child will have at least one teacher with whom he/she relates well.

- Too much to do, and too little time. "The needs of some of these children are so great, I have to be surrogate mother and teacher, and sometimes counselor. Then, just as I am really getting to understand their needs and get a handle on how to meet them, the year is over and I am getting ready for a new group of students."

As our society has changed, the balance of responsibility for nurturing, informing, and empowering our children and youth has shifted from the home to the school. Neither the resources allocated nor the time committed to education have been adequately changed to enable teachers to address these additional expectations. However, the continuing four-teacher team is more productive because is allows the team of teachers to draw on their collective knowledge and nurturing skills over an extended period of time with the same children. It also eliminates the loneliness and reduces the extent to which teaching is too confining.

These are promising beginnings in the reinvention of schools. A not fully anticipated positive outcome of the newly invented and now evolving model is the extent
to which it facilitates the inclusion of children with disabilities in the houses.
Approximately 20 percent of children at Centennial Elementary have some form
of disability. Special education teachers work collaboratively with regular teachers
to include children with disabilities. The multiaged cooperative-learning environment creates a context in which children with disabilities can be included and supported by the other students. When students function as co-teachers, the learning of
students with disabilities is incorporated into the regular patterns of teachers and
students working together and celebrating the achievement of each student. This
is done with a sense of pride and accomplishment for the achievement of students
with disabilities that would not be likely to occur in the competitive classroom.

SUMMARY

The past fifty years have been a time of rapid change in our society. These changes
have restructured the rules, roles, and relationships which prevailed when our existing system of schooling was invented. Responding effectively to the needs of children and society in our time requires a rethinking of our assumptions about
education, and a restructuring of the rules, roles, and relationships among administrators, district staff, teachers, parents, and the larger community. Reallocation of
resources and redefinition of the role of leadership in education are logical outcomes. The goal is the invention of a new educational system. By modeling the
power of working together toward shared positive goals, this new system will help
children recognize the interconnectedness of us all and understand the power that
we have together to make a better world. Such a system will provide superior educational opportunities for all of America's children and present them to our society
as superior human capital ready for investment in our information society. Through
their worthy citizenship, we can create a better world and provide leadership
toward creating a better quality of life for all people.

The old "right things to do" are not good enough. We must identify a new set of
"right things to do" which are appropriate to our time. Six "right things to do" have
been identified which can organize our efforts to restructure in ways that respond
effectively to the needs of children and society.

These key strategies are: 1) restructuring in ways that will provide a continuity of
caring for all children; 2) reinvention of the learning environment to create positive interdependence among students and between students and teachers—an environment in which it is appropriate and expected for students to work together in
groups as mutual learners, carers, and sharers; 3) providing all students access to the
full range of technology and using technology as the primary system for the delivery of information; 4) creating a high-option environment for students, parents, and
teachers; 5) reinventing the teaching profession in ways that will enable the profession to attract and retain more of the best and brightest talent; and 6) creating a

level playing field in expectations for world-class educational outcomes which are paired with world-class standards for our educational infrastructure. The success of the change agenda depends on the simultaneous, or at least coordinated, implementation of the key strategies. The reinvented learning environment contributes to the creation of a continuity of caring. The high-option environment for teachers, students, and parents is needed to create a climate in which alternatives can be tested. Using the technology for information delivery frees teachers to invest more of their time in helping students think with information and for creating a context in which students function as mutually supportive learners. Reinventing the teaching profession will assure the availability of the quality human resources needed to create America's schools as self-renewing organizations. Achievement of world-class standards for our educational infrastructure provides the foundation on which the other "right things to do" rest.

The implications for special education are challenging. Within the field, creative thinking about how educational practice could better serve the interests of handicapped children has blurred the lines of demarcation between special and general education. Changing the "the habits of the mind and heart" which treasure the traditional distinctions between general and special education is difficult enough. Fear that further blurring of the lines between general and special education might result in a loss or dilution of supplemental funding now available for handicapped children provides an even more daunting obstacle to change. We must find a way to affirm the moral mission of inclusion, while maintaining the technical and resource capacity, and the will to nurture and teach all children. Together we can teach all children; together we can find a way.

We believe that America can once again lead the world in the quality of its educational system and the quality of life of its people. We also believe that our nation, and all nations for that matter, have a globally sensitive mission to exercise responsible stewardship of the human resources now in our care. The best interests of all of us are served if we fully develop the potential of each of us. To this end we make our statement of faith in the teachers of today, and our commitment to excellence in the schools of tomorrow.

REFERENCES

Barrett, M. J. (1990). The case for more school days. *The Atlantic.* p. 80.

Bennis, W., & Naus, B. (1985). *Leaders: The strategies for taking charge.* New York: Harper & Row.

Florida Commision on Education Reform and Accountability (1992). *Blueprint 2000.*

Goodlad, J. (1990). *Teachers for our nation's schools.* San Francisco: Jossey-Bass.

Katzenmeyer, W. (1993). *Inventing the schools of tomorrow.* Unpublished manuscript, University of South Florida, College of Education, Tampa.

U. S. Department of Labor. (1991). *What work requires of schools: A SCANS report for America 2000.* Report of the Secretaries' Commission on Achieving Necessary Skills. Washington, DC.

U. S. Department of Labor. (April, 1992). *Learning a living: A blueprint for high performance.* Report of the Secretaries' Commission on Achieving Necessary Skills. Washington, DC.

CHAPTER 13

EDUCATING TEACHERS
FOR ALL CHILDREN
Clinical, Political, and Social
Constructions of Teacher Education

JAMES PAUL, HOWARD JOHNSTON, & SHIRLEY RAINES

INTRODUCTION

AS chairs of the Departments of Special Education, Secondary Education, and Childhood Language Arts/Reading Education respectively at the University of South Florida, we work in a creative environment of academic and school leaders committed to restructuring education. The diverse urban area surrounding the university is serving as a laboratory in which to test the collaborative and inventive capacity of the College of Education. The faculty, led by an imaginative dean who is committed to education reform, are attempting to address the principles of school reform, which challenge the core values and practices of traditional teacher education and leadership training programs. The essence of faculty work and the nature of research, as well as the basic moral and technical conceptions of curriculum, are being reexamined in light of those principles.

The College of Education is seeking to blur institutional boundaries that separate the work of teacher educators and educational researchers from the work of teachers and other school leaders by developing serious university-school collaborations. Central to these collaborative initiatives is a commitment to integrating the perspectives and activities of departments within the university that have been separated by philosophies and practices that reflect educational models no longer considered viable. The separation of special education from general education is an example.

The focus of the discussion that follows is on ideological, ethical, bureaucratic, and operational issues we and our colleagues are addressing as partners with local school leaders as we change ourselves and the schools with which we work. We are attempting to create an integrated collaborative program among our departments and between our departments and public schools. The chapter is divided into discussions of the complexity and both the local and national contexts for collaboration, how the authors came together to form a productive partnership, the forces that have facilitated and those that have challenged the partnership, and gains we are realizing from our work together.

THE NATURE OF COLLABORATION

If restructuring is the trademark of school reform, partnership is the trademark of reforming the teacher education system. There is wide consensus that the education of teachers must change to support the philosophy and meet the needs of restructured schools. There is equally wide support for the idea that the needed changes must be brought about through partnerships.

The interest in partnerships, in all of their complexity, has focused mostly on university-school relationships. Equally complex, however, are the partnerships that must be effected within the university. In order for the university to bring a common voice to the discussion of interests with schools, there is a great deal of work that needs to be done within the university.

Serious partnerships are complex and difficult to effect. Unlike traditional interagency forums in which the vested interests of each agency are protected from the actions of the whole, partnerships that place philosophy, values, resources, and standard practice on the line are difficult to develop. The difficulty comes from the complex ethical, psychological, and political issues often faced in working openly and in solidarity with colleagues as partners.

The ethical issues derive largely from the self-interest which always operates in collaborative relationships. The question is not whether or not there is self-interest but rather the way it is understood and managed. In order for trusting partnerships to work, self-interest has to be redefined so that the common interest reflects the interest of each partner. The interest of the partnership, the common good, has to become the central interest of each partner if the relationship is to move beyond competition and cunning, however gracious and sophisticated the acts aimed at advantaging one's own position may be.

The collective interest can define and take precedence over the individual or self-interest when at least two conditions are met. First, the individual interest is perceived to be in jeopardy, and there is understanding that an ethic of solidarity in fact enhances and secures the individual interest more than an ethic of competition. This can occur, for example, when it is understood that the synergistic by-product of joining forces can, in fact, create new resources for all partners. It can also create a political advantage of speaking with a common voice. Second, the members must be able to trust one another. The conditions and chemistry of trust vary with the character and personality of the individuals.

In addition to the ethical, psychological, and political issues, partnerships occur in organizational contexts. Whatever the perceived highest good, the psychological predisposition of the participants, or the political agendas, the organizational environment must be capable of supporting partnership initiatives. A "business as usual" and rule-driven organizational ethos is not likely to invent or be receptive to serious partnerships. Partnerships are more likely to be nurtured and to thrive in open and principle-guided environments.

Centrifugal and Centripetal Forces Impacting Partnerships

There are strong centrifugal forces within the education environment that tend to disunite and pull us away from any common, integrated, holistic perspective. Among these forces are our organization of knowledge in the university, entrenched professional guilds, and the politics of certification.

Knowledge has traditionally been organized and divided into distinct categories with clear boundaries. There are, for example, pedagogy, social foundations, psychological foundations, special education, elementary education, early childhood education, reading, secondary education, research methods, and so forth. The blurring of the traditional boundaries of these bodies of knowledge and practice poses philosophical and guild challenges. There are real differences in the assumptions and practices of different departments within colleges of education. How can these fundamental differences be resolved?

While philosophers of science have moved beyond understanding knowledge as discrete and compartmentalized entities, most educators have not been prepared to integrate knowledge or to deal with the fundamental issues of foundations or foundationalism. Philosophers whose work focuses on the nature of knowledge and values, for the most part, have not been interested in working on educational problems. This has resulted in moral and epistemological conundrums in educational thought.

Closely related to the hegemonies of selective perspectives within the sciences and arts of education are the politics of professional guilds. Each of the guilds has its national organization(s), journal(s), history, philosophy(s) of practice, and so forth. Deeply linked to the domain-specific knowledge structure reflected in the university's organizational pattern and the independent professional guilds, is the complex political system for certification. It is doubtful that many would consider the present system for certification to be rational. It varies by state, and there is considerable variability within states in specific definitions and certification requirements. Yet, partnerships that would yield productive program development are stymied by the system created to control and maintain standards. These features combine to form a significant political force that must be addressed in any serious partnership.

Equally strong are the centripetal forces that are now tending to coalesce the perspectives and forces within education. These include political and economic forces and deep changes in philosophy. One of the basic reasons for restructuring schools is to reduce our economic risk as a nation. The political forces, described in

Chapter 1, are requiring educators to be accountable for outcomes that better serve the competitive international interest of the country. The political infrastructure of education, with guilds tightly formed around questionable assumptions about their independence, are finding it difficult to bear the weight of public accountability for outcomes. The difficulty is compounded by the complex philosophical differences within the guilds. For example, special education is a subsystem of public education that has been characterized more by its separateness from than its connectedness to general education. A major policy question now facing special and general educators is the appropriate relationship between the two. This involves ethical (what is the right thing to do?) as well as empirical (how well are we doing what we intend?) questions. While efficacy data questioning pull-out programs have been available for almost three decades, the school reform movement since the early 1980s has produced an inclusion movement that would, if fully implemented, end pull-out in schools. The questions of practicality and moral questions having to do with the best interests of children with disabilities are now being debated. The debate is troubled by the fact that some are arguing data while others are arguing interests, and policy makers are forced to bring together and integrate empirical and moral arguments.

Educational philosophy and the epistemology of traditional educational research have not developed a discourse for this kind of integration. However, policy makers, practitioners, and researchers are now getting some help in recasting the arguments. There is a growing number of educators who are beginning to address the foundational paradigmatic and ethical problems, largely within the general context of postmodern philosophy (Noblit, 1992; Noddings, 1992; Poplin, 1992; Rhodes, 1993; Skrtic, 1991; Stone, 1992; 1993). Others are helping address the ethical issues within the general post-positive discourse and moral perspectives of education (Howe & Miramontes, 1992; Paul et al., 1993).

The paradigm shift that is occurring is freeing the thinking about education and empowering its malcontents. There is an ethos for educational research dramatically different from that found in most colleges of education only a decade ago. Educational researchers and practitioners have not rushed to feast at the postmodern banquet. Those who have, however, have created a different menu of askable questions and thinkable thoughts that have profound implications for both inquiry and practice. Others have gathered at another table. They have focused attention on particular critical stances—feminist, Marxist, advocacy, and so on—and have examined education from those stances. Both postmodern philosophers and critical theorists have challenged the tenets and the moral and pedagogical consequences of post-positivism. While advocates of these general perspectives have drawn out paradigmatic differences, they have at the same time created a discourse in which traditional boundaries have faded and new intellectual unions are being created. There are no "postmodern" or "postpositive" or "critical" departments. Individuals within traditional departments are finding new colleagues and creating new intellectual pacts, where there are common questions about practice and similar interests in creating new and different understandings.

We have viewed our growing partnership in this broad philosophical context. There have been clear, and some not so clear, centripetal forces that have helped us create a strong working partnership. These have occurred in spite of equally strong centrifugal forces that, if permitted, would have had us conducting competitive business as usual.

Our analysis of the forces that have impacted our collaboration included personal, professional, philosophical, and political dimensions. Realizing that these dimensions are relevant as contributors or distracters to any serious collaboration, we thought it reasonable to share what we are learning about ourselves and our work as chairs in this context.

BACKGROUND OF THE USF COLLABORATION AMONG THE DEPARTMENTS OF ELEMENTARY, SECONDARY, AND SPECIAL EDUCATION

All three of us have come to USF within the past five years. We came from major research universities, including the University of Cincinnati, George Mason University, and the University of North Carolina, where there were strong teacher education programs. We came, in large part, because we were captured by a spirit of invention and a vision of possibilities in addressing complex issues in school reform in a high-energy environment at one of the largest colleges of education in the country. Each of us was attracted to the idea of working in a dynamic transformational process with a visionary dean committed to serious collaboration with public schools and to reinventing teacher education to meet the needs of restructured schools of the future. The vision of the college, described by Katzenmeyer in chapter 10, included a climate of positive collegial regard and decentralized management which offered flexibility to departments and to individual faculty. There were enormous barriers, including inadequate resources and the cumbersome bureaucracy of a large (about 35,000 students) and relatively young university (about 35 years old). These barriers notwithstanding, it seemed clear to us that the university and the area it serves, including two of the 20 largest school systems in the country, afforded unique experimental and innovative opportunities. We have pursued these opportunities in partnership with chairs of other departments in the College of Education and with our colleagues in public schools.

Each of us has been working from a particular moral stance relative to the educational and social welfare of children. As we have told each other bits and pieces of our stories over the past few years, essentially what we believe about children, education, research, schools, change, and other topics of moral import, we have become aware of the values and philosophical perspectives we share that have made our work together productive and meaningful. As we have worked together in the midst of revenue shortfalls, which could bring out the competitive side of otherwise cooperative and generous colleagues, and in an academic environment typically characterized more by territoriality than by shared missions and resources, we have found ourselves working harder to avoid the pitfalls each of us knew in our own experiences.

Each of us had considerable experience in teacher education and had, we later discovered, similar philosophical roots in the advocacy-oriented reforms for children dating back to the 1960s. We had worked with children who were poor and children with disabilities. More recently, we had worked in higher education long enough to appreciate most of the barriers to change but not long enough to become cynical about possibilities for change.

Reflecting on the historical context of our individual perspectives, the environment in which we now work, and the professional and personal relationships that have emerged all have been instructive. This reflection has led us to approach the topic of clinical, social, and political constructions of teacher education from a narrative perspective. Each of us is a part of a story of educational change. As this book indicates, especially in Section Two, much has been accomplished together. The accomplishments—works in progress—reflect complex stories of individuals and small groups bringing thoughtful and informed perspectives to bear on commonly perceived problems. There are no "answers" that were "discovered" along the way. Rather, there are working understandings, products of the imaginative and value-driven constructions of those seeking to know more and, frequently, to know differently.

The process in which we are participating has an explicit ethic of challenging every assumption of teacher education as we have known it, from the methods of practice to the nature of the knowledge we seek. This process could be hostile and discouraging if it were not accompanied by another explicit ethic—namely, an ethic of caring and positive regard for those who hold onto questionable assumptions and beliefs as well as those who challenge them. This involves living with uncertainty, doing things very differently, giving up the pretense of knowing all we need to, or even are expected to know, and trusting the process. We find the new challenges include basic things like blurring the boundaries of well-established traditional territories, trying new ways of working, becoming a close ally with individuals from disciplines unfamiliar to us, and thinking differently about basic aspects of our work, such as how we do research and how we understand the research we do. Most of us were not "trained" or educated to work this way. If we were fortunate enough to have good models and mentors, they did not do business this way. We share a commitment to work toward the realization of a mature, reflective, and caring community that can look deeply, critically, and sympathetically at itself. We have found this vision to be meaningful as a guide for our work together.

Our work has been situated within several contexts. We will discuss three of those contexts—how we came together in our work, how our own personal stories helped get us together (because of space limitations, we will tell only one of the stories), the college and university in which we work, and the professional areas of which each of us is a part.

Coming Together

Inside of most higher education institutions, the deck is pretty thoroughly stacked against department chairs who would attempt to consolidate their efforts, integrate their preparation programs, and, ultimately, blur the distinctions between and among their units and their functions. Even people of supreme good will and noble intention will be thwarted by institutional policies, practices, traditions, and role expectations which reinforce a view that universities are collections of expert systems and that the organization of these systems is a logical and rational product of the inherent logic of the disciplines themselves.

Department chairs are rewarded by their faculties for the extent to which they reinforce the department's boundaries, operationally defined as protecting resources, the integrity of its discipline, and the intellectual territory in which they reap their student enrollments. Attempts to integrate programs or share resources are often accompanied by protests about what the collaborating departments must give up, or, worse, how the integrity, wholeness, breadth, and depth of their academic program will suffer. Clearly, if a special educator is to learn about technology, or a secondary educator to learn about disabilities, something must be taken out of the existing (and presumably rigorous) program.

Such is the nature of expert systems. No one is as expert as someone inside the system; thus, no one knows better what an expert-in-training must know than those who are already expert. Chairs tamper with such beliefs at their peril.

Why would three intelligent chairs, with over half a century of higher education experience among them, each respected in their fields, all in congenial relations with their departmental faculty attempt to integrate programs, blur boundaries, and prepare students by crossing traditional academic lines? Obviously, there is a rational argument for pursuing the course of action laid out in this chapter. However, even high value congruence, a strong sense of advocacy for children, and deep commitment to an ethic of caring might not have been enough to encourage risky behavior inside of the academy. We had all been in other environments and contexts where, despite shared values and deep commitments, our progress toward integration was notably difficult and inadequate.

After considerable reflection over more lunches and meetings than we can probably count, we agreed that there is a teleological dimension to relationships that produces substantial and revolutionary change inside of institutions. Somehow, we had to come to share a deep faith in an ultimate purpose in our work. At the risk of disclosing more than can be easily borne by an institution that prizes rationality above all else, there is a commonality of spirit which produces a judicious level of zealousness in pursuing a common agenda. Our shared view of purpose had led to a deep and trusting friendship, and just as friends might share a passion for the Yankees or the Bears, we share a passion about child advocacy and the centrality of teachers in the lives of children that compels us, sometimes at some cost, toward common goals.

We came together not because the institution required us to do so, but because we were drawn toward one another in ways that made us major investors in each other's success. One of us was hired, in part to produce a revolution, by a dean who believed that it is best to select people with whom you share deep commitments and beliefs and let them design the job they are best able to perform. That chair participated, albeit indirectly, in the hiring of the next chair, and he presided over the search that found the third. Frankly, and simply, we liked each other.

That is, of course, too simple an explanation for why experienced academics would undertake the enterprise of integration described here. Moreover, it is such an ephemeral condition that it makes the University of South Florida experience seem nontransportable. If, in fact, it is necessary for all interested parties to have strong personal affinities, other institutions can easily dismiss our experience as being much too dependent upon personal relationship and not sufficiently faithful to the dictums of organizational development or systems change theory.

There are conditions of friendship and commitment, though, which can be described and perhaps even replicated inside of institutions. They are the kinds of relationships that fuel profound developments because they permit everyone to focus on the agenda before them and not upon the nuances of utterances or agendas that are hidden. The qualities that characterize these relationships are trust, commitment, affirmation, affection, and vulnerability.

Trust means, in essence, that we each believe the other is committed to the agenda before us and does not use it to gain some form of advantage over the other. In short, we believe that each of us has set aside the competitive agenda which will benefit our individual units at the expense of another and that our actions are predicated on a shared view of the common good. This trust is manifested in both word and deed. We have had to commit precious and scarce resources to the common agenda (including sharing the cost of jointly appointed faculty or bearing the very real fiscal and personnel costs of developing joint ventures), advocate policy and procedural changes in institutional governance forums which might affect the resource position of our own units, and advance sometimes unpopular agendas inside of our own units to promote a collaborative enterprise. Trust among this group was an a priori decision. We decided to trust each other and hoped that we would have evidence that our trust was well placed. Fortunately, it has been.

Commitment is the rational side of a friendship. It is an awareness that attachment to an individual or group is, in the long run, in our own best interest. Because each of us reads the educational landscape in similar ways, we believe that an integrated, collaborative approach is the best hope for successful individual and collective futures.

Affirmation is the simple act of dusting each other off when we take a nasty spill. Because we are all operating in ways that are unfamiliar inside of traditional institutions and which are unlikely to be rewarded in conventional ways, we have accepted the responsibility for affirming one another in both college-wide forums and within our own units. This means that we celebrate our individual and collective successes, cite one another as exemplars of a new way of doing our work, and help one another succeed professionally. We collaborate on research, in teaching, on the solicitation of funding, and on pursuing cultural and policy changes within the college and university.

Affection seems to be a quaint dimension in a thoroughly systematized, organized, and managed world. However, we attribute some of our success, or at least our commitment, to the fact that we genuinely like each other. And that affection, instead of affecting our ability to make objective judgments about collaborative enterprises, helps us to know that what we are hearing from one another is honest, direct, and in our own best interest.

Vulnerability, when shared, reduces the need for defenses. Because we share (indeed, display) our vulnerabilities, uncertainties, and difficulties with one another, we become invested in each other's lives in ways that engender trust. If you know that your collaborator is as vulnerable as you are, there is no need to protect yourself from him or her. If you know that you share weaknesses, it is easier to find strength in collaboration.

It would be easier to write this chapter if we thought that meaningful collaboration was based on an entirely rational model with discrete steps and clear phases. Our own experiences seem to indicate that it is not, however, and that substantive and successful collaboration in an effort to reinvent education for all children will come from those who share a commitment to one another, a passion for their mission, and a willingness to disclose and address their own uncertainty in this revolutionary process.

While it has been useful to reflect on how we came together, it has been necessary to understand how our work is impacted by the professional guilds we represent. Each of these guilds—secondary education, elementary and early childhood education, special education, and so forth—has been going through its own metamorphosis, each propelled by the centrifugal forces and impelled by the centripetal forces that now constitute the dynamic intellectual and political environment of education reform. Following is a brief discussion of the status of these professional areas.

Challenges Facing Secondary Education

Secondary education is faced with challenges which may preclude the full inclusion of students into existing schools. The challenges may, indeed, render as obsolete the current training model used in virtually all secondary education programs.

No educational institution has been as carefully scrutinized in recent history as the secondary school. Beginning with *A Nation at Risk* in 1983, no fewer than 40 major reports on the status of secondary schools and adolescent students have been issued from governments, foundations, and highly placed, ad hoc, blue-ribbon committees. All paint a pretty grim picture. All prescribe revolutionary changes. Many of them promote contradictory missions, roles and remedies for the school.

At the same time, public policy, from graduation requirements to teacher certification regulations, promotes a view of schooling which is congruent with the national competitiveness model articulated in *A Nation at Risk*. Teacher certification regulations in virtually all states mandate a content-rich, pedagogically poor program for the preparation of secondary school teachers. The result is that secondary students, in particular, by virtue of increasingly rigorous selection and early segregation into domain-specific areas, rarely encounter peers who have difficulty learning in that given area. Competent in the field throughout high school, selected to study with others who share that competence, trained by those who are both passionate about their content and devoted to its study, most secondary students never develop a profound empathy for people who do experience difficulty with their field. (Although, ironically, in earlier studies, we found that secondary students are somewhat more likely than almost anyone else to segment talent and attribute performance to ability rather than effort. In other words, they are more likely to say, "I'm good at math, but I could never do English [itself an interesting observation for an English speaker to make]. It doesn't matter how hard I work, I just don't have the ability.")

Further, public accountability is achieved, primarily, through publicized, standardized test scores. (America recently breathed a collective sigh of relief to see that the 25-year-long slide in SAT scores may have hit bottom and started to rise a bit. It is still unclear whether that represents improvement or simply reflects a drop-out rate that is now high enough to assure that only the more affluent, more able, or more tenacious take the test at all.) Given this very clear accountability model, it is in the best interests of the institution to partition the testing population into as many discrete segments as possible, allowing them to report that students who are most comparable to those found in the less-than-egalitarian Japanese, German, British, and French systems are doing as well as or better than their foreign counterparts.

Now that the number of households with children in school has dropped to a national average of about 16 percent (down from a high of about 60% in the 1960s), fewer members of the public have a "child's eye view" of school. Fewer are in a position to assess its performance in more ephemeral terms, such as how it treats children, whether it engages them in significant activity, or whether it attends to all of their needs in a caring, compassionate way.

Despite the politically correct rhetoric of public policy makers about salvaging dropouts, addressing social concerns, and reducing the stresses of teen life, secondary schools and teachers operate under public policies which constrain all but the most innocuous efforts to reinvent schools. Accountability models were developed and integrated into public policy to assess schools' performance in areas that are linked to a national agenda of economic supremacy. Given the reciprocity that exists between public policy and public institutions, a test-driven accountability system forced the schools to become *more* like other systems that are producing problems for special needs populations.

Secondary education must simultaneously alter its own practices and, through action research and site-based inquiry, demonstrate to policy makers the effectiveness and wisdom of innovations. Further, school professionals have to become active partners, with their boards, communities, and legislatures, in the formation of public policy regarding secondary school accountability.

The challenge for the secondary school is to create both a sense of community and shared obligation for all of its learners and an instructional model which addresses the vast and complex array of talents found in a typically large school.

Challenges Facing Elementary Education

Elementary education remains a strong degree program in colleges and universities. There are greater enrollments in these programs than any others in colleges of education. However, major changes in elementary education have splintered the field. Changes include expanded expectations of the background knowledge needed to become an elementary teacher, erosion of identity because of the expansion of early childhood and middle education, appeal of specialty organizations, and roles of specialists in schools.

The basic premise of elementary education is that one teacher with a solid undergraduate background in arts and sciences is sufficiently prepared in the foundations of different disciplines to be able to teach children the content they need to know and understand. However, in recent years, the assumption that two years of coursework, usually referred to as the general education requirement, is sufficient preparation has been questioned by the Holmes Group and other state and national boards. The result is more fifth- and sixth-year teacher preparation programs or a growth in the overall numbers of required courses, so that the elementary education major is now taking five years to complete a bachelor's degree. From all sides, the elementary program is being challenged to add requirements—add more liberal arts, add more basic sciences, add more mathematics in the first two years of general education. The amount, quality, and expansiveness of the knowledge elementary teachers need in the arts and sciences is being questioned. With more students coming into college and university systems from the community colleges, particularly elementary education majors, the changes in requirements for the first two years must be communicated with changes in articulation agreements.

There is a demand from many state agencies that the teacher preparation program start field experiences at the freshman and sophomore levels, so that students can find out if they are suited for teaching. In addition, concerns for special needs of families and children have resulted in added courses in mainstreaming, more assessment courses, additional work in English as a Second Language, and a call for teachers to learn more foreign languages, to name only a few trends.

Elementary education is often called upon to be all things to all educators. However, even the identity of an "elementary school teacher" is being challenged. In the past, most states had certification systems with grade 1–8 endorsements. Usually one could add early childhood certification by taking additional coursework for teaching kindergarten. Because early childhood education has grown rapidly since the mid-60s, the definition of early childhood has been expanded to include from birth to age 8, or through grade 3. Similarly, middle grades education has also come to the forefront with concerns about the special developmental needs of sixth–ninth graders. In some instances the definition of middle grades includes fifth grade. If there are strong early childhood programs that go through third grade and middle grade education shifts down to fifth grade, taken at its extreme, the fourth grade may be considered the only elementary grade. In reality, however, both early childhood and middle grades education remain smaller programs than elementary education. In most states, elementary education continues to be defined for certification purposes as grades 1–6.

Elementary education can be so large that it loses its identity. A loss of identity is also clear in the ways professional elementary teacher organizations are formed. Aside from ACEI, which is one of the smaller national organizations and whose roots are in early childhood, there is no one elementary teacher organization. Each of the specialty organizations has elementary divisions. Yet, the elementary division remains a part of the larger groups of National Council of Teachers of English, National Council of Teachers of Mathematics, International Reading Association, and so forth.

The identity of elementary educators as a group has also been challenged by the addition of specialists in the schools. There are reading, mathematics, and physical education specialists, a variety of special education specialists, English as a Second Language, technology, art, and music specialists. Traditionally, elementary school was the place where the curriculum was connected, and instruction was planned based on the developmental needs of children in a small class with one teacher. With the addition of all of these specialists, the child's day is splintered, and the curriculum seems to many people hopelessly fractured. Yet, elementary teacher preparation is the one place where integrated curriculum, instruction based on holistic assessment, and the leadership of a teacher with a balanced background of content and methodology could orchestrate a connectedness between the world of the child and the way the world has organized disciplines, or ways of knowing.

Somehow, like Humpty-Dumpty, the splinters and fractures of preparation and actual classrooms must be put back together again.

Challenges Facing Special Education

Special education has undergone basic changes during the past 30 years. The formulation of public policies supporting special education practices during the last trimester of the twentieth century has been propelled by an increased public sense of moral responsibility for the welfare of individuals with disabilities. At the same time, it has been impeded by conflicting values guiding the development of policies to implement that responsibility.

Special education is so embedded in economic and social circumstances that policy initiatives reflect the political will and values of a period. Policy changes, therefore, may or may not be enduring or reflect the most reasoned positions. An example is the argument about an "appropriate" education for children with disabilities which has progressed through several iterations including mainstreaming, least restrictive educational environment, regular education initiative, and inclusion. The names have changed and, while there have been nuances of change in the conceptualization of "appropriate practice," the names do not reflect conceptually distinct or internally consistent views. Both the advocates for full inclusion and those for a continuum of services (what Fuchs and Fuchs [1991] called the "abolitionists" and the "conservationists") argue the data. The empirical case is not definitive for either view. The alternative case to be made is moral in nature. Again, moral arguments can be made to support both views. Part of the issue here, of course, is the value-ladenness of data understood as factual. Since Polanyi (1959), the argument that data are value-free has been problematic. The separation of the moral and empirical arguments creates pretentious political discourse and policy conundrums.

Special education policies reflect a somewhat tenuous, and sometimes fragile, interface between science and public interest. As such, these policies maintain a dynamic resonance with changes in what we know, and the regard we have for knowledge, as well as the economy, social priorities, values, and the commonly perceived work and status of public institutions. The challenge for policy makers is to maintain a balance of public interests in affordable, morally defensible, and programmatically feasible services for children with disabilities and their families.

Unfortunately, even though special education policies and practices, from the beginning, have rested on moral grounds of interest and equity, most of the professional debates historically have been on the basis of empirical and rational arguments. It is easier to argue the data than the values. Special education leaders are professionally socialized to approach issues empirically, rationally, and politically. They are not typically educated and trained in ethics and moral arguments. Most of the moral arguments addressing rights and interests are found in the literature on special education law, where efficacy arguments are used selectively with reference to particular legal and constitutional principles.

In addition to the sensitivity of special education policies to the political will, the special interests, and the moral visions of a period of history, there are two related issues that have contributed to the complexity of policy making. First, the theoretical foundations are external to and separated from school-based practice. Policy and programmatic changes are dependent on philosophical perspectives in psychology. "Schools of thought," or models, in psychology have had a profound impact on special education practices. During the past 30 years, fundamental changes in practice have occurred as special education shifted its philosophical orientation from a medical model to behavioral and ecological models, and more recently to cognitive and systems models. These changes have modified our professional practices, approaches to teacher education, beliefs about the science of education, and views about whether professionals in other clinical disciplines are necessary collaborators in our work. While the direction of change is generally supportable, the separation of practice from the technical and moral perspectives that ground the science of practice creates a "thin" foundation from which practitioners can work to renew, reform, and make meaning of their work.

This situation has contributed to the tendency in special education to implement artifacts of ideas, that is, to separate the practice from the theory or the principles that gave meaning and purpose to the practice. Practice devoid of theory has no algorithm for rational change and is likely to become functionally autonomous (Allport, 1937), continuing indefinitely without meeting any particular understood need.

The second, and related, challenge has to do with our tendency toward fads. The limitations of our science, the inconsistencies in the art of practice, the predisposition to value the practical and devalue theory, and the social altruism that has given so much force to "doing the right thing" for children with disabilities predispose special educators and parents of children with disabilities to well-marketed products, whether curriculum materials, behavioral interventions, or ideas about etiology. Practitioners and parents, especially, are vulnerable to the persuasive rhetoric of peddlers and salespeople.

When viewed in this context, the dynamic state of change in special education, whether transitional or transformational, is both exciting and cause for caution. The kinds of things that worry me are "salespeople" who are passionately committed to overly simple solutions to complex problems (magical solutions), agents for changing everything without any clear regard for anything that might be working well at present (throwing out the baby with the bath water). I worry about advocates for major systemic change who do not appear to have a clear vision of the interests of individual children and families.

The professional literature now is exciting, with dramatically different perspectives being advanced which depart from the familiar frameworks that have guided research and practice. However, the enthusiasm many of us have for alternative voices is muted by the absence of any basis for a coherent philosophical discourse on the grounding principles of knowledge upon which our research and theories of learning and teaching are erected. There is a tension between and among those who advance paradigmatic arguments, which is disconcerting when one considers the vague or ambiguous understandings associated with position taking. While there is considerable disenchantment with the epistemological and moral arguments of traditional empiricism, acceptance of an alternative requires a kind of decision for which we have not been professionally socialized and to which we are unaccustomed—namely, deciding on grounds other than data or logic. Deciding among paradigmatic alternatives requires a level of self-reflection and an examination of the nature of our beliefs and our science that involves our values and our views of reality. In the absence of empirical or logical criteria for accepting or rejecting positivistic views, our decisions become morally reasoned positions and faith commitments that resonate to our intuitive sense of what is real and true.

The personal context of our work is deeply impacted by a larger philosophical context that holds the possibility of defining different terms for contracts and substantially creating a different reality for partnerships and for teacher education. This book is a veritable lexicon of issues that form the philosophical context of educational reform. Following are reflections on two of the major issues that will change professional practice in schools and in the university in the future. These are the paradigmatic changes and changes in the nature of faculty work in colleges of education.

Changing Paradigms, Changing Education

The paradigmatic dialogues and debates about educational reform that are taking the problematic nature of knowledge seriously are bringing a richness to the texture of thought in education. This is part of the foundational change being sought and hoped for in restructuring schools. It is at the level of paradigmatic thought that some of the current policy conundrums in education, such as inclusion, are created and the level at which they must be resolved. Knowing what we value and how we choose to ground our arguments about the schooling and society, and about educational practice, is an essential precondition for thoughtful and morally defensible positions on educational policies that are sensitive to the diverse interests in our culturally complex and pluralistic society.

In the absence of uncritical acceptance of the traditional paradigmatic orientation, and having no common criteria for alternatives, how do we talk with one another in meaningful ways about our work? How do we agree on the framework(s) for reforming the substantive foundations of educational practice?

We believe one important approach to this aspect of reform is in the collaborative and collegial construction of educational thought which must address the ethical as well as the preceptual and conceptual grounding of practice. That is not to suggest that constructivism alone is necessarily an adequate set of premises from which to work. Critical and deconstructive methodologies are especially helpful in examining common dogmata and opening up (or closing down) familiar and relatively unexamined arguments.

One of the dilemmas for educational philosophers, theorists, and reflective practitioners is in the area of systematics. How consistent must one be in the current intellectual environment? Can post-positivists be selectively constructive or critical, for example? Is there a philosophically defensible eclecticism, albeit internally inconsistent? Or, is eclecticism on paradigmatic issues intellectually "soft" and, therefore, unacceptable, even if it is in defense of social values backed by sound technical arguments? On pragmatic grounds, how do we ignore or refuse to accept useful views, even if they are based on assumptions we do not accept. The arguments between and among experimental and interpretive researchers illustrate this dilemma. The debate about outcome assessment is another example.

This intellectual context for school reform is especially acute in universities. The nature of research and the curriculum for educating teachers and leaders are now the focus of intense debate, and the issues are fundamentally paradigmatic in nature. What is research? What is acceptable for doctoral dissertations and for publication? What should be the content of the research training curriculum? What must teachers know about knowledge and ethics? There is not the consensus on answers to these questions that there was only a decade ago. The answers, or working understandings, must come from both self-reflection and from such fields of thought and inquiry as ethics, epistemology, and aesthetics. Neither the self nor these sources of understanding have commonly constituted our formal and shared knowledge about practice.

The Nature of Faculty Work in Education: Personnel and Knowledge Workers

While professors do not typically think of themselves as personnel, we are employees of an organization, the university, which has rules governing expected professorial behavior and rewards for valued behavior. The criteria employed for promotion, tenure, and merit pay reveal the core values of the institution. The traditional reward system in most universities is partitioned into three areas: research, teaching, and service—usually in that order. The academic culture and the institutional self-image maintain the values manifested in these priorities and the definitions of each of these areas of faculty work.

In colleges of education, professorial work has mimicked the work of professors in other colleges and departments in the university. Whether one is appointed, and ultimately tenured, in a department of chemistry, English, psychology, or education, the expectations and values associated with faculty work are similar. Unlike a faculty in history, for example, which has its own research methodologies, or in dance, which may have performance expectations, most education faculty members have been expected to conduct and disseminate research within the epistemological tradition of the physical sciences, i.e. logical empiricism. This philosophy of inquiry, rooted in the paradigm of classic science, has governed educational research until very recently. Questions that could not be answered using the reductionistic methods of logic and empiricism could not be asked meaningfully. These questions were, as Wittgenstein said, "passed over quietly."

So much has been "passed over" that it no longer occurs quietly. The necessity of participating in a relevant way in the reform of public schools requires casting a much broader, more robust, and sensitive net. Fortunately, changes in the philosophy of science guiding research in the social sciences and the loosening of the hegemonic grasp of logical empiricism on educational research have begun to create an epistemological environment that is more open and sensitive to different traditions of inquiry. Research in education is increasingly adopting the methods of other disciplines such as anthropology, philosophy, history, and literature. The study of the nature of knowledge and of inquiry is being addressed more directly, in some universities, as the basis from which to pursue training in one or more modes of inquiry.

Different research orientations are necessary to help professors address relevant and meaningful questions about educational practice and school change. Faculties in education are divided in their views about these different methodologies and their use. Faculty members are typically not trained in philosophy of science and in different methodologies. This creates the condition in which there are differences about research approaches on doctoral committees and publication panels, and some of the research in methods from outside the traditional purview of education is poorly conducted because the faculty are not adequately trained; thus, doctoral students are not adequately supervised. In the absence of a basic course on the nature of knowledge, faculty and students sometimes find themselves with inadequate grounding for the epistemological pluralism many of them seek.

This has implications for the faculty reward system. What counts as research? Which journals are acceptable? What about "research" that is not "data based"? How many "data-based" articles are necessary, whatever the nature and extent of other faculty productivity, for promotion/tenure? These are value questions premised upon paradigmatic preferences.

Another issue in understanding and evaluating faculty work has to do with the concept of service, traditionally the least valued form of faculty work. Service is what everyone can and must do to be promoted and tenured, but it is the loosely defined, devalued, "pound of flesh" extracted by the university and, if you are in education, by the field. It is required as part of being a good citizen in the university, but "it takes time away from your research and teaching."

This view is one of the most troubling when universities get serious about collaborating with public schools. Collaboration takes time. Professors must be present in schools if they are ever to be trusted and accepted as a part of a collaborative endeavor such as a Professional Development School. The professor must participate in activities that demonstrate competence and sincerity in her/his commitment to the values and work of the school. Early morning hours when teachers start their day, faculty meetings, time in the classroom with the children, informal time in the lounge, after-school and evening time in special school events—all of these are important to the school-based professor communicating her/his values and commitment to the school.

There is no faculty reward code for this time other than "service." In anthropology, this might be considered a part of the research process in gaining acceptance to a setting as a participant-observer. In education, it is helping out, getting ready for real and valued work, i.e., research. The net effect of this situation is that time invested in schools does not count except as students are assigned to be supervised, or as research papers are published and/or presented at professional meetings. The professor has a full-time assignment which includes teaching and research. The "down time" of development in schools, then, is extra. It is the time spent beyond the 100 percent assignment. For untenured faculty, this is a serious issue. Politically it serves their own interests best if they stay out of schools except to use the schools as places to conduct time-limited studies. Their time is most prudently spent designing studies, writing research grants, collecting and analyzing data, and writing research reports for publication and presentation.

It is most efficient for the professor to work alone, which means that the research is conceived and designed apart from schools and is, therefore, not as likely to be perceived as relevant to practice by practitioners. Collaborative research takes more time, requires sharing of credit, and is more complex. To compound the problem of relevant and useful research, the language for publication is likely to be incomprehensible to practitioners—researchers talk to researchers in the literature.

The culture for university-based research in education reflected in this analysis keeps the knowledge work of faculty—research and teaching—separated from the school. It practically guarantees that educational research and the education of teachers will be only loosely connected to the reform of schools.

The traditional antipathy between universities and public schools is both ideological and political. Professors are "experts" on education, children, and schooling. Teachers have taken their courses, however, and have often found that they do not reflect the realities of the classroom. Similarly, educational research, the professor's highest priority as indicated by the values in the reward system, is frequently not perceived as relevant to teachers. If it is relevant, professors generally do not accept responsibility for translating it for practitioners who may view the language of educational science as esoteric. Further, the journals valued by researchers in education are not those widely read by teachers.

Professional Development Schools are politically constructed systems that connect the knowledge work of public schools and universities. They are attempts to remove the social and philosophical partitions that have kept university and public school cultures incompatible and, in many instances, antagonistic. These institutional inventions will require a major rethinking of the faculty reward system and a new understanding of faculty work.

It is essential that the work of faculty in education be recodified to reflect the real work of collaboration with schools. This has implications for the time faculty members spend in schools and out of schools doing school-related work, such as preparing for school meetings. It has implications for the kinds of activities in which they engage, such as counseling teachers, planning, meetings with school and university staff, substituting for teachers, and other collaborative work.

It is also essential that the recodification address the issue of what constitutes research and scholarship. This has implications for what counts as research process, in which the professor invests time, and what is a research product, which is the evidence provided for knowledge work.

What Are Teacher Educators to Do?

The modern history of preparing educational professionals has been characterized by a rather long period of formal study in a university-based program followed by a period of induction into the profession, both during a structured "field experience" and, ultimately, as a novice teacher. This assumes that there is a relatively large, fixed body of knowledge, the mastery of which is essential for even minimal functioning in the school. This model is one which we find reassuring in the training of pilots, for example, or scuba divers. In both cases, there are minimal technical skills, which, if not mastered, will kill the practitioner and, possibly, innocent bystanders. We have tended to assume that, unless teachers had all of their essential skills before interacting with children, they will do irreparable harm to the child, themselves, or the integrity of the content.

These fears are groundless. Most adults who opt into teaching have some measure of common sense and sensitivity in working with children and adolescents, and are, therefore, unlikely to do any harm either to the students or themselves that an apology or explanation cannot correct. Further, it is also likely that, given the affinity for study that brought a student into an education program in the first place, this will also assure a certain level of competence and not many egregious errors in content will be made. Besides, a mistake can be corrected by a subsequent explanation or correction. (We, for example, were taught with absolute certainty by certified teachers that the molecule was the smallest particle of matter. This bit of wisdom came a decade after the first atom was split with some alacrity.) In short, later adolescents (i.e., those enrolled in the early stages of a teacher education program) are probably pretty well equipped to work with children and younger adolescents. The older students now being attracted to the profession seem, at first glance, to also possess the same level of good sense that an 'unschooled' scoutmaster or Sunday school teacher has.

What all of this leads to is our evolving belief that we need to replace the pilot model of teacher education with an anthropologist's model, one where the anthropologist enters and hangs around in the site for a while in order to figure out what he or she needs to learn more about. In essence, we need to reverse the preparation and socialization sequence. Or, if not reverse them, integrate them so thoroughly that the students begin their training with some basic anthropological research methods— designed to help them figure out what's going on in the school. Then, using a reciprocating schedule of some sort, the students need to remain in "the field" as participant-observers, carrying the results of this inquiry to those who can tutor him or her in the content that is needed for effective mastery, deep study and research on learning, profound inquiry into the social conditions of America's youth and special needs of diverse populations, and a personal understanding of the evolution of educational institutions as reflections of a society's beliefs about its children, its collective mission, and its common future.

Is this likely to happen? It might, and soon, but three things must change. First, the message must come through very clearly to those that teach and those that prepare teachers that this nation's agenda is to raise decent, intelligent, self-sufficient, well-adjusted people who can adapt to and prosper in any evolving economic system. Second, public policy must be altered to focus accountability on these multiple missions of schooling. Finally, new collaborations must arise within the university and between the university and the schools. Critical to these new kinds of collaborations is the reinvention of a funding and accounting model which focuses attention on the children of America, rather than the preservation of institutions. For example, enrollment-driven state reimbursement systems, in which the unit of accountability is the program or department, assures that no department which values its resource base will collaborate with another in the preparation of teachers. Further, an accreditation model which assures institutional compliance with specific procedures rather than performance on outcomes will assure only that nothing ever changes and more public resources will be spent to place another layer of coordination on systems which, by design, must fail to respond to one another's needs.

Collaboration to What Ends?

Our work together with faculty and colleagues in public schools has led to a rich and productive environment. The spirit of invention and reform has stimulated initiatives designed to steer us—learning as we go—along unfamiliar paths. Listed below are 11 of the constructive products of the partnerships formed by our departments and schools:

- *Work in professional development schools*. The Professional Development Schools are the primary medium for our collaborative work with schools. They provide a laboratory for collegial work among faculty in our departments and school personnel. They are the epicenter of our collaborative research, training, staff development, and model development.

- *Collaborative research groups.* We have several collaborative research groups which form the center of our on-campus research collaborations. These groups work intensively on research themes related to school reform. The current groups are working on school restructuring and university-school collaboration, teaching case research and development, inclusion policy and ethics, and families and young children. These groups, which involve interdisciplinary faculty and doctoral students, are designing and implementing the research that is guiding our work with schools and our decisions to restructure our own programs.

- *Collaboration on graduate research and training policies in education.* We and our colleagues in other departments have made a major commitment to designing and implementing graduate education programs that reflect the richness and diversity of current philosophical perspectives and the interest of school reform. This is fundamentally a culture-building process that involves all of the leadership of the college.

- *Joint training and education programs.* We have initiated several joint education and training ventures aimed at empowering professionals and scholars to occupy new roles and to make significant contributions to school reform. These include: a joint doctoral program in elementary education, reading, and special education; a joint doctoral program in secondary and special education; a joint doctoral program in elementary, secondary, and special education focused on preparing school-based teacher educators who can complement university-based faculty and provide leadership in professional development schools; and a joint undergraduate program in secondary and special education.

- *Co-development of a new course on inquiry.* We are planning a new course on inquiry that will address the basic paradigmatic issues of knowledge and knowing. This course, which will be offered at the beginning of the doctoral research sequence, will promote an informed respect for different research traditions and support student pursuits of both quantitative and interpretive inquiry.

- *Redefining faculty work.* We are aware that our experimental initiatives in schools, which are our highest priorities, require a great deal of investment of time by untenured as well as tenured faculty in building trust and earning a place of value in the school. The scholarly productivity from these investments are not as predictable as efficient studies designed and conducted by faculty to meet criteria for promotion and tenure. Much of what has traditionally been regarded as service has to be recast as part of the research process. Perhaps models are to be found in the fields of anthropology, when one must devote extended periods of time preparing for observations, or of history, or philosophy, when so much time must be devoted to preparation and reflection. We are working on recodifying faculty work to reflect the values of a professional college whose primary mission involves work with and in schools.

- *Reinventing funding formulas.* One of the most challenging issues we face in a college of education is the FTE model of funding. There are several serious issues involved in the typical FTE funding formula. Departments are pitted against one another in competing for scarce resources. They are expected to increase student hour enrollment in classes in order to maintain the same level of funding, which ultimately erodes quality if the course is offered in the same format. One major consequence of the current FTE formula is that, as more time is committed to producing additional FTE, time needed for faculty reflection and research in schools is lost. Restructuring the funding formula is one of the most difficult challenges we face since it is so embedded in university-wide fiscal policy. We are limited primarily to alternatives that change the funding within the college.

- *Shared technology agenda.* Certainly one of the approaches to changing the resources picture is to deliver each unit of instruction more efficiently. The infusion of technology is one logical approach to accomplish this end. We are, therefore, developing a specific collaborative initiative to infuse technology into our courses and to deliver them more efficiently.

- *University-school consortia.* We have established consortia with public schools in order to accomplish two goals. The first is to more effectively monitor and respond to the research, teacher education, staff development, and technical assistance needs of schools. The second is to more efficiently deliver courses to the largest number of teachers who need the courses and in the locations and at the times they can access.

- *Co-teaching in schools with teachers and other school leaders.* One of the most important strategies we have for assuring some practical validity in the content of our own curriculum is to assign our faculty to co-teach in schools with teachers and other school leaders. This involves mutual learning, and it is helping us understand how to restructure our own delivery of instruction.

- *Developing a teaching case foundation for integrating general and special education.* We are developing and evaluating teaching cases based on our collaborative work in professional development schools. These cases reflect a constructive perspective and capture the complexity and multiple dimensions of clinical, instructional, policy, and ethical isues embedded in developing inclusive schools. The cases will become the basis for integrating our teacher education curriculum.

CONCLUSION: WORK IN PROGRESS

Partnerships are not easy, but they are essential if we are to participate in the reform of public education. There are many forces that work against serious collaboration. There are also many forces now working to promote and facilitate collaborative efforts.

In this chapter we have described the meaning and productivity we have sought to find in our work together, and we have shared what we believe are successful outcomes. We have also described territorial and competitive alternatives which we believe are more easily pursued.

Some of our work is intellectually renewing because, at the deepest level, educational reform is one aspect of a much larger reform in understanding knowledge, the knowledge industries, and the institutions tethered to the prevailing norms and perspectives on knowledge and learning, including public schools. Serious partnerships are windows on reform; through them we can see the larger multilayered complexity of changing the public education system. This is the context in which the distinction between transition and transformation is understood as personal as well as intellectual, institutional, or policy constructs.

We experience much of our work as exciting because of the new and vigorous dialogue between those seeking to advance the sciences informing education and those new artists and scholars who are recreating their work in constructing holistic understandings and hermeneutic perspectives. On the other hand, some of our work is extraordinarily mundane because it involves the minutiae of bureaucracies, red ink on budgets, and the comfortable habits of those who are "doing their jobs."

We have shared personal stories that, we believe, brought the three of us together in what we experience as a gratifying and productive partnership. And we have shared our thoughts about what our collaboration means and how it works. Finally, we have described the specific productive consequences of our work together with our colleagues.

There is no presumption that our work is unique or that we have found lasting answers to the questions we have raised about partnerships in educational reform. We do believe, however, that the demographically complex urban environment and the large college of education in which we are working has provided us the opportunity to observe and to learn about most of the challenges facing teacher educators who would, together, seek new and higher paths for their work in the context of school reform. Many of the working understandings we share and have found useful in guiding our collaborative efforts are described in this chapter.

REFERENCES

Allport, G. W. (1959). *Personality: A psychological interpretation.* New Haven: Yale University Press.

Fuchs, D., & Fuchs, L. (1991). Framing the REI debate: Abolitionist versus conservationists. In Lloyd, J. Singh, N., & Repp, A. *The regular education initiative: Alternative perspectives on concepts, issues, and models.* Sycamore, IL: Sycamore Publishing Co.

Howe, K., & Miramontes, O. (1992). *The ethics of special education.* NY: Teachers College Press.

Noblit, G. (1993). Power and caring. *American Educational Research Journal, 30*(1), 23–38.

Noddings, N. (1992). *The challenge to care in schools: An alternative approach to education.* Berkeley: University of California Press.

Paul, J., Gallagher, J., Kendrick, B., Thomas, D., & Young, J. (1993). *Handbook for ethical policy making.* Chapel Hill, NC: North Carolina Institute for Policy Studies.

Polanyi, M. (1959). *The study of man.* Chicago: University of Chicago Press.

Poplin, M. (1992). *Voices from the inside: A report on schooling from inside the classroom.* The Institute for Education in Transformation. Claremont Graduate School, Claremont, CA. Funded by John Kluge Foundation.

Rhodes, W. (1993). *Special education and the post-modern shift.* Tampa, FL: Paper presented at the Rhodes Collegium, University of South Florida.

Skrtic, T. (1991). *Behind special education: A critical analysis of professional culture and school organization.* Denver, CO: Love.

Stone, L. (1992). Philosophy, meaning constructs and teacher theorizing. In E. W. Ross, J. Cornett, and G. McCutcheon (Eds.), *Teacher personal theorizing: Connecting curriculum practice, theory, and research* (pp. 19–34). Albany: State University of New York Press.

BUILDING PARTNERSHIPS
FOR REFORM

HILDA ROSSELLI AND JAMES L. PAUL

OVER three years ago, the Department of Special Education at the University of South Florida began partnerships with six school systems on the west-central coast of Florida. We started our work with four basic beliefs. We believed that: 1) we had ample evidence that our traditional approach to teacher education in special education had not been adequate; 2) our research was not addressing the questions teachers and other school leaders were asking; 3) the school reform movement was amplifying the discontinuity between what we, as a university-based program, were doing and what schools needed; and 4) while we worked with restructuring schools we needed to restructure ourselves as well.

These beliefs led us to decide that we would not pursue a course of designing and evaluating interventions in schools. Rather, we would seek partnerships with schools and attempt to develop a context in which we could participate in restructuring activities as colleagues. We gave a great deal of control to the schools and followed the leads they provided. We expressed a wish to focus our work in at least one school in each district with the hope that these sites could become collaborative centers for our working partnerships with the school systems. This basic commitment has continued and has produced partnerships that now range from training affiliations with several schools to well-developed professional development schools.

One of the critical aspects of our work has been the emergence of a collaborative research group (CRG), which includes each faculty member who serves as a liaison between the department and a school system, plus doctoral students who are working with those faculty members. The purpose of the CRG is to provide technical assistance and support for each member of the group. We knew many barriers in the university and in the schools would challenge our work. We also knew that we did not know how to do what we had set out to do. The group continues to meet two hours each week, and attendance is given the priority of a course. In this way, the CRG has provided a safe environment in which to try out new ideas.

The group offers a forum for discussing partnership progress, evaluating and reacting to ideas and proposals, reviewing literature, problem solving, and collaborating on proposals, articles, and—most ambitiously—this book.

Although the partnerships are now at various stages of development, the chapters in this section report on some of the outcomes, more specifically, teacher preparation programs, restructuring initiatives and inclusion efforts that have resulted from the university/school partnerships. Chapter 14 discusses the importance of collaborative planning involving university, school, and district personnel in designing restructured teacher education programs at both undergraduate and graduate levels. The involvement of the partners in collaborative initiatives such as the Teacher Assistance Teams and Focus Groups became important vehicles by which the visions and goals for restructured teacher education programs could be developed and revised. Although representing two distinct school districts and partnerships, the authors draw across their experiences to suggest common principles of collaborative planning that have helped span differences between stakeholders. Particular attention is given in this chapter to the unique needs of the small regional campus that may have limited faculty resources to engage in such a partnership.

Encouraging both general and special education teachers to take responsibility for children with special learning needs is only one of the goals of a partnership involving the university and a local elementary school, described in chapter 15. Insights are offered from the university faculty member on the changing role of professors who elect to move from traditional models of expert, researcher, and teacher trainer to the role of collaborator. Examples and viewpoints are offered by school faculty as they gained confidence and experience in their emergent roles as action researchers, decision makers, mentors for student teachers, and consultants on methods of improving the inclusion of students with disabilities in the regular classroom.

The progress and lessons learned from a university/district partnership involved in developing an inclusion program in a large urban district is the focus of chapter 16. Goals evolving from the partnership planning as well as assumptions guiding the direction of the collaboration are discussed. A description is offered of the collaborative teaching model used in this partnership to serve students with mild disabilities within the regular classroom. The authors identify philosophical, political, procedural, and policy challenges that can be anticipated in such a project, and they define and discuss factors that appear to influence the outcomes of such a large-scale inclusion project. Alignment with school restructuring, use of a change strategy, policy reconciliation, and training for teachers and administrators are just a few of the areas emphasized.

Chapter 17 describes a partnership at a professional development school (PDS) as told by a university faculty member, a special education teacher at the PDS, and a doctoral student from the university. Goals and assumptions of the PDS are reviewed within the context of the district's support for inclusion and integration. Initiatives such as demonstration teaching, involvement with disenfranchised students, and activities to reconnect schools with families of SED and at-risk students are discussed. Highlights from case studies of three interns at the PDS are shared to emphasize the frustration experienced by general education majors who receive little or no preparation for teaching students with special needs. The chapter closes with a discussion of insights derived from the authors' experiences at the PDS that include such issues as: fairness, orderliness and individualized caring, school culture, benefits of a team, and time as a resource.

Acute teacher shortages in special education programs present a special challenge to rural areas. The authors in chapter 18 describe a university district collaborative teacher preparation program designed to recruit trainees from the local community, improve access to university training while experimenting with alternative instructional approaches, and supporting trainees with survival skills pertinent for working in rural at-risk settings.

The use of a strategic planning model is viewed as critical in order to build an agenda that addresses the needs, values, and visions of both partners. A constructivist view has shaped the program curriculum, and the authors share examples of how this approach has impacted students in the training cohorts. Results of formative evaluative data from reflective journals and questionnaires provide insights into the complex changes occurring during the program as well as some of the ethical dilemmas encountered by the trainees and mentor teachers in the program.

Researchers who wish to examine the process of restructuring in projects such as those described in this section will have to accommodate their research protocols to an already existing phenomenon of change. The authors of chapter 19 examine some of the methodological challenges that exist for this type of inquiry. No single paradigm of inquiry appears to be robust enough to adequately investigate the process. The chapter reviews and critiques the relevant literature, examining the process of determining outcomes to be measured by schools, and presenting strategies that can guide research in this area. The authors also discuss the methodology and preliminary results of a federally funded restructuring/inclusion demonstration project which is being conducted by the authors in the five school districts described in chapters 14–18.

The nature of the narrative process enables researchers to examine their work using a wide-angle lens extending the focus to include not only the progression and results of their efforts, but also the contextual setting and uniqueness of the situation in which the researchers are involved with actual events. The next chapter describes what the authors learned as researchers about the culture of collaborative projects, about the selection of methods for doing their research work in the schools, and the ethical issues that evolved as a result of their collaboration. Two narratives are presented and analyzed by the authors around the themes of equity, trust, and confidentiality.

The last chapter presents a discussion by doctoral students of their experiences in a doctoral program focusing on school reform and the restructuring of special education, combined with intensive work in professional development sites. Doctoral education is a challenge for students who are expected to formulate a meaningful intellectual path in their preparation for roles yet to be created. The authors examine their different intellectual journeys, discontinuities of views among faculty and with their own cohort, the impact of paradigm issues in seminars on their personal perspectives, and the challenge of integrating these views in practice. The authors discuss these issues with a focus on implications for leadership education in restructured special education programs of the future.

14

PREPARING AND INITIATING A COLLABORATIVE TEACHER EDUCATION PROGRAM

LEE SMITH, LINDA HOUCK, FRAN ARCHER,
RAY CIEMNIECKI, WILLIAM DELP, & WILMA HAMILTON

INTRODUCTION

IN order to meet special education personnel and training needs, the University of South Florida's regional campus at Sarasota has formed partnerships with two local school districts. This chapter describes the processes of developing these collaborative initiatives through four stages: 1) establishing commitment; 2) developing relationships; 3) visioning and goal setting; and 4) implementing initiatives. Within these stages, issues of institutional awareness, trust building, collaboration, and overcoming possible barriers are discussed. At the conclusion of each section is a short retrospective given by the first author in which an analysis of the step is presented. In the chapter summary, the unique nature of a partnership from a small regional campus with limited resources is given particular attention.

One may be tempted to believe that four identified stages would be likely to occur almost anywhere. However, in this case, the stages reflect an organizational style to help the reader and not necessarily the belief that these stages would be common to all projects. It should be noted that the partnerships described in this chapter have been formed around ideas and did not always follow a linear path. Ann Lieberman (in Lewis, 1989, p.118) cautions against the belief in "rational-linear ideas" and states that "collaboration can start with some ideas that mobilize people."

STAGE ONE: ESTABLISHING COMMITMENT

In August of 1991, responding to an invitation by the director of special education in Manatee County, Florida, the chairman of the special education department from the main campus and a recently employed faculty member from the regional campus met. Later that same day, about twenty miles south in Sarasota County, a similar meeting with the director of special education took place. At each meeting, the chair of the university's special education department explained a vision of school-based teacher training programs and the willingness of the department to work with districts in establishing such programs (Paul, Duchnowski, & Danforth, 1993). The new faculty member shared his visions of field-based programs and his belief in collaborative efforts with local districts. The directors expressed enthusiasm about working with the university. Each of the special education program directors expressed his opinion that there were benefits to the local education of teachers who would be employed within their districts. Also, each director expressed concerns about the number of persons who were not presently certified in special education and about problems in getting recent university graduates to apply for positions in their districts. In addition, the teachers in the districts' classes for students with disabilities who had been hired without special education degrees were having difficulty obtaining the required certification courses at the regional campus. The issues discussed at these introductory meetings provided an initial forum for future work and discussions.

Despite the innocuous appearance of these first encounters, it was here that several important processes began. First, these were the initial commitments for the school districts and the department of special education to collaborate. The new faculty member was implicitly pledging to work with the districts in establishing a special education program at the regional campus. The department chair was lending his support and commiting department resources, despite the fact that the districts were an hour and a half drive from the main campus. The directors of special education were expressing a willingness to participate in developing the special education program on the regional campus. These commitments were the tacit first steps in establishing institutional partnerships.

Secondly, the meetings established an implicit core group of participants who would be relatively stable stakeholders in the coming months. Ultimately, these were also the gatekeepers. Each person, by virtue of his position, became obligated to consider ramifications of any proposed programs. The effects of any initiatives would have to be duly considered for their organizational impact at each respective institution: school districts or university. Each person would, to some degree, control access to their respective systems.

Thus, an initial stage to the development of partnerships was the establishment of a commitment to explore the ideas and visions of the others. Through this commitment, several unspoken questions arose: What would the role of each person be in the establishment of partnerships? What demands would be placed on the regional campus staff, school districts, and, perhaps, individual schools? Could a program in special education be established at a regional campus with collaboration between the university and districts? What resources would be needed and from where would they come? Would it really happen? How long would it take? What were the possible benefits and disadvantages to established systems and structures?

Retrospective on Stage One

Establishing commitments may be necessary only when there is not any past working relationship between districts and departments in universities or colleges. This stage may also be unnecessary and avoided when the university has had a history of responsiveness to district concerns. In many cases, prior reputation of university faculty, the past work of other faculty members, and formal or informal networks have given new university faculty established entry points to forming partnerships with districts and with district programs. Few of these factors were present in this case.

Although the department chair was very supportive, the role of others within the special education department was not clear. Neither of these counties' teachers or staffs had immediate access to the main campus resources, and hence very few of the district people were known to the more established departmental faculty. In effect, in the initial meeting and as the partnerships progressed, the new university faculty member often acted as the lone representative of the regional campus. In small departments or on regional campuses, this may be the norm.

In this case there was a departmental support vehicle for the new university staff through the departmental collaborative research group (CRGs). However, it was a 100-mile round-trip to the meetings, and it took literally half a day to attend. In this situation, the lack of geographic proximity to university colleagues was one issue that was underestimated. Geographic proximity may be an important factor in establishing support from the university community. In the later stages, support was developed from the community and district staff.

In hindsight, our meetings probably should have involved other critical stakeholders, such as the regional deans and assistant superintendents. A wide knowledge and support base in the beginning would have enhanced the next step in the projects as well as avoiding some purely informational meetings later.

STAGE TWO: DEVELOPING RELATIONSHIPS

The regional campus special education faculty member began in the fall with the idea that the undergraduate teacher education program to be developed at the regional campus would soon incorporate staff at school sites. The chosen sites would hopefully evolve into learning centers for teachers in training, the resident teachers, and the university faculty who elected to participate. However, several pragmatic factors quickly arose. Historically, on the regional campus, undergraduate students in special education could obtain some coursework on the regional campus but had to travel a distance to obtain any courses within their major. Graduate courses were only offered on occasion.

Organizationally, regional campus faculty members are responsible to the regional campus dean, although they are also members of main campus departments. Faculty are assigned courses at the regional campus by the regional administrators. Discussions with the dean of the regional campus were needed to clarify the regional campus commitment, which later included discretionary funds from an endowment at the regional campus.

Although the faculty member shared his department's vision of training education professionals at school-based sites, it was his intent to initially approach the establishment of collaborative initiatives and his work in the districts with no preconceived ideas. In effect, his work would be wholly determined by the visions of those in the school district.

It was with this in mind that follow-up meetings were held with the special education directors of each district. In Sarasota County, the discussions focused on district programs which could be enhanced by the skills of the university faculty. A new program for students with autism and related disorders was being implemented, and the faculty member who had expertise in working with students with autism was asked to join the district's advisory group and assist in its development. In this capacity, he became involved in the traditional role of offering technical assistance at the school with the program for students with autism and at other district schools.

Over the course of the next year, a stronger relationship began to develop as the university faculty member began serving on various committees within the district. District staff began to contribute to the newly implemented special education program on the regional campus. During this first year, teachers and staff from the district's special education program began co-instructing selected sessions of the university's course on mainstreaming. This arrangement allowed more time for the university member to meet district teachers and collaborate on interventions. These activities began to create a mutual working and trusting relationship and introduced each partner to the others' environments.

In addition, a large number of teachers from elementary and secondary education in the county began to take courses at the regional campus. With statewide budget cuts, districts such as Sarasota County were forced to reduce the number of general education teachers. Rather than having experienced teachers leave the district, they were given an opportunity to retrain to teach special education classes. As such, a fair number were taking university courses to acquire expertise and certification.

In Manatee County, meetings with the director of special education resulted in the explicit and implicit sharing of visions. At one of these meetings, the university faculty member and the district director shared the features of what they believed a district-based undergraduate teacher education program would entail. The district director expressed a strong desire to recruit paraprofessionals and other school district staff. Both the director and the university faculty member saw the inclusion of these persons as optimal, since these people had previous experience with students with disabilities, were familiar with school culture, and were likely to remain in the district. Other common visions included offering credit for experiential components,incorporating traditional university students in district special education programs, and, initially, basing the program at one school within the district. With these ideas, an agreement was reached to produce a working document which would include goal statements of the program. (See Appendix 1.)

While these talks were occurring, a school was suggested for the partnership site. The school selected had recently merged with a nine-year-old special education center, which created the opportunity for more integrated services for students with disabilities. A number of the school's teachers had need for certification in special education. After a presentation to the school staff, informal weekly meetings were scheduled to plan for a university-district collaborative teacher training. Eight people—teachers, paraprofessionals, and university faculty—became a core group for discussions and activities that were initiated at the school over the course of the first year. A school-based resource consultant for the teachers of persons with low-incidence disabilities soon took the lead in organizing the school faculty for each meeting. Topics at these "agenda-less" meetings were pertinent issues relating to the combining of the two schools, in-service needs and desires, and, on some occasions, discussions of particular students with challenging educational issues. The university faculty member served as a facilitator in discussions and, on occasion, gave technical assistance to the school's personnel. In addition, a doctoral student from the area began coming on occasion to participate in the discussions.

At the end of the first year, the initiatives in the two school districts were distinctly different. In Manatee County, a clearly defined goal of developing a field-based undergraduate teacher education program at a school site had been articulated. In Sarasota County, the goals of the partnership were less defined. The faculty member's work with the autism task force and technical assistance to individual teachers was helping make him known to district staff and administrators. The monthly discussions with the district director and the program director were about common district and university issues, and sometimes focused on the district's recently announced restructuring initiative.

Retrospective on Stage Two

An oversight on the part of the university faculty lay in a misconception of the institutional pressures of the university culture. For example, while approaching the initial collaboration with no preconceived ideas seemed acceptable, it also meant there were no preconceived goals or plans. University culture demands that faculty work be of some benefit, however indirect, to the university, such as recognition through publication or recognition in the local community. Because there was a belief that partnerships are long lasting and would take time to develop, there were no immediate products or projects valued by the university. A more astute awareness of the institutional culture would have allowed the partnership to formalize some goals for meeting the self-interest of *both* the districts and the university (Goodlad, 1988).

Although the partnership was still developing, issues began to arise around the resource of time. Time is a recurring issue across the partnerships described in chapters 14–18 as well as in the literature (Shive, 1984). It has been suggested that, among school leaders, the difference between those who are effective and not may be in how they prioritize their time (Duke, 1990).

Unintentionally, by the second year, the university member had begun assuming traditional roles in both districts. This may have helped as a step in establishing trust. In cases where partners are unknown entities to each other, it may be easier to start with a role that is comfortable for both. Technical assistance is a familiar and traditional role for both the giver (university) and the receiver (school personnel). Perhaps, traditional roles must be established for credibility prior to participating in any risk taking.

The technical assistance role served the purpose of allowing each partner access to the others' institutional patterns. The university faculty member was bound by the schedule of classes he taught, routines of advising, scheduling courses for the special education program, and by faculty meetings. The district staff had similar expectations, and the two cycles did not match.

One of the commonalties that began to appear in the partnership was that both districts were interested in restructuring and in inclusion of children with disabilities. Recently, many schools have been encouraged to educate all students in more inclusive settings (Biklen, 1985; Reynolds, Wang, & Walberg, 1987; Stainback & Stainback, 1990). At the same time, there is evidence that some teachers may not be prepared to serve all children in mainstreamed settings (Kearney & Durand, 1992). The issues of teacher training for more inclusive environments became evident as the partnerships moved forward.

However, there were also differences developing. Sarasota County staff were initially unclear about what they wanted from the university faculty outside of technical assistance roles. They were interested in brainstorming and talking about a variety of issues. Manatee County staff were, conversely, collaboratively defining the goals of partnership.

STAGE THREE: VISIONING AND GOAL SETTINGS

Sarasota County

During the next year the county school board and superintendent established restructuring goals for the district in response to a state policy initiative. The school board adopted a local plan, Project ReDesign, to encourage change from within each school and each administrative department. Each school was required to write school improvement plans and examine programs to respond to the goals of the restructuring plan. Schools in the district wrote plans initiating reforms which included authentic assessment, continuous progress classrooms, team teaching, portfolio assessment and evaluation, and an emphasis on teaching thinking skills. In many cases, teachers would need new skills and retraining to initiate the goals delineated in these plans. The district's restructuring initiatives provided schools with an invitation to change (David, 1991).

It was within this context that the idea of collaboratively designing a graduate teacher education program developed. The university-district partnership worked to design a graduate program for Sarasota County schoolteachers (Teacher 2000) which would enhance their professional abilities to provide optimal educational services to all children and which would help in meeting the district's goals in restructuring.

One of the first steps needed was setting program goals. Over the course of the next several months of meetings, visions were discussed, goals were written, and revisions were made. The program goals of the Teacher 2000 graduate program were intended to put into practice some novel components of teacher education (Appendix 2). The program design included a focus on cohort participation and collaboration, a high standard of competency in both knowledge and application, and participant evaluation through authentic assessment methods.

The design also reflected the five emphases of the Department of Special Education: preparing reflective and ethical practitioners, preparing professionals who can be collaborative, preparing professionals who are affirming of diversity, preparing professionals who are competent in instructional methods, and preparing professionals who are able to utilize technology in teaching and instruction.

During the development process, there were several immediate issues which required permission or resources from the larger institutional bodies. One of the first issues addressed was tuition payment. In a survey of the district's teachers, financial concerns were found to be a primary reason for possible nonparticipation in the program. Subsequently, the superintendent developed and the board approved an innovative plan to assist in tuition payments for its employee participants. Evidence of continuous progress in meeting established objectives and criteria of the Teacher 2000 program became the criteria for continued assistance.

The admission requirements of the university's College of Education became another area to consider. Although persons to be recruited would be exemplary practitioners, some would probably not meet the traditional criteria for admissions. In conjunction with the Department of Special Education's Teacher Education Committee, a proposal was made to the College of Education to implement an experimental system for admission based on criteria other than the Graduate Record Exam (GRE) and past grade point average (GPA). The proposal recommended using GPA and GRE scores as components in a matrix which also included teaching experience, observations by university or district staff letters of recommendation from other teachers, parents, principals, district staff, and colleagues, an admissions portfolio, and, if warranted, a structured interview by the admissions committee. However, in order to ensure that admissions standards and policies were met and evaluated, even within an experimental context, the University of South Florida's College of Education and Department of Special Education retained the right to make all admissions decisions. The college administrators agreed, in principle, to examine all applicants suggested by the departmental committee. Twenty-eight teachers were invited to participate in the first cohort of the Teacher 2000 graduate program.

The Teacher 2000 project also developed a collaborative model for providing instruction involving both university and school district faculty and staff. District teachers and staff will be able to become credentialled as Facilitating Clinical

Instructors (FCI), a new form of credentialled staff within the Department of Special Education. FCI credentialling recognizes outstanding practitioners' abilities and formalizes district participation in instruction of university courses in specific content or skill areas in collaboration with a university instructor of record. The application process for FCI includes recommendations from both district personnel and university faculty, a recommendation from the core faculty or a subcommittee of the departmental Teacher Education Committee, and final approval by the chair of the Department of Special Education. As FCI, a much-needed role for district personnel as teacher educators will be created (Troen & Boles, 1994).

Manatee County

During the fall of the second year in Manatee County, much of the work was focused on the restructured elementary school. The university faculty had made a commitment to spend one day a week at the school site. Some of the endowment money awarded by the regional campus dean was used to financially support a doctoral student who made a commitment to be at the school for two half-days a week. Besides the weekly meetings, the university faculty and doctoral student spent much of the time during the first few months just "hanging out" in the teachers' lounge, cafeteria, office, and hallways. They began to become familiar to the staff and to learn the culture of the school. Professional dialogues began to develop between the university people and the school faculty (Voltz, 1993). As they became more familiar with the staff and the culture of the school, opportunities for future work and relationships began to become more apparent.

Over the course of the next year, two active Teachers' Assistance Teams (Chalfant, Pysh, & Moultrie, 1979; Hayek, 1987; and, Chalfant & Pysh, 1989) developed. Both the university faculty and doctoral student were included on the school's subcommittees which were established to form their school improvement plan. Focus groups with teachers were held to address the curricular content of two university classes. Pre-intern students began working with special education students. A grant-writing group was formed and was successful in obtaining service and training grants.

It seemed to both the university faculty and district director that a school-based training site might eventually impact plans for staff development and human resources. The discussions with the core group at the school were also beginning to focus on ideas for teacher and aide in-services and technical assistance. Pretty soon, the district's director of human resources and staff development support was added to the project.

A survey was sent to all teachers, paraprofessionals, and clerical personnel in the district to identify which areas of education were of interest to district personnel and to better understand any barriers for participation in subsequent professional development programs. The survey provided objective data to confirm that there was an interest in a field-based program in education. The data also indicated that the majority of persons interested were not yet ready to enter junior or senior level classes at the university, thus guiding the next stages of planning for the developing partnership. The next fall saw two courses offered at school sites in the district: one to meet certification needs and the other for the special education cohort participating in the school-based undergraduate program.

Retrospective for Stage Three

Stage three is the current stage of the partnerships. The identification and inclusion of additional stakeholders in both districts has occurred. In the Teacher 2000 project, the district administrators have played major roles, serving as gatekeepers for resources and further development. The College of Education and departmental members have become involved in the admissions committee, as trainers for the FCI, and as reviewers of the documents for the Teacher 2000 program. The first cohort should begin their course of study soon.

In the Manatee County partnership, a school staff has become involved in implementing an effective problem-solving collaboration practice; university classes are occurring within the district; pre-intern students are actively involved in learning at the school; teachers are writing grants; and the teachers are helping to shape the university curricula.

District staff are involved in the education of college students, and the university member is spending more time in the district schools. Roles are beginning to change as a blurring of the lines begins to occur.

STAGE FOUR: IMPLEMENTING PROGRAMS

There have been a number of specific initiatives developed as a result of the partnership arrangements in both counties. In many cases, the partnership arrangements only added a component to these programs, as they were initiated by school or district personnel.

Inclusion Grant Demonstration Sites

Several researchers (see chapter 19) within the university's department of special education had been awarded a federal grant to study inclusion. This provided limited, but important, technical assistance and resources to the teacher-training site.

Technical Support

The doctoral student was employed in a half-time position at the university, but assigned to the Orange Ridge Bullock school. She worked at the school two days per week and taught an undergraduate class on campus on another day. She also began to work with individual teachers and students, addressing very specific needs. She tutored students in reading skills and visited classrooms to offer suggestions on improving student learning, when requested.

Planning Support

Both the university faculty member and doctoral student were included on the restructured school's subcommittees to help develop the school's improvement plan. In addition to serving on specific committees, they provided assistance and research background to several other teams, assisted teams in processing issues, and helped with goal planning. The research grant staff at the main campus assisted in literature reviews and in forming research questions for potential studies at the school site. Monetary resources from the inclusion research grant were used to enhance planning of the final school improvement document in the second and third years.

Release Time and Role Identification

The Manatee County school district provided funds for an adjunct instructor to teach one of the university faculty member's classes, allowing him to spend more time on the development of the partnership.

The Teacher's Assistance Team

The teacher's assistance team (TAT) began serving students from both regular and special education classes. The scheduling of the TAT was handed over to school personnel. Although there was still a core of involved teachers, any teacher in the school could ask to discuss a problem. The TAT members became strong leaders within the school's improvement teams. There were several instances where the informal discussions of this group led to the eventual implementation of programs having a wider influence. For example, after alternatives to office referrals were discussed for one child in the TAT meeting (see Chalfant, Pysh, & Moultrie, 1979; Hayek, 1987; Chalfant & Pysh, 1989), a skill-streaming program was implemented with several students by the school special education resource teacher and the school social worker. Thus, the team developed into a viable option for teachers seeking help.

University Planning

The university faculty also began to address issues of importance to the special education program development at the regional campus. Approximately 10 pre-intern special education students were placed at the school for their practicum experience. The supervision and monitoring of these students became easier and more convenient for the university faculty member because of time spent at the school in his other functions.

University Course Goals.   The teachers at the school participated in focus groups held to discuss teacher education issues. One focus group considered the undergraduate mainstreaming course required of all regular educators. The questions examined were: What should we be teaching? What experiences should the teacher education program be providing? The teachers at Orange Ridge Bullock overwhelmingly believed that experiential learning would be the most beneficial. They believed that more hours of contact with exceptional children were needed. Also there was strong advocacy to include methods of curriculum and lesson modification. It was in this meeting that the teachers voiced concerns about their own teacher education program's lack of attention to special education issues and expressed a strong desire for in-service training in this area.

The second focus group dealt with the practicum experiences of the special education pre-interns. Teachers criticized the university for not providing more guidance to supervising teachers. Also, they suggested that the university could do better in providing more reflective processing time and skill development for the students in the teacher education program.

Grant Writing

There was an interest in obtaining funding which would help meet some of the goals of the school improvement plan. To this end, a meeting for further planning was held during the summer of 1993, and a grant-writing group was planned for the 1993–94 school year. The group has submitted about $50,000 in funding requests for state and local grants and been awarded about $16,000 to date.

Autism Task Force

The Sarasota County Autism Task Force was formed to help bring together the parents and professionals in the newly created program. The university faculty member helped produce the first year's report and served on curriculum writing and community committees, while providing technical assistance to both the integrated setting classes and to the center school.

Teacher 2000

This graduate program in special education redefines, to some extent, the roles of both district personnel and university professors. It utilizes university and district practice and standards. The program is just beginning its first cohort and will be closely monitored to ensure continuing improvement. Designed with a constructivist paradigm (Poplin, 1993), it proposes the development of new models for instruction in communities served by the regional campus.

LOOKING BACK

After the initial commitment to collaboration was made, many questions arose. As the story of the partnerships reveals, only some of these questions have been sufficiently answered to date.

Q. How do roles change in a partnership?

A. Both school districts and universities are exploring different roles but are slow to change. Hard and fast roles are still unclear. Each person has assumed, to a large degree, their traditional roles, since institutional rewards are allocated according to those traditional roles. Despite a major change in what the university faculty member is doing compared to many who enter academia, the tenure rules and course-load assignments have been unchanged. The district administrators are not rewarded for working with universities.

Q. Could a regional campus program in special education be established collaboratively with local districts?

A. Yet to be determined, but ultimately we believe—YES. A traditional undergraduate program is currently underway. This may be a necessary step in our community's development, as it serves as a known base. The Teacher 2000 program establishes a collaborative program at the graduate level.

Q. What resources are needed and from where do they come?

A. People and time resources are needed. Money helps, but it is truly not the answer. Individuals with dreams, convictions, and shared visions can go a long way with minimal funds. Shared visions and reallocated resources help more than do additional people. Local people are knowledgeable of the local system and its values. Utilizing them in new roles may be better than bringing in additional outside resources. The danger is in becoming too parochial.

Q. What are the possible benefits and disadvantages that partnerships offer?

A. Partnerships between universities and school districts should improve pedagogy so that benefits in services to children improve through better-educated teachers and better supports to teachers. Another advantage is that school districts and universities share and participate in dialogue which includes a wider experiential base. The duality of theory and practice, which has been much criticized (Barth, 1990), may begin to diminish. With all partners developing a common base of application, research and teaching may become more relevant and focused at all levels.

A disadvantage to a partnership is that it may threaten the underlying values and workings of existing systems. By developing new roles and expectations of university faculty, teachers, and school administrators, traditional roles may become obsolete. Individuals in organizations may begin to institute structures to protect these roles. It is also possible that a partnership could develop its own bureaucracy.

From a university perspective, forming and developing partnerships is very difficult work. It includes compromise and collaboration and dedicated time. Traditional university work, such as writing and teaching, is usually easier work and more likely to be viewed by the university as a productive activity.

WHAT WE HAVE LEARNED

Collaboration has been affected by many circumstantial occurrences. The mere fact that there was a staff member in special education on the regional campus increased communication on matters of concern to both the districts and the universities. Within the districts, there was a push to reorganize and change. District personnel began examining their resources from a new perspective. An emphasis on continuing teacher education and improving the workforce began to emerge in the districts. Previously, continuing education had been viewed as the sole responsibility of the teacher. However, with changes in state policy, districts were able to develop in-service components in certain areas of exceptional student education.

As the collaborators reflected on processes in forming the partnerships, there were several factors identified which were instrumental in enhancing the development process, as well as several areas which challenged the planning process. Areas instrumental in enhancing the process were trust building and confidence in the other institutions, and mutual respect. Areas which challenged the process were lack of time and lack of knowledge about the structures and limitations of the others' institutional workings.

The process of developing trust and mutual respect requires cultivating. In a relationship with no previous history, there are no established working rules, expectations, or accountability structures. Even though everyone is a professional, the process of establishing trust still must occur. Each time another player is introduced, the process of developing trust must start again. Within the process, the need for open and honest communication remains imperative. Suggestions or ideas which may be brought to the table within an organization that has worked together may be held back in a newly formed partnership.

Associated with communication is ego development. Each side must be able to tolerate constructive criticism, openly admit limitations, and accept different points of view. In this case, the early successful experiences between the districts and university in areas related to technical assistance and co-teaching a course demonstrated the potential for successful collaboration and flexibility and helped to establish trust.

Also, each respective party must continually share information about the workings, policies, procedures, values, mores, and bureaucracy of their organizations, school district, or university department. Initially, it seemed that every goal should be attainable and every problem should have a solution. As the process of development continued, some limits of time, staff, and institutional thinking were found.

Sometimes unnecessary duplication in efforts occurred. One of the solutions was open discussion and priority setting. Only through open communication has the process of developing partnerships been successful. Even then, unforeseen conflict sometimes arose. One specific case arose when a university intern approached a problem in her school by dealing with a third agency. The university and district disagreed on the degree of sanctions to apply. Turf issues arose which could have been a problem. However, the trust and respect issues were established well enough that the process moved forward.

Another issue which impeded a quick process of development was bureaucracy. In this area, universities and school districts have a number of similarities. There are channels to obtain approvals from department chairs and deans and associate superintendents and superintendents. Until superintendents, school boards, university presidents, and deans begin regular communication, complete cooperation may not be possible, and there is a potential of stifling some very innovative restructuring initiatives.

The major barriers to development were, and continue to be, time related. Sometimes, a lack of time to develop the partnerships caused delays in program implementation. Scheduling meetings and coordinating calendars *within* agencies with frequently seen colleagues is difficult. Scheduling these *between* the school districts and university seemed sometimes impossible. School districts and universities have not always been adept at collaborating on long-term projects, perhaps due to time issues. An issue as simple as the calendars being defined differently in semesters and events can make scheduling time for meetings between district and university personnel very difficult.

Time was an underestimated factor in the process of development. As a planning step, it would have been better to jointly list priorities and methods to achieve them. This prior knowledge might have increased the possibility of the university faculty member's release from some other duties. For both district and university staff, there was never a true realization of how much time, thought, and effort the development process took away from other responsibilities. At some point, a regrouping of priorities must be done so that systematic development of new and innovative ideas will become an expected product.

There are long-standing beliefs from both university and school district personnel that must change if education is to be restructured and if it is to include all the established societal institutions. If teacher education programs are to reflect and nurture restructuring, both local school districts and universities must support the developments at all administrative and delivery levels. This must be done through the creation and implementation of new roles for teachers, university professors, and school district administrators. To a very small extent, this has occurred within the initial planning stages in these district-university collaborative projects. Both the districts' administrators and teachers have been able to contribute to development goals of this initiative. They have assumed roles in grant writing and research which are not part of the traditional role of a teacher. With these few exceptions, the roles and expectations for teachers involved in these endeavors have not been altered.

At the university, there has been a great deal of support within the Department of Special Education, as evidenced by other chapters in this book. Outside of the department there has been little change in the faculty assignment patterns and expectations. There is little recognition of the time-consuming nature of restructuring initiatives. It has been largely unrecognized that there is a distinct difference, in both time and skills, between *working for schools* and *working in collaboration with schools*. Both school district personnel and university faculty who are working on restructuring initiatives generally do so because of their own belief and with time which would ordinarily be devoted to more traditionally assigned duties and roles. The need for support to both teachers and faculty involved in partnership relationships is crucial (see Gross, 1988).

REFERENCES

Barth, R.S. (1991). *Improving schools from within*. San Francisco: Jossey-Bass.

Biklen, D. (1985). *Achieving the complete school: Strategies for effective mainstreaming*. New York: Teachers College Press.

Chalfant, J. C., Pysh, M., & Moultrie, R. (1979). Teacher assistance teams: a model for within-building problem solving. *Learning Disability Quarterly, 2*, 85–96.

Chalfant, J. C., & Pysh, M. (1989). Teacher assistance teams: Five descriptive studies on 963 teams. *Remedial and Special Education. 10*(6), 49–58.

David, J. L. (1991). What it takes to restructure education. *Educational Leadership, 48*(8), 11–15.

Duke, D. L. (1990). School leadership for the nineties: A matter of time and vision. *Principal, 69*(4), 22–27.

Goodlad, J. I. (1988). School-university partnerships: A social experiment. *Kappa Delta Pi Record* (Spring), 77–80.

Gross, T. L. (1988). *Partners in education: How colleges can work with schools to improve teaching and learning*. San Francisco: Jossey-Bass.

Hayek, R. A. (1987). The teacher assistance team: A preferable support. *Focus on Exceptional Children, 20*(1) 1–7.

Kearney, C. A., & Durand, V.M. (1992). How prepared are our teachers for mainstreamed classroom settings? A survey of postsecondary schools in New York State. *Exceptional Children, 59*, 6–11.

Lewis, A. (1989). *Restructuring America's schools*. Arlington, VA: American Association of School Administrators.

Paul, J. L., Duchnowski, A. J., & Danforth, S. (1993). Changing the way we do our business: One department's story of collaboration with public schools. *Teacher Education and Special Education, 16*, 95–109.

Poplin, M. (1993). *A practical theory of teaching and learning: The view from inside the new transformative classroom: Contributions of constructivism*. Paper presented at the Florida Teacher Education Division of the Council of Exceptional Children, Tampa, FL. Available from the author: The Claremont Graduate School.

Pugach, M. C. (1992). Unifying the preservice preparation of teachers in W. Stainback and S. Stainback (Eds.), *Controversial issues confronting special education: Divergent perspectives* (pp. 255–267). Boston: Allyn and Bacon.

Reynolds, M. C., Wang, M. C., & Walberg, H. J. (1987). The necessary restructuring of special and regular education. *Exceptional Children, 53*, 391–397.

Schlechty, P. C., & Whitford, B. L. (1988). Shared problems and shared vision: Organic collaboration. In K. A. Sirotnik and J. I. Goodlad (Eds.), *School-University partnerships in action: Concepts, cases and concerns* (pp.191–204). New York: Teachers College Press.

Schlechty, P. C. (1990). *Schools for the 21st century*. San Francisco: Jossey-Bass.

Shive, J. (1984). School-university partnerships: Meeting common needs. *Improving College and University Teaching, 3*, 119–122.

Stainback, W., & Stainback, S. (1990). *Support networks for inclusive schooling: Interdependent integrated education*. Baltimore: Brookes.

Troen, V., & Boles, K. (1994). A time to lead. *Teacher* (February), 40–41.

Voltz, D. (1993). Collaboration. Just what do you mean, "collaborate?" *Learning Disabilities Forum, 17*(4), 32–24.

APPENDIX 1

MISSION STATEMENT FOR THE ESTABLISHMENT OF A UNIVERSITY AND DISTRICT COLLABORATIVE TRAINING PROJECT: The mission of the University of South Florida and Manatee County Schools Collaborative Project is to design and implement community-based post-secondary professional training experiences in careers related to the instruction of at-risk students and students with special learning needs.

Program Goals:

1. Provide a degree-earning program which will be available to teachers, paraprofessionals, and working community members, as well as traditional university students.
2. Provide an integrated transdisciplinary teacher education curriculum which emphasizes applied field components and practice.
3. Provide an educational experience which will incorporate inquiry and research skills into classroom and school settings.
4. Provide structured mentoring and peer teaching experiences for the modeling of innovative and effective instructional approaches and related strategies.
5. Incorporate best practices in accountability of instruction and in measurement of educational outcomes.
6. Provide opportunities for teachers and teachers in training to improve pedagogy, which may or may not lead to a university degree.

APPENDIX 2

TEACHER 2000: AN OUTCOME-BASED MASTERS DEGREE PROGRAM

Mission Statement

The Teacher 2000 Program involves a collaborative partnership between the School Board of Sarasota County and the University of South Florida. This partnership's purpose is to design a graduate program for current teachers which will enhance their professional abilities in providing services to *all* children.

Program Goals

The designed program will:
1. Increase the competence of district-level staff by assisting them in obtaining a master's degree.
2. Include the Sarasota County School District's focus on restructuring education, Project ReDesign, and the competencies and standards of the state of Florida as well as those standard in the university and professional organizations, such as the Council for Exceptional Children.
3. Emphasize the instructional goals and standards of the Sarasota School District's restructuring plan, Project ReDesign and of Blueprint 2000.
4. Seek innovative sources of tuition funding for program participants.
5. Seek teachers from underrepresented groups as program participants.
6. Utilize a collaborative instructional model by having university personnel and district practitioners provide instruction.
7. Determine graduation by demonstration of the achievement of program objectives, utilizing experiential methods and authentic assessment throughout the program.
8. Address the Department of Special Education goals for all program graduates: that they be prepared as reflective practitioners and collaborative professionals who affirm diversity and are professionally competent.

15

EMPOWERING TEACHERS
TO BE RESPONSIVE TO
INDIVIDUAL DIFFERENCES

KIM STODDARD & SCOT DANFORTH

INTRODUCTION

HOW does one write a story of success and a story of failure within the same narrative without unjustly blotting out the evocative essence of one or the other? This is our initial purpose for telling the story of a challenging student named Chris. His journey through joyful educational successes and painful failure serves as a fitting example of the efforts undertaken within a university/school collaboration at Pinellas Park Elementary School.

Chris was celebrating his eleventh birthday on a locked psychiatric unit. Two teachers and a university doctoral student were awkward and apprehensive as they carried a cake and some gifts into the hospital. They feared that they would never have Chris back in their elementary school again. And, indeed, he didn't return. Chris was a student in the special education class for the emotionally handicapped (EH) who had struggled with a chaotic home life that included poverty and the drug abuse of his single parent. He had recently been removed from his home and placed in a temporary shelter by the Florida Department of Health and Rehabilitative Services (HRS), due to charges of parental neglect. Suddenly, as too often happens with troubled children, he found himself whisked away from both home and school to strange surroundings. Then his behavior deteriorated further and he was hospitalized.

The two teachers carrying the cake were Sally and Maxine. Sally had been Chris's general education teacher during the previous year. She had worked closely with him and his classmates to create ways for Chris to remain in the mainstream, despite his often bizarre and disruptive behavior. Maxine was Chris's current teacher in the EH class. After struggling through a year in Sally's mainstream class, Chris had been placed in Maxine's special education class. She tried to help him cope when his

301

mother went away to a substance abuse treatment facility. The third person at their side was a doctoral student who had come to know Chris through a research project chronicling this child's unique and painful path.

Despite their caring efforts to serve Chris's educational and emotional needs, each felt that they had somehow failed him. Each had wonderful successes in their work with this child. They had united themselves and even reeled in a third compatriot as a devoted advocacy force for this boy who chewed holes in his shirt and hid under the table in the back of the class. Yet, on Chris's eleventh birthday, they shared a guilt and sadness for what they had not been able to accomplish and for the child they had not been able to help.

Although uncertain about his future, these professionals also knew that Chris had achieved many classroom victories within the creative collaboration of a project called BRIDGE (Being Responsive to Individual Differences in General Education). The unification of general and special educators, as well as university personnel in this collaborative project had created a supportive alliance working with Chris on specific academic and social problems.

When Chris had initially entered Sally's third-grade class the previous fall, she observed in puzzled amazement as he climbed up on tables and leaped to the ground in flying helicopter twirls. He often picked his nose and chewed wet holes in the front of his shirt, two clown-like exhibitions which both excited and disgusted his peers. He was treated by his peers as a delightful court jester and a rude sideshow attraction. He seemed to form no genuine friendships with the other students.

Working closely together, Sally and the university faculty member devised two plans: a behavioral intervention plan to address Chris's disruptive actions and lack of social connection, and a research plan for the collection of data to follow Chris's progress and growth within the context of the intervention. In the following months, Sally and her colleagues created a broad three-part revision in Chris's general education program: 1) a placement switch from splitting the school day in two teachers' classrooms to residing completely in Sally's class, by far his most successful environment; 2) replacing the basal-based literacy instruction with a more student-centered, constructivist approach (Willinsky, 1990), which included writing and publishing Chris's own books; 3) developing a peer buddy, peer monitoring system in which Chris chose a supportive peer to help him monitor his nose-picking and shirt-chewing behaviors. These three interventions resulted in a dramatic improvement in Chris's academic performance, behavior, degree of social acceptance among peers, and sense of self-worth. We offer this introductory narrative not to merely tell a problematic story but to illustrate what has become the central ethos of the BRIDGE project: *a sense of communal responsibility among general and special educators alike for the care and education of even the most challenging students.* The responsibility for the care and education of struggling students is shifting in this one elementary school from the tradition of special education being called upon somehow to "cure the ailing" to a more comprehensive, united address of students' needs.

Perhaps it is a simple matter to combine professional forces when success and achievement come easily. Such a fairy-tale collaboration would be self-sustaining due to constant success. Yet, the challenge of working in unison to teach and support those students who struggle academically and socially brings, at best, intermittent rewards for the professionals involved. In undertaking this difficult task, the BRIDGE teachers accept not just the successes and failures of their efforts but the shared responsibility for the education of these students.

In this chapter, we will describe the BRIDGE project, a joint endeavor involving the College of Education at the University of South Florida and Pinellas Park Elementary School in Pinellas County. This collaboration unites general and special educators to better meet the needs of students considered to have disabilities and those considered at risk for educational failure. We will tell how the collaboration started, how it developed, and how the roles of both public school teachers and university personnel changed dramatically in the process of working together.

Central to the partnership was our desire to learn about the process of collaboration specific to this growing project. We wanted to learn:

- How do the roles of university faculty change in the development of a partnership with a public elementary school?
- How do the roles of teachers change when expanded opportunities and resources are provided for professional exploration, strategy development, and strategy implementation?
- How does a practicum experience in a school setting involving general and exceptional education teachers actively collaborating impact the teaching skills and attitudes of undergraduate student-teachers?
- What happens when a university exceptional education department collaborates with a public school from a position of facilitation (How can we help?) rather than authority (We know what you should do.)?

Our assumptions underlying the framework of the project included the following:

- Learning within collaborative work is an ongoing, flexible process of individual and communal growth involving social interaction, conflict, caring relationships, and personal reflection.
- Teachers are professionals who, if allowed adequate resources and support, will combine art, science, and self in the development of their craft.
- Teachers share a sense of communal responsibility for the care and education of the most challenging students.
- Teachers are capable decision makers who, if provided with the chance to investigate and learn within a supportive environment, will find ways to make a positive difference in the lives and learning of children.
- Teachers need to feel a sense of ownership in the care and education of students.
- Within their daily activities, teachers can do research which informs and improves their practice.
- University faculty and teachers can work as supportive colleagues, each bringing a unique expertise and perspective to the collaborative process.
- University faculty need to be active, on-site partners in the school setting, playing numerous social roles within their daily activities, spanning from knowledgeable leader to supportive follower.

THE BRIDGE PROJECT: HISTORY AND DAILY PRACTICE

In this section, how the school-university partnership emerged at this elementary school will be discussed in relation to the following three topic areas: 1) the planning stage; 2) the initial entry into the school; and 3) the development of initiatives.

Planning Stage

This school-university partnership program was created after many meetings among the numerous stakeholders within the school district and university. At one such meeting, the department chairperson's question to the superintendent was simply stated, "How can we help?" Five months of planning sessions with an advisory committee followed to determine how the university could help the school system. An advisory committee was formed consisting of the associate superintendent of exceptional student education, the supervisor of the specific learning disabilities program, the director of the district exceptional education resource center, the director of student-teacher placement in the district, the school principal, the chairperson of the department of special education at the university, and a special education university faculty member.

This core group met bi-weekly to discuss issues of concern shared by both the school district and the university, to outline the needs of each institution as shown in Table 15.1, and to make plans for a collaboration which would mutually address needs on both sides.

As discussions progressed, a project emerged that could benefit both groups. Although the needs of each institution were unique, the discussions enabled both groups to realize the similarities of those needs and the value of a cooperative venture.

Traditionally, the role of the university has been one of distant "expert" (Schultz, Laine, & Savage, 1988). University faculty functioned as consultants to the schools and provided "best practice" models in strategies or curricular agendas. Knowing that the expert or consultant role often does not provide ongoing, invested support to school districts in their areas of weakness or need, BRIDGE project members set out to invent a more vital and relevant role for university faculty in relation to schools.

The district identified the high incidence of referrals and placement of students in exceptional education programs, specifically noting learning disabilities programs as a significant concern. The determination was made to explore alternatives at the elementary school level where general education and exceptional education student-teachers might be better prepared for meeting the needs of a challenging population of students. The county selected an elementary school with a challenging, diverse population of students. Many of the students within the school qualified for free lunch (63% of the population) and lived in the surrounding working-class area. The advisory group's premise in the selection of this school was that a collaborative program should be created in a fairly typical elementary school, not in a school already benefiting from considerable outside support and resources.

TABLE 15.1
Outline of the Needs of Each Institution

School's Needs	University's Needs
• Response to significant increase in the number of students qualifying for exceptional education programs	• Better prepare teachers to meet the needs of a more diversified population of students
• More of a match between learning style and delivery model of instruction	• Development of school-based research agenda
• Involve teachers as researchers and decision makers	• Development of a teacher education program where research by teachers is practiced
• Need for collaboration between general and exceptional education	• Development of a program where student-teachers work collaboratively

Initial Entry into the School

Teachers at the school were told this partnership would provide them with the opportunity for general and exceptional education teachers to develop methods to better educate their diverse population of students. The primary goal of the project would be to assist them in developing a keener awareness of students' individual needs and better equip them to address those needs. Students who had been unsuccessful in school and those with specific disabilities were particularly targeted for this project.

Teachers were also told they would be free to explore ways of addressing the above goal. Neither the school district nor the university was mandating any changes as part of the project. However, provisions were to be made in which the teachers could work collaboratively with their colleagues at the university and within the school to explore options. The only stipulation for involvement in the project was a willingness to work collaboratively with the university in the student-teacher mentoring program. This met the needs of the university to place students into supervised student-teaching situations.

Development of Initiatives

After the initial presentation, 65 percent of the teachers volunteered to be involved in the project. The faculty member then met with the teachers individually and in small groups to understand their concerns about the students they taught. The question explored in those meetings was, "What do you think we can do to better meet the needs of students here at this school?" These meetings occurred before school, after school, and during the teachers' planning times throughout the day.

The teachers came up with a wide and diverse range of ideas which were formulated into five program initiatives:

- Collaboration between general education and exceptional education
- Exploration of alternative class models
- Development of family liaison programs
- Mentoring of student-teachers
- Research into the effectiveness of programs

Teachers volunteered to work more specifically in their primary area of interest, and one teacher from each subgroup served as the facilitator for each initiative. This enabled subgroups to meet and focus more specifically on their initiative. Each facilitator was responsible for coordinating the work of each initiative and reporting once a week at the larger group meeting that was held before school. In addition, the facilitators of each initiative met bi-weekly with the faculty member to brainstorm and maintain a focus for the larger group. Under each initiative, teachers (with technical assistance and support from the university faculty member) determined training needs, ideas for implementation, and a means for determining the effectiveness of a particular strategy or larger curriculum issue. Table 15.2 presents highlights of activities explored within each initiative.

CHANGES IN THE FACULTY ROLE IN THIS SCHOOL/ UNIVERSITY PARTNERSHIP

School/university partnerships have created a dilemma for new untenured faculty members who are typically rewarded for activities which produce publications, not "service" projects such as BRIDGE. This dilemma will continue to be problematic for all new faculty unless the emphasis within the specific departments, the education colleges, and the overall university program changes (Lieberman, 1992, Roemer, 1991; Smith, 1992). This section will address the traditional role of university faculty, the new role for a faculty member that has been established by this partnership, and the inherent problems in establishing this new role.

Traditional Roles of Faculty

The philosophy and "practice" to which doctoral students are exposed during their program consists of a considerable emphasis on writing grants and writing up research for publication. Teaching effectively is important, and service is required, but each doctoral student knows that to receive tenure at any "credible" university, publication is a must. The doctoral student's major professor encourages the selection of an area of research in which the doctoral student begins active investigation that can be immediately turned over to publications. This practice is modeled by senior faculty members and reinforced when doctoral students are

TABLE 15.2
Summary of Activities Explored Within Initiatives

Collaboration Between General Education and Exceptional Education

Mini-workshops were developed in which teachers within the school shared strategies they found successful with challenging students.

Collaborative Teaching was implemented with exceptional education teachers and general education teachers in the general education classroom.

Workshops in Strategies were conducted by university faculty on strategies the teachers identified as lacking in their teaching repertoire.

Exploration of Alternative Class Models

Teachers Researched various models of instruction in which students are grouped together for extended periods of time to enhance a positive classroom climate.

Teachers Developed an Instructional Model for grades kindergarten through grade four in which the above plan could be implemented at the school.

Family Liaison

A Family Survey was developed by the teachers, and information was collected on the needs of families concerning school life.

A Make and Take Night for Families was completed in which child care was provided and parents moved from center to center for an array of activities provided by the teachers.

A Family Reading Program was implemented by a first-grade teacher which emphasized practical techniques for parents to enhance reading at home.

Mentoring of Student Teachers

Mentoring Workshops were conducted throughout the semester for all teachers to enhance their communication, coaching, and observation skills in working with student-teachers.

Weekly Student-Teacher Meetings were held throughout the semester, in which teachers presented their area of "expertise" to both the general and exceptional education student-teachers placed at the school.

An Intern Teaching Exchange program was implemented to enable general and exceptional education student-teachers to teach in another discipline.

Research Agenda

An Alternative Data Collection Workshop was conducted to assist teachers in the development of their research projects.

Teacher-Research Projects were developed, implemented, analyzed, and disseminated on various strategies of programs the teachers utilized within their classroom.

Perception Journals were completed by the student-teachers to determine if an attitude of collaboration was evidenced within their classroom and within the school.

applying for positions and beginning their careers as new faculty members. Working with the schools is typically comprised of in-service or consulting work. Work with schools helps faculty meet the minimal "service" requirements of their positions, functions as a supplement to their salary, or gives the faculty member access to captive research subjects.

In traditional doctoral studies, no real training or experience is completed to enhance the skills needed to be an effective participant in collaborative partnerships. Smith and Auger (1985–1986) highlight critical components of successful collaborative projects: a sense of good timing, development of trust and mutuality, and outcomes. The skills needed to ensure that the above components take place require changes in traditional roles and relationships of all participants (Goodlad, 1990). Senior faculty mentors have not practiced these critical skills. Thus, new faculty are not encouraged to expend their energy in enhancing partnerships but are supported to complete traditional research.

A new faculty member deciding to spend additional time in building partnerships often receives criticism from senior colleagues that too much time is being spent in "service" and not in research. The time spent at a school site rather than on the university campus can cause further deterioration of relationships with other colleagues at the university. Administrators may lament that the faculty member has been hired to "teach" at the university and not to work for a school system.

The traditional role of faculty members have been altered by the BRIDGE project. The three major changes in the role of the university faculty in this partnership are as follows:

Traditionally	Changes in Role
• Teach in an "expert" model with little practical knowledge base • Traditional partnership focuses on student-teacher placement; primary goal is to meet self-interest • University faculty are researchers and impart knowledge	• Teach students to be problem solvers and critical analysts based on classroom experience • Partnership encompasses more global objectives, self-interest secondary • Students are researchers; teacher education develops the teacher as researcher

The Expert Model

What is taught in university coursework does not often parallel what university students are exposed to while student-teaching or beginning their teaching careers. Traditionally faculty members are considered the "experts" and defend their assertions through the support of numerous research investigations within the professional literature or from their own professional pursuits. In turn, students return dejected from their initial teaching settings and complain that "it doesn't work that way in the real world." Thus, university faculty complain about the inadequate job the school system is doing and personnel in the school system complain that university faculty have lost touch with reality (Schultz, Laine, & Savage, 1988).

Traditional Partnerships: Student-Teacher Placements

In many instances, the traditional partnership between the school system and the university consists of the placement of student-teachers in settings within the school district. Lasley, Matczynski, and Williams (1992) have described these partnerships as "noncollaborative." In a noncollaborative venture, communication among the parties occurs, but each participant is solely looking out for their own best interest rather than encompassing a more expansive goal for the partnership. The futile attempt at partnerships is further eroded by the fact that student-teaching supervision is considered the least respected role for a faculty member and often the responsibility is delegated to doctoral students, with little guidance given on effective mentoring skills. Thus the faculty member does not actively observe what is going on in the schools and cannot offer feasible solutions to the student-teacher. This lack of "firsthand" knowledge by the university faculty member reduces the credibility of the faculty member, and the cycle of distrust and disjointed efforts continues to erode the possibility of building a collaborative partnership with the school system (Lasley, 1984).

Role as Researcher

Faculty members are expected to complete research investigations and disseminate their findings in professional forums, as well as impart this information to their university students. The faculty member's role is traditionally established as imparter of knowledge, while the student's role is to take this information and utilize it in their setting. Faculty members do not typically encourage student-teachers to view themselves as researchers. The established belief is that research is conducted by faculty and doctoral students, while practical implementation is completed by students and student-teachers (Gage, 1978). Most university teacher education programs require students to take, at most, one research course during their teacher education program. The content of the course emphasizes the understanding of simple statistical information to assist the student in interpreting formal assessment information. The student often begins a teaching career with a strong belief that research is an intrusive process that is only completed by university faculty. These faculty members are often viewed as "outsiders" who come into a school, implement a strategy or method, collect data on the effectiveness of the plan, and leave the research setting without creating positive change or offering suggestions for improved practice.

NEW ROLE FOR UNIVERSITY FACULTY IN THE BRIDGE PROJECT

The traditional roles of university faculty have been altered and expanded by the willingness of both stakeholders to take a risk. As Smith (1992) asserts, the development of trust and risk taking may be the most challenging task for both groups to develop because of past adversarial relationships between school districts and universities. Smith and Auger (1985–1986) reiterate the importance of mutuality and trust in building successful partnerships. This trust can only be developed over time while working within the school.

On-Site Teaching

The time spent in the school, in classrooms, and talking to students and parents has enabled university faculty involved in BRIDGE to provide more plausible suggestions to student-teachers on what to do when "the perfect scenario" plan fails. In addition, the student-teachers receive valuable insight into the importance of "problem solving" that university faculty model while on site. Additionally, university faculty can bring "real" and current case studies to the university classroom. Through observations of student-teachers at the school and candid discussions with the teachers and student-teachers, university faculty develop a better understanding of the weaknesses of the current university program and have a basis for making necessary adjustments.

Mentoring Program for Student-Teachers

In collaborative projects like BRIDGE, university faculty members spend more time on site; thus, the relationship between the supervising teachers and the university faculty members develops beyond the traditional teacher-university role. Teachers and university faculty are viewed as colleagues. In BRIDGE general and exceptional education teachers, student-teachers, and university faculty work in collaboration to determine the progress of a student-teacher and develop a plan for building strengths and addressing weaknesses. The general and exceptional education teachers and university faculty together conduct seminars for student-teachers, equally sharing the responsibility and content of the seminar. This collaborative venture provides an excellent model for student-teachers by demonstrating collaboration across many disciplines.

From Research Expert to Collaborative Research Ventures

The role of faculty members as imparters of knowledge has slowly evolved to one of collaborators in research through the BRIDGE partnership. The research investigated at the school is conducted in many different forms and for many different reasons. The role of research is not conducted to help faculty members write for another publication but to further the knowledge base for teachers. As Ginger Weade (1992) states, "Teacher researchers are viewed as an emergent community of educators who position themselves for leadership and change in the traditional, role-based distinctions that divide research and practice" (p. 60). Furthermore, the classroom-based research fills a void that is missing in traditional research. Through the work of collaborative research ventures, teachers and university faculty members model to student-teachers that teachers and university faculty are professional colleagues and that one role of a teacher is researcher.

University Faculty Perspective

The following section is written in the first person to express the personal perspective of the faculty member involved in the project.

My faculty assignment at the school was in replacement of teaching one university course. I made the decision to physically be present at the school for one full day and come back to the school as needed on other days throughout the week. Although this was considerably more time consuming than a university course load, I felt that my commitment to the project and the teachers needed to be evidenced by my physical presence at the school. This commitment also required me to be actively involved in the school restructuring efforts. Thus, I volunteered to be one of the community members of the School Advisory Council (SAC), a planning and governing body directing restructuring at that site.

A typical day for me would usually begin with a meeting before school with the teachers involved in the BRIDGE project to discuss upcoming activities and the direction of each initiative. In addition, brainstorming sessions and group discussions were conducted if an issue needed further exploration. The other weekly meeting was an informational update session with the principal.

The remainder of the school day consisted of individual and small group meetings with teachers, observations of student-teachers, follow-up meetings with directing teachers, and conferences with student-teachers. Additionally, I would substitute teach for short periods of the time throughout the day to provide teachers the opportunity to conference with other colleagues, work on one of the initiatives, or further their research project. As the student-teachers took over more responsibility in the classroom, additional time was available to teachers for 45-minute mini-sessions to be held when needed throughout the day. Finding the time for completion of all the many aspects of the BRIDGE project was and continues to be a constant challenge for the teachers, the student-teachers, the principal, and myself. For this reason, a new initiative was introduced in year two of the project devoted to the exploration of alternative time schedules.

Although time-consuming, the many meetings provided a supportive, informative, and enjoyable social structure which enabled an improved sense of professional community to develop. Teachers in both general and exceptional education used this time to develop their own research agenda, examine their own teaching strategies, and explore their own belief systems. Their commitment to the BRIDGE project was sincere because it was their project, not a mandate from the county, or the university, or another "professional." In this project, the teachers were identified as the "professionals" and were allowed the resources and support to develop their craft.

As the teachers began the BRIDGE project, it was evident to me that the teachers lacked confidence and a sense of their own professional competence. They seemed to have fallen into a habit of dependency, often looking to others for direction and approval. The following scenario reoccurred several times throughout the day for the first two months of the project. Jan and I were meeting to discuss the Family Liaison Initiative. As we discussed the various possibilities that the teachers had developed for a Family Fun Night, she continued to ask me, "Is this what you want?" I would always answer, "What do you think we should do?" At our bi-weekly facilitator meetings, each facilitator would end their update session by asking me if what they had suggested was what I wanted or thought needed to be done. Gradually, they began to understand that what I wanted was to follow them as they dared to be self-directed and innovative.

Through their interactions with other teachers and myself, the teachers were able to develop a community which supported them through both failures and successes, a community which thrived on asking, "What if we do this?" or "Why don't we try it this way?"

Teacher-Initiated Research Projects

Topics discussed in our meeting often included individual teacher research projects. I would provide feedback to these teachers to assist them with developing and implementing their research ventures. As a facilitator, I provided information on alternative means for collecting data and offered additional readings in their area of investigation. I also acted as a "sounding board" for musings and "from the hip" theorizing about their particular study.

Perhaps the most prohibitive aspect of the research studies was producing final research documents. Upon completion of their data collection, the process of writing up results for dissemination consumed a great deal of time. But, through financial resources provided in the project, teachers were able to dedicate time to work on writing and editing. In addition, the opportunity for the teachers to earn credit toward their recertification area added further support for completion of their investigations.

These teachers are now neither afraid nor unable to do research, as many of my colleagues at the university contend. It is important that I did not initially introduce research to the teachers and say professional research is completed "this way," in a formal manner using only approved social science methodology. Instead, I asked them if there was any aspect of their teaching lives that they would like to more fully explore. They identified the area of investigation, and together we determined the practical possibilities for data collection and analysis. As illustrated

TABLE 15.3
Titles of Teacher-Initiated Research Projects

The use of portfolio assessment as a means to assess the reading ability of selected kindergarten, first- and second-grade students

The effect of the reading program BALANCE on the reading attitude, self-esteem, and reading skills of selected third-grade students

An examination of teacher perceptions about the Early Success Reading program for first-grade students

A qualitative study of building relationships between nursing home residents and students in an exceptional education program

The effect of a self-monitoring program on specific behaviors of selected first-grade students

Audio tapes as a means for assessing the language development of selected kindergarten students

The effectiveness of cooperative grouping for mathematics on the social skills of selected kindergarten students

A case study of the inclusive education of a third-grade student labeled emotionally handicapped

in the titles of the research investigations in Table 15.3, a wide range of areas were explored.

As the project evolved, a support system among the group developed which enabled all of us to continue our efforts although we were not really sure where we were heading. No history had been developed or recorded in which we could read a definitive set of "best practices" for successful collaborative ventures. The support system impacted my willingness to take the risks necessary to direct an emergent project in a "foreign" setting. I often felt as if I were a salesperson without a product. Initially, the teachers looked to me for support in their endeavors, but as time went on a more reciprocal relationship developed which provided a strong mutual support system for all of us. A secondary support system was the weekly Collaborative Research Group (CRG) with other faculty involved in collaborative projects. This forum provided a "sounding board" for me to determine project direction and focus.

During the first year of the project I was the only faculty member actively involved in the BRIDGE project. Although I received support from the weekly CRG meetings and the teachers were strong supporters, I often felt alone in my dual professional roles at the school and the university. I was a junior faculty member without tenure. I was the only faculty member in the elementary school, and I also was the only faculty member on the regional campus involved in such a project. This dilemma was remedied in year two when a doctoral student was assigned to the project, and I was able to bring in another faculty member in elementary education to work on the project. These two individuals added new perspectives, new expertise, and much needed daily support for the continuation of the project.

As our project is now well into its third year, the issue of trust and risk taking continues to influence all that we do. I believe the teachers trust that what I am doing at their school is not to serve my own best interest or some "hidden research agenda" but to provide them with the opportunity to determine how we can work together toward helping all students.

When conflicts and misunderstandings occur among the participants, it primarily is due to poor communication and a temporary breakdown in the sense of trust among all the participants. This challenge to continuously build this sense of trust and risk taking continues to be important to the success of the project.

CHALLENGES IN THE NEW FACULTY ROLE

The changes in faculty role have resulted in some new problems which would not surface if a more traditional university role for faculty were imparted. In traditional roles, participants in partnerships know the expectations and boundaries. With this new partnership, questions emerge due to a shift in roles and responsibility. The roles have not been firmly established, as evidenced by the varied roles that university faculty hold in each unique partnership (chapters 14–18). As Ann Lieberman (1992) concludes, partnerships take considerable energy, time through meetings, paper shuffles, and general bureaucratic red tape. This problem multiplies when two large bureaucracies are involved. The amount of time necessary to establish and maintain a collaborative partnership requires that other more traditional faculty roles are not given top priority. If untenured faculty take the risk of involving themselves in partnerships, a new means for determining tenure may be necessary. The unchartered nature of this partnership often causes a sense of uneasiness that comes with any new endeavor. Support from the mentors, chairs, and deans at the university is critical if the ventures are to continue.

The key to the continued success of this project has been the willingness of the school district and the university chair to take a risk on a project that had no proven history. Traditionally, both school districts and universities shunned projects that did not have clear objectives up front with measurable results. Due to the financial consequences and the public nature of both institutions, only those projects that were guaranteed to produce success could be ventured. This partnership continues to evolve as year three begins. The reason for its success could be summed up in Lieberman's (1992) statement that "the looser nature of collaborative partnerships seems to make them more resilient, allowing for greater risk taking and the possibility of truly learning from errors and failures" (p. 152).

A new perspective of the role of faculty has emerged due to the BRIDGE project. The teacher-education program and the role of university faculty have undergone dramatic changes which more clearly reflect a true collaborative partnership with the school district and teachers within the district. Finally, the transformation of the university faculty's role has resulted in a change in the role we envision for teachers. These changes include a much stronger emphasis in the curriculum on the development of the teacher as an advocate, a life-long learner, and a researcher.

TEACHERS' NEW ROLES

BECAUSE OF BRIDGE, FOR THE FIRST TIME EVER I FEEL LIKE A PROFESSIONAL.

—A BRIDGE TEACHER

As teachers take on and gain confident mastery over new, nontraditional roles in the operation of their schools, they gain a sense of professional pride and dignity. They feel the accomplishment of utilizing their previously untapped talents toward the improved education of their students. These new roles go beyond the traditional teaching capacity of delivering instructional content within the classroom.

Within the context of nationwide school restructuring efforts, many educators have begun to outline a change in the nature of the teaching profession, an expansion of professional roles and occupational power. They have described this shift as "teacher empowerment" (Buswell, 1980; Fagan, 1989; Foster, 1990; Kincheloe, 1991; Duffy, 1992). A national educational policy poll of elementary school teachers found that teacher empowerment was a major priority among that group (Instructor, 1986). Many teachers have become aware of the pervasive impact of the various levels of educational decision making upon their own classroom and now seek a voice in those system processes. As one BRIDGE teacher commented, "My classroom and my kids are the most important. We can't forget them. But we need to do many things to improve our school. And everything we do comes back to help our classrooms and our kids. That's why we have to think big." Certainly, this is a time of big thinking for teachers as their work lives broaden to include many additional roles.

The expanded roles of the BRIDGE teachers are always developing and growing as they think of new paths and take new chances. Currently, those expanded roles include work in the following areas: 1) school decision making; 2) research; 3) mentorship with student interns; and 4) consulting and professional development.

We will briefly describe the work of the BRIDGE teachers in each of these areas with particular emphasis on the prominent issues of trust, risk taking, progress, and frustration.

Teachers as School Decision Makers

Many leaders at the state and national level are calling for a shift of decision-making power, a movement away from the traditional top-down organization of schools to a more participatory form of school decision making in which teachers play a major role (Barth, 1990; Schlechty, 1990). In Florida, the state's restructuring plan, Blueprint 2000, calls for site-based management at each building, ostensibly allowing for an increased role for teachers, parents, and community members in the formation of school goals. According to this plan, the teachers and administration of each school in the state must write a School Improvement Plan (SIP) to direct the further development and growth of programs at that site.

The BRIDGE teachers have found both elation and frustration in their roles as decision makers. They have taken on decision-making roles both in the Blueprint 2000 process and within their BRIDGE project work. Although it is difficult to separate out teacher work into neat piles labelled "BRIDGE Leadership Experiences" and "Blueprint 2000 Leadership Experiences," we will do so to facilitate our discussion.

As participants in the Blueprint 2000 process of writing their SIP, they have valued the opportunity to clarify the priorities of their school and to map out a direction for the future. Yet they have often found the process to be a dance without sufficient music, a set of half-empty bureaucratic steps dictated by the state.

The entire school staff has struggled with the many time-consuming meetings brought on by this process. However, the teachers have typically felt that these meetings and the required extra effort would be worthwhile, if the final product would be an SIP which would allow them to develop and implement innovative new programs. Yet they reported the planning process to be time consuming and inefficient. They felt that they expended a great amount of energy and received little in the way of reform to show for it. Clearly, the decision-making role which was initially prized by the teachers at this school lost value as they struggled through the cumbersome SIP development process.

In contrast, the teachers speak highly of their opportunities to lead and control the various BRIDGE initiatives. The university's open-ended approach offered the support of faculty members and students to follow the lead of teachers at the school. Since the university entered the school with no agenda beyond the placement of student interns at the school, all other initiatives have been created and developed by the teachers with university support. The university has given expertise, time, and encouragement to the ideas of teachers, often the well-kept, secret wishes of what might be done in the best of all possible worlds. The BRIDGE teachers appreciated the opportunity to follow their own inclinations and professional knowledge, to be leaders in their own work.

The primary limitation expressed by teachers in reference to either the Blueprint 2000 process or the BRIDGE initiatives was time. The expansion of teacher work into decision making involves the addition of tasks on top of the traditional classroom instructional responsibilities. They complain of being weighted down with "too much busywork," a plethora of paperwork and noninstructional tasks which keep them constantly racing to merely keep up.

This issue of time and responsibilities is one manifestation of the difficulties caused by the traditional temporal and spatial structure of teacher work. Teachers often spend many hours in their classrooms with their students, isolated from colleagues, with little opportunity to collaborate, learn from one another, and provide mutual support. In many ways, BRIDGE has helped to alleviate the ill affects of this professional isolation by providing ways for teachers to come together in supportive collaboration. Nonetheless, even a good thing like BRIDGE takes time, a scarce commodity in a teacher's tightly structured day. There are obviously some more basic issues of personal time, space, and freedom within the teaching profession which have yet to be adequately addressed on a broad scale.

Teachers as Researchers

One afternoon at a meeting of one of the BRIDGE initiatives, a teacher who had recently joined BRIDGE was attempting to gain her bearings by asking general questions about the kind of work BRIDGE teachers do. When she inquired less than enthusiastically about doing research in her classroom, she was met with a forceful, "You have to do research. BRIDGE teachers do research and that's that." The new member shyly asked about how this research was to be done. She received some direction from the other teachers and arranged a meeting with university personnel to help her set up a study that met her needs and followed her professional interests.

It is important to understand that the one teacher's fierce declaration that "BRIDGE teachers do research" was not merely an echoing of a policy laid down by university faculty. There is no such BRIDGE policy. In fact, BRIDGE has no policies. Common educational wisdom holds that the power of the university faculty member's devotion to research is matched only by the public school teacher's disinterest in educational research. University faculty members relish their roles as knowledge producers while the public school teacher serves as an extremely reluctant knowledge consumer. Yet this one BRIDGE teacher captured in her somewhat demonstrative words the growing sense of professional pride felt by BRIDGE teachers who have become knowledge producers, teachers conducting research on problems and topics of their own professional practice.

"Bridge teachers do research" is a statement that this elementary school is now a knowledge-making place, a community of investigation and active learning. The BRIDGE teacher-researchers have created their own research projects which place the various dimensions of their professional practice under close self-scrutiny. Is this working? Is this the best way? How might I better serve my students? These have been the general questions which have found specificity in the teacher research projects. With the guidance of university personnel, these teachers have begun to incorporate data collection and analysis within their usual teaching activities. They are making research part of their work.

One teacher decided to switch her students to a portfolio assessment system which aggregated student work products as demonstration of learning and progress. She hypothesized that the portfolios would provide useful data for her communication with parents and for planning of instructional activities. During a research consultation session with university personnel, she looked up from her student portfolios and her months of anecdotal notes and asked, "Is this really research? I mean, this has been so helpful to me, but it just seems like reflection." This comment and the conversation that ensued demonstrate the common conception of research as stiff, overly formal, necessarily statistical, and generally removed from the concerns of teachers.

This one teacher had arrived at a personal valuing of her research because it served as an organized approach to reflective teaching practice. She had found a way to analyze and rethink her work. Perhaps this is the greatest gain made by the BRIDGE teachers in their research projects. They have taken on an empowering, exciting strategy for reflecting and reforming their own professional practice.

Teachers as Mentors for Student-Teachers

In the BRIDGE partnership, both general and exceptional education teachers provide mentoring to their own student-teacher and also provide expertise and support for the other general and exceptional education student-teachers. There is a strong emphasis on the practice of active collaboration between general and exceptional education teachers.

Interns assigned to this setting apply to be placed at the school, knowing that extra assignments will be required beyond the traditional student-teacher expectations. In addition, the interns are notified that the philosophy of teachers involved in the BRIDGE project is one of active collaboration between general and exceptional education, that teachers are researchers, and that an emphasis is placed on involving families in the education process.

The additional assignments for the student-teachers are contained within a manual developed in a collaborative effort by the teachers and university faculty. The additional assignments primarily focus on projects that enhance collaboration between the general and exceptional education student-teachers. These include critiquing videotapes of one's own teaching and teaching in each other's discipline. Students turn in weekly journals to the university faculty member at the school. The journal enables the student-teacher to provide candid feedback to the university faculty member and insight into the progress of the skills of the student-teacher.

Teachers and University Faculty as Co-Mentors

In BRIDGE, student-teachers view the classroom teacher and the university faculty as co-mentors. The teachers direct mini-seminars at the school each week in an area of their chosen expertise. In these seminars, the student-teachers have an opportunity to share with both disciplines and learn a new technique or perspective from different teachers. The students meet in an update session with the university faculty member every other week for a 30-minute period during the school day. At this meeting, the students are given the opportunity to discuss schedules and assignments and receive feedback on their journal entries, or discuss any other concerns that may be pertinent.

Enhancement of Mentoring Skills

The teachers meet in mini-sessions to review practices or discuss problems that may be occurring during the student-teaching experience. These 30- to 45-minute sessions are held during the school day when the student-teachers have taken over full responsibility for the teaching load. In addition, methods for enhancing communication and means for providing feedback and direction to student-teachers are presented by both the university faculty and the teachers.

This collaborative venture provides an excellent model for the student-teachers demonstrating collaboration across the disciplines of general and exceptional education and the university and school district. The goal of the mentoring program is to instill in future teachers an attitude of collaboration and professionalism that crosses all disciplines. Perhaps one student-teacher's journal entry typifies the effectiveness of the mentoring program."Teachers demonstrate the essence of BRIDGE. They are involved and concerned with each child's individual situation. Teachers feel they are out to fix things. They seem empowered."

Teachers as Consultants

The teachers within the BRIDGE project have grown dramatically in the area of professional development. Traditionally, when universities and school districts work collaboratively, the university faculty members disseminate the information at local, state, and national forums. In this partnership, the faculty, teachers, principal, and district staff all have interdependent roles in the presentation of the perspectives and findings of this collaborative venture. These presentations have been made to numerous audiences both locally and nationally.

Most of the teachers involved in the project had not presented at a professional conference and were unsure and insecure in their new role. However, as their experiences grew, their self-confidence and sense of personal professionalism emerged. As the project continues to expand through networking with other teachers, the title of one of their presentations aptly sums up their sense of spirit and determination: "Teachers do know best."

This partnership has taught us many important lessons about the influence and interconnection between and among professional and personal variables. On a professional level, we found that teachers were not afraid to do research; in fact, they enjoyed investigating meaningful aspects of their work. However, this finding was influenced in large part by the personal variables of trust and the ability to take risks established in the BRIDGE project. Changes were made in school curriculum, daily lesson plans, and university coursework because the professionals involved were willing to take risks and look beyond their own self-interests and traditional territories to seek communal objectives.

Time and a willingness to extend the extra effort also influenced all aspects of the relationship. Time was needed to complete professional projects such as teacher research projects or the planning and implementation of more inclusive learning settings. In addition, time was needed to develop a mutual relationship built on trust, open communication, and support for risk taking. These professional and personal variables seem to be intertwined throughout the process of developing good partnerships.

CONCLUSION

Despite the encouraging progress of BRIDGE over these past three years, it often seems that the journey ahead is longer and more arduous than the path already traversed. Looking ahead, we see many formidable challenges awaiting our address:

- Given the limited number of university faculty, how can the partnership expand to additional school settings without abandoning our original premise that university faculty need to be actively involved as on-site partners?
- How can we effectively use a "bottom-up" approach to program development in a way that ensures the support and involvement of administrators at the top?
- How can university faculty and teachers continue to maintain a high level of involvement given limited time and uncertain resources?
- How can doctoral students be effectively immersed in the partnership given the constraints of time and responsibility?
- How do we evaluate the value and benefits of this type of multi-faceted, multi-directional project? (See chapter 19.)

Successful inclusion of exceptional students, which we assume to be our ultimate goal of the project, still remains a hopeful future. Currently the staff are implementing a number of practices which increase the likelihood of success for all students. Although general and special educators have come together with increasing communication and comaraderie, the exceptional student services at Pinellas Park Elementary continue to be primarily of the pull-out genre. Additionally, issues of teacher time and the professional control over school-wide policies and directions remain as stumbling blocks for our continued contention. In BRIDGE, it is often uncertain what innovations teachers will actually have time to do.

THE FUTURE

Moving forward into future challenges, BRIDGE teachers carry with them an improved sense of professional self-esteem and unity. They report feeling more powerful and able to trust themselves and each other as they continue moving forward into risky terrain. The progress is slow, but the feeling of group support and togetherness in that progress is currently the glue that holds it all together. We are trusting that glue to hold us firm in our united resolve to reach our most challenging students as we continue working in partnership.

REFERENCES

Barth, R. S. (1990). *Improving schools from within: Teachers, parents, and principals can make a difference*. San Francisco: Jossey-Bass.

Buswell, C. (1980). Pedagogic change and social change. *British Journal of Sociology in Education, 1*, 293–306.

Duffy, G. (1992). Let's free teachers to be inspired. *Phi Delta Kappan, 73*(6), 442–447.

Fagan, W. T. (1989). Empowered students; Empowered teachers. *Reading Teacher, 42*(8), 572–578.

Foster, K. (1990). Small steps on the way to teacher empowerment. *Educational Leadership* (May, 1990), pp. 38–41.

Gage, N.L. (1978). *The scientific basis of the art of teaching*. New York: Teachers College Press.

Goodlad, J. (1990). *Teachers for our nation's schools*. San Francisco: Jossey-Bass.

Instructor. (1986). Here's what you care about most. *Instructor, 95*(9), 30–32.

Kincheloe, J. (1991). *Teachers as researchers: Qualitative inquiry as a path to empowerment*. New York: Falmer Press.

Lasley, T. J. (1984). Editorial. *Journal of Teacher Education, 35*, (inside cover).

Lasley, T. J., Matczynski, T. J., & Williams, J. A. (1992). Collaborative and noncollaborative partnership structures in teacher education. *Journal of Teacher Education, 43*, 257–261.

Lieberman, A. (1992). School/university collaboration: A view from the inside. *Phi Delta Kappan, 74*, 147–156.

Roemer, M. (1991). What we talk about when we talk about school reform. *Harvard Educational Review, 61*, 434–488.

Schlechty, P. (1990). *Schools for the twenty-first century: Leadership imperatives for educational reform*. San Francisco: Jossey-Bass.

Schultz, L., Laine, C., & Savage, M. (1988). Interaction among school and college writing teachers: Toward recognizing and remaking old patterns. *College Composition and Communication, 39*, 139–153.

Smith, S. (1992). Professional partnerships and educational change: Effective collaboration over time. *Journal of Teacher Education, 43*, 243–256.

Smith, S. D., & Auger, K. (1985–1986). Conflict or cooperation? Keys to success in partnerships in teacher education. *Action in Teacher Education, 7*(4), 1–9.

Weade, G. (1992). Insiders and outsiders in classroom research: Blurring the boundaries. *Florida Journal of Educational Research, 32*(1), 60–72.

Willinsky, J. (1990). *The new literacy: Redefining reading and writing in the schools*. New York: Routledge, Chapman & Hall.

16

RESTRUCTURING FOR INCLUSION

DEBORAH HARRIS & DONNIE EVANS

INTRODUCTION

As discussed in previous chapters, the nation is currently immersed in an effort to restructure its entire public education system. Murphy (1991) suggests the major components of school restructuring to be: 1) changes in organizational and governance structures (changes from centralized control structures to site-based management); 2) work redesign (changes in the roles and responsibilities of teachers, administrators, and, parents); and 3) changes in core technology (changes in the way we teach and what we teach). Among the new metaphors of education are "superintendents as enablers," "principals as facilitators," "teachers as leaders," and "parents as partners" (Murphy, 1991).

As these changes are unfolding in general education, parallel efforts are underway in special education (Sailor, 1991). The inclusion of students with mild disabilities in general education classrooms and a reduction in the use of pull-out programs for these students has been a major focus of reform in special education (Sailor, 1991). Various collaboration and consultation strategies designed to expand the continuum of services for students with disabilities to include instruction in regular classrooms have been studied. These include: consulting teachers, collaborative consultation, collaborative teaching, and prereferral consultation (Evans, 1990; West & Idol, 1990; Wiedmeyer & Lehman, 1991; Simpson & Myles, 1990; Reisberg & Wolf, 1986; Huefner, l988).

The multifaceted restructuring efforts currently underway in the nation's schools have significantly contributed to the changing roles of teachers and teacher trainers. The changing roles of teachers and teacher trainers serve as a catalyst for establishing school district and university partnerships. These partnerships are essential to understanding how, who, where, and what we teach. Stoddard and Danforth state in their chapter that the university professor is moving from the traditional model of expert researcher and teacher trainer to collaborator. Teachers are moving from roles of individual responsibility to shared responsibility.

Many challenges exist as teaching professionals in the schools and universities move from living in separate worlds (see chapter 17) to cohabiting in one world for the greater benefit of children. Various aspects of the restructuring process have been addressed in previous chapters. This chapter will describe Florida Uniting Students in Education (FUSE), a public school/university partnership designed to develop and institute an inclusion program in a large public school system that is actively involved in school restructuring. We will discuss the experiences and lessons learned in moving teachers from separate instructional responsibility to collaborative partners delivering instruction in the general education classroom to all students, including those with disabilities.

The goals and underlying assumptions of the program will be outlined. Implementation challenges that evolved, factors critical to successful implementation, and implications for future research will be presented.

THE DISTRICT AND ITS CHALLENGES

The Hillsborough County public schools form a large urban/rural school district located in west-central Florida. With a total enrollment in excess of 130,000, it is the twelfth largest school district in the nation. More than 23,000 students are identified as exceptional and are receiving special education services administered by the district's department of Exceptional Student Education (ESE). Over 1200 teachers are employed by the district to deliver services to students with exceptionalities.

All students with disabilities are identified categorically for specific programs as required by the Florida Department of Education. Each program area provides a continuum of services ranging from least restrictive (consultation with regular education teachers) to most restrictive (full-day services in locations other than the student's home school). The vast majority of students with disabilities are served in resource programs.

The overwhelming number of children being pulled out for special educational services has caused the district considerable concern about meeting the needs of its ever-growing population of students with disabilities. The identification of needs in the district and an agreement to work together in developing strategies for addressing those needs represented the first step in developing FUSE.

Discussions between university faculty, district teachers, and administrators led to the identification of service delivery to students with mild disabilities in the least restrictive environment as a high priority need. More specifically, district teachers and administrators had great concerns about large numbers of students, who were disproportionately minority children, being pulled out of regular classrooms to receive special services in resource rooms. Also, there was concern that special education had become a "dumping ground" for students whom general education teachers had difficulty teaching, though there was a genuine desire among these teachers to help all their students. Furthermore, the maintenance of a system that relied almost totally on special educators to identify and meet the needs of one segment of the district's population appeared to contradict the principles of shared decision making and shared responsibility generally associated with site-based management and school improvement initiatives.

Other major restructuring initiatives underway in the district include the institution of a state-legislated education accountability system, full-service schools, reorganization of central office administration, and realignment and redistricting of schools. Each of these initiatives lended support to the development of inclusive service delivery options for students with disabilities.

The Process

FUSE began with commitments from the school district and the university's College of Education and Department of Special Education to work together to meet the needs of the district as it restructures and reorganizes its schools. It also presented a unique opportunity to contribute to the university's realization of its mission to "improve the schools of today and invent the schools of tomorrow."

Critical to planning associated with the development of FUSE was the establishment of a districtwide steering committee. The committee, comprised of general and special education teachers, building and district-level administrators, parents, and university faculty, agreed upon four major goals for Project FUSE:

- To establish a university/school district partnership to (a) assist the university in restructuring its teacher programs, and (b) assist the district in its efforts to restructure its schools for the benefit of *all* students;
- To establish a mechanism for ongoing training and technical assistance for teachers and administrators specific to implementing inclusion strategies in the district;
- To develop and institute instructional techniques and strategies for serving students with mild disabilities in integrated general education classrooms; and
- To study the change process (planning and implementation), identify stages of change related to inclusion, and determine the impact of this change on school and district personnel and students.

Embedded in each of these goals are a set of assumptions that have guided the process. The assumptions included the belief that: 1) school districts and universities can each benefit more from collaboratively approaching school restructuring rather than undertaking it separately and independently; 2) since the school site is the focal point of education reform, the needs of the schools should "drive the effort" (Evans, Harris, Adeigbola, Houston, & Argott, 1993); 3) inclusive services will provide as much or more benefits to many students with disabilities as resource pull-out programs; 4) general education students, particularly those who are at risk but do not qualify for special education services, will benefit from inclusive services; 5) while there is a climate for change in the school district and the university, tremendous resistance to the change is expected; 6) the district and university would alter traditional methods of operation in order to support the change; and 7) the state of Florida is developing support systems for inclusive programs.

With mutually agreed-upon goals and a clear understanding of assumptions, the steering committee began to make decisions about the design of an inclusive model for servicing students with disabilities. The steering committee decided to promote "collaborative teaching" as the means of reducing pull-out services and to make available to a limited number of schools training and technical assistance to test the techniques.

Support was secured from the district's Board of Education and other constituent groups in the school district. Board approval was acquired in one of its regularly scheduled meetings. Additionally, in separate meetings of building principals and teachers and parents, the work of the steering committee was shared, input was sought, and volunteers were solicited.

During the first year of the program (1991–92), four elementary schools volunteered to pilot the collaborative teaching (co-teaching) model. In each school, two to three teachers of children with disabilities were each paired with general education teachers as co-teachers for selected general education classes. Initially, teachers were paired as a result of their common interest in co-teaching strategies. During training, teachers were given the opportunity to evaluate their teaching styles and discuss adjustments they would need to make to ensure a successful, collaborative relationship. In subsequent years of the project, schools expressing interest in participating were provided a school collaboration readiness checklist which evaluated, among other things, teacher selection criteria and pairing strategies.

The general education classes selected to participate included four to eight students with mild learning or emotional disabilities who would otherwise have been pulled out for resource room services. Ongoing technical assistance and monitoring of project implementation was provided by university faculty.

Florida Uniting Students in Education

Co-teaching, as defined by FUSE, involves general education teachers and special education teachers delivering instruction to students, including identified students with disabilities, in regular classroom settings. Both teachers are responsible for and share equally in the planning, delivery, and evaluation of instruction to *all* students, including identified students with disabilities who have been integrated into regular classroom settings.

In FUSE schools, building-level Child Study Teams (CST) have been used to select students with disabilities for placement in classes with co-teachers. Generally, students selected were those whose special education needs could be met through modified curricula or alternative (collaborative) instructional strategies. Additionally, a student selection checklist was developed to assist Child Study Teams in making decisions about which students could be served in general education classrooms, using collaborative strategies. The checklist was completed by two or three teachers who could evaluate the students' classroom behaviors, organizational skills, social skills, and work habits.

Collaborative instructional strategies used by FUSE teachers include, but are not limited to: one teach/one monitor, teacher-directed centers, cooperative learning, remedial teaching, dialogue teaching, parallel teaching, instruct and outline, mastery learning, and shared presentation. Each of the strategies is designed to enhance collaborative teaching partnerships and ensure optimal educational benefit for all students.

All FUSE teachers received in-service training prior to assuming co-teaching responsibilities. The focus of the training included research associated with collaboration and consultation; interpersonal skills necessary for collaboration; strategies and techniques for co-teaching, co-planning, and co-evaluating; problem-solving strategies; and precollaboration activities critical to successful implementation. Follow-up coaching and modeling was also provided throughout the year.

Planning and coordination of FUSE within each school has been the function of a building task force. Members include a building administrator, general education teachers, special education teachers, and instructional support professionals (guidance counselor, school social worker, and so on). The assurance of alignment between FUSE activities and other restructuring initiatives in the school is also a responsibility of the task force. The task force was crucial to empowering schools and establishing ownership for project goals and objectives in relationship to individual school needs.

Implementation Challenges

Evans et al. (1993) suggests that philosophical, political, policy/procedural, and logistical challenges are associated with developing and instituting inclusion programs for students with disabilities in public school districts. Philosophically, many Hillsborough County district and school administrators and teachers believed that special educational needs of students should be met in segregated settings rather than in regular classrooms and that special educators, not general educators, should be solely responsible for meeting those needs. Reflective of this position was a heavy reliance on resource-room programs for students with mild disabilities and the existence of center schools in the district for students with moderate and severe disabilities. In some instances, there were no other service delivery options for students except in segregated center schools. Also, there were teachers and administrators who expressed doubt about the effectiveness of collaborative instruction because it was their belief that exceptional students could not function in the general education classroom, even with supplemental supports. One teacher stated that she agreed to participate in the project to show her principal that it would not work. This teacher is now among the greatest supporters of collaborative instruction. One very cautious administrator is now convinced that a "new philosophy is needed in his school."

Political challenges associated with developing and implementing FUSE were related to legitimizing the program and securing input, support, and involvement of inside and outside constituents in view of numerous other restructuring or reorganization initiatives underway. Confronted with numerous challenges growing out of the site-based management, accountability, school redistricting, and English as Second or Other Language requirements, principals and teachers were concerned that FUSE was yet another "top-down" add-on to their already overflowing cup. Principals also questioned whether FUSE would lose momentum in time, as had many other change initiatives undertaken in the district. Of additional concern for university faculty was an apparent lack of trust for the motives of university faculty among district personnel.

Policy and procedural challenges associated with FUSE had to do with established procedures and practices for writing student individual education plans (IEPs), managing student information, generating and utilizing ESE funding, and alignment with other restructuring efforts. Computerized IEPs used by the schools were not adequate for recording all mainstreamed service delivery options provided to identified students by special education teachers in general education classrooms. Similarly, the student information management system did not include provisions to account for these students beyond consultation.

District procedures for accounting for student funding were also of concern because it was perceived that funds needed for this "new" initiative could be more wisely invested in existing programs, considering current statewide budget shortfalls. The Florida Education Finance Plan (FEFP) incorporates "full-time equivalent" (FTE) in its funding formula to generate funds and allocate these funds to school districts. In the district, FTE and direct contact hours with students provided the basis for generating ESE funds and allocating special education teachers to schools. These teachers are required to have direct contact with students with disabilities to receive FTE credit for the student. This has also generally been interpreted to mean that students had to be served in separate settings (part- or full-time) and that the teachers paid solely from ESE funds could not have instructional contact with students without disabilities.

Additionally, because of severe budget shortfalls at the state level, the district's budget was cut severely as compared to the previous year's allocation. The result was the release of large numbers of teachers and paraprofessionals, a significant increase in class sizes, and fewer funds for instructional materials and professional development.

Logistically, planning and implementing FUSE offered numerous challenges, the greatest of which were time and resources to perform FUSE-related tasks and responsibilities. Already confronted with changing roles and increased duties growing out of other restructuring initiatives, teachers and building administrators were feeling overwhelmed. Questions to be answered included when would co-teachers meet to plan and engage in problem solving? When would training be scheduled? How and when would students with disabilities be scheduled in general education classes? What personnel and financial resources would be available to support them?

University faculty were concerned with time requirements for assisting with program coordination, in-service training, coaching and modeling, and data collection.

Since the university relies heavily on FTE to generate state funds, faculty involved in FUSE continued to be responsible for teaching, advising, and serving special functions with limited release time for service. Exacerbating this condition was the absence of funds from the university, school district, or grant sources to support university faculty participation.

A logistical challenge that continues to be faced is student progression. Because of the voluntary nature of the program, FUSE is available in 50 percent of the district's schools. Students served in FUSE classrooms in elementary schools will ultimately progress to middle and senior high schools, or families may move within the district requiring a transfer to a non-FUSE school during the year. After having been successfully mainstreamed for all or most of their day, the only special services that may exist for transferred students may be through pull-out programs. As other schools institute FUSE strategies and more students receive services in general education classrooms, this condition is likely to become more challenging.

Confronting and overcoming philosophical, political, policy, and logistical challenges requires the support and commitment of district and building administrators, general and special education teachers, and university administrators and faculty. Equally challenging is designing research and evaluation methods that promote the evolution of teachers as researchers. Even with numerous implementation challenges, contributions have been made to what is known about implementing inclusive models of service delivery.

CRITICAL SUCCESS FACTORS FOR IMPLEMENTATION

In implementing FUSE, ten factors have been identified as critical to successful implementation. These "critical success factors" have evolved from our work at the district office level and in the schools, as well as our review of current inclusion literature. A discussion of each follows.

Alignment with School Restructuring Efforts

The use of inclusive delivery options should be a component of a school's overall restructuring or school improvement plan. By doing so, teachers and administrators are less likely to view inclusive programming as yet another responsibility over and beyond their current duties. Rather, they are more likely to see it as a part of a larger school or district effort to restructure their schools for the purpose of improving the performance of all students.

All schools implementing FUSE are engaged in substantive restructuring. Each is moving toward site-based management and has developed school improvement plans as mandated by the state. Additionally, they are either instituting curricula changes, moving toward "full-service" status, or realigning grade levels.

By design, strategies associated with FUSE are aligned with these efforts. School improvement plans developed in these schools include the integration of students with disabilities in general education settings and collaboration between general and special educators in serving all students. Decision making for FUSE is shared among teachers, administrators, and parents. Curriculum content for general education classes is being used in all FUSE classrooms, and the academic and social outcomes for both general education students and students with disabilities are the same, though there may be some variance in expected levels of mastery.

Strong Administrative Support

Strong administrative support is essential to successful implementation of collaboration programs (Gersten & Woodward, 1990; Evans, 1990; Idol & West, 1987; Reisberg & Wolf, 1986). Without it, attempts at inclusion are very likely to meet with obstacles that will be difficult, if not impossible, to overcome.

In FUSE, building and district office administrators demonstrate their support by providing financial and human resources, allowing flexibility in student and teacher scheduling, providing time for teachers to collaboratively plan, encouraging and permitting risk taking among teachers, and allowing all teachers to share in schoolwide decision making. Additionally, the direct involvement of these administrators in planning and implementing collaboration has enhanced implementation (Reisberg & Wolf, 1986).

Change Strategy

Guiding any major educational change effort should be a change strategy or model. Models such as the Elaborated Leadership Obstacle Course (ELOC) provide a vehicle for establishing purpose and process and provide a framework for program planning and implementation (Herriot & Gross, 1979). Additionally, ELOC aids in the identification of potential obstacles and facilitators to implementation. Through its five stages (exploration, strategic planning, initiation, implementation, and incorporation), ELOC offers program planners a road map for successful implementation.

The implementation of FUSE was guided by ELOC. Since administrators and teachers knew what to expect in moving through each stage, anxieties were minimized, obstacles were more easily overcome, and resistance to the change was significantly reduced. Without a change strategy or model, educators instituting inclusion may lack direction and may not anticipate and overcome obstacles before they become insurmountable.

Policy Reconciliation

Many preexisting local and state policies or procedures associated with personnel assignments or duties, teacher certification, student scheduling, distribution of funds, student evaluation, and so on, tend to impede or discourage inclusion efforts. Additionally, local practices and procedures that have evolved over the years encourage and strongly support the continued maintenance of a dual system of education for general education and for students with disabilities.

With FUSE, district and state administrators have been receptive to reexamination of such policies and procedures and have altered them locally or are permitting waivers of state policies as needed. For example, district administrators have approved a waiver to state rules for process testing (to determine if process deficits exist) for students being evaluated for learning disabilities. Additionally, the district has changed its student information system and IEP format to support inclusion and is permitting experimentation with alternative models for distributing special education funds. At the building level, principals are reexamining policies and practices regarding student/teacher assignments, noninstructional duties, and distribution of funds for instructional materials and equipment.

District or school policies inconsistent with inclusion should be reexamined and modified, or abolished as necessary. In particular, fiscal and personnel policies that tend to influence program design and delivery should give way to policies and procedures that encourage, rather than discourage, inclusive practices.

Voluntary Participation

Too often, change in schools and school districts is forced by top-level administrators or state legislators on teachers and principals who have little or no say regarding their participation. Teachers and principals are more likely to passively resist such change.

For this reason, all schools participating in FUSE do so voluntarily, and in most instances general and special education teachers also volunteer. In situations where teacher participation is voluntary, there has been a reduction in inappropriate referrals for special education. Additionally, social interactions between general education students and students with disabilities are maximized. Cross-discipline collaboration between teachers is also affected when teacher participation is voluntary; generally there is less anxiety and stress in the collaborative relationship. Voluntary participation of teachers and administrators in FUSE has increased the likelihood that students and teachers will realize the benefits of inclusion.

Training for Program Teachers and Administrators

It is unreasonable to expect teachers and administrators to change behavior or practice without substantive training. Also, it should not be assumed that existing special education and general education teachers will possess skills or experiences necessary to successfully collaborate and co-teach. Without training, teachers are more likely to be frustrated and less confident, thus reducing the potential benefits of the intervention.

For this reason, in-service or preservice training should be provided to ensure the acquisition of necessary skills. Such training should focus on instruction, involve potential participants in planning and development, include provisions for follow-up, and should take place as close to the instructional setting (the classroom) as possible. The utilization of colleague special education and general education teachers as trainers can also prove useful.

In FUSE, both in-service and preservice training is provided. "Consultation and Collaboration in Special Education," a university graduate-level course, has been offered to teachers from participating schools. Students enrolled in the university's teacher training program have the option of taking the course at a school site or on the university campus. Additionally, all participant teachers are encouraged to participate in five days of district-sponsored in-service training prior to beginning co-teaching. Assisting in the delivery of the in-service is a cadre of special education and general education teachers who are trained to train other teachers.

Technical Assistance for Teachers and Administrators

As teachers begin to employ collaboration strategies in classrooms and planning meetings, they may need guidance and feedback, especially during the initial stages. Principals and central office administrators may also need assistance in problem solving with teachers, exploring alternatives for scheduling students and teachers, or in reviewing literature in support of inclusion.

In FUSE, technical assistance is provided for both teachers and administrators. Teachers are observed periodically, and feedback is offered relevant to their use of FUSE strategies. On occasion, instructional strategies are modeled for teachers, or training is developed and provided in areas of special need. Regular meetings are held with principals, individually, to discuss administrative issues or problems specific to their schools, and assistance is provided in problem resolution. Through the provision of technical assistance, teachers and administrators feel supported, their confidence levels increase more rapidly, and student and teacher gains are realized earlier.

Teacher Networks to Facilitate the Development of Collegial Relationships

Typically ESE and general education teachers perform their trade in isolation, though most have the benefit of interacting with subject or grade-level colleagues daily. For the teachers who may not have subject or grade-level colleagues in their building (special education teachers, for example), interacting with others who teach the same content may occur once or twice annually in district-level meetings. In these settings, the opportunity for meaningful collegial exchanges may be minimal at best. For these individuals, the benefits of sharing successes, problems, instructional strategies, and so on, often go unrealized.

During quarterly in-service meetings, FUSE teachers are afforded time to interact with each other, to exchange challenges and successes, and seek advice from one another. For additional support, schools and teachers new to the project are paired with experienced FUSE schools to facilitate ongoing exchanges beyond these meetings. The establishment of collegial relationships between and within schools has proven to be an important tool in providing training and support for teachers engaged in inclusion.

Participation of Teachers and Parents in Decision Making

With site-based management has come teacher empowerment, community involvement, and parent participation in schoolwide decision making. At a more practical level, top-down change without the decision-making participation and ownership of teachers, who ultimately are responsible for implementation in the classroom, will likely meet with much resistance and may not result in a lasting change in practice. Also, the public outcry for educational change and a demand for citizen participation in the change is evidenced by state legislation requiring community participation in the development of school improvement plans. This has resulted in citizen advisory boards or school improvement teams, of which parents are members, having tremendous influence on school programs.

In FUSE, the participation of general education and special education teachers in all decisions is strongly encouraged and, with few exceptions, teachers are involved at all levels of decision making. Whether as members of the district's steering committee, the school FUSE task force, or as a pair of co-teachers making instructional decisions for their students, ESE and classroom teachers are involved.

Parent participation at the school level is evolving more slowly. While the district's steering committee includes parents, their involvement at the building level is generally limited to participating in the decision for their child to be served in an inclusive classroom. In some instances, school citizen advisory committees or Parent-Teacher Associations were consulted before the school decided to join the project. In any event, the lack of involvement of teachers and parents in making decisions relevant to inclusion activities can result in a lack of ownership of the program and can seriously impede implementation.

Preparation of Students for Inclusion

Like other reform initiatives, inclusion is intended to improve instructional outcomes for students. Too often, however, in preparing for the change, particularly in relation to the change process, the needs of students are not fully considered. Serious consideration is often not given to the initial impact of placing students with disabilities in instructional settings with nondisabled peers. We simply, and sometimes falsely, assume that they will adjust.

As important as it is to prepare and train teachers, it is equally important to prepare students. Careful attention should be given to making general education students aware that there are students whose learning and behavior patterns and needs are different from theirs. Students with disabilities moving into mainstreamed classrooms should be reassured that their special needs will not be overlooked and that classroom and special education teachers will provide them with the support and assistance they need. They may also need remedial instruction in social skills areas.

In FUSE, both general education students and students with disabilities are prepared prior to being integrated. The amount of preparation varies, depending on the needs and experiences of the students. For the most part, however, general education students participate in a teacher-directed sensitivity training module, and special education students are taught skills for successful mainstreaming in addition to the sensitivity training. The sensitivity training module focuses on accepting and accomodating individual differences. FUSE has taught us that the absence of adequate student preparation for inclusion can increase anxiety and frustration for students with disabilities, heightened unfounded fears of general education students, and impact negatively on potential results of the intervention.

FUTURE CONSIDERATIONS

During the first three years of FUSE, the major focus of attention was on the development and institution of collaborative instructional techniques to address problems identified by the school district. In doing so, the growing body of special education literature on inclusive schooling and school restructuring provided the knowledge base for the efforts. As previously mentioned, there was an assumption that both general education students and students with disabilities would benefit from collaborative instruction. Attention was also given to the development of trusting relationships between university faculty and district personnel to reduce the impact of anticipated resistance to the change.

FUSE is currently being implemented in at least 80 of the district's 161 schools and is expanding rapidly. Next steps in implementing FUSE include placing more emphasis on the research component of the program, continual expansion of the program into other schools, and the permanent institutionalization or incorporation of the program in the district's continuum of services for special education programs. Potential topics for research include:

- outcomes or impact of co-teaching on students, teachers, administrators, and families
- teacher competencies for effective co-teaching or collaboration
- implementation issues and solutions
- leadership skills for administrators of inclusive programs
- family involvement in inclusive programs
- university support of school/university partnerships
- evaluation of inclusive programs

It is anticipated that research in these and other areas will not only add to the literature on inclusion and inclusive service delivery options for students with disabilities, but will also provide valuable evaluation data to district administrators for decision-making purposes. Additionally, this information should be useful to the university in re-examining and perhaps redefining the role of its faculty to encourage or reward their involvement in university/school district partnerships.

REFERENCES

Evans, D., Harris, D., Adeigbola, M., Houston, D., & Argott, L. (l993). Restructuring special education services: A multidimensional approach. *Teacher Education and Special Education, 16*(2), 137–145.

Evans, R. (1990). Making mainstreaming work through prereferral consultation. *Educational Leadership, 48*(1), 73–77.

Friend, M., & McNutt, G. (1984). Resource room programs: Where are we now? *Exceptional Children, 51*(2), 150–155.

Gersten, R., & Woodward, J. (1990). Rethinking the regular education initiative. *Remedial and Special Education, 11*(3), 7–16.

Harrison, C. R., Killon, J. P., & Mitchell, J. E. (1989). Site-based management: The realities of implementation. *Educational Leadership, 46*(8), 55–58.

Herriott, R. E., & Gross, N. (1979). *The dynamics of planned educational change.* Berkeley, CA: McCutchan.

Huefner, D. S. (1988). The consulting teacher model: Risks and opportunities. *Exceptional Children, 54*(5), 403–414.

Idol, L., & West, J. F. (1987). Consultation in special education (Part II): Training and practice. *Journal of Learning Disabilities, 20*, 474–494.

Murphy, J. (1991). Bridging the gap between professors and practitioners. *NASSP Bulletin, 75*(539), 22–30.

Reisberg, L., & Wolf, R. (1986). Developing a consulting program in special education: Implementation and interventions. *Focus on Exceptional Children, 19*(3), 1–12.

Sailor, W. (1991). Special education in the restructured school. *Remedial and Special Education, 12*(6), 8–22.

Simpson, R. L., & Myles, B. S. (1990). The general education collaboration model: A model for successful mainstreaming. *Focus on Exceptional Children, 23*(4), 1–10.

Wiedmeyer, D., & Lehman, J. (1991). The "house plan" approach to collaborative teaching and consultation. *Teaching Exceptional Children. 23*(3), 6–10.

West, F. J., & Idol, L. (1990). Collaborative consultation in the education of mildly handicapped and at-risk students. *Remedial and Special Education, 11*(1), 22–31.

17

BECOMING A TEACHER FOR ALL CHILDREN IN A PROFESSIONAL DEVELOPMENT SCHOOL

Hilda Rosselli, Susan Perez, & Kass Claggett

INTRODUCTION

THE concurrent reform agendas in special and general education have created a unique opportunity for a shared educational agenda (Sailor, 1991). Although there has already been considerable discussion, at least in the field of special education, regarding the obvious absence of special education from the general education reform landscapes (see chapter 3), there remains a need for proactive responses from those who have historically advocated for our nation's students with disabilities. In our opinion, however, the task now must involve both school-based personnel and university teacher preparation programs, deliberately involving individuals from both regular and special education. In this way, we can work simultaneously to ensure that within current school restructuring efforts, "all" children means what it means: "all." At the same time, we can begin the parallel task of restructuring our teacher preparation programs to make "all" children the responsibility of "all" teachers.

This chapter describes a collaborative effort involving a professional development school (PDS) as told from the experiences (voices) of a university faculty member appointed .50 FTE to the PDS, a faculty member at the PDS who serves as the special education department chair, and a third-year doctoral student who works at the PDS on a number of technical assistance, research, and grant-related activities. Our intent in this chapter is to recount a variety of initiatives in our collaboration that we believe have helped teachers, both preservice and in-service levels, to meet the diverse needs of students in inclusive learning environments. Although some activities initially evolved from special education and some from general education, we have, in fact, attempted to deliberately "blur" the lines.

Our organizational framework for this chapter includes a summary of our goals and assumptions followed by a discussion of: a) the PDS site; b) the district's support for inclusion and integration; c) collaborative initiatives benefitting students with special needs; d) teacher preparation efforts aimed at blurring the lines between special and general education; and e) the results of three case studies examining the perceptions of student teachers during their final internships. We will close with a summary of our findings and discuss selected questions that have emerged from our collaboration.

Goals and Assumptions

Our goals in the PDS included:

- Restructuring preservice level education in ways that enable future personnel to better meet the needs of all students;
- Supporting the professional development of faculty at the professional development school in ways that encourage reflection and collaborative inquiry; and
- Collaborating on mutually defined areas of school improvement and restructuring.

Our (university) assumptions were that:

- University personnel would not assume the role of "experts" in the professional development school;
- Collaborative initiatives would need to be mutually agreed upon and mutually beneficial;
- Student-teacher involvement and research activities would be sensitive to the school's daily operation; and
- The university was invested in the partnership for more than a short-term arrangement; thus, immediate cost benefits could not be expected.

SCHOOL DEMOGRAPHICS

The site selected for the Professional Development School was a new middle school that, as a result of a district rezoning plan, drew a more diverse spectrum of students than most schools in the district. Located in a rural area of the county and distanced approximately 25 minutes from a large university, the school serves students from rural migrant communities, low-income housing projects, suburban-style housing communities, as well as an exclusive golf and tennis resort. The location of the school in an undeveloped area of the county presented its own unique challenges. The faculty, having agreed upon the importance of community building as part of their vision statement, had to deal with a lack of connection to any nearby community, transportation provisions for 98% of their students, and the perspectives of parents who felt removed and distanced from daily school life.

Approximately 10 percent of the student population (N=1,000) is Hispanic, 10 percent African American, and 80 percent Caucasian. The county's overall ethnic percentages are much less diverse: 3 percent Hispanic, 5 percent African American, and 92 percent Caucasian. Consequently, during the school's first year of operation, a Diversity Committee was formed. During the second year, five additional minority staff members were hired, the faculty participated in a diversity awareness workshop, and the school sponsored its first annual Culture Fair. A peer mediation program and skill-streaming training are also offered now to help students develop skills in interacting with diversity.

The school's student mobility rate (22.4%) is higher than either the district (17.93) or the state (14.84) average while the percentage of students who are eligible to receive free or reduced lunch is 43.36 percent, again higher than the district (37.38%) and the state (36.25%) averages.

SPECIAL PROGRAMS AND SERVICES

Paralleling the trends emerging in Florida demographics (Hodgkinson, 1988), close to 50 percent of the school's population could be identified as having special needs. Special programs include the English for Speakers of Other Languages (ESOL), classes for severely disturbed students, SLD resource classes, EH classes, Gifted resource class, and three different Graduation Enhancement Programs funded through Dropout Prevention funds. In its fourth year now, the school offers students with disabilities team-taught classes that include science, geography, and math. Students with disabilities are also served by the Mainstream Consult teacher as they are mainstreamed into the regular classroom.

DISTRICT SUPPORT FOR INCLUSION AND INTEGRATION

The district in which the PDS exists has progressed from the early special education consultation models of the 70s towards more collaborative models which downplay the expert role and encourage more collegial relationships. This parallels a broader societal trend towards collaboration as evidenced in the workplace, in educational partnerships, and in aspects of school reform calling for empowerment, participatory management, and site-based decision making (Friend & Cook, 1992). Prior to the opening of the PDS, the district invested considerable state and local resources into developing a collaborative consultation program and implementing a co-teaching model for students with mild disabilities to more fully integrate students into general education. This was also seen as a benefit for the many university student-teachers who would be working in the professional development school context. In addition to direct services, a number of initiatives began as a result of the partnership that impacted the ability of the school to better work with all students. These are described from the perspective of the doctoral student assigned to the PDS.

COLLABORATIVE PROJECTS

Diversity surfaced in many ways as the school opened and teaching began. As university partners, we entered the school community with the offer to be helpful in a meaningful way. We looked to the faculty and students for direction, and we followed their needs. As a doctoral student assigned to the professional development middle school, I found an instantaneous niche.

Emotional Diversity

The district had 50 percent out-of-field teachers for EH/SED classrooms, and the school felt the impact of that with their own team. Within the first few days, students from this population of adolescents were being suspended from a school that had made the decision during preplanning to avoid suspending students. Since I had years of experience with students that had been considered too emotionally disturbed to be with children in regular school classrooms or settings, I headed back to the special education classrooms.

I immediately gravitated to the students and offered to work with them in any way that would be helpful to the teachers. My own style of teaching was to model what I am teaching, and that was what I began to do. My presence and authentic pleasure in being able to spend time with these students was meant to offer a perspective for consideration. The nature of entering into relationships with the students was based on an ethic of care. All through the first semester of the first year, I spent my time getting to know the members of the class and giving them time to know me. I was interested in developing trusting relationships through ongoing interaction.

Second semester, I developed a series of classes in drama and photography offered weekly. The teachers and students were delightful participants, and we often had an enjoyable time. The last four weeks the classes were designed to create an awareness of separating, saying good-bye. My experience in the mental health system had strengthened my belief that attaching and separating were important aspects of human interaction.

With talk about inclusion back at the university, I wondered how these students who seemed so isolated from the rest of the student population would fare in such an arrangement. I decided to have lunch with those students who had earned behavior levels that entitled them to have lunch in the cafeteria. Early in the school year, we sat as a group with very little recognition from other students. Over the school year, I made a conscious effort to see how I could entice other students to sit at our table. Sometimes I brought special edible treats like home-baked cookies, individual bags of chips, cans of soda and/or bite-sized Cuban sandwiches that slowly lured students outside of the SED classroom to sit and partake with us. Toward the second half of the school year, we had several students who became regulars at our table. One girl from the same neighborhood as one of our SED students shared letters with us that she had received from a student in Russia to whom she was writing in her language arts class. Following my suggestions, this young lady and one of our students obtained permission from the teachers to spend time walking around the campus taking pictures that Martha could send to her pen pal to give him a visual idea of what one middle school looked like in the United States. As our student had demonstrated competence in using my 35 mm camera, he was designated the photographer while Martha decided what composition she wanted to have captured on film.

Encouraged by this teaming of special education and regular education students, I tried to find other ways to engage a mix of students from the school. Making some inroads, I felt that this focus had advantages to bridging the gap, blurring the lines between groups of students at the school, particularly general and special education students.

Adolescence as Diversity

My experience working with adolescents became another area into which I found myself drawn. Although many of the teachers had previously taught middle grades, some seemed unprepared for such a concentration of adolescent students, all probing, questioning, and exploring the mysteries of life in ways that frequently could be misperceived as inappropriate. In the Graduation Enhancement Program (dropout prevention classes), class size had already been made smaller, and a specialized focus on computers and physical education had been introduced. But the teachers expressed bewilderment about how to teach students who seemed to be starving for attention, struggling to get along, and experiencing aspects of life that were totally unfamiliar to them.

In the spirit of partnership, the school social worker and I provided weekly seminars with the students focusing on what was going on in their lives. This arrangement was an example of how we viewed the "freeing up of time" for teachers as an immediate need, as it provided the computer teacher additional time to provide technical assistance to other faculty members at the school who needed support.

As our seminars progressed and adolescents began to express an eagerness about attending the seminars, the teachers asked for monthly meetings with us to better understand adolescent issues and to plan strategies that would enhance the supportive and caring aspects of the classroom environment. As a result, revisions were made to enhance both the curricular content and relationships between the teachers and students.

Concerned about the use of drugs in the adolescent culture, we began the school year with a focus on drug prevention. As a way of introducing the school population to the partnership between the university and the school, the university took an active role in creating a Drug-Free Week. Culminating this week of activities was a schoolwide basketball game between the middle school students and members of the men and women's university basketball team. As part of the celebration in the gym, each of the university basketball team members talked to the student population about their own struggles as adolescents and their ultimate goals of becoming college graduates. Their talks were moving and inspiring.

Racial Diversity

The school's rezoning plan had created a more diverse student body than what most of the staff or students had previously experienced. This was especially true for a small group of African-American female students who found themselves amongst a predominantly Caucasian population with only one African-American teacher in the school (a male PE coach). Early in the year, these adolescent females were frequently involved in fights on campus. One of our female African-American faculty members from the Department of Special Education teamed up with the school social worker to meet weekly with this group in order to provide a supportive forum for them to discuss their feelings about being black in a predominantly white school. Sensitive to the needs of both students and teachers, the university faculty rotated her visits to a different period each week rather than have students miss the same class on a regular basis.

   With the opportunity to voice their feelings, the girls began to take on leadership roles. Encouraged by this university female role model, they began to carve out a place for themselves and introduced ideas to the school that included an appropriate focus on their culture.

Ethnic Diversity

Within the school community, there existed a migrant population who were identified by various teachers in the school as needing specialized assistance. This resulted in a collaborative effort between the school and the university's High School Equivalency Program. Students in this program were older migrant students who had dropped out of school and later elected to participate in a university program designed to help them get their GED. The union of these migrant populations at the PDS led to tutoring opportunities and several field trips designed to familiarize students with options that would break the cycle of becoming adult field workers. Students visited the university to get a flavor of campus life. They were introduced to programs intended to assist migrant students in pursuing higher education.

Parent Survey

At the end of our first year together in the partnership, our university research faculty member designed a study in which we interviewed school faculty, staff, students, and parents to examine their thoughts about the school as a professional development school. I was asked to survey a sample of parents that represented the diverseness in the school population. These groups included parents who served as volunteers, parents of students in the Graduation Enhancement Program, parents of African-American students, parents of honor students, parents of students whose stanines put them in the low achievement category, parents of students in EH/SED classes, parents of Hispanic students, and parents of students who were identified as having demonstrated leadership qualities.

The majority of parents I interviewed commented on the beauty of the brand new school. Several parents remarked about specific resources like the darkroom, broadcasting room, state-of-the-art media center, and tennis courts. In fact, many parents stated they would like it if the school were open to families after school hours and on weekends. One mother suggested the school should become more of a community center when classes were not in session. Almost all minority parents and a sprinkling of others felt that the school was too far from home. These parents reported that transportation made it difficult to attend events, allow students to stay after school, get involved with the school, and pick their children up from school when they were sick. In almost all cases, these parents expressed feeling isolated from school.

Many parents were pleased that the university had joined the school in a partnership. They stated that the connection with the university brought in numbers of individuals who modeled for students the importance of education. In fact, some parents expressed a strong desire that their children do "better" than they did. They wanted the school to emphasize academics and homework so their children would be prepared for high school and college. They wanted students to learn study habits to help them in the future.

These interviews were conducted by telephone. I would much rather have interviewed people personally, preferably in their homes, but for the most part the interviews were fruitful and pleasant. A few parents, not restricted to any particular group, did not seem pleased about participating but answered a question or two and then got off the phone. However, the majority of parents talked at great length about their feelings toward the school and toward society with regard to the education of their child. These parents expressed appreciation at being able to talk about their thoughts and concerns. They stated they were glad that the school wanted to hear what they as parents were thinking.

It occurred to me that while the university and school had joined in a partnership, it was equally important that parents become partners.

CASSP

During my third year I was selected to coordinate a grant that helped fulfill that vision. A state-funded initiative CASSP (Child and Adolescent Special Services Program) is intended to reach out to parents who feel disenfranchised from the school community in an effort to help them become advocates for their children. The intent is to work with families who have children at risk of not finishing school, particularly due to problems that involve the mental health system, the juvenile justice system, and the school system. The idea is to develop a local system of care that works together to provide coordinated services to families. This focus stems from the belief that parents, as well as professionals, are experts with regard to their own children and should be integrally involved in the planning and providing of their children's needs.

As a doctoral student who has spent over three years in this professional development school, I believe that my experiences at the PDS have provided me with a good background from which to begin my next stages of professional work through this grant. I spent one year working in classrooms with at-risk populations, I conducted a survey of parents to better understand their feelings toward the school, and I have come to know a variety of people in the surrounding community. Now I am ready to extend our partnership and seek ways to work collaboratively with parents for the benefit of all students.

TEACHER PREPARATION EFFORTS—THE UNIVERSITY PERSPECTIVE

One of the failings often attributed to teacher preparation programs is the gap between theory and practice experienced by preservice-level teachers. Whether real or imagined, our university believes that this discrepancy can at least be diminished through initiatives that blend classroom experiences and reflection with the daily challenges and responsibilities faced by teachers. To do this, we (university personnel) must be able to personally conceptualize the work of teachers in today's schools and assist novice teachers in making meaning of their site-based experiences in schools by using journals, teaching cases, and other tools. Today's teachers have even more of a challenge as they figure out what's going on (student, class, content, team, school, community, nation), figure out what needs to happen (outcomes, goals, needs of students, families, and so on), figure out what paths are available to "get there," choose accordingly, and finally reflect on the impact of their visions, choices, and actions. This view of reflective practice has helped to guide an array of preservice-level experiences provided at the PDS for university student-teachers.

Internships at the PDS

Each semester, approximately 12 student-teachers have interned at the PDS. These interns represent a variety of areas and are supervised by the university's special education faculty member assigned to the PDS. The interns have regularly scheduled time to converse and share ideas. They also are encouraged to observe each other and to visit different classroom structures/programs. The Senior Seminar, which is held on the PDS campus each week, offers another opportunity for blurring the lines between general and special education. "Guest" experts from the PDS staff join us for collaborative problem-solving sessions, interns write and share teaching cases based on real teaching dilemmas, and the university professor selects issues and discussion points that emerge from the interns' weekly reflective journals.

Practicums at the PDS

The placement of special education pre-intern students in the professional development school has also had a significant impact on the school's ability to meet the individual needs of students with disabilities. Approximately 12 practicum student-teachers per semester are placed in a variety of classes of students with disabilities or students at risk. Practicum students placed with the mainstream consultation teacher are paired with individual students and participate in reviewing cumulative records, observing the student in the mainstream and special education environment, conferencing with basic education teachers regarding the students' needs, establishing and adjusting a schedule of services for the student, and monitoring progress. Practicum students are guided in establishing a caring rapport with each student and assisted in devising and testing strategies and interventions to help these students achieve success. Many of the practicum students have established reward systems and written contracts for student performance. The mainstream consultation teacher oversees the process and provides guidance and evaluations. In some cases, particularly strong bonds have been established between student-teacher and middle-school student. In these instances, every effort is made to provide a practicum student the following semester for that student. In light of these positive experiences, several practicum students have requested that they be assigned to the school for their internship.

Being a professional development school ensures that the mainstream consultation teacher can anticipate practicum students each semester, unlike at other schools where they may be placed more sporadically. This is advantageous for both the practicum student and the teacher with whom they are placed. With each successive placement, there is an opportunity for reflection and continuous improvement. In addition, with the continued flow of practicum students and interns, the cooperating teachers have been able to reflect on their own teacher education experiences and contribute to the improvement of teacher training practices at the university.

On-Site Courses

As mentioned previously, our efforts in this project included the intentional blurring of boundaries in order to bridge the gap between special and regular education. During year one, we created a hybrid course that combined special education majors taking *Introduction to Special Education* with secondary education majors taking the university's required mainstreaming course. Typically, these groups are seldom together during their training programs, but upon graduating they are placed in the same environment and expected to collaborate together. Our intent was to begin the collaborative dialogue much earlier while both groups were relatively unentrenched in the old models that separated general and special educators (Rosselli, Perez, Piersall, & Pantridge, 1993). An experiential approach was used to acquaint the prospective teachers with a variety of students who had special learning needs.

Student-teachers in the pilot group attended weekly hour-long lectures at the school site provided by a variety of university and school personnel, including the social worker, the ESOL teacher, the behavior specialist, the SLD teacher, the guidance counselor, and the mainstream consult teacher. Their remaining time on campus, approximately two hours, was spent observing in various classrooms, shadowing individual students and faculty members, collecting data on mainstreamed students in both special and general education environments, and attending school staffings. The course was arranged around a contract that provided choices of assignments, all with different weights, but which all met the university instructor's course goals. As the student-teachers progressed through the initial stages of understanding the school context, they identified volunteer opportunities to tutor students or select a student for an in-depth case study. Weekly journals and activity logs were kept by the student-teachers and shared with the instructor. Besides giving the student-teachers written responses and feedback, the instructor used this information to individualize topics or activities for the following week. Although time-consuming on the instructor's part, it provided for the varying levels of knowledge and expertise that the student-teachers brought to the course. Informal comparisons showed that the students who volunteered to participate in the pilot scored as well on the quarterly content exams as the rest of their class who were taught on campus in a large lecture format. They were also able to demonstrate a more professional and caring attitude toward students with special needs. The students helped us monitor the course and suggested improvements for future offerings of the course. Their insights were particularly helpful in identifying trends and issues that were not necessarily part of traditional textbooks used to teach this class. A common observation by the student-teachers was that the number of students considered at risk in today's schools is so large that we may, out of necessity, *have* to blur the traditional boundaries. They asked, "When is a student a special student or just one with special needs?" "Do all students have special needs?"

CASE STUDIES OF INTERNS

During the first semester of our second year, we had a mix of 15 students from special and regular education who came to our professional development school as interns. This clustering of full-time student-teachers provided an opportunity to examine the expectations interns hold of teaching to their actual experience during internship. Three regular education interns were randomly selected to be involved in this qualitative case study. From the perspective of a special education researcher, the findings were quite interesting. All three interns reported they felt totally unprepared to deal with the behavioral problems they encountered in their classrooms. They each stated that 90 percent of their time was spent getting students to pay attention, follow directions, and behave according to school policy. Unlike special education training, these teachers lamented during interviews that they were not prepared for the disruptive nature of students. They each said they expected students to be eager to learn if the material was presented in an interesting manner. They did not find this to be true. They expressed frustration in their lack of preparedness and disappointment when they felt they had become nags.

While special education focuses heavily on teaching students with special learning needs, the general education interns felt totally unprepared for the diversity of student ability they found in the classroom. They had not expected to find such a range of capabilities. In all their classes they had students who had great difficulty reading, writing, and understanding the English language. Initially they floundered in handling such academic diversity and spent much of their time attempting to develop ways to reach all students. The stories told by the interns suggested, perhaps, that both regular and special education students could benefit from more classes together, in which they could explore behavioral techniques and curriculum modification.

CONCLUSIONS AND INSIGHTS—THE PDS FACULTY MEMBER'S PERSPECTIVE

Fairness

Many issues and dilemmas face a school that is moving in the direction of fullest possible inclusion of students with disabilities. A number of these center around the basic philosophy that "Fairness does not always mean equal." This philosophy crosses varying classroom policies regarding modifications for students with disabilities, allowances for make-up work and homework, task analysis in grading, and alternatives to suspensions for students with emotional handicaps.

Generally, concerns have centered around the struggle between protecting the high standards of the classroom that the basic education teachers have set for all students and the need for modifications and adaptations for the success of mainstreamed students. Grading has posed special dilemmas for teachers of these students; yet, the school and district's movement toward portfolio assessment, integrated teaming, and outcome-based education have had a positive impact on this area of policy. Each of these restructuring efforts focuses on assessing the student's individual progress as opposed to grading using set standards for whole classes.

Orderly Versus Student-Centered Schools

Because the school opened in its first year with a mainstream Consult Teacher, the concept of mainstreaming was part of the school's philosophy from the start. Most faculty members were open to having students with specific learning disabilities in their classes with support. Attitudes toward mainstreaming students with emotional handicaps were not, however, as open initially, as teachers struggled with the concept of an orderly versus an individual approach. For example, within the class for students with emotional handicaps, teachers expect that there will be times that the student will be unable to maintain a certain standard of behavior and they make provisions for setting the student back on track with opportunities to be successful. Unfortunately, at times in the regular class, these students will diminish their chances for success with a suspension or outcome that could result in failing grades. A student with a 65 percent completion rate for homework may be viewed by special education teachers as being very successful based on previous records. In the basic education class, this would be considered a failing grade if the student were to be measured with the same criteria applied to the rest of the class.

A School Culture Supporting Inclusion

The philosophy of inclusion is conveyed at the school through the representation of special education faculty on a variety of committees, an assistant principal assigned to special education, a guidance counselor who handles all referrals for service, and a written commitment to *all* students in the school's vision statement which reads: (The school) "will offer a nurturing and safe environment that provides an academic focus, values diversity, and challenges all students to achieve their full potential with the support of its home, staff, university, and community partnerships."

In keeping with this philosophy, special education classes are purposely housed in several buildings, which allows for more integration and collegiality for faculty as well as students. The faculty mingle together across teams, grade levels, disciplines, and specialty areas. This is seen in faculty meetings, team meetings, and in the faculty lounge. Of the two faculty elected to serve as representatives for the professional development school issues, one was in special education and one in regular education. Recognition of the accomplishments of special education faculty and students can be found in the school newsletter. A large number of the school's students with disabilities receive recognition and distinction at the awards assemblies. Special education faculty are encouraged to attend regular education staff development opportunities and vice versa. When one of the university's intern and clinical faculty meetings was dedicated to strategies that can help students with disabilities achieve success in the regular classroom, the meeting was facilitated by members of the school's special education department.

Further evidence of the school's philosophy appeared in a faculty poll supporting five priorities for the 1993–94 school year: 1) support services to meet students' personal/social, health, academic, and career needs; 2) curriculum that enables students to demonstrate high academic performance; 3) curriculum that improves vocational preparation; 4) scheduling and staffing to help each student achieve success; and 5) curriculum to enhance graduation rates/student mastery prior to leaving the school system. Embedded also in these priorities was a commitment to continuity of caring for students. During the third year, both 7th grade teams stayed with their students while 8th grade teachers moved to 7th grade and will follow their students for the next two years.

Individual Commitment and Vision

We have noted as the school continues in its fourth year of operation, more and more teachers have begun incorporating modifications into their instructional practice that can increase the success of mainstreamed students with disabilities or students at risk. These include developing separate assessments for students with disabilities when appropriate, collaborating with the mainstream consultation teacher to revise assessments, allowing students to redo missed test questions as homework for partial credit, and modifying the length and criteria for assignments. This awareness is evidenced by the fact that some teachers have included "better meeting the needs of their students with disabilities" as one of their individually determined professional development goals for the upcoming year.

Benefits of a Team

Particularly at the secondary level where wider gaps may exist between the skills of mildly handicapped pupils and the instructional setting (Schumaker & Deshler, 1988), systems for collaboration such as the cooperative consultation model can help support students as they are integrated into the general education classroom. In a middle school organized by academic teams, this process involves not only being there for the student, but consistent collaboration between special education faculty and general education team members on curriculum planning and modification. Ultimately, all students can benefit from the collaborative efforts of a team with various areas of expertise who have time to work together to plan and provide instruction that meet students' needs.

Time as a Resource

The lack of sufficient common planning time between the special education and basic education teachers has in some situations resulted in the special education teacher being more of an aide to the classroom environment as opposed to an equal partner in the classroom instruction. Possible solutions that we are exploring include the increased use of interns from the university during team teaching assignments, more co-teaching time, and more co-planning time. A state-funded collaborative training grant has been awarded that will provide all team teach faculty with more training and planning time. Regularly scheduled forums throughout the year will also facilitate communication of ideas and concerns as they arise.

Review, Re-Vision, and Refine

Team teaching has expanded from no team teach classes during the first semester of the 91–92 school year to 17 during the 94–95 school year. As the team teach model of instruction expands, the staff are seeking ways to improve and refine it. Placement of students in a team teach situation is based on parent input at the Individual Educational Plan conference, teacher acceptance of the concept, and information derived from SAT and other assessments. As a result, one team-taught reading class has been disbanded as we found that students who were in the lower 25 percent on the SAT did not possess the skill levels necessary to be successful in the type of reading curriculum offered, even though modifications were being made. These students were then taught reading in a more structured format in the resource room.

Personnel Needs

Although a district may commit to the philosophy of mainstreaming and initiate varying models of integration, successful implementation still relies on cooperation between regular and special educators within individual schools (Bogdan, 1983). Coordinating these efforts at the school site requires extensive public relations strengths as well as collaborative problem-solving skills.

In promoting the rights of students with disabilities, the role of the advocate can be delicate at times. Some faculty perceive the special education advocate as placing the needs of students with disabilities above the needs of the classroom or school as a whole. The advocate must, when at all possible, allow the classroom teacher to preserve individual integrity in regard to the classroom parameters and standards, yet, represent students with disabilities in their right to be educated with nondisabled peers.

CONCLUSIONS AND INSIGHTS—THE UNIVERSITY FACULTY MEMBER'S PERSPECTIVE

As I look back now at the three and a half years that I have been assigned to the PDS, I have tried to find a pattern of involvement that could assist another university in implementing a similar partnership. The subtleties of my job often go beyond the traditional job description of a university faculty member. Although generic in nature, many of these aspects of my job responsibility help support an inclusion agenda, as well as a broader middle school restructuring agenda. These job activities also vary between university agenda, district/school agenda, and both as indicated in Table 17.1.

The fact that these responsibilities represent only 50 percent of my assigned faculty load presents challenges to manage my time efficiently, maintain constant communication and presence at both sites, avoid overcommitment, select research and publication activities that are already embedded in my job responsibilities, and be alert to early signs of schizophrenia! I find myself developing a more middle-of-the-road orientation to my two lives: quicker to question the usefulness of traditional university research agendas, more compassionate to the daily demands placed on teachers, and less receptive to big reform ideas that come packaged in three-ring binders published by $5,000 a day consultants who fail to hang around for the implementation stages.

My teaching back at the university links me more closely now to the teachers who drive in at the end of an exhausting day. I often arrive only minutes before they do. My examples embedded in the courses now relate more to teachers' daily experiences. I filter the concepts and theories that I present in class by evaluating them first from the perspective of teachers trying to implement them in classes of 35 sometimes not overly motivated students. The resulting mutations come from heart-to-heart discussions in class in which we try to answer: "What can we really do with this idea/theory?" "What can we combine with what we already know?" Without even consciously trying, I find myself adopting a constructivist approach to teaching teachers. Also critical now is the modeling of what I would want to see happen in classrooms. I treat my students as individuals and try to be attuned to what their nonverbal behaviors are telling me about their response to the course. I use contracts for assignments that can be renegotiated should the need occur. When an idea or concept seems distant from the realities of the classroom, I invite their interpretation and construction.

On the other hand, my time at the school provokes an increasingly painful sensitivity to the ways in which students are treated in even well-meaning contexts of education. The issues of power and control seem obvious to my eyes and ears as I watch and listen in classrooms. In the course of "covering" material, maintaining order, and calculating final grades, teachers often waste valuable time. When working with student-teachers, I sometimes feel a breath of hope as they enter with rather altruistic views of teaching as acts of "lighting fires" rather than "filling pails." Many quickly acquire the habits of their mentors, who on teacher performance evaluations are marked as "effective" teachers but who leave students with only glimmers of what learning is all about. Sometimes the pain of watching this transpire is too much. I think about what must be my obvious hypocrisy when I let certain practices fly in the face of what my intuition and feeling for students as humans tells me is powerfully harmful. I worry about how far away meaningful learning really is in the schools, I wonder if parents really know how boring the curriculum is, and I resign myself to looking for bright spots and modeling a caring relationship with my interns.

All of this has led to a level of cynicism that must be guarded back at the university. Yet, I listen with chagrin as doctoral students share examples in which students are treated without regard to their rights, and I ask myself the painful question: Am I doing a longer term good by plugging the dike one finger at a time and selecting my battles strategically? When is it time to report that the emperor is not wearing many clothes?

FINDINGS PERTINENT TO THE PDS ARRANGEMENT

In addition to the insights discussed, there were a number of other "discoveries" worth noting that have evolved from our collaboration in a PDS.

TABLE 17.1
University Faculty Responsibilities at the PDS

University Faculty Activity	Inclusion Agenda	Middle School Agenda	University Agenda	District or School Agenda
Coordinate and schedule student-teacher placements at all levels at PDS	X	X	X	X
Maintain an ongoing analysis of program activities and concerns	X	X	X	
Serve as a spokesperson for the PDS			X	X
Support research and program development initiatives at the PDS	X	X	X	
Coordinate ongoing staff development offerings sponsored by the university	X	X	X	X
Assist in writing and implementing grants designed to support PDS activities	X	X	X	X
Teach university courses on site at undergraduate and graduate levels	X	X	X	
Supervise 9–15 full-time interns per semester at the PDS	X	X	X	

TABLE 17.1—*Continued*
University Faculty Responsibilities at the PDS

University Faculty Activity	Inclusion Agenda	Middle School Agenda	University Agenda	District or School Agenda
Teach Senior Seminar on PDS site	X	X	X	
Facilitate the development of publications involving staff that inform others of PDS activities	X		X	X
Participate in the PDS School Advisory Council and school committees	X	X		X
Assist faculty in locating instructional resources as requested	X	X		X
Actively support district restructuring initiatives	X	X		X
Actively support university restructuring initiatives in Secondary Education and Special Education departments	X	X	X	

- Not all university personnel may find collaborative involvement with schools easy or rewarding.
- A period of time is critical for university personnel to gain entrée to a school and develop rapport with school-based personnel.
- As a result of gaining entrée and developing rapport, one is likely to feel compromised and embroiled in ethical dilemmas.

- A number of university policies may need to be reexamined when faculty are actively involved in a PDS, e.g. calendar and load adjustments, revision of tenure and promotion policies, and support for the type of complexity encountered when living in two systems.
- The typical results and findings expected in research and development are more elusive and harder to objectify when the observer (researcher) is also a participant and community member.
- The payoffs for partnerships are evident but probably require a longer wait time than universities are used to expecting on the traditional cost/benefits model.

QUESTIONS EMERGING FROM OUR COLLABORATION

Although we are well into our fourth year of the PDS collaboration, we still feel that there is much to learn and that our questions that have emerged will guide our next stages of involvement. Several of significance to this article include:

- How long can the momentum be sustained in a collaborative partnership?
- Is there a natural limit for a PDS collaboration, either in length of time or capacity of activity?
- What happens to restructuring efforts in a school when the partnership ends?
- How can personnel effectively continue to work in a PDS when ethical dilemmas emerge, e.g., nonexemplary practices?
- Do preservice-level teachers who are involved in a PDS differ significantly from those who have a traditional internship?

REFERENCES

Bogdan, R. (1983, Summer). A closer look at mainstreaming. *Educational Forum*, 425–434.

Friend, M., & Cook, L. (1992). *Interactions: Collaboration skills for school professionals*. White Plains, NY: Longman.

Hodgkinson, J. L. (1988). *Florida: The state and its educational system*. Washington, DC: Institute for Educational Leadership.

Rosselli, H., Perez, S., Piersall, C., & Pantridge, O. (1993). Evolution of a professional development school: The story of a partnership. *Teacher Education and Special Education, 16*(2), 124–136.

Sailor, W. (1991). Special education in the restructured school. *Remedial and Special Education, 12*(6), 8–22.

Schumaker, J. B., & Deshler, D. D. (1988). Implementing the regular education initiative in secondary schools: A different ball game. *Journal of Learning Disabilities, 21*, 36–42.

18

SHARING THE RESPONSIBILITY FOR EDUCATING "HOMEGROWN TEACHERS"

Betty Epanchin & Cathy Wooley-Brown

THE collaborative project described in this chapter grew out of the need to reduce an acute shortage of special education teachers in a large rural school district. To address this need, the school district and university planned and implemented an experimental, undergraduate teacher training program that was intended to prepare "homegrown" teachers. The project was funded for three years by the U.S. Office of Education, during which time 50 teachers were educated in the program. Additionally, all departments in the College of Education and many schools within the school district participated in the implementation of the project.

BACKGROUND OF PROJECT

Called the USF/Polk County Collaborative Teacher Preparation Program for Paraprofessionals, this project was established in response to the shared needs of a university and a public school district. From the beginning, the goal was to create a mutually beneficial situation. For the university, the collaboration provided opportunities to implement an experimental teacher preparation program, access relevant and authentic clinical training sites, and work with practitioners in inventing better ways of educating children. For the school district, the collaboration significantly reduced the critical teacher shortages in special education, contributed to school improvement efforts, and created professional development opportunities.

Work reported in this chapter was supported by U.S. Department of Education Grant #HO29B10234.

When the project was conceived, the school district had been experiencing a period of rapid growth. In the previous two years, over 5,000 additional students had enrolled in the district and approximately 30 percent of those new children came from backgrounds of poverty and limited education. Additionally, almost 40 percent of the children already enrolled in the district's schools were receiving free or reduced-price lunches.

In the previous year, 126 teachers of children with disabilities were teaching "out of field." The district ranked second in the state in the number of employed, out-of-field special education teachers. Dade County (Miami) was first. To further compound the district's training needs, 11 percent of the teachers who were employed in special education were first-year teachers. Like out-of-field teachers, beginning teachers also need attention, mentoring, and support in order to continue their professional development.

Prior to this project, the district spent approximately $25,000 annually to recruit special education graduates from colleges of education in the north, midwest, and west, but these new recruits averaged only two years of teaching in the county before they moved to other areas. The problem of retaining teachers in rural areas has been noted by Cheney, Cummings, and Royce (1990). They observed that "students preparing to become special education teachers typically attend classes at universities in urban settings. Once they are certified and relocate in rural communities, they often find themselves unprepared for the rural lifestyle and experience 'rural culture shock'. As a result of this problem, many of these teachers leave rural areas after a short time" (p. 210). Likewise in this district, informal surveys conducted with teachers who were leaving the rural area indicated that many had found the area to be isolated and lacking in stimulating community activities. High turnover rates are a strain on a school system, both financially and in terms of morale.

Another area of need was recruitment of minority teachers. Like many school districts in the nation, the district had a discrepancy between the number of minority children who populated special education classes and the number of minority teachers employed by the system. While 30 percent of the children in the special education programs came from minority backgrounds, only 7 percent of the special education teachers were from minority backgrounds.

INITIATION OF THE PROJECT

The project grew out of an informal conversation involving the chair and the director of Teacher Education from the Department of Special Education and the school district's director of Exceptional Student Education (ESE). The chair asked if the school district would be interested in working collaboratively on a mutual problem or need, which was to be specified by the district. The ESE Director immediately indicated an interest in collaborating on the teacher recruitment and retention problems in her district, and steps were taken to actualize the project.

Shortly after this initial discussion, a series of meetings were held to negotiate the nature of the work. From the beginning, it was evident that the task was a challenging one because ambivalence, skepticism, and criticalness were evident among both school district leaders and members of the college of education faculty. Nonetheless, a committed core of interested persons persisted in planning the project. In retrospect, there were several factors that appear to have contributed to the success of the initial planning period. They are briefly described below.

Supportive Stakeholders

Invitations to the initial planning meeting were extended to approximately 25 key people from the university faculty and administration, the school district central administration, and principals and teachers from district schools. These people held jobs relevant to the project, but more importantly, they were also likely to be interested in and enthusiastic about designing an experimental teacher preparation program for special educators. Called the Steering Committee, this group was initially charged with the task of establishing the direction of the project. Once a focus and design for the project had been approved, the Steering Committee expanded to include a few skeptics and critics so that optimism about the project would not cause the group to overlook important issues. This mix of enthusiastic support tempered by a few skeptics proved to be helpful. In the beginning, the project needed affirmation to proceed, thus a supportive steering committee was important in launching the project. As obstacles were encountered, people in pivotal positions to deal with the obstacles were invited to be members of the Steering Committee. Through this strategy, people who had opposed the project sometimes became allies and always became sources of valuable information.

To maintain support from the Steering Committee, it was important that the structure of the committee and scope of the work fit the realities of members' lives. While all of the members were committed to the project's success, some had neither the time nor interest in becoming involved in the day-to-day operations of the project. By choice, these persons limited themselves to only being members of the Steering Committee. Smaller subcommittees were identified to develop the project in greater detail. People who were interested in the specific operation of the project volunteered for the subcommittee work. The subcommittees met frequently, were diligent in their work (read the professional literature and discussed issues at length), and successful in developing creative plans. They became the "workhorses" of the project. Work from the subcommittees was submitted to the Steering Committee for approval annually.

A Shared Mission

For the first meeting of the Steering Committee, a facilitator was hired to lead a discussion of values, visions of the future, and beliefs about education and teacher training. This format was patterned after Pfeiffer, Goodstein and Nolan's (1985) strategic planning model that posits organizations must be clear about their mission, vision, beliefs, and values before they begin planning specific strategies. The first planning meeting, when the facilitator managed the discussion, was uneventful. School personnel, district administrators, and university personnel all voiced many of the same goals. Concerns about the inadequacy of traditional university approaches to training and the shortages of skilled teachers were shared by all.

From the vision and mission discussions came the suggestion that the project should prepare "homegrown" teachers. By concentrating recruitment efforts on paraprofessionals currently working in the district, individuals would be identified who had long-term ties to the community and were likely to stay in the area. Additionally, paraprofessionals would already have experience with children. It was also hoped that by recruiting paraprofessionals, the pool of minority applicants might be increased. This suggestion provided a mission that the Steering Committee could enthusiastically support because it was so relevant to the needs of the district and the university.

Authentic Communication

Once the project had an organizational structure and a vision and mission, the project was launched. However, some of the challenges that arose as the project was starting were instrumental in shaping its future. These challenges had to do with creating authentic communication among the persons in charge of the project. The second planning meeting was intended to extend plans and clarify direction. During this meeting, fears and concerns about the project began to emerge. Each stakeholder had a set of expectations for school district/university collaborations based on his or her previous experiences, and some of these were negative. School personnel expected to be told what to do and sold on a plan. At one point, a principal asked, "If you don't have a plan, why am I here? I'm just wasting my time." University personnel were aware that a plan developed without collaboration would be flawed because many school realities would be overlooked; however, the lack of clear structure frustrated the school people.

At several points, the discussion became heated as school district and university personnel struggled with issues of mistrust, territory, control, and beliefs about educational practice. For example, a teacher proposed that student-teachers would have to understand that teachers could tell them to leave the classroom when children began misbehaving. University personnel interpreted this suggestion as an indication that the teacher was viewing the student-teachers as outsiders and potential problems. Furthermore, such practice would deprive student-teachers of valuable opportunities to learn. University personnel pointed out that this stipulation reflected a lack of trust and unwillingness to collaborate, which precipitated a rather heated discussion. It took most of the two-hour meeting to agree upon basic tenets about the project's operation. The turning point in the discussion came when the ESE director reaffirmed her commitment to the collaboration by saying, "Look guys. I know these people (referring to the university contingent) and they are good people. I asked them to get involved with us. This project can help us a lot!" Her unambivalent commitment to the collaboration helped to silence the fears and advance the planning. By the end of the meeting, the idea of "we" rather than "they" began to develop, and planning for the next steps proceeded.

In retrospect, these early disagreements were instrumental in clarifying participants' concerns and establishing more authentic communication. By openly expressing their concerns, participants ensured that the negotiations covered the issues of greatest importance to the people who would implement the project. During the three years of funding, the project encountered a number of challenges, but communication was always open, so that issues were discussed and no one within the project resorted to subversive opposition.

STRUCTURE OF THE PROJECT

After several months of frequent subcommittee meetings, a plan was presented to the Steering Committee for approval and then to the Office of Special Education Programs in the U.S. Department of Education for funding. The principal features of the project to "home grow" special education teachers for a rural school district are briefly described below. The program of study is depicted in Table 18.1.

- Recruitment of paraprofessionals and secretaries, especially persons from minority cultures, who currently live in rural Florida and therefore are likely to stay in the area;
- Development of two professional practice schools to provide students with learning environments that encourage active learning and a work environment for teachers and administrators that is rich in continuous inquiry, peer discussion, and opportunities for adult learning;
- Delivery of university courses in geographically accessible locations to accommodate the students' needs;
- Experimentation with alternative instructional approaches, including the infusion of computer technology and demonstration of teaching approaches; and
- Focused, individualized efforts to help trainees acquire survival skills needed to thrive in rural schools serving at-risk children.

CHALLENGES AND SUCCESSES

The project has given us some valuable insights regarding the benefits of collaborating with a school district on teacher preparation. We have organized our discussion of these insights around the following topics: recruitment and admission barriers, the teacher education curriculum, professional practice schools, the impact of the peer group or training cohort, and the challenges of university restructuring.

TABLE 18.1
Program of Study

Semester 1 (fall)
 Introduction to Exceptional Children
 Computers in Education
 Curriculum and Instruction

Semester 2 (spring)
 Introduction to Teaching Reading and Introduction to Teaching Language Arts (two
  3-hour courses that were linked and taught in a condensed format before and after
  the practicum)
 Introduction to Teaching Math and Introduction to Teaching Science
 (two 3-hour courses that were linked and taught in a condensed format before and
  after the practicum)
 Practicum
 (9 weeks of 5 days, full-time work in a regular education setting)
 Introduction to Learning Disabilities or Introduction to Mental Retardation

Semester 3 (summer)
 Psychological Foundations
 Measurement
 Corrective Reading

Semester 4 (fall)
 Programming for Exceptional Adolescents and Young Adults
 Introduction to Behavior Disorders and Behavior Management
 (two 3-hour courses linked with a full-day every week practicum at the secondary
  vocational professional practice school)

Semester 5 (condensed spring)
 Clinical Teaching and Assessment
 (two 3-hour courses linked with a practicum that was typically conducted in the
  student's home school)

Semester 6 (atypical summer session)
 Student Teaching
 Senior Seminar
 Social Foundations

Recruitment and Admission Barriers

The first goal set by the Steering Committee was to recruit two cohorts of 30 paraprofessionals who lived and worked in rural Florida and who already had an A.A.
degree. Particular attention was to be given to recruiting persons from minority
backgrounds. An assumption was made that there was an untapped source of talented, motivated people working in the district who would like to be teachers, if the

training opportunity existed. Thus, project staff undertook a goal of learning more about effective recruitment strategies.

Experience with this project suggests that indeed there is an untapped source of talented and motivated persons working in the schools who would like to be teachers. The problem is not locating or recruiting them, rather it is helping them navigate the maze of bureaucratic requirements to be admitted to the university. Effective recruitment strategies are relatively easy to develop and implement. For example, the following strategies were found to be both effective, easy, and relatively inexpensive: public service announcements on the radio, articles in the local newspaper, school bulletins, program brochures distributed to community organizations, solicitation of principals' help in identifying good candidates, and personal letters to employees of the system.

Within several months of receiving funding notification, an applicant pool of approximimately 38 people had been recruited; however several had serious problems with their admission credentials, and several lost their motivation when they learned more about the level of commitment that would be required of them. For the remaining group of applicants, admission decisions were based upon recommendations, interviews, job evaluations, grade point averages from their A.A. degree, and standardized test scores (ACT or SAT). Over half of the applicants to the first cohort did not have all their application credentials processed when the program began; consequently, preliminary admission decisions were based primarily upon recommendations, interviews, and job evaluations. Thirty people started the program and 29 eventually were admitted to the first cohort. Their characteristics are summarized in Table 18.2.

One of the most significant barriers encountered by the project was helping students meet university admission standards, a barrier mentioned by other programs working with paraprofessionals. The university adheres to state board rules that specify all graduates from community colleges within Florida must be admitted to state universities if they have attained the admission standard. Upper-level programs may set higher admission standards, but all students who meet the specified criteria are admitted. Likewise, all students who do not meet the criteria are denied admission. College officials were supportive of this project and willing to allow modifications of many practices to accommodate the needs of the project, but because of legal ramifications, they were not willing to alter the admission standards. Each year many students are denied admission on the basis of their test scores and grade point averages. The university would have faced legal complications if standards had been relaxed for some students and not for others.

The admission standards created a formidable challenge to this project. Although the standards were intended to ensure equity and fairness, they sometimes served as barriers to recruiting persons who came from backgrounds that have traditionally been excluded from the teaching profession. In many instances, the wisdom and fairness of these admission requirements were questioned as the credentials and circumstances of an individual were examined. For example, one of the applicants was a member of the school board. For many years, she had served as an able school

TABLE 18.2
Characteristics of Participants in Cohort #1 and #2

	Cohort 1	Cohort 2
Gender		
Female	26	24
Male	3	1
Ethnic Identity		
African American	6	1
Euro-American	21	24
Hispanic American	1	
Native American	1	
Age		
Mean	36	28
Range	19* to 49	20 to 47
Number who live in Polk County	26	19
Current employment status		
Paraprofessional or related educational role (school nurse, vocational ed. teacher, substitute teacher)	19	12
Full-time student**	8	5
School board member	1	
Electrician	1	
Store clerk/cashier		3
Secretary		3
Pharmacy technician		1
Self-employed		1

*The nineteen year old was the mother of a four-year-old.
**All of the full-time students have had experience with children and have lived in the area for some time.

volunteer and as an effective advocate for the school district. Her service record was uniquely impressive, and her test scores were respectable; however, her grade point average from 20+ years earlier was low. In her words, she was young, immature, and more interested in her social life than her academic work. She had not done well during her first two years in college, and those grades served as an impediment to her admission. Had project staff not taken an individual interest in her, she would have been denied admission.

Of the 10 initial applicants from minority backgrounds, only one initially met the requirements. As has been well-documented in the literature, standardized tests are frequently a barrier for people from minority backgrounds. The personnel in the project and the admissions office worked cooperatively to advise these students how to meet the admission standards. The school district paid for a course to help applicants prepare for the tests. The combined efforts of all these groups sustained students as they grappled with requirements that often appeared to them to be irrelevant and insulting. Without such support, students report they would have given up.

It should be noted that there was no intent or interest in admitting persons to the project who might not be good teachers or who could not successfully complete the program of study. Issue was taken with a policy that had been developed for traditional students moving through the traditional system with very few provisions for individual variations.

Some of the paraprofessionals who applied or expressed interest in the project had been out of school for a number of years, had not been outstanding students in high school (often because of poverty and family problems), had not taken strong college preparation courses, and were anxious about their ability to perform on standardized tests. Not surprisingly, some did not perform well on norm-referenced, national tests that were standardized on a youthful, more traditional population than the applicants in this project. These applicants were, however, highly motivated, mature persons with a wealth of experience working with children and other adults. To assist the project in recruiting a full cohort of students, the college allowed students in the first cohort to take courses even though they had not been officially admitted— an exception to university practice. This exception was justified on the basis of late notification of funding. However, such exceptions were not permissible with the second cohort. Thus, with the second cohort, if students did not meet the admission standards upon their application, there was very little time to sort out how the applicants might work to meet the requirements. It is noteworthy that the second cohort consisted of younger, less experienced, and almost all Euro-American applicants—persons more typical of college of education applicant pools.

Based on experiences with this project, it would appear that current, fairly standard university admission practices may provide institutional barriers to nontraditional and minority applicants. In fields such as special education, if we indeed want to recruit nontraditional students and persons from minority backgrounds, serious and careful attention needs to be given to university structures and policies. The real challenge to recruitment of minority and nontraditional applicants appears to be in reforming ourselves, not creating innovative recruitment strategies.

THE TEACHER EDUCATION CURRICULUM

During the first meeting of the Curriculum Subcommittee, members shared some of their own frustrations with their training programs. Even though some had been out of school for many years, their disappointments and hurts were still vivid memories. Their reaction is not unusual (Barth, 1991). Many people enter education highly motivated and excited about teaching, but are quickly disappointed by what they perceive as irrelevant content in their training program. Likewise with this group, they recalled theories and research studies that were interesting, but in their opinions, irrelevant. Thus, one of the guiding principles of this project became the importance of enabling student-teachers to become actively involved in their own learning and not to be merely told what to do.

Because project planners were committed to an adult learning model that featured relevance and individualized learning, questions were raised about the *meaning* and *value* of traditional teacher training content. Although no labels were used, as members of the subcommittee discussed their views on learning, they were endorsing principles that are now associated with constructivism or holism.

Holistic, constructivist views have changed the meaning of learning from acquiring knowledge to constructing knowledge, from a receptive act to a creative one. This "change of lens," as Poplin (1993) describes it, means that teachers interact with children in authentic ways as they make meaning of learning experiences. Knowledge is not viewed as static, something the experts know and students have to learn; rather it is created. As we learn, we change old knowledge with our new understandings.

In the constructivist approach, teachers are co-learners and facilitators of others' learning, not the ones who give knowledge to students. The single most important function of a teacher is to know how her students think so that she can create new experiences that can be related to the students' ways of thinking. From the constructivist approach, curriculum is connected to what students already know. It is geared toward the students' developmental needs (e.g., what they are developmentally ready to learn). To the extent possible, it should be experientially based, and it should be interesting to the students.

Another tenet of holistic or constructivist approach is that errors are opportunities to teach, not behaviors to punish. Learning occurs when students' understandings are challenged, not when the proper answer is recorded on a piece of paper. One of the students described this process in her reflective journal:

> I seem to be the kind of learner who does not learn well by only memorizing and recalling. I seem to need discussion, rules or reasons for certain things, and application or practice of what I am taught. I also want an explanation of my mistakes. I can't learn this stuff if it isn't explained to me.

She clearly describes how she learns, and it seems she is typical, not atypical.

From the start of this project, an effort was made to protect learning experiences and allow students to experiment, take risks, and make mistakes. Mentors were identified who were responsible for helping student-teachers reflect upon their practice and learn how to deal with their errors. As Noddings (1992) explains, "We do not need to cram their heads with specific information and rules. Instead we should help them learn how to inquire, to seek connections between their chosen subject and other subjects, to give up the notion of teaching their subject only for its own sake" (p. 178).

By following the needs of individual students, knowledge and skills were included that are not typically found in teacher education curricula. For example, some students were coached in being sensitive to school culture, others in personal appearance or interpersonal communication skills. This flexibility in responding to individual students' needs probably had a significant impact on students' successes as teachers. Student-teachers, like children in our schools, are not all alike. They have different needs as they learn to become effective teachers; therefore the teacher education curriculum should have mechanisms that enable flexibility in program planning.

Pace of the program was another important curriculum issue. Most of the participants were working full-time jobs, carrying the equivalent of a full-time course load, and dealing with family concerns. During the program several students shared that they were frequently in conflict with their spouses, and virtually all of the student-teachers who still had children in their homes were concerned about their children's well-being. Project coordinators often discussed the function of stress in the curriculum and whether the program should be spread over a longer period of time to make it less intense. Each time the question was considered, the decision was made that the intensity seemed to be counterbalanced by the speed with which students were able to finish the program. Although the two years required to complete the program were stressful, that time period was very efficient. Furthermore, it seemed that as long as the stress was tolerable, it served as a catalyst for students to seek support and help from each other. Most students had "study buddies," and many assignments were completed by cooperative teams. The relationships developed during the training program were important sources of learning and growth. Furthermore, project graduates maintained these relationships after graduation and now have a solid network that is providing support and assistance during the first year of teaching.

When students reached the end of their program, project directors felt the students had become thoughtful, confident teachers who were eager to teach. Most of the students attributed their growth to the rich and varied clinical experiences they had, while faculty emphasized the importance of the individualized curriculum and the cooperative learning approaches. Students in the project often wanted straightforward, simple answers about how to teach and clear directions about what to do. Instead, they were presented with questions and problems. While some information was directly taught, more often students were encouraged to read and investigate independently, to write reflective journals, to collaborate with others, and to experiment during their clinical experiences. Clearly, more information is needed about how adults learn to teach and what they need to know in order to be good teachers.

PROFESSIONAL PRACTICE SCHOOLS

From the start, an assumption was made that some of the content that teachers need to learn is best learned in the library and university classroom, but methods and strategies of teaching need to be learned in ecologically valid settings. Student-teachers need opportunities to apply their thoughts through teaching. Recognizing the transformative nature of teaching, John Dewey is reported to have ended a lecture by saying "Ladies and gentlemen, I thank you very much. I think I understand it all a lot better now" (Poplin, 1993).

Creating environments that allow such experimentation, however, is a major undertaking. In her excellent paper on the socialization of beginning teachers, Marleen Pugach (1992) cites teacher education literature that suggests novice teachers inevitably acquire the characteristics of their veteran counterparts. These studies portray the novice teacher as learning from and fitting into the existing school structures. The novice teacher is seen as essentially powerless and passive. Lortie's classic, *Schoolteacher* (1975), fits this tradition. In this work, Lortie cites the 12 or more years students spend in classrooms prior to entering teacher training as a "powerful apprenticeship of observation." During this time individuals acquire beliefs and understandings about being a teacher; however, their ideas are often narrow, limited, and not carefully examined. Lortie also notes that people entering other occupations are more likely to realize how much they still need to know because they feel less familiar with the professional role they are entering. People entering teaching, however, think they know the role, and this illusion may limit their learning.

Traditionally, most teacher preparation programs have not been able to counteract the powerful and enduring influences of the 12-year apprenticeship. It, therefore, is not surprising that the "power of what currently exists tends to dominate the thinking and actions of those who enter" our profession (Pugach, 1992, p. 134). In this project the two Professional Practice Schools were intended to be a primary vehicle for overcoming the powerful influence of the 12-year apprenticeship.

In this project, there were two professional practice schools to which all students in the training project were assigned a practicum for a major portion of the semester. Because there were 25 to 30 student-teachers at the school on a regular basis, this arrangement necessitated the schools defining roles for the student-teachers, training teachers in the supervision of student-teachers, developing strategies for dealing with differences of opinion, and generally planning and creating a place for the students in the school structure. For example, schools had to develop policies and procedures for parking and bathroom breaks because existing practices were disrupted by the infusion of so many new people. This in itself was an improvement over the typical practice of leaving the orientation of student-teachers to the cooperating teacher, who may or may not think about introducing the student-teacher to the school. The principals also met with the students on a regular basis, providing a forum to ask questions and express concerns.

One of the professional practice schools was an elementary site, and one was a secondary, vocational education site. At the elementary school, student-teachers were assigned to work with general education teachers. While in general education settings at the elementary school, students were either assigned to work with children who were considered at risk or exceptional, or they could teach the entire class while the teacher worked with a few children with special needs. At the secondary site, students were assigned both to vocational teachers and to teachers of exceptional children.

Having all students assigned to the same professional practice school had important advantages. Since everyone was at the same site and regularly shared their perceptions of teaching and learning, project and school staff were able to get to know students on a more personal basis than is often the case when students are assigned to different schools within a large geographic area. This knowledge enabled project staff to individualize training experiences for each student. For example, one woman had difficulty with her written work, and another had difficulty with the math that she was expected to teach. After several conferences with them and with their cooperating teachers, the project staff encouraged them to take additional coursework in writing and in math so they would be more adequately prepared.

The ever-present questioning of student-teachers also benefitted staff in the school. The principal and assistant principal often commented on the fact that the school was sharing "its dirty linen," and student teachers were remarkably perceptive in seeing these shortcomings. Fortunately most students were able to raise their concerns in tactful ways so that teachers often learned from their observations. In a few instances, however, the communication was not so smooth in spite of efforts to be tactful and diplomatic. One student wrote in her journal of her own unhappy childhood and the insensitivity of her own teachers to her personal problems. When she witnessed her cooperating teacher practicing many of the same exclusionary practices that she suffered through during her own childhood, she voiced her concerns. The teacher took offense, and within a matter of days, the two were barely speaking. The principal, assistant principal, and project coordinator all tried to help, as did peers of the teacher and the student, but none were successful in working out the conflict between the two. However, the conflict did provide the principal with an opportunity to review the student-teacher's concerns with the teacher. As a result of the discussion, the teacher began to question her attitudes toward students from backgrounds different from her own. This conflict did not end the teacher's prejudices, but it did start a dialogue about them. Had there been plans to continue the professional practice school, there would have been additional incentives to focus on this issue. The teacher is a capable, creative teacher with children from backgrounds similar to her own, and, with support and encouragement, may well learn how to use these same strengths with children from less advantaged backgrounds.

Experiences at the secondary professional practice school helped to underscore and emphasize advantages and liabilities of professional practice schools. The first cohort was assigned to the secondary professional practice school for summer school. Many of the teachers on the school staff elected not to teach that summer, so teachers from all over the district were hired. While all were highly recommended, they were unfamiliar with the school and its practices, thus they had difficulty orienting student-teachers to the school. There had not been enough time to train the teachers in how to deal with their project responsibilities because summer school hiring was not finalized until shortly before summer school started. Students felt somewhat abandoned, in spite of several built-in project supports. Furthermore, when conflict arose, there were no structures to help work out the conflicts; thus, scapegoating and blaming were common and very little reflection about practice was evident. The second cohort was placed at the same school during a regular semester when the principal had time to plan with the staff how to involve the students. Accordingly, the experience was entirely different and much more positive for the second cohort.

In watching the schools work with the students, project staff were impressed with the role that leadership plays in determining the success of a professional practice school. Although the leadership in both schools differed sometimes in style, both were committed to the project, incorporated students into the school structure, and provided support to students and staff as they worked on conflicts and differences. When a school embraces a training mission, it must be willing to support experimentation which involves mistakes as well as successes. Faculty and students need to feel supported and protected in their efforts to learn and explore. The principal of one of the schools noted that behavioral referrals increased the week that most of the student-teachers began assuming more responsibility in the classrooms. When a parent complained, he protected the student-teacher who was the target of the complaint. He dealt with the parent's anger and provided assistance and support to the student-teacher. When conflicts arose between teachers and student-teachers, the principal listened to both sides and mediated, but never took sides or judged. He often praised practices that impressed him; he emphatically supported a system of in-service that involved teachers teaching teachers; he encouraged teachers to try new techniques; and he set an example of continuously wanting to improve and learn. This principal was frequently heard saying, "We don't have to wait until it's broken to improve it."

In the other school, the principal allotted funds to employ some of the students as paraprofessionals in his school. He and his staff were actively involved in teaching a course and in teaching many specific instructional and behavior management skills. They clearly communicated that they loved their work and welcomed the opportunity to involve others in it. In both schools, when problems arose, the leadership was strongly committed to supporting both the training and service missions of their schools, and this commitment provided important momentum.

The teacher-training literature has consistently underscored the importance of clinical experiences during training programs, but coordinating fieldwork with content in classes has consistently posed problems. Professional practice schools hold much promise for meeting that need, but they require trust and respect between university personnel and school district personnel. To be successful, they also require talented, visionary leaders who can create opportunities and benefits from having large numbers of student-teachers in their schools.

IMPACT OF THE PEER GROUP

From the beginning of the project, students were given cooperative learning assignments, were encouraged to have study buddies, and had team presentations in classes. A supportive, cooperative atmosphere was encouraged among project participants because project directors believed students learn a great deal from each other. They also obtain significant support and motivation to sustain a high level of effort from their peer group. Support for this assumption was found repeatedly in comments written by students in the first cohort. During one of the seminars attached to their final internship, students were asked to complete the stem, "Being a member of a cohort has taught me. . . . " Representative responses to this activity are listed below.

> Being a member of this cohort has taught me to be a team player. Like in sports, various types of people make up a team and even though each is a different individual, they are all working towards a common goal. On the field they combine their talents for the benefit of the team, while off the field they live completely different lives. The same holds true for this cohort. When we are together, we have a common goal or interest. Outside of the cohort, we each have very different lifestyles. When I am on a school faculty and am working in a group, I know I must be a part of the "team." I will contribute to the group by sharing ideas and being an open-minded listener. Working together is the best way to achieve success.
>
> Being a member of this cohort has taught me to be a better friend to more people at the same time. I have developed some wonderful relationships that I will cherish deeply and will work to keep them growing.
>
> Being a member of this cohort has taught me to actively choose to be a part of solutions, not problems.
>
> Being a member of this cohort has taught me to be more accepting and tolerant of others. I feel that I am a better person after this experience.

However, emphasis on the peer group also creates challenges to the training program. As previously noted, project staff encouraged the first cohort to work together, but no interventions were implemented to ensure this cooperation. The first cohort was diverse in a number of ways: ethnicity, social class, religion, geographic heritage, gender, age, and basic personality types. Early in the project, cliques formed within the cohort, and project coordinators and school staffs heard hostile, critical statements from some students about other students. For the most part, such comments were heard but publicly ignored. During the first cohort's two-year program, project staff often questioned how best to deal with this issue. In a group of 29, subgroups are to be expected. Furthermore, individual differences were respected, and no one felt students could or should be forced to like another person; yet the differences created strife within the group. As one student wrote, "I have learned that it is almost impossible for this many women to get along." Because the situation represented a microcosm of the types of problems that might arise in a school, project staff felt it was important to help students learn how to deal with their differences, but staff were never able to agree upon how this should be done. While some attempts were made, the first cohort graduated without dealing with this issue to the extent that project coordinators would have liked. Cliques remained, and caustic comments about each other continued.

Experiences with the second cohort were different, and these differences were noticed by everyone closely associated with the project. Several explanations were advanced, and all seem plausible. The second cohort was a less diverse group, thus they did not need to learn how to deal with people different from themselves in order to be harmonious. Another explanation had to do with a significant event that occurred early in their program. Shortly after the second semester started, one of the members of the cohort was in a very serious automobile accident. Naturally, the group was upset and eager to do whatever they could to help. Since there was not another group following the second cohort, the injured student had to complete her program of study with her cohort or drop out of the project. Efforts to help the member who was injured stimulated discussion about values, and a commitment to each other emerged from the discussions.

Another explanation for why the second cohort was more cohesive and supportive of each other focused on the different program structure for the second cohort. The first cohort spent their fourth semester in a professional practice school. Most of their work until that semester had been fairly traditional university coursework. For most of the members of the cohort, traditional university coursework was anxiety producing. They had been out of school for some time and were apprehensive about returning. Although they were all assigned to the secondary professional practice school during semester #3 (the summer), many did not get to do much teaching. It was not until their fourth semester in the program that they really had the opportunity to teach, to see if indeed they were going to enjoy this new role. It was also during this semester that potential deficits were really noted. Given the significance of this experience, it was decided that students should spend a semester in a professional practice school as early in the program as possible, affording students with an opportunity to do what they like best and the project with opportunities to be certain that participants are likely to be good teachers. Thus, the schedule was changed for the second cohort so they could spend their second semester in the elementary professional practice school. This structure may have eliminated a lot of pressure and anxiety for most of the members of the cohort. Whatever the reason, the second cohort seemed to gel early on, and, with the exception of a very few people, the cohort was accepting and supportive of each other. The few peripheral members of the group were clearly different from the majority of the group and seemed comfortable being on the periphery.

The fact that the second cohort had so few problems working as a cohort raised additional questions for further exploration. Were there program structures that caused the first cohort to be more anxious? If so, what? Were the obvious differences in the two groups primarily due to personality differences? Is it more desirable to have diverse groups that have to learn to work together or cohesive groups that naturally seem to gel? Should training programs promote harmony and cooperation among members of the cohort, or should programs work with cohorts to understand their conflicts? What ethical boundaries should be considered in making such decisions?

All of these questions remain for future consideration, but they do underscore how much we do not know about teacher training. It is commonly accepted that training cohorts are beneficial for several reasons: they allow programs to have better control over their curriculum and students learn a great deal from their peers. However, it must be acknowledged that we know very little about how to work with and use training cohorts as important components of our teacher preparation programs.

CHALLENGES OF UNIVERSITY RESTRUCTURING

In an effort to accommodate students' need to work, the project developed and offered several courses using different formats. Content from several courses was condensed during class lectures and discussions, and students worked with facilitators to implement the practices and test the theories. One course was taught by weekly assessment of mastery of learning principles through computer-administered and -scored tests. Not surprisingly, students reacted differently to the different approaches, but generally they all agreed that they benefitted from the experience of different instructional techniques.

Project personnel, however, were impressed by the difficulties encountered in changing the traditional way of offering university coursework. Even faculty who wanted to experiment with different approaches had difficulty participating because their schedules were set up to follow traditional class schedules. Faculty also had difficulty collaborating with other faculty to the degree they wanted, again because their schedules did not permit. Coordinating class lectures and discussion with the field activities also presented challenges. Some instructors were able to establish good working relationships with the facilitators early in the course, and together they offered an outstanding program. Other instructors approached the collaborative task with traditional attitudes (professor telling school personnel what to do) and, not surprisingly, encountered resistance when working with the facilitators.

Project personnel realized that although change is difficult for all, school personnel seemed to realize that it was inevitable, and they were struggling to adapt to new and different expectations. School systems are modifying their structures to accommodate such change. Universities, however, may not be so well positioned for restructuring. Many university personnel seemed to be interested in the project goals and the prospect of innovation, but the institutional practices and structures are not prepared for such change.

Based on experiences with this project, it appears that universities need to focus on their own institutional structures if they are to effectively accommodate the changing needs of schools. Issues such as faculty time, assignments, criteria for promotion, the creation of faculty positions for personnel within the schools, appointments from the field, and creation of shared, jointly funded positions are all important areas that need to be studied and developed. Until these issues are addressed, projects such as this are likely to face serious impediments during their implementation, and university/school district collaborations will be hindered.

CONCLUSIONS

After three years of working with the USF/Polk County Collaborative Teacher Training Program for Paraprofessionals, one cohort of students has graduated and another will graduate soon. The project reduced significantly the number of out-of-field teachers that Polk County employed. Project coordinators and district personnel generally believe the project was very successful, and at graduation, students reported feeling confident and ready to teach. In spite of the enthusiasm the project has generated, project coordinators still have more questions than answers.

We do not know how this group compares with our "traditional" students, thus we cannot determine whether this program was at least as good as the traditional program on campus. Our impressions are that, as a group, project students may not perform as well as traditional groups on standardized tests, but in the classroom, they will be more confident in their ability to teach and more satisfied with the preparation they received in their training program. Plans are underway to compare the two groups.

We do not know whether the graduates of this project will stay in the area. One of the basic assumptions of this project was the belief that there was an untapped source of talented persons who could become "homegrown teachers." We have demonstrated that there are persons working in schools who can be prepared to be effective teachers, but if these people leave the area after receiving their training, the project will not have accomplished the primary goal of recruiting teachers who will remain in the area. If, however, graduates continue to teach in Polk County, as most of the first cohort are now doing, this model shows promise as a recruitment strategy for districts in rural or difficult-to-recruit areas.

Although we believe the program was successful in preparing the cohort to be good teachers of exceptional children, we do not know what aspects of the program contributed to its success. By the time members of the first cohort graduated, it was clear that many had undergone major transformations in the way they thought about teaching. One woman who had worked as a paraprofessional for many years prior to entering the program wrote in her journal that she was now dressing like a teacher, so she knew she looked different on the outside, but she felt different on the inside too. She proceeded to describe how much more confident and self-assured she felt. Project staff all agreed that she looked almost like a different person when comparing pictures taken at the beginning of the program and at graduation. She also behaved differently. When the project began, she was quiet, compliant, and somewhat obsequious. By graduation, the entire group had learned to enjoy her sense of humor, spirit, creativeness, and clear ability. It seemed as though this woman had survived many years as a paraprofessional, often one of the least respected roles in a school. As she became a teacher, many of her dormant talents became more evident. Upon graduation, she was offered six jobs within the school district!

Most of the students had developed clear images of the type of teacher they wanted to be, and most were concerned about how to care for individual children. Some of their journal entries illustrate this point.

> One of the lowest achievers in our class tugs at my heart. She has so little to draw from in her life. She has such a poor home life that she lacks many of the basic skills. What she does not lack, however, is the desire to do and to learn. Because she tries so hard and even asks me for homework, I do all I can whenever I can to help her.
>
> Today I went to the office to pick up picture money for a student. I turned around to leave and there she was, standing with a blue note. She was crying and hurt because a student laughed at her. She had pushed the other girl. I immediately had to take the child and discuss the incident. After our talk, I suggested ways she could handle this situation in the future. This was from the heart. I didn't learn this from a textbook. I could have walked away and let the office handle the situation, but I think a teacher should be sensitive and flexible, eager to help children.
>
> One morning (a student) had an ugly incident happen at home. He was brought to school late by the same person who caused the incident. He was full of hostility and anger. The classroom teacher said nothing to him upon his entry or at any other time of the day—even though the teacher had been told about the incident. I took the time to talk to the student, or rather, to let him talk to me about the incident. I feel this was a good thing to do because the child was in no frame of mind to learn as long as all of those feelings were boiling inside of him.

During the program, students were often resistant to new ideas, but as one person explained, she had learned a lot during her 15 years as a paraprofessional. It was difficult to unlearn what she had learned. She had to test and examine new ideas before she was willing to give up comfortable ways. Project staff, however, were impressed by how well she learned new ideas. Another participant wrote:

> During the course of this program, I have changed in many ways. In the past, I was set in my ways for doing things one way, whereas now I will try different ways. . . . Now, I am comfortable with working with new teachers and sharing ideas and techniques. I feel very confident about my abilities and also expressing my weaknesses.

Project staff agreed with her self-assessment; however, we still do not know what made this group change. What transformed them from passive followers to confident teachers? The project deliberately incorporated techniques designed to accomplish this goal, but the participants rarely mentioned these activities as being among the most influential in their development. They typically cited their extensive and diversified clinical experiences and the cohort experience as the most important part of their training. It may be the case that more formal university-based learning experiences prepared the foundation that enabled students to profit from their applied experiences, or it may be that the content was not as relevant or was not taught as effectively as it needed to be. More projects of this nature are needed so that these issues can be explored more fully.

One clear outcome is that university and school district personnel benefitted from the collaboration. In spite of the stresses and differences of opinion, both groups believe that the shared experience was enriching, enlightening, and worthy of continuation. A proposal for continued funding has been submitted, with an overarching goal of institutionalizing the project within the community. Specific objectives have to do with refining and improving components of the project and continuing to study the process collaboratively so that together we can develop a relevant, quality program for preparing "homegrown" special education teachers.

REFERENCES

Barth, R. (1991). *Improving schools from within*. San Francisco: Jossey-Bass.

Cheney, C.O., Cummings, R.W., & Royce, P.P. (1990). Training rural early childhood special educators: A model of effective distance learning. *Teacher Education and Special Education, 13*, 210–212.

Lortie, D. (1975). *Schoolteacher: A sociological study*. Chicago: The University of Chicago Press.

Noddings, N. (1992). *The challenge to care in schools: Advances in contemporary educational thought, Vol. 8*. New York: Teachers College Press.

Pfeiffer, J.W., Goodstein, L.D., & Nolan, T.M. (1985). *Applied strategic planning*. San Diego, CA: University Associates.

Poplin, M. (1993). *A practical theory of teaching and learning: The view from inside the new transformative classroom: Contributions of constructivism*. Paper presented at the Florida Teacher Education Division of the Council of Exceptional Children. Tampa, FL. Available from the author: The Claremont Graduate School.

Pugach, M. C. (1992). Uncharted territory: Research on the socialization of special education teachers. *Teacher Education and Special Education, 15*, 133–147.

19

DESIGNING STUDIES THAT ARE SENSITIVE TO THE COMPLEXITY OF INCLUSION
Creating a Knowledge Base

ALBERT DUCHNOWSKI, BRENDA TOWNSEND,
ANN HOCUTT, & JAMES MCKINNEY

INTRODUCTION

RESEARCHERS who wish to study the restructuring of the nation's schools need to be prepared to board a moving train. Since the publication of America 2000, (1990) schools across the country have almost immediately begun to change the way they are organized and administered, as well as how they teach children. Today, there are few schools that have not begun at least some aspect of restructuring. Consequently, researchers who wish to examine the process will have to accommodate their research protocols to an existing phenomenon of change.

The database on restructuring and inclusion is new, relatively small, and has many methodological challenges. For example: Can true experimental designs be employed in field studies of restructuring and inclusion? How is restructuring defined and operationalized? What are the dependent variables?

No single paradigm of inquiry appears to be robust enough to adequately investigate the process. Qualitative as well as quantitative methods are needed to document the ongoing and dynamic changes that will occur as we explore any causal relationships that may exist. Sound evaluation research is needed as much as experimental studies.

This chapter will identify specific challenges facing researchers, examine the process of determining outcomes to be measured by schools, and present several strategies that may guide research in this area. The chapter will close with a presentation of a restructuring/inclusion demonstration project being conducted by the authors. A federally funded project, it is being conducted in the five school districts described in chapters 14–18. The authors will discuss the methodology, the outcomes to be measured, and the planning process.

RESEARCHING RESTRUCTURING SCHOOLS

Many challenges are presented for researchers of restructuring schools. Defining restructuring is an arduous task in and of itself. To further compound the difficulties in research efforts, goals are often developed in accordance with the varied interests advanced by the initiative. Therefore, they lack consistency and may even be incongruent. As researchers, we are challenged to identify outcomes and evaluation methods for the complex process of restructuring. Studies have been conducted on various reform features in isolation: alternative curricula (Deno, Maruyama, Espin, & Cohen, 1990), alternative assessment models (Fuchs & Deno, 1991), students with disabilities in general education settings (Schulte, Osborne, & McKinney, 1990). However, there is a paucity of data on the efficacy of school reform efforts involving multiple innovations. Thus, evaluation methods are needed to clearly identify changes responsible for achieving school improvement goals. Educators and researchers must be able to determine whether outcomes do improve for all students, including students with disabilities.

The authors are currently involved in a multi-site school restructuring demonstration project involving schools at various stages of the process. The demonstration project was not designed to intervene in school efforts at restructuring, but to support and identify the systemic changes that must be made to improve outcomes for all students, including those with disabilities.

State goals of school reform have emerged from the nine national goals (Goals America 2000, 1993) and guide the reform movement we are studying. They specifically address: 1) readiness to start school; 2) improved graduation rates and postsecondary education and employment; 3) increased student performance; 4) learning environment conducive to teaching and learning; 5) adequate school safety and healthy environment; 6) professional teachers and staff; 7) improved adult literacy; 8) professional development; and 9) partnerships with communities and family.

Each school has a school advisory council composed of administrators, faculty and staff, parents, students, and community members. These school councils, as building-level authorities, determine the goals for the improvement of their schools. Table 19.1 presents which of these seven goals each school targeted for school improvement.

For the most part, it appears that the schools in the project only selected goals that were adopted by the state from the national goals. Absent from the national and state goals is an articulation of goals involving the inclusion of students with disabilities. These omissions are also reflected among the goals identified by the participating schools. Thus, national, state, and local goals appear to drive individual school goals. As inclusion was not a national, state, or local goal, individual schools did not identify it as their goal.

TABLE 19.1
School Improvement Goals

Goals

State: (across)	Goal 1	Goal 2	Goal 3	Goal 4	Goal 5	Goal 6	Goal 7
School A	x	x	x	x	x		
School B			x	x	x		
School C			x	x	x		x
School D			x	x	x		
School E		x	x	x	x		x

*Data analyzed prior to passage of Goals 2000.

A lack of specific reference to students with disabilities in school reform efforts is not uncommon. For example, much of the effective schools literature fails to clearly address the education of students with disabilities (Lilly, 1987; Pugach & Sapon-Shevin, 1987). Children who are at risk have received some attention in school reform movements (Murphy, 1991), while students with identified disabilities have received little.

Based on our observations, several challenges face researchers of school transformation. Research is complicated by an inability to clearly define dependent variables that are common to restructuring schools. These problems of definition are exacerbated when researching intervention effects on students with disabilities; efforts to characterize features of restructuring schools are often futile. In responding to the various national, state, or local goals, schools have developed many strategies, and it becomes difficult to determine which components, or combinations of components, can be attributed to improved student outcomes.

As school restructuring is designed to increase the involvement of parents, community members, and students in school improvement, evaluation methods must target the stakeholders. In effect, schools can no longer assess only students for improved outcomes. Evaluation procedures must be developed to include family and community members in the evaluation of restructuring efforts, but the field is just at the stage of developing the methodology for this process (Winton & Bailey, 1993).

MULTIPLE MODELS OF INTERVENTION

The difficulties caused by lack of clarity of definitions are not the only sources of challenge to researchers in this field. The task of developing rigorous designs to study restructuring is further complicated by the fact that interventions or change can be focused at several levels. The literature contains reports of demonstration projects that are grade level, schoolwide (elementary, middle, or high school), curriculum focused, districtwide and even statewide. Some projects represent a combination of these approaches.

The possible range of dependent measures or outcomes is also extensive. Some studies have clearly defined quantitative outcomes such as achievement scores. Others focus on governance and decision making, while still others may measure attitudinal change in administrators, faculty, students, and/or parents.

Another difficulty is associated with the types of "subjects" chosen to be studied. The range of children in regular education as well as those with disabilities is clearly diverse, not only in their physical and mental challenges but in their ethnic and cultural representation. A researcher will be faced with the difficult problem of deciding how to select subjects in studies that almost preclude random assignment because of ethical and logistic considerations. The difficulties resulting from biased or uncontrolled subject selection are well known. Kavale, Forness, and Alper (1986), for example, examined research on children who have behavioral disorders and pointed out how the inconsistencies in definitions and methods of subject selection have virtually rendered the results of more than 100 studies useless in contributing to the knowledge base and furthering our understanding in this field. The problem is magnified when we desire information about *all* children or when we mix children with severe disabilities with those who have mild or moderate problems.

The current literature on restructuring is composed of studies that contain the varieties of design and focus described above. As this literature grows, the potential for advancing the knowledge base, understanding restructuring, and for applying the results of this research to practice will be enhanced if these studies are judged to have an acceptable level of validity by the scientific community, policy makers, advocates, and the general public.

WHICH QUESTIONS TO ASK: HOW TO ASK THEM

Social science, of which we consider special education to be a part, has traditionally been guided by concerns for validity and reliability. There are, however, several threats to validity in special education research arising from many sources, including: sampling problems, imprecise assessments, poor control in field settings, and lack of specificity of interventions. In addition, much of special education research has been retrospective, limiting the explication of causal relations.

Several remedies to these threats have been developed, ranging from the use of quasi-experimental designs to structural equation modeling (Switzky & Heal, 1990). Each generation of methodologists and statisticians has produced new approaches and techniques, such as multivariate methods and, more recently, growth curve analysis (Bryk & Raudenbush, 1992), all aimed at reducing threats to the data caused by situations that the investigator could not or did not control. This battery of data analyses has enabled special education researchers to continue a systematic pursuit of the objective truth of how to best teach children who have disabilities.

Another solution to these problems of methodology requires the adoption of an entirely different method of inquiry. Influenced by B.F. Skinner and his colleagues (see, for example, Skinner, 1957), many special education researchers adopted the technique of single subject designs (Kazdin, 1982). In this approach, each subject serves as his/her own control, reducing the confounds arising from sampling error or flawed group comparisons. Single subject designs have much greater specificity of the intervention, and only observable, quantifiable behaviors are used to avoid the problems associated with imprecise measures of mediating constructs such as self-esteem. The use of the techniques of the experimental analysis of behavior has had a significant effect on the practice of special education (see for example, Peacock Hill Working Group, 1991). Yet the zeal for experimental control in the behavioral approach has been traded, frequently, for a reduction in generalization of results (Stokes & Bear, 1977). The adoption and implementation of university-originated behavioral programs has not been as successful in the field as desired (Duchnowski, in press). Consequently, the search goes on.

The Paradigm Shift

While the use of qualitative research methods in special education is not new, there has been a sharp increase in interest in the last few years (Peck & Furman, 1992). Some of this interest has come from investigators looking for new techniques to examine research questions that do not lend themselves to designs in the positivist tradition. For example, Weatherley and Lipsky (1992) used qualitative methods to describe the richness of social policy implementation as related to the bureaucracy of school reform. In trying to examine how things happen at "the street level" after centralized decrees are made, they abandoned experimental designs as not feasible and developed a qualitative methodology that collected data in a more ethnographic manner.

Others have promoted qualitative designs from a more fundamental perspective, viz., a shift in the philosophy of science away from logical positivism toward the relativism of post-positivism (see for example, Lincoln & Guba, 1985). In this point of view, experimental methods are incomplete and fundamentally incompatible with the qualitative paradigm (Lincoln & Guba, 1985; Smith & Heshusius, 1986). While the authors understand the need for holistic analysis, we do not support the development of an either-or position, but rather one in which both methodologies are used to contribute their unique data to an understanding of the phenomenon under investigation. While it is beyond the scope of this chapter to fully compare the two paradigms, the reader is referred to an excellent review of these issues by Peck & Furman (1992).

Interpretivism

Our use of the term *paradigm* in the discussion above is not technically accurate. We have really been discussing methods of inquiry within the objectivist paradigm. A substantive paradigm shift in research occurs when the tenets of interpretivism are embraced with its nonobjectivist worldview and different standards of truth. In this approach, stories are told by the researcher to an audience. The *telling* of the story is as important as the story itself because the interpretation is fostered by the inclusion of a speaker and an audience (Ferguson, Ferguson, & Taylor, 1992). For a full discussion of this paradigm shift, the reader is referred to a book by Guba and Lincoln (1989).

Available Options

We would propose that the special education researcher has several options available in planning how to examine the processes of school reform and particularly how they affect children with disabilities and their families. Experimental and quasi-experimental designs, single subject methods, and the broad range of qualitative research, including interpretavistic methods, are all described and reported upon in the special education literature. We propose a true pluralistic strategy and will describe a study with such an approach a little later in this chapter.

What Do We Need to Know?

Our assessment of the current body of research examining restructured schools and special education is that it is very rough around the edges. The research community has moved rapidly in several directions and a base of information, not necessarily knowledge, is growing. It is time to answer the very common sense question, "What is restructuring?" This is a fundamental question for researchers to include in their projects, and a similar task exists for "inclusion."

It is not sufficient for this type of policy analysis to be dependent upon a snapshot when we need a video. The question of what happens in the long run is fundamental to implementing effective school reform—thus, longitudinal data are sorely needed in this endeavor. The danger for applied researchers is that policy makers are off to the next issue before the data are all collected and analyzed.

We need to know how children from the diverse cultures that constitute our schools are differentially effected by reform policies. We know that children from nondominant cultures are overrepresented and poorly served in special education programs. Their families are even more disempowered than those from the dominant culture (Harry, 1992). Studies of school reform need to include analyses of children from diverse cultures.

Finally, we need to ask the primary recipients of the proposed benefits of school reform, the students, what is their perception of and their involvement in school reform. This can be done through the adoption of participatory research and evaluation methods (Fenton, Batavia, & Roody, 1993).

In the final section of this chapter, we present the design of an ongoing study of school reform and its effects (if any) on children who have a disability. The authors and their colleagues are attempting to follow the recommendations suggested in this chapter and look forward to the completion of data collection and the analysis of the results.

METHODOLOGY

Currently, we are conducting a study of systemic changes made in restructuring schools to increase the inclusion of students with disabilities in the general education program and to improve outcomes for *all* students in the schools, including those with disabilities. Our research sites consist of five schools that are at various stages of restructuring, are committed to the concept of increased inclusion of students with disabilities, and serve students with a range of conditions. Additionally, the five schools have different demographic characteristics.

Our research questions are as follows:

a. What systemic changes must be made in schools that are restructuring to foster both increased inclusion and improved outcomes?
b. How are these changes made?
c. Why are these changes made?
d. To what extent do these changes result in increased inclusion for students with disabilities?
e. To what degree do these changes result in improved outcomes for *all* students, including those with disabilities?

These questions clearly demand a research methodology very different from the traditional experimental and quasi-experimental designs. They indicate that this is a policy study which focuses on the relationship between ends (goals and objectives of the policy of inclusion), means (systemic changes made by the schools to achieve these goals and objectives), and actual outcomes (increased inclusion and improved outcomes in a variety of domains). As investigators, we have no control over events, e.g., decisions regarding what specific systemic changes need to be made or how the changes are implemented in these schools. Consequently, traditional designs that call for manipulation of variables by the investigator are not appropriate for addressing these questions.

Fortunately, there is a research approach appropriate for addressing the questions: the case study as conceptualized by Yin (1989, 1993), combined with a quantitative description of outcomes in the areas of inclusion and specific outcome domains.

The Case Study

As described by Yin (1989), the case study is not the pre-experimental, one-shot case study design described by Campbell and Stanley (1966). Instead, a case study is an "empirical inquiry that investigates a contemporary phenomenon within its real life context when the boundaries between the phenomenon and context are not evident and in which multiple sources of evidence are used" (page 23).

That is, the case study as defined above is the research strategy of choice when one wishes to study a contemporary (as opposed to historical) phenomenon when relevant variables either cannot or should not be manipulated.

A major difference between this research strategy and other more "qualitative" strategies (e.g., ethnography) is Yin's (1989, 1993) focus on theory. He argues that theory development and/or testing is essential in case studies to drive data collection, analysis, and interpretation. In a policy study such as ours, the theory focuses on the "means," the "how" and "why" a policy is implemented. Theoretical considerations determine what data/information are gathered, which sources provide the data and information, and how the data/information are analyzed. In effect, a case is analogous to an entire experiment in the traditional paradigm, not to a subject in an experiment. Further, the findings and conclusions of a case generalize to the theory being developed and/or tested by the case, not to a population of subjects. Our study on inclusion within the context of restructuring is exploratory because there is insufficient information/data with which to develop an a priori theory of what systemic changes in schools foster increased inclusion and simultaneously improve student outcomes. However, we have used the strategic planning process in place in the five cases (schools) as well as observations made by key personnel in the schools to develop an initial theory of what systemic changes take place for the purpose of achieving the desired outcomes.

We will test (and undoubtedly revise) this initial theory over a three-year period. We will develop a case study protocol that clearly and directly relates our information/data collection effort (consisting primarily of interviews and examination of records) to the research questions and our initial theory. Specifically, we will gather information and data regarding what systemic changes have in fact been made in each school for the purpose of fostering inclusion and improving student outcomes, how these changes have been made, and why these changes have been made. In asking these questions, we will probe deeply into those systemic changes that, based on the school improvement plans and our own observations, we believe the schools intend to make, e.g. changes in some faculty roles. However, our questions will be designed to allow for other systemic changes that are not now part of the initial theory to be noted and, if made across most schools, become part of a revised theory. (Research questions regarding the outcomes will be addressed below).

The major data analysis strategy in case studies using Yin's approach is pattern matching, i.e., looking for patterns of findings across multiple cases and comparing the empirical patterns to posited theoretical patterns. (Single cases are used only when there is but one case or when a case is in some way unique.) For this study, we are writing annual, individual case study reports for each school. These reports contain only those data and that information that has been independently corroborated by at least three sources and pertains directly to the research questions and theory of systemic change. We will compare the findings of the individual cases across all five cases on an annual basis to draw conclusions about what systemic changes are being implemented, and how and why they are being implemented. We will compare these findings and conclusions with the initial theory and modify the theory based on the empirical data. This process will be followed for three years and will result in a final model of the systemic changes that are made in restructuring schools and how and why they are implemented.

This methodology not only takes advantage of the excellent information that can be obtained through a carefully planned and implemented case study, but meets scientific standards of reliability and validity as well. To avoid charges that subjective judgment has been used by an investigator, or that a good set of measures for conceptualization of the phenomena being studied have not been developed, we

- use multiple sources of evidence to corroborate information;
- establish a chain of evidence (the individual case study reports) and have key informants review the report to ensure that the systemic changes selected for study do indeed reflect the changes that have been made in the school to foster inclusion and improve outcomes.

To deal with threats to internal validity in an explanatory case study, a pattern-matching technique can be used. (It should be noted that the study we are conducting is exploratory in nature, for we are *developing* a theory based on findings and conclusions in these five schools. Another study would be needed for purely explanatory purposes, i.e. to determine the causal relationship between systemic change and desired outcomes.) In explanatory studies with multiple dependent variables (a variety of outcomes), the analysis focuses on whether, for each outcome, an initially predicted pattern has been found while at the same time alternative patterns have not been found. Similarly, in explanatory studies with a known dependent outcome, the analysis focuses on whether a predicted pattern (the presence of multiple independent variables) is found, and alternative patterns (mutually exclusive sets of variables) have not been found.

Issues of external validity have been dealt with above in that the case study as conceptualized by Yin generalizes to a theory, not to a population. Use of multiple cases and a replication logic, which looks for patterns predicted by theory(ies), ensures that the findings and conclusions of the cross-case analysis generalize to theory. Finally, issues of reliability are met by using the case study protocol to collect data and develop a case study data base (the case study report). This enables other investigators to follow the same procedures used in the study. These other investigators should arrive at the same findings and conclusions as the initial investigators.

Quantitative Analysis of Outcomes

As stated above, the case study methodology allows us to determine the means by which a policy such as increased inclusion is implemented. However, to be complete, a policy study must also consider the nature and extent of the empirical outcomes and assess the relation of these outcomes to the ends (goals and objectives) of the policy.

We have adopted the model developed by the National Center for Educational Outcomes (NCEO) at the University of Minnesota (Ysseldyke, Thurlow, & Gilman, 1992). A consensus-building process has been used to develop this model, and many educators, administrators, policy makers and parents from multiple organizations (education, mental health, public welfare) have been involved in the development of the outcome domains and indicators of achievement in these domains. Thus, there is assurance that the outcomes in this model are those valued by society. Further, they apply to *all* children, including those with disabilities.

The NCEO model posits that educational resources (inputs and context) influence learning opportunity and process which, in turn, influence student outcomes in six functional domains: physical health, responsibility and independence, contribution and citizenship, academic and functional literacy, personal and social adjustment, and satisfaction. Meaningful participation of students, family involvement, and accommodations/adaptations (e.g., service delivery processes) are viewed as enabling outcomes which are necessary to assure opportunity and process.

Assessment of the extent to which students with disabilities participate in general education and assessment of the degree to which various domains of outcomes are achieved clearly requires quantified data. Addressing the first issue involves analysis of the extent to which students with disabilities receive their schooling in, or adjacent to, general education classes and are involved in "typical" school functions, e.g., plays, clubs. The data on these variables will be assessed longitudinally for students collectively at each school.

Assessment of the degree to which all students in the schools, including those with disabilities, have achieved improved educational outcomes will be assessed using specific indicators for outcomes in each of the six domains. An example of an indicator for each domain of educational outcomes is as follows:

- percent of students who use and comprehend oral and written language that effectively accomplishes the purpose of communication (functional/academic literacy);
- percent of students who comply with school rules (contribution/citizenship);
- percent of students who know when, where, and how to access health care (physical health);
- percent of students who have a record of disciplinary actions (responsibility/independence);
- percent of students who have lasting and positive peer interactions (personal/social);

- percent of students who are happy to be in school, or of parents who are satisfied with their child's education (satisfaction).

Most of these indicators, which are measured by rates and proportions, are readily available from school records (e.g., cumulative folders, Individualized Education Plans). We have collected data on the indicators for these six domains of outcomes and will run distributional statistics to assess the quality of the measures of each outcome, enabling us to select the most robust of several alternative indicators. The reduced data set for each of the five schools will constitute the baseline measures for assessing longitudinally change in outcomes for students at each school since the unit of analysis is the school, not individual students within each school.

INITIAL MODEL: PROPOSITIONS RELATED TO SYSTEMIC CHANGES THAT MUST BE MADE IN SCHOOLS TO FOSTER INCREASED INCLUSION AND IMPROVED OUTCOMES

Under Florida's initiative to develop a statewide system of school improvement and accountability, five participating schools developed their school improvement plans. The plans follow a strategic planning model, in which each school and school system develop their vision and mission statements and set their goals accordingly. Action plans were developed to achieve each goal. In keeping with the project's aim to identify and describe the systemic changes being made in schools to foster increased inclusion of students with exceptionalities and improved outcomes for all students, three methods were used to observe school change activity.

Specifically, they were: a) observations during meetings of School Improvement Teams (SIT) and School Advisory Council (SAC) meetings; b) school improvement plans; and c) interviews and materials provided by USF special education faculty and graduate students working collaboratively with the participating schools. An initial model describing the changes has been developed based on the information obtained through the above methods.

The initial model identifies propositions and subpropositions regarding systemic changes related to school restructuring. Each proposition and subproposition is a testable hypothesis that can be confirmed or disconfirmed over the next three years. Modifications will be based on the continuous planning and implementation of changes in the five schools. Based on our observations to date and the nature of the plans developed in this first year, we anticipate that the final model will reflect the context in which decisions are made in restructuring schools as well as the systemic changes which are planned and implemented to achieve school goals. We further anticipate that the final model may be developmental in nature: that is, it may show that restructuring is evolutionary and focuses on more fundamental systemic changes in its later stages. (Our assumption is that school restructuring implies a transformation from one kind of school to another kind of school.) The final model will reflect *patterns* that project staff have observed in at least three of the five schools or that have appeared in at least three school's improvement plans.

For this chapter, we have included an initial conceptual framework for the types of systemic changes that may be made to achieve increased inclusion and improved outcomes for students. We are using this conceptual framework to organize our thinking about the types of systemic changes that might be made in one or more schools.

Propositions and Subpropositions

A. Context of Restructuring.
  1. The nature of national, state, and local goals is the primary determinant of the nature of individual school goals. For example, if national, state, or local goals include a goal related to school safety, a school is highly likely to develop a safety-related goal. Conversely, if national, state and local goals do not specifically include a goal (e.g., increased inclusion), a school is not likely to develop a goal in that area.
  2. Environmental forces working for school-level restructuring include:
     a. concepts, e.g., site-based management or teacher empowerment, in the larger reform effort that appeal to educators working in individual schools;
     b. personnel at the local school district or school building levels who want to change "business as usual" in education.
  3. Environmental forces working against school-level restructuring include:
     a. the lack of education/training of educators with regard to planning—especially strategic planning, which requires planners to go beyond "business as usual";
     b. a concern on the part of principals about situations in which they share decision making on the one hand but are held responsible for results of those decisions on the other; and
     c. a concern on the part of principals that visionary goals will not be achievable and consequently they will be considered "failures" by educators at the local and state levels. Risk taking and accountability are viewed as potentially incompatible.
B. Nature of the planning process to foster increased inclusion and improved outcomes in restructuring schools.
  1. At least initially, planning team members who teach or are parents of disabled students do not advocate for specific goals/strategies regarding inclusion in the initial school improvement plans.
     a. One possible reason for this is that initial school improvement goals relate to state and national priorities that do not mention inclusion.
     b. Another possible reason is that members of the SIT and/or SAC believe that all goals in the plan apply equally to general and special education students.

c. Another possible reason is that members of any school improvement committee are selected/elected because they are considered team players rather than outspoken advocates for a particular group of students.

d. Another possible reason is that some parents and/or special educators are comfortable with current levels of inclusion.

2. "Restructuring" is a developmental process in which long-range planning based on current educational procedures and practices precedes strategic planning, which goes beyond "business as usual." Building-level self-study does not initially or automatically result in either a basic reorganization or a transformation from one kind of school to another kind of school.

3. The degree to which members of the school improvement teams actually develop the strategic plans (a shared decision-making process) is inversely related to the extent to which the principal's leadership style is autocratic.

C. Systemic changes to facilitate increased inclusion and improved outcomes.

1. Changes regarding philosophy of inclusion/beliefs/values/attitudes.

a. Greater acceptance of increased inclusion for exceptional students is related to increases in interaction between ESE teachers and general education teachers (see Governance/Organization).

b. The nature of the disability impacts on the extent to which school-level educators accept changes in school organization/structure.

- Changes leading to greater inclusion are more accepted for students who have learning problems, but no serious behavior problems (e.g., MR students).

- Conversely, changes leading to greater inclusion for students with serious behavior problems (e.g., SED students) are less accepted.

- The limited acceptance of inclusion for students with serious behavior problems is related to the emphasis at the national, state, local, and school levels on a "safe and orderly climate" in schools, including a decrease in discipline problems so that teachers will have "more quality instructional time."

2. Changes regarding policies.

a. Greater flexibility with regard to existing policies rather than totally different policies, appear to be more prevalent, at least initially. (Example: when an ESE student fails a test, that student may retake the test with additional aids such as notes, calculators, and so on.)

b. At least initially in the restructuring/inclusion process, greater flexibility does not involve waivers of existing rules/regulations.

3. Changes regarding utilization of resources.

a. Assignment to specific general education staff (e.g., one assistant principal, one guidance counselor) of major duties relating to ESE students (e.g., attending staff meetings dealing with specific discipline issues) helps foster general/special education interaction and therefore may be helpful regarding greater inclusion and/or improved outcomes.

     b. Increased use of resources available to the general school faculty (e.g., faculty from USF in professional development schools, TA from the SED network or the LEA network of cooperative consultation teachers) provides support to general educators who teach ESE students.

     c. At least initially, team teaching and cooperative consultation are the major strategies that are used in school to facilitate inclusion and improved outcomes.

     d. Increased instructional time (e.g., intersession schooling, more time for instruction due to fewer disruptions) is a major strategy of educators for improving outcomes for all students.

4. Changes regarding governance structure/school organization.

     a. The major systemic change facilitating greater inclusion (and perhaps better outcomes) in restructuring schools is increased interaction between general and special educators.

       • Greater interaction is facilitated informally by greater physical proximity of general and special education teachers (e.g., ESE classrooms are next to general education classrooms).

       • Greater interaction occurs formally by use of the team concept (e.g., joint service on a variety of committees, regularly scheduled meetings involving both ESE and general education faculty, use of a consulting teacher model, team teaching, and professional development discussions).

       • Greater interaction focuses on both academic (e.g., team teaching in specified topics such as science, reading, geography, math) and on behavior (e.g., use of skill-streaming model).

       • The interaction between ESE and general education teachers must constitute a win/win situation in which both types of teachers get something they value (e.g., general education students do peer tutoring while ESE teachers help with general education problems without demands for reciprocal exchange and no paperwork involved).

     b. Restructuring does lead to new relationships with groups external to the school. However, these relationships initially are limited to community representatives who serve on school advisory committees or other organizations.

       • Community representatives on advisory committees typically reflect practical considerations (who is interested/available) rather than service-oriented considerations (the need for a variety of organizations/businesses to be represented).

SUMMARY

We believe that the combination of case study methods as described by Yin (1989, 1993), which are more qualitative than traditional research methods, combined with quantitative assessment of outcomes is the research strategy of choice when studying policy implementation. Specifically, this methodology allows for comprehensive study of the means by which the policy is implemented and the outcomes of those means. For our study of school inclusion within the context of restructuring, we will know what systemic changes were made in all five schools to foster increased inclusion and improved outcomes for all students, how these changes were implemented, and why. Additionally, we will have data about the outcomes for all students in these schools, including those with disabilities, and will be able to compare empirical outcomes with desired outcomes (the ends of the policy). The findings and conclusions of the study will provide sound information to policy makers and others who are interested in this important issue.

REFERENCES

Bryk, A., & Raudenbush, S. (1992). *Hierarchical linear models*. Newbury Park, CA: Sage.

Campbell, D. T., & Stanley, J. (1966). *Experimental and quasi-experimental designs for research*. Chicago: Rand McNally.

Deno S., Maruyama, G., Espin, C., & Cohen, C. (1990). Educating students with mild disabilities in general education classrooms: Minnesota alternatives. *Exceptional Children*, 57(2), 150–161.

Duchnowski, A. J. (in press). Innovative service models: Education. *Special Issue, Journal of Clinical Child Psychology*.

Fenton, J., Batavia, A., & Roody, D. (1993). *Constituency-oriented research and dissemination*. Washington, DC: National Institute on Disability and Rehabilitation Research.

Ferguson, P., & Ferguson, D., & Taylor, S. (1992). Introduction. In P. Ferguson, D. Ferguson, & S. Taylor (Eds.), *Interpreting disability, a qualitative reader*. New York: Teachers College Press.

Fuchs, D., & Deno, S. L. (1991). Paradigmatic distinctions between instructionally relevant measurement models. *Exceptional Children*, 57(6), 488–500.

Guba, E., & Lincoln, Y. (1989). *Fourth generation evaluation*. Newbury Park, CA: Sage.

Harry, B. (1992). Cultural diversity, families, and the special education system. New York: Teachers College Press.

Kavale, K., Forness, S., & Alper, A. (1986). Research in behavioral disorders and emotional disturbance: A survey of subject identification criteria. *Behavioral Disorders*, 11, 159–167.

Kazdin, A. (1982). *Single case research designs: Methods for clinical and applied settings*. New York: Oxford Press.

Lilly, M.S. (1987). Lack of focus on special education in literature on educational reform. *Exceptional Children*, 53(4), 325–329.

Lincoln, Y., & Guba, E. (1985). *Naturalistic inquiry*. Beverly Hills, CA: Sage.

Murphy, J. (1991). *Restructuring schools: Capturing and assessing the phenomena*. New York: Teachers College Press.

Peacock Hill Working Group (1991). Problems and promises in special education and related services for children and youth with emotional or behavioral disorders. *Behavioral Disorders*, 16, 299–313.

Peck, C., & Furman, F. (1992). Qualitative research in special education: An evaluative review. In R. Gaylord-Ross (Ed.), *Issues and research in special education* (Vol. 2, pp. 1–42). New York: Teachers College Press.

Pugach, M., & Sapon-Shevin, M. (1987). New agendas for special education policy: What the national reports haven't said. *Exceptional Children*, 53(4), 295–299.

Schulte, A.C., Osborne, S.S., & McKinney, J.D. (1990). Academic outcomes for students with learning disabilities in consultation and resource programs. *Exceptional Children, 57*(2), 162–172.

Skinner, B. F. (1957). The experimental analysis of behavior. *American Scientist, 45,* 343–371.

Smith, J., & Heshusius L. (1986). Closing down the conversation: The end of the qualitative-quantitative debate among educational inquirers. *Educational Researchers, 15,* 4–12.

Stokes T., & Bear, D. (1977). An implicit technology of generalization. *Journal of Applied Behavior Analysis, 10,* 349–367.

Switzky, H., & Heal, L. (1990). Research methods in special education. In R. Gaylord-Ross (Ed.), *Issues and research in special education* (Vol.1, pp. 1–82). New York: Teachers College Press.

U.S. Department of Education. (1990). *America 2000: An education strategy sourcebook.* Washington, DC: U. S. Government Printing Office.

Weatherley, R., & Lipsky, M. (1992). Street-level bureaucrats and institutional innovation. *Harvard Educational Review, 47,* 171–197.

Winton, P. J., & Bailey, D. B. (1993). Communicating with families: Examining practices and facilitating change. In J. L. Paul & R. J. Simeonsson (Eds.), *Children with special needs: Family, culture, and society* (pp, 210–230). Fort Worth, TX: Harcourt, Brace, Jovanovich.

Yin, R. (1989). *Case study research: Design and methods.* Newberry Park, CA: Sage.

Yin, R. (1993). *Case study research: Design and methods.* 2nd Edition. Newberry Park, CA: Sage.

Ysseldyke, J., Thurlow, M., & Gilman, C. (1992). Expected educational outcomes for students with disabilities. *Remedial and Special Education, 13,* 19–30.

20

UNDERSTANDING OUR COLLABORATIVE WORK WITH SCHOOLS
Reading and Interpreting the Stories

JAMES KING, HILDA ROSSELLI, JOANNE ARHAR,
SCOT DANFORTH, & SUSAN PEREZ

INTRODUCTION

THIS chapter is a look at some of the ethical dilemmas that are encountered in partnerships involving university and school district personnel. The group of authors in this chapter participated as the "university half" of a professional development school project or PDS (Holmes Group, 1986) who reported their first year of development as a research endeavour. Some of the authors were on site daily, and some were infrequent visitors. One was primarily responsible for supervision of student-teachers. Another assisted with students who had severe emotional difficulties. Still another conducted a case study of the PDS and involved a colleague on the project who later became an important facilitator for the group's discussion which resulted in this chapter. Only one of the authors was not directly involved at this PDS but was participating in a similar university/district venture in a nearby district.

For this chapter, we worked together, telling each other stories that represented the ethical dilemmas that we all faced in collaborative research. The dilemmas in these stories emerged at the juncture of two educational cultures: a university teacher-training program and a nearby middle school that shared a commitment to school restructuring at both the university and the school site. As participating observers, we wrote fieldnotes and journals, collected documents, held and attended meetings, and participated in other "in-context" methods of assembling data.

As we wrote this chapter about our experiences as researchers in a collaboration, we told each other stories that helped us look for the deeper patterns of meaning.

We learned that trust-building, defined as shared intimacies in caring environments, can lead to relationships that promote the risk taking needed for change. We now understand that while developing trust is a prerequisite for taking risks, building that trust also places the participants at risk. We begin with a story that we believe illustrates this paradox inherent in building trust.

SUSAN'S STORY

I walked toward the university office in our professional development school with a mixture of feelings. Kelly Davis, one of the teachers, and I had just finished a series of classes focused on ways of dealing with separation. In the last quarter of the school year, the goal of the group was to explore how we say good-bye to one another. The students had started off the discussion with smart aleck remarks sprinkled with profanity, the ways of saying good-bye with which they were familiar. Kelly had threatened them with point deductions for inappropriate behavior while I had worked at pulling them back into discussion. I felt, as I had often felt during the school year, that I was walking a tightrope between supporting classroom policies that I did not value and building positive relationships with students through my acceptance and understanding. Their quips about saying good-bye such as, "See ya, wouldn't want to be ya," or "Yeah, one less faggot in the classroom," said more about their discomfort than about their presumed cruelty and bigotry. I knew that throughout their relatively short lives most of them had been repeatedly placed in residential care, juvenile detention, foster care, and crisis stabilization units. From my own years of experience in education and mental health, I knew that troubled children and adolescents were often moved with little notice. Placements were grabbed when there were openings. Likewise, discharges were made the moment funds ran out. These disjunctive living arrangements were hardships the students knew all too well. Yet, communicating honestly about their separation fears was unknown territory to them as a group. What we were asking our students to explore was foreign, uncomfortable, and awkward.

Bobby was the first one to bring up death as a kind of separation. He told us about his dog who had been his companion for years. Bobby's dog would run to the school bus when he saw it coming down the road to drop Bobby off at the end of the driveway. And he told us how his father had taken the dog out behind the house and shot him when the family had to move and couldn't take the dog along.

His classmates began to suggest that he was lying. "Your father didn't shoot your dog," Larry scoffed. "I saw your dog last week."

"Not that dog," Bobby defended. "It was when we lived in Alabama, and we were moving here. I dug a big hole and buried him under a shady tree and made a marker for his grave," Bobby said with a quiver in his voice.

I leaned toward Bobby and touched him. As I tried to legitimize feelings about death as a way of understanding separation, Kelly Davis interrupted me and gave the class a quick lecture on telling the truth and not using this time to make up stories. She told Bobby that she was not accusing him of lying but she wanted to make sure that what he told was not a "tall tale." As soon as I sensed that Kelly had finished, I praised Bobby for his bravery in telling the group such a painful story.

With the pressure released, the students began to share personal accounts of separation. Donald told us about when his older brother joined the Army. Larry briefly talked about his parents' divorce and never having seen his father again. Sprinkled throughout their personal narratives were insults directed at each other. Accusations of lying and insensitive quips sailed through the room like arrows. Kelly talked to the students about losing points. She talked about their cruelty and threatened to end the lesson.

When the students left for the bus, Kelly and I talked with each other about the group. "What a joke!" she said when I asked her how she felt it went. "They were absolutely obnoxious and I didn't believe half of what they first told us. But then I guess *you* thought it was great. You and I just see things very differently." I agreed and told her how I thought the students struggled to share personal experiences in a setting that provided only tenuous personal safety and that I was proud of them. We parted in a stalemate.

Hilda was in the university office when I entered. I closed the door behind me, something I rarely did. But I needed a safe place to sort out my feelings. Seeing me close the door, Hilda stopped what she was doing and listened to me as I recounted the last forty-five minutes.

"What am I supposed to do when she suggests a student is lying when he tells us about his dog being shot? Just as I am recovering from Bobby's story, Kelly lands a punch challenging his integrity. I felt the breath knocked out of me. Even worse, I feel like a witness to abuse. I feel like an accomplice because I don't tell her *SHE* is inappropriate. If *I* feel this way can you imagine how the kids must feel?"

Hilda shared with me that Kelly's supervisors have concerns about her as well, and that she has been scheduled for additional observation. These types of stories help to illustrate to Kelly's supervisors what is occurring in the classroom.

I got a sick feeling in my stomach as though I had violated my own sense of honesty. I felt like a spy, a snitch. Kelly was tearful when later she told me about the observations, and I remembered feeling the same empathy for her as I did for the students in her class. Then, still later in the school year, she invited me to have dinner at her house some evening.

I wondered if I had avoided dealing directly with Kelly because of my own discomfort with what might be perceived as confrontational. Instead, I had chosen to be a model of my beliefs about how to interact with children. I had used photography to demonstrate the trust that could be developed with students whom she felt were irresponsible, when I allowed them to use my camera. I had used drama to show the joy and fun that students could experience in a classroom. I had used creative writing to provide examples of how students could write about feelings that were difficult for them to discuss verbally.

My second year of doctoral studies helped me understand what others had theorized about caring in a postmodern era. I embraced the notion of multiple perspectives. I recognized that we are all complex individuals with assorted beliefs and values. And that our beliefs are based on a multitude of experiences over our lifetime.

Thinking About Susan's Story: Multiple Points of View

Susan's story about Kelly is not the most extreme example of conflict of values, nor is her story unique. Susan wrote it from memory with help from fieldnotes. Any of the researchers could and did have similar narrative analyses. When Susan discussed the significance of the narrative, she confided that there were limitless ways for her to tell the events in the preceding story. As researchers with caring ties to a real school with real people, we all nodded. We think the story has a great deal to tell us about trust and loyalty in collaborative research contexts.

Susan feels she has witnessed child abuse. Her instincts and identification with children tell her to stop the abuse. Yet, special education requires a great deal of teamwork, and the need to develop and maintain professional relationships can be problematic (Howe & Miramontes, 1992). If Kelly Davis had been a more likable teacher, perhaps Susan would have been more willing to take the risks necessary to talk with her. But since Susan isn't sure if she likes her or trusts her, she is not willing to overlook Kelly's behavior and to understand the causes of her mistreatment of students. Unsure of how the school will respond to such information, Susan may also be fearful that letting an administrator know what is going on will impact on Kelly, or, more problematically, that nothing would come of it (Howe & Miramontes, 1992).

As professional educators we are obligated to report abusive behavior toward children. In our collaborative relationships, there seemed to be a gray area that was not so exacting. Susan had/has loyalties beyond the students. She was part of a larger collaboration between a school district and a university. The university wanted to keep Susan in classrooms where she could model therapeutic teaching. Susan was then caught between institutional loyalties (the school and the university) and personal loyalties (to the students and to Kelly). When faced with such conflicts, what choices does Susan have?

Another way of looking at the meaning in Susan's story is to consider her social stance. She was paralyzed by role confusion. One assumption we used to understand our collaborative issues is the notion of *equity*. Susan was operating in a space that closed the distance between the roles of teacher and student, between the roles of university and school. Yet, the reality of school settings is that these are very distinct roles, with power differentials associated with the roles. So while she struggled for more representation for students, she felt guilty for not representing Kelly.

Yet another issue associated with Susan's story is *confidentiality*. She felt somewhat responsible for the fact that Kelly's teaching would be monitored. Susan questioned her intentions for discussing Kelly. In her work back at the university, Susan was encouraged to share her interpretations, frustrations, and evaluations of Kelly's abusive interactions with students. To what extent does debriefing at the university break confidence with Kelly? To what extent does Susan's debriefing off-site lessen or relieve her need to work issues out directly with Kelly? Further, to what extent does discussion in context change the relationships? In a larger sense, we wondered how we address issues *anywhere* in a collaborative partnership without breaking trust.

Susan's story also pointed out to us the importance of relationships in our collaboration. Susan owned her feelings toward Kelly, yet was troubled that there remained unresolved feelings, ones that were not shared with Kelly but with others. Susan claimed to care, but felt pressured to pass on an opportunity to act in a caring way toward Kelly. Kelly's right to refuse Susan's help remains a dilemma for us. In fact, Susan suggested that neither she nor Kelly could refuse, as there was no mechanism for withdrawal. One of the emerging issues from our experience is whether an organization's blanket consent to participate in collaborative activities adequately protects the rights of individuals to choose. Our use of Susan's story about Kelly is problematic. And finally, our choice to textualize Kelly without her consent or knowledge is ethically questionable. And sharing this story puts us at risk as well.

Susan's story points to the issues of equity, confidentiality, and informed consent within the contexts of collaborative relationships. What these issues have in common is a breached sense of *trust*. Hilda's story points out the importance of trust in our collaboration.

HILDA'S STORY: IS THIS COLLABORATIVE RESEARCH?

The paper was part of a master's degree requirement. It was identified on the cover sheet as a case study of a professional development school (PDS) collaboration. When the author, who was a teacher at the PDS, handed it to me, he explained that he would turn in the final copy that evening. As I accepted the paper, I was plagued by many questions.

The research questions were direct. "How does the university affect the organizational structure of the school?" and "What are the attitudes of the staff toward the university's involvement?" His research questions addressed issues similar to ones that my university colleague had pursued in her open-ended study to understand stakeholders' perceptions of school needs. Based on that study, there was no evidence to suggest that there was teacher dissatisfaction with the university involvement at the school. Further, no mention was made of dissatisfaction by the School Improvement Team or the School Advisory Committee when the results of Joanne's study were presented to them.

Yet, the study initiated and conducted by this middle-school teacher pointed to teachers' discomfort with the university's presence in the middle school. His study included a survey given to all the faculty and staff, interviews with 10 percent of the faculty, and an analysis of documents from the principal's files. In his paper, he explained that he had chosen to focus on the perceptions of the faculty and staff, and therefore excluded the university participants and the principal.

When I read that some of his informants felt that their school was a "dumping ground" for the university student-teachers, I was shocked. Though my personal feelings were hurt, I also realized that the survey represented an example of teachers taking risks to shape "their school." In some ways, I could even see the findings as an example of the kind of dialogue we hoped to have. "But was this collaboration?" I felt betrayed. "Why didn't he involve us [university people] in the study?" "Why did I feel like something had gone on in our school that I had totally missed?" "Was there truly this feeling of discontent among the faculty regarding the university role, as described in his paper?" "How would this affect the future of our partnership?" "What *is* our relationship?"

Thinking About Hilda's Story

The major ethical theme we found in Hilda's story was *trust*, and what it means when it is broken. We felt, as a university team, that we had earnestly made an effort to include teachers in the activities of the professional development school. As Hilda wrote, we felt betrayed by the teachers' perceptions. It seemed an unfair response to our attempts to be collaborative. We used what we saw as a collaborative approach to include teachers in decisions, but when one of the teachers chose to research the issue of university effect, we were left out.

Another perspective related to trust is the control of information. We were not consulted about our impressions regarding the university effect on the school culture. One could argue that since the study was about our presence, exclusion was a reasonable approach to finding the "real story." Yet, the underlying assumption then becomes that the university team members would have concealed information or withheld it. This seemed like an implicit lack of trust.

Working from the notion of covert research (Bogdan & Biklen, 1992), we suspect that the researching teacher's choice to exclude the university group may also be related to equity issues. In a relationship characterized by equity, there is equal and open sharing of information that participants may find useful. Yet, if there is a perception of power differences, information can be withheld. Is our exclusion a backlash in response to the "favored status" historically given to universities in their relationships with schools?

When we examined (and reexamined) both Susan's and Hilda's stories, several themes emerged. These themes lead us to investigate how we functioned in the research context and upon what we based our ethical and social positionings. Before we analyze these themes, it is also important to explain how we came to the larger context of our work.

ON TELLING STORIES (OUR STORY)

From the beginning of our work in a PDS, we understood that we were in the business of making sense out of the experience. And from the beginning, making that sense, or telling "the story" was a problem with which we struggled. In the rest of this chapter, we propose several issues that characterized our collaboration in the PDS. We think that these same issues made writing about the collaboration a problem for us.

To write this chapter we tried to understand the struggles that characterized our collaborative work. We sat in Joanne's living room and told each other about times when we were uncomfortable in our roles, in our settings, in our multiple commitments, as we worked in two different education cultures, the school setting and the college of education. What we remembered were issues, important events, embarrassments, and joyful experiences. We relied on our collective memory for points of significance. As we each shared, the other authors listened, asked for clarification, offered alternative interpretations, became animated, interrupted, and interrogated. One of us took notes during this interaction, and the whole session was audiotaped and transcribed. During a second meeting, we revisited the themes developed during the first meeting. We focused on these themes and looked for examples and nonexamples from our respective sets of data. Next, we examined the transcripts from our first meeting for the match between the tape and our synthesized categories. With some modification, these categories became the issues for this paper. The text you are now reading is the result of our recursive analysis.

Relationships in Collaboration

A common issue raised in the field of collaborative research and ethnography is the shift in social positioning between the researcher and the researched (Rosaldo, 1989). As collaborative researchers, we worked to intentionally reduce the social distance between participants and the power hierarchies that separate us and often result in "research others" (Hooks, 1990). The collaboration model attempts to close the political distances, yet makes more space for the emerging relationships (Berkey et al., 1990). Our initial purpose in the context of the collaboration was the construction of relationships. We saw shared intimacy as the touchstone of these relationships. Often this was a subjective, felt sense of closeness. We noticed when we became more than visitors by the level of complexity of our shared experience (continuing stories, inside humor, personal invitations). Other times, intimacy was delineated by what was missing, such as losing our honorific titles. Less-frequent visitors from the university retained their titles ("Dr." or "Professor") and were given dedicated meeting time to discuss their issues and ideas.

Unlike more traditional approaches to qualitative inquiry, our roles were not to observe and sit back. We were continually involved, and our continued involvement in these relationships depended on our developing intimacy with the participants. A researcher's self-representation shifts from "expert" to a "trustworthy" person. At one point Joanne described herself as "someone a teacher or principal could confide in and know that that information would not be used against them." In fact, keeping confidence became one of the important conflicts in Susan's introductory story.

We also recognized that we withheld feedback that might be perceived as critical. Adler and Adler (1987) call this habit "role pretense." Joanne recalls that she did not speak up in meetings where she "not only disagreed strongly with the procedures and policies for dealing with issues such as discipline, but also in the manner in which the meeting was conducted, where I felt the voices of some were silenced." Silencing of others and ourselves was common practice, particularly during the first two years. Hilda recalled cringing when she heard students referred to by descriptors that condensed their individuality to a categorical label. However, by the third year, she was able to describe her feelings about that incident to a group of 20 faculty and administrators and even suggest this lack of professionalism be addressed as a area of focus on next year's School Improvement Plan.

We also realized that we were less likely to share critical information when the subject of the feedback held a position of power. At one of our sites, an administrator's management style became a stumbling block for progress and created a chasm between the administration and the faculty, as well as a split among the faculty. One of the writers remembers feeling frustrated and powerless when the principal denied any problem.

This is a particular problem for us because from an intimacy-building perspective, honesty is presumably valuable. Yet, we found ourselves compromising honesty to keep participants (all of us) invested in the collaboration. It seems like a paradox. On one hand, it is more likely that we can help each other if we give honest feedback. On the other hand, we saw ourselves withholding feedback to preserve relationships. Withholding and disclosing information in caring relationships is influenced by power differences. Is equity in collaborative relationships possible between hierarchically ordered institutions?

Trust: Stories in the Bank

In our view, trust is constructed when intimacy is exchanged. According to Spacks (1986), relationships are built and maintained by sharing intimate or otherwise personal bits of information. The relationship is enhanced when the information is self-revealing, and trust is the outcome. But the trust that is developed exists on a foundation of paradox. Sharing self-referential information (gossip, as noun) puts the sharer at risk that the recipient will further share the information (gossip, as verb). Yet, sharing personal information is essential for developing the intimacy that characterized our relationships. The sharer and the recipient of the intimate confidence implicitly engage in a trusting relationship, whose rules are implicit, yet binding (Tannen, 1990; Spacks, 1986).

Our first realization of intimacy was in sorting out that some participants share and some don't. Those who choose not to share are concomitantly seen as withholding, an active role. Withholding preempts trusting, and therefore intimacy. Our second realization was that we all choose to withhold. Since we were able to examine our own unwillingness to share, we learned it is sometimes done to protect relationships. Hilda bites her tougue when she is criticized in a meeting for presenting a grant proposal for approval late in an advisory council meeting. Earlier, she had "thought for a moment about putting the proposal earlier in the council's agenda, but discarded that thought as it might look like [she] was taking advantage."

Another way to put intimacy at risk is to break trust and share information outside of the social group from which it emerges. This realization put us in yet another paradoxical situation. We recognized the need to share secrets to develop intimacy and trust. Yet, we also recognized that in sharing, we willingly give away the right to control the information. Essentially, we recognize that information we share is public domain. Again, the value of the secret, as a commodity, is related to the power of its subject and its potential to break trust. In our discussion, we chose not to tell because "they couldn't handle it," "because of our own baggage," "because we didn't trust [the person]," or "because we might damage the relationship." In general, trust breaking became not holding to the intimacy contract which involved secrets and honesty. Further, our decisions about what the participants "can handle" deserve our attention for their inherent patriarchal positioning.

In another round of analysis and interpretation, the issue of communication style and implicit rules was interrogated. Rather than an act of intimacy, the sharing of small secrets (Tannen, 1990; Spacks, 1986) might be known and purposely manipulated. If we are aware that our secrets will be shared, then we can purposefully circulate desired rumors in the social context. While the rules of intimacy and trust were, for us, direct comunication and caring attitude, another set of communication rules also operated. Susan's confidences about Kelly which were shared with Hilda are only one of many examples. We saw that we accepted a pattern of telling tales to higher levels of the school's social hierarchy.

Who's Telling Whom This Story?

As a team, we examined several ways that we implicitly and explicitly enacted our collaboration along power differentials. It was difficult for us to own these hegemonies, especially in an intentionally collaborative project. One way that we preserved distance and maintained control of the research part of the project was to structure analysis and talk around decontextualized topics. "The nature of knowledge" as a discussion, however, only included those participants who had no direct links to the university community. Once we realized this separation of "us" and "them," we defended it with our self-perceived roles as researchers charged by the university, whereas, our school-based colleagues had not been so charged.

Another basis for differences was our need to make text out of experience. This operated as an overt agenda that shaped our activity with the other participants. Like other professional development schools, we were responsible for initiating most occasions where writing about the project occurred (Thompson, 1993). We also presided over analysis and revision of texts. This ownership of the text became very evident when a simultaneous research agenda emerged from the middle school that excluded the university collaborators. Friend and Cook (1991) have defined collaboration as a *style* in order to emphasize the nature of the interpersonal relationships that must transpire. Regardless of the task, direct interaction between two or more individuals occurs when collaboration takes place. A sense of trust, shared resources, and mutual goals are important characteristics that either define or emerge from successful collaboration (Friend & Cook, 1991).

Whose Stories Count? Power Differentials

Barth (1991) describes the issues of being both an "insider" and an "outsider" at the same time. Our protective attitude toward the school had been challenged, and the challenge was from within. Our operating definitions for collaboration, rapport, and trust were tested. Our sense of school climate and faculty satisfaction were questioned. And, once again, we had an opportunity to review our position on what "collaboration" means.

Our previous research efforts at the school had been fashioned to be "useful" to the local site. At the time, we saw this intent of higher utility in contrast to more traditional research relationships between universities and public schools. We were in it for the long run, and we recognized the importance of building a common sense of trust, ownership, and mutuality that we thought would ensure collaboration. Yet, we also carried with us what Barth (1991) calls "the baggage of the past." All of the previous relationships that the teachers had had with the university culture were brought into this relationship. Further, all the relationships the university group had had as teachers and with teachers also came into our emerging relationship. Our experiences with "ivory tower experts" who penetrated our school contexts, who took away our lives as data, who made reports about our idiosyncracies were also part of what was emerging.

In fact, we now recognize that, in a subtle way, we were doing something very similar. Text making was an implicit agenda that permeated interviews, fieldnotes, and discussion. "Would this make a good story?" changed how we responded to other participants (Blagg, 1989). Our focus on text making set us apart from participants who were less interested in textualizing our mutual experiences.

Another form of power differential was the issue of informed consent. While all participants were aware that a collaborative study was happening, it is safe to say that not all actions and conversations were constrained by that agreement. For us, the recurrent question was "When is it data?" We were trading between trust and deception when we made choices about what was acceptable and what was not acceptable as data. Because teachers have consented to be part of a large descriptive study, have they also agreed to an analysis of their personal teaching, social interactions, values, as well as their attitudes toward children? We did attempt to respond to this dilemma by making all published material available for faculty review. In many ways, we looked to make equitable relationships with the school collaborators. But we also participated in many historically scripted relations that depended on implicit notions of power and its distribution in the "collaboration." When our relationships with members of the school community involved hierarchy, permission, authority, or other instances of embedded power differences, we were more likely to have conflicts.

Confidentiality and Information as Tokens of Care

A second theme that has helped us understand our experiences in this collaboration is the notion of confidentiality and participants' right to privacy. We were very aware about breaches in individuals' privacy. This was most critical when we perceived what we considered inappropriate, unprofessional and even damaging treatment of children. We were most confused about our rights and responsibilities in confronting "bad teaching." And always, the most immediate result of our abuse of these delicate, implicit contracts of confidentiality was our loss of trust with our collaborators. These situations threw us into ethical dilemmas that we are still struggling to understand. Susan's story illustrates the paralyzing sense we experienced when we were caught between advocating for students and maintaining our relationships with their teachers. We wonder about taking the information about Kelly outside of the research site to discuss it with university colleagues. We continue to struggle with the problem of how do you take an issue, a problem, a story anywhere without breaking confidence. Perhaps it becomes an issue of intent on the part of the teller. And so it is with this chapter.

The Moral of the Story or Caring in Research Relationships

All of us involved in this paper follow what we believe to be strong moral and value-informed practices in teaching and research. We base our beliefs on an ethic of caring. But these assertions were certainly problematized in our experiences as collaborators. Ethical decisions in this project rose from conflicts in values. Diener and Crandall (1978) suggest that ethics are just that: The expression of our values. For Noddings (1992, 1984) ethics are embedded in an intention of caring and in the social construction of relationships. In our collaboration, we experienced a synthesis of these two approaches to ethics. Initially, we naively believed that "our collaboration" was progressing smoothly, in what we thought was a shared set of valuing. Yet, when we experienced instances where that assumption was challenged, so too was our understanding of how we were actually interacting.

Now, we think that the shared agenda was not a fact. We were brought into the school "to do a collaboration." While our values were for the most part congruent with those of the teachers in the school (for example, we all believed in nonabusive relationships with other people) we could not make the claim to have a shared set of assumptions and values that drove the collaboration. In fact, now we understand the disruption, the breaches in trust, the ethical dilemmas, as the occasions for the development of shared direction, values, and ethical premises. From a costs and benefits analysis, we could claim to be doing "greater good" by staying in the context and influencing the greater mass of teachers over a period of time. But this seems an unsatisfying rationale for problematic ethical decisions. Ethics in postmodern culture is itself a problem. Whose sense of right and wrong? Whose interpretation of an issue? Whose perspective? More traditional qualitative research has opted for the emic perspective, the voice of the insiders. What we have here are different camps of insiders with different versions of right and wrong. What we also have is a shift in anthropology and interpretive research that strongly suggests that an "insider's view" never was that (Clifford, 1988). Rather, what we have had are researchers' subjective constructions masquerading as "emic view." And finally, representing all the voices in text (the politically correct polyvocal text) does little to guide the day-to-day social constructions that make intimacy.

Our personal ethical positioning became the most problematic when we stopped seeing the injustices. When we started singing the school songs, we began to "understand" mistreatment, disregard, and accept in emic ways. As advocates for our own understanding of ethics, we were at risk. When students voiced complaints about their treatment, we could shift towards seeing them as immature and thus, disregard the validity of their complaints. Yet, when those same student complaints were made in a context of racial inequality, we listened. Is this because we are sensitized to racial inequality or because we are sensitized to the social consequences of not attending to perceptions of racism?

THE END(S) OF INTIMACY (CAN ETHICS BE COLLABORATIVE?)

As collaborative researchers, we are ethically committed to an intimate relationship with the context in which we research. As we have told this story, it is the construction and maintenance of these relationships that guides the course of our continued interaction within the context. Yet, entering into interpersonal space makes decisions involving ethical issues highly troubling. As we acclimate to the research climate or the social context of the project, we change, as does the context. This is the goal of collaboration. But the steps of change are always ones on contested ground. We do not mean to suggest that interaction is characteristically contentious (though this does happen), but rather the construction of "solutions" to the daily "problems" of collaborative research is an ambiguous and subjective experience. We believe that looking at the ambiguity that surrounds the disruptions in our social relationships is productive work. We think it helped us understand how progress toward collaboration is made. Noddings (1992) suggests "An ethic of care starts with the study of relation. It is fundamentally concerned with how human beings meet and treat one another. It is not unconcerned with individual rights, the common good, or community traditions, but it re-emphasizes these concepts and recasts them in terms of relations" (p. 45). From a socioconstructivist perspective, we have consistently asked ourselves what it means to have a relationship in a collaborative research endeavor. If all the voices of participants are equally valued, how do we choose one for an particular instantiation? How are conflicts resolved when power is shared? How is a vision created in a social system (e.g., a middle school) without clearly established leaders (e.g., site-based management)?

Initially, we believed that trust was embodied in things going well, not stepping on toes, and including as many participants as we could. If we were to stay at the school, we felt this was our posture. What we have learned is that our initial definition of trust was a platonic one. We now understand that trust is something that is constructed out of breaches of trust. Trust, caring, confidence, relationships, and equity come from making those constructs on the occasions when they are needed to understand what has gone "wrong."

REFERENCES

Adler, P. A., & Adler, P. (1987). *Membership roles in field research*. Sage University Paper series on Quantitative Research Methods (Vol. 2). Newbury Park, CA: Sage.

Barth. R. S. (1991). *Improving schools from within*. San Francisco: Jossey-Bass.

Berkey, R., Curtis, T., Minnick, F., Zietlow, K., Campbell, D., & Kirschner, B. (1990). Collaborating for reflective practice: Voice of teachers, administrators, and researchers. *Education and Urban Society, 22*(2), 204–232.

Blagg. S. B. (1989, November). *The interviewer as critic: Distortion of the voice in the collection of oral narratives*. Paper presented at the annual meeting of the Speech Communication Association. (75th, San Francisco) (ERIC Document Reproduction Service No. ED 319 078).

Bogdan, R., & Biklen, S. K. (1992). *Qualitative research for education: An introduction to theory and methods* (2nd ed.). Boston: Allyn & Bacon.

Clifford, J. (1988). *The predicament of culture: Twentieth-century ethnography, literature, and art*. Cambridge, MA: Harvard University.

Diener, E. & Crandall, R. (1978). *Ethics in social and behavioral research*. Chicago: The University of Chicago Press.

Friend, M., & Cook, L. (1991). *Interactions: Collaboration skills for school professionals*. White Plains, NY: Longman.

Holmes Group. (1986). *Tomorrow's teachers: A report of the Holmes Group*. East Lansing, MI: Holmes Group, Inc.

Holmes Group (1990). *Tomorrow's schools: Principles for the design of professional development schools*. East Lansing, MI: The Holmes Group.

Hooks, B. (1990). *Yearning: Race, gender, cultural politics*. Boston: South End Press.

Howe, K. R., & Miramontes, B. (1992). *The ethics of special education*. New York: Teachers College Press.

Noddings, N. (1992). *The challenge of care in schools: An alternative approach to education*. New York: Teachers College Press.

Noddings, N. (1984). *Caring: A feminine approach to ethics and moral education*. Berkeley, CA: The University of California Press.

Rosaldo, R. (1989). *Culture and truth: The remaking of social analysis*. Boston: Beacon Press.

Spacks, P. M. (1986). *Gossip*. Chicago: University of Chicago Press.

Tannen, D. (1990). *You just don't understand: Women and men in conversation*. NY: Morrow.

Thompson, C. (1993). *Issues involved in PDS research*. Unpublished manuscript.

CHAPTER

21

EDUCATING LEADERS IN SPECIAL EDUCATION FOR INCLUSIVE SCHOOLS
The Experience of Doctoral Study in a Partnership Environment

SUSAN PEREZ, SCOT DANFORTH, YOLANDA MARTINEZ,
LINDA HOUCK, & KAREN COLUCCI

INTRODUCTION

IN this chapter, we seek to provide insight into our experiences as doctoral students in the Department of Special Education at the University of South Florida. Our coursework and graduate assistantship experiences have taken place within the shifting folds and tensions of dramatic structural and conceptual reconstruction. Our goal in this text is twofold. First, we will describe the theoretical and social context in which our learning has taken place. This involves describing the atmosphere of questioning and change in the College of Education and the nature of the full-time doctoral program in special education. Additionally, we will provide three separate experiential narratives, allowing the reader access to our personal and professional wonderings, crises, and developments. These three reflections describe our work as graduate assistants, collaborative ventures between our College of Education and the various local school districts.

THEORETICAL AND SOCIAL CONTEXTS OF OUR EXPERIENCES

As doctoral students, we have received firsthand benefits from the many facets of the restructuring at both the College of Education and in the public schools. Entering the doctoral program somewhat naively, we quickly found ourselves living and learning in the midst of a rapid flurry of change and uncertainty. Our department, and indeed the entire College of Education, was engaged in an intense questioning of previous assumptions about knowledge, practice, politics, and ethics. Theoretical and reflective unrest seemed to be the crucible for moving ahead toward an improved professional space that includes greater creativity, personal reflection, and increased practical relevance in educational work.

The areas of questioning, conceptual tension, and growth may be said to contain four parts: 1) paradigmatic; 2) programmatic; 3) practical; and 4) personal. A brief explication of these problematic spheres will serve as an introduction to the various layers of change and conflict surrounding our individual doctoral experiences.

Paradigmatic issues involve investigations of the nature of knowledge and knowledge making. The status of objective knowledge and the researcher's ability to remain detached and accurate in observing and representing social reality have been questioned on many fronts (Heshusius, 1989; Guba, 1990; Guba & Lincoln, 1994; Skrtic, 1991). In our experience, we have discovered that active critique of the apparent bulwark of positivism/post-positivism in educational research quickly leads to questions concerning many political and ethical aspects of knowledge production. Who creates knowledge? How is it legitimized, accepted, or "made true?" What research methods should a researcher employ? How shall research knowledge be interpreted and evaluated? In our professional knowledge production, what knowledges are we missing, ignoring, silencing? What ethical dilemmas and responsibilities become central to research as we move into collaborative, school-based research? Our discussions in class, in the hallways, and in local restaurants were a crude microcosm of the entire paradigm conversation in the social sciences. We learned of both our personal epistemological predispositions while becoming tolerant and even appreciative of alternative worldviews.

Programmatic reforms bring practicality and structure to paradigm issues, implicating the College of Education and its faculty members in ongoing, practical problems and efforts in the local school districts. From the fertile atmosphere of epistemological critique and paradigmatic conversation at the university, the traditional separation of academy and public school is problematized on moral and practical grounds.

At our university, a desire for reasoned relevance in a time of change has brought about a series of programmatic reconstructions which draw together faculty teaching, research, doctoral study, and the daily efforts of teachers and administrators in nearby schools. For example, our professors and graduate assistantship supervisors maintained responsibilities at both the university and in public schools. A series of professional development schools which united the university and public schools were growing in the surrounding districts, each a distinct program offering unique opportunities for our professional growth in the areas of collaborative research, technical assistance, program development, and teacher education.

Practical concerns are predicated upon our getting "down to earth" by taking our experience, knowledge, and theory into active educational settings—our assistantship placements. Most of us originally gave up practitioner positions to become full-time doctoral students. After diving into the reform stew of paradigms and programmatic change at the university, our second-year placements sent us back to the public schools we previously knew so well. Freshly armed with theories, hopes, and doubts, we sought to contribute to the daily work of teachers in collaborative school sites. Our ideals met the limitations of the practical, a necessary but not problem-free experience.

Perhaps the final area is the most crucial. As demonstrated in the three reflections to follow, we accepted and struggled with our experiences in fully personal ways. Our work in the collaborative school sites touched upon emotions of joy, hope, and despair. We found success and roadblocks. We felt encouraged by prospects and challenged as to the base of our own inadequacies and fears.

THE DOCTORAL PROGRAM IN SPECIAL EDUCATION

The full-time doctoral program in the Department of Special Education features a curricular focus on the challenges of significant policy and programmatic issues embedded in restructuring. A major goal of the program is the integration of university teaching and research into local school-based settings. Thus, the graduates of the program are being specifically trained to provide leadership within the state restructuring mandate and in universities throughout the nation.

For this purpose, first-year doctoral students whose research interests match the projects in process are encouraged to spend 20 hours per week of their total training at a collaborative school site working closely with a university faculty member. During the second year of studies, these students have the opportunity to engage in a 20-hour research apprenticeship at a partnership site. Finally, third-year students have the opportunity to pursue a full-time career development placement at one of the sites.

The intent of the doctoral program is to bring together, in each cadre of new students, a group of individuals from diverse areas of interest and professional backgrounds but who share one goal—the improvement of educational opportunities for all children. This group of students is a cohort, a community of learners who progress through the coursework together.

Within the program, students are encouraged to explore as many areas of interest as they are willing to handle, given time constraints and program requirements. The training itself is a combination of traditional educational theories and postmodern thought that provides a fertile ground for the development of ideas that can be applied to the restructuring movement. The hope is that all of these elements combined will contribute to the unfolding of new ideas in applied and research areas.

To foster the feeling of community, cohort members actively seek opportunities to gather to share newly acquired knowledge and experiences. Thus, each doctoral cohort at the University of South Florida's Department of Special Education can be thought of as a "think tank" in which new ideas can be explored and exchanged, with the primary goal of contributing to the restructuring of special and regular education.

PERSONAL PERSPECTIVES

When we first came together as a cohort, we each were apprehensive about the program and our role in the department. The department chair outlined 9 points that he felt guided our doctoral program. Although we were so diverse, we each listened to the items without knowing how much they would guide our lives.

Early on it became evident that the support of our cohort would be the sustenance that would get us through the journey we were all beginning. The community we established through proximity, common goals, and shared frustrations helped to solidify us into a group ready to support and nurture each other. The idea of cohort cannot be taken lightly within the philosophy of restructuring. The need for community support is essential.

To each of us who have authored this chapter, the following points have guided our thinking and transformation:

1. Your relationship to the cohort is vital.
2. Build a sense of community among yourselves.
3. Your feelings will change; trust the process.
4. Your thinking will change; trust yourself, and allow yourself to grow. Be open to new ideas.
5. Compete only with yourself.
6. Doctoral study is a wonderful opportunity; don't waste it.
7. Use mentors and other resources.
8. Learn respect for the ideas of others.
9. Leave the community better than you found it.

In the following sections, we present three personal professional stories: three accounts of the individual experiences of doctoral students working in collaborative schools. While each narrative is unique to the individual voice, common themes run through all three: hope in the face of uncertain demands, a self-assigned mission of furthering efforts on behalf of children and families, and a drive to make theory and practice one.

The Ivory Tower

Before beginning doctoral study, I had a clear notion of what I thought a professor was. Professors were experts who lectured, quoted a vast array of researchers, and were able to talk about a subject for hours. Professors also lived at universities, far removed from daily teaching with its behavior management, lesson plans, irate parents, imposed curriculums, principals, and central office administrators. They had moved from that whirlwind of activity to the ivy-covered walls of academia. That had pretty much been my experience with higher education.

I also believed that students were the recipients of this expert wisdom, and theirs was a world of philosophical, theory-driven discussions with these learned people.

Yes, it was intellectually stimulating and enlightening. Yes, the center of the student's world was the library. But, I would soon find out that this was only part of my doctoral education. I was off on an adventure that brought academia into the practical arena. I decided to begin this "terminal degree" at the same time that school reform was rising. "Ladies and gentlemen, welcome to a new breed of higher education. You are not leaving the ranks of school personnel. In fact, you will blaze a path for this new professional." So much for my naive notion of doctoral study.

Looking back, being assigned to a professional development school was both a blessing and a burden. I felt like the bat in Jarrell's (1963) story, *The Bat Poet*, who decided to stay awake during the day and see what the world was like. He left his safe bat community and experienced new sights and sounds in a daytime world. The school-based experiences allowed me to view the school world and teaching from a different perspective. It allowed me to leave the safe confines of the university community and develop relationships with teachers, try ideas, experiment with philosophies in the reality of the school world. As academicians we can write the poems, just as the bat-poet did. But, the problem is getting someone to listen to them in the reality of their existence. How many teachers actually read those professional journals full of statistical research? Collaborative schools may be our avenue to get the word out. It may also be the place to research what teachers really care about rather than our university agenda. But, this avenue is still riddled with stones and holes and in need of a smooth finish.

My early days were difficult. What was my role? What was I to do? Many of the teachers looked to me as an expert because I was from the university. I wanted to say, "Hold it! It wasn't too long ago that I was in the classroom like you. I don't have all the answers. That's not my job!" I didn't want to fix holes in the dike. I wasn't ready. I needed time to move from teacher to doctoral student and then to expert—or so I thought! As a result, I spent days just hanging around the school—the office, cafeteria, teachers' lounge, hallways, media center, and so on. I didn't know how to break into the culture. I was a visitor; I wasn't "one of them." I knew my ultimate goal was not to be "the expert," but that seemed to be what the teachers wanted.

The other problem I encountered was the lack of teacher time to collaborate. Although the concept has both professional and personal merit, the reality is that teachers are busy teaching all day. When they are not teaching, there are many other duties such as calls to parents, lesson plans, tutoring students, counseling children, and so on that demand their time. Although the idea of action research was intriguing, the constraints of time were great.

Since I didn't want to be the expert and time was at a premium, what could my role be? The idea of a Teacher Assistance Team seemed to be viable. We could work together to problem-solve. It would be a service needed by the staff, and I would not be expected to have all the answers. I began to look forward to these Thursday morning sessions. The problems were varied and the solutions were not always anchored in research, but the camaraderie grew. Opportunities to really collaborate arose. Technical assistance grew out of these needs, and I was once again collaborating with teachers and working with students. Together we would plan the types of experiences the children needed. It opened up opportunities to try new ways, to share journal articles, to blend my new knowledge from coursework into the school environment. Yet, it was different from what I had imagined. I wasn't there to say, "This is how you should teach this child to read." Rather, "Do you think this might work? Let's try to adapt this together." I developed a strong working relationship with one teacher. We felt safe. She asked me to work with more of her children and was always interested in what I was doing. I, too, wanted to know what made her feel successful. We learned from each other. We both had talents; we both were professionals. Neither of us had all the answers, but together our joint knowledge began to smooth out the avenue known as collaboration. Some of the debris was swept away.

I feel good about the poem or story or knowledge inside me. Like the bat-poet, I'm starting to get the words right, if not the tune! I've learned to appreciate the emergent nature of this kind of working relationship. How can we as university folk best serve the school community? It's tempting to jump in and "tell them what should be done." We may have information that can help in the decision making but those choices must be made by those within that reality—namely, that school staff. Partnership schools are also a necessary reality check for university faculty and doctoral students. Only by being in the trenches can one truly understand the impact of the research we hold dear.

I do not believe that a school site is a mecca for teacher training. We may be sending our novice teachers into situations that may not be model ones. We may be making great demands on our university faculties. Yet, school reform is placing responsibilities on classroom teachers beyond what they had ever bargained for. It seems to me that the burden of solution lies at the university and the school site. It is a call to be responsive and to ethically look at what we define as teacher, professor, and collaborator. It is a call to ethically look at the work we do, especially in a social context. As our department chair told us at our doctoral orientation, "Doctoral study is an opportunity, don't waste it. Learn to respect ideas. And, leave a community better than you found it." I hope that I made a difference at the school site. I believe it was a beginning for professional change within me and for the teachers with whom I worked. I'm glad I had the chance to trail blaze, write bat poems, and collaborate within this community.

A Foot in Both Camps

I got my master's degree when my children were preschoolers and I was married. Fifteen years have since passed. Now my daughters are themselves in college, I am no longer married, and I have had a rich and diverse history of working with parents and the students of children we call severely emotionally disturbed. Coming into the doctoral program, I was looking for a sense of belonging, a place where I could stretch myself and take a fresh turn in my professional career. I wanted to teach college students. So I came to the Department of Special Education at the University of South Florida.

During our first year I was teamed with a mentor who represented the university in a partnership with the school district. The school was brand new, so the entire community came together for the first time, at the same time. In the spirit of the professional development school concept, we supported the belief that university and public school could work together to educate all students. We consciously decided not to enter the school as experts. Rather we entered to provide service in any way the school felt we could be of help.

I accepted the invitation to join the SED teachers who were both out of field and working with adolescents whose behaviors were volatile and oppositional. The students continually provoked each other while the teachers worked at maintaining order and an academic focus. At times it felt painful to be in the classroom, and I didn't know quite what to do. Unsure of just what my role should be, I squirmed in my skin as I tried to understand how to be of help without taking over.

In our coursework, our cohort was immersed in a philosophical whitewater ride down the nature of inquiry and across the nature of knowledge. We read, we talked, we wrote, we argued, we wrote, we had beers, we read, we wrote, we reeled with information and dialogue that caused us to question our beliefs and assumptions. While we struggled with the notion of reality, I had fresh images of wounded students feeling misunderstood and weary teachers feeling much the same. I struggled personally between being a practitioner and a theorist. As students continued to lose points in the classroom for inappropriate behavior, my doctoral papers continued to be returned with written encouragement to be more abstract. I felt like someone tied to two horses pointed in opposite directions.

At the university we talked new paradigm, in the classroom we lived the old. In my courses we talked about the construction of knowledge, multiple perspectives, and an ethic of care. In the classroom we spent much of our time dealing with points, level systems, and appropriate on-task behavior.

Back at the university, I feared we were engaged in rhetoric rather than restructuring. When we entered into dialogue about inclusion I could only wonder, inclusion in what? I was riveted at looking at the nature of education. I could not understand how we could be considering the effects of inclusion or exclusion when the greater considerations seemed to be about the relationships between students and teachers. In the school I heard teachers talking about undisciplined and resistant learners while students talked about being controlled and bored.

I came to our weekly department research meetings confused, upset, and uncertain. Like my camera zoom lens, my focus pulled in and out of the plight of the members of the school community and the philosophical beliefs and assumptions about the nature of knowledge. On one occasion I reminded myself of Khrushchev banging his shoe on the table at the United Nations as I pounded my fist to emphasize a point. As we dealt with what seemed like abstractions, I feared we would lose sight of what was actually happening in the schools.

During our second year, I remained at the same professional development school feeling comfortable in my familiar surroundings. Throughout my first year,

I had developed good working relationships with teachers, support staff, administrators, and county officials. I felt like an accepted member of the school community. It was here that I conducted a qualitative research case study on three preservice teachers during their internship. In-depth interviews focused on the disparity between their expectations and their experiences. They expressed feelings about being expected to take over someone else's class and to teach students who had limited skills, were unable to follow directions, and who rarely retained what they were taught. They each lamented that they spent too much of their time disciplining students in order to keep them focused on a curriculum that often seemed irrelevant in the lives of these individuals.

As a second-year doctoral student, I struggled with my professional identity. Much like a snake working to shed its skin, I searched for an understanding of the nature of education, the purpose of schools, and the intent of learning. I traveled in and out of educational cultures, institutions, and environments finding my way.

In the fall of our second year I taught a course at the university. I felt wonderful being back in the classroom. Each Wednesday I would come bursting into our cohort office after a 4-hour class, animated and full of wonderful stories about what was happening in our class. And there my cohort would sit sharing my pleasure about the feelings of connection among people. I began to imagine myself teaching in a college tucked away in a beautiful setting. I pictured an office that was comfortable and inviting to students who were involved in their own personal transformation. I felt that by teaching cohorts of teachers through modeling my own reflecting on the process, I could make an impact on our restructuring efforts.

With the approach of our third year, I began to catch a glimpse of my new skin. I realized that the rub between theory and practice, university and school, abstraction and practicality had provided a context rich with tensions that enabled me to construct my own philosophy of education. Spending time in both educational settings, I began to feel torn between teaching at the university and being a principal of a school. For me the issues of restructuring have to do with the sense of community that is developed in the educational setting. I could imagine myself being principal of a school creating a community based on an orientation of care (Noddings, 1984, 1992). I could visualize myself teaching my faculty while engaging with students and parents to build relationships among all members of the school community.

And now it is almost my third year. I am equally comfortable at both the university and our professional development school. The course I teach this fall at the university has been reshaped based on what I have learned by being in the professional development school. Many educators are struggling in the schools to keep students under control in order to teach them. This seems to be fundamentally different from talking about teaching as connecting and relating to students with a holistic approach to learning. In my course, I am able to draw from my experiences in and allegiances to both camps in order to provide an opportunity for university students to develop themselves as caring teachers.

Now What Do I Do?: A Critical Theorist in a Collaborative School

In our first doctoral seminar at the University of South Florida, our cohort took on Guba's *Paradigm Dialogue* (1990). We confronted many issues concerning philosophy of social scientific inquiry, digging into our own epistemological assumptions and sorting through our various paradigmatic alternatives. I found myself to have certain constructivist inclinations but, above all, I found that I was comfortable in critical theory, interpreting various aspects of pedagogy and educational institutions in terms of inequalities of power. The critical stance had always served as one of my primary lenses upon social reality and education. I just never had a word to describe this approach to my profession. Now I had a word and an entire literature for my own self-development.

Critical educators, following in the tradition of Marx, neo-Marxist analysis, and the work of the Frankfurt School of Critical Theory, typically see American education as existing within the institutional tension of democratic and capitalistic principles. Critical educators are concerned with the unequal distribution of power within society and within education, often analyzing situations in light of power differences based on gender, ethnicity, race, and socioeconomic status (Apple, 1990; Giroux 1982; Giroux, 1988; Aronowitz & Giroux, 1991).

From this perspective, America is a modern Western society that structures the activities and political expressions of persons through a liberal democratic political system and a profit-motive, market economy.

Often these forms of social structure conflict. Many issues arise in this conflict. Most basically, what personal freedoms can democracy ensure when financial constraints limit the actions of many? What political equality can democracy offer in a society of great financial inequality? Is there not a link between all forms of power, position, gender, finances, knowledge, and so on? And what role do American schools play in the unequal distribution of power in our society?

I entered my position as a graduate assistant in a collaborative school site eager to put my newfound self-knowledge into professional practice, ready to critically analyze ongoing practice in terms of hegemony and the asymmetrical production of cultural capital. I came upon four key observations about my own use of a critical theory lens in my assistantship.

First. I had no one at my site who spoke my language or understood my ideas. Despite my six years of teaching experience, I felt like an immigrant in the school. I tried making a few comments in my critical theory "native tongue" to my supervising professor, but she struggled to fathom why anyone would examine the political implications of a reading curriculum or a behavior management program. I could speak her language—primarily behavioral or developmental theories—but she could not speak mine.

Second. I was given thoroughly mixed messages from university faculty members about my critical theory stances on various issues in our work in the public schools. On the one hand, the faculty members were devoted to opening up the field of special education to alternative paradigm views. Often my interpretations of the inequalities of power evident in various relationships among participants in the collaborative school sites were heard respectfully by faculty members. And they were always heard with a serious and respectful ear by my fellow doctoral students who had come to know me and felt my opinions were worth hearing.

On the other hand, despite their claims of a progressive epistemological openness, some faculty members obviously felt more comfortable with behavioral or cognitive psychology talk. They seemed to fear that critical theory was too openly political.

Third. As my knowledge of the central concepts of critical theory grew through reading, I struggled to understand how to put the ideas into practice. Critical educators often point to the emancipatory literacy work of Paulo Freire or Eliot Wigginton's grass roots Foxfire program in the Appalachian Mountains as examples of critical pedagogy. Yet it seems that for every critical educator bringing the theories to life, there must be 50 writing and talking the stuff at universities. In my own experience in the collaborative school site, I found that I could learn to analyze social phenomena through a critical lens, but I could envision little space for cultural action. I learned that dancing is a far more complex task than intelligently explaining the motions of the dancers.

Fourth. Thankfully, I found the critical theory view of my school to be a valuable and insightful way of understanding the actions taking place before and around me. I found it to be not the only way, but certainly an important way of seeing educational process and practice. I saw administrators, university faculty, teachers, front office staff, paraprofessionals, parents, and children struggling within a social setting, struggling in valuing certain actions, certain words, and certain artifacts of culture above others. The school was a place of constant value determinations and redeterminations. To read this way is better than to read that way. To stand this way is better than to stand that way. To speak. To walk. To dress. To be. All day long, children (and adults) simultaneously conformed to and contested the social pressures which followed what was understood or believed to be "best," "positive," and "normal." I observed the often conflictual negotiation of positions, space, language, and symbols of meaning in the interactions of educators and children. I was pleased to have come upon the writings of the critical educators.

CONCLUSION: REFLECTIONS ON OUR COHORT

When we entered the doctoral program at the University of South Florida we were told that we were being prepared for careers that did not exist. The volatile nature of education fueled by restructuring had made the role of special education as we know it an uncertainty. The future could bring a vastly different conception of education and special education into reality. How then could leaders in special education be prepared for a future no one could accurately predict? The faculty at the University of South Florida envisioned and established a doctoral program that addressed this uncertainty. As doctoral students, we were guided down a path we had never been down before. Through readings and discussions, we began to see a whole different "way of knowing" legitimized. Our focus became wider and more abstract, and we began to embrace conflict and celebrate the idea of multiple perspectives. We began to question and explore the grounding assumptions of the field in which we had lived so closely in the past. We had to explore and resolve the conflicts that arose between our past experiences and conceptions and our current revelations. A feeling of discomfort and uncertainty drove us to find our own inner balance and to develop a personal philosophy of special education. As diverse individuals within a group, we looked at things through different lenses and developed our philosophies from various perspectives such as critical theory and constructivism. This diversity, however, did not act as a stumbling block in our own personal development or in the development of a sense of community within the group. Instead it served to enrich our developing philosophies and made us see the value of conflict and the joy of celebrating diversity.

Our philosophies were further refined and solidified when we entered the realm of the partnership schools. We no longer had the luxury of endless debates and analyses to help us deal with inconsistencies we encountered. We had to put our philosophies to the test. We had to leave the nurturing nest of cohort support and forge new relationships within the schools. We experienced frustration, self-doubt, and a sense of alienation. Through frequent cohort meetings we examined our experiences and our philosophies, and dealt with inconsistencies. These meetings were not guided by the faculty but were instead an outgrowth of our own needs. As time progressed, we further refined our philosophies and roles. We became more confident in our collective ability to deal with the diversity and multiple perspectives we encountered. We began to meet less and less, and in an evolutionary process we found our own footing on the ever-changing terrain of special education. Even though we have chosen different branches of that original path to explore, there will always remain a special bond between us and a quiet knowing that support is there for the asking.

At the time it seemed that so much of our training was left to chance. Looking back now, however, it seems like a well-orchestrated dance. Experiences were provided to create dissonance against a background of multiple perspectives and diversity. A sense of community was fostered. Personal philosophies emerged, were challenged, and refined. Consequently a sense of confidence in dealing with uncertainty, conflict, and diversity fueled this cohort of doctoral students eager to face the challenges of tomorrow.

If we are to bring together a concluding observation which may be meaningful to university faculty who plan and operate doctoral programs, we must emphasize the crucial themes of dissonance and community. For us, dissonance occurred on many levels. We found our own cosmologies and assumptions confronted with provocative alternatives. The certain grounds were shaken, and we struggled to reformulate our understandings of ourselves, our world, and our work with children. An additional sense of dissonance was created as these newly fabricated theoretical positions met with the daily realities of the collaborative school sites. Ideals and practicalities seemed to meet with bared teeth, bringing each of us again to wonder and question ourselves and our knowledge.

The key to allowing dissonance to foster learning is the context of supportive community. In our cohort, we fortunately remained united and steadfast through the many experiences of self-doubt. It was this very unity which allowed us each to turn self-doubt and uncertainty into growth experiences. Unsettling tensions and contradictions which may have overwhelmed us individually became fecund challenges within the bustling support of the cohort.

We were fortunate. From the start, we felt like co-learners completing an extended cooperative learning assignment. The cohort provided a consistent source of comfort and learning, laughter and critique. It gave us a social space in which to try out new ideas and challenge concepts. Even more, it gave us a warm web of friendship in which to grow and take the personal risks necessary to change ourselves, a necessary prerequisite to moving forth to change educational programs.

REFERENCES

Apple, M. (1990). *Ideology and curriculum.* New York: Routledge.

Aronowitz, S., & Giroux, H. (1991). *Postmodern education: Politics, culture and social criticism.* Minneapolis: University of Minnesota Press.

Giroux, H. (1982). *Theory and resistance in education: A pedagogy for the opposition.* South Hadley, MA: Bergin and Garvey.

Giroux, H. (1988). *Teachers as intellectuals: Toward a critical pedagogy of learning.* Granby, MA: Bergin and Garvey.

Guba, E. (1990). *The paradigm dialog.* Newbury Park, CA: Sage.

Guba, E. G., & Lincoln, Y. S. (1994). Competing Paradigms in Qualitative Research. In N. K. Denzin & Y. S. Lincoln (Eds.), *Handbook of qualitative research* (pp. 105–117). Thousand Oaks, CA: Sage.

Heshusius, L. (1989). The Newtonian mechanistic paradigm, special education, and contours of alternatives: An overview. *Journal of Learning Disabilities, 22*(7), 403–415.

Jarrell, R. (1963). *The bat-poet.* New York: Collier.

Noddings, N. (1984). *Caring, a feminine approach to ethics and moral education.* Berkeley: University of California Press.

Noddings, N. (1992). *The challenge to care in schools: An alternative approach to education.* New York: Teachers College Press.

Skrtic, T. M. (1991). *Behind special education: A critical analysis of professional culture and school organization.* Denver, CO: Love.

REFLECTIONS ON CHAPTERS 14–21

DONNIE EVANS AND HILDA ROSSELLI

EACH of the public school/university partnerships discussed in this chapters 14–18 has developed in large measure because of the university's desire to collaborate with schools in their effort to restructure. An underlying assumption across the partnerships has been that the university's teacher preparation programs would become more relevant and available. Also, these partnerships would involve university faculty in collaborations with school personnel that extended beyond the university's traditional faculty assignments and productivity expectations.

Although the six public school/university partnerships described in this section have evolved in very distinct ways,, the goals, assumptions, and principles guiding the partnerships have been similar in most instances.

Partnership Goals

The primary goal of *restructuring the teacher education programs* was consistent across the partnerships but accomplished through different vehicles that included the establishment of professional development schools, new degree programs, and professional development opportunities. In some cases, teachers became partners in the venture of professional development: co-developing, co-implementing, and co-refining the process as it emerged. Regardless of the design, the partnership was the mechanism through which this goal was achieved.

Although the *development of professional development schools* (PDSs) was envisioned within each partnership, importance for achieving this goal varied depending on the context of the partnership. Even where it was a primary focus (chapter 17), the very nature of a PDS became a point for clarification. Subsequently, a collegewide task force at the university has been charged to clarify the nature of professional development schools in the context of our work. As the remaining partnerships move toward this goal, much of the preliminary groundwork, sometimes semantic in nature, will have already been established.

Also common across projects was a *focus on inclusive programming* for students with disabilities. In one district, this was the major purpose of the partnership. Other partnerships focused on inclusive programs either as an emphasis for professional development within the partnership or the basis for a restructured teacher preparation program.

A final goal common to each partnership related to research. Associated with each project is an evolving research agenda. Topical areas of interest include the change process, the nature and evolution of professional development schools, teachers as researchers (a major focus in most projects), teacher competencies for inclusive schooling, teacher education initiatives that result in these competencies, and the integration of school restructuring and special education reform. In common was *a commitment to sustained collaborative arrangements that fostered research* related to these areas of interest.

Assumptions Related to the Partnerships

Common assumptions across projects related to the longevity of the partnership, new roles for the partners, and common understandings between each district and the university. The first assumption or understanding was that the *partnerships represent long-term commitments* for both the university and the school districts.. Though there were no written contracts, and in most instances no formal letters of agreement, district administrators and university faculty clearly invested together for the long haul. Tangential to that assumption was a recognition of the importance of developing mutually trusting relationships between teachers, administrators, and university personnel.

Secondly, since the school site is the focal point of educational reform, it was a common assumption that *the focus of the partnerships should relate to the school/district needs rather than the university's agenda.* In fact, there was agreement that the needs of schools in the respective districts should drive the projects, even though these needs varied from school to school and district to district. Furthermore, each of the partnerships involved university faculty working with teachers and administrators at the school site and their roles varied from leader to follower depending on the individual needs of the school community.

Third, there was an assumption that *the collaboration would be mutually agreed upon and thus, mutually beneficial.* As more and more stakeholders became involved in the partnerships, new understandings emerged of what was mutually beneficial, and the process of determining mutually beneficial activities sometimes required redefinition. However, there was a common belief that school districts and universities would benefit more from collaboratively approaching school restructuring rather than approaching it as separate entities.

Fourth, *each partnership assumed a cost-sharing approach particular to its own resources and needs.* This helped diminish tensions that can occur if one partner feels they are putting significantly more into the partnership than the other. Resources incurred across most of the partnerships included salary for the university liaisons, graduate assistants, travel costs, computer costs, printing, and supplies. Each partnership developed plans for fiscal arrangements that met the unique needs of the site and personnel involved. At least one partnership was able to secure substantial federal funding, while another secured private endowment funds. The use of university faculty or graduate assistants to supervise student interns was a common vehicle used for funding salaries.

WHAT WE HAVE LEARNED AND ARE CONTINUING TO LEARN

From each partnership, we gained new understandings about our work in progress. These are discussed in each chapter (see chapters 14–18). However, as we met and examined our experiences in the six partnerships, we found a number of common realizations that generalized across partnerships. Not surprising was the identification of time as a critical need. *Because of the time commitment required and the resources that must be invested, the benefits must be clearly perceived and a high priority assigned by both universities and schools seeking to collaborate.* Even if a university faculty person's workload is adjusted to provide sustained time at a school site, the partners with whom we seek to collaborate are often still meeting the pressures of everyday classroom teaching and school administration. This can promote feelings of resentment when extra effort is not compensated or considered within the workload of the school personnel. Thus, we believe that the absence of adequate time can be a major obstacle to collaboration and larger restructuring efforts. This still is a challenge to our projects as we reflect on the lifetime of a partnership.

We also believe the *time needed to build rapport and develop mutually beneficial plans requires a sustained partnership of at least three to five years.* During this time, it is necessary to define and redefine the goals or intended outcomes of the partnership. This process is tested and readjusted only after a period of collaboration. We are still uncertain how a partnership will end. The formal and extended planning process by which most of the partnerships began suggests that any endings will be different from other types of collaborative initiatives, e.g., a grant ends, a research study culminates, etc. *Partnerships infer membership in a collaborative community, thus suggesting a different set of protocols from those found in traditional research arrangements.*

Related to this issue is an important need for ongoing dialogue and reflection. *Restructuring and reinventing the way we do our work can sometimes challenge the beliefs and philosophies held by one or more of the partners.* If ignored, these differences can become subtle threats to the partnership. In the busy daily world of schools, a lack of time to dialogue and reflect can stifle change and innovation before it starts.

University support for faculty to participate in school/university partnerships was also found to be a critical element (chapters 14, 15, 16, 17). *University faculty must have assignments to partnerships of this nature as well as more flexible use of university resources that support non-FTE-driven outcomes or immediate cost-benefits.* This is especially critical in larger school districts and in rural areas where, for example, travel costs can often be substantial. Additionally, considering the time necessary to establish and maintain partnerships, *it is essential for the university to incorporate this work into the criteria for promotion and tenure.* Too much is expected and required of faculty in this context for their work not to be valued and rewarded. A task force at our university is currently examining this issue in order to suggest revisions of policies and procedures.

We found that building trust between university faculty and school faculty or administrators is critical and requires extensive communication, constant attention, and time in order to achieve the level of collaboration that can result in major restructuring efforts. *Building rapport and learning more about each other's culture is also an important step in the process of collaboration* (chapters 14–18). Several university faculty reported that this period of "hanging out" felt strange at first as it was not characterized by high levels of visible productivity. Yet it is during this stage that philosophies and agendas are slowly refined to the satisfaction of both parties. Also, this process was useful for identifying those individuals at the school or district sites who would later become important collaborators on the partnership's initiatives (chapters 14, 15).

It is important to note that each of our partnerships experienced conflict in some form, e.g., philosophical differences, policy issues, or use of resources. Some reported these conflicts as initial barriers to collaboration that needed to be worked through before further collaboration was possible (chapters 14, 15, 18). Others describe conflicts that slowly emerged from daily events and decisions which posed ethical dilemmas for the university personnel (chapters 17, 20, 21). We believe that these ethical dilemmas become even harder to ignore in professional development sites where a dual mission for educating students and student teachers exists. We found there was an ongoing need for discussing issues from multiple perspectives, including those of students, families, university faculty, student teachers, school personnel, and district personnel. *Conflicts or crises may be symptomatic of a lack of perspective of the multiple realities of stakeholders in the collaborative process.*

Research efforts within the contexts of partnerships face some unique challenges as evidenced in chapters 19–20. This may pose a dilemma for university faculty who are accustomed to meeting the demands for academic productivity and scholarly efforts toward the development of a knowledge base. *When working in partnerships, questions emerge, such as who owns the knowledge, who has the power/authority to report findings, and what impact will the reporting have on the continued partnership.* In the past, researchers were expected to keep a distance from their subjects in order to stay objective. When they shared a copy of their research findings with the school or district, it often signaled the end of their involvement. Our work is very different. We have tried to co-determine what research will be done, we have acknowledged that we often became participant observers, and our results became a working agenda for our collaborative work. This has not been without complications, however. *Researchers working within partnerships may find that the very relationships which afforded them entry can present risks to objectivity and challenge predetermined research protocols.* When the researcher intends to stay at a school site, the nature and design of a research study may be affected. When results from a study are perceived as negative by the school personnel, the researcher runs the risk of losing the trust and rapport that had previously been established.

Although the partnerships are in various stages of development and we anticipate more findings as our work continues, we believe that what we have already learned may be of use to others who are engaging in similiar school/university collaboration efforts. Consistent with the qualitative nature of inquiry that governs much of our work, the research described in these chapters is iterative; we attempt to improve our understanding and discernment about inclusion in schools with successive approximations of our goal to form a truly collegial collaboration.

22

AMERICAN EDUCATION IN THE POSTMODERN ERA

Wayne Sailor & Thomas M. Skrtic

COSMOLOGIES

We are clearly living in a time of sweeping change. Often, those who describe the processes of change within scientific disciplines refer to Kuhn's (1962) classic work in which he proclaims a paradigm shift. However, there are growing indications that the term *paradigm* is of insufficient conceptual magnitude to adequately describe the phenomenon (Goerner, 1994). The German language has a term that may fit more closely the scale and scope of change, and it has no English equivalent. The word is *Weltanschauung,* and it is usually translated as worldview, but with a disclaimer that English has no adequate descriptions for the term.

One way to view the significance of the change is to consider attributions of causation in human history. Throughout earliest recorded history, the fate of humanity was felt to be in the hands of one or more deities. The period of *spiritual determination* lasted until the Copernican revolution and the "Age of Enlightenment." The period of *natural determination* has lasted to the present time. Now, some feel a new era is emerging, one with 2000 A.D. as its temporal marker in the Christian calendar. By this reasoning, the new age is increasingly characterized by *self/social determination.*

Each of these periods presents a different perspective on humanity. Under spiritual determinism, human problems are resolvable only through faith in divine powers. In the age of natural determinism, the relative position of power occupied by humanity in the universe is improved somewhat. If all things are lawfully ordered and ultimately knowable, then human problems can be addressed through discovery of the underlying laws and manipulation of their consequences through scientific endeavor.

In the age of self/social determinism, it is recognized that all is not orderly and lawfully governed in the universe and that human problems can be addressed only through interpretation and political processes. The burden of responsibility on humanity increases with the progression through each of these periods of interpretation of causation or worldview.

A more complex progression was described by the philosopher Stephen Pepper (1946; Goerner, 1994) in a discourse on world hypotheses. In Pepper's progression, humanity's interpretation of the cosmos has progressed through the following six hypotheses: animism, mysticism, formism, mechanism, organicism, and contextualism. In this progression, mysticism is roughly an analog for spiritual determinism. Formism is Aristotelianism: the attempt to classify and name all things, and the search for absolute categories. Mechanism is the view that espouses natural determinism and is reflected in scientific thought from the time of Galileo through Newton (perhaps its zenith) and represented in contemporary thought in Skinnerian psychology.

The beginnings of the present transformation are anticipated in Pepper's system by organicism. Systems in the universe are evolving toward some end, according to this view, and knowledge must progress through discovery of the underlying change processes. Examples from philosophy include the dialectic, the thesis-antithesis process described by Hegel (Goerner, 1994). Finally, contextualism emerged, wherein humanity, according to Pepper, discovered that all things exist in a dynamic state of change with an interdependent relationship to all other things. Contextualism is manifest in the present through pragmatism and, in science, through applications of "chaos theory" (Guess & Sailor, 1993) and other sophisticated models of systems analysis (i.e., Gleick, 1987).

MODERN AND POSTMODERN

One argument, albeit controversial (Danforth, Rhodes, & Smith, this volume; Rowland, in press, Skrtic, 1991a), is that the transformation in worldview, paradigm shift, or whatever is represented in contemporary thought in a progression from "modern" systems and ideas to "postmodernism." In essence, according to this analysis, our modern foundations of knowledge are grounded philosophically in Pepper's (1946) hypothesis of formism and mechanism. We have behaved scientifically as if there is a reality that exists "out there" (epistemology) and that we can improve the human condition (axiology) by revealing and thus understanding its underlying laws and natural order (Rowland, in press). Modern foundations of knowledge are predicated on cognitive, rational processes (discourse and understanding). The very hallmark of humanity, that which separates us from the remainder of the organic world, is rationality. Through rational processes we discover truth, and truth shall set us free.

In postmodern thought, cognitive or technical rationality goes out the window. With it goes all of the bases for foundations of modern knowledge (Derrida, 1976; Searle, 1983). For this reason, postmodernists are regarded as antifoundational. If there is no permanently describable "out there" out there and it cannot be plumbed rationally, then how can we ever hope to solve human problems? The laws that describe order in a rational universe are not really laws at all, but are rather political constructions that are subject to reformulation with the changing ethos of social organization (Derrida, 1976). By Derrida's argument, there is no way to "know" outside of the manipulation of symbols ("text") (Derrida, 1976). Because no particular symbol system exists independent of social consensus in interpretation and of change, no system of description can be privileged over another. There is then no means of arriving at "truth" because there are no facts apart from some point of view that is transient in time (Rorty, 1991a). In the social sciences, the modern tradition of positivism is under challenge from interpretive or constructivist social science which assumes there is no objective truth, but rather that "reality" is socially constructed (Berger & Luckmann, 1967). Objectivity is replaced by intersubjective agreement reached not through rational discourse, but through communication and participation in evolving social settings and corresponding systems of meaning (Rorty, 1982; 1991a).

If the cognitive or technical rationality basis for knowledge is called into question, and that basis provides the foundation for the discovery of "truths" with which to benefit humankind, then from an axiological perspective, what hope is there for humankind and the preservation of social order? An answer can be found in the shift to a cultural rationality, a perspective on knowledge which is premised on understanding the evolving culture in which actions, practices, and premises are constructed and agreed upon. Such a view emphasizes the values, norms, and interpretations of participants in context (Skrtic, 1990; 1991a).

But what of epistemology? If there are no facts and no immutable laws that govern the "known," then how can we build a scientific process of discovery? The answer lies in shifting our standard from discovering truths to problem-solving. Under pragmatism (Dewey, 1982, 1990; James, 1948) the standard for what is true becomes what works, not in the narrow, uncritical sense of expediency, but in the critical sense of moving social systems and practices closer to democratic ideals of liberty, equality, social justice, and community. Ideas do not become facts under pragmatism, but rather hold "true" to the extent that they serve some human purpose for which they were constructed. Thus, knowledge is not about facts, but rather is concerned with symbolic descriptions of the universe that work when employed in the service of humankind (Rorty, 1982; Rowland, in press).

Pragmatism, because it sidesteps rational foundationalism, becomes a way to guide decisions about what to do and how to act in a postmodern world. The use of inter-subjectivist research methods, such as critical ethnography and naturalistic inquiry (e.g., Lincoln & Guba, 1985; Gitlin, 1990; Skrtic, 1985, 1990) engage the researcher in interpretive dialogues with research participants. The goal of social research is to understand how those studied "contextualize" their social reality. Constructivist research, by enabling researchers to be privy to "insiders'" interpretation of reality, affords an opportunity to facilitate recontextualization and thus to promote change (Kelly & Maynard-Moody, 1993; Rorty, 1991b; below).

POSTMODERN/MODERN BORDER TENSIONS

School reform in recent times can be seen to be shifting from the technical rationality approach to change (Cuban, 1989; Elmore & McLaughlin, 1988; Wise, 1988) in the first "wave" of educational reform, the so-called "excellence" movement to the cultural rationality perspective embodied in the current "school restructuring" movement (Cuban, 1993; Skrtic, 1991b). Under the excellence movement, a rational-technical (linear) relationship between government policy inputs and local program outputs was assumed (McLaughlin, 1990). Such an externally driven (rather than internally motivated) approach led less to higher standards than to greater standardization (Skrtic, 1991b; Ware, 1994).

This approach to higher standards resulted in larger numbers of students failing and large resultant increases in special support programs such as special education and chapter one. Only at the beginning of the present decade did educational policy makers begin to realize that meaningful reform, that is, one that pertains to all students and that injects equality into the excellence standard (Cuban, 1990a), requires an understanding of the contexts in which teaching and learning occur. Our ability to change the teaching/learning process requires changing the way that people view and subsequently act within these contexts (Skrtic, 1991a).

From this cultural point of view, teachers are valued as contributors to the policy processes that guide educational reform. Meaningful change in schools requires cultural change rather than mandates from the central office or school board (Gitlin, 1990). Since culture is dependent upon interpretation, we need research that promotes understanding of how teachers interpret their practices in context, how those interpretations affect their practice, and the manner in which they change (Skrtic, 1991a). A postmodern study of education transformations thus would seem to require a constructivistic approach, one grounded in qualitative or interpretivist research methods (Denzin & Lincoln, 1994; Krueger, 1994; Stewart & Shamdasani, 1990).

The transformation from technical (modern) to cultural (postmodern) rationality precipitates various stresses ("border tensions") across virtually all processes that make up the field of education as a whole. In the paragraphs that follow, we examine some of these border tensions in pedagogy, and then finally we present a partial description of the emerging development of a postmodern elementary school.

Program Evaluation

Educational research is a case in point. As Hines and Kromrey (this volume) point out, a postmodern school agenda necessitates a pragmatic strategy, one that recognizes the legitimacy (indeed, the necessity) of interpretivist research methods. Not everyone agrees with this position. Modernists, arguing from the perspective of technical rationality consider interpretivist research to be "soft," "subjective," and to "lack vigor and utility" (e.g., Ullman & Rosenberg, 1986; discussed in Fergusen, 1993, p. 37).

Interpretivists have their resident challengers who take equally strident positions in response to positivism. Smith and Heshusius (1986), for example, argue that subjectivism is a fundamentally different view of the world and that only interpretivist methods can build a base of knowledge with which to benefit humanity. Others, (e.g., Howe, 1988; Shulman, 1987) approach such paradigmatic border tensions by offering compromise positions. Howe (1988) advances the case for pragmatism and argues that competing paradigms can coexist through problem solving and that each approach can bring something of value to the knowledge base. Others argue that interpretivist research methods can generate new hypotheses, which can then be subjected to empirical (positivistic) validation through combinations of methods (Cronbach, 1982). And there are those who take a more postmodern position, arguing that no single paradigm can investigate the full range of social phenomena and that a social inquiry must encompass competing schools of thought (Fergusen, 1993; Shulman, 1987).

Educational Placements

Nowhere have border tensions in the field of education become more visible than in the recent controversy over "inclusion" (Sailor, Skrtic & Kleinhammer-Tramill, in press). Inclusion is a tremendously important educational concept because it embodies two of the most radical aspects of postmodernism—voice and collaboration.

As Kuhn (1970) points out, when paradigms change, the entire structure of reality changes. "Facts" remain or become so only in the social context in which they are commonly understood, that is, within their paradigm of understanding. Whether one's perspective is psychology (i.e., Sampson, 1993; Flax, 1990), women's studies (i.e., Riger, 1992), education (i.e., Rhodes, Danforth, & Smith, in press; Skrtic, 1986), rhetoric (Rowland, in press), or anthropology (i.e., Schwartz, White & Lutz, 1992), changes in perspective are attributed to paradigm-level processes, and entire epistemologies are undergoing conceptual revolutions. These changes are principally and in common characterized by the legitimization of voice (social constructivism) in the construction of knowledge, and by recognition of interdependency among categorical "disciplines" of knowledge in defining truth (collaboration).

If special education and general education are coming finally to share a common agenda, and there is increasing evidence that this is so (Sailor, 1991; York, 1994; Paul & Rosselli, this volume), it is because of transformations in both disciplines. The transformations intersect at their respective evolutions toward the postmodern agenda of collaborative, team-driven processes (site management/shared decision making), and recognition of the need to include the voices of those who are different and/or disempowered in restructuring education. In the latter case, the child participates interactively in the construction of subject matter, as for example in the case of hermeneutics (Bernstein, 1983), wherein the child partially defines the "reality" of subject matter by challenging the assumptions of the author. In both special and general education, strong shifts of relatively recent origin are now apparent away from the passivity of radical behaviorism (i.e., Kohn, 1993) and toward social constructivism, where the child is very much an active participant in the learning process. As Rhodes et al. (in press) point out, the classic, modern view of children with disabilities is that they should be regarded as a "host of differences within a difference." Each category of learning "problem" requires a discrete, fragmented, and isolationistic solution. Postmodernism, by contrast, views disability within a broader context of valued diversity among participants in the process of education. The postmodern trend in education is reflected in the current manifestations of "detracking, degrouping, destreaming, inclusion, collaboration, cooperation, etc." (p.27).

Implicit in these trends is the growing unification of special education (and other categorical special needs programs) and general education, so that all of the challenges presented by their respective populations' inherent diversity can be addressed by a workforce of shared abilities, values, and perspectives. In addition, the postmodern processes of collaboration and voice (or empowerment) are reflected in similar reform strategies within the community at large, such as the services integration movement, which promotes the restructuring of health and social welfare systems and their integration with the educational system (see Sailor, Gerry, & Wilson, 1993; Sailor, Skrtic, & Kleinhammer-Tramill, in press).

The mid-to-late 1980s brought a shift in general education reform initiatives from a narrow concern for "excellence" to increased interest in equity and instructional efficacy for the growing number of students at risk for educational failure (Cuban, 1989, 1990a). Likewise, realization of the need for major reform of social services organization and delivery systems to address the needs of these children and their families, many of whom are living in crisis because of poverty, racial and ethnic discrimination, violence, and disenfranchisement. These events created the context for a broader and more pragmatic special education reform effort—inclusive education.

The components of inclusive education variously defined by Sailor (1991); Snell (1991); York (1994), stress: (a) inclusion of all students with disabilities in the schools which they would attend if they had no disability; (b) representation of students with disabilities in schools and classrooms in natural proportion to their incidence in the district at large; (c) zero rejection and heterogeneous grouping; (d) age- and grade-appropriate placements of students with disabilities; (e) site-based coordination and management of instruction and resources; and (f) "effective schools" style decentralized instructional models (Sailor, Gerry, & Wilson, 1993).

These definitions of inclusive education differ somewhat in focus from proponents of "full inclusion" (i.e., Stainback & Stainback, 1994). The emphasis in full inclusion models tends to be heavily driven by professionals and parent advocacy organizations identified with severe disability programs (see Fuchs & Fuchs, 1994, for a discussion of the role of TASH in the process). The issues seem almost wholly focused on full-time, regular classroom placement of students with severe disabilities. Discussions of "inclusive education," on the other hand, have tended to be more focused on different educational arrangements for all students and thus are more identified with school restructuring rather than a strict focus on special education service delivery. Both full inclusion and inclusive education proponents have in common a push toward the elimination of strictly segregated educational programs for students identified for special education (but see Sailor et al., 1989, for a discussion of special concerns in inclusive programs for students with deafness and hard-of-hearing conditions).

Inclusion has been treated in the media as if it were about putting students with severe intellectual disabilities in regular classrooms and not much else. Inclusive education, however, is a definitive postmodern agenda in the terms described earlier in this chapter. Collaboration among parents and professionals in a context of school restructuring is the driving force. Implicit in these collaborative mechanisms is the collective voice of consumers (children and families) and of the "worker bees" in the system, the teachers. The outcome is increasingly described as the "unification" of education (i.e., McLaughlin & Warren, 1992; Sailor, Skrtic & Kleinhammer–Tramill, in press). Through processes characterized by voice and collaboration, all formerly fragmented, isolated, categorical subsystems (within and outside the school) are brought together and reorganized in a manner that benefits all of the students at the school. Including children with severe disabilities in a general education classroom can be viewed as an effort to integrate special education resources into general education as much as to enhance the cognitive and social development of the students with disabilities.

Teacher Education

Just as border tensions are felt in school restructuring approaches, so they are felt at least as acutely in colleges and schools of education. McLaughlin and Warren (1992), commenting on special education policy reform under postmodern transformations suggest that staff development for special educators should be undertaken in the context of restructured schools as the only viable personnel preparation policy.

Under the emerging implications of collaboration and voice, such preparation should be undertaken as an interdisciplinary team effort and should include participation by family members and members of the community through school/community partnerships (i.e., Duchnowski, Dunlap, Berg & Adiegbola, this volume). Team-governed staff development allows professionals and others to focus on common goals for all students and to share expertise. Where present training practices reinforce the "special" nature of skills held by special educators, team staff development approaches enable more fluid information and resource exchanges to occur across all disciplines, to the benefit of all children at the school site.

Examples of the need for this type of staff development abound in restructured schools. Teachers of "regular" students grapple with the need to individualize instruction for all students relative to the shift to outcomes-based education and curriculum-based, portfolio assessment. Special educators have historically been trained in these methods and have much to offer other teachers in making these transitions. General education teachers have much to offer special education teachers in facilitating the integration of "special" children and in making functional adaptations to facilitate the special education child's participation in the general education classroom. The special education teacher has much to offer their general education colleagues in performing functional analyses and instituting positive behavior management practices. This "bottled up" expertise can benefit all students under team-driven staff development models. Compare this to categorical personnel preparation models which actually retard progress in school restructuring by fostering isolation and dependency among teachers (Pugach, 1988).

Johnson and Pugach (1992) argue that the central question of inclusive education, that is, how to accommodate students with disabilities, may best be understood in the broader context of accommodating increasing diversity in American classrooms. The ability of professionals to collaborate in schools depends upon the commonality of their respective teacher education experiences (Su, 1990). Mason and Good (1993) argue that changing demographics are creating the need for more flexible grouping patterns in schools. These patterns, in turn, require expertise from both general and special educators relative to accommodating to diversity in situations where disability is but one aspect of a range of individual differences (also see Ware, 1994).

A number of the chapters that constitute Section Two, Part Two of this volume can be regarded as voices from the field in interpreting within a social constructivist framework the experiences of higher education students and faculty and the staff with whom they work in schools. These experiences are encountered daily in helping to transform teacher education from university-based, categorical training to school-based, team-driven growth and development.

Not the least of the border tensions reflected in personnel preparation programs are those encountered by faculty who are held to a modern standard of evaluation for promotion and tenure (i.e., number of referreed publications; participation on university committees, and so on). How can these field-based, team-participant faculty compete with colleagues from departments in which career advancement depends only on publishing (i.e., Paul, Johnston & Raines, this volume): As Paul et al. point out, preparing personnel for restructured schools in the postmodern era means that the preparation programs themselves must be restructured. If they are not, square pegs will go on being produced in the hope that they can somehow be fitted into the round holes of a different and evolving system.

Other border tensions can be felt across the entire spectrum of education. In school finance, for example, arguments abound over which kind of state funding formula is more likely to enhance inclusive practices (Greyerbiehl, 1993; Moore, Walker, & Holland, 1982; Parrish, 1993a, 1993b; Shriner, Ysseldyke & Thurlow, 1994). In early childhood education, the argument is focused on shared arrangements between schools and their communities (i.e., Smith & Rose, 1991), and on the role of families in the implementation of Part H service delivery (Dunst, Trivette & Deal, 1988; Hanson & Lynch, 1989; Turnbull & Turnbull, 1990). What is clear from a comparative look across these issues is that a set of transformations are underway in education and, for that matter, across all human service arenas (Sailor, Skrtic & Kleinhammer–Tramill, in press), transformations that reflect the postmodern thesis of this book. The border tensions are likely to continue for some time but the transformation agenda is underway.

SCHOOLS IN THE POSTMODERN ERA

A community not far from the University of Kansas offers a glimpse at the transformation from modern to postmodern schooling in one school district. Consider School A, a medium-sized elementary school in a lower-middle class neighborhood in a small city. School A is a traditional modern elementary school. Its program begins at kindergarten and continues through grade 6. Children are in self-contained classrooms all day except for kindergarten, which operates two separate half-day sessions. There are no ties with preschool providers and no formal transition planning for movement of students into junior high school.

School A has two special education classrooms for students with behavior disorders. Some of the children in these "BD" classes are partially mainstreamed for some regular class periods (art, PE, and others). The district has traditionally considered School A to be "the BD school." Other children with different types of disabilities who would otherwise be expected to attend School A are bused to other schools in the district. Some regular classroom children are encouraged to be "peer tutors" and to spend some small time in the BD classes doing relatively nonfunctional assistance tasks with some of the special education students. When the special education students reach the age equivalence for grade 7, they are passed along to the special BD classes at two junior high schools in the city, only one of which typically receives students from School A.

School A also operates two chapter one pull-out classes, a pull-out program for gifted instruction, and a resource room program for students with learning disabilities. The school is "governed" by a principal and a site advisory committee that meets once a month, but all school policies are set by central district office administrators. Similarly, although the principal is responsible for the day-to-day operation of the school, the categorical programs, including special education, are the responsibility of a special programs administrative staff at the central office. School A has no mechanisms in place for including teachers, parents, and community members in decision making regarding utilization of school resources. Attendance at the school's parent-teacher organization meetings is light and fund-raising efforts have been only marginally successful. The school has a high number of minority students, even though the proportion of minority students in the surrounding community is low.

Consider now School B. This school has been undergoing significant transformations for about three years. In terms of size and demographics, School B is comparable to School A except that a relatively higher percentage of School B students qualify for the free lunch program, and the school operates a schoolwide chapter one program.

Things began to happen at School B in earnest when it began a process of rapid compliance with the new state school restructuring initiative passed by the Kansas State Board of Education and called Quality Performance Accreditation, or QPA for short. This initiative calls for transformation to site-based management, team-governed processes at the school, and movement toward outcomes-based assessment and curriculum planning. The principal at School B additionally applied for and received a number of small state-level incentive grants (including one on special education inclusion). The principal further applied for status as one of the Professional Development School sites in conjunction with the University of Kansas School of Education, Professional Development School project. Finally, the principal and teaching staff requested and have been receiving technical assistance from the KU University Affiliated Program (UAP) which provides technical assistance in partnership with the KU Department of Special Education.

These and other efforts by the administration, staff, and parents of School B have led to some remarkable transformations in the way that children receive their education. When School B opened in the Fall of 1994 it exhibited, among many others, the features described in the paragraphs to follow.

School B voluntarily surrendered its isolation and self-containment within its community. It has reorganized to form partnerships with community agencies, with the nearby university, with its community of families and businesses, and internally with its full panoply of specialized support services.

School B now has a preschool program on the campus. Funded by a variety of sources, the program affords children and families who will attend the school a chance to become familiar with the school's staff and program in advance of regular attendance. It provides school staff the opportunity to assess and plan for the specialized support needs of students before they arrive in kindergarten (which is now a full day program). Both the preschool program and the grade level programs are fully inclusive for all students. Gone are the special education classes and the pull-out programs. The students who would normally attend School B are no longer sent elsewhere, and the school, with very few exceptions, serves only those students from its designated service area.

School B has a site resource management council that consists of teachers, other staff, and parents. Governance at the site is an interactive process between the principal and the site council, and the principal represents the interests of the school to the central district office. Smaller "preassessment teams" examine the needs of students who require special assistance and make recommendations to the site council. Supports are arranged in terms of the "best fit" among school staff and the particular support needs of students. No student is designated for special education simply on the basis of test results. There are no special classes and all students, including those with severe disabilities are "unlabeled" members of regular classes. All extra-classroom support services are operated as interdisciplinary, integrated resource environments, where specialized therapies can be integrated into cooperative learning groups, peer tutorials, and other peer-mediated integrative approaches.

The school develops transition planning mechanisms for students with special support needs in the year before graduation to junior high school. Junior high staff visit the classes at School B and get to know the incoming students with special needs. All sixth graders get field experience visits to the junior high school, and some take one or more classes such as advanced mathematics at the school.

School B opened in the fall with both a hot lunch and supper program and operates an inclusive, after-school "latchkey" program, again funded from a variety of school and nonschool sources. The school is open in the evenings on a frequent basis for community/school planning sessions, attended by school staff, school board members, district staff, parents, and members of the community.

The school hosts a Family Resource Center which operates in conjunction with a community/school partnership program for school-linked integrated services (see Sailor, Skrtic, & Kleinhammer–Tramill, in press). Under this arrangement, services coordinators (called "family advocates") participate on the school site governance council and help to plan special support services for students who need them. They also represent the school on the "community integrated services planning council" and look after the needs of students and their families for specialized support services in the community.

The Family Resource Center is a "one-stop-shopping" center for all support services including health and social welfare services for families in need of such assistance for any reason. A health clinic associated with the Family Resource Center provides vaccinations, EPSDT screenings and referrals, and other school/community health programs.

The University of Kansas places practicum student trainees in a variety of educational programs at School B. Faculty from KU participate directly with the school program in providing supervision and instruction for their university students. As a result, the transformations occurring in School B have an interactive effect with the university. Departments (i.e., Special Education, Educational Psychology, Curriculum and Instruction, Human Development and Family Life) that normally operate independently and with autonomy now hold interdisciplinary sessions in conjunction with the UAP to facilitate combined teacher training and staff development efforts at School B.

School B is well on the way to becoming a postmodern school. The contrast with School A is striking. In this community, as in many others around the country (including those described in various chapters in this volume), transformational processes have begun that will likely go to scale to the extent that they produce better educational outcomes for students. More time is required to adequately evaluate the outcomes question, but the underlying change processes clearly "lead lives of their own" and are linked to the broader changes that are affecting all aspects of human endeavor.

MOVING FROM A TO B

Operating under constructivist principles, policy analysts (e.g., Jennings, 1987; Kelly & Maynard-Moody, 1993; Lindblom, 1990), program evaluators (e.g., Guba & Lincoln, 1989; Sirotnik, 1984) and implementation researchers from a variety of fields—including general education (Gitlin, 1990; Sirotnik & Oakes, 1986) and special education (Skrtic, Guba & Knowlton, 1985; Skrtic, 1985, 1990, 1991a)—have begun to transform the process of studying change into one of promoting change. Given the goal of understanding how research participants construct or contextualize their social reality, constructivist research necessarily engages researchers in interpretive dialogues with research participants. Besides making researchers privy to the insiders' interpretation of reality, this creates a unique opportunity for them to influence the participants' contextualizations and thus to facilitate change through recontextualization.

Writing from the perspective of constructivist policy analysis, Kelly and Maynard-Moody (1993) noted that, "outsiders can facilitate the recontextualization of insiders' [constructions] by bringing together different subnarratives so that all concerned can gain a better understanding of the larger narrative of which they are all a part" (p.3). Given a conceptualization of change as recontextualization, the goal of the researcher is to facilitate change in social settings by broadening and enriching inter-subjective agreement through methods geared to "probing, not proving" (Lindblom, 1990, p.21). The role of researchers is to "facilitate. . .deliberation, to bring together multiple perspectives, to assist in the process of exploring alternative courses of action, and to aid [participants and themselves]. . .in understanding the possible limitation of their current perspectives" (Kelly & Maynard-Moody, 1993, p.4).

The advantage today is that implementation researchers and program evaluators in education have begun to conceptualize educational change research as "educative" rather than merely evaluative (e.g., Gitlin, 1990; Guba & Lincoln, 1989; Sirotnik & Oakes, 1986). They are calling for a dialogical approach to inquiry, an educative process characterized by a mutually shaping relationship among researchers and research participants. Under this approach, the very criteria by which educational research is judged has changed to "the degree to which the research process enabled disenfranchised groups to participate in the decision-making process; examine their beliefs, actions, and the school context; and make changes based on this [recontex-tualized] understanding" (Gitlin, 1990, p. 446).

REFERENCES

Berger, P. & Luckmann, T. (1967). *The social construction of reality.* Garden City, NY: Doubleday.

Bernstein, R. J. (1983). *Beyond objectivism and relativism: Science, hermeneutics, and praxis.* Philadelphia: University of Pennsylvania Press.

Cronbach, L.J. (1982). Prudent aspirations for social inquiry. In W. Kruskal (Ed.), *The social sciences: Their nature and uses.* Chicago: University of Chicago Press.

Cuban, L. (1989). The "at-risk" label and the problem of urban school reform. *Phi Delta Kappan, 70*(10), 780–784, 799–801.

Cuban, L. (1990a). Cycles of history: Equity versus excellence. In S.B. Bacharach (Ed.), *Education reform: Making sense of it all* (pp. 135–140). Boston: Allyn & Bacon.

Cuban, L. (1990b) Reforming again, again, and again. *Educational Researcher, 19*(1), 3–13.

Cuban, L. (1993). The lure of curricular reform and its pitiful history. *Phi Delta Kappan, 75*(2), 182–185.

Danforth, S., Rhodes, W., & Smith, T. (this volume). Inventing the future: Postmodern challenges in educational reform. (Chapter 21).

Denzin, N.K., & Lincoln, Y.S. (Eds.) (1994). *Handbook of qualitative research.* Thousand Oaks, CA: Sage Publications.

Derrida, J. (1976). *Of grammatology.* Baltimore: Johns Hopkins University Press.

Dewey, J. (1982). The development of American pragmatism. In H.S. Thayer (Ed.), *Pragmatism: The classic readings.* Indianapolis: Hackett.

Dewey, J. (1990). *The school and society* and *The child and the curriculum.* Chicago: University of Chicago Press.

Duchnowski, A., Dunlap, G., Berg, K., & Adiegbola, M. (this volume). Rethinking the participation of families in the education of children: Clinical and policy issues. (Chapter 5).

Dunst, C.J., Trivette, C.M., & Deal, A.G. (1988). *Enabling and empowering families: Principles and guidelines for practice.* Cambridge, MA: Brookline Books.

Elmore, R. F., & McLaughlin, M. W. (1988). *Steady work: Policy, practice, and the reform of American education.* Santa Monica, CA: Rand Corporation.

Ferguson, D.L. (1993). Something a little out of the ordinary: Reflections on becoming an interpretivist researcher in special education. *Remedial and Special Education, 14*(4), 35–43, 51.

Flax, J. (1990). *Thinking fragments: Psychoanalysis, feminism, and postmodernism in the contemporary west.* Berkeley: University of California Press.

Fuchs, D., & Fuchs, L.S. (1994). Inclusive schools movement and the radicalization of special education reform. *Exceptional Children, 60*(4), 294–309.

Gitlin, A. D. (1990). Educative research, voice, and school change. *Harvard Educational Review, 60*(4), 443–466.

Gleick, J. (1987). *Chaos: Making a new science.* New York: Viking.

Goerner, S.J. (Ed.) (1994). *Chaos and the evolving ecological universe.* Langhorne, PA: Gordon and Breach.

Greyerbiehl, D. (1993). *Educational policies and practices that support the inclusion of students with disabilities in the general education classroom.* Charleston, WV: West Virginia Developmental Disabilities Planning Council.

Guba, E.G., & Lincoln, Y.S. (1989). *Fourth generation evaluation.* San Francisco: Jossey-Bass.

Guess, D., & Sailor, W. (1993). Chaos theory and the study of human behavior: Implications for special education. *Journal of Special Education, 27*(1), 16–34.

Hanson, M.J., & Lynch, E.W. (1989). *Early intervention: Implementing child and family services for infants and toddlers who are at-risk or disabled.* Austin, TX: Pro-Ed.

Hines, C., & Kromrey, J. (this volume). Re-examining research in teacher education: Paradigmatic and technical issues. (Chapter 9).

Howe, K.R. (1988). Against the quantitative-qualitative incompatibility thesis (or dogmas die hard). *Educational Researcher, 17*(8), 10–16.

James, W. (1948). Pragmatism's conception of truth. In A. Castell (Ed.), *Essays in Pragmatism.* New York: Hafner.

Jennings, B. (1987). Interpretation and the practice of policy analysis. In F. Fischer & J. Forester (Eds.), *Confronting values in policy analysis: The politics of criteria* (pp. 128–152). Newbury Park, CA: Sage Publications.

Johnson, L. J., & Pugach, M.C. (1992). Continuing the dialogue: Embracing a more expansive understanding of collaborative relationships. In W. Stainback & S. Stainback (Eds.), *Controversial issues confronting special education.* Boston: Allyn & Bacon.

Kauffman, J.M. (1991). Restructuring in sociopolitical context: Reservations about the effects of current reform proposals on students with disabilities. In J.W. Lloyd, A.C. Rapp, & N.N. Singh (Eds.), *The Regular Education Initiative: Alternative perspectives on concepts, issues and models* (pp. 57–66). Sycamore, IL: Sycamore.

Kelly, M., & Maynard-Moody, S. (1993). Policy analysis in the post-positivist era: Engaging stakeholders in evaluating the Economic Development Districts program. *Public Administration Review, 53*(2), 135–142.

Kohn, A. (1993). *Punished by rewards.* Boston: Houghton Mifflin.

Krueger, R.A. (1994). *Focus groups: A practical guide for applied research,* (2nd ed.). Thousand Oaks, CA: Sage Publications.

Kuhn, T. S. (1962). *The structure of scientific revolutions* (1st ed.). Chicago: University of Chicago Press.

Kuhn, T. (1970). *The structure of scientific revolutions* (2nd ed.). Chicago: University of Chicago Press.

Lincoln, Y.S., & Guba, E.G., (1985). *Naturalistic Inquiry.* Beverly Hills, CA: Sage Publications.

Lindblom, C. (1990). *Inquiry and change: The troubled attempt to understand and shape society.* New Haven: Yale University Press.

Mason, D.A., & Good, T.L. (1993). Effects of two-group and whole-class teaching on regrouped elementary students' mathematical achievement. *American Educational Research Journal, 30*, 328–360.

McLaughlin, M. W. (1990). The Rand change agent study revisited: Macro perspectives and micro realities. *Educational Researcher, 19*(9), 11–16.

McLaughlin, M.J., & Warren, S.H. (1992). *Issues & options in restructuring schools and special education programs.* Reston, VA: Council for Exceptional Children.

Moore, M.T., Walker, L.J., & Holland, R.P. (1982). *Fine-tuning special education finance: A guide for state policy makers.* Washington, DC: Education Policy Research Institute of Educational Testing Service.

Parrish, T.B. (1993a). Federal policy options for funding special education. *CSEF Resource, 1*(2), Policy Brief No. 1.

Parrish, T.B. (1993b). State funding provisions and least restrictive environment: Implications for federal policy. *CSEF Resource, 1*(2), Policy Brief No. 2.

Paul, J., Evans, D., & Rosselli, H. (in press). *Integrating school restructuring and special education reform.*

Paul, J., Johnston, H., & Raines, S. (this volume). Educating teachers for all children: Clinical, political, and social constructions of teacher education. (Chapter 11).

Paul, J., & Rosselli, H. (this volume). Integrating the parallel reforms in general and special education. (Chapter 9).

Pepper, S. (1946). *World hypotheses: Prolegomena to systematic philosophy and a complete survey of metaphysics.* Berkeley: University of California Press.

Pugach, M. (1988). Special education as a constraint on teacher education reform. *Journal of Teacher Education, 39*(3), 52–59.

Rhodes, W., Danforth, S., & Smith, T. (in press). Inventing the future: Paradigmatic, programmatic and political challenges in restructuring education. In J. Paul, D. Evans, & H. Rosselli (Eds.), *Integrating school restructuring and special education reform.* (Chapter 23).

Riger, S. (1992). Epistemological debates, feminist voices: Science, social values, and the study of women. *American Psychologist, 47*, 730–740.

Rorty, R. (1982). *Consequences of pragmatism.* Minneapolis: University of Minnesota Press.

Rorty, R. (1991a). *Objectivity, relativism, and truth: Philosophical papers, volume 1.* Cambridge, England: Cambridge University Press.

Rorty, R. (1991b). Inquiry as recontextualization: An anti-dualist account of interpretation. In D. Hiley, J. Bohman, and R. Shusterman (Eds.), *The interpretive turn: Philosophy, science, culture* (pp. 59–80). Ithaca, NY: Cornell University Press.

Rowland, R.C. (in press). *In defense of rational argument: A pragmatic justification of argumentation theory and response to the postmodern critique.* Communication Studies, University of Kansas, Lawrence, KS.

Sailor, W. (1991). Special education in the restructured school. *Remedial and Special Education, 12*(6), 8–22.

Sailor, W., Anderson, J., Halvorsen, A.T., Doering, K., Filler, J., & Goetz, L. (1989). *The comprehensive local school: Regular education for all students with disabilities.* Baltimore, MD: Paul H. Brookes Publishing Co.

Sailor, W., Gerry, M., & Wilson, W.C. (1993). Disability and school integration. In T. Husen & T.N. Postlethwaite (Eds.), *International encyclopedia of education: Research and studies* (2nd suppl.). New York: Pergamon Press.

Sailor, W., Skrtic, T., & Kleinhammer-Tramill, J. (in press). *New community schools.* Lawrence, KS: Beach Center on Families and Disability.

Sampson, E.E. (1993). Identity politics: Challenges to psychology's understanding. *American Psychologist, 48*(12), 1219–1230.

Schwartz, T., White, G.M., & Lutz, C.A. (Eds.) (1992). *New directions in psychological anthropology*. Cambridge, England: Cambridge University Press.

Searle, J. (1983). The world turned upside down. *New York Review of Books*, Oct. 27, 74–79.

Shriner, J.G., Ysseldyke, J.E., & Thurlow, M.L. (1994). Standards for all American students. *Focus on Exceptional Children, 26*(5).

Shulman, L. (1987). Knowledge and teaching: Foundations of the new reform. *Harvard Educational Review, 57*(1), 1–22.

Sirotnik, K.A. (1984). An outcome-free conception of schooling : Implications for school-based inquiry and information systems. *Educational Evaluation and Policy Analysis, 6*, 227–239.

Sirotnik, K.A., & Oakes, J. (1986). *Critical perspectives on the organization and improvement of schooling*. Boston: Kluwer-Nijhoff Publishing.

Skrtic, T. (1985). Doing naturalistic research into educational organizations. In Y.S. Lincoln (Ed.), *Organizational theory and inquiry: The paradigm revolution* (pp. 185–220). Beverly Hills, CA: Sage Publications.

Skrtic, T. (1986). The crisis in special education knowledge: A perspective on perspective. *Focus on Exceptional Children, 18* (7), 1–16.

Skrtic, T.M., Guba, E.G., & Knowlton, H.E. (1985). *Interorganizational special education programming in rural areas: Technical report on the multisite naturalistic field study*. Washington: National Institute of Education.

Skrtic, T. M. (1990). Social accommodation: Toward a dialogical discourse in educational inquiry (pp. 125–135). In E. Guba (Ed.), *The paradigm dialog*. Newbury Park, CA: Sage Publications.

Skrtic, T. M. (1991a). *Behind special education: A critical analysis of professional culture and school organization*. Denver: Love Publishing.

Skrtic, T. M. (1991b). The special education paradox: Equity as the way to excellence. *Harvard Educational Review, 61*(2), 148–206.

Smith, J.K., & Heshusius, L. (1986). Closing down the conversation: The end of the quantitative-qualitative debate among educational inquirers. *Educational Researcher, 15*(1), 4–12.

Smith, B.J., & Rose, D.F. (1991). *Administrator's policy handbook for preschool mainstreaming*. Cambridge, MA: Brookline Books.

Snell, M.E. (1991). Schools care for all kids: The importance of integration for students with severe disabilities and their peers. In J.W. Lloyd, A.C. Rapp, & N.N. Singh (Eds.), *The Regular Education Initiative: Alternative perspectives on concepts, issues and models*. Sycamore, IL: Sycamore.

Stainback, W., & Stainback, S. (1984). A rationale for the merger of special and regular education. *Exceptional Children, 51*, 102–111.

Stewart, D.W., & Shamdasani, P.N. (1990). *Focus groups: Theory and practice*. Newbury Park, CA: Sage Publications.

Su, Z. (1990). The function of the peer group in teacher socialization. *Phi Delta Kappan*.

Turnbull, A.P., & Turnbull, H.R. (1990). *Families, professionals, and exceptionality*. Columbus, OH: Merrill Publishing Co.

Ullman, J.D., & Rosenberg, M.S. (1986). Science and superstition in special education. *Exceptional Children, 52*(5), 459–460.

Ware, L. P. (1994). Contextual barriers to collaboration. *Journal of Educational and Psychological Consultation, 5* (4), 339–357.

Wise, A. E. (1988). The two conflicting trends in school reform: Legislated learning revisited. *Phi Delta Kappan, 69*(5), 328–333.

York, J. (1994). A shared agenda for educational change. *TASH Newsletter, 20*(2), 10–11.

Name Index

Subject Index